LET THE GAMES BEGIN!

Widely acknowledged as the best guide of its kind, this is the book that millions of Olympics enthusiasts have turned to when they want the most extensive, up-to-date, and entertaining collection of Olympic records, facts, and statistics. This all-new guide to the 1992 Winter and Summer Olympics features:

- A roll of all medalists and their records from 1896 to the present
- A complete schedule of all 1992 winter and summer events
- A detailed history of each Olympic sport, including a list of the names and nationalities of every medal winner
- A record of each country's participation in the games
- Fascinating stories about the most dramatic, heart-breaking, awe-inspiring moments in Olympic history

Packed with facts and trivia, *The Guinness Book of Olympic Records* is a guaranteed gold-medal winner—the essential guide to enjoying the 1992 games!

GUINNESS BOOK OF OLYMPIC RECORDS

COMPLETE ROLL OF
OLYMPIC MEDAL WINNERS (1896–1988,
including 1906) FOR THE SPORTS (7 WINTER
and 25 SUMMER) CONTESTED IN THE
1992 CELEBRATIONS AND OTHER
USEFUL INFORMATION

Editors and Compilers

STAN GREENBERG, editor-in-chief
PETER MATTHEWS
NORRIS McWHIRTER
DAVID A. BOEHM

BANTAM BOOKS
NEW YORK • TORONTO • LONDON • SYDNEY • AUCKLAND

GUINNESS BOOK OF OLYMPIC RECORDS

*A Bantam Book / published by arrangement with
Guinness Publishing Limited*

PRINTING HISTORY

*Original Sterling edition published May 1964
Revised edition / October 1975
Revised Bantam edition / June 1967
New Revised Bantam edition / December 1971
New Revised Bantam edition / February 1976
New Revised Bantam edition / November 1979
New Revised Bantam edition / December 1983
New Revised Bantam edition / February 1988
New Revised Bantam edition / January 1992*

TABLE OF SUPERLATIVES

Most gold medals (men)	10	Ray Ewry (USA)	1900–1908
Most gold medals (women)	9	Larissa Latynina (URS)	1956–1964
Most medals (men)	15	Nikolai Andrianov (URS)	1972–1980
Most medals (women)	18	Larissa Latynina (URS)	1956–1964
Oldest gold medalist (men)	64 yr 258 days	Oscar Swahn (SWE)	1912
Oldest gold medalist (women)	45 yr 13 days	Liselott Linsenhoff (GER)	1972
Oldest medalist (men)	72 yr 280 days	Oscar Swahn (SWE)	1920
Oldest medalist (women)	46 yr 258 days	Maud Van Rosen (SWE)	1972
Youngest gold medalist (men)	7–10 yr	Unknown French boy	1900
Youngest gold medalist (women)	13 yr 267 days	Marjorie Gestring (USA)	1936
Youngest medalist (men)	7–10 yr	Unknown French boy	1900
Youngest medalist (women)	12 yr 24 days	Inge Sörensen (DEN)	1936
Most gold medals in one Games (men)	7	Mark Spitz (USA)	1972
Most gold medals in one Games (women)	4	Six women	1980
Most medals in one Games (men)	8	Alexandr Dititain (URS)	1980
Most medals in one Games (women)	7	Maria Gorochowskaya (URS)	1952
Most Games attended (men)	8	Raimondo d'Inzeo (ITA)	1948–1976
Most Games attended (women)	7	Kerstin Palm (SWE)	1964–1988
Longest span (men)	40 yr	Ivan Osiier (DEN)	1908–1948
	40 yr	Magnus Konow (NOR)	1908–1948
	40 yr	Durward Knowles (GBR/BAH)	1948–1988
	40 yr	Paul Elvström (DEN)	1948–1988
Longest span (women)	24 yr	Ellen Müller-Preis (AUT)	1932–1956
	24 yr	Kerstin Palm (SWE)	1964–1988
Oldest competitor (men)	72 yr 280 days	Oscar Swahn (SWE)	1920
Oldest competitor (women)	70 yr 5 days	Lorna Johnstone (GBR)	1972
Youngest competitor (men)	7–10 yr	Unknown French boy	1920
Youngest competitor (women)	11 yr 73 days	Cecilia Colledge (GBR)	1932

PICTURE CREDITS

The editors and publisher wish to thank the following for pictures used in this book: Aitken Ltd.; Allsport Photographic; Associated Press; Canoeing Magazine; Central Press; Gerry Cranham; Tony Duffy; European Picture Union; Mary Evans; International News Photo; Keystone Press Agency; E.D. Lacey; London & Wide World Photos; Don Morley; Planet News; Radio Times Hulton Picture Library; Popperfoto; Sports and General Press Agency; United Press International; World Sports; Dave Terry.

TABLE OF CONTENTS

TABLE OF MEDAL WINNERS
BY NATIONS 1896 TO 1988

Note: These totals include all first, second and third places including those in events no longer on the current schedule. (Not included are medals for the official Olympic art competitions of 1912 to 1948.) The 1906 Games which were officially staged by the International Olympic Committee have been included.

OLYMPIC GAMES (Summer)

		GOLD	SILVER	BRONZE	TOTAL
1.	U.S.A.	752	569	481	1,802
2.	U.S.S.R.	397	323	304	1,024
3.	Great Britain	172	221	206	599
4.	East Germany[1]	154	131	126	411
5.	Germany[2]	153	206	208	567
6.	France	153	170	175	498
7.	Italy	147	121	123	391
8.	Sweden	132	142	167	441
9.	Hungary	125	112	137	374
10.	Finland	97	75	110	282
11.	Japan	87	75	82	244
12.	Australia	71	67	87	225
13.	Romania	55	64	82	201
14.	Czechoslovakia	45	48	49	142
15.	Netherlands	43	46	65	154
16.	Switzerland	41	63	58	162
17.	Norway	41	33	33	107
18.	Poland	40	56	95	191
19.	Canada	39	62	73	174
20.	Bulgaria	35	62	49	146
21.	Belgium	35	46	42	123

1. East Germany (GDR) 1968–1988
2. Germany 1896–1964, West Germany from 1968–1988

Development of the Olympic Games

These figures relate to the Summer Games and exclude Demonstration Sports.

	Countries Represented	Number of Sports	Number of Competitors	
			Male	Female
1896	13	9	311	0
1900	22	17	1,319	11
1904	13	14	617	8
1906	20	11	877	7
1908	22	21	1,999	36
1912	28	14	2,490	57
1920	29	22	2,543	64
1924	44	18	2,956	136
1928	46	15	2,724	290
1932	37	15	1,281	127
1936	49	20	3,738	328
1948	59	18	3,714	385
1952	69	17	4,407	518
1956	71	17	2,958	384
1960	83	17	4,738	610
1964	93	19	4,457	683
1968	112	18	4,750	781
1972	122	21	6,077	1,070
1976	92	21	4,834	1,251
1980	81	21	4,265	1,088
1984	140	21	5,458	1,620
1988	159	23	6,279	2,186
1992		25	—	—

For the Winter Olympics see tables on page 233.

Celebrations of the Modern Olympic Games

I	1896	Athens	April 6–15
II	1900	Paris	May 20–Oct. 28
III	1904	St. Louis	July 1–Nov. 23
*	1906	Athens	April 22–May 2
IV	1908	London	April 27–Oct. 31
V	1912	Stockholm	May 5–July 22
VI	1916	Berlin	not celebrated owing to war
VII	1920	Antwerp	April 20–Sept. 12
VIII	1924	Paris	May 4–July 27
IX	1928	Amsterdam	May 17–Aug. 12
X	1932	Los Angeles	July 30–Aug. 14
XI	1936	Berlin	Aug. 1–16
XII	1940	Tokyo, then Helsinki	not celebrated owing to war
XIII	1944	London	not celebrated owing to war
XIV	1948	London	July 29–Aug. 14
XV	1952	Helsinki	July 19–Aug. 3
XVI	1956	Melbourne[1]	Nov. 22–Dec. 8
XVII	1960	Rome	Aug. 25–Sept. 11
XVIII	1964	Tokyo	Oct. 10–24
XIX	1968	Mexico	Oct. 12–27
XX	1972	Munich	Aug. 26–Sept. 10
XXI	1976	Montreal	July 17–Aug. 1
XXII	1980	Moscow	July 19–Aug. 3
XXIII	1984	Los Angeles	July 28–Aug. 12
XXIV	1988	Seoul	Sept. 17–Oct. 2
XXV	1992	Barcelona	July 25–Aug. 9

* *This celebration (to mark the 10th anniversary of the modern Games) was officially intercalated but is not numbered.*
[1] *The equestrian events were held in Stockholm June 10–17, 1956.*

The Winter Olympic Games

I	1924	Chamonix, France	Jan. 25–Feb. 4
II	1928	St. Moritz, Switzerland	Feb. 11–19
III	1932	Lake Placid, U.S.A.	Feb. 4–15
IV	1936	Garmisch-Partenkirchen, Germany	Feb. 6–16
V	1948	St. Moritz, Switzerland	Jan. 30–Feb. 8
VI	1952	Oslo, Norway	Feb. 14–25
VII	1956	Cortina d'Ampezzo, Italy	Jan. 26–Feb. 5
VIII	1960	Squaw Valley, California	Feb. 18–28
IX	1964	Innsbrück, Austria	Jan. 29–Feb. 9
X	1968	Grenoble, France	Feb. 6–18
XI	1972	Sapporo, Japan	Feb. 3–13
XII	1976	Innsbrück, Austria[2]	Feb. 4–15
XIII	1980	Lake Placid, U.S.A.	Feb. 14–23
XIV	1984	Sarajevo, Yugoslavia	Feb. 8–19
XV	1988	Calgary, Canada	Feb. 13–28
XVI	1992	Albertville	Feb. 8–23

[2] *Originally awarded to Denver, U.S.A.*

PREFACE

Students of the modern Olympic Games movement seem to be offered in existing books either a bare Roll of Champions since 1896, or else a highly detailed and expensive (and in the case of the earlier Games, very rare) report of a single celebration. We have attempted, in an inexpensive form and in as much detail as space permits, to set out *all* the medal winners of all time—that is, the holders of the gold, silver, and bronze awards for every event on the 1992 program.

The Olympics have many fascinations to those who follow them round the world for television, radio, or the press, but there are two peculiarities perhaps above all others.

First, the competitors themselves make friendships that will last for the rest of their lives. This happens despite the tendencies of some commentators to overemphasize any disagreement that inevitably occurs in such a highly charged competitive atmosphere. Occasionally there are even Olympic marriages. Olympic friendships, particularly notable since the custom started in 1932 of lodging the participants in an Olympic village, transcend the mere difficulties of conflicting language, race and creed. The Olympic spirit of common interest in the techniques of sport makes rather light of nationalistic differences, which so often leave professional diplomats in deadlock.

Secondly, especially in those sports that enjoy a dependence on absolute measurement of either time, distance, or weight to determine their results—such as track and field athletics, swimming, and weightlifting—the continuous urge to improve on previous high-water marks is most evident. It is practically a law of the Olympics that every record set in previous Games will be in great jeopardy when the next celebration takes place four years later.

This work has been again revised in the light of continuing research, including attention to the earlier Games. The leading authority is Erich Kamper whose *Enzyklopädie der Olympischen Spiele* (Römer, 1972) and *Lexikon der Olympischen Winter Spiele* (Union Verlag Stuttgart, 1964) should be recognized as the most complete text of Olympic results yet compiled of the first 18 Games.

NORRIS MCWHIRTER

GUINNESS
BOOK OF
OLYMPIC RECORDS

HISTORY OF THE OLYMPIC GAMES

1. THE ANCIENT GAMES

Few human institutions can even remotely approach the antiquity of the Olympic Games. Though precise records of the Ancient Games began only in 776 B.C., there is abundant evidence of their occasional celebration up to six centuries earlier. A date conservatively attributed to the Games at Olympia sponsored by Pelops is 1370 B.C. This date is, of course, subject to adjustment in the light of evidence of new archaeological techniques. All the signs are, however, that Olympic history spans some thirty-three centuries.

The Olympic Games faded away about the middle of the 9th Century B.C., but were reputedly revived by King Iphitos of Elis. During this period came the idea of a temporary truce among all the warring factions in Greece: the Olympic peace or *ekecheiria* was proclaimed to last for about three months before the Games (which themselves lasted for five days) and long enough after them for the competitors to enjoy a safe passage back to their homes.

The Games of 776 B.C.—the first of which there is an actual record of the name of a champion—seem to have consisted of merely one event: the stadium race (about 190 meters or 209 yd), won by Coroibos of Elis. But the Games rapidly expanded in scope—with longer races, plus a penthathlon of running, discus throwing (about 9lb *4 kg* in weight), long jump with weights, javelin throwing with a lever, and wrestling; as well as boxing and wrestling. Moreover, the Greeks had to compete soon against the challenge of both Sicilians and Cretans.

Even in those days each celebration had its hero. There were winners of what would now be called the sprint double, there were heats for the shorter events, and eventually women had their own Games.

A famous champion, Chionis, in the middle of the 7th century B.C. is credited by modern researchers to have long jumped, almost certainly with the aid of hand-held weights, *7 m 05 cm* or 23 feet 1½ in.

From this time onward, the names and feats of many champions are recorded and competitions in the fine arts were added.

The original prizes were only olive wreaths, but gradually the champions began to acquire valuable rewards and the Games became corrupted. The long Roll of Champions ends in A.D. 369, and in 393 the Emperor Theodosius decreed from Milan the end of the Olympic Games. So the Olympic torch went out for 1,503 summers.

2. THE MODERN (OR REVIVED) GAMES

The germ of the idea of reviving the Ancient Olympic Games was born in Germany. Johann Guts-Muths (1759–1839), the founder of

Pierre, Baron de Coubertin (1863–1937), the founder of the Olympic movement, stated the ideals of the Modern Olympic Games that have inspired succeeding generations.

the notable German gymnastics movement, put forward the idea. Ernst Curtius (1814–96) gave a lecture on the Ancient Games in Berlin on January 10, 1852. His researches aroused interest in Greece where the wealthy Major Evangelis Zappas organized the first "Pan-Hellenic Games," in 1859 watched by 20,000 spectators. These games—a purely national affair—were repeated in 1870, 1875, 1888 and 1889. They at least kindled a spark of interest in other countries.

It is Baron Pierre de Coubertin (1863–1937) of France, however, who is rightly styled the "Founder of the Modern Olympic Games." This wealthy young nobleman was commissioned by the French Government in 1889 to study physical culture throughout the civilized world. His inquiries produced a disquieting picture of feuding and dissension between sport and sport, nation and nation, and the already apparent commercial spirit in sport.

On November 25, 1892, de Coubertin in a lecture at the Sorbonne in Paris for the first time publicly advanced his conviction that there should be a modern revival of the Ancient Games. His lecture was received with an ovation. In 1893, de Coubertin convened an international conference at the Hall of Sciences at the Sorbonne from June 16–23, 1894. Thirteen countries sent representatives and 21 others sent messages of support. On the last day a resolution was passed that "sport competitions should be held every fourth year on the lines of the Greek Olympic Games and every nation should be invited to participate."

De Coubertin envisaged the first Games being in Paris at the beginning of the century, but a Greek motion was passed giving the Greeks the privilege of holding the First Celebration at Athens in 1896. Accordingly, the International Olympic Committee (IOC)—then 12 strong—was formed.

1896—The Ist Games at Athens

On April 6, after a gap of 1,503 years 80,000 Athenians witnessed the revival of the Olympics.

Despite the support of 34 nations at the Paris Conference only 13 sent representatives to Athens. The white marble stadium was a splendid sight, but too long and narrow for track events. The small American team won 9 out of the 12 track and field events, while the Germans dominated the gymnastics, and the French the cycling. The Greeks became depressed as the titles, even those which they regarded as their national specialties, such as the discus throw, were won by foreigners. Happily, the last event—the Marathon—(24 miles 1503 yd *40 km*) was dramatically won by Spyridon Louis, a post office messenger from Marusi near Athens, one of 21 Greek starters.

1900—The IInd Games at Paris

It was feared that the Second Games would rival the World Exhibition in Paris in the same year, so de Coubertin was subdued and the Games were allowed to be nothing more than a sideshow. Another factor that reduced interest was that the Games in the Bois de Boulogne, Paris, were spread over more than five months. Despite these drawbacks, the standards shot up and quite a few world best performances were set. The hero of the Games was Alvin Kraenzlein (U.S.A.) who won the 60 meters, 100 meters hurdles, 200 meters hurdles, and long jump.

1904—The IIIrd Games at St. Louis

Again the Olympics were organized as a mere sideshow to a World's Fair. Because of the distance and expense of travel, only eight European and five other countries were represented. Interest in the 85 Olympic events was minimal: the record crowd was 2,000.

Despite the rather crude facilities, mostly at Washington University, the competitive spirit and advancing skill of the contestants—the golden thread of the whole Olympic tapestry—was undiminished. There was a major scandal in the Marathon when an American (Lorz) got a clandestine 10 mile lift in a car in the middle section of the race and naturally arrived in the Stadium first. When the truth dawned, wild applause soon thinned to vituperative abuse and immediate expulsion.

1906—The Intercalated Games at Athens

These Games were to mark the tenth anniversary of the Ist Games at Athens in 1896.

They were in no sense unofficial—the International Olympic Committee sanctioned them—but they were unnumbered because they did not conform to the regular Olympic four-year cycle.

The Games were far more successful than the Exhibition sideshow type of Games in 1900 or 1904. Twenty nations were represented by 884 competitors. Great crowds, including a galaxy of royalty, thronged to the marble stadium.

There were 11 sports including 22 track and field, 16 shooting and 8 fencing events.

The individual hero was Paul H. Pilgrim (U.S.A.) who financed his own journey to Athens and won the 400 and 800 meters double.

Reginald Walker turned in a time under 11 seconds in the 100 meters event at the 1908 Games.

1908—The IVth Games at London

Italy was originally awarded the IVth Games but resigned them and London took on the job. With the White City Stadium that could hold 100,000, full royal patronage, a vast schedule, good publicity, and 2,056 competitors from 22 nations, the Olympics at last broke through as a world event.

The two most memorable incidents were in the track and field athletics, and both sadly involved disqualification. There was an unfortunate rumpus over the 400 meters final in which the U.S. runner Carpenter was disqualified for obstruction. His compatriots Robbins and Taylor then scratched in protest, so the only remaining competitor, Lt. Wyndham Halswell (GBR), had a 50.0 sec. walk-over for the gold medal.

The marathon from Windsor to the Stadium was watched by the then world's largest recorded sports crowd—an estimated 250,000 people. The leader, a frail looking little Italian, Dorando Pietri, tottered into the Stadium in the last stages of exhaustion. Harassed officials aided him when he fell for the fifth time, so he had to be disqualified for receiving aid, and the race went to the U.S. runner Johnny Hayes, who took the gold medal while Pietri got a gold cup from a sympathetic Queen Alexandra.

1912—The Vth Games at Stockholm

Following the success of the London Games, this celebration at Stockholm confirmed and cemented worldwide interest in the Olympics. The number of participants rose to 2,546, drawn from 28 countries. The hero of the Games was the American Indian, Jim Thorpe, who won both the pentathlon and the decathlon. Thorpe was later discovered by the A.A.U. to have rather thoughtlessly transgressed their amateur rules by earlier acceptance of payment for some minor baseball appearances. Inevitably he was struck off the Roll of Champions and his two gold medals were re-awarded to his runners-up. But he was reinstated as an amateur in 1973 by the A.A.U. twenty years after his death. In 1982 the IOC pardoned him and the medals were presented to his family.

1916—The VIth Games, awarded to Berlin

Owing to the World War which developed following Germany's invasion of Belgium and part of France, in August, 1914, the Games inevitably had to be canceled.

1920—The VIIth Games at Antwerp

The Olympics were resumed at Antwerp but were without any representation from the defeated central European countries or the Russians, who remained absent until 1952. The Games were highly successful, with the Finns challenging even the Americans in the track events.

Forty years elapsed between the appearance of Czarist Russia's last Olympic team in 1912, shown above, and the first Soviet team in 1952.

1924—The VIIIth Games at Paris

The Olympic Games again leapt forward in growth—44 countries entered 3,092 competitors. The Finn, Paavo Nurmi, won 5 gold medals—for the 1,500 meters, 5,000 meters, 10,000 meters cross-country race (both team and individual), and the 3,000 meters team event. The American, Johnny Weissmuller, later to be the most famous of Hollywood's dynasty of Tarzans, won 3 gold medals for sprint swimming.

1928—The IXth Games at Amsterdam

At Amsterdam the Germans reappeared. Olympic medals tended to be more widely distributed among the nations. The Finns were again dominant in distance running, but this time Nurmi won only the 10,000 meters. Weissmuller won two more swimming gold medals. Women's events were successfully introduced in track and field with world records being set in all five events.

1932—The Xth Games at Los Angeles

Under the famous sunny California climatic conditions a profusion of Olympic and world records were set. Every single track and field Olympic record, except the long jump, was improved. America's black sprinters and jumpers excelled while the Japanese collected five gold medals in the men's swimming events. It was wrongly predicted that records made under these "freak California conditions" would remain unbroken for years.

1936—The XIth Games at Berlin

At Berlin the Nazi government of Germany disgracefully attempted to turn the Olympic movement into a propaganda vehicle for the glorification of their creed. The strong internationalism of the Games prevented complete subversion. The levels of performance in most events left many of the 1932 "super-records" well behind, against all prediction. The hero of the Games was the modest American Jesse Owens, who won the 100 meters, 200 meters, 4 × 100 meters relay, and the long jump. The Japanese (actually Korean) marathon runners (gold and bronze medals) and the Dutch women swimmers made a strong impression.

Paavo Nurmi, the Flying Finn, is the most successful medal winner in Olympic track and field history, with 9 gold and 3 silver medals in the 1920, 1924, and 1928 Games.

Jim Thorpe, the American Indian (USA), shown here in the pole vault, won the gold medal in the 1912 decathlon with 6,845 points, but was disqualified later when it was discovered that he had received $25 once for playing semipro baseball. In 1982, after 70 years, his medals (2 golds) were restored post-mortem.

1940–44—The XIIth Games, awarded to Tokyo and then Helsinki; the XIIIth Games awarded to London

Neither of these two celebrations could be held because of the World War. The 1940 Games were originally awarded to Tokyo but when the Japanese became involved in war with China, they were re-awarded to Helsinki. The 1944 Games were hopefully given to London but the war still had a year to run.

1948—The XIVth Games at London

London and the Wembley Stadium attracted 4,099 competitors from 59 countries. For the first time a woman became the Victrix Ludorum and Fanny Blankers-Koen, the mother of two children, won the 100 meters, 200 meters, 80 meter hurdles, and the 4 × 100 meters relay for the Netherlands. Other athletes who attracted great interest were Harrison Dillard (USA) in the 100 meters and 4 × 100 meters relay; Emil Zatopek (Czechoslovakia) in the 10,000 meters; Bob Mathias (USA) in the decathlon; and Willi Grut (Sweden) in the modern pentathlon.

1952—The XVth Games at Helsinki

Sixty-nine nations and 4,925 competitors came to the Finnish capital city, Helsinki (population 350,000) in 1952. The Games were notable for the reappearance of the Russians after an absence of 40 years. The undoubted heroes of the Games were the Zatopeks of Czechoslovakia. Emil won the unprecedented triple—the 5,000 meters, 10,000 meters, and the marathon—all in Olympic record time. On the day he won the 5,000 meters, his wife, Dana, won the women's javelin throwing title, also with an Olympic record.

1956—The XVIth Games at Melbourne

The Games were celebrated in the Southern Hemisphere for the first and so far only time. Inevitably, the difficulties of season, distances, and expense reduced the entries, but only slightly. The equestrian events had to be held separately in Stockholm because of rigid horse quarantine laws in Australia. Outstanding on the track was Vladimir Kuts (U.S.S.R.) with a great 5,000 meters and 10,000 meters double victory; and the sprinters Bobby Joe Morrow (USA) and Betty Cuthbert of Australia, each of whom won three gold medals in the 100 meters, 200 meters and 4 × 100 meters relay. The Australians dominated the swimming, winning 8 out of 13 events.

1960—The XVIIth Games at Rome

Rome, which missed its opportunity of staging the Games in 1908, made a magnificent setting for the XVIIth Games. Eighty-three nations contributed 5,346 competitors to a fortnight of the most intense competition, for the most part in exceptionally hot conditions. Awards were widely spread with 23 countries gaining at least one gold medal. Outstanding achievements were the 1,500 meters world record by the Australian, Herbert Elliott, and the unexpected marathon success of the Ethiopian, Abebe Bikila. In the women's events, Wilma Rudolph, a black American runner, dominated the sprints and won three gold medals. The Australians in equestrianism and the Soviet girl gymnasts left a great impression.

1964—The XVIIIth Games at Tokyo

The first celebration in Asia was the organizational high-water mark of the Games, thanks to meticulous attention to detail by the Japanese. A conservative estimate is that the cost of all the public works and other expenses with a direct bearing on the Games was $560,000,000.

Vast crowds, undeterred by frequent rain, added atmosphere to a celebration in which Olympic records again fell wholesale, though, perhaps significantly, the number of world records set was fewer than in past Games. The highlights included the unique marathon double by Abebe Bikila (Ethiopia); a blazing finish in the 10,000 meters by Billy Mills (USA) with less than 1½ seconds between the three medalists; the four swimming gold medals won by Don Schollander (USA); and the third successive win in the 100 meters free-style by Dawn Fraser (Australia).

1968—XIXth Games at Mexico City

A record 5,530 competitors from one hundred and twelve nations did battle at nearly seven and a half thousand feet above sea level: these are the two salient figures to remember for the first Games in Latin America—the size and the height.

The technical organization in Mexico was excellent, while the brilliantly colorful fiesta atmosphere excused the few flaws in the ancillary arrangements for programs, information to the public and transport.

Because nobody dropped dead it did not mean that the altitude problem was insignificant. Just as predicted the performances in the "explosive" events—memorably Bob Beamon's incredible long jump of 29 ft 2½ in (8.90 m)—were records, while those involving more than three minutes' continuous effort were in some cases back to standards achieved as long ago as 1948.

Bob Mathias (USA) won the decathlon title in 1948 when he was only 17 years old. He successfully defended his crown at Helsinki in 1952—the only man ever to retain this championship.

Up 90 steps to the Olympic flame caldron in 1968 in Mexico City ran the first woman to take the final pass of the torch and to light the Olympic flame.

Olga Korbut was the darling of the spectators at the Munich Games in 1972. The elfin Russian gymnast won a silver and 3 gold medals.

1972—XXth Games at Munich

West Germany's massive effort to provide perfect and efficient Olympic conditions was marred by the murder of 11 members of the Israeli team by Palestinian terrorists on September 5th.

The great show stumbled, some commentators mistakenly predicted the death of the whole Olympic movement. After a stunned 24-hour pause the Games started off again and the entire program was fulfilled.

The Olympics, which attracted over 4,000 "media men" and an estimated 1,000,000,000 world television viewership, had become an irresistible stage for murderous protesters. Obviously the Olympics were becoming too large but the IOC was finding it very difficult to hold the program to its present size.

The heroine of the Games was the diminutive Russian gymnast, Olga Korbut, who was the darling of the crowds and the despair of the judges. The male hero was the swimmer Mark Spitz (USA) who won 7 gold medals each in a world record time.

In the stadium there were two sprint doubles by Valeriy Borzov (U.S.S.R.) and East Germany's Renate Stecher, but the greatest acclaim went rightly to Finland's Lasse Viren who won the 5,000 and 10,000 meters double. The almost traditional United States dominance suffered a partial eclipse and the termination of its famous pole-vault monopoly.

The Soviet team won ten more medals than the United States including 17 more golds than their traditional rivals. The efficiency of the U.S.S.R.'s deployment of their strength over the entire Olympic program certainly produced handsome dividends.

1976—XXIst Games at Montreal

The 1976 Games, the first in Canada, saw some substantial changes in the program but all attempts to reduce the number of events from the 1972 record of 195 were frustrated and in fact there were 198 Olympic titles open for competition.

The program changes included the elimination of the 50 kilometer walk, tandem cycling, slalom canoeing events, the free rifle event and three swimming events.

But the pruning was more than canceled by the introduction of women's basketball, four canoeing events over 500 meters, women's handball and no less than seven new rowing events, six of them for women.

The run-up to the Games was beset by financial, constructional and political disputes. The excessive costs of the facilities, the industrial problems, and then the withdrawal of 22 Third World countries, mainly African, seemed destined to diminish the Games. However, once they were underway, the quality of performance was exceptionally high and provided, in the petite form of gymnast Nadia Comaneci of Romania, and the powerful Cuban runner, Alberto Juantorena, two athletes whose deeds will far outlive a single Olympiad.

1980—XXIInd Games at Moscow

There had been only a little dissent in 1974 when the IOC voted by a substantial majority to award the 1980 Games to Moscow. Tsarist Russia had competed in 1900 and from 1906 to 1912. Athletes from Estonia and Latvia, which had been provinces of Russia prior to 1918 and were taken over by the Soviet Union in 1940, had competed independently from 1920 to 1936. The Soviet Union had entered the Games in force in 1952 and was now the second highest medal scorer of all time.

In December 1979 the Soviet Union invaded Afghanistan, and much of the non-Communist world, led by the United States, tried to impose a boycott on the Games—but not, it should be noted, on trade and other economic activity. Not all countries supported the boycott, although sports within those countries sometimes did. It is difficult to finalize a list of those who did not go to Moscow in support of the boycott, as a number of those previously included were unlikely to attend anyway for other, usually financial, reasons. The most reliable estimate is 45–50, of which the most important in sporting terms were the United States, the Federal Republic of (West) Germany, and Japan. When the Games were officially opened by Leonid Brezhnev, President of the U.S.S.R., there were eight first time entries to the Games, not including Zimbabwe which had previously been at the Olympics as Rhodesia.

Facilities, including the 103,000 capacity Lenin Stadium, were excellent and large crowds attended most sports. New competitions such as women's hockey, two extra judo classes, one extra weightlifting class and reintroduced events brought the total of gold medals available to a record 203 (barring ties).

The heroine of Montreal, Nadia Comaneci (ROM) returned but was not the force she had been, and the star of the gymnastics was a male, Alexandr Ditiatin (URS). By winning three golds, four silvers and one bronze he set a record for the most medals ever won by a competitor, of any sport, in a single Games. He also was awarded a maximum 10.00 in the horse vault, the first such score ever to a man in the Olympics. His teammate Nikolai Andrianov brought his total of medals to a men's record 15, comprising seven golds, five silvers and three bronze, in three Games. This total has only ever been exceeded in Olympic history by Larissa Latynina (URS), also a gymnast.

1984—XXIIIrd Games at Los Angeles

The IOC awarded the Games of 1984 to Los Angeles only after involved negotiations about the financial guarantees usually required from a host city. Various innovations to protect Los Angeles from a Montreal-like deficit proved highly successful. These included widespread sponsorship by private corporations. Television rights amounted to some $287 million, of which the major part came from the ABC network for US rights.

Against current thinking the program was expanded to 221 events, including an extra 12 events for women, while tennis and baseball were demonstration sports.

The Memorial Coliseum, main site of the 1932 Games, was refurbished, and many other venues, famous in their own right, were utilized. There were complaints that some of these venues were too far-flung, but the overall good weather and the enthusiasm, at times overwhelming, of the American crowds offset most problems. Smog and traffic congestion did not materialize to anything like the degree predicted. One unfortunate phenomenon, however, was the orgy of American chauvinism displayed—especially by the media. Attendances at all sports were quite remarkable with the highest single figure 101,799 for the final of the soccer tournament at the famed Rose Bowl. The one, albeit major, disaster of these Games was the last-minute boycott by the Soviet Union and other Socialist countries, although of 159 official invitations sent out, a record 140 countries accepted and competed—notably including Romania. Nevertheless standards in most sports were generally high.

Aided enormously by the absence of Soviet and East German opposition, the U.S. gained the lion's share of the medals. Leading the gold rush were sprinter/jumper Carl Lewis, who equaled the feat of Jesse Owens in 1936, with four golds, and another track star, Valerie Brisco-Hooks, and five swimmers who all won three golds each.

At the end of the Games the organizers reported a profit of $215 million.

1988—XXIVth Games at Seoul, Korea

The capital of Korea, Seoul, has one of the largest populations of any city on earth—an estimated 9,000,000. Nearly all facilities for the Games were in place by the end of 1986 when the Asian Games were held there. Most major installations were part of the sports complex on the bank of the Han River, including a 100,000-capacity stadium.

Once again the program was expanded, with the reintroduction of tennis (for the first time since 1924), the addition of table tennis, and the inclusion of extra events which brought the total to a record 237. Badminton, tae-kwon-do and women's judo were demonstration sports. American television companies offered incredible sums (up to $750 million) for the USA rights, provided that major sports finals take place during American prime-time viewing. That would have required that track and field finals take place 9:00–11:00 AM Korean time. This was opposed by the International Amateur Athletic Federation and the IOC, although some compromise was reached. Television income was still immense. Though there were threats of possible boycotts, the most tenacious problem was the claim of North Korea to host half of the Games. Against IOC rules, but with their blessing, some sports were offered to them, but they remained intransigent. Finally, they refused to attend and attempted to get Eastern bloc support. However, only six countries backed them; the most important being Cuba. Record totals of 8,465 competitors from 159 countries turned up.

Despite outstanding performances by Kristin Otto (GDR), who won six swimming gold medals, and sprinter Florence Griffith-Joyner (USA), with three golds and a silver, the focus of most attention was the winner of the men's 100 m title, Ben Johnson (CAN). Three days after destroying a superlative field in world record time it was disclosed that he had failed a drug test, and was disqualified. The repurcussions of that continued to affect sport for the next four years.

1992—XXVth Games at Barcelona, Spain

After intense 'politicking' the 1992 Summer Games were awarded to Barcelona, Spain in October 1986. The city, the birthplace of the current President of the IOC, Juan Antonio Samaranch, had been promised the Games in 1924 but Baron de Coubertin had changed his mind and opted for Paris. It was then suggested for 1936 but by then the spectre of civil war decided the IOC in favor of Berlin. The stadium intended for those Games, built in 1929 on Montjuic, has been completely refurbished, and will be the main venue. Most of the other venues are within the city limits, with only football (preliminary games), rowing, canoeing and road cycling sites at any great distance. Television revenue has already set a record with NBC paying $401 million for the American rights. Two new sports have been added, badminton and baseball, and there are also a number of additional events within existing sports. Thus the total number of medal events will be 257, an increase of 20 over Seoul. There will also be three demonstration sports; pelota Basque, taekwondo and rink hockey.

1996—XXVIth Games at Atlanta, USA

The somewhat surprising decision was made in September 1990 to award these Games—the 100th anniversary of the rebirth of the Modern Olympics—to Atlanta. The emotional favorite had been Athens, with other bids from Manchester, Toronto, Melbourne and Belgrade. It has been decided that demonstration sports will no longer be held, and that there may be some cutting back on the number of sports and events.

Official Olympic International
Abbreviations of Names of Countries

AFG — Afghanistan
AHO — Netherlands Antilles
ALB — Albania
ALG — Algeria
AND — Andorra
ANG — Angola
ANT — Antigua
ARG — Argentina
ARU — Aruba
ASA — American Samoa
AUS — Australia
AUT — Austria
BAH — Bahamas
BAN — Bangladesh
BAR — Barbados
BEL — Belgium
BEN — Benin
BER — Bermuda
BHU — Bhutan
BIR — Burma
BIZ — Belize
BOH — Bohemia
BOL — Bolivia
BOT — Botswana
BRA — Brazil
BRN — Bahrain
BRU — Brunei
BUL — Bulgaria
BUR — Burkina Faso
CAF — Central Africa
CAN — Canada
CAY — Cayman Islands
CEY — Ceylon (now Sri Lanka)
CGO — Congo
CHA — Chad
CHI — Chile
CHN — China
CIV — Ivory Coast
CMR — Cameroun
COK — Cook Islands
COL — Columbia
CRC — Costa Rica
CUB — Cuba
CYP — Cyprus
DAH — Dahomey
DEN — Denmark
DJI — Djibouti
DOM — Dominican Republic
ECU — Ecuador
EGY — Egypt
ESA — El Salvador
ESP — Spain
EST — Estonia
ETH — Ethiopia
FIJ — Fiji Islands
FIN — Finland
FRA — France
FRG — Federal Republic of Germany
GAB — Gabon
GAM — Gambia
GBR — United Kingdom
GDR — German Democratic Republic
GEQ — Equatorial Guinea
GER — Germany (prior to 1968)
GHA — Ghana

GRE — Greece
GRN — Grenada
GUA — Guatemala
GUI — Guinea
GUM — Guam
GUY — Guyana
HAI — Haiti
HBR — British Honduras (now BIZ)
HKG — Hong Kong
HOL — Netherlands
HON — Honduras
HUN — Hungary
INA — Indonesia
IND — India
IRL — Ireland
IRN — Iran
IRQ — Iraq
ISL — Iceland
ISR — Israel
ISV — Virgin Islands
ITA — Italy
IVB — British Virgin Islands
JAM — Jamaica
JOR — Jordan
JPN — Japan
KEN — Kenya
KHM — Cambodia
KOR — Korea
KSA — Saudi Arabia
KUW — Kuwait
LAO — Laos
LAT — Latvia
LBA — Libya
LBR — Liberia
LES — Lesotho
LIB — Lebanon
LIE — Liechtenstein
LIT — Lithuania
LUX — Luxembourg
MAD — Madagascar
MAL — Malaysia
MAR — Morocco
MAW — Malawi
MDV — Maldives
MEX — Mexico
MGL — Mongolia
MLI — Mali
MLT — Malta
MON — Monaco
MOZ — Mozambique
MRI — Mauritius
MTN — Mauritania
NCA — Nicaragua
NEP — Nepal
NGR — Nigeria
NGU — Papua New Guinea
NIG — Niger
NOR — Norway
NZL — New Zealand
OMA — Oman
PAK — Pakistan
PAN — Panama
PAR — Paraguay
PER — Peru
PHI — Philippines

POL — Poland
POR — Portugal
PRK — Dem. People's Rep. of Korea
PUR — Puerto Rico
QAT — Qatar
RHO — Rhodesia (now Zimbabwe)
ROM — Romania
RWA — Rwanda
SAF — South Africa
SAM — Western Samoa
SEN — Senegal
SEY — Seychelles
SIN — Singapore
SLE — Sierra Leone
SMR — San Marino
SOL — Solomon Islands
SOM — Somali Republic
SRI — Sri Lanka
SUD — Sudan
SUI — Switzerland
SUR — Surinam
SWE — Sweden
SWZ — Swaziland
SYR — Syria
TAN — Tanzania

TCH — Czechoslovakia
THA — Thailand
TOG — Togo
TON — Tonga
TPE — Taiwan
TRI — Trinidad and Tobago
TUN — Tunisia
TUR — Turkey
UAE — United Arab Emirates
UGA — Uganda
URS — U.S.S.R.
URU — Uruguay
USA — United States of America
VAN — Vanuatu
VEN — Venezuela
VIE — Vietnam
VIN — St Vincent
VOL — Upper Volta
YAR — Yemen Arab Republic
YMD — Yemen Democratic Republic
YUG — Yugoslavia
ZAI — Zaire
ZAM — Zambia
ZIM — Zimbabwe

ROLL OF OLYMPIC MEDAL WINNERS SINCE 1896 IN THE 25 CURRENT SPORTS

*throughout indicates an Olympic record or best performance.
d.n.a. indicates data not available.

1. Archery

MEN'S DOUBLE F.I.T.A. ROUND

(2 × 36 arrows at 90, 70, 50 and 30 meters. Possible is 2,880 points.)
In 1988 medals were decided by the scores in the final round of 36 arrows

	GOLD	SILVER	BRONZE
1972	John C. Williams (USA) 2,528	Gunnar Jarvil (SWE) 2,481	Kyoesti Laasonen (FIN) 2,467
1976	Darrell Pace (USA) 2,571	Hiroshi Michinaga (JPN) 2,502	Giancarlo Ferrari (ITA) 2,495
1980	Tomi Polkolainen (FIN) 2,455	Boris Isachenko (URS) 2,452	Giancarlo Ferrari (ITA) 2,449
1984	Darrell Pace (USA) 2,616*	Richard McKinney (USA) 2,564	Hiroshi Yamamoto (JPN) 2,563
1988	Jay Barrs (USA) 338 (2,605)	Park Sung-Soo (KOR) 336 (2,614)	Vladimir Yecheyev (URS) 335 (2,600)

WOMEN'S DOUBLE F.I.T.A. ROUND

(2 × 36 arrows at 70, 60, 50 and 30 meters. Possible is 2,880 points)

1972	Doreen Wilbur (USA) 2,424	Irena Szydlwska (POL) 2,407	Emma Gapchenko (URS) 2,403
1976	Luann Ryon (USA) 2,499	Valentina Kovpan (URS) 2,460	Zebiniso Rustamova (URS) 2,407
1980	Keto Losaberidze (URS) 2,491	Natalya Butuzova (URS) 2,477	Paivi Meriluoto (FIN) 2,449
1984	Seo Hyang-Soon (KOR) 2,568	Li Lingjuan (CHN) 2,559	Kim Jin-Ho (KOR) 2,555
1988	Kim Soo-Nyung (KOR) 344 (2,683*)	Wang Hee-Kyung (KOR) 332 (2,612)	Yung Young-Sook (KOR) 327 (2,603)

MEN'S TEAM

1988	Korea	United States	Great Britain

WOMEN'S TEAM

	GOLD	SILVER	BRONZE
1988	Korea	Indonesia	United States

(Archery was included in the Games of 1900, 1904, 1908 and 1920. But none of the events in those celebrations compare with the championship events of 1972–88.)

---

2. Badminton

A new Olympic sport introduced in 1992. It was a demonstration sport in 1972.

---

3. Baseball

A new Olympic sport introduced in 1992. It has been a demonstration sport on six occasions—1912, 1936, 1956, 1964, 1984 and 1988.

---

4. Basketball (Men)

1896–1932 Event not held[1]

1936 UNITED STATES	CANADA	MEXICO
Francis Johnson	James Stewart	Carlos Borja Morco
Carl S. Knowles	Jan Allison	Victor H. Borja Morco
Joe Fortenberry	Charles Chapman	Luis I. de la Vega Leija
William Wheatly	Malcolm Wiseman	José Pamplona
Jack W. Ragland	Gordon Aitchison	Lecuanda
Ralph Bishop	Douglas Peden	Rodolfo Choperanna
Carl Shy	Arthur Chapman	Irizarri
Duane A. Swanson	Irving Meretsky	Jesus Olmos Moreno
Samuel Balter	Edward J. Dawson	Raul Fernández Robert
John H. Gibbons		Greer Skousen
Frank J. Lubin		Spilsbury
Arthur O. Mollner		Francisco Martinez
Donald A. Piper		Cordero
Willard Schmidt		Silvio Hernandez del
		Valle
		Andrés Gómez
		Domingues

---

[1] There were basketball competitions in the 1904 and 1928 Games, but they were only demonstration events.

Action in the 1948 basketball finals between the United States (in white) and France. From the introduction of the sport in the Olympic program in 1936 to the disputed title of 1972, the USA never lost a single Olympic match.

	GOLD	SILVER	BRONZE
1948	**UNITED STATES**	**FRANCE**	**BRAZIL**
	Clifford Barker	André Barrais	Zenny de Azevedo
	Donald Barksdale	Michel Bonnevie	João F. Braz
	Ralph Beard	André Buffière	Marcus V. Dias
	Louis Beck	René Chocat	Alfonso A. Evora
	Vincent Boryla	René Dérency	Ruy de Freitas
	Gordon Carpenter	Maurice Desaymonnet	Alexandre Gemignani
	Alexander Groza	André Even	Alberto Marson
	Wallace Jones	Fernand Guillou	Alfredo R. da Mota
	Robert Kurland	Maurice Girardot	Nilton P. de Oliveira
	Raymond Lumpp	Raymond Offner	Massinet Sorcinelli
	Robert C. Pitts	Jacques Perrier	
	Jesse Renick	Yvan Quénin	
	R. Jackie Robinson	Lucien Rebuffic	
	Kenneth Rollins	Pierre Thiolon	
1952	**UNITED STATES**	**U.S.S.R.**	**URUGUAY**
	Charles Hoag	Viktor Vlassov	Martin Acosta y Lara
	William Hougland	Styapas Butautas	Enrique Boliño
	John Keller	Yvan Lysov	Victorio Cieslinkas
	M. Dean Kelley	Kazis Petkyavitschus	Héctor Costa
	Robert Kenney	Nodar Dzhordzhikiya	Nelson Demarco
	William Lienhard	Anatoliy Konyev	Héctor Garcia Otero
	Clyde Lovelette	Otar Korkiya	Tabaré Larre Borges
	Marcus Frieberger	Ilmar Kullam	Adesio Lombardo
	V. Wayne Glasgow	Yuriy Ozerov	Roberto Lovera
	Frank McCabe	Aleksandr Moiseyev	Sergio Matto
	Daniel Pippin	Heino Kruus	Wilfredo Pelaez
	Howard Williams	Yustinas Lagunavichus	Carlos Roselló
	Ronald Bontemps	Maigonis Valdmanis	
	Robert Kurland	Stassis Stonkus	

GOLD	SILVER	BRONZE
1956 UNITED STATES	**U.S.S.R.**	**URUGUAY**
Carl C. Cain	Valdis Muizhnieks	Carlos Blixen
William Hougland	Maigonis Valdmanis	Ramiro Cortes
K. C. Jones	Vladimir Torban	Héctor Costa
William Russell	Stassis Stonkus	Nelson Chelle
James P. Walsh	Kazis Petkyavitschus	Nelson Demarco
William Evans	Arkhadiy Bochkaryev	Héctor Garcia Otero
Burdette Haldorson	Yanis Kruminsch	Carlos Gonzalez
Ronald Tomsic	Mikhail Semyonov	Sergio Matto
Richard J. Boushka	Alguirdas Lauritenas	Oscar Moglia
Gilbert Ford	Yuriy Ozerov	Raúl Mera
Robert E. Jeangerard	Viktor Zoubkov	Ariel Olascoaga
Charles F. Darling	Mikhail Studenetskiy	Milton Scarón
1960 UNITED STATES	**U.S.S.R.**	**BRAZIL**
Jerry West	Valdis Muizhnieks	Zenny de Azevedo
Walter Bellamy	Maigonis Valdmanis	Amaury A. Pasos
Robert Boozer	Tsezars Ozers	Wlamir Marques
Terry Dischinger	Guram Minashvili	Moyses Blas
Burdette Haldorson	Viktor Zoubkov	Carlos Domingos
Darrall Imhoff	Vladimir Ugrekhelidze	Massoni
Allen Kelley	Yanis Kruminsch	Fernando Pereira
Lester Lane	Mikhail Semyonov	de Freitas
Jerry Lucas	Yuriy Korneyev	Carmo de Souza
Adrian Smith	Aleksandr Petrov	Jatyr E. Schall
Jay Arnette	Albert Valtin	Edson Bispo dos Santos
Oscar Robertson	Gennady Volnov	Antônio Salvador Sucar
		Waldyr Geraldo
		Boccardo
		Waldemar Blatkauskas
1964 UNITED STATES	**U.S.S.R.**	**BRAZIL**
Jim Barnes	Valdis Muizhnieks	Amaury A. Pasos
William Bradley	Nikolay Bagley	Wlamir Marques
Lawrence Brown	Armenak Alachachian	Ubiratan P. Maciel
Joe Caldwell	Aleksandr Travin	Carlos Domingos
Mel Counts	Vyacheslav Khrynin	Massoni
Richard Davies	Yanis Kruminsch	Friedrich Wilhelm Brauñ
Walter Hazzard	Levan Mosheshvili	Carmo de Souza
Lucius Jackson	Yuriy Korneyev	Jatyr E. Schall
John McCaffrey	Aleksandr Petrov	Edson Bispo dos Santos
Jeffrey Mullins	Gennady Volnov	Antônio Salvador Sucar
Jerry Shipp	Yaak Lipso	Victor Mirshawka
George Wilson	Yuris Kalninsh	Sergio de Toledo
		Machado
		José Edvar Simões
1968 UNITED STATES	**YUGOSLAVIA**	**U.S.S.R.**
Michael Barrett	Dragutin Čermac	Vladimir Andreyev
John Clawson	Krešimir Ćošič	Sergei Belov
Donald Dee	Vladimir Cvetković	Vadim Kapranov
Calvin Fowler	Ivo Daneu	Sergei Kovalenko
Spencer Haywood	Radivoje Korač	Anatoly Krikun
William Hoskett	Zoran Maroevič	Yaak Lipso
James King	Nikola Plečas	Anatoly Polivoda
Glynn Saulters	Trajko Rajkovič	Modestas Paulauskas
Charles Scott	Dragoslav Raznatovič	Zurab Sakandelidze
Michael Silliman	Petar Skansi	Yuri Selikhov
Kenneth Spain	Damir Šolman	Priit Tomson
Joseph White	Aljoša Zorga	Gennady Volnov

The 1972 USA basketball squad (dark uniforms), seen here against Brazil, lost to the U.S.S.R. in a highly controversial final match.

GOLD	SILVER	BRONZE
1972 U.S.S.R.	**UNITED STATES**	**CUBA**
Anatoli Polivoda	Kenneth Davis	Juan Domecq
Modestas Paulauskas	Douglas Collins	Ruperto Herrera
Zurab Sakandelidze	Thomas Henderson	Juan Roca
Alshan Sharmukhamedov	Michael Bantom	Pedro Chappe
	Robert Jones	José M. Alvarez
Aleksander Boloshev	Dwight Jones	Rafael Camizares
Ivan Edeshko	James Forbes	Conrado Perez
Sergei Belov	James Brewer	Miguel Calderon
Mishako Korkia	Tommy Burleson	Tomas Herrera
Yvan Dvorni	Thomas McMillen	Oscar Varona
Gennadi Volnov	Kevin Joyce	Alejandro Urgelles
Aleksander Belov	Ed Ratleff	Franklin Standard
Sergei Kovalenko	Henry Iba	Juan C. Ortega
Vladimir Kondrashin		
1976 UNITED STATES	**YUGOSLAVIA**	**U.S.S.R.**
Phil Ford	Blagoye Georgijevski	Vladimir Arzamaskov
Steve Sheppard	Dragan Kicanovic	Alexandr Salnikov
Adrian Dantley	Vinko Jelovac	Valeriy Miloserdov
Walter Davis	Rajko Zizic	Alshan Shamukhamedov
William Buckner	Zeljko Jerkov	Andrei Makeyev
Ernie Grunfeld	Andro Knego	Ivan Edeshko
Kenneth Carr	Zoran Slavnic	Sergei Belov
Scott May	Kresimir Cosic	Vladimir Tkachenko
Michel Armstrong	Damir Solman	Anatoli Mychkin
Thomas La Garde	Zarko Varajic	Mikhail Korkiya
Philip Hubbard	Drazen Dalipagic	Aleksander Belov
Mitchell Kupchak	Mirza Delibasic	Vladimir Zhigiliy
1980 YUGOSLAVIA	**ITALY**	**U.S.S.R.**
Andro Knego	Romeo Sacchetti	Stanislav Yeremin
Dragan Kicanovic	Roberto Brunamonti	Valeriy Miloserdov
Rajko Zizic	Michael Sylvester	Sergey Tarakanov
Minovil Nakic	Enrico Gilardi	Aleksandr Salnikov
Zeljko Jerkov	Fabizio Della Fiori	Andrei Lopatov
Branko Skroce	Marco Solfrini	Nikolai Deryugin
Zoran Slavnic	Marco Bonamico	Sergei Belov
Kresimir Cosic	Dino Meneghin	Vladimir Tkachenko
Ratko Radovanovic	Renato Villalta	Anatoliy Mishkin
Duje Krstulovic	Renzo Vecchaito	Sergey Yovaysha
Drazen Dalipagic	Pier Luigi Marzorati	Aleksandr Belostenny
Mirza Delibasic	Pietro Generali	Vladimir Shigili

GOLD	SILVER	BRONZE
1984 UNITED STATES	**SPAIN**	**YUGOSLAVIA**
Steve Alford	Jose Manuel Beiran	Drazen Petrovic
Leon Wood	Jose Luis Llorente	Aleksandar Petrovic
Patrick Ewing	Fernando Arcega	Nebojsa Zorkic
Vern Fleming	Jose Maria Margall	Rajko Zizic
Alvin Robertson	Andres Jiminez	Ian Sunara
Michael Jordan	Fernando Romay	Emir Mutapcic
Joseph Kleine	Fernando Martin	Saabit Hadzic
Jon Koncak	Juan Antonio Corbalan	Andro Knego
Wayman Tisdale	Ignacio Solozabal	Ratko Radovanovic
Chris Mullin	Juan Domingo de la	Mihovil Nakic-Vojnovic
Samuel Perkins	Cruz	Drazen Dalipagic
Jeffrey Turner	Juan Maria Lopez	Branko Vukicevic
	Juan Antonio San	
	Epifanio	

GOLD	SILVER	BRONZE
1988 U.S.S.R.	**YUGOSLAVIA**	**UNITED STATES**
Alexandr Volkov	Drazen Petrovic	Mitchell Richmond
Tiit Sokk	Zdravko Radulovic	Charles E. Smith
Savuras Tarakanov	Zoran Cutura	Vernell Coles
Raimondas	Toni Kukoc	Hersey Hawkins
Marchioullenis	Zarko Paspali	Jeff Grayer
Igor Migliniex	Stojan Vrankovic	Charles D. Smith
Valeriy Tikhonenko	Vlada Divac	Willie Anderson
Rimas Kourtinaitis	Franjo Arapovic	Stacey Augmon
Arvidas Sabonis	Juru Zdovc	Daniel Majerle
Viktor Pankrachkine	Dino Radja	Danny Manning
Valdemaras	Danko Cvjeticanin	Herman Reid
Khomitchious	Zelimir Obradovic	David Robinson
Alexandr Belostennyi		
Valeriy Goborov		

Basketball (Women)

GOLD	SILVER	BRONZE
1896–1972 Event not held		
1976 U.S.S.R.	**UNITED STATES**	**BULGARIA**
Angele Rupshene	Cindy Brogdon	Nadka Goltcheva
Tatyana Zakharova	Susan Rojcewicz	Penka Methodieva
Raisa Kurvyakova	Ann Meyers	Petkana Makaveyeva
Olga Barisheva	Lusia Harris	Snejana Mikhailova
Tatyana Ovetchkina	Nancy Dunkle	Krassim Guiourova
Nadyezhda Shuvayeva	Charlotte Lewis	Krassim Bogdanova
Iuliyana Semenova	Nancy Lieberman	Todorka Yardanova
Nadyezhda Zakharova	Gail Marquis	Diana Dilova
Nelli Feryabnikova	Patricia Roberts	Margari Shtarkelova
Olga Sukharnova	Mary Anne O'Connor	Maria Stoyanova
Tamara Daunene	Patricia Head	Guirgui Skerlatova
Natalia Klimova	Juliene Simpson	Penka Stoyanova

GOLD	SILVER	BRONZE
1980 U.S.S.R.	**BULGARIA**	**YUGOSLAVIA**
Angele Rupshene	Nadka Goltcheva	Vera Djuraskovic
Lubov Sharmay	Penka Methodieva	Mersada Berhirspahic
Vida Besselene	Petkana Makaveyeva	Jelica Komnenovic
Olga Korosteleva	Snejana Mikhailova	Mir Bjedov
Tatiana Ovechkina	Vania Dermenoyieva	Vukica Mitic
Nadezda Olkhova	Krassim Bogdanova	Sanja Ozegovic
Iuliana Semenova	Angelina Mikhailova	Sofija Pekic
Ludmila Rogozina	Diana Brainova	Marija Tonkovic
Nelly Feriabnikova	Evladia Slavcheva	Zorica Djurkovic
Olga Sukharnova	Kostadinka Radkova	Vesna Despotovic
Tatiana Nadyrova	Silvia Ghermanova	Biljana Majstorovic
Tatiana Ivinskaya	Penka Stoyanova	Jasmina Perazic

GOLD	SILVER	BRONZE
1984 UNITED STATES	KOREA	CHINA
Teresa Edwards	Aei-Young Choi	Yuefang Chen
Lea Henry	Yang-Gae Park	Xiaoqin Li
Lynette Woodard	Eun-Sook Kim	Yan Ba
Anne Donovan	Hyung-Sook Lee	Xiaobo Song
Cathy Boswell	Kyung-Hee Choi	Chen Qiu
Cheryl Miller	Mi-Ja Lee	Jun Wang
Janice Lawrence	Kyung-Ja Moon	Lijuan Xiu
Cindy Noble	Hwa-Soon Kim	Haixia Zheng
Kim Mulkey	Myung-Hee Jeong	Xuedi Cong
Denise Curry	Young-Hee Kim	Hui Zhang
Pamela McGee	Jung-A Sung	Qing Liu
Carol Menken-Schaudt	Chan-Sook Park	Yueqin Zhang
1988 UNITED STATES	YUGOSLAVIA	U.S.S.R.
Teresa Edwards	Stojna Vangelovska	Olga Evkova
Mary Ethridge	Mara Lakic	Irina Guerlits
Cynthia Brown	Zana Lelas	Olessia Barel
Anne Donovan	Eleonora Wild	Irina Soumnikova
Teresa Weatherspoon	Kornelia Kvesic	Olga Bouryakina
Bridgette Gordon	Damira Nakic	Irina Minkh
Victoria Bullett	Sludjana Golic	Alexandra Leonova
Andrea Lloyd	Polona Dornik	Yelena Khoudachova
Katrina McClain	Razija Mijanovic	Vitalia Touomaite
Jennifer Gillam	Vesna Bajkvisa	Olga Yakovleva
Cynthia Cooper	Andjelija Arbutina	Natalya Zassoulskaya
Suzanne McConnell	Bojana Milosevic	Galina Savitskaya

---

5. Boxing

From 1952 each losing semi-finalist was awarded a bronze medal.

LIGHT FLYWEIGHT
Weight up to *48 kg* 105.8 lb

1896–1964 Event not held		
1968 Francisco Rodriguez (VEN)	Yong-ju jee (KOR)	Harlan Marbley (USA)
		Hubert Skrzypczak (POL)
1972 Gyoergy Gedo (HUN)	U. Gil Kim (PRK)	Ralph Evans (GBR)
		Enrique Rodriguez (ESP)
1976 Jorge Hernandez (CUB)	Byong Uk Li (PRK)	Payao Pooltarat (THA)
1980 Shamil Sabyrov (URS)	Hipolito Ramos (CUB)	Byong Uk Li (PRK)
		Ismail Moustafov (BUL)
1984 Paul Gonzales (USA)	Salvatore Todisco (ITA)	Keith Mwila (ZAM)
		Jose Marcelino Bolivar (VEN)
1988 Ivailo Hristov (BUL)	Michael Carbajal (USA)	Robert Isaszegi (HUN)
		Leopoldo Serantes (PHI)

FLYWEIGHT

From 1948 the weight limit has been *51 kg* 112½ lb. In 1904 it was 105 lb *47,6 kg*. From 1920–1936 it was 112 lb *50,8 kg*.

GOLD	SILVER	BRONZE
1896–1900 Event not held		
1904 George Finnegan (USA)	Miles Burke (USA)	d.n.a.
1906–1912 Event not held		
1920 Frank De Genaro (USA)	Anders Petersen (DEN)	William Cuthbertson (GBR)
1924 Fidel LaBarba (USA)	James McKenzie (GBR)	Raymond Fee (USA)
1928 Antal Kocsis (HUN)	Armand Appel (FRA)	Carlo Cavagnoli (ITA)
1932 István Énekes (HUN)	Francisco Cabañas (MEX)	Louis Salica (USA)
1936 Willi Kaiser (GER)	Gavino Matta (ITA)	Louis D. Laurie (USA)
1948 Pascual Perez (ARG)	Spartaco Bandinelli (ITA)	Soo-Ann Han (KOR)
1952 Nathan Brooks (USA)	Edgar Basel (GER)	Anatoliy Bulakov (URS) William Toweel (SAF)
1956 Terence Spinks (GBR)	Mircea Dobrescu (ROM)	John Caldwell (IRL) René Libeer (FRA)
1960 Gyula Török (HUN)	Sergey Sivko (URS)	Kiyoshi Tanabe (JPN) Abdelmoneim Elguindi (EGY)
1964 Fernando Atzori (ITA)	Artur Olech (POL)	Robert Carmody (USA) Stanislav Sorokin (URS)
1968 Ricardo Delgado (MEX)	Artur Olech (POL)	Servilio Oliveira (BRA) Leo Rwabwogo (UGA)
1972 Gheorghi Kostadinov (BUL)	Leo Rwabwogo (UGA)	Leszek Blazynski (POL) Douglas Rodriguez (CUB)

Willi Kaiser (GER), the winner of the flyweight championship at the Berlin Games in 1936, rests in his corner between rounds.

	GOLD	SILVER	BRONZE
1976	Leo Randolph (USA)	Ramon Duvalon (CUB)	Leszek Blazynski (POL) David Torosyan (URS)
1980	Petar Lessov (BUL)	Viktor Miroshnickenko (URS)	Hugh Russell (IRL) Janos Varadi (HUN)
1984	Steven McCrory (USA)	Redzep Redzerovski (YUG)	Eyup Can (TUR) Ibrahim Bilali (KEN)
1988	Kim Kwang-Sun (KOR)	Andreas Tews (GDR)	Mario Gonzalez (MEX) Timofey Skriabin (URS)

BANTAMWEIGHT

From 1948 the weight limit has been *54 kg* 119 lb. In 1904 it was 115 lb *52,16 kg*. In 1908 it was 116 lb *52,62 kg* From 1920 to 1936 118 lb *53,52 kg*.

	GOLD	SILVER	BRONZE
1896–1900	Event not held		
1904	Oliver L. Kirk (USA)	George Finnegan (USA)	d.n.a.
1906	Event not held		
1908	A. H. Thomas (GBR)	John Condon (GBR)	W. Webb (GBR)
1912	Event not held		
1920	Clarence Walker (SAF)	Christopher J. Graham (CAN)	James McKenzie (GBR)
1924	William Smith (SAF)	Salvatore Tripoli (USA)	Jean Ces (FRA)
1928	Vittorio Tamagnini (ITA)	John Daley (USA)	Harry Isaacs (SAF)
1932	Horace Gwynne (CAN)	Hans Ziglarski (GER)	José Villanueva (PHI)
1936	Ulderico Sergo (ITA)	Jack Wilson (USA)	Fidel Ortiz (MEX)
1948	Tibor Csik (HUN)	Giovanni B. Zuddas (ITA)	Juan Venegas (PUR)
1952	Pentti Hämäläinen (FIN)	John McNally (IRL)	Gennadiy Garbuzov (URS) Joon-Ho Kang (KOR)
1956	Wolfgang Behrendt (GER)	Soon-Chun Song (KOR)	Frederick Gilroy (IRL) Claudio Barrientos (CHI)
1960	Olyeg Grigoryev (URS)	Primo Zamparini (ITA)	Brunoh Bendig (POL) Oliver Taylor (AUS)
1964	Takao Sakurai (JPN)	Shin Cho Chung (KOR)	Juan Fabila Mendoza (MEX) Washington Rodriguez (URU)
1968	Valeriy Sokolov (URS)	Eridadi Mukwanga (UGA)	Eiji Morioka (JPN) Kyou-Chull Chang (KOR)

	GOLD	SILVER	BRONZE
1972	Orlando Martinez (CUB)	Alfonso Zamora (MEX)	George Turpin (GBR)
			Ricardo Carreras (USA)
1976	Yong Jo Gu (PRK)	Charles Mooney (USA)	Patrick Cowdell (GBR)
			Viktor Rybakov (URS)
1980	Juan Hernandez (CUB)	Bernardo Pinango (VEN)	Michael Anthony (GUY)
			Dumitru Cipere (ROM)
1984	Maurizio Stecca (ITA)	Hector Lopez (MEX)	Dale Walters (CAN)
			Pedro Nolasco (DOM)
1988	Kennedy McKinney (USA)	Alexandar Hristov (BUL)	Jorge Julio Rocha (COL)
			Phajol Moolsan (THA)

FEATHERWEIGHT

From 1952 the weight limit has been *57 kg* 126 lb. In 1904 it was 125 lb *56,70 kg*. From 1908 to 1936 it was 126 lb *57,15 kg*. In 1948 it was *58 kg* 127¾ lb.

	GOLD	SILVER	BRONZE
1896–1900	Event not held		
1904	Oliver L. Kirk (USA)	Frank Haller (USA)	d.n.a.
1906	Event not held		
1908	Richard Gunn (GBR)	C. W. Morris (GBR)	Hugh Roddin (GBR)
1912	Event not held		
1920	Paul Fritsch (FRA)	Jean Gachet (FRA)	Edoardo Garzena (ITA)
1924	John Fields (USA)	Joseph Salas (USA)	Pedro Quartucci (ARG)
1928	Lambertus van Klaveren (HOL)	Victor Peralta (ARG)	Harold Devine (USA)
1932	Carmelo Robledo (ARG)	Josef Schleinkofer (GER)	Carl Carlsson (SWE)
1936	Oscar Casanovas (ARG)	Charles Catterall (SAF)	Josef Miner (GER)
1948	Ernesto Formenti (ITA)	Denis Shepherd (SAF)	Aleksey Antkiewicz (POL)
1952	Jan Zachara (TCH)	Sergio Caprari (ITA)	Joseph Ventaja (FRA)
			Leonard Leisching (SAF)
1956	Vladimir Safronov (URS)	Thomas Nicholls (GBR)	Henryk Niedzwiedzki (POL)
			Pentti Hämäläinen (FIN)
1960	Francesco Musso (ITA)	Jerzy Adamski (POL)	William Meyers (SAF)
			Jorma Limmonen (FIN)
1964	Stanislav Stepashkin (URS)	Antony Villaneuva (PHI)	Charles Brown (USA)
			Heinz Schultz (GER)

	GOLD	SILVER	BRONZE
1968	Antonio Roldan (MEX)	Albert Robinson (USA)	Philip Waruinge (KEN) Ivan Michailov (BUL)
1972	Boris Kousnetsov (URS)	Philip Waruinge (KEN)	Clemente Rojas (COL) András Botos (HUN)
1976	Angel Herrera (CUB)	Richard Nowakowski (GDR)	Juan Paredes (MEX) Leszek Kosedowski (POL)
1980	Rudi Fink (GDR)	Adolfo Horta (CUB)	Viktor Rybakov (URS) Krzysztof Kosedowski (POL)
1984	Meldrick Taylor (USA)	Peter Konyegwachie (NGR)	Turgut Aykac (TUR) Omar Catari Peraza (VEN)
1988	Giovanni Parisi (ITA)	Daniel Dumitrescu (ROM)	Lee Jae-Hyuk (KOR) Abdelhak Achik (MAR)

LIGHTWEIGHT

From 1952 the weight has been *60 kg* 132 lb. In 1904 and from 1920 to 1936 it was 135 lb *61,24 kg*. In 1908 it was 140 lb *63,50 kg*. In 1948 it was *62 kg* 136½ lb.

	GOLD	SILVER	BRONZE
1896–1900	Event not held		
1904	Harry J. Spanger (USA)	James Eagan (USA)	Russel Van Horn (USA)
1906	Event not held		
1908	Frederick Grace (GBR)	Frederick Spiller (GBR)	H. H. Johnson (GBR)
1912	Event not held		
1920	Samuel Mosberg (USA)	Gotfred Johansen (DEN)	Clarence Newton (CAN)
1924	Hans Nielsen (DEN)	Alfredo Coppello (ARG)	Frederick Boylstein (USA)
1928	Carlo Orlandi (ITA)	Stephen M. Halaiko (USA)	Gunnar Berggren (SWE)
1932	Lawrence Stevens (SAF)	Thure Ahlqvist (SWE)	Nathan Bor (USA)
1936	Imre Harangi (HUN)	Nikolai Stepulov (EST)	Erik Agren (SWE)
1948	Gerald Dreyer (SAF)	Joseph Vissers (BEL)	Svend Wad (DEN)
1952	Aureliano Bolognesi (ITA)	Aleksey Antkiewicz (POL)	Gheorghe Fiat (ROM) Erkki Pakkanen (FIN)
1956	Richard McTaggart (GBR)	Harry Kurschat (GER)	Anthony Byrne (IRL) Anatoliy Lagetko (URS)
1960	Kazimierz Pazdzior (POL)	Sandro Lopopoli (ITA)	Richard McTaggart (GBR) Abel Laudonio (ARG)

GOLD	SILVER	BRONZE
1964 Józef Grudzien (POL)	Vellikton Barannikov (URS)	Ronald Harris (USA) James McCourt (IRL)
1968 Ronald Harris (USA)	Józef Grudzien (POL)	Calistrat Cutov (ROM) Zvonimir Vujin (YUG)
1972 Jan Szczepanski (POL)	László Orban (HUN)	Samuel Mbugua (KEN) Alfonso Perez (COL)
1976 Howard Davis (USA)	Simion Cutov (ROM)	Ace Rusevski (YUG) Vasiliy Solomin (URS)
1980 Angel Herrera (CUB)	Viktor Demianenko (URS)	Kazimierz Adach (POL) Richard Nowakowski (GDR)
1984 Pernell Whitaker (USA)	Luis Ortiz (PUR)	Martin Ebanga (CMR) Chun Chi-Sung (KOR)
1988 Andreas Zülow (GDR)	George Cramne (SWE)	Nerguy Enkhbat (MGL) Romallis Ellis (USA)

LIGHT-WELTERWEIGHT

Weight up to *63,5 kg* 140 lb.

GOLD	SILVER	BRONZE
1896–1948 Event not held		
1952 Charles Adkins (USA)	Viktor Mednov (URS)	Erkki Mallenius (FIN) Bruno Visintin (ITA)
1956 Vladimir Yengibaryan (URS)	Franco Nenci (ITA)	Henry Loubscher (SAF) Constantin Dumitrescu (ROM)
1960 Bohumil Nemeček (TCH)	Clement Quartey (GHA)	Quincy Daniels (USA) Marian Kasprzyk (POL)
1964 Jerzy Kulej (POL)	Yvgeniy Frolov (URS)	Eddie Blay (GHA) Habib Galhia (TUN)
1968 Jerzy Kulej (POL)	Enrique Regueiferos (CUB)	Arto Nilsson (FIN) James Wallington (USA)
1972 Ray Seales (USA)	Anghel Anghelov (BUL)	Zvonimir Vujin (YUG) Issaaka Daborg (NIG)
1976 Ray Leonard (USA)	Andres Aldama (CUB)	Vladimir Kolev (BUL) Kazimier Szczerba (POL)
1980 Patrizio Oliva (ITA)	Serik Konakbaev (URS)	Anthony Willis (GBR) Jose Aguilar (CUB)

GOLD	SILVER	BRONZE
1984 Jerry Page (USA)	Dhawee Umponmaha (THA)	Mircea Fulger (ROM) Mirko Puzovic (YUG)
1988 Vyacheslav Janovski (URS)	Grahame Cheney (USA)	Lars Myrberg (SWE) Reiner Gies (FRG)

WELTERWEIGHT

From 1948 the weight limit has been *67 kg* 148 lb. In 1904 it was 143¾ lb *65,27 kg*. From 1920 to 1936 it was 147 lb *66,68* kg.

GOLD	SILVER	BRONZE
1896–1900 Event not held		
1904 Albert Young (USA)	Harry J. Spanger (USA)	Joseph Lydon (USA)
1906–1912 Event not held		
1920 Albert Schneider (CAN)	Alexander Ireland (GBR)	Frederick Colberg (USA)
1924 Jean Delarge (BEL)	Héctor Mendez (ARG)	Douglas Lewis (CAN)
1928 Edward Morgan (NZL)	Raul Landini (ARG)	Raymond Smillie (CAN)
1932 Edward Flynn (USA)	Erich Campe (GER)	Bruno Ahlberg (FIN)
1936 Sten Suvio (FIN)	Michael Murach (GER)	Gerhard Petersen (DEN)
1948 Julius Torma (TCH)	Horace Herring (USA)	Alessandro D'Ottavio (ITA)
1952 Zygmunt Chychla (POL)	Sergey Schtscherbakov (URS)	Victor Jörgensen (DEN) Günther Heidemann (GER)
1956 Nicholae Linca (ROM)	Frederick Tiedt (IRL)	Kevin J. Hogarth (AUS) Nicholas Gargano (GBR)
1960 Giovanni Benvenuti (ITA)	Yuriy Radonyak (URS)	Leszek Drogosz (POL) James Lloyd (GBR)
1964 Marian Kasprzyk (POL)	Ritschardas Tamulis (URS)	Pertti Purhonen (FIN) Silvano Bertini (ITA)
1968 Manfred Wolke (GDR)	Joseph Bessala (CMR)	Vladimir Musalinov (URS) Mario Guilloti (ARG)
1972 Emilio Correa (CUB)	Janos Kajdi (HUN)	Dick T. Murunga (KEN) Jesse Valdez (USA)
1976 Jochen Bachfeld (GDR)	Pedro J. Gamarro (VEN)	Reinhard Skricek (FRG) Victor Zilberman (ROM)
1980 Andres Aldama (CUB)	John Mugabi (UGA)	Karl-Heinz Kruger (GDR) Kazimierz Szcezerba (POL)

	GOLD	SILVER	BRONZE
1984	Mark Breland (USA)	An Young-Su (KOR)	Joni Nyman (FIN) Luciano Bruno (ITA)
1988	Robert Wanglia (KEN)	Laurent Boudouani (FRA)	Jan Dydak (POL) Kenneth Gould (USA)

LIGHT-MIDDLEWEIGHT

Weight up to *71 kg* 157 lb.

	GOLD	SILVER	BRONZE
1896–1948 Event not held			
1952	László Papp (HUN)	Theunis van Schalkwyk (SAF)	Boris Tishin (URS) Eladio Herrera (ARG)
1956	László Papp (HUN)	José Torres (USA)	John McCormack (GBR) Zbigniew Pietrzykowski (POL)
1960	Wilbert McClure (USA)	Carmelo Bossi (ITA)	Boris Lagutin (URS) William Fisher (GBR)
1964	Boris Lagutin (URS)	Josef Gonzales (FRA)	Nojim Maiyegun (NGR) Jozef Grzesiak (POL)
1968	Boris Lagutin (URS)	Rolando Garbey (CUB)	John Baldwin (USA) Günther Meier (GER)
1972	Dieter Kottysch (FRG)	Wieslaw Rudkowski (POL)	Alan Minter (GBR) Peter Tiepold (GDR)
1976	Jerzy Rybicki (POL)	Tadija Kacar (YUG)	Rolando Garbey (CUB) Victor Savchenko (URS)
1980	Armando Martinez (CUB)	Aleksandr Koshkin (URS)	Jan Franek (TCH) Detlef Kastner (GDR)
1984	Frank Tate (USA)	Shawn O'Sullivan (CAN)	Manfred Zielonka (FRG) Christophe Tiozzo (FRA)
1988	Park Si-Hun (KOR)	Roy Jones (USA)	Richard Woodhall (GBR) Raymond Downey (CAN)

MIDDLEWEIGHT

From 1952 the weight limit has been *75 kg* 165 lb. From 1904 to 1908 it was 158 lb *71,68 kg*. From 1920 to 1936 it was 160 lb *72,57 kg*. In 1948 it was *73 kg* 161 lb.

GOLD	SILVER	BRONZE
1896–1900 Event not held		
1904 Charles Mayer (USA)	Benjamin Spradley (USA)	d.n.a.
1906 Event not held		
1908 John Douglas (GBR)	Reginald Baker (AUS/NZL)	W. Philo (GBR)
1912 Event not held		
1920 Harry W. Mallin (GBR)	Georges A. Prud'homme (CAN)	Moe H. Herscovitch (CAN)
1924 Harry W. Mallin (GBR)	John Elliott (GBR)	Joseph Beecken (BEL)
1928 Piero Toscani (ITA)	Jan Hermánek (TCH)	Léonard Steyaert (BEL)
1932 Carmen Barth (USA)	Amado Azar (ARG)	Ernest Pierce (SAF)
1936 Jean Despeaux (FRA)	Henry Tiller (NOR)	Raúl Villareal (ARG)
1948 László Papp (HUN)	John Wright (GBR)	Ivano Fontana (ITA)
1952 Floyd Patterson (USA)	Vasile Tita (ROM)	Boris Nikolov (BUL) Stig Sjolin (SWE)
1956 Genadiy Schatkov (URS)	Ramón Tapia (CHI)	Gilbert Chapron (FRA) Victor Zalazar (ARG)
1960 Edward Crook (USA)	Tadeusz Walasek (POL)	Iona Monea (ROM) Evgeniy Feofanov (URS)
1964 Valeriy Popentschenko (URS)	Emil Schultz (GER)	Franco Valle (ITA) Tadeusz Walasek (POL)

Laszlo Papp (HUN), a southpaw, is the first of two boxers to win three gold medals. He took the middleweight title in 1948, and the light-middleweight title in 1952 and 1956.

GOLD	SILVER	BRONZE
1968 Christopher Finnegan (GBR)	Aleksey Kisselyov (URS)	Agustin Zaragoza (MEX) Alfred Jones (USA)
1972 Viatcheslav Lemechev (URS)	Reima Virtanen (FIN)	Prince Amartey (GHA) Marvin Johnson (USA)
1976 Michael Spinks (USA)	Rufat Riskiev (URS)	Alec Nastac (ROM) Luis Martinez (CUB)
1980 Jose Gomez (CUB)	Viktor Savchenko (URS)	Valentin Silaghi (ROM) Jerzy Rybicki (POL)
1984 Shin Joon-Sup (KOR)	Virgil Hill (USA)	Mohamed Zaoui (ALG) Aristides Gonzalez (PUR)
1988 Henry Maske (GDR)	Egerton Marcus (CAN)	Chris Sande (KEN) Hussain Shah Syed (PAK)

The future professional champion Floyd Patterson (USA) captured the middleweight title at Helsinki in 1952.

LIGHT-HEAVYWEIGHT

From 1952 the weight limit has been *81 kg* 178½ lb. From 1920 to 1936 it was 175 lb. *79,38 kg.* In 1948 it was *80 kg* 176¼ lb.

GOLD	SILVER	BRONZE
1896–1912 Event not held		
1920 Edward Eagen (USA)	Sverre Sörsdal (NOR)	H. Franks (GBR)
1924 Harry Mitchell (GBR)	Thyge Petersen (DEN)	Sverre Sörsdal (NOR)
1928 Victor Avendaño (ARG)	Ernst Pistulla (GER)	Karel L. Miljon (HOL)
1932 David Carstens (SAF)	Gino Rossi (ITA)	Peter Jörgensen (DEN)
1936 Roger Michelot (FRA)	Richard Vogt (GER)	Francisco Risiglione (ARG)
1948 George Hunter (SAF)	Donald Scott (GBR)	Maurio Cia (ARG)
1952 Norvel Lee (USA)	Antonio Pacenza (ARG)	Anotiliy Perov (URS) Harri Siljander (FIN)
1956 James F. Boyd (USA)	Gheorghe Negrea (ROM)	Carlos Lucas (CHI) Romualdas Murauskas (URS)
1960 Cassius Clay (USA)	Zbigniew Pietrzykowski (POL)	Anthony Madigan (AUS) Giulio Saraudi (ITA)
1964 Cosimo Pinto (ITA)	Aleksey Kisselyov (URS)	Aleksandar Nikolov (BUL) Zbigniew Pietrzykowski (POL)

Cassius M. Clay (USA), then an 18-year-old schoolboy, and later three-time heavyweight champion of the world, is shown on the way to his 1960 Olympic lightheavyweight gold medal, bouncing a right off the head of Tony Madigan (AUS), the bronze-medal winner.

	GOLD	SILVER	BRONZE
1968	Dan Poznyak (URS)	Ion Monea (ROM)	Georgy Stankov (BUL) Stanislav Dragan (POL)
1972	Mate Parlov (YUG)	Gilberto Carrillo (CUB)	Isaac Ikhouria (NGR) Janusz Gortat (POL)
1976	Leon Spinks (USA)	Sixto Soria (CUB)	Costica Dafinoiu (ROM) Janusz Gortat (POL)
1980	Slobodan Kacar (YUG)	Pawel Skrzecz (POL)	Herbert Bauch (GDR) Ricardo Rojas (CUB)
1984	Anton Josipovic (YUG)	Kevin Barry (NZL)	Mustapha Moussa (ALG) Evander Holyfield (USA)
1988	Andrew Maynard (USA)	Nourmagomed Chanavazov (URS)	Damor Skaro (YUG) Henryk Petrich (POL)

HEAVYWEIGHT

From 1984 the weight limit has been *91 kg* 200½ lb. From 1952 to 1980 the class was for those over *81 kg* 178½ lb. From 1904 to 1908 it was over 158 lb *71,67 kg*. From 1920 to 1936 it was over 175 lb *79,38 kg*. In 1948 it was over *80 kg* 176¼ lb.

	GOLD	SILVER	BRONZE
1896–1900	Event not held		
1904	Samuel Berger (USA)	Charles Mayer (USA)	d.n.a.
1906	Event not held		
1908	A. L. Oldhan (GBR)	S. C. H. Evans (GBR)	Frederick Parks (GBR)
1912	Event not held		
1920	Ronald Rawson (GBR)	Sören Petersen (DEN)	Xavier Eluère (FRA)
1924	Otto von Porat (NOR)	Sören Petersen (DEN)	Alfredo Porzio (ARG)
1928	Arturo Rodriguez Jurado (ARG)	Nils Ramm (SWE)	M. Jacob Michaelsen (DEN)
1932	Santiago Lovell (ARG)	Luigi Rovati (ITA)	Frederick Feary (USA)
1936	Herbert Runge (GER)	Guillermo Lovell (ARG)	Erling Nilsen (NOR)
1948	Rafael Iglesias (ARG)	Gunnar Nilsson (SWE)	John Arthur (SAF)
1952	Hayes Edward Sanders (USA)	Ingemar Johansson (SWE)*	Andries Nieman (SAF) Ilkka Koski (FIN)
1956	T. Peter Rademacher (USA)	Lev Mukhin (URS)	Daniel Bekker (SAF) Giacomo Bozzano (ITA)
1960	Franco de Piccoli (ITA)	Daniel Bekker (SAF)	Josef Nemec (TCH) Günter Siegmund (GER)

---

*Medal awarded in October 1981 after initial disqualification

	GOLD	SILVER	BRONZE
1964	Joe Frazier (USA)	Hans Huber (GER)	Giuseppe Ros (ITA) Vadim Yemelyanov (URS)
1968	George Foreman (USA)	Ionas Tschepulis (URS)	Giorgio Bambini (ITA) Joaquin Rocha (MEX)
1972	Teofilo Stevenson (CUB)	Ion Alexe (ROM)	Peter Hussing (FRG) Hasse Thomsen (SWE)
1976	Teofilo Stevenson (CUB)	Mircea Simon (ROM)	Johnny Tate (USA) Clarence Hill (BER)
1980	Teofilo Stevenson (CUB)	Pyotr Zaev (URS)	Istvan Levai (HUN) Jurgen Fanghanel (GDR)
1984	Henry Tillman (USA)	Willie Dewit (CAN)	Angelo Musone (ITA) Arnold Vanderlijde (HOL)
1988	Lennox Lewis (CAN)	Riddick Bowe (USA)	Alexandr Mirochnitchenko (URS) Janusz Zarenkiewicz (POL)

Teofilo Stevenson (CUB) won the heavyweight title three times. No other heavyweight ever successfully defended the title even once.

SUPER-HEAVYWEIGHT

From 1984 the class has been for those over *91 kg* 200½ lb.

	GOLD	SILVER	BRONZE
1984	Tyrell Biggs (USA)	Francesco Damiani (ITA)	Robert Wells (GBR) Salihu Azis (YUG)
1988	Ray Mercer (USA)	Baik Hyun-Man (KOR)	Andrzej Golota (POL) Arnold Vanderlijde (HOL)

---

6. Canoeing (Men)

500 METERS KAYAK SINGLES (K-1)

1896–1972 Event not held

	GOLD	SILVER	BRONZE
1976	Vasile Diba (ROM) 1:46.41	Zoltan Szytanity (HUN) 1:46.95	Rudiger Helm (GDR) 1:48.30
1980	Vladimir Parfenovich (URS) 1:43.43	John Sumegi (AUS) 1:44.12	Vasile Diba (ROM) 1:44.90
1984	Ian Ferguson (NZL) 1:47.84	Lars-Erik Moberg (SWE) 1:48.18	Bernard Bregeon (FRA) 1:48.41
1988	Zsolt Gyulay (HUN) 1:44.82	Andreas Stähle (GDR) 1:46.38	Paul McDonald (NZL) 1:46.46

1,000 METERS KAYAK SINGLES (K-1)

1896–1932 Event not held

	GOLD	SILVER	BRONZE
1936	Gregor Hradetzky (AUT) 4:22.9	Helmut Cämmerer (GER) 4:25.6	Jacob Kraaier (HOL) 4:35.1
1948	Gert Fredriksson (SWE) 4:33.2	Johan F. Kobberup (DEN) 4:39.9	Henri Eberhardt (FRA) 4:41.4
1952	Gert Fredriksson (SWE) 4:07.9	Thorvald Strömberg (FIN) 4:09.7	Louis Gantois (FRA) 4:20.1
1956	Gert Fredriksson (SWE) 4:12.8	Igor Pissaryev (URS) 4:15.3	Lajos Kiss (HUN) 4:16.2
1960	Erik Hansen (DEN) 3:53.00	Imre Szöllösi (HUN) 3:54.02	Gert Fredriksson (SWE) 3:55.89
1964	Rolf Peterson (SWE) 3:57.13	Mihály Hesz (HUN) 3:57.28	Aurel Vernescu (ROM) 4:00.77
1968	Mihály Hesz (HUN) 4:02.63	Aleksandr Shaparenko (URS) 4:03.58	Erik Hansen (DEN) 4:04.39
1972	Aleksandr Shaparenko (URS) 3:48.06	Rolf Peterson (SWE) 3:48.35	Geza Csapo (HUN) 3:49.38
1976	Rudiger Helm (GDR) 3:48.20	Geza Csapo (HUN) 3:48.84	Vassile Diba (ROM) 3:49.65
1980	Rudiger Helm (GDR) 3:48.77	Alain Lebas (FRA) 3:50.20	Ion Birladeanu (ROM) 3:50.49
1984	Alan Thompson (NZL) 3:45.73	Milan Janic (YUG) 3:46.88	Greg Barton (USA) 3:47.38
1988	Greg Barton (USA) 3:55.27	Grant Davies (AUS) 3:55.28	Andre Wohllebe (GDR) 3:55.55

Nine canoes run head-to-head during one of the 1,000 meters K-2 preliminary heats at Munich in 1972.

500 METERS KAYAK PAIRS (K-2)

GOLD	SILVER	BRONZE
1896–1972 Event not held		
1976 EAST GERMANY 1:35.87	U.S.S.R. 1:36.81	RUMANIA 1:37.43
Joachim Mattern	Sergei Nagorny	Larion Serghei
Bernd Olbricht	Vladimir Romanovski	Policarp Malihin
1980 U.S.S.R. 1:32.38	SPAIN 1:33.65	EAST GERMANY 1:34.00
Vladimir Parfenovich	Herminio Menendez	Bernd Olbricht
Sergey Chukhrai	Guillermo Del Riego	Rudiger Helm
1984 NEW ZEALAND 1:34.21	SWEDEN 1:35.26	CANADA 1:35.41
Ian Ferguson	Per-Inge Bengtsson	Hugh Fisher
Paul MacDonald	Lars-Erik Moberg	Alwyn Morris
1988 NEW ZEALAND 1:33.98	USSR 1:34.15	HUNGARY 1:34.32
Ian Ferguson	Igor Nagayev	Attila Abraham
Paul McDonald	Viktor Denissov	Ferenc Csipes

1,000 METERS KAYAK PAIRS (K-2)

GOLD	SILVER	BRONZE
1896–1932 Event not held		
1936 AUSTRIA 4:03.8	GERMANY 4:08.9	NETHERLANDS 4:12.2
Adolf Kainz	Ewald Tilker	Nicolaas Tates
Alfons Dorfner	Fritz Bondroit	Willem van der Kroft
1948 SWEDEN 4:07.3	DENMARK 4:07.5	FINLAND 4:08.7
Hans Berglund	Ejvind Hansen	Thor Axelsson
Lennart Klingström	Bernhard Jensen	Nils Björklöf
1952 FINLAND 3:51.1	SWEDEN 3:51.1	AUSTRIA 3:51.4
Kurt Wires	Lars Glassér	Max Raub
Yrjö Hietanen	Ingemar Hedberg	Herbert Wiedermann

GOLD	SILVER	BRONZE
1956 GERMANY 3:49.6	U.S.S.R. 3:51.4	AUSTRIA 3:55.8
Michael Scheuer	Mikhail Kaaleste	Max Raub
Meinrad Miltenberger	Antoliy Demitkov	Herbert Wiedermann
1960 SWEDEN 3:34.7	HUNGARY 3:34.91	POLAND 3:37.34
Gert Fredriksson	András Szente	Stefan Kaplaniak
Sven-Olov Sjödelius	György Mészáros	Wladyslaw Zielinski
1964 SWEDEN 3:38.4	NETHERLANDS 3:39.30	GERMANY 3:40.69
Sven-Olov Sjödelius	Antonius Geurts	Heinz Buker
Nils Utterberg	Paul Hoekstra	Holger Zander
1968 U.S.S.R. 3:37.54	HUNGARY 3:38.44	AUSTRIA 3:40.71
Aleksandr Shaparenko	Csaba Giczi	Gerhard Seibold
Vladimir Morozov	István Timár	Gunther Pfaff
1972 U.S.S.R. 3:31.23	HUNGARY 3:32.00	POLAND 3:33.83
Nikolai Gorbachev	Jozsef Deme	Wladyslaw Szuszkiewicz
Viktor Kratassyuk	Janos Ratkai	Rafal Piszez
1976 U.S.S.R. 3:29.01	EAST GERMANY 3:29.33	HUNGARY 3:30.56
Sergei Nagorny	Joachim Mattern	Zoltan Bako
Vladimir Romanovski	Bernd Olbricht	Istvan Szabo
1980 U.S.S.R. 3:26.72	HUNGARY 3:28.49	SPAIN 3:28.66
Vladimir Perfenovich	Istvan Szabo	Luis Ramos-Misione
Sergey Chukhrai	Istvan Joos	Herminio Menendez
1984 CANADA 3:24.22	FRANCE 3:25.97	AUSTRALIA 3:26.80
Hugh Fisher	Bernard Bregeon	Terry Kent
Alwyn Morris	Patrick Lefoulon	Terry White
1988 USA 3:32.42	NEW ZEALAND 3:32.71	AUSTRALIA 3:33.76
Greg Barton	Ian Ferguson	Peter Foster
Norman Bellington	Paul McDonald	Kelvin Graham

1,000 METERS KAYAK FOURS (K-4)

GOLD	SILVER	BRONZE
1896–1960 Event not held		
1964 U.S.S.R. 3:14.67	GERMANY 3:15.39	ROMANIA 3:15.51
Nikolay Chuzhikov	Günther Perleberg	Simion Cuciuc
Anatoly Grishin	Bernhard Schulze	Atanase Sciotnic
Vyatscheslav Ionov	Friedhelm Wentzke	Mihai Turcas
Vladimir Morozov	Holger Zander	Aurel Vernescu
1968 NORWAY 3:14.38	ROMANIA 3:14.81	HUNGARY 3:15.10
Steinar Amundsen	Anton Calenic	Csaba Giczi
Egil W. Söby	Dimitrie Ivanov	István Timár
Tore Berger	Haralambie Ivanov	Imre Szöllösi
Jan Johansen	Mihai Turcas	István Csizmadia
1972 U.S.S.R. 3:14.02	ROMANIA 3:15.07	NORWAY 3:15.27
Yuri Filatov	Aurel Vernescu	Egil W. Söby
Yuri Stezenko	Mihai Zafiu	Steinar Amundsen
Vladimir Morozov	Roman Vartolomeu	Tore Berger
Valeri Didenko	Atanase Sciotnic	Jan Johansen
1976 U.S.S.R. 3:08.69	SPAIN 3:08.95	EAST GERMANY 3:10.76
Sergei Chuhray	Jose Celorrio	Peter Bischof
Aleksandr Degtiarev	Jose Diaz-Flor	Bernd Duvigneau
Yuri Filatov	Herminio Menendez	Rudiger Helm
Vladimir Morozov	Luis Misone	Jurgen Lehnert
1980 EAST GERMANY 3:13.76	ROMANIA 3:15.35	BULGARIA 3:15.46
Bernd Olbricht	Mihai Zafiu	Boleslaw Borissov
Bernd Duvigneau	Vasile Diba	Boshidar Milenkov
Rudiger Helm	Ion Geanta	Lazar Christov
Harald Marg	Esanu Nicusor	Ivan Manev

GOLD	SILVER	BRONZE
1984 **NEW ZEALAND** 3:02.28	**SWEDEN** 3:02.81	**FRANCE** 3:03.94
Grant Bramwell	Per-Inge Bengtsson	Francois Barouh
Ian Ferguson	Tommy Karls	Philippe Boccara
Paul MacDonald	Lars-Erik Moberg	Pascal Boucherit
Alan Thompson	Thomas Ohlsson	Didier Vavasseur
1988 **HUNGARY** 3:00.20	**USSR** 3:01.40	**EAST GERMANY** 3:02.37
Zsolt Gyulay	Alexandr Motouzenko	Kay Bluhm
Ferenc Csipes	Sergey Kirsanov	Andre Wohllebe
Sandor Hodosi	Igor Nagayev	Andreas Stähle
Attila Abraham	Viktor Denissov	Hans-Jörg Bliesener

500 METERS CANADIAN SINGLES (C-1)

1896–1972 Event not held		
1976 Aleksandr Rogov (URS) 1:59.23	John Wood (CAN) 1:59.58	Matija Ljubek (YUG) 1:59.60
1980 Sergei Postrekhin (URS) 1:53.37	Lubomir Lubenov (BUL) 1:53.49	Olaf Heukrodt (GDR) 1:54.38
1984 Larry Cain (CAN) 1:57.01	Henning Jakobsen (DEN) 1:58.45	Costica Olaru (ROM) 1:59.86
1988 Olaf Heukrodt (GDR) 1:56.42	Mikhail Slivinski (URS) 1:57.26	Martin Marinov (BUL) 1:57.27

1,000 METERS CANADIAN SINGLES (C-1)

1896–1932 Event not held		
1936 Francis Amyot (CAN) 5:32.1	Bohuslav Karlik (TCH) 5:36.9	Erich Koschik (GER) 5:39.0
1948 Josef Holeček (TCH) 5:42.0	Douglas Bennett (CAN) 5:53.3	Robert Boutigny (FRA) 5:55.9
1952 Josef Holeček (TCH) 4:56.3	János Parti (HUN) 5:03.6	Olavi Ojanperä (FIN) 5:08.5
1956 Leon Rotman (ROM) 5:05.3	István Hernek (HUN) 5:06.2	Gennadiy Bukharin (URS) 5:12.7
1960 János Parti (HUN) 4:33.93	Aleksandr Silayev (URS) 4:34.41	Leon Rotman (ROM) 4:35.87
1964 Jürgen Eschert (GER) 4:35.14	Andrei Igorov (ROM) 4:37.89	Yevgeny Penyayev (URS) 4:38.31
1968 Tibor Tatai (HUN) 4:36.14	Detlef Lewe (GER) 4:38.31	Vitaly Galkov (URS) 4:40.42
1972 Ivan Patzaichin (ROM) 4:08.94	Tamas Wichmann (HUN) 4:12.42	Detlef Lewe (FRG) 4:13.63
1976 Matija Ljubek (YUG) 4:09.51	Vasiliy Urchenko (URS) 4:12.57	Tamas Wichmann (HUN) 4:14.11
1980 Lubomir Lubenov (BUL) 4:12.38	Sergei Postrekhin (URS) 4:13.53	Eckhard Leue (GDR) 4:15.02
1984 Ulrich Eicke (FRG) 4:06.32	Larry Cain (CAN) 4:08.67	Henning Jakobsen (DEN) 4:09.51
1988 Ivan Klementyev (URS) 4:12.78	Jörg Schmidt (GDR) 4:15.83	Nikolay Boukhalov (URS) 4:18.94

500 METERS CANADIAN PAIRS (C-2)

1896–1972 Event not held		
1976 **U.S.S.R.** 1:45.81	**POLAND** 1:47.77	**HUNGARY** 1:48.35
Sergei Petrenko	Jerzy Opara	Tamas Buday
Aleksandr Vinogradov	Andrzej Gronowicz	Oszkar Frey
1980 **HUNGARY** 1:43.39	**ROMANIA** 1:44.12	**BULGARIA** 1:44.83
Laszlo Foltan	Ivan Patzaichin	Borislaw Ananiev
Istvan Vaskuti	Istvan Capusta	Nikolai Ilkov

The Rumanian pair, Patzaichin and Covaliov, winning the 1968 Canadian Pairs event on the artificial lake, Canal de Quemanco, which was also used for rowing.

	GOLD	SILVER	BRONZE
1984	YUGOSLAVIA 1:43.67	ROMANIA 1:45.68	SPAIN 1:47.71
	Matija Ljubek	Ivan Potzaichin	Enrique Miguez
	Mirko Nisovic	Toma Simionov	Narcisco Suarez
1988	USSR 1:41.77	POLAND 1:43.61	FRANCE 1:43.81
	Viktor Reneiski	Marek Dopierala	Philippe Renaud
	Nikolay Jouravski	Marek Lbik	Joel Bettin

1,000 METERS CANADIAN PAIRS (C-2)

1896–1932	Event not held		
1936	CZECHOSLOVAKIA 4:50.1	AUSTRIA 4:53.8	CANADA 4:56.7
	Vladimir Syrovátka	Rupert Weinstabl	Frank Saker
	Jan-Felix Brzák	Karl Proisl	Harvey Charters
1948	CZECHOSLOVAKIA 5:07.1	U.S.A. 5:08.2	FRANCE 5:15.2
	Jan-Felix Brzák	Stephen Lysak	Georges Dransart
	Bohumil Kudrna	Stephan Macknowski	Georges Gandil
1952	DENMARK 4:38.3	CZECHOSLOVAKIA 4:42.9	GERMANY 4:48.3
	Bent Peder Rasch	Jan-Felix Brzák	Egon Drews
	Finn Haunstoft	Bohumil Kudrna	Wilfried Soltau
1956	ROMANIA 4:47.4	U.S.S.R. 4:48.6	HUNGARY 4:54.3
	Alexe Dumitru	Pavel Kharin	Károly Wieland
	Simion Ismailciuc	Gratsian Botev	Ferenc Mohácsi
1960	U.S.S.R. 4:17.94	ITALY 4:20.77	HUNGARY 4:20.89
	Leonid Geyshtor	Aldo Dezi	Imre Farkas
	Sergey Makarenko	Francesco La Macchia	András Törö
1964	U.S.S.R. 4:04.64	FRANCE 4:06.52	DENMARK 4:07.48
	Andrey Khimich	Jean Boudehen	Peer N. Nielsen
	Stepan Oschepkov	Michel Chapuis	John Sorenson
1968	ROMANIA 4:07.18	HUNGARY 4:08.77	U.S.S.R. 4:11.30
	Ivan Patzaichin	Tamás Wichmann	Naum Prokupets
	Serghei Covaliov	Gyula Petrikovics	Mikhail Zamotin

	GOLD	SILVER	BRONZE
1972	U.S.S.R. 3:52.60	ROMANIA 3:52.63	BULGARIA 3:58.10
	Vlados Chessyunas	Ivan Patzaichin	Fedia Damianov
	Yuri Lobanov	Serghei Covaliov	Ivan Bourtchine
1976	U.S.S.R. 3:52.76	ROMANIA 3:54.28	HUNGARY 3:55.66
	Sergei Petrenko	Gheorghe Danielov	Tamas Buday
	Aleksandr Vinogradov	Gheorghe Simionov	Oszkar Frey
1980	ROMANIA 3:47.65	EAST GERMANY	U.S.S.R. 3:51.28
		3:49.93	
	Ivan Patzaichin	Olaf Heukrodt	Vasiliy Yurchenko
	Toma Simionov	Uwe Madeja	Yuriy Lobanov
1984	ROMANIA 3:40.60	YUGOSLAVIA 3:41.56	FRANCE 3:48.01
	Ivan Potzaichin	Matija Ljubek	Didier Hoyer
	Toma Simionov	Mirko Nisovic	Eric Renaud
1988	USSR 3:48.36	EAST GERMANY	POLAND 3:54.33
		3:51.44	
	Viktor Reneiski	Olaf Heukrodt	Marek Dopierala
	Nikolay Jouravski	Ingo Spelly	Marek Lbik

Canoeing (Women)

500 METERS KAYAK SINGLES (K-1)

	GOLD	SILVER	BRONZE
1896–1936	Event not held		
1948	Karen Hoff (DEN) 2:31.9	Alide Van de Anker-Doedans (HOL) 2:32.8	Fritzi Schwingl (AUT) 2:32.9
1952	Sylvi Saimo (FIN) 2:18.4	Gertrude Liebhart (AUT) 2:18.8	Nina Savina (URS) 2:21.6
1956	Elisaveta Dementyeva (URS) 2:18.9	Therese Zenz (GER) 2:19.6	Tove Söby (DEN) 2:22.3
1960	Antonina Seredina (URS) 2:08.08	Therese Zenz (GER) 2:08.22	Daniela Walkowiak (POL) 2:10.46
1964	Ludmila Khvedosyuk (URS) 2:12.87	Hilde Lauer (ROM) 2:15.35	Marcia Jones (USA) 2:15.68
1968	Ludmila Pinayeva-Khvedosyuk (URS) 2:11.09	Renate Breuer (GER) 2:12.71	Viorica Dumitru (ROM) 2:13.22
1972	Yulia Ryabchlinskaya (URS) 2:03.17	Mieke Jaapies (HOL) 2:04.03	Anna Pfeffer (HUN) 2:05.50
1976	Carola Zirzow (GDR) 2:01.05	Tatyana Korshunova (URS) 2:03.07	Klara Rajnai (HUN) 2:05.01
1980	Birgit Fischer (GDR) 1:57.96	Vania Checheva (BUL) 1:59.48	Antonina Melnikova 1:59.66
1984	Agneta Andersson (SWE) 1:58.72	Barbara Schuttpelz (FRG) 1:59.93	Annemiek Derckx (HOL) 2:00.11
1988	Ivana Guecheva (BUL) 1:55.19	Birgit Schmidt (GDR) 1:55.31	Isabela Dylewska (POL) 1:57.38

500 METERS KAYAK PAIRS (K-2)

	GOLD	SILVER	BRONZE
1896–1956	Event not held		
1960	U.S.S.R. 1:54.76	GERMANY 1:56.66	HUNGARY 1:58.22
	Maria Zhubina	Therese Zenz	Vilma Egresi
	Antonina Seredina	Ingrid Hartmann	Klára Fried-Bánfalvi
1964	GERMANY 1:56.95	UNITED STATES	ROMANIA 2:00.25
		1:59.16	
	Roswitha Esser	Francine Fox	Hilde Lauer
	Annemarie Zimmermann	Gloriane Perrier	Cornelia Sideri
1968	GERMANY 1:56.44	HUNGARY 1:58.60	U.S.S.R. 1:58.61
	Annemarie Zimmermann	Anna Pfeffer	Ludmila Pinayeva
	Roswitha Esser	Katalin Rosznyói	Antonina Seredina

GOLD	SILVER	BRONZE
1972 U.S.S.R. 1:53.50	EAST GERMANY 1:54.30	ROMANIA 1:55.01
Ludmila Pinayeva	Ilse Kaschube	Maria Nichiforov
Ekaterina Kuryshko	Petra Grabowsky	Viorica Dumitru
1976 U.S.S.R. 1:51.15	HUNGARY 1:51.69	EAST GERMANY 1:51.81
Nina Gopova	Anna Pfeffer	Barbel Koster
Galina Kreft	Klara Rajnai	Carola Zirzow
1980 EAST GERMANY 1:43.88	U.S.S.R. 1:46.91	HUNGARY 1:47.95
Carsta Genauss	Galina Alexeyeva	Eva Rakusz
Martina Bischof	Nina Trofimova	Maria Zakarias
1984 SWEDEN 1:45.25	CANADA 1:47.13	FEDERAL REPUBLIC OF GERMANY 1:47.32
Agneta Andersson	Alexandra Barre	Josefa Idem
Anna Olsson	Sue Holloway	Barbara Schuttpelz
1988 EAST GERMANY 1:43.46	BULGARIA 1:44.06	NETHERLANDS 1:46.00
Birgit Schmidt	Ivana Guecheva	Annemiek Derckx
Anke Nothnagel	Diana Paliska	Annemarie Cox

500 METERS KAYAK FOURS

GOLD	SILVER	BRONZE
1984 ROMANIA 1:38.34	SWEDEN 1:38.87	CANADA 1:39.40
Agafia Constantin	Agneta Andersson	Alexandra Barre
Nastasia Ionescu	Anna Olsson	Lucie Guay
Tecla Marinescu	Eva Karlsson	Sue Holloway
Maria Stefan	Susanne Wiberg	Barb Olmsted
1988 EAST GERMANY 1:40.78	HUNGARY 1:41.88	BULGARIA 1:42.63
Birgit Schmidt	Erika Geczi	Ivana Guecheva
Anke Nothnagel	Erika Meszaros	Diana Paliska
Ramona Portwich	Eva Rakusz	Ogniana Petkova
Heike Singer	Rita Koban	Borislava Ivanova

7. Cycling (Men)

1,000 METERS SPRINT

GOLD	SILVER	BRONZE
1896–1904 Event not held		
1906 Francesco Verri (ITA) 1:42.2	H. C. Bouffler (GBR)	Eugène Debougnie (BEL)
1908[1]–1912 Event not held		
1920 Maurice Peeters (HOL) 1:38.3	H. Thomas Johnson (GBR)	Harry Ryan (GBR)
1924[2] Lucien Michard (FRA) 12.8	Jacob Meijer (HOL)	Jean Cugnot (FRA)
1928 René Beaufrand (FRA) 13.2	Antoine Mazairac (HOL)	Willy Falck-Hansen (DEN)
1932 Jacobus van Egmond (HOL) 12.6	Louis Chaillot (FRA)	Bruno Pellizzari (ITA)
1936 Toni Merkens (GER) 11.8	Arie Van Vliet (HOL)	Louis Chaillot (FRA)

[1] There was a 1,000 meters sprint event in the 1908 Games, but it was declared void because "the riders exceeded the time limit, in spite of repeated warnings."
[2] Since 1924 only times over the last 200 meters of the event have been recorded.

	GOLD	SILVER	BRONZE
1948	Mario Ghella (ITA) 12.0	Reginald Harris (GBR)	Axel Schandorff (DEN)
1952	Enzo Sacchi (ITA) 12.0	Lionel Cox (AUS)	Werner Potzernheim (GER)
1956	Michel Rousseau (FRA) 11.4	Guglielmo Pesenti (ITA)	Richard Ploog (AUS)
1960	Sante Gaiardoni (ITA) 11.1	Leo Sterckx (BEL)	Valentino Gasparella (ITA)
1964	Giovanni Pettenella (ITA) 13.69	Sergio Bianchetto (ITA)	Daniel Morelon (FRA)
1968	Daniel Morelon (FRA) 10.68	Giordano Turrini (ITA)	Pierre Trentin (FRA)
1972	Daniel Morelon (FRA) 11 .25	John M. Nicholson (AUS)	Omari Phakadze (URS)
1976	Anton Tkac (TCH) 10.78	Daniel Morelon (FRA)	Hans-Jurgen Geschke (GDR)
1980	Lutz Hesslich (GDR) 11.40	Yave Cahard (FRA)	Sergei Kopylov (URS)
1984	Mark Gorski (USA) 10.49	Nelson Vails (USA)	Tsutomu Sakamoto (JPN)
1988	Lutz Hesslich (GDR)	Nikolay Kovche (URS)	Gary Neiwand (AUS)

1,000 METERS TIME-TRIAL

	GOLD	SILVER	BRONZE
1896–1924	Event not held		
1928	Willy Falck-Hansen (DEN) 1:14.4*	Gerard D. H. Bosch van Drakestein (HOL) 1:15.2	Edgar Gray (AUS) 1:15.6
1932	Edgar Gray (AUS) 1:13.0*	Jacobus van Egmond (HOL) 1:13.3	Charles Rampelberg (FRA) 1:13.4
1936	Arie van Vliet (HOL) 1:12.0*	Pierre Georget (FRA) 1:12.8	Rudolf Karsch (GER) 1:13.2
1948	Jacques Dupont (FRA) 1:13.5	Pierre Nihant (BEL) 1:14.5	Thomas Godwin (GBR) 1:15.0
1952	Russell Mockridge (AUS) 1:11.1*	Marino Morettini (ITA) 1:12.7	Raymond Robinson (SAF) 1:13.0
1956	Leandro Faggin (ITA) 1:09.8*	Ladislav Foucek (TCH) 1:11.4	J. Alfred Swift (SAF) 1:11.6
1960	Sante Gaiardoni (ITA) 1:07.27*	Dieter Gieseler (GER) 1:08.75	Rotislav Vargashkin (URS) 1:08.86
1964	Patrick Sercu (BEL) 1:09.59	Giovanni Pettenella (ITA) 1:10.09	Pierre Trentin (FRA) 1:10.42
1968	Pierre Trentin (FRA) 1:03.91*	Niels-Christian Fredborg (DEN) 1:04.61	Janusz Kierzkowski (POL) 1:04.63
1972	Niels-Christian Fredborg (DEN) 1:06.44	Daniel Clark (AUS) 1:06.87	Juergen Schuetze (GDR) 1:07.02
1976	Klaus-Jurgen Grunke (GDR) 1:05.93	Michel Vaarten (BEL) 1:07.52	Niels Fredborg (DEN) 1:07.62
1980	Lothar Thoms (GDR) 1:02.955	Alexandr Panfilov (URS) 1:04.845	David Weller (JAM) 1:05.241
1984	Fredy Schmidtke (FRG) 1:06.10	Curtis Harnett (CAN) 1:06.44	Fabrice Colas (FRA) 1:06.65
1988	Alexandr Kiritchenko (URS) 1:04.499	Martin Vinnicombe (AUS) 1:04.784	Robert Lechner (FRG) 1:05.114

4,000 METERS INDIVIDUAL PURSUIT

Note: Bronze medal times are set in a third place race, so can be faster than those set in the race for first and second place.

GOLD	SILVER	BRONZE
1896–1960 Event not held		
1964 Jiři Daler (TCH) 5:04.75	Giorgio Ursi (ITA) 5:05.96	Preben Isaksson (DEN) 5:01.90
1968 Daniel Rebillard (FRA) 4:41.71	Mogens Frey Jensen (DEN) 4:42.43	Xaver Kurmann (SUI) 4:39.42
1972 Knut Knudsen (NOR) 4:45.74	Xaver Kurmann (SUI) 4:51.96	Hans Lutz (GER) 4:50.80
1976 Gregor Braun (GDR) 4:47.61	Herman Ponsteen (HOL) 4:49.72	Thomas Huschke (GDR) 4:52.71
1980 Robert Dill-Bundi (SUI) 4:35.66	Alain Bondue (FRA) 4:42.96	Hans-Henrik Orsted (DEN) 4:36.54
1984 Steve Hegg (USA) 4:39.35	Rolf Golz (FRG) 4:43.82	Leonard Nitz (USA) 4:44.03
1988 Gintaoutas Umaras (URS) 4:32.00*	Dean Woods (AUS) 4:35.00	Bernd Dittert (GDR) 4:34.17

4,000 METERS TEAM PURSUIT

Note: Bronze medal times are set in a third place race, so can be faster than those set in the race for first and second place.

1896–1912 Event not held		
1920 ITALY 5:20.0	GREAT BRITAIN	SOUTH AFRICA
Franco Giorgetti	Albert White	James R. Walker
Ruggero Ferrario	H. Thomas Johnson	William R. Smith
Arnaldo Carli	William Stewart	Henry J. Kaltenbrun
Primo Magnani	C. Albert Alden	Harry W. Goosen
1924 ITALY 5:15.0	POLAND	BELGIUM
Alfredo Dinale	Jósef Lange	Léon Dahelinczky
Francesco Zucchetti	Franciszek Szymeczyk	Henry Hoevenaers
Angelo de Martino	Jan Lazarski	Fernand Saive
Aleardo Menegazzi	Tomas Sztankiewicz	Jean van den Bosch
1928 ITALY 5:01.8	NETHERLANDS 5:06.2	GREAT BRITAIN
Luigi Tasselli	Adriann Braspenninx	Frank Wyld
Giacomo Gaioni	Jan Maas	Leonard Wyld
Cesare Facciani	Johannes B. N. Pijnenburg	Percy Wyld
Mario Lusiani	Piet van der Horst	M. George Southall
1932 ITALY 4:53.0	FRANCE 4:55.7	GREAT BRITAIN 4:56.0
Marco Cimatti	Amédé Fournier	Ernest A. Johnson
Paolo Pedretti	René Legrèves	William Harvell
Alberto Ghilardi	Henri Mouillefarine	Frank W. Southall
Nino Borsari	Paul Chocque	Charles Holland
1936 FRANCE 4:45.0	ITALY 4:51.0	GREAT BRITAIN 4.52.6
Robert Charpentier	Bianco Bianchi	Harry H. Hill
Jean Goujon	Mario Gentili	Ernest A. Johnson
Guy Lapébie	Armando Latini	Charles T. King
Roger Le Nizerhy	Severino Rigoni	Ernest V. Mills
1948 FRANCE 4:57.8	ITALY 5:36.7	GREAT BRITAIN 4:55.8
Pierre Adam	Arnaldo Benefenati	Alan Geldard
Serge Blusson	Guido Bernardi	Thomas Godwin
Charles Coste	Anselmo Citterio	David Ricketts
Ferdinand Decanali	Rino Pucci	Wilfred Waters

	GOLD	SILVER	BRONZE
1952	ITALY 4:46.1	S. AFRICA 4:53.6	GREAT BRITAIN 4:51.5
	Marino Morettini	Thomas F. Shardelow	Ronald C. Stretton
	Guido Messina	Alfred J. Swift	Alan Newton
	Mino de Rossi	Robert G. Fowler	George A. Newberry
	Loris Campana	George Estman	Donald C. Burgess
1956	ITALY 4:37.4	FRANCE 4:39.4	GREAT BRITAIN 4:42.2
	Leandro Faggin	René Bianchi	Thomas Simpson
	Valentino Gasparella	Jean Graczyk	Donald Burgess
	Franco Gandini	Jean-Claude Lecante	John Geddes
	Tonino Domenicali	Michel Vermeulin	Michael Gambrill
1960	ITALY 4:30.90	GERMANY 4:35.78	U.S.S.R. 4:34.05
	Luigi Arienti	Peter Gröning	Stanislav Moskvin
	Franco Testa	Manfred Klieme	Viktor Romanov
	Mario Vallotto	Siegfried Köhler	Leonid Kolumbet
	Marino Vigna	Bernd Barleben	Arnold Belgardt
1964	GERMANY 4:35.67	ITALY 4:35.74	NETHERLANDS 4:38.99
	Lothar Claesges	Luigi Roncaglia	Gerard Koel
	Karl-Heinz Henrichs	Vincenzo Mantovani	Hendrik Cornelisse
	Karl Link	Carlo Rancati	Jacob Oudkerk
	Ernest Streng	Franco Testa	Cornelis Schururing
1968	DENMARK 4:22.44	GERMANY 4:18.94[1]	ITALY 4:18.35
	Gunnar Asmussen	Udo Hempel	Lorenzo Bossio
	Per. P. Lyngemark	Karl Link	Cipirano Chemello
	Reno B. Olsen	Karl-Heinz Henrichs	Luigi Roncaglia
	Mogens Frey Jensen	Jürgen Kissner	Giorgio Morbiato
1972	WEST GERMANY 4:22.14	EAST GERMANY 4:25.25	GREAT BRITAIN 4:23.78
	Jurgen Colombo	Thomas Huschke	Michael Bennett
	Günter Haritz	Heinz Richter	Ian Hallam
	Udo Hempel	Herbert Richter	Ronald Keeble
	Günther Schumacher	Uwe Unterwalder	William Moore
1976	WEST GERMANY 4:21.06	U.S.S.R. 4:27.15	GREAT BRITAIN 4:22.41
	Gregor Braun	Vladimir Osokin	Ian Banbury
	Hans Lutz	Aleksandr Perov	Michael Bennett
	Günther Schumacher	Vitaly Petrakov	Robin Croker
	Peter Vonhof	Victor Sokolov	Ian Hallam
1980	U.S.S.R. 4:15.70	EAST GERMANY 4:19.67	CZECHOSLOVAKIA[2]
	Viktor Manakov	Gerald Mortag	Teodor Cerny
	Valeriy Movchan	Uwe Unterwalder	Martin Penc
	Vladimir Osokin	Matthias Wiegand	Jiri Pokorny
	Vitaliy Petrakov	Volker Winkler	Igor Slama
1984	AUSTRALIA 4:25.99	USA 4:29.85	FEDERAL REPUBLIC OF GERMANY 4:25.60
	Michael Grenda	David Grylls	Reinhard Alber
	Kevin Nichols	Steve Hegg	Rolf Golz
	Michael Turtur	Patrick McDonough	Roland Gunther
	Dean Woods	Leonard Nitz	Michael Marx
1988	USSR 4:13.31*	EAST GERMANY 4:14.09	AUSTRALIA 4:16.02
	Vyatcheslav Ekimov	Steffen Blochwitz	Brett Dutton
	Artouras Kaspoutis	Roland Hennig	Wayne McCarney
	Dmitriy Nelubine	Dirk Meier	Steve McGlede
	Gintaoutas Umaras	Carsten Wolf	Dean Woods

---

[1] Won final but disqualified.
[2] Italy disqualified in third place race.

POINTS RACE

	GOLD	SILVER	BRONZE
1984	Roger Ilegems (BEL)	Uwe Messerschmidt (FRG)	Jose Manuel Youshimatz (MEX)
1988	Dan Frost (DEN)	Leo Peelen (HOL)	Marat Ganeyev (URS)

INDIVIDUAL ROAD RACE

	GOLD	SILVER	BRONZE
1896	Aristides Konstantinidis (GRE) 3h 22:31.0	August Goedrich (GER) 3h 42:18.0	F. Battel (GBR) d.n.a.
1900–1904	Event not held		
1906	Fernand Vast (FRA) 2h 41:28.0	Maurice Bardonneau (FRA) 2h 41:28.4	Edmond Luguet (FRA) 2h 41:28.6
1908	Event not held		
1912	Rudolph Lewis (SAF) 10h 42:39.0	Frederick Grubb (GBR) 10h 51:24.2	Carl Schutte (USA) 10h 52:38.8
1920	Harry Stenqvist (SWE) 4h 40:01.8	Henry J. Kaltenbrun (SAF) 4h 41:26.6	Fernand Canteloube (FRA) 4h 42:54.4
1924	Armand Blanchonnet (FRA) 6h 20:48.0	Henry Hoevenaers (BEL) 6h 30:27.0	René Hamel (FRA) 6h 40:51.6
1928	Henry Hansen (DEN) 4h 47:18.0	Frank W. Southall (GBR) 4h 55:06.0	Gösta Carlsson (SWE) 5h 00:17.0
1932	Attilio Pavesi (ITA) 2h 28:05.6	Guglielmo Segato (ITA) 2h 29:21.4	Bernhard Britz (SWE) 2h 29:45.2
1936	Robert Charpentier (FRA) 2h 33:05.0	Guy Lapébie (FRA) 2h 33:05.2	Ernst Nievergelt (SUI) 2h 33:05.8
1948	José Beyaert (FRA) 5h 18:12.6	Gerardus P. Voorting (HOL) 5h 18:16.2	Lode Wouters (BEL) 5h 18:16.2
1952	André Noyelle (BEL) 5h 06:03.4	Robert Grondelaers (BEL) 5h 06:51.2	Edi Ziegler (GER) 5h 07:47.5
1956	Ercole Baldini (ITA) 5h 21:17.0	Arnaud Geyre (FRA) 5h 23:16.0	Alan Jackson (GBR) 5h 23:16.0
1960	Viktor Kapitonov (URS) 4h 20:37.0	Livio Trapè (ITA) 4h 20:37.0	Willy van den Berghen (BEL) 4h 20:57.0
1964	Mario Zanin (ITA) 4h 39:51.63	Kjell A. Rodian (DEN) 4h 39:51.65	Walter Godefroot (BEL) 4h 39:51.74
1968	Pierfranco Vianelli (ITA) 4h 41:25.24	Leif Mortensen (DEN) 4h 42:49.71	Gösta Pettersson (SWE) 4h 43:15.24
1972	Hennie Kuiper (HOL) 4h 14:37.0	Kevin C. Sefton (AUS) 4h 15:04.0	Jaime Huelamo (disq) (ESP) 4h 15:04.0
1976	Bernt Johansson (SWE) 4h 46:52.0	Giuseppe Martinelli (ITA) 4h 47:23.0	Mieczysl Nowicki (POL) 4h 47:23.0
1980	Sergei Sukhoruchenkov (URS) 4h 48:28.9	Czeslaw Lang (POL) 4h 51:26.9	Yuri Barinov (URS) 4h 51:26.9
1984	Alexi Grewal (USA) 4:59.57	Steve Bauer (CAN) close	Dag Otto Lauritzen (NOR) 5:00.18
1988	Olaf Ludwig (GDR) 4:32.22	Bernd Gröne (FRG) 4:32.25	Christian Henn (FRG) 4:32.46

This event has been held over the following distances:—1896—87 km; 1906—84 km; 1912—320 km; 1920—175 km; 1924—188 km; 1928—168 km; 1932 and 1936—100 km; 1948—194,63 km; 1952—190,4 km; 1956—187,73 km; 1960—175,38 km; 1964—194,83 km; 1968—196,2 km; 1972—200 km; 1976—176 km; 1980—189 km; 1984—190 km; 1988—196.8 km.

ROAD TEAM TIME-TRIAL

Held over 100 km except in 1964 (109,89 km), 1968 (104 km), 1980 (101 km).

1896–1956	Event not held		
1960	**ITALY** 2h 14:33.53	**GERMANY** 2h 16:56.31	**U.S.S.R.** 2h 18:41.67
	Antonio Bailetti	Gustav-Adolf Schur	Viktor Kapitonov
	Ottavio Cogliati	Egon Adler	Yevgeny Klevzov
	Giacomo Fornoni	Erich Hagen	Yuriy Melikhov
	Livio Trapè	Günter Lörke	Aleksey Petrov

	GOLD	SILVER	BRONZE
1964	**NETHERLANDS** 2h 26:31.19	**ITALY** 2h 26:55.39	**SWEDEN** 2h 27:11.52
	Gerben Karstens	Severino Andreoli	Sven Hamrin
	Evert G. Dolman	Luciano dalla Bona	Erik Pettersson
	Johannes Pieterse	Pietro Guerra	Gösta Pettersson
	Hubertus Zoet	Ferrucio Manza	Sture Pettersson
1968	**NETHERLANDS** 2h 07:49.06	**SWEDEN** 2h 09:26.60	**ITALY** 2h 10:18.74
	Marinus Pijnen	Gösta Pettersson	Vittorio Marcelli
	Fedor den Hertog	Sture Pettersson	Mauro Simonetti
	Jan Krekels	Erik Pettersson	Pierfranco Vianelli
	Henk Zoetemelk	Tomas Pettersson	Giovanni Bramucci
1972	**U.S.S.R.** 2h 11:17.8	**POLAND** 2h 11:47.5	**NETHERLANDS** 2h 12:27.1
	Boris Chouhov	Lucjan Lis	Fedor den Hertog
	Valeri Iardy	Edward Barcik	Hennie Kuiper
	Gennady Komnatov	Stanislaw Szozda	Cees Priem
	Valery Likhachev	Ryszard Szurkowski	Aad van den Hoek
1976	**U.S.S.R.** 2h 08:53.0	**POLAND** 2h 09:13.0	**DENMARK** 2h 12:20.0
	Anatoli Chukanov	Tadeusz Mytnik	Verner Blaudzun
	Valeriy Chaplygin	Mieczysl Nowicki	Gert Frank
	Vladimir Kaminski	Stanisla Szozda	Jorgen Hansen
	Aavo Pikkuus	Ryszard Szurkowski	Jorn Lund
1980	**U.S.S.R.** 2h 01:21.7	**EAST GERMANY** 2h 02:53.2	**CZECHOSLOVAKIA** 2h 02:53.9
	Yuriy Kashirin	Falk Boden	Michal Klasa
	Oleg Logwin	Bernd Drogan	Vlastibor Konecny
	Sergey Shelpakov	Olaf Ludwig	Alipi Kostadinov
	Anatoliy Yarkin	Hans-Joachin Hartnick	Jiri Skoda
1984	**ITALY** 1:58.28	**SWITZERLAND** 2:02.38	**USA** 2:02.46
	Marcello Bartalini	2:02.38	Ronald Kiefel
	Marco Giovannetti	Alfred Acherman	Roy Knickman
	Eros Poli	Richard Trinkler	Davis Phinney
	Claudio Vandelli	Laurent Vial	Andrew Weaver
		Benno Wiss	
1988	**EAST GERMANY** 1:57:47.7	**POLAND** 1:57:54.2	**SWEDEN** 1:59:47.3
	Uwe Ampler	Joachim Halupczok	Bjorn Johansson
	Mario Kummer	Zenon Jaskula	Jan Karlsson
	Maik Landsmann	Marek Lesniewski	Michel Lars
	Jan Schur	Andrzej Sypytkowski	Anders Jarl

Cycling (Women)

INDIVIDUAL ROAD RACE

	GOLD	SILVER	BRONZE
1984	Connie Carpenter-Phinney (USA) 2:11:14	Rebecca Twigg (USA) close	Sandra Schumacher (FRG) close
1988	Monique Knol (HOL) 2:00.52	Jutta Niehaus (FRG) close	Laima Zilporitee (URS) close

Held over a distance of 79.2 km in 1984 and 82 km in 1988.

SPRINT

	GOLD	SILVER	BRONZE
1988	Erika Saloumae (URS)	Christa Rothenburger-Luding (GDR)	Connie Young (USA)

8. Equestrian Sports

GRAND PRIX (JUMPING)

GOLD	SILVER	BRONZE
1896 Event not held		
1900 Aimé Haegeman (BEL) *Benton II*	Georges van de Poele (BEL) *Windsor Squire*	de Champsavin (FRA) *Terpischore*
1904–1908 Event not held		
1912 Jean Cariou	Rabod W. von Kröcher	Emanuel de Blommaert de Soye
(FRA) 186 *Mignon*	(GER) 186 *Dohna*	(BEL) 185 *Clonmore*
Teams—SWEDEN 545 pts.	FRANCE 538	GERMANY 530
C. Gustav Lewenhaupt	Jean Cariou	Sigismund Freyer
Hans von Rosen	Michel d'Astafort	William Graf von Hohenau
Gustaf Kilman	Bernard Meyer	Ernst-Hubertus Deloch
1920 Tommaso Lequio (ITA) 2 faults *Trebecco*	Alessandro Valerio (ITA) 3 faults *Cento*	C. Gustaf Lewenhaupt (SWE) 4 faults *Mon Coeur*
Teams—SWEDEN 114 faults	BELGIUM 16.25	ITALY 18.75
Hans von Rosen	Count Herman d'Oultremont	Ettore Caffaratti
Claes König	André Commans	Guilio Cacciandra
Daniel Norling	Baron Herman de Gaiffier d'Hestroy	Alessandro Alvisi
1924 Alphonse Gemuseus (SUI) 6 faults *Lucette*	Tommaso Lequio (ITA) 8.75 *Trebecco*	Adam Królikiewicz (POL) 10 *Picador*
Teams—SWEDEN 42.25 pts.	SWITZERLAND 50	PORTUGAL 53
Ake Thelning	Alphonse Gemuseus	Antonio Borges d'Almeida
Axel Ståhle	Werner Stüber	Helder de Souza Martins
Age Lundström	Hans Bühler	José Mouzinho d'Albuquerque
1928 František Ventura (TCH) no faults *Eliot*	Pierre Bertrand de Balanda (FRA) 2 *Papillon*	Charles Kuhn (SUI) 4 *Pepita*
Teams—SPAIN 4 faults	POLAND 8	SWEDEN 10
Marquis José Alvarez de los Trujillos	Kazimierz Gzowski	Karl Hansen
José Navarro Morenés	Kazimierz Szosland	Carl Björnstjerna
Julio Garcia Fernández	Michal Antoniewicz	Ernst Hallberg
1932[1] Takeichi Nishi (JPN) 8 pts. *Uranus*	Harry Chamberlin (USA) 212 *Show Girl*	Clarence von Rosen jr. (SWE) 16 *Empire*
1936 Kurt Hasse (GER) 4 faults *Tora*	Henri Rang (ROM) 4 *Delfis*	József von Platthy (HUN) 8 *Sellö*
Teams—GERMANY 44 faults	NETHERLANDS 51.5	PORTUGAL 56
Kurt Hasse	Jan A. de Bruine	Luis Mena e Silva
Marten von Barnekow	Johan J. Greter	Luis Marquéz do Funchal
Heinz Brandt	Henri L. M. van Schaik	José Beltrão
1948 Humberto Mariles Cortés (MEX) 6.25 faults *Arete*	Rubén Uriza (MEX) 8 *Harvey*	Jean F. d'Orgeix (FRA) 8 *Sucre de Pomme*

---

[1] There was also a teams competition, but there was no nation of which all three riders completed the course.

Alwin Schockemöhle (GER) won the individual Grand Prix gold medal on "Warwick Rex" in 1976. He has also won 3 team medals, in 1960, 1968 and 1976.

GOLD	SILVER	BRONZE
Teams—MEXICO 34.25 faults	SPAIN 56.50	GREAT BRITAIN 67
Humberto Mariles Cortés	Jaime Garcia Cruz	Henry M. V. Nicoll
Rubén Uriza	Marcelino Gavilán y Ponce de Leon	Arthur Carr
Alberto Valdés	José Navarro Morenés	Harry M. Llewellyn
1952 Pierre Jonquières d'Oriola	Oscar Cristi	Fritz Thiedemann
(FRA) no faults *Ali Baba*	(CHI) 4 *Bambi*	(GER) 8 *Meteor*
Teams—GREAT BRITAIN 40.75 faults	CHILE 45.75	UNITED STATES 52.25
Douglas Stewart	Oscar Cristi	Arthur J. McCashin
Wilfred H. White	Ricardo Echeverria	John Russell
Harry M. Llewellyn	Cesar Mendoza	William Steinkraus
1956 Hans Günter Winkler	Raimondo d'Inzeo	Piero d'Inzeo
(GER) 4 faults *Halla*	(ITA) 8 *Merano*	(ITA) 11 *Uruguay*
Teams—GERMANY 40	ITALY 66	GREAT BRITAIN 69
Hans Günter Winkler	Raimondo d'Inzeo	Wilfred H. White
Fritz Thiedemann	Piero d'Inzeo	Patricia Smythe
Alfons Lütke-Westheus	Salvatore Oppes	Peter Robeson
1960 Raimondo d'Inzeo	Piero d'Inzeo	David Broome
(ITA) 12 faults *Posillippo*	(ITA) 16 *The Rock*	(GBR) 23 *Sunsalve*
Teams—GERMANY 46.50	UNITED STATES 66	ITALY 80.50
Alwin Schockemöhle	George Morris	Riamondo d'Inzeo
Fritz Thiedemann	Frank Chapot	Piero d'Inzeo
Hans Günter Winkler	William Steinkraus	Antonio Oppes
1964 Pierre Jonquières d'Oriola	Hermann Schridde	Peter Robeson
(FRA) 9 faults *Lutteur*	(GER) 13.75 faults *Dozen*	(GBR) 16 faults *Firecrest*
Teams—GERMANY 68.50	FRANCE 77.75	ITALY 88.50
Hermann Schridde	Pierre Jonquières d'Oriola	Piero d'Inzeo
Kurt Jarasinksi	Janou Lefebvre	Raimondo d'Inzeo
Hans Günter Winkler	Guy Lefrant	Graziano Mancinelli

	GOLD	SILVER	BRONZE
1968	William Steinkraus (USA) 4 faults *Snowbound*	Marian Coakes (GBR) 8 faults *Stroller*	David Broome (GBR) 12 faults *Mister Softee*
	Teams—CANADA 102.75 Thomas Gayford James Day James Elder	FRANCE 110.50 Marcel Rozier Jánou Lefebvre Pierre Jonquières d'Oriola	GERMANY 117.25 Hermann Schridde Alwin Schockemöhle Hans Günter Winkler
1972	Graziano Mancinelli (ITA) 8 faults *Ambassador*	Ann Moore (GBR) 9 faults *Psalm*	Neal Shapiro (USA) 8 faults *Sloopy*
	Teams—WEST GERMANY 32 Fritz Ligges Gerhard Wiltfang Hartwig Steenken Hans Günter Winkler	UNITED STATES 32.25 William Steinkraus Neal Shapiro Kathryn Kusner Frank Chapot	ITALY 48 Vittorio Orlando Raimondo d'Inzeo Graziano Mancinelli Piero d'Inzeo
1976	Alwin Schockemöhle (GER) No faults *Warwick Rex*	Michael Vaillancourt (CAN) 12 faults *Branch County*	Francois Mathy (BEL) 12 faults *Gai Luron*
	Teams—FRANCE 40 Hubert Parot Marcel Rozier Michel Roche Marc Roguet	WEST GERMANY 44 Hans Günter Winkler Paul Schockemöhle Alwin Shockemöhle Soenke Soenksen	BELGIUM 63 Eric Wauters Francois Mathy Edgar Guepper Stanny Van Paeschen
1980	Jan Kowalczyk (POL) 8 faults *Artemor*	Nikolai Korolkov (URS) 9.5 faults *Espadron*	Joaquin Perez Heras[2] (MEX) 12 faults *Alymony*
	Teams—U.S.S.R. 20.25 Vyacheslav Chukanov Viktor Poganovsky Viktor Asmayev Nikolai Korolkov	POLAND 56 Marian Kozicki Jan Kowalczyk Wieslaw Hartman Janusz Bobik	MEXICO 59.75 Joaquin Perez Heras Alberto Valdes Lacarra Gerardo Tazzer Valencia Jesus Gomez Portugal
1984	Joe Fargis (USA) 4 faults *Touch of Class*	Conrad Homfeld (USA) 4 faults *Abdullah*	Heidi Robbiani (SUI) 8 faults *Jessica V*
	Teams—USA 12.00 Joe Fargis Conrad Homfeld Leslie Burr Melanie Smith	GREAT BRITAIN 36.75 Michael Whitaker John Whitaker Steven Smith Timothy Grubb	WEST GERMANY 39.25 Paul Schockemohle Peter Luther Franke Sloothaak Fritz Ligges
1988	Pierre Durand (FRA) 1.25 faults *Jappeloup*	Greg Best (USA) 4 faults *Gem Twist*	Karsten Huck (FRG) 4 faults *Nepomuk 8*
	Teams—WEST GERMANY 17.25 faults Lüdger Beerbaum Wolfgang Brinkmann Dirk Hafemeister Franke Sloothaati	USA 20.50 faults Greg Best Lisa Jacquin Anne Kursinski Joe Fargis	FRANCE 27.50 faults Hubert Bourdy Frederic Cottier Michel Robert Pierre Durand

[2] Won jump off.

GRAND PRIX (DRESSAGE)

1896–1908	Event not held		
1912	Carl Bonde (SWE) 15 pts. *Emperor*	Gustaf-Adolf Boltenstern Sr. (SWE) 21 *Neptun*	Hans von Blixen-Finecke (SWE) 32 *Maggie*
1920	Janne Lundblad (SWE) 27,937 pts. *Uno*	Bertil Sandström (SWE) 26,312 *Sabel*	Hans von Rosen (SWE) 25,125 *Running Sister*
1924	Ernst Linder (SWE) 276.4 pts. *Piccolomini*	Bertil Sandström (SWE) 275.8 *Sabel*	Xavier Lesage (FRA) 265.8 *Plumard*

1928 Carl F. F. von Langen   Charles Marion   Ragnar Olsson
     (GER) 237.42 pts.   (FRA) 231.00   *Limon*   (SWE) 229.78
              Draufgänger   *Günstling*
Teams—GERMANY   SWEDEN 650.86   NETHERLANDS
         669.72 pts.   642.96
     Carl von Langen   Ragnar Olsson   Jan van Reede
     Hermann Linkenbach   Carl Bonde   Pierre Vesteegh
     Eugen von Lotzbeck   Janne Lundblad   Gérard le Heux
1932 Xavier Lesage   Charles Marion   Hiram Tuttle
     (FRA) 1,031.25 pts   (FRA) 916.25   *Linon*   (USA) 901.50 *Olympic*
              Taine

Teams—FRANCE   SWEDEN 2,678.00   UNITED STATES
       2,818.75 pts.   2,576.75
     Xavier Lesage   Thomas Byström   Hiram Tuttle
     Charles Marion   Gustaf-Adolf   Isaac Kitts
     André Jousseaume   Boltenstern Jr.   Alvin Moore
                             Bertil Sandström
1936 Heinz Pollay   Friedrich Gerhard   Alois Podhajsky
     (GER) 1,760 *Kronos*   (GER) 1,745.5 *Absinth* (AUT) 1,721.5 *Nero*
Teams—GERMANY   FRANCE 4,846   SWEDEN 4,660.5
         5,074 pts.
     Heinz Pollay   André Jousseaume   Gregor von Aldercreutz
     Freidrich Gerhard   Daniel Gillois   Folke Sandström
     Hermann von Oppeln   Gérard de Ballorre   Sven Colliander
       Bronikowski
1948 Hans Moser   André Jousseaume   Gustaf-Adolf
     (SUI) 492.5 pts.   (FRA) 480.0   Boltenstern Jr.
          Hummer   *Harpagon*   (SWE) 477.5 *Trumpf*
Teams—FRANCE 1,269 pts.¹ UNITED STATES 1,256   PORTUGAL 1,182
     André Jousseaume   Robert Borg   Fernando da Silva Paes
     Jean Paillard   Earl Thomson   Francisco Valadas
     Maurice Buret   Frank Henry   Luis Mena e Silva
1952 Henri St. Cyr   Lis Hartel   André Jousseaume
     (SWE) 561 pts.   (DEN) 541.5 *Jubilee* (FRA) 541.0 *Harpagon*
       Master Rufus
Teams—SWEDEN   SWITZERLAND   GERMANY 1,501.0
       1,597.5 pts.   1,759.0
     Gustaf-Adolf   Gustav Fischer   Ida von Nagel
       Boltenstern Jr.   Gottfried Trachsel   Fritz Thiedemann
     Henri St. Cyr   Henri Chammartin   Heinrich Pollay
     Gehnäll Persson
1956 Henri St. Cyr   Lis Hartel   Liselott Lisenhoff
     (SWE) 860 pts.   *Juli* (DEN) 850   *Jubilee* (GER) 832   *Adular*
Teams—SWEDEN, 2,475 pts. GERMANY 2,346   SWITZERLAND 2,346
     Henri St. Cyr   Liselott Lisenhoff   Gustav Fischer
     Gehnäll Persson   Hannelore Weygand   Gottfried Trachsel
     Gustaf-Adolf   Anneliese Küppers   Henri Chammartin
       Boltenstern Jr.
1960 Sergey Filatov   Gustav Fischer   Josef Neckermann
     (URS)2,144pts.*Absent*   (SUI) 2,087   *Wald*   (GER) 2,082 *Asbach*
                             Team event not held
1964 Henri Chammartin   Harry Boldt   Sergey Filatov
     (SUI) 1,504 pts.   (GER) 1,503 *Remus*   (URS) 1,486   *Absent*
          Woermann
Teams—GERMANY   SWITZERLAND   U.S.S.R. 2,311
       2,558 pts.   2,526
     Harry Boldt   Henri Chammartin   Sergey Filatov
     Josef Neckermann   Gustav Fischer   Ivan Kizimov
     Reiner Klimke   Marianne Gossweiler   Ivan Kalita
1968 Ivan Kizimov   Josef Neckermann   Reiner Klimke
     (URS) 1,572 pts.*Ikhor* (GER) 1,546 *Mariano* (GER) 1,537   *Dux*
Teams—GERMANY   U.S.S.R. 2,657   SWITZERLAND 2,547
       2,699 pts.
     Josef Neckermann   Elena Petuchkova   Henri Chammartin
     Liselott Linsenhoff   Ivan Kizimov   Marianne Gossweiler
     Dr. Reiner Klimke   Ivan Kalita   Gustav Fischer

GOLD	SILVER	BRONZE
1972 Liselott Linsenhoff (GER) 1,229 pts. *Piaff*	Elena Petuchkova (URS) 1,185 *Pepel*	Josef Neckermann (GER) 1,177 *Venetia*
Teams—U.S.S.R. 5,095 pts.	WEST GERMANY 5,083	SWEDEN 4,849
Elena Petuchkova	Liselott Linsenhoff	Ulla Hakansson
Ivan Kizimov	Josef Neckermann	Ninna Swaab
Ivan Kalita	Karin Schlüter	Maud van Rosen
1976 Christine Stückelberger (SUI) 1,486 pts.	Harry Boldt (GER) 1,432	Reiner Klimke (GER) 1,395
Teams—WEST GERMANY 5,155 pts.	SWITZERLAND 4,684	USA 4,670
Harry Boldt	Christine Stückelberger	Hilda Gurney
Reiner Klimke	Ulrich Lehmann	Dorothy Morkis
Gabriela Grillo	Doris Ramseier	Edith Master
1980 Elizabeth Theurer (AUT) 1,370 pts. *Mon Cherie*	Yuri Kovshov (URS) 1,300 *Igrok*	Viktor Ugryumov (URS) 1,234 *Shkval*
Teams—U.S.S.R. 4,383 pts.	BULGARIA 3,580	ROMANIA 3,346
Yuriy Kovshov	Petar Mandajiev	Anghelache Donescu
Viktor Ugryumov	Svetoslav Ivanov	Dumitru Veliku
Vera Misevich	Gheorghi Gadjev	Petre Rosca
1984 (FRG) 1,504 pts. *Ahlerich*	Reiner Klimke (DEN) 1,442 *Marzog*	Otto Hofer (SUI) 1,364 *Limandus*
Teams—WEST GERMANY 4,955 pts.	SWITZERLAND 4,673	SWEDEN 4,630
Reiner Klimke	Otto Hofer	Ulla Hakansson
Uwe Sauer	Christine Stückelberger	Ingamay Bylund
Herbert Krug	Amy De Bary	Louise Nathhorst
1988 Nicole Uphoff (FRG) 1,521 pts. *Rembrandt 24*	Margit Otto Crepin (FRA) 1,462 *Corlandus*	Christine Stückelberger (SUI) 1,417 *Gauguin De Lully*
Teams—WEST GERMANY 4,302 pts.	SWITZERLAND 4,164	CANADA 3,969
Reiner Klimke	Otto Hofer	Cynthia Ishoy
AnnKathrin Linsenhoff	Christine Stückelberger	Eva Maria Pracht
Monica Theodorescu	Daniel Ramseier	Gina Smith
Nicole Uphoff	Samuel Schatzmann	Ashley Nicoll

[1] SWEDEN was originally declared the winner with 1,366 pts., but was disqualified subsequently—five years later.

THREE-DAY EVENT

GOLD	SILVER	BRONZE
1896–1908 Event not held		
1912 Axel Nordlander (SWE) 46.59 pts. *Lady Artist*	Friedrich von Rochow (GER) 46.42 *Idealist*	Jean Cariou (FRA) 46.32 *Cocotte*
Teams—SWEDEN 139.06 pts.	GERMANY 138.48	UNITED STATES 137.33
Nils Adlercreutz	Friedrich von Rochow	Benjamin Lear
Axel Nordlander	Eduard von Lütcken	John C. Montgomery
Ernst G. Casparsson	Richard G. von Schaesberg-Thannheim	Guy Henry
1920 Helmer Mörner (SWE) 1,775 pts. *Germania*	Age Lundström (SWE) 1,738.75 *Yrsa*	Ettore Caffaratti (ITA) 1,733.75 *Traditore*
Teams—SWEDEN 5.057.5 pts.	ITALY 4,735	BELGIUM 4,560
Helmer Mörner	Ettore Caffaratti	Roger Moremans d'Emaus
Age Lundström	Garibaldi Spighi	
George von Braun	Guilio Cacciandra	Oswald Lints
		Jules Bonvalet

The first winners of the Three-Day Event team competition were this Swedish trio at Stockholm in 1912.

	GOLD	SILVER	BRONZE
1924	Adolph D. C. van der Voort van Zijp (HOL) 1,976 pts. *Silver Piece*	Fröde Kirkebjerg (DEN) 1,853.5 *Meteor*	Sloan Doak (USA) 1,845.5 *Pathfinder*
Teams—	NETHERLANDS 5,297.5 pts.	SWEDEN 4,743.5	ITALY 4,512.5
	Adolph D. C. van der Voort van Zijp	Claes König Torsten Sylvan	Alberto Lombardi Alessandro Alvisi
	Charles F. Pahud de Mortanges	Gustaf Hagelin	Emanuele di Pralormo
	Gerard P. C. de Kruyff		
1928	Charles F. Pahud de Mortanges (HOL) 1,969.82 pts. *Marcoix*	Gerard P. C. de Kruyff (HOL) 1,967.26 *Va-t-en*	Bruno Neumann (GER) 1,944.42 *Ilja*
Teams—	NETHERLANDS 5,865.68 pts.	NORWAY 5,395.68	POLAND 5,067.92
	Charles F. Pahud de Mortanges	Arthur Quist Bjart Ording	Jósef Trenkwald Michal Antoniewicz
	Gerard P. C. de Kruyff	Eugen Johansen	Karol de Rómmel
	Adolph D. C. van der Voort van Zijp		
1932	Charles F. Pahud de Mortanges (HOL) 1,813.83 pts. *Marcoix*	Earl Thomson (USA) 1,811 *Jenny Camp*	Clarence von Rosen Jr. (SWE) 1,809.42 *Sunnyside Maid*
Teams—	UNITED STATES 5,038.08 pts.	NETHERLANDS 4,689.08	—
	Earl Thomson Harry Chamberlin Edwin Argo	Charles F. Pahud de Mortanges Karel J. Schummelketel Aernout van Lennep	

GOLD	SILVER	BRONZE

1936 Ludwig Stubbendorff (GER) 37.7 faults *Nurmi*

Earl Thomson (USA) 99.9 *Jenny Camp*

Hans Mathiesen-Lunding (DEN) 102.2 *Jason*

Teams—**GERMANY** 676.75 pts.

POLAND 991.70

GREAT BRITAIN 9,195.50

Ludwig Stubbendorff
Rudolf Lippert
Konrad von Wangenheim

Severyn Kulesza
Henryk Rojcewicz
Zdislaw Kawecki

Edward Howard-Vyse
Alec Scott
Richard Fanshawe

1948 Bernard Chevallier (FRA) plus 4 pts. *Aiglonne*

Frank Henry (USA) minus 21 *Swing Low*

J. Robert Selfelt (SWE) minus 25 *Claque*

Teams—**UNITED STATES** 161.50 faults

SWEDEN 165.00

MEXICO 305.25

Frank Henry
Charles Anderson
Earl Thomson

J. Robert Selfelt
Nils Olof Stahre
Sigurd Svensson

Humberto Mariles Cortés
Raúl Campero
Joaquin Solano Chagoya

1952 Hans von Blixen-Finecke (SWE) 28.33 faults *Jubal*

Guy Lefrant (FRA) 54.50 *Verdun*

Wilhelm Büsing (GER) 55.50 *Hubertus*

Teams—**SWEDEN** 221.49 pts.

GERMANY 235.49

UNITED STATES 587.16

Hans von Blixen-Finecke
Nils Olof Stahre
Karl F. Frölén

Wilhelm Büsing
Klaus Wagner
Otto Rothe

Charles Hough
Walter Staley Jr.
John Wofford

1956 Petrus Kastenman (SWE) 66.53 faults *Iluster*

August Lütke-Westhues (GER) 84.87 *Trux von Kamax*

Francis Weldon (GBR) 85.48 *Kilbarry*

Teams—**GREAT BRITAIN** 355.48 pts.

GERMANY 475.61

CANADA 572.72

Albert E. Hill
Francis Weldon
A. Lawrence Rook

August Lütke-Westhues
Klaus Wagner
Otto Rothe

James Elder
Brian Herbinson
John Rumble

1960 Lawrence Morgan (AUS) plus 7.15 pts. *Salad Days*

Neale Lavis (AUS) minus 16.50 *Mirrabooka*

Anton Bühler (SUI) minus 51.21 *Gay Spark*

Teams—**AUSTRALIA** 128.18 pts.

SWITZERLAND 386.02

FRANCE 515.71

Lawrence Morgan
Neale Lavis
William Roycroft

Anton Bühler
Hans Schwarzenbach
Rudolf Günthardt

Jack L. Le Goff
Jean R. Le Roy
Guy Lefrant

1964 Mauro Checcoli (ITA) 64.40 pts. *Surbean*

Carlos Moratorio (ARG) 56.40 *Chalan*

Fritz Ligges (GER) 49.20 *Donkosak*

Teams—**ITALY** 85.80 pts.

UNITED STATES 65.86

GERMANY 56.73

Mauro Checcoli
Paolo Angioni
Giuseppe Ravano

Michael Page
Kevin Freeman
J. Michael Plumb

Fritz Ligges
Horst Karsten
Gerhard Schultz

1968 Jean-Jacques Guyon (FRA) 38.86 pts. *Pitou*

Derek Allhusen (GBR) 41.61 *Lochinvar*

Michael Page (USA) 52.31 *Faster*

Teams—**GREAT BRITAIN** 175.93 pts.

UNITED STATES 245.87

AUSTRALIA 331.26

Derek Allhusen
Richard H. Meade
Reuben Jones

Michael Page
James Wofford
J. Micheal Plumb

Wayne Roycroft
Brian Cobcroft
William Roycroft

1972 Richard H. Meade (GBR) 57.73 pts. *Laurieston*

Alessa Argenton (ITA) 43.33 *Woodland*

Jan Jonsson (SWE) 39.67 *Sarajevo*

Teams—**GREAT BRITAIN** 95.53 pts.

UNITED STATES 10.81

WEST GERMANY minus 18.00

Mary D. Gordon-Watson
Bridget Parker
Richard H. Meade
Mark A. Phillips (non-scorer)

Kevin Freeman
Bruce Davidson
Michael Plumb

Harry Klugmann
Karl Schultz
Ludwig Goessing

	GOLD	SILVER	BRONZE
1976	Edmund Coffin (US) 114.99 pts. *Bally—Cor*	Michael Plumb (USA) 125.85 *Better & Better*	Karl Schultz (GER) 129.45 *Madrigal*
	Teams—UNITED STATES 441.00 pts.	WEST GERMANY 584.60	AUSTRALIA 599.54
	Edmund Coffin	Karl Schultz	Wayne Roycroft
	Michael Plumb	Herbert Bloecker	Mervyn Bennett
	Bruce Davidson	Helmut Rethemeier	William Roycroft
	Mary Tauskey	Otto Ammermann	Denis Pigott
1980	Frederico Euro Roman (ITA) 108.60 pts. *Rossinan*	Aleksandr Blinov (URS) 120.80 *Galzun*	Yuri Salnikov (URS) 151.60 *Pintset*
	Teams—U.S.S.R. 457.00 pts.	ITALY 656.20	MEXICO 1,172.85
	Aleksandr Blinov	Frederico Euro Roman	Manuel Mendivil Yocupicio
	Yuri Salnikov	Anna Casagrande	David Barcena Rios
	Valeriy Volkov	Mauro Roman	Jose Luis Perez Soto
	Sergey Roghozhin	Marina Sciocchetti	Fabian Vazquez Lopez
1984	Mark Todd (NZL) 51.60 *Charisma*	Karen Stives (USA) 54.20 *Ben Arthur*	Virginia Holgate (GBR) 56.80 *Priceless*
	Teams—UNITED STATES 186.00	GREAT BRITAIN 189.20	WEST GERMANY 234.00
	Michael Plumb	Virginia Holgate	Dietmar Hogrefe
	Karen Stives	Ian Stark	Bettina Overesch
	Torrance Fleischmann	Diana Clapham	Burkhard Tesdorpf
	Bruce Davidson	Lucinda Green	Claus Erhorn
1988	Mark Todd (NZL) 42.60 pts. *Charisma*	Ian Stark (GBR) 52.80 pts. *Sir Wattie*	Virginia Leng (GBR) 62.00 *Master Craftsman*
	Teams—WEST GERMANY 225.95 pts.	GREAT BRITAIN 256.80	NEW ZEALAND 271.20
	Claus Erhorn	Mark Phillips	Mark Todd
	Matthias Baumann	Karen Straker	Marges Knighton
	Thies Kaspareit	Virginia Leng	Andrew Bennie
	Ralf Ehrenbrink	Ian Stark	Tinks Pottinger

9. Fencing (Men)

FOIL (INDIVIDUAL)

Wins are assessed on both wins (2 pts.) *and* draws (1 pt.) so, as in 1928, the winner does not necessarily have most wins.

	GOLD	SILVER	BRONZE
1896	Emile Gravelotte (FRA) 4 wins	Henri Callott (FRA) 3	Perikles Mavromichalis-Pierrakos (GRE) 2
1900	Emile Coste (FRA) 6 wins	Henri Masson (FRA) 5	Jacques Boulenger (FRA) 4
1904	Ramón Fonst (CUB) 3 wins	Albertson Van Zo Post (USA) 2	Charles Tatham (USA) 1
1906	Georges Dillon-Kavanagh (FRA) d.n.a.	Gustav Casmir (GER) d.n.a.	Pierre d'Hugues (FRA) d.n.a.
1908	Event not held		
1912	Nedo Nadi (ITA) 7 wins	Pietro Speciale (ITA) 5	Richard Verderber (AUT) 4
1920	Nedo Nadi (ITA) 10 wins	Phillippe Cattiau (FRA) 9	Roger Ducret (FRA) 9

Jean Buhan of France (right), the winner of the individual foil event in 1948, is shown in an early bout with John Emrys Lloyd (GBR).

	GOLD	SILVER	BRONZE
1924	Roger Ducret (FRA) 6 wins	Philippe Cattiau (FRA) 5	Maurice van Damme (BEL) 4
1928	Lucien Gaudin (FRA) 9 wins	Erwin Casmir (GER) 9	Giulio Gaudini (ITA) 9
1932	Gustavo Marzi (ITA) 9 wins	Joseph Levis (USA) 6	Giulio Gaudini (ITA) 5
1936	Giulio Gaudini (ITA) 7 wins	Edouard Gardère (FRA) 6	Giorgio Bocchino (ITA) 4
1948	Jean Buhan (FRA) 7 wins	Christian d'Oriola (FRA) 5	Lajos Maszlay (HUN) 4
1952	Christian d'Oriola (FRA) 8 wins	Edoardo Mangiarotti (ITA) 6	Manlino di Rosa (ITA) 5
1956	Christian d'Oriola (FRA) 6 wins	Giancarlo Bergamini (ITA) 5	Antonio Spallino (ITA) 5
1960	Viktor Zhdanovich (URS) 7 wins	Yuriy Sissikin (URS) 4	Albert Axelrod (USA) 3
1964	Egon Franke (POL) 3 wins	Jean-Claude Magnan (FRA) 2	Daniel Revenu (FRA) 1
1968	Ion Drimba (ROM) 4 wins	Jenö Kamuti (HUN) 3	Daniel Revenu (FRA) 3
1972	Witold Woyda (POL) 5 wins	Jenö Kamuti (HUN) 4	Christian Noël (FRA) 2
1976	Fabio Dal Zotto (ITA) 4 wins	Aleksandr Romankov (URS) 4	Bernard Talvard (FRA) 3
1980	Vladimir Smirnov (URS) 5 wins	Paskal Jolyot (FRA) 5	Aleksandr Romankov (URS) 5
1984	Mauro Numa (ITA)	Matthias Behr (FRG)	Stefano Cerioni (ITA)
1988	Stefano Cerioni (ITA)	Udo Wagner (GDR)	Alexandr Romankov (URS)

FOIL (TEAM)

GOLD	SILVER	BRONZE
1896–1900 Event not held		
1904 CUBA/USA	**UNITED STATES**	
Ramón Fonst	Charles Tatham	
Albertson Van Zo Post	Charles Townsend	
Manuel Diaz	Arthur Fox	
1906–1912 Event not held		
1920 ITALY	**FRANCE**	**UNITED STATES**
Nedo Nadi	Lionel Bony de	Francis W. Honeycutt
Aldo Nadi	Castellane	Henry Breckinridge
Abelardo Olivier	Gaston Amson	Arthur Lyon
Pietro Speciale	André Labatut	Robert V. Sears
Rodolfo Terlizzi	Georges Trombert	Harold Rayner
Tomasso Costantino	Marcel Perrot	
Baldo Baldi	Lucien Gaudin	
Oreste Puliti	Philippe Cattiau	
	Roger Ducret	
1924 FRANCE	**BELGIUM**	**HUNGARY**
Lucien Gaudin	Désiré Beaurain	László Berti
Roger Ducret	Charles Crahay	István Lichteneckert
Philippe Cattiau	Fernand de Montigny	Sándor Posta
Henri Jobier	Maurice van Damme	Zoltán Schenker
Jacques Coutrot	Marcel Berré	Ödön Tersztyánszky
Guy de Luget	Albert de Roocker	
André Labatut		
Joseph Peroteaux		
1928 ITALY	**FRANCE**	**ARGENTINA**
Ugo Pignotti	Lucien Gaudin	Roberto Larraz
Oreste Puliti	Philippe Cattiau	Raúl Anganuzzi
Giulio Gaudini	Roger Ducret	Luis Lucchetti
Giorgio Pessina	André Labatut	Hector Lucchetti
Giorgio Chiavacci	Raymond Flacher	Carmelo Camet
Gioacchino Guaragna	André Gaboriaud	
1932 FRANCE	**ITALY**	**UNITED STATES**
Edouard Gardère	Gustavo Marzi	George C. Calnan
René Lemoine	Ugo Pignotti	Frank Righeimer Jr.
René Bougnol	Gioacchino Guaragna	Richard Steere
Philippe Cattiau	Giulio Gaudini	Hugh Alessandroni
René Bondoux	Giorgio Pessina	Dernell Every
Jean Piot	Rodolfo Terlizzi	Joseph Levis
1936 ITALY	**FRANCE**	**GERMANY**
Gustavo Marzi	André Gardère	Erwin Casmir
Gioacchino Guaragna	René Bougnol	Julius Eisenecker
Manlio di Rosa	René Lemoine	August Heim
Ciro Verratti	Jacques Coutrot	Seigfrid Lerdon
Giulio Gaudini	Edouard Gardère	Otto Adam
Giorgio Bocchino	René Bondoux	Stefan Rosenbauer
1948 FRANCE	**ITALY**	**BELGIUM**
André Bonin	Renzo Nostini	Georges de Bourguignon
Christian d'Oriola	Manlio di Rosa	Henry Paternoster
Jean Buhan	Edoardo Mangiarotti	Edoardo Yves
René Bougnol	Giuliano Nostini	Raymond Bru
Jacques Lataste	Giorgio Pellini	André van de W. de
Adrien Rommel	Saverio Ragno	Vorsselaer
		Paul Valcke
1952 FRANCE	**ITALY**	**HUNGARY**
Jean Buhan	Giancarlo Bergamini	Endre Tilli
Christian d'Oriola	Antonio Spallino	Aladár Gerevich
Adrien Rommel	Manlio di Rosa	Endre Palócz
Claude Netter	Edoardo Mangiarotti	Lajos Maszlay
Jacques Nöel	Renzo Nostini	Tibor Berczelly
Jacques Lataste	Giorgio Pellini	József Sákovics

Christian d'Oriola (FRA) (left) won 2 gold medals in the individual foil event and a gold and a silver medal in the team event, in 1952 and 1956.

	GOLD	SILVER	BRONZE
1956	**ITALY**	**FRANCE**	**HUNGARY**
	Edoardo Mangiarotti	Christian d'Oriola	Lajos Somodi
	Giancarlo Bergamini	Jacques Lataste	József Gyuricza
	Antonio Spallino	René Coicaud	Endre Tilli
	Vittorio Lucarelli	Claude Netter	József Marosi
	Manlio di Rosa	Roger Closset	Mihály Fülöp
	Luigi Carpaneda	Bernard Baudoux	József Sákovics
1960	**U.S.S.R.**	**ITALY**	**GERMANY**
	Viktor Zhadanovich	Alberto Pellegrino	Jürgen Theuerkauff
	Mark Midler	Luigi Carpaneda	Tim Gerresheim
	Yuriy Sissikin	Mario Curletto	Eberhard Mehl
	Gherman Sveshnikov	Aldo Aureggi	Jürgen Brecht
	Yuriy Rudov	Edoardo Mangiarotti	
1964	**U.S.S.R.**	**POLAND**	**FRANCE**
	Gherman Sveshnikov	Zbigniew Skrudik	Daniel Revenu
	Yuriy Sissikin	Witold Woyda	Jacky Courtillat
	Viktor Zhadanovich	Ryszard Parulski	Pierre Rodacanachi
	Mark Midler	Egon Franke	Christian Noël
	Yury Scharov	Janusz Rózycki	Jean-Claude Magnan
1968	**FRANCE**	**U.S.S.R.**	**POLAND**
	Daniel Revenu	Gherman Sveshnikov	Witold Woyda
	Gilles Berolatti	Yury Scharov	Zbigniew Skrudlik
	Christian Noël	Vassily Stankovich	Ryszard Parulski
	Jean-Claude Magnan	Viktor Putiatin	Egon Franke
	Jacques Dimont	Yuriy Sissikin	Adam Lisewski
1972	**POLAND**	**U.S.S.R.**	**FRANCE**
	Witold Woyda	Vassily Stankovich	Daniel Revenu
	Lech Koziejowski	Anatoly Kotescev	Christian Noël
	Jerzy Kaczmarek	Vladimir Demissov	Bernard Talvard
	Marek Dabrowski	Leonid Romanov	Jean-Claude Magnan
	Arkadiusz Godel	Viktor Putiatin	Gilles Berolatti
1976	**WEST GERMANY**	**ITALY**	**FRANCE**
	Matthias Behr	Fabio Dal Zotto	Christian Noël
	Thomas Bach	Carlo Montano	Bernard Talvard
	Harald Hein	Stefano Simoncelli	Didier Flament
	Klaus Reichert	Giovanni B. Coletti	Frederic Pietruska

	GOLD	SILVER	BRONZE
1980	**FRANCE**	**U.S.S.R.**	**POLAND**
	Didier Flament	Aleksandr Romankov	Adam Robak
	Paskal Jolyot	Vladimir Smirnov	Boguslaw Zych
	Bruno Boscherie	Sabiryan Rusiyev	Lech Koziejowski
	Philippe Bonnin	Aschot Karagyan	Marian Sypniewski
1984	**ITALY**	**WEST GERMANY**	**FRANCE**
	Mauro Numa	Matthias Behr	Philippe Omnes
	Andrea Borella	Mathias Gey	Patrick Groc
	Stefano Cerioni	Harald Hein	Frederick Pietruszka
	Angelo Scuri	Frank Beck	Pascal Jolyot
	Andrea Cipressa	Klaus Reichert	Marc Cerboni
1988	**U.S.S.R.**	**WEST GERMANY**	**HUNGARY**
	Vladimir Aptsiaouri	Matthias Behr	Istvan Busa
	Anvar Ibragumov	Thomas Endres	Zsolt Ersek
	Boris Koretskii	Mathias Gey	Robert Gatai
	Ilgar Mamedov	Ulrich Schreck	Pal Szekeres
	Alexandr Romankov	Thorsten Weidner	Istvan Szelei

ÉPÉE (INDIVIDUAL)

	GOLD	SILVER	BRONZE
1896	Event not held		
1900	Ramón Fonst (CUB)	Louis Perrée (FRA)	Léon Sée (FRA)
1904	Ramón Fonst (CUB)	Charles Tatham (USA)	Albertson Van Zo Post (USA)
1906	Georges de la Falaise (FRA)	Georges Dillon-Kavanagh (FRA)	Alexander van Blijenburgh (HOL)
1908	Gaston Alibert (FRA) 5 wins	Alexandre Lippmann (FRA) 4	Eugène Olivier (FRA) 4
1912	Paul Anspach (BEL) 6 wins	Ivan Osiier (DEN) 5	Philippe Le Hardy de Beaulieu (BEL) 4
1920	Armand Massard (FRA) 9 wins	Alexandre Lippmann (FRA) 7	Gustave Buchard (FRA) 6
1924	Charles Delporte (BEL) 8 wins	Roger Ducret (FRA) 7	Nils Hellsten (SWE) 7
1928	Lucien Gaudin (FRA) 8 wins	Georges Buchard (FRA) 7	George Calnan (USA) 6
1932	Giancarlo Cornaggia-Medici (ITA) 8 wins	Georges Buchard (FRA) 7	Carlo Agostoni (ITA) 7
1936	Franco Riccardi (ITA) 5 wins	Saverio Ragno (ITA) 6	Giancarlo Cornaggia-Medici (ITA) 6
1948	Luigi Cantone (ITA) 7 wins	Oswald Zappelli (SUI) 5	Edoardo Mangiarotti (ITA) 5
1952	Edoardo Mangiarotti (ITA) 7 wins	Dario Mangiarotti (ITA) 6	Oswarld Zappelli (SUI) 6
1956	Carlo Pavesi (ITA) 5 wins	Giuseppe Delfino (ITA) 5	Edoardo Mangiarotti (ITA) 5
1960	Giuseppe Delfino (ITA) 5 wins	Allan L. N. Jay (GBR) 5	Bruno Khabarov (URS) 4
1964	Grigory Kriss (URS) 2 wins	H. William F. Hoskyns (GBR) 2	Guram Kostava (URS) 1
1968	Gyözö Kulcsár (HUN) 4 wins	Grigory Kriss (URS) 4	Gianluigi Saccaro (ITA) 4
1972	Csaba Fenyvesi (HUN) 4 wins	Jacques la Degaillerie (FRA) 3	Gyözö Kulcsár (HUN) 3
1976	Alexander Pusch (GER) 3 wins	Jurgen Hehn (GER) 3	Gyözö Kulcsár (HUN) 3
1980	Johan Harmenberg (SWE) 4 wins	Erno Kolczonay (HUN) 3	Philippe Riboud (FRA) 3
1984	Philippe Boisse (FRA)	Bjorne Vaggo (SWE)	Philippe Riboud (FRA)

GOLD	SILVER	BRONZE
1988 Arnd Schmitt (FRG)	Philippe Riboud (FRA)	Andrey Chouvalov (URS)

ÉPÉE (TEAM)

1896–1904 Event not held

GOLD	SILVER	BRONZE
1906 **FRANCE** Pierre d'Hugues George Dillon-Kavanagh Mohr Georges de la Falaise	**GREAT BRITAIN** William H. Derborough Cosmo E. Duff-Gordon Charles N. Robinson Edgar Seligman	**BELGIUM** Constant Cloquet Fernard de Montigny Edmond Grahay Philippe Le Hardy de Beaulieu
1908 **FRANCE** Gaston Alibert Bernard Gravier Alexandre Lippmann Eugène Olivier Jean Stern Henri-Georges Berger Charles Collignon	**GREAT BRITAIN** C. Leaf Daniell Cecil Haig Martin Holt Robert Montgomerie Edward Amphlett Edgar Seligman Sydney Martineau	**BELGIUM** Paul Anspach Désiré Beaurain Ferdinand Feyerick François Rom Fernand de Montigny Victor Willems Ferdnand Bosmans
1912 **BELGIUM** Paul Anspach Henri Anspach Fernand de Montigny Jacques Ochs Gaston Salmon Francois Rom Victor Willems Robert Hennet	**GREAT BRITAIN** Edgar Seligman Edward Amphlett Robert Montgomerie John Blake Percival Davson Arthur Everitt Sydney Martineau Martin Holt	**NETHERLANDS** Adrianus E. W. de Jong W. P. Hubert van Blijenburgh Jetze Doorman George van Rossem Leo Nardus
1920 **ITALY** Nedo Nadi Aldo Nadi Abelardo Olivier Giovanni Canova Dino Urbani Tullio Bozza Andrea Marrazzi Antonio Allocchio Paolo Thaón di Revel	**BELGIUM** Paul Anspach Léon Tom Ernest Gevers Felix G. d'Alviella Victor Boin Joseph de Craecker Maurice de Wée Philippe Le Hardy de Beaulieu	**FRANCE** Armand Massard Alexandre Lippmann Gustave Buchard Casanova Georges Trombert Gaston Amson Moreau
1924 **FRANCE** Lucien Gaudin Roger Ducret Alexandre Lippmann Georges Buchard André Labatut Georges Tainturier Lioteel Lioteel	**BELGIUM** Fernand de Montigny Joseph de Craecker Paul Anspach Ernest Gevers Léon Tom Charles Delporte	**ITALY** Vincenzo Cuccia Giovanni Canova Giulio Basletta Marcello Bertinetti Virgilio Mantegazza Oreste Moricca
1928 **ITALY** Carlo Agostoni Marcello Bartinetti Giancarlo Cornaggia-Medici Renzo Minoli Giulio Basletta Franco Riccardi	**FRANCE** Armand Massard Georges Buchard Gaston Amson Emile Cornic Bernard Schmetz René Barbier	**PORTUGAL** Paolo d'Eca Leal Mário de Noronha Jorge Paiva Frederico Paredes João Sassetti Henrique da Silveira
1932 **FRANCE** Bernard Schmetz Philippe Cattiau Georges Buchard Jean Piot Fernand Jourdant Georges Tainturier	**ITALY** Carlo Agostoni Franco Riccardi Saverio Ragno Giancarlo Cornaggia-Medici Renzo Minoli	**UNITED STATES** George Calnan Gustave Heiss Tracy Jaeckel Frank Righeimer Jr. Curtis Shears Miguel de Capriles

	GOLD	SILVER	BRONZE
1936	**ITALY**	**SWEDEN**	**FRANCE**
	Giancarlo Cornaggia-Medici	Sven Thofelt	Georges Buchard
		Gustaf Dyrssen	Paul Wormser
	Edoardo Mangiarotti	Gösta Almgren	Philippe Cattiau
	Saverio Ragno	Hans Granfelt	Henri Dulieux
	Alfredo Pezzano	Birger Cederin	Bernard Schmetz
	Giancarlo Brusati	Hans van Drakenberg	Michel Pécheux
	Franco Riccardi		
1948	**FRANCE**	**ITALY**	**SWEDEN**
	Henri Guérin	Edoardo Mangiarotti	Carl Forssell
	Henri Lepage	Carlo Agostoni	Arne Tolbom
	Marcel Desprets	Fiorenzo Marini	Bengt H. Ljungquist
	Michel Pécheux	Antonio Mandruzzato	Sven Thofelt
	Maurice Huet	Luigi Cantone	Frank Cervell
	Edouard Artigas	Dario Mangiarotti	Per H. Carleson
1952	**ITALY**	**SWEDEN**	**SWITZERLAND**
	Edoardo Mangiarotti	Lennart Magnusson	Willy Fitting
	Dario Mangiarotti	Carl Forssell	Otto Rüfenacht
	Carlo Pavesi	Berndt-Otto Rehbinder	Oswald Zappelli
	Giuseppe Delfino	Per H. Carleson	Paul Barth
	Franco Bertinetti	Sven Fahlman	Marlo Valota
	Roberto Battaglia	Bengt H. Ljungquist	Paul Meister
1956	**ITALY**	**HUNGARY**	**FRANCE**
	Giuseppe Delfino	Béla Rerrich	Yves Dreyfus
	Franco Bertinetti	Ambrus Nagy	René Queyroux
	Alberto Pellegrino	Barnabás Berszenyi	Daniel Dagallier
	Giorgio Anglesio	József Marosi	Claude Nigon
	Carlo Pavesi	József Sákovics	Armand Mouyal
	Edoardo Mangiarotti	Lajos Balthazár	
1960	**ITALY**	**GREAT BRITAIN**	**U.S.S.R.**
	Alberto Pellegrino	Allan L. N. Jay	Valentin Chernikov
	Carlo Pavesi	Michael Howard	Arnold Chernusevich
	Giuseppe Delfino	John Pelling	Guram Kostava
	Edoardo Mangiarotti	H. William F. Hoskyns	Bruno Khabarov
	Gianluigi Saccaro	Michael Alexander	Aleksandr Pavlovsky
	Fiorenzo Marini	Raymond Harrison	
1964	**HUNGARY**	**ITALY**	**FRANCE**
	Győző Kulcsár	Gianluigi Saccaro	Jacques Brodin
	Zoltán Nemere	Giovanni Battista Breda	Yves Dreyfus
	Tamás Gabor	Gianfranco Paolucci	Claude Bourquard
	István Kausz	Giuseppe Delfino	Jack Guittet
	Árpád Bárány	Alberto Pellegrino	Claude Brodin
1968	**HUNGARY**	**U.S.S.R.**	**POLAND**
	Csaba Fenyvesi	Grigory Kriss	Bogdan Andrzejewski
	Zoltán Nemere	Iosif Vitebsky	Michal Butkiewicz
	Pál Schmitt	Aleksey Nikanchikov	Bogdan Gonsior
	Győző Kulcsár	Yury Smolyakov	Henryk Nielaba
	Pál Nagy	Viktor Modzalevsky	Kazimierz Barburski
1972	**HUNGARY**	**SWITZERLAND**	**U.S.S.R.**
	Sandor Erdoes	Guy Evequoz	Viktor Modzalevsky
	Győző Kulcsár	Peter Lötscher	Sergei Paramonov
	Csaba Fenyvesi	Daniel Giger	Igor Valetov
	Pál Schmitt	Christian Kanter	Georgy Zajitsky
	Istvan Osztrics	François Suchanecki	Grigory Kriss
1976	**SWEDEN**	**WEST GERMNY**	**SWITZERLAND**
	Carl Von Essen	Alexander Pusch	Francois Suchanecki
	Hans Jacobson	Jurgen Hehn	Michel Poffet
	Leif Hogstrom	Reinhold Behr	Daniel Giger
	Rolf Edling	Volker Fischer	Christian Kauter
1980	**FRANCE**	**POLAND**	**U.S.S.R.**
	Philippe Riboud	Pyotr Jablowski	Aschot Karagyan
	Patrick Picot	Andrzej Lis	Boris Lukomski
	Hubert Gardas	Leszek Swornowski	Aleksandr Abushakhmetov
	Philippe Boisse	Ludomir Chronowski	Aleksandr Moshayev

GOLD	SILVER	BRONZE
1984 **WEST GERMANY**	**FRANCE**	**ITALY**
Elmar Borrmann	Philippe Boisse	Stefano Bellone
Volker Fischer	Jean Michel Henry	Sandro Cuomo
Gerhard Heer	Olivier Lenglet	Cosimo Ferro
Rafael Nickel	Philippe Riboud	Roberto Manzi
Alexander Pusch	Michel Salesse	Angelo Mazzoni
1988 **FRANCE**	**WEST GERMANY**	**U.S.S.R.**
Frederic Delpla	Elmar Borrmann	Andrey Chouvalov
Jean Michel Henry	Volker Fischer	Pavel Kolobkov
Olivier Lenglet	Thomas Gerull	Vladimir Reznitchenko
Philippe Riboud	Alexander Pusch	Mikhail Tichko
Eric Srecki	Arnd Schmitt	Igor Tikhomirov

SABRE (INDIVIDUAL)

1896 Jean Georgiadis	Telemachos Karakalos	Holger Nielsen
(GRE) 4 wins	(GRE) 3	(DEN) 2
1900 Georges de la Falaise	Léon Thiébaut	Siegfried Flesch
(FRA) d.n.a.	(FRA) d.n.a.	(AUT) d.n.a.
1904 Manuel Diaz	William Grebe	Albertson Van Zo Post
(CUB) d.n.a.	(USA) d.n.a.	(USA) d.n.a.
1906 Jean Georgiadis	Gustav Casmir	Federico Cesarano
(GR) d.n.a.	(GER) d.n.a.	(ITA) d.n.a.
1908 Jenö Fuchs	Béla Zulavsky	Vilem Goppold von
(HUN) 6 wins	(HUN) 6	Lobsdorf
		(BOH) 4
1912 Jenö Fuchs	Béla Békéssy	Ervin Mészáros
(HUN) 6 wins	(HUN) 5	(HUN) 5
1920 Nedo Nadi	Aldo Nadi	Adrianus E. W. de Jong
(ITA) 11 wins	(ITA) 9	(HOL) 7
1924 Sándor Posta	Rogert Ducret	János Garai
(HUN) 5 wins	(FRA) 5	(HUN) 5
1928 Ödön Tersztyánszky	Attila Petschauer	Bino Bini
(HUN) 9 wins	(HUN) 9	(ITA) 8
1932 György Piller	Giulio Gaudini	Endre Kabos
(HUN) 8 wins	(ITA) 7	(HUN) 5
1936 Endre Kabos	Gustavo Marzi	Aladár Gerevich
(HUN) 7 wins	(ITA) 6	(HUN) 6
1948 Aladár Gerevich	Vincenzo Pinton	Pál Kovács
(HUN) 7 wins	(ITA) 5	(HUN) 5
1952 Pál Kovács	Aladár Gerevich	Tibor Berczelly
(HUN) 8 wins	(HUN) 7	(HUN) 5
1956 Rudolf Kárpáti	Jerzy Pawlowski	Lev Kuznyetsov
(HUN) 6 wins	(POL) 5	(URS) 4
1960 Rudolf Kárpáti	Zoltán Horvath	Wladimiro Calarese
(HUN) 5 wins	(HUN) 4	(ITA) 4
1964 Tibor Pézsa	Claude Arabo	Umar Mavlikhanov
(HUN) 2 wins	(FRA) 2	(URS) 1
1968 Jerzy Powlowski	Mark Rakita	Tibor Pézsa
(POL) 4 wins	(URS) 4	(HUN) 3
1972 Viktor Sidiak	Peter Maroth	Vladimir Nazlimov
(URS) 4 wins	(HUN) 3	(URS) 3
1976 Viktor Krovopouskov	Vladimir Nazlimov	Viktor Sidiak
(URS) 5 wins	(URS) 4	(URS) 3
1980 Viktor Krovopuskov	Mikhail Burtsev	Imre Gedovari
(URS) 5 wins	(URS) 4	(HUN) 3
1984 Jean Francois Lamour	Marco Marin	Peter Westbrook
(FRA)	(ITA)	(USA)
1988 Jean Francois Lamour	Janusz Olech	Giovanni Scalzo
(FRA)	(POL)	(ITA)

SABRE (TEAM)

GOLD	SILVER	BRONZE

1896–1904 Event not held

1906 GERMANY
Gustav Casmir
Jacob Erckrath de Bary
August Petri
Emil Schön

GREECE
Jean Georgiadis
Menelaos Sakorraphos
C. Zorbas
Triantaphylos Kordogannis

NETHERLANDS
James A. H. L. Melvill
    van Carnbée
Johannes Franciscus
    Osten
George van Rossem
Maurits Jacob van
    Löben Sels

1908 HUNGARY
Jenö Fuchs
Oszkár Gerde
Péter Tóth
Lajos Werkner
Dezsö Földes

ITALY
Riccardo Nowak
Alessandro Pirzio-Biroli
Abelardo Olivier
Marcello Bertinetti
Sante Ceccherini

BOHEMIA
Vilém Goppold von
    Lobsdorf
Jaroslav Tucek
Vlastimil Lada-
    Sázavsky
Otakar Lada
Bedřich Schéjbal

1912 HUNGARY
László Berti
Jenö Fuchs
Ervin Mészáros
Zoltán Schenker
Dezsö Földes
Oszkár Gerde
Péter Tóth
Lajos Werkner

AUSTRIA
Richard Verderber
Otto Herschmann
Rudolf Cvetko
Friedrich Golling
Andreas Suttner
Albert Bogen
Reinhold Trampler

NETHERLANDS
William P. Hubert
    van Blijenburgh
Adrianus E. W. de Jong
Daik Scalongne
Jetze Doorman
George van Rossem
Hendrik de Iongh

1920 ITALY
Nedo Nadi
Aldo Nadi
Oreste Puliti
Dino Urbani
Baldo Baldi
Francesco Gargano
Giorgio Santelli

FRANCE
Marc Perrodon
Georges Trombert
J. Margraff
Henri de Saint Germain
Jean Lacroix Mondielli

NETHERLANDS
Jan van der Wiele
Adrianus E. W. de Jong
Jetze Doorman
William P. Hubert van
    Blijenburgh
Louis A. Delaunoy
Salomon Zeldenrust
Henri J. M. Wijnoldij-
    Daniels

1924 ITALY
Oreste Puliti
Giulio Sarrocchi
Marcello Bertinetti
Oreste Moricca
Renato Anselmi
Guido Balzarini
Bino Bini
Vincenzo Cuccia

HUNGARY
László Berti
János Garai
Sándor Posta
József Rády
Zoltán Schenker
Jeno Uhlyárik
László Széchy
Ödön Tersztyánszky

NETHERLANDS
Adrianus E. W. De Jong
Jetzc Doorman
Hendrik D.
    Scherpenhuysen
Jan van der Wiele
Maarten H. van Dulm

1928 HUNGARY
János Garai
Gyula Glykais
Sándor Gombos
József Rády
Ödön Tersztyánszky
Attila Petschauer

ITALY
Renato Anselmi
Bino Bini
Gustavo Marzi
Oreste Puliti
Emilio Salafia
Giulio Sarrocchi

POLAND
Kazimierz Laskowski
Aleksander Malecki
Adam Papée
Wladyslaw Segda
Tadeusz Friedrich
Jerzy Zabielski

1932 HUNGARY
Endre Kabos
Aladár Gerevich
György Piller
Gyula Glykais
Attila Petschauer
Ernö Nagy

ITALY
Renato Anselmi
Gustavo Marzi
Arturo de Vecchi
Giulio Gaudini
Ugo Pignotti
Emilio Salafia

POLAND
Leszek Lubicz-Nycz
Marian Suski
Wladyslaw Dobrowolski
Adam Papée
Tadeusz Friedrich
Wladyslaw Segda

1936 HUNGARY
Tibor Berczelly
Aladár Gerevich
Endre Kabos
László Rajcsányi
Imre Rajczy
Pál Kovács

ITALY
Giulio Gaudini
Gustavo Marzi
Aldo Masciotta
Aldo Montano
Vincenzo Pinton
Athos Tanzini

GERMANY
Richard Wahl
Erwin Casmir
Julius Eisenecker
August Heim
Hans Jörger
Hans Esser

Rudolf Karpati (HUN) (left) won the individual sabre competition in 1956 and 1960, one of 3 men who have won the gold medal twice.

Part of Hungary's successful sabre team poses in London in 1908. Since then, Hungarian teams have amassed 8 gold medals, a silver medal, and 3 bronze medals in this event.

GOLD	SILVER	BRONZE
1948 **HUNGARY**	**ITALY**	**UNITED STATES**
Aladár Gerevich	Gastone Darè	Norman Armitage
Rudolf Kárpáti	Carlo Turcato	George Worth
Pál Kovács	Vincenzo Pinton	Tibor Nyilas
Tibor Berczelly	Mauro Racca	Dean V. Cetrulo
László Rajcsányi	Renzo Nostini	Miguel de Capriles
Bertalan Papp	Aldo Montano	James Flynn
1952 **HUNGARY**	**ITALY**	**FRANCE**
Rudolf Kárpáti	Gastone Daré	Jean Laroyenne
Pál Kovács	Robert Ferrari	Jacques Lefèvre
Tibor Berczelly	Renzo Nostini	Jean Levavasseur
Aladár Gerevich	Giorgio Pellini	Bernard Morel
László Rajcsányi	Vincenzo Pinton	Maurice Piot
Bertalan Papp	Mauro Racca	Jean-François Tournon
1956 **HUNGARY**	**POLAND**	**U.S.S.R.**
Atilla Keresztes	Zygmunt Pawlas	Yakov Rylskiy
Aladár Gerevich	Jerzy Pawlowski	David Tychler
Rudolf Kárpáti	Wojciech Zablocki	Lev Kuznyetsov
Jenö Hámori	Andrzej Piatkowski	Evgeniy Cherepovskiy
Pál Kovács	Marek Kuszewski	Leonid Bogdanov
Dániel Magai	Ryszard Zub	
1960 **HUNGARY**	**POLAND**	**ITALY**
Zoltán Horváth	Jerzy Pawlowski	Pierluigi Chicca
Rudolf Kárpáti	Wojciech Zablocki	Wladimiro Calarese
Tamás Mendelényi	Ryszard Zub	Mario Ravagnan
Pál Kovács	Emil Ochyra	Roberto Ferrari
Gabor Delneki	Andrzej Piatkowski	Gianpaolo Calanchini
Aladár Gerevich	Marek Kuszewski	
1964 **U.S.S.R.**	**ITALY**	**POLAND**
Nugzar Asatiani	Wladimiro Calarese	Emil Ochyra
Yakov Rylsky	Cesare Salvadori	Jerzy Pawlowski
Mark Rakita	Gianpaolo Calanchini	Ryszard Zub
Umar Mavlikhanov	Pierluigi Chicca	Andrzej Piatowski
Boris Melnikov	Mario Ravagnan	Wojciech Zablocki
1968 **U.S.S.R.**	**ITALY**	**HUNGARY**
Vladimir Nazlimov	Wladimiro Calarese	Tamás Kovács
Viktor Sidiak	Michele Maffei	János Kalamár
Eduard Vinokurov	Cesare Salvadori	Péter Bakonyi
Mark Rakita	Pierluigi Chicca	Miklós Meszéna
Umar Mavlikhanov	Rolando Rigoli	Tibor Pezsa

Aladár Gerevich (right), the Hungarian sabreur, won 7 gold, 1 silver, and 2 bronze medals from 1932 to 1960. This action took place in 1948.

Action during the sabre event in Rome, 1960, with Fimamizu of Japan (right), dueling with Van Celden of Israel.

	GOLD	SILVER	BRONZE
1972	**ITALY**	**U.S.S.R.**	**HUNGARY**
	Michele Maffei	Vladimir Nazlimov	Pál Gerevich
	Mario A. Montano	Eduard Vinokurov	Tamás Kovács
	Rolando Rigoli	Viktor Sidiak	Peter Maroth
	Mario T. Montano	Viktor Bajenov	Tibor Pezsa
	Cesare Salvadori	Mark Rakita	Péter Bakonyi
1976	**U.S.S.R.**	**ITALY**	**ROMANIA**
	Viktor Krovopouskov	Mario A. Montano	Dan Irimiciuc
	Eduard Vinokurov	Michele Maffei	Ioan Pop
	Viktor Sidiak	Angelo Arcidiacono	Marin Mustata
	Vladimir Nazlimov	Tommaso Montano	Cornel Marin
1980	**U.S.S.R.**	**ITALY**	**HUNGARY**
	Mikhail Burtsev	Michele Maffei	Imre Gedovari
	Viktor Krovopouskov	Mario Montano	Rudolf Nebald
	Viktor Sidyak	Marco Romano	Pal Gerevich
	Vladimir Nazlymov	Ferdinando Meglio	Ferenc Hammang
1984	**ITALY**	**FRANCE**	**ROMANIA**
	Marco Marin	Jean Francois Lamour	Marin Mustata
	Gianfranco Dalla Barba	Pierre Guichot	Ioan Pop
	Giovanni Scalzo	Herve Granger-Veyron	Alexandru Chiculita
	Ferdinando Meglio	Philippe Delrieu	Corneliu Marin
	Angelo Arcidiacono	Franck Ducheix	
1988	**HUNGARY**	**U.S.S.R.**	**ITALY**
	Imre Bujdoso	Andrey Alchan	Massimo Cavaliere
	Laszlo Csongradi	Mikhail Burtsev	Gianfranco Dalla Barba
	Imre Gedovari	Sergey Noriakine	Marco Marin
	Gyorgy Nebald	Sergey Mindirgassov	Ferdinando Meglio
	Bence Szabo	Gueorgui Pogossov	Giovanni Scalzo

Fencing (Women)

FOIL (INDIVIDUAL)

1896–1920	Event not held		
1924	Ellen Osiier	Gladys M. Davis	Grete Heckscher
	(DEN) 5 wins	(GBR) 4	(DEN) 3
1928	Helène Mayer	Muriel B. Freeman	Olga Oelkers
	(GER) 7 wins	(GBR) 6	(GER) 4
1932	Ellen Preis	J. Heather Guinness	Ena Bogen
	(AUT) 9 wins	(GBR) 8	(HUN) 7

Nedo Nadi (ITA), winner of an unprecedented 5 gold medals at the 1920 Games, poses here with Helène Mayer (GER), gold medalist in the women's fencing event at the 1928 Games.

	GOLD	SILVER	BRONZE
1936	Ilona Elek (HUN) 6 wins	Helène Mayer (GER) 5	Ellen Preis (AUT) 5
1948	Ilona Elek (HUN) 6 wins	Karen Lachmann (DEN) 5	Ellen Müller-Preis (AUT) 5
1952	Irene Camber (ITA) 5 wins	Ilona Elek (HUN) 5	Karen Lachmann (DEN) 4
1956	Gillian M. Sheen (GBR) 6 wins	Olga Orban (ROM) 6	Renée Garilhe (FRA) 5
1960	Heidi Schmid (GER) 6 wins	Valentina Rastvorova (URS) 5	Maria Vicol (ROM) 4
1964	Ildikó Ujlaki-Rejtö (HUN) 2 wins	Helga Mees (GER) 2	Antonella Ragno (ITA) 2
1968	Elena Novikova (URS) 4 wins	Pilar Roldan (MEX) 3	Ildikó Ujlaki-Rejtö (HUN) 3
1972	Antonella Ragno-Lonzi (ITA) 4 wins	Ildikó Bóbis (HUN) 3	Galina Gorokhova (URS) 3
1976	Ildikó Schwarczenberger (HUN) 4 wins	Maria C. Collino (ITA) 4	Elene Novikova-Belova (URS) 3
1980	Pascale Trinquet (FRA) 4 wins	Magda Maros (HUN) 3	Barbara Wysoczanska (POL) 3
1984	Jujie Luan (CHN)	Cornelia Hanisch (FRG)	Dorina Vaccaroni (ITA)
1988	Anja Fichtel (FRG)	Sabine Bau (FRG)	Zita Funkenhauser (FRG)

FOIL (TEAM)

1896–1956	Event not held		
1960	U.S.S.R.	HUNGARY	ITALY
	Valentina Rastvorova	Katalin Juhász-Nagy	Irene Camber
	Tatyana Petrenko	Lidia Dömölky	Velleda Cesari
	Valentina Prudskova	Ildikó Ujlaki-Rejtö	Antonella Ragno
	Lyudmila Shishova	Magda Kovács-Nyári	Bruna Colombetti
	Galina Gorokhova	Tiborné Székely	Claudia Pasini
	Alexandra Zabelina		

	GOLD	SILVER	BRONZE
1964	**HUNGARY**	**U.S.S.R.**	**GERMANY**
	Ilkidó Ujlaki-Rejtö	Galina Gorokhova	Heidi Schmid
	Katalin Juhász-Nagy	Valentina Prudskova	Helga Mees
	Lidia Dömölky-Sakovics	Tatyana Samusenko	Rosemarie Scherberger
	Judit Medelényi-Agoston	Lyudmila Shishova	Gudrun Theuerkauff
	Paula Földessy-Marosi	Valentina Rastvorova	
1968	**U.S.S.R.**	**HUNGARY**	**ROMANIA**
	Alexandra Zabelina	Lidia Dömölky-Sakovics	Clara Stahl-Iencic
	Tatyana Samusenko		Ileana Drimba
	Elena Novikova	Ildikó Bóbis	Maria Vicol
	Galina Gorokhova	Ildikó Ujlaki-Rejtö	Olga Szabo
	Svetlana Chirkova	Mária Gulácsy	Ana Ene-Dersidan
		Paula Földessy-Marosi	
1972	**U.S.S.R.**	**HUNGARY**	**ROMANIA**
	Elena Novikova-Belova	Ildikó Sagine-Retjo	Olga Szabo
	Alexandra Zabelina	Ildikó Schwarczenberger	Ileana Gyulai
	Galina Gorokhova	Maria Szolnoki	Ana Pascu
	Tatyana Samusenko	Ildikó Bóbis	Ecaterina Stahl
	Svetlana Chirkova	Ildikó Matuscakene-Ronay	
1976	**U.S.S.R.**	**FRANCE**	**HUNGARY**
	Elena Novikova-Belova	Brigitte Latrille	Ildikó Schwarczenberger
	Olga Kniazeva	Brigitte Dumont	Edit Kovacs
	Valentina Sidorova	Christi Muzio	Magda Maros
	Nailia Guilazova	Veronique Trinquet	Ildikó Sagi-Retjö
1980	**FRANCE**	**U.S.S.R.**	**HUNGARY**
	Brigitte Gaudin	Valentina Sidorova	Ildikó Schwarczenberger
	Pascale Trinquet	Vailia Gilyasova	Magda Maros
	Isabelle Boeri-Begard	Yelena Belova	Gertrud Stefanek
	Veronique Brouquier	Irina Ushakova	Zsuzsa Szocs
1984	**WEST GERMANY**	**ROMANIA**	**FRANCE**
	Christiane Weber	Aurora Dan	Laurence Modaine
	Cornelia Hanisch	Koszto Veber	Pascale Trinquet-Hachin
	Sabine Bischoff	Rozalia Oros	Brigitte Gaudin
	Zita Funkenhauser	Marcela Zsak	Veronique Brouquier
	Ute Wessel	Elisabeta Guzganu	Anne Meygret
1988	**WEST GERMANY**	**ITALY**	**HUNGARY**
	Sabine Bau	Francesca Bortolozzi	Zsuzsanna Janosi
	Anja Fichtel	Annapia Gandolfi	Edit Kovacs
	Zita Funkenhauser	Lucia Traversa	Getrud Stefanek
	Annette Klug	Dorina Vaccaroni	Zsuzsa Szocs
	Christiane Weber	Margherita Zalaffi	Katalin Tuschak

10. Gymnastics (Men)

In gymnastics there are eight events for men which are interlinked. First is the Team Competition which comprises one compulsory and one optional exercise for each of the six events: Floor Exercises, Side Horse, Rings, Horse Vault, Parallel Bars and Horizontal Bars. Each team competitor gets marks out of 10 for both his compulsory and optional exercise for each of the six events. The team of six with the greatest *total* of marks wins the gold medal.

Next, the best 36 competitors from the Team Competition qualify for the Individual All-Round Competition. They each complete a further optional exercise for each of the six events and gain new marks (out of 10) per event. These are then added to the *average* (not total) of their previous total marks in the compulsory and optional sections brought forward from the Team Competition previously decided.

Finally, the six best on each apparatus in the Team Competition qualify for the individual Final on that apparatus. This is decided by adding a new mark (out of 10)

Viktor Chukarin (URS), shown here on the pommeled horse, won a total of 7 gold medals in the gymnastics competitions of 1952 and 1956.

for a further optional exercise on that apparatus to the *average* (not total) of their previous marks in the compulsory and optional performances on that apparatus within the Team Competition previously decided.

In 1948 points for an event were marked out of 20 instead of 10 as in other recent years; otherwise scores since 1936 are of same comparative value.

TEAM COMPETITION

There was no team event in 1896 and 1900. From 1904 to 1932 this event often differed substantially from the current event as to program content, number of competitors and scoring values.

	GOLD	SILVER	BRONZE
1936	**GERMANY** 657.430 pts.	SWITZERLAND 654.802	FINLAND 638.468
	Franz Beckert	Walter Bach	Martti Uosikinen
	Konrad Frey	Albert Bachmann	Heikki Savolainen
	Alfred Schwarzmann	Eugen Mack	Mauri Noroma-Nyberg
	Willi Stadel	Georges Miez	Aleksanteri Saarvala
	Walter Steffens	Michael Reusch	Esa Seeste
	Matthias Volz	Edi Seinemann	Veikkö Pakarinen
1948	**FINLAND** 1,358.3 pts.	SWITZERLAND 1,356.7	HUNGARY 1,330.35
	A. Veikkö Huhtanen	Walter Lehmann	Lajos Tóth
	Paavo Aaltonen	Josef Stalder	Lajos Sántha
	Heikki Savolainen	Christian Kipfer	László Baranyai
	Olavi Rove	Emil Studer	Ferenc Pataki
	Einari Teräsvirta	Robert Lucy	János Mogyorósi-
	Kalevi Laitinen	Michael Reusch	Klencs
			Ferenc Várköi
1952[1]	**U.S.S.R.** 574.4 pts.	SWITZERLAND 567.5	FINLAND 564.2
	Viktor Chukarin	Josef Stalder	Onni Lappalainen
	Grant Shaginyan	Hans Eugster	Berndt Lindfors
	Valentin Muratov	Jean Tschabold	Paavo Aaltonen
	Yevgeniy Korolkov	Jack Günthard	Kaino Lempinen
	Vladimir Belyakov	Melchior Thalmann	Heikki Savolainen
	Yosif Berdiyev	Ernst Gebendinger	Kalevi Laitinen
	Mikhail Perelman	Hans Schwarzentruber	Kalevi Viskari
	Dimitriy Leonkin	Ernst Fivian	Olavi Rove

---

[1] In 1952 eight competitors counted instead of 6 as in other years.

	GOLD	SILVER	BRONZE
1956	**U.S.S.R.** 568.25 pts.	**JAPAN** 566.40	**FINLAND** 555.95
	Viktor Chukarin	Takashi Ono	Raimo Heinonen
	Valentin Muratov	Masao Takemoto	Onni Lappalainen
	Boris Shakhlin	Akira Kono	Olavi Leimuvirta
	Albert Azaryan	Nobuyuki Aihara	Berndt Lindfors
	Yuriy Titov	Shinsaku Tsukawaki	Martti Mansikka
	Pavel Stolbov	Masami Kubota	Kelevi Suoniemi
1960	**JAPAN** 575.20 pts.	**U.S.S.R.** 572.70	**ITALY** 559.05
	Takashi Ono	Boris Shakhlin	Franco Menichelli
	Shuji Tsurumi	Yuriy Titov	Giovanni Carminucci
	Yukio Endo	Albert Azaryan	Gianfranco Marzolla
	Masao Takemoto	Vladimir Portnoi	Angelo Vicardi
	Nobuyuki Aihara	Valeriy Kerdemilidi	Orlando Polmonari
	Takashi Mitsukuri	Nikolaya Miligulo	Pasquale Carminucci
1964	**JAPAN** 577.95 pts.	**U.S.S.R.** 575.45	**GERMANY** 565.10
	Yukio Endo	Yury Tsapenko	Siegfried Fülle
	Shuji Tsurumi	Boris Shakhlin	Klaus Köste
	Haruhiro Yamashita	Victor Leontyev	Erwin Koppe
	Takashi Mitsukuri	Victor Lisitsky	Peter Weber
	Takuji Hayata	Sergey Diomidov	Philipp Fürst
	Takashi Ono	Yuriy Titov	Günter Lyhs
1968	**JAPAN** 575.90 pts.	**U.S.S.R.** 571.10	**E. GERMANY** 557.15
	Sawao Kato	Mikhail Voronin	Matthias Brehme
	Akinori Nakayama	Sergey Diomidov	Klaus Köste
	Eizo Kenmotsu	Vladimir Klimenko	Siegfried Fülle
	Takeshi Kato	Valeryi Karassev	Peter Weber
	Yukio Endo	Victor Lisitsky	Gerhard Dietrich
	Mitsuo Tsukahara	Valeryi Iljinykh	Günter Beier
1972	**JAPAN** 571.25 pts.	**U.S.S.R.** 564.05	**E. GERMANY** 559.70
	Sawao Kato	Nikolai Andrianov	Klaus Köste
	Eizo Kenmotsu	Mikhail Voronin	Matthias Brehme
	Shigeru Kasamatsu	Viktor Klimenko	Wolfgang Thune
	Akinori Nakayama	Edvard Mikhaelian	Wolfgang Klotz
	Mitsuo Tsukahara	Aleksandre Maleev	Reinhard Rychly
	Teriuihi Okamura	Vladimir Schukin	Jürgen Paeke
1976	**JAPAN** 576.85 pts.	**U.S.S.R.** 576.45	**E. GERMANY** 564.65
	Hisato Igarashi	Vladimir Tikhonov	Bernd Jager
	Shun Fujimoto	Gennadi Kryssin	Wolfgang Klotz
	Sawao Kato	Alexandr Ditiatin	Rainer Hanschke
	Hiroshi Kajiyama	Vladimir Marchenko	Michail Nikolay
	Eizo Kenmotsu	Vladimir Markelov	Lutz Mack
	Mitsuo Tsukahara	Nikolai Andrianov	Roland Bruckner
1980	**U.S.S.R.** 589.60 pts.	**E. GERMANY** 581.15	**HUNGARY** 575.00
	Nikolai Andrianov	Roland Bruckner	Ferenc Donath
	Alexandr Ditiatin	Michael Nikolay	Zoltan Magyar
	Eduard Asaryan	Lutz Hoffmann	Peter Kovacs
	Alexandr Tkachyov	Ralf-Peter Hemmann	Gyorgy Guczoghy
	Bogdan Makuts	Andreas Bronst	Istvan Vamos
	Vladimir Markelov	Lutz Mack	Zoltan Kelemen
1984	**USA** 591.40	**CHINA** 590.80	**JAPAN** 586.70
	Timothy Daggett	Yun Lou	Shinji Morisue
	Scott Johnson	Li Yuejiu	Noritoshi Hirata
	Mitchell Gaylord	Xu Zhiqiang	Koji Sotomura
	James Hartung	Tong Fei	Nobuyuki Kajitani
	Peter Vidmar	Li Ning	Kyoji Yamawaki
	Bart Conner	Li Xiaoping	Koji Gushiken
1988	**U.S.S.R.** 593.35	**E. GERMANY** 588.45	**JAPAN** 585.60
	Vladimir Gogoladze	Ulf Hoffmann	Hiroyuki Konishi
	Vladimir Nouvikov	Andreas Wecker	Takahiro Yamada
	Sergey Kharikov	Sven Tippelt	Toshiharu Sato
	Dmitry Bilozertsev	Ralf Büchner	Daisuke Nishikawa
	Vladimir Artemov	Holger Behrendt	Koichi Mizushima
	Valeriy Lyukine	Sylvio Kroll	Yukio Iketani

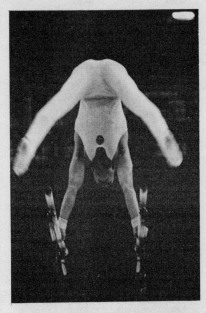

Soviet gymnast Alexandr Sitiatin won a medal in each of the eight gymnastics categories in 1980, setting an all-Olympic record for the most medals won at one Games.

COMBINED EXERCISES (INDIVIDUAL)

This event was not held in 1896. From 1900 to 1932 this event often differed substantially from the current event as to program content and scoring values.

	GOLD	SILVER	BRONZE
1936	Alfred Schwarzmann (GER) 113.100	Eugen Mack (SUI) 112.334	Konrad Frey (GER) 111.532
1948	A. Veikkö Huhtanen (FIN) 229.7	Walter Lehmann (SUI) 229.0	Paavo Aaltonen (FIN) 228.8
1952	Viktor Chukarin (URS) 115.70	Grant Shaginyan (URS) 114.95	Josef Stalder (SUI) 114.75
1956	Viktor Chukarin (URS) 114.25	Takashi Ono (JPN) 114.20	Yuriy Titov (URS) 113.80
1960	Boris Shakhlin (URS) 115.95	Takashi Ono (JPN) 115.90	Yuriy Titov (URS) 115.60
1964	Yukio Endo (JPN) 115.95	Shuji Tsurumi (JPN) 115.40 Boris Shakhlin (URS) 115.40 Victor Lisitsky (URS) 115.40	
1968	Sawao Kato (JPN) 115.90	Mikhail Voronin (URS) 115.85	Akinori Nakayama (JPN) 115.65
1972	Sawao Kato (JPN) 114.650	Eizo Kenmotsu (JPN) 114.575	Akinori Nakayama (JPN) 114.325
1976	Nikolai Andrianov (URS) 116.650	Sawao Kato (JPN) 115.650	Mitsuo Tsukahara (JPN) 115.575
1980	Alexandr Ditiatin (URS) 118.650	Nikolai Andrianov (URS) 118.225	Stoyan Deltchev (BUL) 118.000

GOLD	SILVER	BRONZE
1984 Koji Gushiken (JPN) 118.700	Peter Vidmar (USA) 118.675	Li Ning (CHN) 118.575
1988 Vladimir Artemov (URS) 119.125	Valeriy Lyukine (URS) 119.025	Dmitry Bilozertsev (URS) 118.975

FLOOR COMPETITION

1896–1928 Event not held		
1932 István Pelle (HUN) 9.60	Georges Miez (SUI) 9.47	Mario Lertora (ITA) 9.23
1936 Georges Miez (SUI) 18.666	Josef Walter (SUI) 18.5	Konrad Frey (GER) 18.466 Eugen Mack (SUI) 18.466
1948 Ferenc Pataki (HUN) 38.7	János Mogyorósi-Klencs (HUN) 38.4	Zdenek Ružička (TCH) 38.1
1952 William Thoresson (SWE) 19.25	Tadao Uesako (JPN) 19.15 Jerzy Jokiel (POL) 19.15	
1956 Valentin Muratov (URS) 19.20	Nobuyuki Aihara (JPN) 19.10 William Thoresson (SWE) 19.10 Viktor Chukarin (URS) 19.10	—
1960 Nobuyuki Aihara (JPN) 19.450	Yuriy Titov (URS) 19.325	Franco Menichelli (ITA) 19.275
1964 Franco Menichelli (ITA) 19.45	Victor Lisitsky (URS) 19.35 Yukio Endo (JPN) 19.35	—
1968 Sawao Kato (JPN) 19.475	Akinori Nakayama (JPN) 19.400	Takeshi Kato (JPN) 19.275
1972 Nikolai Andrianov (URS) 19.175	Akinori Nakayama (JPN) 19.125	Shigeru Kasamatsu (JPN) 19.025
1976 Nikolai Andrianov (URS) 19.450	Vladimir Marchenko (URS) 19.425	Peter Kormann (USA) 19.300
1980 Roland Bruckner (GDR) 19.750	Nikolai Andrianov (URS) 19.725	Alexandr Ditiatin (URS) 19.700
1984 Li Ning (CHN) 19.925	Yun Lou (CHN) 19.775	Koji Sotomura (JPN) 19.700 Philippe Vatuone (FRA) 19.700
1988 Sergey Kharikov (URS) 19.925	Vladimir Artemov (URS) 19.900	Lou Yun (CHN) 19.850 Yukio Iketani (JPN) 19.850

SIDE HORSE

1896 Jules A. Zutter (SUI) d.n.a.	Hermann Weingärtner (GER)	
1900 Event not held		
1904 Anton Heida (USA) 42 pts	George Eyser (USA) 33	William A. Merz (USA)29
1906–1920 Event not held		
1924 Josef Wilhelm (SUI) 21.23	Jean Gutweniger (SUI) 21.13	Antoine Rebetez (SUI) 20.73
1928 Hermann Hänggi (SUI) 19.75	Georges Miez (SUI) 19.25	Heikki Savolainen (FIN) 18.83
1932 István Pelle (HUN) 19.07	Omero Bonoli (ITA) 18.87	Frank Haubold (USA) 18.57
1936 Konrad Frey (GER) 19.333	Eugen Mack (SUI) 19.167	Albert Bachmann (SUI) 19.067

	GOLD	SILVER	BRONZE
1948	Paavo Aaltonen (FIN) 38.7 A. Veikkö Huhtanen (FIN) 38.7 Heikki Savolainen (FIN) 38.7	Luigi Zanetti (ITA) 38.3	Guido Figone (ITA) 38.2
1952	Viktor Chukarin (URS) 19.50	Yevgeniy Korolkov (URS) 19.40 Grant Shaginyan (URS) 19.40	—
1956	Boris Shakhlin (URS) 19.25	Takashi Ono (JPN) 19.20	Viktor Chukarin (URS) 19.10

RIGHT: Nikolai Andrianov (URS) has won more Olympic medals than any other male competitor, earning 15 in three Games from 1972 through 1980.

LEFT: Boris Shakhlin (URS) dominated the 1960 gymnastics competition with his 1 bronze, 2 silver, and 4 gold medals.

	GOLD	SILVER	BRONZE
1960	Eugen Ekman (FIN) 19.375 Boris Shakhlin (URS) 19.375		Shuji Tsurumi (JPN) 19.150
1964	Miroslav Cerar (YUG) 19.525	Shuji Tsurumi (JPN) 19.325	Yury Tsapenko (URS) 19.200
1968	Miroslav Cerar (YUG) 19.325	Olli E. Laiho (FIN) 19.225	Mikhail Voronin (URS) 19.200
1972	Viktor Klimenko (URS) 19.125	Sawao Kato (JPN) 19.000	Eizo Kenmotsu (JPN) 18.950
1976	Zoltan Magyar (HUN) 19.700	Eizo Kenmotsu (JPN) 19.575	Nikolai Andrianov (URS) 19.525
1980	Zoltan Magyar (HUN) 19.925	Alexandr Ditiatin (URS) 19.800	Michael Nikolay (GDR) 19.775
1984	Li Ning (CHN) 19.950 Peter Vidmar (USA) 19.950	—	Timothy Daggett (USA) 19.825
1988	Lubomir Gueraskov (URS) 19.950 Zsolt Borkai (HUN) 19.950 Dmitry Bilozertsev (URS) 19.950	—	

RINGS

	GOLD	SILVER	BRONZE
1896	Ioannis Mitropoulos (GRE) d.n.a.	Hermann Weingärtner (GER)	Petros Persakis (GRE)
1900	Event not held		
1904	Herman Glass (USA) 45	William A. Merz (USA) 35	Emil Voight (USA) 32
1906–1920	Event not held		
1924	Franco Martino (ITA) 21.553	Robert Pražák (TCH) 21.483	Ladislav Vácha (TCH) 21.430
1928	Leon Škutelj (YUG) 19.25	Ladislav Vácha (TCH) 19.17	Emanuel Löffler (TCH) 18.83
1932	George Gulack (USA) 18.97	William Denton (USA) 18.60	Giovanni Lattuada (ITA) 18.50
1936	Alois Hudec (TCH) 19.433	Leon Škutelj (YUG) 18.867	Matthias Volz (GER) 18.667
1948	Karl Frei (SUI) 39.60	Michael Reusch (SUI) 39.10	Zdenek Ružička (TCH) 38.50
1952	Grant Shaginyan (URS) 19.75	Viktor Chukarin (URS) 19.55	Hans Eugster (SUI) 19.40 Dimitriy Leonkin (URS) 19.40
1956	Albert Azaryan (URS) 19.35	Valentin Muratov (URS) 19.15	Masao Takemoto (JPN) 19.10 Masami Kubota (JPN) 19.10
1960	Albert Azaryan (URS) 19.725	Boris Shakhlin (URS) 19.500	Velik Kapsazov (BUL) 19.425 Takashi Ono (JPN) 19.425
1964	Takuji Hayata (JPN) 19.475	Franco Menichelli (ITA) 19.425	Boris Shakhlin (URS) 19.400
1968	Akinori Nakayama (JPN) 19.450	Mikhail Voronin (URS) 19.325	Sawao Kato (JPN) 19.225
1972	Akinori Nakayama (JPN) 19.350	Mikhail Voronin (URS) 19.275	Mitsuo Tsukahara (JPN) 19.225
1976	Nikolai Andrianov (URS) 19.650	Aleksandr Ditiatin (URS) 19.550	Danut Grecu (ROM) 19.500
1980	Alexandr Ditiatin (URS) 19.875	Alexandr Tkachyov (URS) 19.725	Jiri Tabak (TCH) 19.600

ABOVE: Olympic champion of the rings in both 1956 and 1960 was Albert Azaryan of Russia.

RIGHT: Akinori Nakayama (JPN) repeated his 1968 triumph on the rings in 1972 at Munich.

	GOLD	SILVER	BRONZE
1984	Koji Gushiken (JPN) 19.850 Li Ning (CHN) 19.850	—	Mitchell Gaylord (USA) 19.825
1988	Holger Behrendt (GDR) 19.925 Dmitry Bilozertsev (URS) 19.925	—	Sven Tippelt (GDR) 19.875

HORSE VAULT

	GOLD	SILVER	BRONZE
1896	Karl Schumann (GER) d.n.a.	Jules A. Zutter (SUI)	—
1900	Event not held		
1904	Anton Heida (USA) 36 George Eyser (USA) 36	—	William A. Merz (USA) 31
1906–1920	Event not held		
1924	Frank Kriz (USA) 9.98	Jan Koutny (TCH) 9.97	Bohumil Mořkovsky (TCH) 9.93
1928	Eugen Mack (SUI) 9.58	Emanuel Löffler (TCH) 9.50	Stane Derganc (YUG) 9.46
1932	Savino Guglielmetti (ITA) 18.03	Alfred Jochim (GER) 17.77	Edward Carmichael (USA) 17.53
1936	Alfred Schwarzmann (GER) 19.200	Eugen Mack (SUI) 18.967	Matthias Volz (GER) 18.467
1948	Paavo Aaltonen (FIN) 39.10	Olavi Rove (FIN) 39.00	János Mogyorósi-Klencs (HUN) 38.50 Ferenc Pataki (HUN) 38.50 Leos Sotornik (TCH) 38.50
1952	Viktor Chukarin (URS) 19.20	Masao Takemoto (JPN) 19.15	Tadao Uesako (JPN) 19.10 Takashi Ono (JPN) 19.10
1956	Helmuth Bantz (GER) 18.85 Valentin Muratov (URS) 18.85	—	Yuriy Titov (URS) 18.75
1960	Takashi Ono (JPN) 19.350 Boris Shakhlin (URS) 19.350	—	Vladimir Portnoi (URS) 19.225
1964	Haruhiro Yamashita (JPN) 19.600	Victor Lisitsky (URS) 19.325	Hannu Rantakari (FIN) 19.300
1968	Mikhail Voronin (URS) 19.000	Yukio Endo (JPN) 18.950	Sergey Diomidov (URS) 18.925
1972	Klaus Köste (GDR) 18.850	Viktor Klimenko (URS) 18.825	Nikolai Andrianov (URS) 18.800
1976	Nikolai Andrianov (URS) 19.450	Mitsuo Tsukahara (JPN) 19.375	Hiroshi Kajiyama (JPN) 19.275
1980	Nikolai Andrianov (URS) 19.825	Alexandr Ditiatin (URS) 19.800	Roland Bruckner (GDR) 19.775
1984	Yun Lou (CHN) 19.950	Li Ning (CHN) 19.825 Koji Gushiken (JPN) 19.825 Mitchell Gaylord (USA) 19.825 Shinji Morisue (JPN) 19.825	—
1988	Lou Yun (CHN) 19.875	Silvio Kroll (GDR) 19.862	Park Jong-Hoon (KOR) 19.775

PARALLEL BARS

	GOLD	SILVER	BRONZE
1896	Alfred Flatow (GER) d.n.a.	Jules A. Zutter (SUI)	Hermann Weingärtner (GER)
1900	Event not held		
1904	George Eyser (USA) 44	Anton Heida (USA) 43	John Duha (USA) 40
1906–1920	Event not held		
1924	August Güttinger (SUI) 21.63	Robert Pražák (TCH) 21.61	Giorgio Zampori (ITA) 21.45
1928	Ladislav Vácha (TCH) 18.83	Josip Primožič (YUG) 18.50	Hermann Hänggi (SUI) 18.08
1932	Romeo Neri (ITA) 18.97	István Pelle (HUN) 18.60	Heikki Savolainen (FIN) 18.27
1936	Konrad Frey (GER) 19.067	Michael Reusch (SUI) 19.034	Alfred Schwarzmann (GER) 18.967
1948	Michael Reusch (SUI) 39.5	Veikkö Huhtanen (FIN) 39.3	Christian Kipfer (SUI) 39.1 Josef Stalder (SUI) 39.1
1952	Hans Eugster (SUI) 19.65	Viktor Chukarin (URS) 19.60	Josef Stalder (SUI) 19.50
1956	Viktor Chukarin (URS) 19.20	Masami Kubota (JPN) 19.15	Takashi Ono (JPN) 19.10 Masao Takemoto (JPN) 19.10
1960	Boris Shakhlin (URS) 19.400	Giovanni Carminucci (ITA) 19.375	Takashi Ono (JPN) 19.350
1964	Yukio Endo (JPN) 19.675	Shuji Tsurumi (JPN) 19.450	Franco Menichelli (ITA) 19.350
1968	Akinori Nakayama (JPN) 19.475	Mikhail Voronin (URS) 19.425	Vladimir Klimenko (URS) 19.225
1972	Sawao Kato (JPN) 19.475	Shigeru Kasamatsu (JPN) 19.375	Eizo Kenmotsu (JPN) 19.250
1976	Sawao Kato (JPN) 19.675	Nikolai Andrianov (URS) 19.500	Mitsuo Tsukahara (JPN) 19.475
1980	Alexandr Tkachyov (URS) 19.775	Alexandr Ditiatin (URS) 19.750	Roland Bruckner (GDR) 19.650
1984	Bart Conner (USA) 19.950	Nobuyuki Kajitani (JPN) 19.925	Mitchell Gaylord (USA) 19.850
1988	Vladimir Artemov (URS) 19.925	Valeriy Lyukine (URS) 19.900	Sven Tippelt (GDR) 19.750

HORIZONTAL BAR

1896	Hermann Weingärtner (GER) d.n.a.	Alfred Flatow (GER)	
1900	Event not held		
1904	Anton Heida (USA) 40 Edward Hennig (USA) 40	—	George Eyser (USA) 39
1906–1920	Event not held		
1924	Leon Štukelj (YUG) 19.730	Jean Gutweniger (SUI) 19.236	André Higelin (FRA) 19.163
1928	Georges Miez (SUI) 19.17	Romeo Neri (ITA) 19.00	Eugen Mack (SUI) 18.92
1932	Dallas Bixler (USA) 18.33	Heikki Savolainen (FIN) 18.07	Einari Teräsvirta (FIN) 18.07[1]
1936	Aleksanteri Saarvala (FIN) 19.367	Konrad Frey (GER) 19.267	Alfred Schwarzmann (GER) 19.233
1948	Josef Stalder (SUI) 39.7	Walter Lehmann (SUI) 39.4	Veikkö Huhtanen (FIN) 39.2

---

[1]Teräsvirta conceded second place to Savolainen.

GOLD	SILVER	BRONZE
1952 Jack Günthard (SUI) 19.55	Josef Stalder (SUI) 19.50 Alfred Schwarzmann (GER) 19.50	—
1956 Takashi Ono (JPN) 19.60	Yuriy Titov (URS) 19.40	Masao Takemoto (JPN) 19.30
1960 Takashi Ono (JPN) 19.60	Masao Takemoto (JPN) 19.525	Boris Shakhlin (URS) 19.475
1964 Boris Shakhlin (URS) 19.625	Yuriy Titov (URS) 19.55	Miroslav Cerar (YUG) 19.50
1968 Mikhail Voronin (URS) 19.550 Akinori Nakayama (JPN) 19.550	—	Eizo Kenmotsu (JPN) 19.375
1972 Mitsuo Tsukahara (JPN) 19.725	Sawao Kato (JPN) 19.525	Shigeru Kasamatsu (JPN) 19.450
1976 Mitsuo Tsukahara (JPN) 19.675	Eizo Kenmotsu (JPN) 19.500	Henry Böerio (FRA) 19.475
1980 Stoyan Deltchev (BUL) 19.825	Alexandr Ditiatin (URS) 19.750	Nikolai Andrianov (URS) 19.675
1984 Shinji Morisue (JPN) 20.00	Tong Fei (CHN) 19.975	Koji Gushiken (JPN) 19.950
1988 Vladimir Artemov (URS) 19.900 Valeriy Lyukine (URS) 19.900	—	Holger Behrendt (GDR) 19.800 Marius Germann (ROM) 19.800

Gymnastics (Women)

In women's gymnastics there are six events which are interlinked. First is the Team Competition which comprises one compulsory and one optional exercise for each of the four events: Horse Vault, Uneven Bars, Balance Beam and Floor Exercises. Each team competitor gets marks out of 10 for both her compulsory and optional exercise for each of the four events. The team of six with the greatest *total* of marks wins the gold medal.

Next the best 36 competitors from the Team Competition qualify for the Individual All-Round Competition. They each complete a further optional exercise for each of the four events and gain new marks (out of 10) per event. These are then added to the *average* (not total) of their previous total marks in the compulsory and optional sections brought forward from the Team Competition previously decided.

Finally, the six best on each apparatus in the Team Competition qualify for the individual Final on that apparatus. This is decided by adding a new mark (out of 10) for a further optional exercise on that apparatus and the *average* (not total) of their previous marks in the compulsory and optional performances on that apparatus within the Team Competition previously decided.

COMBINED EXERCISES (TEAM)

There was no team event from 1896 to 1924 nor in 1932. A team event was introduced in 1928 and was also held in 1936 to 1956 but the fundamental conditions make the results not comparable with the current event and conditions which started in 1960.

1960 U.S.S.R. 382.320	CZECHOSLOVAKIA 373.323	ROMANIA 372.053
Larissa Latynina	Vera Čáslavská	Sonia Iovan
Sofia Muratova	Eva Bosáková	Elena Leustean
Polina Astakhova	Ludmila Švedová	Antanasia Ionescu
Margarita Nikolayeva	Adolfina Tkačíková	Uta Poreceanu
Lydia Ivanova	Mathydla Matoušková-Šinová	Emilia Lita
Tamara Lyukhina	Hana Ružičková	Elena Niculescu

GOLD	SILVER	BRONZE
1964 U.S.S.R. 380.890	CZECHOSLOVAKIA 379.989	JAPAN 377.889
Larissa Latynina	Vera Čáslavská	Keiko Ikeda-Tanaka
Elena Volchetskaya	Hana Ružičková	Toshiko Aihara-
Polina Astakhova	Jaroslava Sedlačková	Shirasu
Tamara Lyukhina	Adolfina Tkačiková	Kiyoko Ono
Tamara Manina	Mária Krajčírová	Taniko Nakamura
Ludmila Gromova	Jana Posnerová	Hiroko Tsuji
		Ginko Chiba-Abukawa
1968 U.S.S.R. 382.85	CZECHOSLOVAKIA 382.20	E. GERMANY 379.10
Zinaida Voronina	Vera Čáslavská	Erika Zuchold
Natalya Kuchinskaya	Bohumila Rimnácova	Karin Janz
Larissa Petrik	Miroslava Skleničková	Maritta Bauerschmidt
Olga Karasseva	Maria Krajčírová	Ute Starke
Lyudmila Tourischeva	Hana Lišková	Marianne Noack
Ljubov Burda	Jana Kubičková	Magdalena Schmidt
1972 U.S.S.R. 380.50	E. GERMANY 376.55	HUNGARY 368.25
Lyudmila Tourischeva	Karin Janz	Ilona Bekesi
Olga Korbut	Erika Zuchold	Monika Csaszar
Tamara Lazakovitch	Angelika Hellmann	Krisztina Medveczky
Ljubov Burda	Irene Abel	Aniko Kery
Elvira Saadi	Christine Schmitt	Marta Kelemen
Antonina Koshel	Richarda Schmeisser	Zsuzsa Nagy
1976 U.S.S.R. 390.35	ROMANIA 387.15	E. GERMANY 385.10
Svetlana Grozdova	Gabriela Trusca	Angelika Hellmann
Elvira Saadi	Georgeta Gabor	Marion Kische
Maria Filatova	Anca Grigoras	Kerstin Gerschau
Olga Corbut	Mariana Constantin	Gitta Escher
Lyudmila Tourischeva	Teodora Ungureanu	Steffi Kraker
Nelli Kim	Nadia Comaneci	Carola Dombeck
1980 U.S.S.R. 394.90	ROMANIA 393.50	E. GERMANY 392.55
Natalya Shaposhnikova	Emilia Eberle	Maxi Gnauck
Yelena Davydova	Nadia Comaneci	Katharina Rensch
Nelli Kim	Rodica Dunka	Steffi Kraker
Maria Filatova	Melita Ruhn	Birgit Suss
Stella Zacharova	Cristina Grigoras	Silvia Hindorff
Yelena Naimushina	Dumitrita Turner	Karola Sube
1984 ROMANIA 392.20	USA 391.20	CHINA 388.60
Simona Pauca	Pamela Bileck	Qun Huang
Cristina Grigoras	Michelle Dusserre	Qiurui Zhou
Mihaela Stanulet	Kathy Johnson	Jiani Wu
Laura Cutina	Tracee Talavera	Yanhong Ma
Lavinia Agache	Julianne McNamara	Ping Zhou
Ecaterina Szabo	Mary Lou Retton	Yongyan Chen
1988 U.S.S.R. 395.475	ROMANIA 394.125	E. GERMANY 390.875
Svetlana Baitova	Camelia Voinea	Martina Jentsch
Yelena Chevtchenko	Eugenia Golea	Gabriele Fähnrich
Olga Strayeva	Celestina Popa	Ulrike Klotz
Svetlana Bogunskaya	Gabriela Potorac	Bettina Schieferdecker
Natalya Lachtchenova	Daniela Silivas	Dörte Thümmler
Yelena Chouchounova	Aurelia Dobre	Dagmar Kersten

COMBINED EXERCISES (INDIVIDUAL)

1896–1948 Event not held		
1952 Maria Gorokhovskaya (URS) 76.78	Nina Bocharova (URS) 75.94	Margit Korondi (HUN) 75.82
1956 Larissa Latynina (URS) 74.933	Agnes Keleti (HUN) 74.633	Sofia Muratova (URS) 74.466
1960 Larissa Latynina (URS) 77.031	Sofia Muratova (URS) 76.696	Polina Astakhova (URS) 76.164
1964 Vera Časlavská (TCH) 77.564	Larissa Latynina (URS) 76.998	Polina Astakhova (URS) 76.965
1968 Vera Čáslavská (TCH) 78.25	Zinaida Voronina (URS) 76.85	Natalya Kuchinskaya (URS) 76.75

At the 1976 Games in Montreal, 14-year-old Nadia Comaneci of Romania became the first gymnast to be awarded a perfect score in Olympic competition.

Mary Lou Retton (USA) was voted best all-around Olympic gymnast in the 1984 games. She won a gold medal in that category, a silver in the vault and a bronze in the uneven parallel bars.

	GOLD	SILVER	BRONZE
1972	Lyudmila Tourischeva (URS) 77.025	Karin Janz (GDR) 76.875	Tamara Lazakovitch (URS) 76.850
1976	Nadia Comaneci (ROM) 79.275	Nelli Kim (URS) 78.675	Lyudmila Tourischeva (URS) 78.625
1980	Yelena Davydova (URS) 79.150	Maxi Gnauck (GDR) 79.075 Nadia Comaneci (ROM) 79.075	—
1984	Mary Lou Retton (USA) 79.175	Ecaterina Szabo (ROM) 79.125	Simona Pauca (ROM) 78.675
1988	Yelena Chouchounova (URS) 79.662	Daniela Silivas (ROM) 79.637	Svetlana Bogunskaya (URS) 79.400

HORSE VAULT

	GOLD	SILVER	BRONZE
1896–1948	Event not held		
1952	Yekaterina Kalinchuk (URS) 19.20	Maria Gorokhovskaya (URS) 19.19	Galina Minaitscheva (URS) 19.16
1956	Larissa Latynina (URS) 18.833	Tamara Manina (URS) 18.800	Ann-Sofi Colling (SWE) 18.733 Olga Tass (HUN) 18.733
1960	Margarita Nikolayeva (URS) 19.316	Sofia Muratova (URS) 19.049	Larissa Latynina (URS) 19.016
1964	Vera Cáslavská (TCH) 19.483	Larissa Latynina (URS) 19.283 Birgit Radochla (GER) 19.283	—
1968	Vera Cáslavská (TCH) 19.775	Erika Zuchold (GDR) 19.625	Zinaida Voronina (URS) 19.500

GOLD	SILVER	BRONZE
1972 Karin Janz (GDR) 19.525	Erika Zuchold (GDR) 19.275	Lyudmila Tourischeva (URS) 19.250
1976 Nelli Kim (URS) 19.800	Lyudmila Tourischeva (URS) 19.650 Carola Dombeck (GDR) 19.650	—
1980 Natalia Shaposhnikova (URS) 19.725	Steffi Kraker (GDR) 19.675	Melita Ruhn (ROM) 19.650
1984 Ecaterina Szabo (ROM) 19.875	Mary Lou Retton (USA) 19.850	Lavinia Agache (ROM) 19.750
1988 Svetlana Bogunskaya (URS) 19.905	Gabriela Potorac (ROM) 19.830	Daniela Silivas (ROM) 19.818

ASYMMETRICAL BARS

GOLD	SILVER	BRONZE
1896–1948 Event not held		
1952 Margit Korondi (HUN) 19.40	Maria Gorokhovskaya (URS) 19.26	Agnes Keleti (HUN) 19.16
1956 Agnes Keleti (HUN) 18.966	Larissa Latynina (URS) 18.833	Sofia Muratova (URS) 18.800
1960 Polina Astakhova (URS) 19.616	Larissa Latynina (URS) 19.416	Tamara Lyukhina (URS) 19.399
1964 Polina Astakhova (URS) 19.332	Katalin Makray (HUN) 19.216	Larissa Latynina (URS) 19.199
1968 Vera Cáslavská (TCH) 19.650	Karin Janz (GDR) 19.500	Zinaida Voronina (URS) 19.425
1972 Karin Janz (GDR) 19.675	Olga Korbut (URS) 19.450 Erika Zuchold (GDR) 19.450	—
1976 Nadia Comaneci (ROM) 20.000	Teodora Ungureanu (ROM) 19.800	Marta Egervari (HUN) 19.775
1980 Maxi Gnauck (GDR) 19.875	Emilia Eberle (ROM) 19.850	Steffi Kraker (GDR) 19.775 Melita Ruhn (ROM) 19.775 Maria Filatova (URS) 19.775
1984 Ma Yanhong (CHN) 19.950 Julianne McNamara (USA) 19.950	—	Mary Lou Retton (USA) 19.800
1988 Daniela Silivas (ROM) 20.000	Dagmar Kersten (GDR) 19.987	Yelena Chouchounova (URS) 19.962

BALANCE BEAM

GOLD	SILVER	BRONZE
1896–1948 Event not held		
1952 Nina Bocharova (URS) 19.22	Maria Gorokhovskaya (URS) 19.13	Margit Korondi (HUN) 19.02
1956 Agnes Keleti (HUN) 18.80	Eva Bosáková (TCH) 18.63 Tamara Manina (URS) 18.63	—
1960 Eva Bosáková (TCH) 19.283	Larissa Latynina (URS) 19.233	Sofia Muratova (URS) 19.232
1964 Vera Cáslavská (TCH) 19.449	Tamara Manina (URS) 19.399	Larissa Latynina (URS) 19.382
1968 Natalya Kuchinskaya (URS) 19.650	Vera Cáslavská (TCH) 19.575	Larissa Petrik (URS) 19.250
1972 Olga Korbut (URS) 19.575	Tamara Lazakovitch (URS) 19.375	Karin Janz (GDR) 18.975
1976 Nadia Comaneci (ROM) 19.950	Olga Korbut (URS) 19.725	Teodora Ungureanu (ROM) 19.700

RIGHT: The Soviet gymnast Larissa Semyonovna Latynina has won more medals than any other Olympic competitor— 9 gold, 5 silver, and 4 bronze. She now coaches the U.S.S.R. team.

BELOW: Lyudmila Tourischeva (URS), winner of 4 gold medals in 3 Games, married Soviet track and field gold medalist Valery Borzov after the 1976 Olympics.

	GOLD	SILVER	BRONZE
1980	Nadia Comaneci (ROM) 19.800	Yelena Davydova (URS) 19.750	Natalia Shaposhnikova (URS) 19.725
1984	Simona Pauca (ROM) 19.800 Ecaterina Szabo (ROM) 19.800	—	Kathy Johnson (USA) 19.650
1988	Daniela Silivas (ROM) 19.924	Yelena Chouchounova (URS) 19.875	Gabriela Potorac (ROM) 19.837 Phoebe Mills (USA) 19.837

FLOOR EXERCISES

	GOLD	SILVER	BRONZE
1896–1948	Event not held		
1952	Ágnes Keleti (HUN) 19.36	Maria Gorokhovskaya (URS) 19.20	Margit Korondi (HUN) 19.00
1956	Larissa Latynina (URS) 18.733 Ágnes Keleti (HUN) 18.733	—	Elena Leustean (ROM) 18.70
1960	Larissa Latynina (URS) 19.583	Polina Astakhova (URS) 19.532	Tamara Lyukhina (URS) 19.449
1964	Larissa Latynina (URS) 19.599	Polina Astakhova (URS) 19.500	Anikó Jánosi (HUN) 19.300
1968	Larissa Petrik (URS) 19.675 Vera Cáslavská (TCH) 19.675	—	Natalya Kuchinskaya (URS) 19.650
1972	Olga Korbut (URS) 19.575	Lyudmila Tourischeva (URS) 19.550	Tamara Lazakovitch (URS) 19.450
1976	Nelli Kim (URS) 19.850	Lyudmila Tourischeva (URS) 19.825	Nadia Comaneci (ROM) 19.750
1980	Nelli Kim (URS) 19.875 Nadia Comaneci (ROM) 19.875	—	Natalia Shaposhnikova (URS) 19.825 Maxi Gnauck (GDR) 19.825
1984	Ecaterina Szabo (ROM) 19.975	Julianne McNamara (USA) 19.950	Mary Lou Retton (USA) 19.775
1988	Daniela Silivas (ROM) 19.937	Svetlana Bogunskaya (URS) 19.887	Diana Doudeva (BUL) 19.850

RHYTHMIC GYMNASTICS

	GOLD	SILVER	BRONZE
1984	Lori Fung (CAN) 57.950	Doina Staiculescu (ROM) 57.900	Regina Weber (FRG) 57.700
1988	Marina Lobatch (URS) 60.000	Adriana Dounavska (BUL) 59.950	Alexandra Timochenko (URS) 59.875

11. Handball, Men (Indoor)

It should be noted that in 1936 there was a Field Handball (i.e., outdoor) competition. The medals went to Germany (gold), Austria (silver) and Switzerland (bronze).

	GOLD	SILVER	BRONZE
1972	**YUGOSLAVIA**	**CZECHOSLOVAKIA**	**ROMANIA**
	Zoran Zivkovic	František Krabik	Cornel Penu
	Abaz Arslanagic	Peter Pospisil	Alexandru Dinca
	Miroslav Pribanic	Ivan Satrapa	Gavril Kicsid
	Petar Fajfric	Vladimir Jary	Ghita Licu
	Milorad Karalic	Jiri Kavan	Cristian Gatu
	Djoko Lavrnic	Andrej Lukosik	Roland Gunnesch
	Slobodan Miskovic	Vladimir Haber	Radu Voina
	Hrvoje Horvat	Jindrich Krepinal	Simion Schobel
	Branislav Pokrajac	Ladislav Benes	Gheorghe Gruia
	Zdravko Miljak	Vincent Lavko	Werner Stockl
	Milan Lazarevic	Jaroslav Konecny	Dan Marin
	Nebojsa Popovic	Pavel Mikes	Adrian Cosma
1976	**U.S.S.R.**	**ROMANIA**	**POLAND**
	Mikhail Istchenko	Cornel Penu	Andrzej Szymczak
	Anatoli Fedjukin	Gavril Kicsid	Piotr Ciesla
	Vladimir Maximov	Cristian Gatu	Zdzislaw Antczak
	Sergei Kushnirjuk	Ghita Licu	Zygfryd Kuchta
	Vladimir Kravsov	Radu Voina	Jerzy Klempel
	Yuri Klimov	Roland Gunnesch	Janusz Brzozowski
	Aleksandr Anpilogov	Stefan Birtalan	Ryszard Przybysz
	Evgeniy Tchernyshov	Adrian Cosma	Jerzy Melcer
	Valeriy Gassiy	Constantin Tudosie	Andrzej Sokolowski
	Anatoli Tomin	Nicolae Munteanu	Jan Gmyrek
	Yuri Kidjayev	Werner Stockl	Henryk Rozmiarek
	Aleksandr Rezanov	Mircea Grabovschi	Alfred Kaluzinski
1980	**EAST GERMANY**	**U.S.S.R.**	**ROMANIA**
	Siegfried Voigt	Mikhail Istchenko	Nicolae Munteanu
	Gunter Dreibrodt	Viktor Machorin	Marian Dumitru
	Peter Rost	Sergei Kushnirjuk	Iosif Boros
	Klaus Gruner	Aleksandr Karshakevich	Maricel Voinea
	Hans-Georg Beyer	Vladimir Belov	Vasile Stinga
	Dietmar Schmidt	Anatoli Fedjukin	Radu Voina
	Hartmut Kruger	Aleksandr Anpilogov	Cornel Durau
	Lothar Doering	Yevgeniy Cheryshov	Stefan Birtalan
	Ernst Gerlach	Aleksey Zhuk	Alexandru Folker
	Frank Wahl	Nikolai Tomin	Neculai Vasilca
	Ingolf Wiegert	Yuri Kidjayev	Adrian Cosma
	Wieland Schmidt	Valdemar Novitsky	Claudiu Eugen Ionescu
	Rainer Hoft	Vladimir Kravsov	Cezar Draganita
	Georg Jaunich	Vladimir Repiyev	Lucian Vasilache
1984	**YUGOSLAVIA**	**WEST GERMANY**	**ROMANIA**
	Zlatan Amautovic	Andreas Thiel	Nicolae Munteanu
	Veselin Vukovic	Arnulf Meffle	Marian Dumitru
	Milan Kalina	Rudiger Neitzel	Iosif Boros
	Jovan Elezovic	Martin Schwalb	Maricel Voinea
	Zdravko Zovko	Dirk Rauin	Vasile Stinga
	Branko Strbac	Michael Paul	George Dogarescu
	Davo Jurina	Michael Roth	Gheorghe Covaciu
	Veselin Vujovic	Thomas Happe	Cornel Durau
	Slobodan Kuzmanovski	Erhard Wunderlich	Alexandru Folker
	Mirko Basic	Thomas Springel	Alexandru Buligan
	Zdravko Radjenovic	Klaus Woller	Vasile Oprea
	Mile Isakovic	Jochen Fraatz	Mircea Bedivan
	Momir Rnic	Ulrich Roth	Adrian Simion

GOLD	SILVER	BRONZE
1988 U.S.S.R.	KOREA	YUGOSLAVIA
Andrey Lavrov	Yoon Tae-Il	Momir Rinic
Alexandr Toutchkine	Kim Jae-Hwan	Zlatko Saracevic
Alexandr Rymanov	Sin Young-Suk	Iztok Puc
Alexandr Karchakevish	Park Do-Hun	Goran Perkovac
Yuriy Nestorov	Park Young-Dae	Irfan Smajlagic
Guerogui Sviridenko	Koh Suk-Chang	Zlatko Portner
Andrey Tyoumentsev	Roh Hyun-Suk	Vaselin Vujovic
Mikhail Vassilyev	Oh Young-Ki	Jozef Holpert
Yuriy Chevtsov	Choi Suk-Jae	Mirko Basic
Vyacheslav Atavin	Kang Jae-Won	Alvaro Nacinovic
Valdemar Novitsky	Lee Sang-Hyo	Slobodan Kuzmanovski
Igor Tcooumak	Lim Jin-Suk	Ermin Velic

Handball, Women (Indoor)

1896–1972   Event not held

1976 U.S.S.R.	EAST GERMANY	HUNGARY
Natalia Sherstjuk	Hannelore Zober	Agota Bujdoso
Rafiga Shabanova	Gabriele Badorek	Marta Megyeri
Lubov Berezhnaya	Evelyn Matz	Borbala Toth-Harsanyi
Zinaida Turchina	Roswitha Krause	Katalin Laki
Tatyana Makarets	Christina Rost	Amalia Sterbinszky
Maria Litoshenko	Petra Uhlig	Marianna Nagy
Ludmila Bobrus	Christina Voss	Klaru Csik
Tatyana Glustchenko	Liane Michaelis	Rozalia Lelkes
Ludmila Shubina	Silvia Siebert	Maria Vadasz
Galina Zakharova	Marion Tietz	Erzsebet Nemeth
Aldona Chesaitite	Kristina Richter	Eva Angyal
Nina Lobova	Eva Paskuy	Maria Berzsenyi
Ludmila Pantchuk	Waltraud Kretzschmar	Ilona Nagy
Larisa Karlova	Hannelore Burosch	Zsuzsa Kezi

1980 U.S.S.R.	YUGOSLAVIA	EAST GERMANY
Natalia Timoshkina	Ana Titlic	Hannelore Zober
Larisa Karlova	Slavica Jeremic	Katrin Kruger
Irina Palchikova	Zorica Vojinovic	Evelyn Matz
Tatiana Kochergina	Radmila Drljaca	Roswitha Krause
Ludmila Poradnik	Katica Iles	Christina Rost
Larisa Savkina	Mirjana Ognjenovic	Petra Uhlig
Aldona Nenenene	Svetlana Anastasovski	Claudia Wunderlich
Yulia Safina	Svetlana Kitic	Savine Rother
Olga Zubareva	Mirjana Djurica	Kornelia Kunisch
Valentina Lutaeva	Biserka Visnjic	Marion Tietz
Lubov Odinokova	Jasna Merdan	Kristina Richter
Sigita Strechen	Vesna Radovic	Waltraud Kretzschmar
Natalia Lukianenko	Vesna Milosevic	Birgit Heinicke
Zinaida Turchina	Rada Savic	Renate Rudolph

1984 YUGOSLAVIA	KOREA	CHINA
Jasna Ptujec	Son Mi-Na	Wu Xingjiang
Mirjana Ognjenovic	Kim Kyung-Soon	He Jianping
Ljubinka Jankovic	Lee Soon-Ei	Zhu Juefeng
Svetlana Anastasovski	Jeong Hyoi-Soon	Zhang Weihong
Svetlana Dasic-Kitic	Kim Mi-Sook	Gao Xiumin
Alenka Cuderman	Han Hwa-Soo	Wang Linwei
Svetlana Mugosa	Kim Ok-Hwa	Liu Liping
Mirjana Djurica	Kim Choon-Yei	Sun Xiulan
Biserka Visnjic	Jeung Soon-Bok	Liu Yumei
Slavica Djukic	Yoon Byung-Soon	Li Lan
Jasna Kolar-Merdan	Lee Young-Ja	Wang Mingxing
Ljiljana Mugosa	Sung Kyung-Hwa	Chen Zhen
Zorica Pavicevic	Youn Soo-Kyung	Zhang Peijun
Emilija Ercic		

GOLD	SILVER	BRONZE
1988 **KOREA**	**NORWAY**	**U.S.S.R.**
Song Ji-Hyun	Cathrine Svendsen	Natalya Mitryuk
Han Hyun-Sook	Heidi Sundal	Larisa Karlova
Kim Choon-Rye	Hanne Hegh	Svetlana Mankova
Kim Myung-Soon	Susann Goksor	Zinaida Turchina
Lee Ki-Soon	Hanne Hogness	Marina Bazanova
Kim Hyun-Mee	Karin Singstao	Natalya Morskova
Ki Mi-Sook	Trine Haltvik	Tatyana Gorb
Suk Min-Hee	Ingrid Steen	Yevgenia Tovstogan
Son Mi-Na	Karin Pettersen	Yelena Nemachkalo
Lim Mi-Kyung	Annette Skottvoll	Tatyana Dzhandzhgava
Kim Kyung-Soon	Kristin Midthun	Natalya Anissimova
Sung Kyung-Hwa	Kerstin Andersen	Natalya Lapitskaya

---

12. Hockey (Field)

1896–1906 Event not held

1908 **ENGLAND**	**IRELAND**	**SCOTLAND &**
H. I. Wood	E. P. C. Holmes	**WALES**
L. C. Baillon	Henry J. Brown	(tied for third place)
Harold Scott-Freeman	Walter E. Peterson	d.n.a.
Alan H. Noble	Henry L. Murphy	
Edgar W. Page	Walter J. H. Campbell	
John Y. Robinson	William E. Graham	
Eric Green	Robert L. Kennedy	
Reginald G. Pridmore	Frank L. Robinson	
Stanley H. Shoveller	Eric P. Allman-Smith	
Gerald Logan	G. S. Gregg	
Percy M. Rees	C. F. Power	
	W. G. McCormick	

1912 Event not held

Grahannandan Singh (left) scores one of India's four winning goals in the 1948 finals.

GOLD	SILVER	BRONZE
1920 ENGLAND	**DENMARK**	**BELGIUM**
Harry E. Haslam	Andreas Rasmussen	Charles Delelienne
John H. Bennett	Hans-Christian Herlak	Maurice van den
Charles S. Atkin	Frans Faber	Bemden
Harold D. R. Cooke	Erik Husted	Raoul Daufresne de la
Eric B. Crockford	Henning Holst	Chevalerie
Cyril T. A. Wilkinson	Hans-Jörgen Hansen	René Strauwen
William F. Smith	Hans-Adolf Bjerrum	Fernand de Montigny
George F. McGrath	Thorvald Eigenbrod	Adolphe Goemaere
John McBryan	Sven Blach	Pierre Chibert
Stanley H. Shoveller	Steen Due	André Becquet
Rex W. Crummack	Ejvind Blach	Raymond Keppens
Arthur F. Leighton		Pierre Valcke
Colin H. Campbell		Jean van Nerom
Charles Marcon		Robert Gevers
Harold K. Cassels		Louis Diercxens
1924 Event not held		
1928 INDIA	**NETHERLANDS**	**GERMANY**
Richard J. Allen	Adriaan J. L. Katte	George Brunner
Michael E. Rocque	Albert W. Tresling	Werner Proft
Leslie C. Hammond	Reindert B. J. de Waal	Heinz Wöltje
Rex A. Norris	Johannes W. Brand	Werner Freyberg
Broome E. Pinniger	Emile P. J. Duson	Theo Haag
Sayed M. Yusuf	Jan G. Ankerman	Erich Zander
E. John Goodsir-Cullen	Hendrik P. Visser t'Hooft	Friedrich Horn
Maurice A. Gateley	Robert van der Veen	Herbert Müller
George E. Marthins	Paulus van de Rovaert	Bruno Boche
Dhyan Chand	Gerrit J. A. Jannink	Herbert Hobein
Frederick S. Seaman	August J. Kop	Herbert Kemmer
Khair Singh		Erwin Franzkowiak
Jaipal Singh		Hans Haussmann
Shaukat Ali		Karl Heinz Immer
Feroze Khan		Aribert Heymann
		Kurt Haverbeck
		Rolf Wollner
		Gerd Strantzen
		Heinz Förstendorf
1932 INDIA	**JAPAN**	**UNITED STATES**
Sayed Mohammed	Junzo Inohara	David McMullin
Jaffar	Toshio Usami	William Boddington
Roop Singh	Kenichi Konishi	James Gentle
Dhyan Chand	Hiroshi Nagata	Charles Shaeffer
Gurmit Singh	Haruhiko Kon	Lawrence Knapp
Richard J. Carr	Eiichi Nakamura	Horace Disston
Lal Shah Bokhari	Yoshio Sakai	Samuel Ewing
Broome E. Pinniger	Katsumi Shibata	Henry Greer
M. A. K. Minhas	Sadayoshi Kobayashi	Leonard O'Brien
Leslie C. Hammond	Akio Sohda	Frederick Wolters
Carlyle C. Tapsell	Shumkichi Hamada	Harold Brewster
Arthur C. Hind		Amos Deacon
Richard Allen		
Masud Minhas		

	GOLD	SILVER	BRONZE

1936	**INDIA**
	Richard J. Allen
	Carlyle C. Tapsell
	Mohammed Hussain
	Baboo N. Nimal
	E. John Goodsir-Cullen
	Joseph Galibardy
	Shabban Shahab ud Din
	Dara ali Iqtidar Shah
	Dhyan Chand
	Roop Singh
	Sayed Mohammed
	        Jaffar
	Ahmed Sher Khan
	Garewal Gurcharan
	        Singh
	Ahsan Mohomed Khan
	Lionel C. Emmett
	Mirza Nasir ud Din
	        Masood
	Cyril J. Michie
	Fernandes Paul Peter
	Joseph Phillip
		GERMANY
		Karl Dröse
		Erich Zander
		Herbert Kemmer
		Heinz Schmalix
		Erwin Keller
		Alfred Gerdes
		Fritz Messner
		Hans Scherbart
		Kurt Weiss
		Werner Hamel
		Harald Huffmann
		Werner Kubitzki
		Tito Warnholtz
		Detlef Okrent
		Hermann Auf der Heide
		Heinrich Peter
		Carl Menke
		Heinz Raack
		Paul Mehlitz
		Ludwig Beisiegel
		Karl Ruck
		Erich Cuntz
			NETHERLANDS
			Jan de Looper
			Reindert B. J. de Waal
			Max Westerkamp
			Hendrik C. de Looper
			Rudolf J. van der Haar
			Anton R. van Lierop
			Pieter A. Gunning
			Henri C. W. Schnitger
			Ernst W. van den Berg
			Agathon de Roos
			René Sparenberg
			Carl E. Heybroek

1948	**INDIA** Leo H. K. Pinto Trilochan Singh Randhir Singh Gentle Keshav C. Datt Amir C. Kumar Maxie Vaz Kishan Lal Kunwa Digvijai Singh Grahanandan Singh Patrick A. Jansen Lawrie Fernandes Ranganadhan Francis Akhtar Hussain Leslie W. Claudius Jaswant S. Rajput Reginald Rodrigues Latifur Rehman Balbir Singh Walter J. L. D'Souza Gerry R. Glacken	**GREAT BRITAIN** David L. S. Brodie George B. Sime William L. C. Lindsay Michael M. Walford Frank O. Reynolds F. Robin Lindsay John M. Peak W. Neil White Robert E. Adlard Norman F. Borrett William S. Griffiths Ronald Davies G. Hudson R. T. Lake Peter Whitbread	**NETHERLANDS** Antonius M. Richter Henri J. J. Derckx Johan F. Drijver Jenne Langhout Hermanus P. Loggere Edvard H. Tiel Willem van Heel Andries C. Boerstra Pieter M. J. Bromberg Jan H. Kruize Rius T. Esser Henricus N. Bouwman
1952	**INDIA** Ranganadhan Francis Dharam Singh Randhir S. Gentle Leslie W. Claudius Keshav C. Datt Govind Perumal Raghbir Lal Kunwar D. Singh Balbir Singh Udham Singh Muniswamy Rajagopal Meldric St. C. Daluz Grahanandan Singh Chinadorai Deshmutu	**NETHERLANDS** Laurens S. Mulder Henri J. J. Derckx Johan F. Drijver Julius T. Ancion Hermanus P. Loggere Edvard H. Tiel Willem van Heel Rius T. Esser Jan H. Kruize Andries C. Boerstra Leonard H. Wery	**GREAT BRITAIN** Graham B. Dadds Roger K. Midgley Denys J. Carnill John A. Cockett Dennis M. R. Eagan Anthony J. B.Robinson Anthony S. Nunn Robin A. Fletcher Richard O. A. Norris John V. Conroy John P. Taylor Derek M. Day S. T. Theobald

GOLD	SILVER	BRONZE
1956 INDIA	**PAKISTAN**	**GERMANY**
Shankar Laxman	Zakir Hussain	Alfred Lücker
Bakshish Singh	Ghulam Rasul	Helmut Nonn
Randhir S. Gentle	Anwar Ahmad Khan	Günther Ullerich
Leslie W. Claudius	Hussain Mussarat	Günther Brennecke
Amir Kumar	Noor Alam	Werner Delmes
Govind Perumal	Abdul Hamid	Eberhard Ferstl
Charles Stephen	Habibur Rehman	Hugo Dollheiser
Gurdev Singh	Mutih Ullah	Heinz Radzikowski
Balbir Singh	Hussain Akhtar	Wolfgang Nonn
Udham Singh	Nasir Ahmad	Hugo Budinger
Raghbir S. Bhola	Manzur H. Atif	Werner Rozenbaum
Ranganadhan Francis	Habib Alikiddi	
Balkishan Singh	Munir Ahmad Dar	
Amit Singh Bakshi	Latifur Rehman	
Kaushi Haripal		
Hardyal Singh		
Raghbir Lal		
1960 PAKISTAN	**INDIA**	**SPAIN**
Abdul Rashid	Shankar Laxman	Carlos Del Coso Iglesias
Bashir Ahmad	Prithipal Singh	José Colomer Rivas
Manzur H. Atif	Jamanlal Sharma	Rafael Egusquiza
Ghulam Rasul	Leslie W. Claudius	Basterva
Anwar Ahmad Khan	Joseph Antic	Juan Angel Calzado
Ali Habib Kidi	Mohinder Lal	de Castro
Noor Alam	Joginder Singh	José Antonio Dinares
Abdul Hamid	John V. Peter	Massaqué
Abdul Waheed	Jaswant Singh	Edouardo Dualde
Nasir Ahmad	Udham Singh	Santos de Lamadrid
Mutih Ullah	Raghbir S. Bhola	Joachim Dualde
Khurshid Aslam	Charanjit Singh	Santos de Lamadrid
Mushtaq Ahmad	Govind Savant	Pedro Amat Fontanais
Munir Ahmad Dar		Francisco Caballer
		Soteras
		Ignacio Macaya
		Santos de Lamadrid
		Pedro Murúa
		Leguizamón
		Pedro Roig Junyent
		Luis Maria Usoz
		Quintana
		Narciso Ventalló
		Surralles
1964 INDIA	**PAKISTAN**	**AUSTRALIA**
Shankar Laxman	Abdul Hamid	Paul Dearing
Prithipal Singh	Munir Ahmad Dar	Donald McWatters
Dhara M. Singh	Manzur H. Atif	Brian Glencross
Mohinder Lal	Saeed Anwar	John McBride
Charanjit Singh	Anwar Ahmad Khan	Julian Pearce
Gurbux Singh	Muhammad Rashid	Graham Wood
Joginder Singh	Khalid Mahmood Hussain	Robin Hodder
John V. Peter	Zaka-ud-Din	Raymond Evans
Harbinder Singh	Muhammad Afzal	Eric Pearce
Kashik Haripal	Manna	Patrick Nilan
Darshan Singh	Mohammad Asad Malik	Donald Smart
Jagjit Singh	Mutih Ullah	Antony Waters
Bandu Patil	Tariq Niazi	Mervyn Crossman
Udham Singh	Zafar Hayat	Desmond Piper
Ali Sayeed	Khizar Nawaz	
	Kurshid Aslam	

	GOLD	SILVER	BRONZE
1968	**PAKISTAN**	**AUSTRALIA**	**INDIA**
	Zakir Hussain	Paul Dearing	Rajendra A. Christy
	Tanvir A. Dar	James Mason	Gurbux Singh
	Tariq Aziz	Brian Glencross	Prithipal Singh
	Saeed Anwar	Gordon Pearce	Balbir Singh II
	Riaz Ahmed	Julian Pearce	Ajitpal Singh
	Bulrez Akhtar	Robert Haigh	Krishna Murtay
	Khalid Mahmood	Donald Martin	Perumal
	Hussain	Eric Pearce	Balbir Singh III
	Mohammad Ashfaq	Raymond Evans	Balbir Singh I
	Abdul Rashid	Frederick Quinn	Harbinder Singh
	Mohammad Asad Malik	Ronald Riley	Inamur Rehman
	Jahangir Ahmad Butt	Patrick Nilan	Inder Singh
	Riaz Ud Din	Donald Smart	Munir Sait
	Tariq Niazi	Desmond Piper	Harmik Singh
			John V. Peter
			Tarsem Singh
1972	**WEST GERMANY**	**PAKISTAN**	**INDIA**
	Peter Kraus	Saleem Sherwan	Cornelius Charles
	Michael Peter	Akhtarul Islam	Mukhbain Singh
	Dieter Freise	Munawaruz Zaman	Michael Kindo
	Michael Krause	Saeed Anwar	Krishna Murtay
	Eduard Thelen	Riaz Ahmed	Perumal
	Horst Droese	Fazalur Rehman	Ajitpal Singh
	Carsten Keller	Islahud Din	Harmik Singh
	Ulrich Klaes	Mudasser Asqhar	Ganesh
	Wolfgang Baumgart	Abdul Rashid	Mollerapoovayya
	Uli Vos	Mohammad Asad Malik	Harbinder Singh
	Peter Trump	Muhammad Shahnaz	Govin
			Billimogaputtaswamy
			Kumar Ashok
			Harcharn Singh
1976	**NEW ZEALAND**	**AUSTRALIA**	**PAKISTAN**
	Paul Ackerley	Robert Haigh	Saleem Sherwan
	Jeff Archibald	Richard Charlesworth	Manzoor Hassan
	Thur Borren	David Bell	Munawar Zaman Khan
	Alan Chesney	Gregory Browning	Saleem Nazim
	John Christensen	Ian Cooke	Akhtar Rasool
	Greg Dayman	Barry Dancer	Iftikhar Syed
	Tony Ineson	Douglas Golder	Islah Islahuddin
	Alan McIntyre	Wayne Hammond	Manzoor Hussain
	Barry Maister	James Irvine	Abdul Rashid
	Selwyn Maister	Malcolm Poole	Shanaz Sheikh
	Trevor Manning	Robert Proctor	Samiulah Khan
	Arthur Parkin	Graham Reid	Qamar Zia
	Mohan Patel	Ronald Riley	Arshad Mahmood
	Ramesh Patel	Trevor Smith	Arshad Ali Chaudry
		Terry Walsh	Mudassar Asghar
			Haneef Khan
1980	**INDIA**	**SPAIN**	**U.S.S.R.**
	Schofield Allan	Jose Garcia	Vladimir Pleshakov
	Chettri Bir Bhadur	Juan Amat	Vyacheslav Lampeyev
	Dung Dung Sylvanus	Santiago Malgosa	Leonid Pavlovsky
	Rajinder Singh	Rafael Garralda	Sos Airapetyan
	Deavinder Singh	Francisco Fabregas	Farit Ziganganov
	Gurmail Singh	Juan Luis Coghen	Valeriy Belyakov
	Ravinder Pal Singh	Ricardo Cabot	Sergey Klevtsov
	Baskaran Vasudevan	Jaime Arbos	Oleg Zagorodny
	Somaya Maneypanda	Carlos Roca	Aleksandr Gusev
	Maharaj Krishon Kaushik	Miguel Chaves	Sergey Pleshakov
	Charanjit Kumar	Juan Arbos	Mikhail Nichepurenko
	Mervyn Fernandis	Javier Cabot	Aleksandr Sytchev
	Amarjit Rana Singh	Juan Pellon	Aleksandr Myasnikov
	Shahid Mohamed	Miguel De Paz	Minnuela Azizov
	Zafar Iqbal	Paulino Monsalve	Viktor Deputatov
	Surinder Singh	Jaime Zumalacarregui	Aleksandr Goncharov

GOLD	SILVER	BRONZE
1984 **PAKISTAN**	**WEST GERMANY**	**GREAT BRITAIN**
G. Moinuddin	Christian Bassemir	Ian Taylor
Qasim Zia	Yobias Frank	Veryan Pappin
Nasir Ali	Ulrich Hanel	Stephen Martin
A. Rashid	Carsten Fischer	Paul Barber
Ayaz Mehmood	Joachim Hurter	Robert Cattrall
Naeem Akhtar	Ekkhard Schmidt-Opper	Jonathon Potter
Kaleemullah	Reinhard Krull	Richard Dodds
Manzoor Hussain	Michael Peter	William McConnell
Hasan Sardar	Stefan Blocher	Norman Hughes
Hanir Khan	Andreas Keller	David Westcott
Khlid Hameed	Thomas Reck	Richard Leman
Shahid Ali Khan	Maekku Slawyk	Stephen Batchelor
Tauqeer Dar	Thomas Gunst	Sean Kerly
Ishtiaq Ahmed	Heiner Dopp	James Duthie
Salleem Sherwani	Volker Fried	Kulbir Bhaura
Mushtaq Ahmad	Dirk Brinkmann	Mark Precious
1988 **GREAT BRITAIN**	**WEST GERMANY**	**NETHERLANDS**
Ian Taylor	Christian Schliemann	Frank Leistra
Veryan Pappin	Tobias Frank	Marc Benninga
David Faulkner	Ulrich Hänel	Cees Jan Diepeveen
Paul Barber	Carsten Fischer	Maurits Crucg
Stephen Martin	Andreas Mollandrin	Rene Klaassen
Jon Potter	Ekkard Schmidt-Opper	Hendrik Jan Kooyman
Richard Dodds	Dirk Brinkmann	Marc Delissen
Martyn Grimley	Heiner Dopp	Gerrit Jan Schlatmann
Stephen Batchelor	Stefan Blöcher	Tim Steens
Richard Leman	Andreas Keller	Floris Bove Lander
James Kirkwood	Thomas Reck	Patrick Faber
Dulbir Bhaura	Thomas Brinkmann	Ronald Jansen
Sean Kerly	Hanns-Henning Fastrich	Jan Hidde Kruize
Robert Clift	Michael Hilgers	Erik Parlevliet
Imran Sherwani	Volker Fried	Taco Van Den Honert
Russell Garcia	Michael Metz	Jacques Brinkmann

Hockey (Field) Women

1896–1976 Event not held

1980 **ZIMBABWE**	**CZECHOSLOVAKIA**	**U.S.S.R.**
Sarah English	Berta Hruba	Nelli Gorbatkova
Anne Mary Grant	Jirina Kadlecova	Valentina Zazdravnykh
Brenda Joan Phillips	Jirina Cermakova	Nadyezda Ovechkina
Patricia Jean McKillop	Marta Urbanova	Natella Krasnikova
Sonia Robertson	Kveta Petrickova	Natalya Bykova
Patricia Joan Davies	Marie Sykorova	Lidiya Glubokova
Maureen Jean George	Ida Hubackova	Galina Vyuzhanina
Linda Margaret Watson	Milada Blazkova	Natalya Bozunova
Susan Huggett	Jana Lahodova	Lyailya Akhmerova
Gillian Margaret Cowley	Alena Kyselicova	Nadyezda Filipova
Elizabeth Murial Chase	Jirina Hajkova	Tatyana Yembakhtova
Sandra Chick	Viera Podhanyiova	Tatyana Shviganova
Helen Volk	Jarmila Kralickova	Ludmila Frolova
Christine Prinsloo	Iveta Srankova	Galina Inzhuvatova
Arlene Nadine Boxhall	Lenka Vymazalova	Yelena Gureva
Anthea Doreen Stewart	Jirina Krizova	Alina Kham

	GOLD	SILVER	BRONZE
1984	**NETHERLANDS**	**WEST GERMANY**	**UNITED STATES**
	Bernadette De Beus	Ursula Thielemann	Gwen Cheeseman
	Alette Pos	Beate Deininger	Beth Anders
	Margriet Zegers	Christina Moser	Kathleen McGahey
	Laurien Wllemse	Hella Roth	Anita Miller
	Marjolein Eysvogel	Dagmar Breiken	Regina Buggy
	Josephine Boekhorst	Birgit Hagen	Christine Larson-Mason
	Carina Benninga	Birgit Hahn	Beth Beglin
	Alexandra LePoole	Gabriele Appel	Marcella Place
	Francisca Hillen	Andrea Weiermann-Lietz	Julie Staver
	Marieke Van Doorn	Corinna Lingnau	Diane Moyer
	Sophie Von Weiler	Martina Koch	Sheryl Johnson
	Aletta Van Manen	Gabriele Schley	Charlene Morett
	Irene Hendriks	Patricia Ott	Karen Shelton
	Elisabeth Sevens	Susanne Schmid	Brenda Stauffer
	Martine Ohr	Sigrid Landgraf	Leslie Milne
	Anneloes Nieuwenhuizen	Elke Drull	Judy Strong
1988	**AUSTRALIA**	**KOREA**	**NETHERLANDS**
	Kathleen Partridge	Kim Mi-Sun	Bernadette De Beus
	Elspeth Clement	Han Ok-Kyung	Yvonne Buter
	Liane Tooth	Chang Eun-Jung	Willemien Aardenburg
	Loretta Dorman	Han Keum-Sil	Laurien Willemse
	Lorraine Hillas	Choi Choon-Ok	Marjolein Bolhuis
	Michelle Capes	Kim Soon-Duk	Lisanne Lejeune
	Sandra Pisani	Chung Sang-Hyun	Carina Benninga
	Deborah Bowman	Jin Won-Sim	Annemieke Fokke
	Lee Capes	Hwang Keum-Sook	Ingrid Wolff
	Kim Small	Cho Ki-Hyang	Marieke Van Doorn
	Sally Carbon	Seo Kwang-Mi	Sophie Van Weiler
	Jacqueline Pereira	Park Soon-Ja	Aletta Van Manen
	Tracey Belbin	Kim Young-Sook	Noor Holsboer
	Rechelle Hawkes	Seo Hyo-Sun	Helen Van Der Ben
	Sharon Patmore	Lim Kye-Sook	Martine Ohr
	Maree Fish	Chung Eun-Kyung	Anneloes Nieuwenhuizen

---

13. Judo

Sport introduced in 1964.

OPEN CATEGORY, NO WEIGHT LIMIT

1964	Antonius Geesink (HOL)	Akio Kaminaga (JPN)	Theodore Boronovskis (AUS) Klaus Glahn (GER)
1968	Event not held		
1972	Wilhelm Ruska (HOL)	Vitali Kusnezov (URS)	Jean-Claude Brondani (FRA) Angelo Parisi (GBR)
1976	Haruki Uemura (JPN)	Keith Remfry (GBR)	Shota Chochoshvili (URS) Jeaki Cho (KOR)
1980	Dietmar Lorenz (GDR)	Angelo Parisi (FRA)	Arthur Mapp (GBR) Andras Ozsvar (HUN)

	GOLD	SILVER	BRONZE
1984	Yasuhiro Yamashita (JPN)	Mohamed Rashwan (EGY)	Mihai Cioc (ROM) Arthur Schnabel (FRG)
1988	Event not held		

New weight categories were introduced in 1980

OVER 95 kg (209¼ lb)

	GOLD	SILVER	BRONZE
1980	Angelo Parisi (FRA)	Dimitar Zaprianov (BUL)	Vladimir Kocman (TCH) Radomir Kovacevic (YUG)
1984	Hitoshi Saito (JPN)	Angelo Parusi (FRA)	Yong-Chul Cho (KOR) Mark Berger (CAN)
1988	Hitoshi Saito (JPN)	Henry Stöhr (GDR)	Cho Yong-Chul (KOR) Grigoriy Veritchev (URS)

UP TO 95 kg (209¼ lb)

1980	Robert Van De Walle (BEL)	Tengiz Khubuluri (URS)	Dietmar Lorenz (GDR) Henk Numan (HOL)
1984	Ha Hyoung-Zoo (KOR)	Douglas Vieira (BRA)	Bjarni Fridriksson (ISL) Gunter Neureuther (FRG)
1988	Aurelio Miguel (BRA)	Marc Meiling (FRG)	Robert Van De Walle (BEL) Dennis Stewart (GBR)

UP TO 86 kg (189½ lb)

1980	Juerg Roethlisberger (SUI)	Issac Azcuy (CUB)	Alexandr Iatskevich (URS) Detlef Ultsch (GDR)
1984	Peter Seisenbacher (AUT)	Robert Berland (USA)	Seiki Nose (JPN) Walter Carmona (BRA)
1988	Peter Seisenbacher (AUT)	Vladimir Chestakov (URS)	Ben Spijkers (HOL) Akinobu Osako (JPN)

UP TO 78 kg (171¾ lb)

1980	Shota Khabareli (URS)	Juan Ferrer (CUB)	Bernard Tchoullouyan (FRA) Harald Heinke (GDR)

	GOLD	SILVER	BRONZE
1984	Frank Wieneke (FRG)	Neil Adams (GBR)	Michel Nowak (FRA) Mircea Fratica (ROM)
1988	Walter Legien (POL)	Frank Wieneke (FRG)	Torsten Brechot (GDR) Bachir Varayev (URS)

UP TO 71 kg (156½ lb)

	GOLD	SILVER	BRONZE
1980	Ezio Gamba (ITA)	Neil Adams (GBR)	Karl-Heinz Lehmann (GDR) Ravdan Davaadalai (MGL)
1984	Ahn Byeoung-Keun (KOR)	Ezio Gamba (ITA)	Luis Onmura (BRA) Kerrith Brown (GBR)
1988	Marc Alexandre (FRA)	Sven Loll (GDR)	Michael Swain (USA) Guergui Tenadze (URS)

UP TO 65 kg (143¼ lb)

	GOLD	SILVER	BRONZE
1980	Nikolay Solodukhin (URS)	Tsendying Damdin (MGL)	Ilian Nedkov (BUL) Janusz Pawlowski (POL)
1984	Yoshiyuki Matsuoka (JPN)	Hwang Jung-Oh (KOR)	Josef Reiter (AUT) Marc Alexandre (FRA)
1988	Lee Kyung-Keun (KOR)	Janusz Pawlowski (POL)	Bruno Carabetta (FRA) Yosuke Yamamoto (JPN)

UP TO 60 kg (132¼ lb)

	GOLD	SILVER	BRONZE
1980	Thierry Rey (FRA)	Jose Rodriguez (CUB)	Aramby Emizh (URS) Tibor Kinces (HUN)
1984	Shinji Hosokawa (JPN)	Kim Jae-Yup (KOR)	Edward Liddie (USA) Neil Eckersley (GBR)
1988	Kim Jae-Yup (KOR)	Kevin Asano (USA)	Shinji Hosokawa (JPN) Amiran Totikachvili (URS)

Shinobu Sekine of Japan (left) defeated Brian Jacks of Great Britain (right) in this semi-final match and went on to win the gold medal in the middleweight category in 1972.

PREVIOUS WINNERS

OVER 93 kg (205 lb)

	GOLD	SILVER	BRONZE
1964	Isao Inokuma (JPN)	A. H. Douglas Rogers (CAN)	Parnaoz Chikviladze (URS) Anzor Kiknadze (URS)
1968	Event not held		
1972	Wilhelm Ruska (HOL)	Klaus Glahn (GER)	Givi Onashvili (URS) Motoki Nishimura (JPN)
1976	Sergey Novikov (URS)	Gunther Neureuther (GER)	Sumio Endo (JPN) Allen Coage (USA)

80 to 93 kg (176¼ to 205 lb)

	GOLD	SILVER	BRONZE
1964–1968	Event not held		
1972	Shota Chochoshvili (URS)	David C. Starbrook (GBR)	Chiaki Ishii (BRA) Paul Barth (GER)
1976	Kazuhiro Ninomiya (JPN)	Ramaz Harshiladze (URS)	David C. Starbrook (GBR) Juerg Roethlisberger (SUI)

70 to 80 kg (154¼ to 176¼ lb)

	GOLD	SILVER	BRONZE
1964	Isao Okano (JPN)	Wolfgang Hofmann (GER)	James Bregman (USA) Eui Tae Kim (KOR)
1968	Event not held		
1972	Shinobu Sekine (JPN)	Oh Seung-Lip (KOR)	Brian Jacks (GBR) Jean-Paul Coche (FRA)
1976	Isamu Sonoda (JPN)	Valeriy Dvoinikov (URS)	Slavko Obadov (YUG) Youngchul Park (KOR)

63 to 70 kg (138¾ to 154¼ lb)

	GOLD	SILVER	BRONZE
1964–1968	Event not held		
1972	Toyokazu Nomura (JPN)	Anton Zajkowski (POL)	Dietmar Hoetger (GDR) Anatoli Novikov (URS)
1976	Vladimir Nevzorov (URS)	Koji Kuramoto (JPN)	Patrick Vial (FRA) Marian Talaj (POL)

Up to 63 kg (138¾ lb)

	GOLD	SILVER	BRONZE
1964	Takehide Nakatani (JPN)	Eric Haenni (SUI)	Oleg Stepanov (URS) Aron Bogulubov (URS)
1968	Event not held		
1972	Takao Kawaguchi (JPN)	—	Kim Yong Ik (PRK) Jean-Jacques Mounier (FRA)
1976	Hector Rodriguez (CUD)	Chang Eunkyung (KOR)	Felice Mariani (ITA) Jozsef Tuncsik (HUN)

[1]Bakhaavaa Buidaa (MGL) disqualified after positive drug test.

14. Modern Pentathlon

The five events [currently in the order Riding (800 m course), Fencing (epée), Shooting (pistol 25 m), Swimming (300 m free-style), and Cross-country running (4,000 m)] have remained constant although there have inevitably been changes of rules, time allowed and order over the years.

Competitors were placed by lowest number of placing points (e.g., 1 for 1st in an event and 10 for 10th place in another) until an international graduated points scoring table was introduced in 1956.

GOLD	SILVER	BRONZE
1896–1908 Event not held		
1912 Gustaf Lilliehöök (SWE) 27	Gösta Åsbrink (SWE) 28	Georg de Laval (SWE) 30
1920 Gustaf Dryssen (SWE) 18	Erik de Laval (SWE) 23	Gösta Rúno (SWE) 27
1924 Bo Lindman (SWE) 18	Gustaf Dryssen (SWE) 39.5	Bertil Uggla (SWE) 45
1928 Sven Thofelt (SWE) 47	Bo Lindman (SWE) 50	Helmuth Kahl (GER) 52
1932 Johan Gabriel Oxenstierna (SWE) 32	Bo Lindman (SWE) 35.5	Richard Mayo (USA) 38.5
1936 Gotthard Handrick (GER) 31.5	Charles Leonard (USA) 39.5	Silvano Abba (ITA) 45.5
1948 William Grut (SWE) 16	George Moore (USA) 47	Gösta Gärdin (SWE) 49
1952 Lars Hall (SWE) 32	Gábor Benedek (HUN) 39	István Szondi (HUN) 41
Teams—HUNGARY 166	SWEDEN 182	FINLAND 213
Gábor Benedek	Lars Hall	Olavi Mannonen
István Szondi	Torsten Lindqvist	Lauri Vikko
Aladár Kovácsi	Cläes Egnell	Olavi Rokka
1956 Lars Hall (SWE) 4,843	Olavi Mannonen (FIN) 4,774.5	Väinö Korhonen (FIN) 4,750
Teams—U.S.S.R. 13,690.5	UNITED STATES 13,482	FINLAND 13,185.5
Igor Novikov	George H. Lambert	Olavi Mannonen
Aleksandr Tarassov	William Andre	Väinö Korhonen
Ivan Deryugin	Jack T. Daniels	Berndt Katter
1960 Ferenc Németh (HUN) 5,024	Imre Nagy (HUN) 4,988	Robert L. Beck (USA) 4,981
Teams—HUNGARY 14,863	U.S.S.R. 14,309	UNITED STATES 14,192
Ferenc Németh	Igor Novikov	Robert L. Beck
Imre Nagy	Nikolai Tatarinov	George H. Lambert
András Balczó	Hanno Selg	Jack T. Daniels
1964 Ferenc Török (HUN) 5,116	Igor Novikov (URS) 5,067	Albert Mokeyev (URS) 5,039
Teams—U.S.S.R. 14,961	UNITED STATES 14,189	HUNGARY 14,173
Igor Novikov	James Moore	Ferenc Török
Albert Mokeyev	David Kirkwood	Imre Nagy
Victor Mineyev	Paul Pesthy	Otto Török
1968 Björn Ferm (SWE) 4,964	András Balczó (HUN) 4,953	Pavel Lednev (URS) 4,795
Teams—HUNGARY 14,325	U.S.S.R. 14,248	FRANCE 13,289
András Balczó	Boris Onischenko	Raoul Gueguen
István Móna	Pavel Lednev	Lucien Guiguet
Ferenc Török	Stasis Shaparnis	Jean-Pierre Giudicelli
1972 András Balczó (HUN) 5,412	Boris Onischenko (URS) 5,335	Pavel Lednev (URS) 5,328
Teams—U.S.S.R. 15,968	HUNGARY 15,348	FINLAND 14,812
Boris Onischenko	András Balczó	Risto Hurme
Pavel Lednev	Zsigmond Villanyi	Veikko Salminen
Vladimir Shmelev	Pal Bako	Martti Ketelae
1976 Janusz Pyciak-Peciak (POL) 5,520	Pavel Lednev (URS) 5,485	Jan Bartu (TCH) 5,466
Teams—GREAT BRITAIN 15,559	CZECHOSLOVAKIA 15,451	HUNGARY 15,395
Adrian Parker	Jan Bartu	Tamas Kancsal
Robert Nightingale	Bohumil Starnovsky	Tibor Maracsko
Jeremy Fox	Jiri Adam	Szvetiszlav Sasics
1980 Anatoly Starostin (URS) 5,568	Tamas Szmobathelyi (HUN) 5,502	Pavel Lednev (URS) 5,382
Teams—U.S.S.R. 16,126	HUNGARY 15,912	SWEDEN 15,845
Anatoliy Starostin	Tamas Szombathelyi	Svante Rasmuson
Pavel Lednev	Tibor Maracsko	Lennart Pettersson
Yevgeniy Lipeyev	Laszlo Horvath	George Horvath

Andras Balczo (HUN) was the most successful of all modern pentathletes with 3 gold and 2 silver medals.

	GOLD	SILVER	BRONZE
1984	Daniele Masala (ITA) 5,469	Svante Rasmuson (SWE) 5,456	Carlo Massullo (ITA) 5,406
Teams—	**ITALY 16,060**	**USA 15,568**	**FRANCE 15,565**
	Carlo Massullo	Deam Glenesk	Paul Four
	Daniele Masala	Robert Losey	Didier Boube
	Pierpaolo Cristofori	Michael Storm	Joel Bouzou
1988	Janos Martinek (HUN) 5,404	Carlo Massullo (ITA) 5,379	Vakhtang Iagorachvili (URS) 5,367
Teams—	**HUNGARY 15,886**	**ITALY 15,571**	**GREAT BRITAIN 15,276**
	Janos Martinek	Carlo Massullo	Richard Phelps
	Attila Mizser	Daniele Masala	Dominic Mahony
	Laszlo Fabian	Gianluca Tiberti	Graham Brookhouse

15. Rowing (Men)

The standard Olympic course is now 1 mile 427 yards *2 000 m* in length.

In 1904, however, the course was 2 miles *3 218,7 m;* in 1908 1½ miles *2 414 m;* and in 1948 1 mile 350 yards *1 929 m.*

Times: The water conditions can vary sufficiently from one Games to another, even over a course of the same length, so as to make comparison between Games of little value.

There can thus be no Olympic *records* as such, but as a matter of interest the following are the *fastest times* achieved in any Olympic regatta over 2,000 meters:

MEN

Single Sculls	6:49.86	Thomas Lange (GDR)	1988
Double Sculls	6:12.48	Norway	1976
Quadruple Sculls	5:47.50	Italy	1988

Coxless Pairs	6:31.95	Romania	1988
Coxed Pairs	6:56.62	Italy	1988
Coxless Fours	5:53.65	East Germany	1976
Coxed Fours	6:00.75	East Germany	1988
Eights	5:32.17	East Germany	1976

WOMEN

Single Sculls	7:35.47	Magdalena Guerguyeva (BUL)	1988
Double Sculls	7:00.48	East Germany	1988
Quadruple Sculls	6:21.06	East Germany	1988
Coxless Pairs	7:28.13	Romania	1988
Coxed Fours	6:56.00	East Germany	1988
Eights	6:05.50	East Germany	1988

SINGLE SCULLS

The times given of the Bronze medal winners in 1928 are those achieved in a losing semi-final or race between beaten semi-finalists.

	GOLD	SILVER	BRONZE
1896	Event not held		
1900	Henri Barrelet (FRA) 7:35.6	André Gaudin (FRA) 7:41.6	St. George Ashe (GBR) 8:15.6
1904	Frank Greer (USA) 10:08.5	James Juvenal (USA) 2 lengths	Constance Titus (USA) 1 length
1906	Gaston Delaplane (FRA) 5:53.4	Joseph Larran (FRA) 6:07.2	
1908	Harry Blackstaffe (GBR) 9:26.0	Alexander McCulloch (GBR) 1 length	Bernhard von Gaza (GER) d.n.a. Károly Levitzky (HUN) d.n.a.
1912	William D. Kinnear (GBR) 7:47.6	Polydore Veirman (BEL) 1 length	Everard B. Butler (CAN) d.n.a. Mikhail Kusik (URS) d.n.a.
1920	John Kelly (USA) 7:35.0	Jack Beresford (GBR) 7:36.0	Clarence Hadfield d'Arcy (NZL) 7:48.0
1924	Jack Beresford (GBR) 7:49.2	William E. Garrett-Gilmore (USA) 7:54.0	Josef Schneider (SUI) 8:01.1
1928	Henry Pearce (AUS) 7:11.10	Kenneth Myers (USA) 7:20.8	T. David Collet (GBR) 7:19.8
1932	Henry Pearce (AUS) 7:44.4	William Miller (USA) 7:45.2	Guillermo Douglas (URU) 8:13.6
1936	Gustav Schäfer (GER) 8:21.5	Josef Hasenöhrl (AUT) 8:25.8	Daniel Barrow (USA) 8:28.0
1948	Mervyn Wood (AUS) 7:24.4	Eduardo Risso (URU) 7:38.2	Romolo Catasta (ITA) 7:51.4
1952	Yuri Tyukalov (URS) 8:12.8	Mervyn Wood (AUS) 8:14.5	Teodor Kocerka (POL) 8:19.4
1956	Vyacheslav Ivanov (URS) 8:02.5	Stuart Mackenzie (AUS) 8:07.7	John B. Kelly (USA) 8:11.8
1960	Vyacheslav Ivanov (URS) 7:13.96	Achim Hill (GER) 7:20.21	Teodor Kocerka (POL) 7:21.26
1964	Vyacheslav Ivanov (URS) 8:22.51	Achim Hill (GER) 8:26.34	Gottfried Kottmann (SUI) 8:29.68
1968	Henri Jan Wienese (HOL) 7:47.80	Jochen Meissner (GER) 7:52.00	Alberto Demiddi (ARG) 7:57.19
1972	Yuri Malishev (URS) 7:10.12	Alberto Demiddi (ARG) 7:11.53	Wolfgang Gueldenpfennig (GDR) 7:14.45
1976	Pertti Karppinen (FIN) 7:29.03	Peter Kolbe (GER) 7:31.67	Joachim Dreifke (GDR) 7:38.03

One of only five oarsmen to take three gold medals, Jack Beresford of Great Britain won rowing events in 1924, 1932 and 1936.

	GOLD	SILVER	BRONZE
1980	Pertti Karppinen (FIN) 7:09.61	Vasily Yakusha (URS) 7:11.66	Peter Kersten (GDR) 7:14.88
1984	Pertti Karppinen (FIN) 7:00.24	Peter-Michael Kolbe (FRG) 7:02.19	Robert Mills (CAN) 7:10.38
1988	Thomas Lange (GDR) 6:49.86	Peter-Michael Kolbe (FRG) 6:54.77	Eric Verdonk (NZL) 6:58.86

DOUBLE SCULLS

	GOLD	SILVER	BRONZE
1896–1900	Event not held		
1904	UNITED STATES 10:03.2	UNITED STATES d.n.a.	UNITED STATES d.n.a.
	John Mulcahy William Varley	John Hoben James McLoughlin	John Wells Joseph Ravanack
1906–1912	Event not held		
1920	UNITED STATES 7:09.0	ITALY 7:19.0	FRANCE 7:21.0
	John Kelly Paul Costello	Erminio Dones Pietro Annoni	Alfred Plé Gaston Giran
1924	UNITED STATES 7:45.0	FRANCE 7:54.8	SWITZERLAND d.r.a.
	John Kelly Paul Costello	Jean-Pierre Stock Marc Detton	Rudolf Bosshard Heini Thoma
1928	UNITED STATES 6:41.4	CANADA 6:51.0	AUSTRIA 6:48.8
	Charles J. McIlvaine Paul Costello	Jack Guest Joseph Wright	Viktor Flessl Leo Losert
1932	UNITED STATES 7:17.4	GERMANY 7:22.8	CANADA 7:27.6
	William E. Garrett-Gilmore Kenneth Myers	Gerhard Boetzelen Herbert Buhtz	Nöel de Mille Charles Pratt
1936	GREAT BRITAIN 7:20.8	GERMANY 7:26.2	POLAND 7:36.2
	Leslie F. Southwood Jack Beresford	Joachim Pirsch Willy Kaidel	Jerzy Ustupski Roger Verey
1948	GREAT BRITAIN 6:51.3	DENMARK 6:55.3	URUGUAY 7:12.4
	B. Herbert T. Bushnell Richard D. Burnell	Aage E. Larsen Ebbe Parsner	Juan Rodriguez William Jones

	GOLD	SILVER	BRONZE
1952	**ARGENTINA** 7:32.2	**U.S.S.R.** 7:38.3	**URUGUAY** 7:43.7
	Tranquilo Capozzo	Georgiy Zhilin	Miguel Seijas
	Eduardo Guerrero	Igor Emchuk	Juan Rodriguez
1956	**U.S.S.R.** 7:24.0	**UNITED STATES** 7:32.3	**AUSTRALIA** 7:37.4
	Aleksandr Berkutov	Bernard Costello	Murray Riley
	Yuri Tyukalov	James Gardiner	Mervyn Wood
1960	**CZECHOSLOVAKIA** 6:47.50	**U.S.S.R.** 6:50.49	**SWITZERLAND** 6:50.59
	Václav Kozák	Aleksandr Berkutov	Ernst Huerlimann
	Pavel Schmidt	Yuri Tyukalov	Rolf Larcher
1964	**U.S.S.R.** 7:10.66	**UNITED STATES** 7:13.16	**CZECHOSLOVAKIA** 7:14.23
	Oleg Tyurin	Seymour Cromwell	Vladimir Andrs
	Boris Dubrovsky	James Storm	Pavel Hofman
1968	**U.S.S.R.** 6:51.82	**NETHERLANDS** 6:52.80	**UNITED STATES** 6:54.21
	Anatoly Sass	Henricus A. Droog	John Nunn
	Aleksandr Timoshinin	Leendert F. van Dis	William Maher
1972	**U.S.S.R.** 7:01.77	**NORWAY** 7:02.58	**EAST GERMANY** 7:05.55
	Aleksandr Timoshinin	Frank Hansen	Joachim Boehmer
	Gennadi Korshikov	Svein Thogersen	Hans-Ulrich Schmied
1976	**NORWAY** 7:13.20	**GREAT BRITAIN** 7:15.26	**EAST GERMANY** 7:17.45
	Frank Hansen	Chris Baillieu	Hans-Ulrich Schmied
	Alf Hansen	Michael Hart	Jurgen Bertow
1980	**EAST GERMANY** 6:24.33	**YUGOSLAVIA** 6:26.34	**CZECHOSLOVAKIA** 6:29.07
	Joachim Dreifke	Zoran Pancic	Zdenek Pecka
	Klaus Kroppelien	Milorad Stanulov	Vaclav Vochoska
1984	**UNITED STATES** 6:36.87	**BELGIUM** 6:38.19	**YUGOSLAVIA** 6:39.59
	Bradley Lewis	Pierre-Marie Deloof	Zoran Pancic
	Paul Enquist	Dirk Crois	Milorad Stanulov
1988	**NETHERLANDS** 6:21.13	**SWITZERLAND** 6:22.59	**U.S.S.R.** 6:22.87
	Ronald Florijn	Beat Schwertzmann	Alexandr Martchenko
	Nicolaas Rienks	Veli Bodenmann	Vassiliy Yakouchka

COXLESS QUADRUPLE SCULLS

	GOLD	SILVER	BRONZE
1896–1972	Event not held		
1976	**EAST GERMANY** 6:18.65	**U.S.S.R.** 6:19.89	**CZECHOSLOVAKIA** 6:21.77
	Wolfgang Guldenpfennig	Yevgeni Duleyev	Jaroslav Helebrand
	Rudiger Reiche	Yuri Yakimov	Vaclav Vochoska
	Karl-Heinz Bussert	Aivar Lazdenieks	Zdenek Pecka
	Michael Wolfgramm	Vitautas Butkus	Vladek Lacina
1980	**EAST GERMANY** 5:49.81	**U.S.S.R.** 5:51.47	**BULGARIA** 5:52.38
	Frank Dundr	Yuriy Shapochka	Mintscho Nikolov
	Karsten Bunk	Yevgeniy Barbakov	Lubomir Petrov
	Uwe Heppner	Valeriy Kleshnev	Ivo Russev
	Martin Winter	Nikolai Dovgan	Bogdan Dobrev
1984	**WEST GERMANY** 5:57.55	**AUSTRALIA** 5:57.98	**CANADA** 5:59.07
	Albert Hedderich	Paul Reedy	Doug Hamilton
	Raimund Hormann	Gary Gullock	Mike Hughes
	Dieter Wiedenmann	Timothy McLaren	Phil Monckton
	Michael Dursch	Anthony Lovrich	Bruce Ford
1988	**ITALY** 5:53.37	**NORWAY** 5:55.08	**EAST GERMANY** 5:56.13
	Piero Poli	Lars Bjonness	Steffen Bogs
	Gianluca Farina	Vetle Vinje	Steffen Zühlke
	Davide Tizzano	Rolf Bernt Thorsen	Heiko Habermann
	Agostino Abbagnale	Alf John Hansen	Jens Köppen

COXLESS PAIRS

GOLD	SILVER	BRONZE

1896–1906 Event not held

1908 GREAT BRITAIN 9:41.0 / **GREAT BRITAIN** 2½ lengths / **CANADA** Fred Toms
- (Leander I) — (Leander II) — Norman Jackes
- J. R. K. Fenning — George E. Fairbairn — **GERMANY**
- Gordon L. Thomson — Philip E. Verdon — Martin Hanke, Willy Düskow

1912–1920 Event not held

1924 NETHERLANDS 8:19.4 / **FRANCE** 8:21.6 / —
- Wilhelm H. Rösingh — Maurice Bouton
- Antonie C. Beijnen — George Piot

1928 GERMANY 7:06.4 / **GREAT BRITAIN** 7:08.8 / **UNITED STATES** 7:20.4
- Bruno Müller — R. Archibald Nisbet — John Schmitt
- Kurt Moeschter — Terence O'Brien — Paul McDowell

1932 GREAT BRITAIN 8:00.0 / **NEW ZEALAND** 8:02.4 / **POLAND** 8:08.2
- H. R. Arthur Edwards — Frederick Thompson — Janusz Mikolajczyk
- Lewis Clive — Cyril Stiles — Henryk Budzynski

1936 GERMANY 8:16.1 / **DENMARK** 8:19.2 / **ARGENTINA** 8:23.0
- Hugo Strauss — Harry J. Larsen — Julio Curatella
- Willi Eichhorn — Richard Olsen — Horacio Podestá

1948 GREAT BRITAIN 7:21.1 / **SWITZERLAND** 7:23.9 / **ITALY** 7:31.5
- John H. T. Wilson — Josef Kalt — Bruno Boni
- William G. R. M. Laurie — Hans Kalt — Felice Fanetti

1952 UNITED STATES 8:20.7 / **BELGIUM** 8:23.5 / **SWITZERLAND** 8:32.7
- Charles Logg — Michel Knuysen — Kurt Schmid
- Thomas Price — Robert Baetens — Hans Kalt

1956 UNITED STATES 7:55.4 / **U.S.S.R.** 8:03.9 / **AUSTRIA** 8:11.8
- James Fifer — Igor Buldakov — Josef Kloimstein
- Duvall Hecht — Viktor Ivanov — Alfred Sageder

1960 U.S.S.R. 7:02.01 / **AUSTRIA** 7:03.69 / **FINLAND** 7:03.80
- Valentin Boreyko — Josef Kloimstein — Veli Lehtelä
- Olyeg Golovanov — Alfred Sageder — Toimi Pitkänen

1964 CANADA 7:32.94 / **NETHERLANDS** 7:33.40 / **GERMANY** 7:38.63
- George Hungerford — Steven Blaisse — Michael Schwan
- Roger C. Jackson — Ernst W. Veenemans — Wolfgang Hottenrott

1968 EAST GERMANY 7:26.56 / **UNITED STATES** 7:26.71 / **DENMARK** 7:31.84
- Jörg Lucke — Lawrence Hough — Peter F. Christiansen
- Hans-Jürgen Bothe — Philip Johnson — Ib Ivan Larsen

1972 EAST GERMANY 6:53.16 / **SWITZERLAND** 6:57.06 / **NETHERLANDS** 6:58.70
- Siegfried Brietzke — Heinrich Fischer — Roelof Luyernburg
- Wolfgang Mager — Alfred Bachmann — Rund Stokvis

1976 EAST GERMANY 7:23.31 / **UNITED STATES** 7:26.73 / **GERMANY** 7:30.03
- Jorg Landvoigt — Calvin Coffey — Peter Vanroye
- Bernd Landvoigt — Michael Staines — Thomas Strauss

1980 EAST GERMANY 6:48.01 / **U.S.S.R.** 6:50.50 / **GREAT BRITAIN** 6:51.47
- Jorg Landvoigt — Yuriy Pimenov — Charles Wiggin
- Bernd Landvoigt — Nikolai Pimenov — Malcolm Carmichael

1984 ROMANIA 6:45.39 / **SPAIN** 6:48.47 / **NORWAY** 6:51.81
- Petru Iosub — Fernando Climent — Hans Magnus Grepperud
- Valer Toma — Luis Lasurtegui — Sverre Loken

1988 GREAT BRITAIN 6:36.84 / **ROMANIA** 6:38.06 / **YUGOSLAVIA** 6:41.01
- Andrew Holmes — Dragos Neagu — Bojan Presern
- Steven Redgrave — Danut Dobre — Sadik Mukic

COXED PAIRS

	GOLD	SILVER	BRONZE
1896	Event not held		
1900	**NETHERLANDS** 7:34.2	FRANCE I 7:34.4	FRANCE II 7:57.2
	(Minerva, Amsterdam)	(Soc. Nautique de la Marne)	(Rowing Club Castillonais)
1904–1912	Event not held		
1920	**ITALY** 7:56.0	FRANCE 7:57.0	SWITZERLAND d.n.a.
	Ercole Olgeni	Gabriel Poix	Edouard Candeveau
	Giovanni Scatturin	Maurice Bouton	Alfred Felber
	Guido de Filip (cox)	Ernest Barberolle (cox)	Paul Piaget (cox)
1924	**SWITZERLAND** 8:39.0	ITALY 8:39.1	UNITED STATES d.n.a.
	Edouard Candeveau	Ercole Olgeni	Leon Butler
	Alfred Felber	Giovanni Scatturin	Harold Wilson
	Emil Lachapelle (cox)	Gino Sopracordevole (cox)	Edward Jennings (cox)
1928	**SWITZERLAND** 7:42.6	FRANCE 7:48.4	BELGIUM 7:59.4
	Hans Schöchlin	Armand Marcelle	Léon Flament
	Karl Schöchlin	Edouard Marcelle	François de Coninck
	Hans Bourquin (cox)	Henri Préaux (cox)	Georges Anthony (cox)
1932	**UNITED STATES** 8:25.8	POLAND 8:31.2	FRANCE 8:41.2
	Charles Kieffer	Janusz Slazak	André Giriat
	Joseph Schauers	Jerzy Braun	Anselme Brusa
	Edward Jennings (cox)	Jerzy Skolimowski (cox)	Pierre Brunet (cox)
1936	**GERMANY** 8:36.9	ITALY 8:49.7	FRANCE 8:54.0
	Herbert Adamski	Guido Santin	Georges Tapie
	Gerhard Gustmann	Almiro Bergamo	Marceau Fourcade
	Dieter Arend (cox)	Luciano Negrini (cox)	Nöel Vandernotte (cox)
1948	**DENMARK** 8:00.5	ITALY 8:12.2	HUNGARY 8:25.2
	Tage Henriksen	Aldo Tarlao	Béla Zsitnik
	Finn Pedersen	Giovanni Steffe	Antal Szendey
	Carl Ebbe Andersen (cox)	Alberto Radi (cox)	Róbert Zimonyi (cox)
1952	**FRANCE** 8:28.6	GERMANY 8:32.1	DENMARK 8:34.9
	Raymond Salles	Heinz Manchen	Svend Petersen
	Gaston Mercier	Helmut Heinhold	Paul Svendsen
	Bernard Malivoire (cox)	Helmut Noll (cox)	Jörgen Frandsen (cox)
1956	**UNITED STATES** 8:26.1	GERMANY 8:29.2	U.S.S.R. 8:31.0
	Arthur Ayrault	Karl-Heinrich von Groddeck	Igor Yemtschuk
	F. Conn Findlay	Horst Arndt	Georgiy Zhilin
	Kurt Seiffert (cox)	Rainer Borkowsky (cox)	Vladimir Petrov (cox)
1960	**GERMANY** 7:29.14	U.S.S.R. 7:30.17	UNITED STATES 7:34.58
	Bernhard Knubel	Antanas Bogdanavichus	F. Conn Findlay
	Heinz Renneberg	Zigmas Yukna	Richard Draeger
	Klaus Zerta (cox)	Igor Rudakov (cox)	H. Kent Mitchell (cox)
1964	**UNITED STATES** 8:21.23	FRANCE 8:23.15	NETHERLANDS 8:23.42
	Edward Ferry	Georges Morel	Jan J. Bos
	F. Conn Findlay	Jacques Morel	Herman J. Rouwé
	H. Kent Mitchell (cox)	Jean-Claude Darouy (cox)	Frederik Hartsuiker (cox)
1968	**ITALY** 8:04.81	NETHERLANDS 8:06.80	DENMARK 8:08.07
	Primo Baran	Herman J. Suselbeek	Jörn Krab
	Renzo Sambo	Hadriaan van Nes	Harry Jörgensen
	Bruno Cipolla (cox)	Roderick Rijnders (cox)	Preben Krab (cox)
1972	**EAST GERMANY** 7:17.25	CZECHOSLOVAKIA 7:19.57	RUMANIA 7:21.36
	Wolfgang Gunkel	Oldrich Svojanovsky	Stefan Tudor
	Joerg Lucke	Pavel Svojanovsky	Petre Ceapura
	Klaus-Dieter Neubert (cox)	Vladimir Petricek (cox)	Ladislau Lowrenschi (cox)

	GOLD	SILVER	BRONZE
1976	**EAST GERMANY** 7:58.99	**U.S.S.R.** 8:01.82	**CZECHOSLOVAKIA** 8:03.28
	Harald Jahrling	Dmitri Bekhterev	Oldrich Svojanovsky
	Friedrich Ulrich	Yuri Shurkalov	Pavel Svojanovsky
	George Spohr (cox)	Yuri Lorentson (cox)	Ludvik Vebr (cox)
1980	**EAST GERMANY** 7:02.54	**U.S.S.R.** 7:03.35	**YUGOSLAVIA** 7:04.92
	Harald Jahrling	Viktor Prevertsev	Dusko Mrduljas
	Friedrich-Wilhelm Ulrich	Gennadiy Kryuchkin	Zlatko Celent
	Georg Spohr (cox)	Aleksandr Lukyanov (cox)	Josip Reic (cox)
1984	**ITALY** 7:05.99	**ROMANIA** 7:11.21	**UNITED STATES** 7:12.81
	Carmine Abbagnale	Dimitrie Popescu	Kevin Still
	Giuseppe Abbagnale	Vasile Tomoiaga	Robert Espeseth
	Giuseppe Di Capua	Dumitru Raducanu	Douglas Herland
1988	**ITALY** 6:58.79	**EAST GERMANY** 7:00.63	**GREAT BRITAIN** 7:01.95
	Carmine Abbagnale	Mario Streit	Andrew Holmes
	Giusseppe Abbagnale	Detlef Kirchhoff	Steven Redgrave
	Giuseppe Di Capua	Rene Rensch	Patrick Sweeney

COXLESS FOURS

	GOLD	SILVER	BRONZE
1896–1900	Event not held		
1904	**UNITED STATES** 9:53.8	**UNITED STATES** d.n.a.	—
	(Century B.C., St. Louis)	(Mound City R.C., St. Louis)	
	Arthur M. Stockhoff	Frederick Suerig	
	August C. Erker	Martin Fromanack	
	George Dietz	Charles Aman	
	Albert Nasse	Michael Begley	
1906	Event not held		
1908	**GREAT BRITAIN** 8:34.0	**GREAT BRITAIN** 1½ lengths	**NETHERLANDS** Albertus Wielsma
	(Magdalen B.C., Oxford)	(Leander)	Johan Burk
	C. Robert Cudmore	Philip R. Filleul	Karel Jacobi
	James A. Gillan	Harold R. Barker	Bernadus Cronn
	Duncan McKinnon	J. R. K. Fenning	**CANADA**
	John R. Somers-Smith	Gordon L. Thomson	Gordon Balfour
			Beecher Gale
			Charles Riddy
			Geoffrey Taylor
1912–1920	Event not held		
1924	**GREAT BRITAIN** 7:08.6	**CANADA** 7:18.0	**SWITZERLAND** d.n.a.
	Charles R. M. Eley	Archibald C. Black	Emile Albrecht
	James A. McNabb	Colin H. B. Finlayson	Alfred Probst
	Robert E. Morrison	George F. McKay	Eugen Sigg
	T. Robert B. Sanders	William Wood	Hans Walter
1928	**GREAT BRITAIN** 6:36.0	**UNITED STATES** 6:37.0	**ITALY** 6:31.6
	Edward V. Bevan	Charles Karle	Cesare Rossi
	Richard Beesly	William Miller	Pietro Freschi
	Michael H. Warriner	George Heales	Umberto Bonadè
	John G. H. Lander	Ernest Bayer	Paolo Gennari
1932	**GREAT BRITAIN** 6:58.2	**GERMANY** 7:03.0	**ITALY** 7:04.0
	Rowland D. George	Hans Maier	Antonio Provenzani
	Jack Beresford	Walter Flinsch	Giliante d'Este
	Hugh R. A. Edwards	Ernst Gaber	Francesco Cossu
	John C. Badcock	Karl Aletter	Antonio Ghiardello
1936	**GERMANY** 7:01.8	**GREAT BRITAIN** 7:06.5	**SWITZERLAND** 7:10.6
	Wilhelm Menne	Thomas Bristow	Karl Schmid
	Martin Karl	Alan Barrett	Alex Homberger
	Anton Rom	Peter Jackson	Hans Homberger
	Rudolf Eckstein	John D. Sturrock	Hermann Betschart

East Germany, the eventual gold medalist, leads Great Britian in a preliminary heat of coxless fours at the 1972 Games in Munich.

	GOLD	SILVER	BRONZE
1948	**ITALY** 6:39.0	**DENMARK** 6:43.5	**UNITED STATES** 6:47.7
	Franco Faggi	Ib Storm Larsen	Robert Perew
	Giovanni Invernizzi	Helge Schroeder	Gregory Gates
	Elio Morille	A. Bonde Hansen	Stuart Griffing
	Giuseppe Moioli	Helge Halkjaer	F. John Kingsbury
1952	**YUGOSLAVIA** 7:16.0	**FRANCE** 7:18.9	**FINLAND** 7:23.3
	Duje Bonačič	Pierre Blondiaux	Veikko Lommi
	Vleimir Valenta	Jacques Guissart	Kauko Wahlsten
	Mate Trojanovič	Marc Bouissou	Oiva Lommi
	Peter Segvič	Roger Gautier	Lauri Nevalainen
1956	**CANADA** 7:08.8	**UNITED STATES** 7:18.4	**FRANCE** 7:20.9
	Archibald McKinnon	John Welchli	Guy Guillabert
	Lorne Loomer	John McKinlay	Gaston Mercier
	I. Walter d'Hondt	Arthur McKinlay	Yves Delacour
	Donald Arnold	James McIntosh	René Guissart
1960	**UNITES STATES** 6:26.26	**ITALY** 6:28.78	**U.S.S.R.** 6:29.62
	Arthur Ayrault	Tullio Baraglia	Igor Akhremchik
	Theodore Nash	Renato Bosatta	Yuriy Batschurov
	John Sayre	Giancarlo Crosta	Valentin Morkovkin
	Richard Wailes	Giuseppe Galante	Anatoliy Tarabrin
1964	**DENMARK** 6:59.30	**GREAT GRITAIN** 7:00.47	**UNITED STATES** 7:01.37
	John Orsted Hansen	John M. Russell	Geoffrey Picard
	Björn Haslöv	Hugh A. Wardell-Yerburgh	Richard Lyon
	Erik Petersen	William Barry	Theodore Mittet
	Kurt Helmudt	John James	Theodore Nash
1968	**EAST GERMANY** 6:39.18	**HUNGARY** 6:41.64	**ITALY** 6:44.01
	Frank Forberger	Zoltán Melis	Renato Bosatta
	Dieter Grahn	György Sarlós	Tullio Baraglia
	Frank Rühle	József Csermely	Pier Angelo Conti Manzini
	Dieter Schubert	Antal Melis	Abramo Albini
1972	**EAST GERMANY** 6:24.27	**NEW ZEALAND** 6:25.64	**WEST GERMANY** 6:28.41
	Frank Forberger	Dick Tonks	Joachim Ehrig
	Frank Rühle	Dudley Storey	Peter Funnekoetter
	Dieter Grahn	Ross Collinge	Franz Weld
	Dieter Schubert	Noel Mills	Wolfgang Plottke

	GOLD	SILVER	BRONZE
1976	**EAST GERMANY** 6:37.42	**NORWAY** 6:41.22	**U.S.S.R.** 6:42.52
	Siegfried Brietzke	Ole Nafstad	Raul Arnemann
	Andreas Decker	Arne Bergodd	Nikolai Kuznetsov
	Stefan Semmler	Finn Tveter	Valeri Dolinin
	Wolfgang Mager	Rolf Andreassen	Anushavan Gasan-Dzhalalov
1980	**E. GERMANY** 6:08.17	**U.S.S.R.** 6:11.81	**GREAT BRITAIN** 6:16.58
	Jurgen Thiele	Aleksey Kamkin	John Beattie
	Andreas Decker	Valeri Dolinin	Ian McNuff
	Stefan Semmler	Aleksandr Kulagin	David Townsend
	Siegfried Brietzke	Vitaliy Yeliseyev	Martin Cross
1984	**NEW ZEALAND** 6:03.48	**UNITED STATES** 6:06.10	**DENMARK** 6:07.72
	Leslie O'Connell	David Clark	Michael Jessen
	Shane O'Brien	Jonathan Smith	Lars Nielsen
	Conrad Robertson	Philip Stekl	Per Rasmussen
	Keith Trask	Alan Forney	Erik Christiansen
1988	**EAST GERMANY** 6:03.11	**UNITED STATES** 6:05.53	**WEST GERMANY** 6:06.22
	Roland Schröder	Raoul Rodriguez	Norbert Kesslau
	Thomas Greiner	Thomas Bohrer	Volker Grabow
	Ralf Brudel	David Krmpotich	Jörg Puttlitz
	Olaf Förster	Richard Kennelly	Guido Grabow

COXED FOURS

	GOLD	SILVER	BRONZE
1896	Event not held		
1900	**GERMANY** 5:59.0 (Germania, Hamburg)	**NETHERLANDS** 6:33.0 (Minerva, Amsterdam)	**GERMANY** 6:35.0 (Ruderverein, Ludwigshafen)
	Oskar Gossler		
	Katzenstein		
	Tietgens		
	G. Gossler		
	G. Gossler (cox)		
1904	Event not held		
1906	**ITALY** 8:13.0 (Bucintoro)	**FRANCE** d.n.a. (Soc. Nautique de la Basse Siene)	**FRANCE** d.n.a. (Soc. Nautique de Bayonne)
	Enrico Bruna	Gaston Delaplane	Adolphe Bernard
	Emilio Fontanella	Charles Delaporte	Joseph Halcet
	Riccardo Jandinoni	León Deliguières	Jean-Baptiste Laporte
	Giorgio Cesana	Paul Echard	Jean-Baptiste Mathieu
	Giuseppe Poli (cox)	Marcel Frébourg (cox)	Pierre Sourbé (cox)
1908	Event not held		
1912	**GERMANY** 6:59.4 (Ludwigshafener R.C.)	**GREAT BRITAIN** 2 lengths (Thames R.C.)	**NORWAY** d.n.a. (Christiania R.C.)
	Albert Arnheiter	Julius Beresford	Henry Larsen
	Otto Fickeisen	Charles Rought	Matias Torstensen
	Rudolf Fickeisen	Bruce Logan	Theodor Klem
	Herman Wilker	Charles G. Vernon	Haakon Tonsager
	Otto Maier (cox)	Geoffrey Carr (cox)	Ejnar Tonsager (cox)
			DENMARK (Polyteknik R.C.)
			Erik Bisgaard
			Rasmus P. Frandsen
			Magnus Simonsen
			Poul Thymann
			Eigil Clemmensen (cox)
1920	**SWITZERLAND** 6:54.0	**UNITED STATES** 6:58.0	**NORWAY** 7:02.0
	Hans Walter	Kenneth Myers	Henry Larsen
	Max Rudolf	Carl O. Klose	Per Gulbrandsen
	Willy Brüderlin	Franz Federschmidt	Theodor Klem
	Paul Rudolf	Erich Federschmidt	Birger Var
	Paul Staub (cox)	Sherman Clark (cox)	Thoralf Hagen (cox)

GOLD	SILVER	BRONZE

1924 **SWITZERLAND** 7:18.4 | **FRANCE** 7:21.6 | **UNITED STATES**
1 length

Hans Walter	Louis Gressier	Robert Gerhardt
Alfred Probst	Georges Lecointe	Sidney Jelinek
Emile Albrecht	Raymond Thalleux	Edward Mitchell
Eugen Sigg	Eugène Constant	Henry Welsford
Walter Loosli (cox)	Marcel Lepan (cox)	John Kennedy (cox)

1928 **ITALY** 6:47.8 | **SWITZERLAND** 7:03.4 | **POLAND** 7:12.8

Valerio Perentin	Ernst Haas	František Bronikowski
Giliante d'Este	Joseph Meyer	Edmund Jankowski
Nicolo Vittori	Otto Bucher	Leszek Birkholz
Giovanni Delise	Karl Schwegler	Bernard Ormanowski
Renato Petronio (cox)	Fritz Boesch (cox)	Bronislaw Drewek (cox)

1932 **GERMANY** 7:19.0 | **ITALY** 7:19.2 | **POLAND** 7:26.8

Joachim Spemberg	Bruno Parovel	Edward Kobylinski
Walter Meyer	Riccardo Divora	Stanislaw Urban
Horst Hoeck	Giovanni Plazzer	Janusz Slazak
Hans Eller	Bruno Vattovaz	Jerzy Braun
Karlheinz Neumann (cox)	Giovanni Scherl (cox)	Jerzy Skolimowski (cox)

1936 **GERMAY** 7:16.2 | **SWITZERLAND** 7:24.3 | **FRANCE** 7:33.3

Paul Söllner	Karl Schmid	Fernand Vandernotte
Ernst Gaber	Hans Homberger	Marcel Vandernotte
Walter Volle	Alex Homberger	Marcel Cosmat
Hans Maier	Hermann Betschart	Marcel Chauvigné
Fritz Bauer (cox)	Rolf Spring (cox)	Noel Vandernotte (cox)

1948 **UNITED STATES** 6:50.3 | **SWITZERLAND** 6:53.3 | **DENMARK** 6:58.6

Gordon Giovanelli	Pierre Stebler	Harry M. Knudsen
Robert W. Eill	Erich Schriever	Henry C. Larsen
Robert Martin	Emile Knecht	Börge R. Nielsen
Warren Westlund	Rudolf Reichling	Erik C. Larsen
Allen Morgan (cox)	André Moccand (cox)	Jörgen Ib Olsen (cox)

1952 **CZECHOSLOVAKIA** 7:33.4 | **SWITZERLAND** 7:36.5 | **UNITED STATES** 7:37.0

Karel Mejta	Enrico Bianchi	Carl Lovested
Jiří Havlis	Karl Weidmann	Alvin Ulbrickson
Jan Jindra	Heinrich Scheller	Richard Wahlström
Stanislav Lusk	Emile Ess	Matthew Leanderson
Miroslav Koranda (cox)	Walter Leiser (cox)	Albert Rossi (cox)

1956 **ITALY** 7:19.4 | **SWEDEN** 7:22.4 | **FINLAND** 7:30.9

Alberto Winkler	Olof Larsson	Kauko Hänninen
Romano Sgheiz	Gösta Eriksson	Reino Poutanen
Angelo Vanzin	Ivar Aronsson	Veli Lehtelä
Franco Trincavelli	Sven E. Gunnarsson	Toimi Pitkänen
Ivo Stefanoni (cox)	Bertil Göransson (cox)	Matti Niemi (cox)

1960 **GERMANY** 6:39.12 | **FRANCE** 6:41.62 | **ITALY** 6:43.72

Gerd Cintl	Robert Dumantois	Fulvio Balatti
Horst Effertz	Claude Martin	Romano Sgheiz
Jürgen Litz	Jacques Morel	Franco Trincavelli
Klaus Riekemann	Guy Nosbaum	Giovanni Zucchi
Michael Obst (cox)	Jean Klein (cox)	Ivo Stefanoni (cox)

1964 **GERMANY** 7:00.44 | **ITALY** 7:02.84 | **NETHERLANDS** 7:06.46

Peter Neusel	Renato Bosatta	Alex Mullink
Bernhard Britting	Emilio Trivini	Jan van de Graaf
Joachim Werner	Giuseppe Galante	Frederick R. van de Graaf
Egbert Hirschfelder	Franco de Pedrina	
Jürgen Oelke (cox)	Giovanni Spinola (cox)	Robert van de Graaf Marius Klumperbeek (cox)

1968 **N. ZEALAND** 6:45.62 | **E. GERMANY** 6:48.20 | **SWITZERLAND** 6:49.04

Richard J. Joyce	Peter Kremtz	Denis Oswald
Dudley L. Storey	Roland Göhler	Hugo Waser
Warren J. Cole	Klaus Jacob	Jakob Grob
Ross H. Collinge	Manfred Gelpke	Peter Bolliger
Simon C. Dickie (cox)	Dieter Semetzky (cox)	Gottlieb Fröhlich (cox)

	GOLD	SILVER	BRONZE
1972	**W. GERMANY** 6:31.85	**E. GERMANY** 6:33.30	**CZECHOSLOVAKIA** 6:35.64
	Peter Berger	Dietrich Zander	Otakar Marecek
	Hans-Johann Faerber	Reinhard Gust	Karel Neffe
	Gerhard Auer	Eckhard Martens	Vladimir Janos
	Alois Bierl	Rolf Jobst	František Provaznik
	Uwe Benter (cox)	Klaus-Dieter Ludwig (cox)	Vladimir Petricek (cox)
1976	**U.S.S.R.** 6:40.22	**E. GERMANY** 6:42.70	**W. GERMANY** 6:46.96
	Vladimir Eshinov	Andreas Schulz	Johann Faerber
	Nikolai Ivanov	Rudiger Kunze	Ralph Kubail
	Mikhail Kuznetsov	Walter Diessner	Siegfried Frickle
	Alexandr Klepikov	Ullrich Diessner	Peter Niehusen
	Alexandr Lukianov (cox)	Johannes Thomas (cox)	Hartmut Wenzel (cox)
1980	**E. GERMANY** 6:14.5	**U.S.S.R.** 6:19.05	**POLAND** 6:22.52
	Dieter Wendisch	Artur Garonskis	Grzegorz Stellak
	Ullrich Diessner	Dimant Krisianis	Adam Tomasiak
	Walter Diessner	Dzintars Krisianis	Grzegorz Nowak
	Gottfried Dohn	George Tikmers	Ryszard Stadniuk
	Andreas Gregor (cox)	Juris Berzynsh (cox)	Ryszard Kubiak (cox)
1984	**GREAT BRITAIN** 6:18.64	**UNITED STATES** 6:20.28	**NEW ZEALAND** 6:23.68
	Martin Cross	Thomas Kiefer	Kevin Lawton
	Richard Budgett	Gregory Springer	Donald Symon
	Andrew Holmes	Michael Bach	Barrie Mabbott
	Steven Redgrave	Edward Ives	Ross Tong
	Adrian Ellison	John Stillings	Brett Hollister
1988	**E. GERMANY** 6:10.74	**ROMANIA** 6:13.58	**NEW ZEALAND** 6:15.78
	Frank Klawonn	Dimitrie Popescu	George Keys
	Bernd Eichwurzel	Ioan Snep	Ian Wright
	Bernd Niesecke	Valentin Robu	Greg Johnson
	Karsten Schmeling	Vasile Tomoiaga	Chris White
	Hendrik Reiher	Ladislau Lovrenski	Andrew Bird

The United States wins by a nose over Italy, Canada and Great Britain in the final eights race at Los Angeles in 1932.

EIGHTS

	GOLD	SILVER	BRONZE

1896 Event not held

1900 **UNITED STATES** 6:09.8
(Vesper B.C., Philadelphia)
Roscoe Lockwood
Edward Marsh
Edward Hedley
William Carr
John E. Geiger
James Juvenal
Harry Debaecke
John N. Exley
Louis G. Abell

BELGIUM 6:13.8
(Royal Club Nautique de Ghent)
Marcel van Crombrugghe
Maurice Hemelsoet
Oscar de Cock
Maurice Verdonck
Prospère Bruggeman
Oscar de Somville
Frank Odberg
Jules de Bisschop
Alfred Vanlandeghem

NETHERLANDS 6:23.0
(Minerva, Amsterdam)
Walker M. Timmerman Thijssen
Ruurd G. Leegstra
Johannes W. van Djik
Henricus Tromp
Hendrick K. Offerhaus
Roelof Klein
François A. Brandt
Walter Middelberg
Hermanus G. Brockmann

1904 **UNITED STATES** 7:50.0
(Vesper B.C., Philadelphia)
Fred Cresser
M. D. Gleason
Frank Schell
J. S. Flanigan
C. E. Armstrong
H. H. Lott
J. F. Dempsey
John N. Exley
Louis G. Abell

CANADA d.n.a. —
(Argonaut, R.C., Toronto)
Joseph Wright
Donald Mackenzie
William Wadsworth
Geroge Strange
Phil Boyd
C. R. 'Pat' Reiffenstein
W. Rice
R. Bailey
Thomas Loudon

1906 Event not held

1908 **GREAT BRITAIN I** 7:52.0
(Leander Club)
Albert C. Gladstone
Frederick S. Kelly
Banner C. Johnstone
Guy Nickalls
Charles D. Burnell
Ronald H. Sanderson
Raymond B. Etherington-Smith
Henry C. Bucknall
Gilchrist S. Maclagen (cox)

BELGIUM 2 lengths
(Royal C.N. Gand)
Oscar Taelman
Marcel Morimont
Rémy Orban
Georges Mijs
François Vergucht
Polydore Veirman
Oscar de Somville
Rodolphe Poma
Alfred Vanlandeghem (cox)

GREAT BRITAIN II
(Cambridge University B.C.)
Frederick Jerwood
Eric W. Powell
Guy A. Carver
Edward G. Williams
Henry M. Goldsmith
Harold E. Kitching
John S. Burn
Douglas C. R. Stuart
Richard F. Boyle (cox)
CANADA
(Argonaut R. C. (Toronto)
Irvine R. Robertson
George F. Wright
Julius A. Thomson
Walter A. Lewis
Gordon B. Balfour
Becher R. Gale
Charles Riddy
Geoffrey Taylor
Douglas E. Kertland (cox)

1912 **GREAT BRITAIN I** 6:15.0
(Leander Club)
Sidney E. Swann
Leslie G. Wormald
Ewart D. Horsfall
James A. Gillan
Arthur S. Garton
Alister G. Kirby
Philip Fleming
Edgar R. Burgess
Henry B. Wells (cox)

GREAT BRITAIN II 1 length
(New College, Oxford)
Sir William Parker
William Fison
Thomas Gillespie
Beaufort Burdekin
Frederick Pitman
Arthur Wiggins
Charles Littlejohn
Robert Bourne
John Walker (cox)

GERMANY d.n.a.
(Berliner R.V. 1876)
Otto Leibing
Max Broeske
Max Vetter
Wilhelm Bartholomae
Fritz Bartholomae
Werner Dehn
Rudolf Reichelt
Hans Mathiae
Kurt Runge (cox)

	GOLD	SILVER	BRONZE
1920	**UNITED STATES** (Navy) 6:02.6	**GREAT BRITAIN** (Leander Club) 6:05.0	**NORWAY** 6:36.0
	Virgil Jacomini	Rev. Sidney Swann	Theodor Nag
	Edwin Graves	Ralph Shove	Conrad Olsen
	Willian Jordan	Sebastian Earl	Adolf Nilsen
	Edward Moore	John Campbell	Haakon Ellingsen
	Allen Sanborn	Walter James	Thore Michelsen
	Donald Johnston	Richard Lucas	Arne Mortensen
	Vincent Gallagher	Guy O. Nickalls	Karl Nag
	Clyde King	Ewart Horsfall	Tollef Tollefsen
	Sherman Clark (cox)	Robin Johnston (cox)	Thoralf Hagen (cox)
1924	**UNITED STATES** (Yale B.C.) 6:33.4	**CANADA** 6:49.0 (Toronto B.C.)	**ITALY** d.n.a. (Zara R.C.)
	Leonard G. Carpentier	Arthur Bell	Antonio Cattalinich
	Howard T. Kingsbury	Robert Hunter	Francesco Cattalinich
	Alfred M. Wilson	William Langford	Simeone Cattalinich
	J. David Lindley	Harold Little	Guiseppe Crivelli
	John L. Miller	John Smith	Latino Galasso
	James S. Rockefeller	Warren Snyder	Pietro Ivanov
	Frederick Sheffield	Norman Taylor	Bruno Sorich
	Benjamin M. Spock	William Wallace	Carlo Toniatti
	Laurence R. Stoddard (cox)	Ivor Campbell (cox)	Vittorio Gliubich (cox)
1928	**UNITED STATES** (Univ. of Calif.) 6:03.2	**GREAT BRITAIN** (Thames R.C.) 6:05.6	**CANADA** 6:03.8
	Marvin Stalder	Harold West	Frederick Hedges
	John Brinck	Jack Beresford	Frank Fiddes
	Francis Frederick	Gordon Killick	John Hand
	Walter Thompson	Harold Lane	Herbert Richardson
	William Dally	Donald Gollan	Jack Murdock
	James Workman	John Badcock	Athol Meech
	Hubert Caldwell	Guy O. Nickalls	Edgar Norris
	Peter Donlon	James Hamilton	William Ross
	Donald Blessing (cox)	Arthur Sulley (cox)	Jack Donelly (cox)
1932	**UNITED STATES** (Univ. of Calif.) 6:37.6	**ITALY** 6:37.8	**CANADA** 6:40.4
	Winslow Hall	Renato Barbieri	Albert Taylor
	Harold Tower	Enrico Garzelli	Donald Boal
	Charles Chandler	Guglielmo del Bimbo	William Thoburn
	Burton Jastram	Roberto Vestrini	Cedric Liddell
	David Dunlap	Dino Barsotti	Harry Fry
	Duncan Gregg	Renato Bracci	Stanley Stanyar
	James Blair	Mario Balleri	Joseph Harris
	Edwin Salisbury	Vittorio Cioni	Earl Eastwood
	Norris Graham (cox)	Cesare Milani (cox)	George MacDonald (cox)
1936	**UNITED STATES** 6:25.4 (Univ. Washington)	**ITALY** 6:26.0	**GERMANY** 6:26.4
	Donald Hume	Guglielmo del Bimbo	Herbert Schmidt
	Joseph Rantz	Dino Barsotti	Hans-Joachim Hannemann
	George Hunt	Oreste Grossi	
	James McMillin	Enzo Bartolini	Werner Loeckle
	John White	Mario Checcacci	Gerd Völs
	Gordon Adam	Dante Secchi	Hein Kaufmann
	Charles Day	Ottorino Quaglierini	Hans Kuschke
	Herbert Morris	Enrico Garzelli	Helmut Radach
	Robert Moch (cox)	Cesare Milani (cox)	Alfred Rieck
			Wilhelm Mahlow (cox)
1948	**UNITED STATES** (Univ. of Calif.) 5:56.7	**GREAT BRITAIN** 6:06.9	**NORWAY** 6:10.3
	John Stack	Andrew Mellows	Carl H. Monssen
	Justus Smith	David Meyrick	Thor Pedersen
	David Brown	C. Brian Lloyd	Leif Naess
	Lloyd Butler	Paul Massey	Harald Kråkenes
	George Ahlgren	E. A. Paul Bircher	Halfdan Gran-Olsen
	James Hardy	Guy Richardson	Hans E. Hansen

	GOLD	SILVER	BRONZE
1948	**UNITED STATES** (Univ. of Calif.) 5:56.7	**GREAT BRITAIN** 6:06.9	**NORWAY** 6:10.3
	John Stack	Andrew Mellows	Carl H. Monssen
	Justus Smith	David Meyrick	Thor Pedersen
	David Brown	C. Brian Lloyd	Leif Naess
	Lloyd Butler	Paul Massey	Harald Kråkenes
	George Ahlgren	E. A. Paul Bircher	Halfdan Gran-Olsen
	James Hardy	Guy Richardson	Hans E. Hansen
	David Turner	Maurice Lapage	Torstein Kråkenes
	Ian Turner	Christopher Barton	Kristoffer Lepsöe
	Ralph Purchase (cox)	Jack Dearlove(cox)	Sigurd Monssen (cox)
1952	**UNITED STATES** (Navy) 6:25.9	**U.S.S.R.** 6:31.2	**AUSTRALIA** 6:33.1
	Frank Shakespeare	Yevgeniy Brago	Robert Tinning
	William Fields	Vladimir Rodimushkin	Ernest Chapman
	James Dunbar	Aleksey Komarov	Nimrod Greenwood
	Richard Murphy	Igor Borisov	Mervyn Finlay
	Robert Detweiler	Slava Amiragov	Edward Pain
	Henry Proctor	Leonid Gissen	Philip Cayzer
	Wayne Frye	Yevgeniy Samsonov	Thomas Chessel
	Edward Stevens	Vladimir Krukov	David Anderson
	Charles Manring (cox)	Igor Polyakov (cox)	Geoffrey Williamson (cox)
1956	**UNITED STATES** (Yale Univ.) 6:35.2	**CANADA** 6:37.1	**AUSTRALIA** 6:39.2
	Thomas Charlton	Philip Kueber	Michael Aikman
	David Wight	Richard McClure	David Boykett
	John Cooke	Robert Wilson	Angus Benfield
	Donald Beer	David Helliwell	James Howden
	Caldwell Esselstyn	Donald Pretty	Garth Manton
	Charles Grimes	William McKerlich	Walter Howell
	Richard Wailes	Douglas McDonald	Adrian Monger
	Robert Morey	Lawrence West	Bryan Doyle
	William Becklean (cox)	Carlton Ogawa (cox)	Harold Hewitt (cox)
1960	**GERMANY** 5:57.18	**CANADA** 6:01.52	**CZECHOSLOVAKIA** 6:04.84
	Klaus Bittner	Donald Arnold	Josef Ventus
	Karl-Heinz Hopp	I. Walter d'Hondt	Bohumil Janoušek
	Hans Lenk	Nelson Kuhn	Jan Jindra
	Manfred Rulffs	John Lecky	Jiri Lundák
	Frank Schepke	Lorne Loomer	Stanislav Lusk
	Kraft Schepke	Archibald McKinnon	Václav Pavkovič
	Walter Schröeder	William McKerlich	Luděk Pojezny
	Karl-Heinz von Groddeck	Glen Mervyn	Jan Švéda
	Willi Padge (cox)	Sohen Biln (cox)	Miroslav Koniček (cox)
1964	**UNITED STATES** 6:18.23	**GERMANY** 6:23.29	**CZECHOSLOVAKIA** 6:25.11
	Joseph Amlong	Klaus Aeffke	Petr Čermák
	Thomas Amlong	Klaus Bittner	Jiri Lundák
	Harold Budd	Karl-Heinz von Groddeck	Jan Mrvik
	Emory Clark		Julnis Toček
	Stanley Cwiklinski	Hans-Jürgen Wallbrecht	Josef Ventus
	Hugh Foley	Klaus Behrens	Luděk Pojezny
	William Knecht	Jürgen Schroeder	Bohumil Janoušek
	William Stowe	Jürgen Plagemann	Richard Novy
	Robert Zimonyi (cox)	Horst Meyer	Miroslav Koniček (cox)
		Thomas Ahrens (cox)	
1968	**W. GERMANY** 6:07.00	**AUSTRALIA** 6:07.98	**U.S.S.R.** 6:09.11
	Horst Meyer	Alfred Duval	Zigmas Yukna
	Dirk Schreyer	Michael Morgan	Antanas Bagdonavichus
	Ruediger Henning	Joseph Fazio	Vladimir Sterlik
	Lutz Ulbricht	Peter Dickson	Yozanas Yagelavichus
	Wolfgang Hottenrott	David Douglas	Alexander Matryshkin
	Egbert Hirschfelder	John Ranch	Vitautas Briedis
	Joerg Siebert	Gary Pearce	Valentin Kravtschuk
	Nico Ott	Robert Shirlaw	Victor Suslin
	Gunther Thiersch (cox)	Alan Grover (cox)	Yury Lorentsson (cox)

	GOLD	SILVER	BRONZE
1976	**EAST GERMANY** 5:58.29	**GREAT BRITAIN** 6:00.82	**NEW ZEALAND** 6:03.51
	Bernd Baumgart	Richard Lester	Ivan Sutherland
	Gottfried Döhn	John Yallop	Trevor Coker
	Werner Klatt	Timothy Crooks	Peter Dignan
	Hans-Joachim Lück	Hugh Matheson	Lindsay Wilson
	Dieter Wendisch	David Maxwell	Athol Earl
	Roland Kostulski	James Clark	Dave Rodger
	Ulrich Karnatz	Fred Smallbone	Alex McLean
	Karl-Heinz Prudohl	Leonard Robertson	Tony Hurt
	Karl-Heinz Danielowski (cox)	Patrick Sweeney (cox)	Simon Dickie (cox)
1980	**EAST GERMANY** 5:49.05	**GREAT BRITAIN** 5:51.92	**U.S.S.R.** 5:52.66
	Bernd Krauss	Duncan McDougall	Viktor Kokoshkin
	Hans-Peter Koppe	Allan Whitwell	Andrej Tishchenko
	Ulrich Kons	Henry Clay	Aleksandr Tkachenko
	Jorg Friedrich	Chris Mahoney	Ionas Pintskus
	Jens Doberschutz	Andrew Justice	Ionas Normantas
	Ulrich Karnatz	John Pritchard	Andrej Lugin
	Uwe Duhring	Malcolm McGowan	Aleksandr Manzevich
	Bernd Hoing	Richard Stanhope	Igor Maistrenko
	Klaus-Dieter Ludwig (cox)	Colin Moynihan (cox)	Grigori Dmitrenko (cox)
1984	**CANADA** 5:41.32	**UNITED STATES** 5:41.74	**AUSTRALIA** 5:43.40
	Pat Turner	Walter Lubsen Jr	Craig Muller
	Kevin Neufield	Andrew Sudduth	Clyde Hefer
	Mark Evans	John Terwilliger	Sam Patten
	Grant Main	Christopher Penny	Timothy Willoughby
	Paul Steele	Thomas Darling	Ian Edmunds
	Mike Evans	Earl Borchelt	James Battersby
	Dean Crawford	Charles Clapp	Ion Popa
	Blair Horm	Bruce Ibbetson	Steve Evans
	Brian McMahon	Robert Jaugstetter	Gavin Thredgold
1988	**WEST GERMANY** 5:46.05	**U.S.S.R.** 5:48.01	**UNITED STATES** 5:48.26
	Thomas Möllenkamp	Veniamin But	Mike Teti
	Matthias Mellinghaus	Nikolay Komarov	John Smith
	Eckhardt Schultz	Vassiliy Tikhonov	Ted Patton
	Ansgar Wessling	Alexandr Dumchev	John Rusher
	Armin Eichholz	Pavel Gurkovsky	Peter Nordell
	Thomas Domian	Viktor Diduk	Jeff McLaughlin
	Wolfgang Maennig	Viktor Omelyanovich	Doug Burden
	Bahne Rabe	Andrey Vassilyev	John Pescatore
	Manfred Klein	Alexandr Lukyanov	Seth Bauer

Rowing (Women)

Women's rowing was introduced in 1976 over a course of 1,000 meters. Since 1988 the course for women has been over 2000 m, as for the men.

SINGLE SCULLS

	GOLD	SILVER	BRONZE
1976	Christine Scheiblich (GDR) 4:05.56	Joan Lind (USA) 4:06.21	Elena Antonova (URS) 4:10.24
1980	Sanda Toma (ROM) 3:40.69	Antonina Makhina (URS) 3:41.65	Martina Schroter (GDR) 3:43.54
1984	Valeria Racila (ROM) 3:40.68	Charlotte Geer (USA) 3:43.89	Ann Haesebrouck (BEL) 3:45.72
1988	Jutta Behrendt (GDR) 7:47.19	Anne Marden (USA) 7:50.28	Magdalena Guerguyeva (BUL) 7:53.65

DOUBLE SCULLS

	GOLD	SILVER	BRONZE
1976	BULGARIA 3:44.36	EAST GERMANY 3:47.86	U.S.S.R. 3:49.93
	Svetla Otzetova Zdravka Yordanova	Sabine Jahn Petra Boesler	Leonora Kaminskaite Genovate Ramoshkene
1980	U.S.S.R. 3:16.27	EAST GERMANY 3:17.63	ROMANIA 3:18.91
	Elena Khloptseva Larisa Popova	Cornelia Linse Heidi Westphal	Olga Homeghi Valeria Rosca-Racila
1984	ROMANIA 3:26.75	NETHERLANDS 3:29.13	CANADA 3:29.82
	Marioara Popescu Elisabeta Oleniuc	Greet Hellemans Nicolette Hellemans	Daniele Laumann Silken Laumann
1988	EAST GERMANY 7:00.48	ROMANIA 7:04.36	BULGARIA 7:06.03
	Birgit Peter Martina Schroter	Elisabeta Lipa Veronica Cogeanu	Violeta Ninova Stefka Madina

COXLESS PAIRS

	GOLD	SILVER	BRONZE
1976	BULGARIA 4:01.22	EAST GERMANY 4:01.64	WEST GERMANY 4:02.35
	Siika Kelbetcheva Stoyanka Grouitcheva	Angelika Noack Sabine Dahne	Edith Eckbauer Thea Einoeder
1980	EAST GERMANY 3:30.49	POLAND 3:30.95	BULGARIA 3:32.39
	Ute Steindorf Cornelia Klier	Malgorzata Dluzewska Czeslawa Koscianska	Siika Barboulova Stoyanka Kubatova
1984	ROMANIA 3:32.60	CANADA 3:36.06	WEST GERMANY 3:40.50
	Rodica Arba Elena Horvat	Betty Craig Tricia Smith	Ellen Becker Iris Volkner
1988	ROMANIA 7:28.13	BULGARIA 7:31.95	NEW ZEALAND 7:35.68
	Rodica Arba Olga Homeghi	Radka Stoyanova Lalka Berberova	Nicola Payne Lynley Hannen

COXED QUADRUPLE SCULLS

	GOLD	SILVER	BRONZE
1976	EAST GERMANY 3:29.99	U.S.S.R. 3:32.49	ROMANIA 3:32.76
	Anke Borchmann Jutta Lau Viola Poley Roswitha Zobelt Liane Weigelt (cox)	Anna Kondrachina Mira Bryunina Larisa Alexandrova Galina Ermolaeva Nadyezda Chernysheva (cox)	Ioana Tudoran Maria Micsa Felicia Afrasiloaia Elisabeta Lazar Elena Giurca (cox)

GOLD	SILVER	BRONZE
1980 **EAST GERMANY** 3:15.32	**U.S.S.R** 3:15.73	**BULGARIA** 3:16.10
Sybille Reinhardt	Antonina Pustovit	Mariana Serbezova
Jutta Ploch	Yelena Matyevskaya	Rumeliana Boneva
Jutta Lau	Olga Vasilchenko	Dolores Nakova
Roswitha Zobelt	Nadyezda Lubimova	Ani Bakova
Liane Buhr (cox)	Nina Cheremisina (cox)	Anka Georgieva (cox)
1984 **ROMANIA** 3:14.11	**UNITED STATES** 3:15.57	**DENMARK** 3:16.02
Titie Taran	Anne Marden	Hanne Eriksen
Anisoara Sorohan	Lisa Rohde	Birgitte Hanel
Ioana Badea	Joan Lind	Charlotte Koefoed
Sofia Corban	Virginia Gilder	Bodil Rasmussen
Ecaterina Oancia	Kelly Rickon	Jette Soeresen
1988[1] **EAST GERMANY** 6:21.06	**U.S.S.R.** 6:23.47	**ROMANIA** 6:23.81
Kerstin Förster	Irina Kalimbet	Anisoara Balan
Kristina Mundt	Svetlana Mazyi	Anisoara Minea
Beate Schramm	Inna Frolova	Veronica Cogeanu
Jana Sorgers	Antonina Dumcheva	Elisabeta Lipa

[1]without cox

COXED FOURS

GOLD	SILVER	BRONZE
1976 **EAST GERMANY** 3:45.08	**BULGARIA** 3:48.24	**U.S.S.R.** 3:49.38
Karin Metze	Ginka Gurova	Nadyezda Sevostyanova
Bianka Schwede	Liliana Vasseva	Ludmila Krokhina
Gabriele Lohs	Reni Yordanova	Galina Mishenina
Andrea Kurth	Mariika Modeva	Anna Pasokha
Sabine Hess (cox)	Kapka Gueorguieva (cox)	Lidia Krylova (cox)
1980 **EAST GERMANY** 3:19.27	**BULGARIA** 3:20.75	**U.S.S.R.** 3:20.92
Ramona Kapheim	Ginka Gurova	Mariya Fadeyeva
Silvia Frohlich	Mariika Modeva	Galina Sovetnikova
Angelika Noack	Rita Todorova	Marina Studneva
Romy Saalfeld	Iskra Velinova	Svetlana Semyonova
Kristen Wenzel (cox)	Nadelda Filipova (cox)	Nina Cheremisina (cox)
1984 **ROMANIA** 3:19.30	**CANADA** 3:21.55	**AUSTRALIA** 3:23.39
Florica Lavric	Marilyn Brain	Robyn Grey-Gardner
Maria Fricioiu	Angie Schneider	Karen Brancourt
Chira Apostol	Barbara Armbrust	Susan Chapman
Olga Bularda	Jane Tregunno	Margot Foster
Viorica Ioja	Lesley Thompson	Susan Lee
1988 **EAST GERMANY** 6:56.00	**CHINA** 6:58.78	**ROMANIA** 7:01.13
Martina Walther	Zhang Xianghua	Marioara Trasca
Gerlinde Doberschütz	Hu Yadong	Veronica Necula
Carola Hornig	Yang Xiao	Herta Anitas
Birte Siech	Zhou Shouying	Doina Balan
Sylvia Rose	Li Ronghua	Ecaterina Oancia

EIGHTS

	GOLD	SILVER	BRONZE
1976	**EAST GERMANY** 3:33.32	U.S.S.R. 3:36.17	UNITED STATES 3:38.68
	Viola Goretzki	Lubov Tatalayeva	Jacqueline Zoch
	Christiane Knetsch	Nadyezda Roshchina	Anita DeFrantz
	Ilona Richter	Klavdiya Kozenkova	Carie Graves
	Brigitte Ahrenholz	Elena Zubko	Marion Greig
	Monika Kallies	Olga Kolkova	Anne Warner
	Henrietta Ebert	Nelli Tarakanova	Peggy Ann McCarthy
	Helma Lehmann	Nadyezda Rozgon	Carol Brown
	Irina Muller	Olga Guzenko	Gail Ricketson
	Marina Wilke (cox)	Olga Pugovskaya (cox)	Lynn Silliman (cox)
1980	**EAST GERMANY** 3:03.32	U.S.S.R. 3:04.39	ROMANIA 3:05.63
	Martina Boesler	Olga Pivovarova	Angelica Aposteanu
	Kersten Neisser	Nina Umanets	Marlena Zagoni
	Christiane Kopke	Nadyezda Prischepa	Rodica Frintu
	Birgit Schutz	Valentina Zhulina	Florica Bucur
	Gabriele Kuhn	Tatyana Stetzenko	Rodica Puscatu
	Ilona Richter	Yelena Tereshina	Ana Iliuta
	Marita Sandig	Nina Preobrazhenskaya	Maria Constantinescu
	Karin Metze	Maria Pazyun	Elena Bondar
	Marina Wilke (cox)	Nina Frolova (cox)	Elena Dobritoiu (cox)
1984	**UNITED STATES** 5:59.80	ROMANIA 3:00.87	NETHERLANDS 3:02.92
	Shyril O'Steen	Doina Balan	Nicolette Hellemans
	Harriet Metcalf	Marioara Trasca	Lynda Cornet
	Caroll Brewer	Aurora Plesca	Harriet Van Ettekoven
	Carie Graves	Aneta Mihaly	Greet Hellemans
	Jeanne Flanagan	Adriana Chelariu	Marieke Van Drogenbroek
	Kristine Norellus	Minaela Armasescu	Anne Marie Quist
	Kristen Thorsness	Camelia Diaconescu	Catharina Neelissen
	Kathryn Keeler	Lucia Sauca	Willemien Vaandrager
	Betsy Beard	Viorica Ioja	Martha Laurijsen
1988	**EAST GERMANY** 6:15.17	ROMANIA 6:17.44	CHINA 6:21.83
	Annegret Strauch	Doina Balan	Zhou Xiuhua
	Judith Zeidler	Marioara Trasca	Zhang Yali
	Kathrin Haacker	Veronica Necula	He Yanwen
	Ute Wild	Herta Anitas	Han Yaqin
	Anja Kluge	Adriana Bazon	Zhang Xianghua
	Beatrix Schrör	Mihaela Armasescu	Zhou Shouying
	Ramona Balthasar	Rodica Arba	Yang Xiao
	Uta Stange	Olga Homeghi	Hu Yadong
	Daniela Neunast	Ecaterina Oancia	Li Ronghua

16. Shooting

New regulations were introduced in 1988 in accordance with ISU rules. The leading eight competitors at the end of the designated number of rounds take part in a final shoot-out round with the target sub-divided into tenths of a point for rifle and pistol shooting. For trap and skeet each of the leading competitors has 25 extra shots.

FREE PISTOL (50 meters)

	GOLD	SILVER	BRONZE
1896	Summer Paine (USA) 442	Viggo Jensen (DEN) 285	Holger Nielsen (DEN) d.n.a.
1900	Karl Röderer (SUI) 503	Achille Paroche (FRA) 466	Konrad Stäheli (SUI) 453
1904	Event not held		
1906	Georgios Orphanidis (GRE) 221	Jean Fouconnier (FRA) 219	Aristides Rangavis (GRE) 218
1908	Event not held		
1912	Alfred Lane (USA) 499	Peter J. Dolfen (USA) 474	Charles E. Stewart (GBR) 470
1920	Karl T. Frederick (USA) 496	Afranio da Costa (BRA) 489	Alfred P. Lane (USA) 481
1924–1932	Event not held		
1936	Torsten Ullmann (SWE) 559	Erich Krempel (GER) 544	Charles des Jammonières
1948	Edwin Vazquez Cam (PER) 545	Rudolf Schnyder (SUI) 539	Torsten Ullmann (SWE) 539
1952	Huelet Benner (USA) 553	Angel Léon de Gozalo (ESP) 550	Ambrus Balogh (HUN) 549
1956	Pentti Linnosvuo (FIN) 556	Makhmud Oumarov (URS) 556	Offutt Pinion (USA) 551
1960	Aleksey Gushchin (URS) 560	Makhmud Oumarov (URS) 552	Yoshihisa Yoshikawa (JPN) 552
1964	Väinö Markkanen (FIN) 560	Franklin Green (USA) 557	Yoshihisa Yoshikawa (JPN) 554
1968	Grigory Kossykh (URS) 562	Heinz Mertel (GER) 562	Harald Vollmar (GDR) 560
1972	Ragnar Skanakar (SWE) 567*	Dan Iuga (ROM) 562	Rudolf Dollinger (AUT) 560
1976	Uwe Potteck (GDR) 573*	Harald Vollmar (GDR) 567	Rudolf Dollinger (AUT) 562
1980	Aleksandr Melentev (URS) 581*	Harald Vollmar (GDR) 568	Lubtcho Diakov (BUL) 565
1984	Xu Haifeng (CHN) 566	Ragnar Skanaker (SWE) 565	Wang Yifu (CHN) 564
1988	Sorin Babii (ROM) 660(566 + 94)	Ragnar Skanaker (SWE) 657(564 + 93)	Igor Bassinski (URS) 657(570 + 87)

SMALL-BORE RIFLE—PRONE POSITION

1896–1920	Event not held		
1924	Pierre Coquelin de Lisle (FRA) 398	Marcus W. Dinwiddie (USA) 396	Josias Hartmann (SUI) 394
1928	Event not held		
1932	Bertil Rönnmark (SWE) 294	Gustavo Huet (MEX) 294	Zoltán Hradetsky-Soós (HUN) 293
1936	Willy Rögeberg (NOR) 300	Ralph Berzsenyi (HUN) 296	Wladyslaw Karás (POL) 296
1948	Arthur Cook (USA) 599	Walter Tomsen (USA) 599	Jonas Jonsson (SWE) 597
1952	Iosif Sarbu (ROM) 400	Boris Andreyev (URS) 400	Arthur Jackson (USA) 399
1956	Gerald Ouellette (CAN) 600[1]	Vasiliy Borissov (URS) 599	Gilmour S. Boa (CAN) 598
1960	Peter Kohnke (GER) 590	James Hill (USA) 589	Enrico Forcella Pelliccione (VEN) 587
1964	László Hammerl (HUN) 597	Lones Wigger (USA) 597	Tommy Pool (USA) 596
1968	Jan Kurka (TCH) 598	László Hammerl (HUN) 598	Ian Ballinger (NZL) 597

---

[1]Range found to be slightly short—record not allowed.

Lones Wigger (USA) receiving the silver medal for small-bore rifle shooting from the prone position at Tokyo in 1964. He earned a gold medal for small-bore rifle shooting in the three-position event at the same Games.

	GOLD	SILVER	BRONZE
1972	Li Ho Jun (PRK) 599*	Victor Auer (USA) 598	Nicolae Rotaru (ROM) 598
1976	Karlheinz Smieszek (GER) 599*	Ulrich Lind (GER) 597	Gennadi Lushchikov (URS) 595
1980	Karoly Varga (HUN) 599*	Hellfried Heilfort (GDR) 599*	Petar Zaprianov (BUL) 598
1984	Edward Etzel (USA) 599*	Michel Bury (FRA) 596	Michael Sullivan (GBR) 596
1988	Miroslav Varga (TCH) 703.9(600* + 103.9)	Cha Young-Chul (KOR) 702.8(598 + 104.8)	Attila Zahonyi (HUN) 701.9(597 + 104.9)

SMALL-BORE RIFLE—THREE POSITIONS
(prone, kneeling, standing)

	GOLD	SILVER	BRONZE
1896–1948	Event not held		
1952	Erling Kongshaug (NOR) 1,164	Vilho Ylönen (FIN) 1,164	Boris Andreyev (URS) 1,163
1956	Anatoliy Bogdanov (URS) 1,172	Otakar Hořinek (TCH) 1,172	Nils J. Sundberg (SWE) 1,167
1960	Viktor Shamburkin (URS) 1,149	Marat Niyasov (URS) 1,145	Klaus Zähringer (GER) 1,139
1964	Lones Wigger (USA) 1,164	Velitchko Khristov (BUL) 1,152	László Hammerl (HUN) 1,151
1968	Bernd Klingner (GER) 1,157	John Writer (USA) 1,156	Vitaly Parkhimovich (URS) 1,154
1972	John Writer (USA) 1,166*	Lanny Bassham (USA) 1,157	Werner Lippoldt (GDR) 1,153
1976	Lanny Bassham (USA), 1,162	Margaret Murdock (USA) 1,162	Werner Seibold (GER) 1,160

GOLD	SILVER	BRONZE
1980 Viktor Vlasov (URS) 1,173*	Bernd Hartstein (GDR) 1,166	Sven Johansson (SWE) 1,165
1984 Malcolm Cooper (GBR) 1173*	Daniel Nipkow (SUI) 1163	Alister Allan (GBR) 1162
1988 Malcolm Cooper (GBR) 1279.3(1180 + 99.3)	Alister Allan (GBR) 1275.6(1181* + 94.6)	Kirill Ivanov (URS) 1275.0(1173 + 102.0)

RAPID-FIRE PISTOL

1896 Jean Phrangoudis (GRE) 344	Georgios Orphanidis (GRE) 249	Holger Nielsen (DEN) d.n.a.
1900 Maurice Larony (FRA) 58	Léon Moreaux (FRA) 57	Eugène Balne (FRA) 57
1904 Event not held		
1906 Maurice Lecoq (FRA) 250	Léon Moreaux (FRA) 249	Aristides Rangavis (GRE) 245
1908 Paul van Asbroeck (BEL) 490	Réginald Storms (BEL) 487	James E. Gorman (USA) 485
1912 Alfred Lane (USA) 287	Paul Palén (SWE) 286	Johan H. von Holst (SWE) 283
1920 Guilherne Paraense (BRA) 274	Raymond C. Bracken (USA) 272	Fritz Zulauf (SUI) 269
1924 H. M. Bailey (USA) 18	Vilhelm Carlberg (SWE) 18	Lennart Hannelius (FIN) 18
1928 Event hot held		
1932 Renzo Morigi (ITA) 36	Heinz Hax (GER) 36	Domenico Matteucci (ITA) 36
1936 Cornelius van Oyen (GER) 36	Heinz Hax (GER) 35	Torsten Ullmann (SWE) 34
1948 Károly Takács (HUN) 580	Carlos E. Diaz Sáenz Valiente (ARG) 571	Sven Lundqvist (SWE) 569
1952 Károly Takács (HUN) 579	Szilárd Kun (HUN) 578	Gheorghe Lichiardopol (ROM) 578
1956 Stefan Petrescu (ROM) 587	Evgeniy Shcherkasov (URS) 585	Gheorghe Lichiardopol (ROM) 581
1960 William McMillan (USA) 587	Pentti Linnosvuo (FIN) 587	Aleksandr Zabelin (URS) 587
1964 Pentti Linnosvuo (FIN) 592	Ion Tripsa (ROM) 591	Lubomi T. Nacovsky (TCH) 590
1968 Jozef Zapedzki (POL) 593	Marcel Rosca (ROM) 591	Renart Suleimanov (URS) 591
1972 Josef Zapedzki (POL) 595*	Ladislav Faita (TCH) 594	Victor Torshin (URS) 593
1976 Norbert Klaar (GDR) 597*	Jurgen Wiefel (GDR) 596	Roberto Ferraris (ITA) 595
1980 Corneliu Ion (ROM) 596	Jurgen Wiefel (GDR) 596	Gerhard Petritsch (AUT) 596
1984 Takeo Kamachi (JPN) 595	Corneliu Ion (ROM) 593	Rauno Bies (FIN) 591
1988 Afanasi Kouzmine (URS) 698(598* + 100)	Ralf Schumann (GDR) 696(597 + 99)	Zoltan Kovacs (HUN) 693(594 + 99)

OLYMPIC TRAP SHOOTING

1896 Event not held		
1900 Roger de Barbarin (FRA) 17	René Guyot (FRA) 17	Justinien de Clary (FRA) 17
1904 Event not held		
1906 Two events were held under different conditions.		
1908 Walter H. Ewing (CAN) 72	George Beattie (CAN) 60	Alexander Maunder (GBR) 57 Anastassios Metaxas (GRE) 57

GOLD	SILVER	BRONZE
1912 James Graham (USA) 96	Alfred Goeldel (GER) 94	Harry Blau (URS) 91
1920 Mark Arie (USA) 95	Frank Troeh (USA) 93	Frank Wright (USA) 87
1924 Gyula Halasy (HUN) 98	Konrad Huber (FIN) 98	Frank Hughes (USA) 97
1928–1948 Event not held		
1952 George P. Généreux (CAN) 192	Knut Holmqvist (SWE) 191	Hans Liljedahl (SWE) 190
1956 Galliano Rossini (ITA) 195	Adam Smelczynski (POL) 190	Alessandro Ciceri (ITA) 188
1960 Ion Dumitrescu (ROM) 192	Galliano Rossini (ITA) 191	Sergey Kalinin (URS) 190
1964 Ennio Mattarelli (ITA) 198	Pavel Senichev (URS) 194	William Morris (USA) 194
1968 J. Robert Braithwaite (GBR) 198	Thomas Garrigus (USA) 196	Kurt Czekalla (GDR) 196
1972 Angelo Scalzone (ITA) 199*	Michel Carrega (FRA) 198	Silvano Basagni (ITA) 195
1976 Donald Haldeman (USA) 190	Armando Silva Marques (POR) 189	Ubaldesc Baldi (ITA) 189
1980 Luciano Giovannetti (ITA) 198	Rustan Yambulatov (URS) 196	Jorg Damme (GDR) 196
1984 Luciano Giovannetti (ITA) 192	Francisco Boza (PER) 192	Daniel Carlisle (USA) 192
1988 Dimtry Monakov (URS) 222(197 + 25)	Miloslav Bednarik (TCH) 222(197 + 25)	Frans Peeters (BEL) 219(195 + 24)

SKEET SHOOTING

1896–1964 Event not held		
1968 Evgeny Petrov (URS) 198*	Romano Garagnani (ITA) 198*	Konrad Wirnhier (GER) 198*
1972 Konrad Wirnhier (GER) 195	Evgeny Petrov (URS) 195	Michael Buchheim (GDR) 195
1976 Josef Panacek (TCH) 198	Eric Swinkels (HOL) 198	Wieslaw Gawlikowski (POL) 196
1980 Hans Kjeld Rasmussen (DEN) 196	Lars-Goran Carlsson (SWE) 196	Roberto Castrillo (CUB) 196
1984 Matthew Dryke (USA) 198*	Ole Rasmussen (DEN) 196	Luca Scribani Rossi (ITA) 196
1988 Axel Wegner (GDR) 222(198 + 24)	Alfonso de Iruarrizaga (CHI) 221(198 + 23)	Jorge Guardiola (ESP) 220(196 + 24)

RUNNING GAME TARGET

1896 Event not held		
1900 Louis Debray (FRA) 20	P. Nivet (FRA) 20	de Lambert (FRA) 19
1904–1968 Event not held		
1972 Lakov Zhelezniak (URS) 569*	Hanspeter Bellingrodt (COL) 565	John Kynoch (GBR) 562
1976 Alexander Gazov (URS) 579*	Alexander Kedyarov (URS) 576	Jerzy Greszkiewicz (POL) 571
1980 Igor Sokolov (URS) 589*	Thomas Pfeffer (GDR) 589*	Alexandr Gazov (URS) 587
1984 Li Yuwei (CHN) 587	Helmut Bellingrodt (COL) 584	Huang Shiping (CHN) 581
1988 Tor Heiestad (NOR) 689(591* + 98)	Huang Shiping (CHN) 686(589 + 98)	Gennady Avramenko (URS) 685(591* + 95)

AIR RIFLE

	GOLD	SILVER	BRONZE
1984	Philippe Heberle (FRA) 589*	Andreas Kronthaler (AUT) 587	Barry Dagger (GBR) 587
1988	Goran Maksimovic (YUG) 695.6(594* + 101.6)	Nicolas Berthelot (FRA) 694.2(593 + 101.2)	Johann Riederer (FRG) 694.0(592 + 102.0)

Shooting (Women)

SPORT PISTOL

1984	Linda Thom (CAN) 585*	Ruby Fox (USA) 585*	Patricia Dench (AUS) 583
1988	Nino Saloukvadze (URS) 690(591* + 99)	Tomoko Hasegawa (JPN) 686(587 + 99)	Jasna Sekaric (YUG) 686(591* + 95)

STANDARD RIFLE

1984	Wu Xiaoxuan (CHN) 581*	Ulrike Holmer (FRG) 578	Wanda Jewell (USA) 578
1988	Silvia Sperber (FRG) 685.6(590* + 95.6)	Vessela Letcheva (BUL) 683.2(583 + 100.2)	Valentina Tcherkassova (URS) 681.4(586 + 95.4)

AIR PISTOL

1984	Event not held		
1988	Jasna Sekaric (YUG) 489.5(389 + 100.5)	Nino Saloukvadze (URS) 487.9(390* + 97.9)	Marina Dobrantcheva (URS) 485.2(385 + 100.2)

AIR RIFLE

1984	Pat Spurgin (USA) 393*	Edith Gufler (ITA) 391	Wu Xiaoxuan (CHN) 389
1988	Irina Chilova (URS) 498.5(395* + 103.5)	Silvia Sperber (FRG) 497.5(393 + 104.5)	Anna Maloukhina (URS) 495.8(394 + 101.8)

17. Soccer

There was no Soccer event in 1896. In the 1900, 1904 and 1906 Games most of the medal winning teams were merely clubs rather than strictly international teams.

GOLD	SILVER	BRONZE

1896 Event not held

1908 **GREAT BRITAIN** | **DENMARK** | **NETHERLANDS**
GREAT BRITAIN	DENMARK	NETHERLANDS
Harold P. Bailey	Ludwig Drescher	Reinier B. Beeuwkes
Walter S. Corbett	Charles Buchwald	Karel Heijting
Herbert Smith	Harald Hansen	Lou Otten
Kenneth R. G. Hunt	Harald Bohr	Johan W. E. Sol
Frederick W. Chapman	Christian Middelboe	Johannes M. de Korver
Robert M. Hawkes	Nils Middelboe	Emil G. Mundt
Arthur Berry	Oscar Nielsen-Nörland	Jan H. Welcker
Vivian J. Woodward	August Lindgreen	Edu Snethlage
Harold S. Stapley	Sophus Nielsen	Gerard S. Reeman
Claude H. Parnell	Vilhelm Wolffhagen	Jan Thomée
Harold P. Hardman	Björn Rasmussen	Georges F. de
	Marius Andersen	Bruyn Kops
	Johannes Gandil	Johan A. F. Kok

1912
GREAT BRITAIN	DENMARK	NETHERLANDS
Ronald G. Brebner	Sophus Hansen	Marius J. Göbel
Thomas C. Burn	Nils Middelboe	David Wijnfeldt
Arthur E. Knight	Harald Hansen	Piet Bouman
Douglas McWhirter	Charles Buchwald	Gerardus Fortgens
Horace C. Littlewort	Emil Jörgensen	Constant W. Feith
James Dines	Paul Berth	Nicolaas de Wolff
Arthur Berry	Oscar Nielsen-Nörland	Dick N. Lotsy
Vivian J. Woodward	Axel Thufason	Johannes W. Boutmy
Harold A. Walden	Anton Olsen	Jan G. van Bredakolff
Gordon R. Hoare	Sophus Nielsen	Huug F. de Groot
Ivan G. A. Sharpe	Vilhelm Wolffhagen	Caesar H. ten Cate
Edward Hanney	Askel M. Petersen	Jan van der Sluis
Harold Stamper	Hjalmar Christoffersen	Jan Vos
E. Gordon D. Wright	Poul Nielsen	Nico J. Bouvy
	Ivar L. Seidelin-Neilsen	Johannes M. de Korver

1916 Event not held

1920
BELGIUM	SPAIN	NETHERLANDS
Jan de Bie	Ricardo Zamora	Robert McNeill
Armand Swartenbroeks	Pedro Vallana	Henri L. B. Denis
Oscar Verbeek	Mariano Arrate	Leonard F. G. Bosschart
Joseph Musch	Juan Artola	Frederick C. Kuipers
Emile Hanse	Agustin Sancho	Hermanus H. Steeman
André Fierens	Ramón Eguiazábal	Johannes D. de Natris
Louis van Hege	Francisco	Jacob E. Bulder
Robert Coppée	Pagazaurtundúa	Bernardus Groosjohan
Mathieu Bragard	Felix Sesúmaga	Jan L. van Dort
Henri Larnoe	Patricio Arbolaza	Oscar E. van Rappard
Désiré Bastin	Rafael Moreno	Herman C. G. van
Fernand Nisot	Domingo Acedo	Heijden
Georges Hebden	José Samitier	Bernard W. J. Verweij
Félix Balyu	José M. Belausteguigoitia	Evert J. Bulder
	Louis Otero	Adrianus G. Bieshaar
	Joaquin Vázquez	
	Ramón Moncho Gil	
	Sabino Bilbao	
	Silverio Izaguirre	

GOLD	SILVER	BRONZE
1924 URUGUAY	**SWITZERLAND**	**SWEDEN**
Andrés Mazali	Hans Pulver	Sigfrid Lindberg
José Nasazzi	Adolphe Reymond	Axel Alfredsson
Pedro Arispe	Rudolf Ramseyer	Fritjof Hillén
José L. Andrade	August Oberhauser	Sven Friberg
José Vidal	Paul Schmiedlin	Gustaf Carlson
Alfredo Ghierra	Aron Pollitz	Harry Sundberg
Santos Urdinarán	Karl Ehrenbolger	Charles Brommesson
Hector Scarone	Robert Pache	Sven Rydell
Pedro Petrone	Walter Dietrich	Per Kaufeldt
Pedro Céa	Max Abbeglen	Albin Dahl
Alfredo Romano	Paul Fässler	Rudolf Kock
Umberto Tomasina	Paul Sturzenegger	Gunnar Holmberg
Juan Naya	Edmond Kramer	Evert Lundqvist
Alfredo Zibechi	Félix Bédouret	Tore Keller
Antonio Urdinarán	Adolphe Mengotti	Thorsten Svensson
		Konrad Hirsch
		Sven Linqvist
		Sten Mellgren
1928 URUGUAY	**ARGENTINA**	**ITALY**
Andrés Mazali	Angel Bossio	Giampiero Combi
José Nasazzi	Fernando Paternoster	Delfo Bellini
Pedro Arispe	Ludovico Bidoglio	Umberto Caligaris
José L. Andrade	Juan Evaristo	Alfredo Pitto
Lorenzo Fernández	Luis F. Monto	Fulvio Bernardini
Alvaro Gestido	Segundo Medici	Pietro Genovesi
Santos Urdináran	Raimundo Orsi	Adolfo Baloncieri
Hector Castro	Enrique Gainzarain	Elvio Banchero
Pedro Petrone	Manuel Ferreira	Angelo Schiavio
Pedro Céa	Domingo Tarasconi	Mario Magnozzi
Hector Scarone	Adolfo Carricaberri	Virgilio F. Levratto
Antonio Campolo	Feliciano A. Perducca	Giovanni Deprà
Juan Arremón	Saúl Calandra	Antonio Janni
René Borjas	Roberto Cherro	Silvio Pietroboni
Juan Piriz	Rodolfo Orlandini	Enrico Rivolta
Adhemar Canavesi	Octavio Diaz	Virginio Rosetta
Roberto Figueroa		Gino Rossetti
1932 Event not held		
1936 ITALY	**AUSTRIA**	**NORWAY**
Bruno Venturini	Eduard Kainberger	Henry Johansen
Alfredo Foni	Ernst Künz	Nils Eriksen
Pietro Rava	Martin Kargl	Öivind Holmsen
Giuseppe Baldo	Anton Krenn	Frithjof Ulleberg
Achille Piccini	Karl Wahlmüller	Jörgen Juve
Ugo Locatelli	Max Hofmeister	Rolf Holmberg
Annibale Frossi	Walter Werginz	Magdalon Monsen
Libero Marchini	Adolf Laudon	Reidar Kvammen
Sergio Bertoni	Klement Steinmetz	Alf Martinsen
Carlo Biagi	Karl Kainberger	Odd Frantzen
Francesco Gabriotti	Franz Fuchsberger	Arne Brustad
Luigi Scarabello	Josef Kitzmüller	Frederik Horn
Giulio Cappelli	Franz Mandl	Sverre Hansen
Alfonso Negro		Magnar Isaksen

	GOLD	SILVER	BRONZE
1948	**SWEDEN**	**YUGOSLAVIA**	**DENMARK**
	Torsten Lindberg	Ljubomir Lovrič	Ejgil Nielsen
	Knut Nordahl	Miroslav Brozovič	Viggo Jensen
	Erik Nilsson	Branislav Stankovič	Knud B. Overgaard
	Birger Rosengren	Zlatko Cajkoviski	Axel Pilmark
	Bertil Nordahl	Miodrag Jovanovič	Dion Örnvold
	Sune Andersson	Aleksandar Atanakovič	Ivan Jensen
	Kjell Rosén	Zvonko Cimermančič	Johannes Plöger
	Gunnar Grén	Rajko Mitič	Knud Lundberg
	Gunnar Nordahl	Stjepan Bobek	Carl A. Praest
	Henry Carlsson	Željko Čajkovski	John Hansen
	Nils Liedholm	Bernard Vukas	Jörgen Sörensen
	Börje Leander	Franjo Soštarič	Holger Seebach
		Prvoslav Mihajlovič	Karl Aage Hansen
		Franjo Völfl	
		Kosta Tomasevič	

This hard-fought match resulted in a bronze medal for Denmark (dark shirts) in the 1948 Games.

	GOLD	SILVER	BRONZE
1952	**HUNGARY**	**YUGOSLAVIA**	**SWEDEN**
	Gyula Grosics	Vladimir Beara	Karl Svensson
	Jenő Buzánszky	Branko Stankovič	Lennart Samuelsson
	Gyula Lóránt	Tomislav Crnkovič	Erik Nilsson
	Mihály Lantos	Zlatko Cajkovski	Olle Åhlund
	József Bozsik	Ivan Horvat	Bengt Gustavsson
	Nándor Hidegkuti	Vujadin Boškov	Gösta Lindh
	Sándor Kocsis	Tihomir Ognjanov	Sylve Bengtsson
	Péter Palotás	Rajko Mitič	Gösta Löfgren
	Ferenc Puskás	Bernard Vukas	Ingvar Rydell
	Zoltán Csibor	Stjepan Bobek	Yngve Brodd
	József Zakariás	Branko Zebec	Gösta Sandberg
	Jenő Dalnoki		Holger Hansson
	Imre Kovács		
	László Budai		
	Lajos Csordás		

	GOLD	SILVER	BRONZE
1956	**U.S.S.R.**	**YUGOSLAVIA**	**BULGARIA**
	Lev Yashin	Petar Radenkovič	Georgi Naydenov
	Boris Kuznyetsov	Mladen Koščak	Kiril Rakarov
	Mikhail Ogognikov	Nikola Radovič	Yosif Yosifor
	Aleksey Paramanov	Ivan Santek	Stefan Stefanov
	Anatoliy Bashashkin	Ljubiša Spajič	Manol Manolov
	Igor Netto	Dobroslav Krstič	Nikola Kovatchev
	Boris Tatushin	Dragoslav Sekularac	Gavril Stojanov
	Anatoliy Issayev	Zlatko Papec	Miltcho Goranov
	Edouard Streltsov	Sava Antič	Panayot Panayotov
	Sergey Salnikov	Todor Vaselinovič	Ivan Kolev
	Anatoliy Ilin	Muhamed Mujič	Kroum Yanev
	Anatoliy Maslenkin	Blagoje Vidinič	Todor Diyev
	Nikita Simonian	Ibrahim Biogradlič	Dimiter Milanov
	Nikolay Tyshenko	Luka Liposinovič	Georgy Dimitrov
	Vladimir Ryjkin		
	Iosif Betsa		
	Valentin Ivanov		
	Boris Rasinsky		
1960	**YUGOSLAVIA**	**DENMARK**	**HUNGARY**
	Blagoje Vidinič	Poul Andersen	Gábor Török
	Vladimir Djurkovic	Poul Jensen	Zoltán Dudás
	Fahrudin Jusufi	Bent Hansen	Jenő Dalnoki
	Ante Zanetic	Hans C. Nielsen	Ernő Sölymösi
	Novak Roganovič	Flemming Nielsen	Pál Várhidi
	Želijko Perušič	Poul Pedersen	Ferenc Kovács
	Andreja Ankovič	Tommy Troelsen	Imre Sátori
	Zelijko Matuš	Harald Nielsen	János Göröcs
	Milan Galič	Henning Enoksen	Flórián Albert
	Tomislav Knez	Jörn Sörensen	Pál Orosz
	Borivoje Kostič	Henry Fröm	János Dunai
	Velimir Sombolac	John Danielsen	Dezső Novák
	Alexsandar Kozlina		Oszkár Vilezsál
	Dušan Maravič		Gyula Rákosi
	Silvester Takač		Lajos Faragó
	Milutin Soskič		László Pál
			Tibor Pál
1964	**HUNGARY**	**CZECHOSLOVAKIA**	**GERMANY**
	Antal Szentmihàlyi	František Schmucker	Hans J. Heinsch
	Dezső Novák	Anton Urban	Peter Rock
	Kálmán Ihász	Karel Z. Pičman	Manfred Geisler
	Árpád Orban	Josef Vojta	Herbert Pankau
	Ferenc Nógrádi	Vladimir Weiss	Manfred Walter
	János Farkas	Jan Geleta	Gerhard Koerner
	Tibor Csernai	Jan Bramovsky	Hermann Stoeker
	Ferenc Bene	Ivan Mráz	Otto Fraessdorf
	Imre Komora	Karel Lichtnégl	Henning Frenzel
	Gustáv Szepesi	Vojtech Masny	Jürgen Noeldner
	Sándor Katona	František Valošek	Eberhard Vogel
	József Gelei	Anton Svajlen	Horst Weigang
	Károly Palotai	Karel Knesl	Klaus Urbanczyk
	Zoltán Varga	Stefan Matlák	Klaus-Dieter Seehaus
		Karel Nepomucky	Werner Unger
		Ludevit Cvet	Dieter Engelhardt
		František Knebort	Wolfgang Bartels
			Bernd Bauchspiess
			Klaus Lisiewicz

GOLD	SILVER	BRONZE
1968 **HUNGARY**	**BULGARIA**	**JAPAN**
Károly Fatér	Stoyan Yordanov	Kenzo Yokayama
Dezső Novák	Atanas Gerov	Hirosci Katayama
Lajos Dunai	Gueorgui Christakiev	Yoshitada Yamaguchi
Miklós Pancsics	Milko Gaidarski	Mitsuo Kamata
Iván Menczel	Kiril Ivkov	Takaji Mori
Lajos Szücs	Ivailo Georgiev	Aritatsu Ogi
László Fazekas	Tzvetan Dimitrov	Teruki Miyamoto
Antal Dunai	Evgueni Yantchovski	Masashi Watanabe
László Nagy	Petar Jekov	Kunishige Kamamoto
Ernö Noskó	Atanas Christov	Ikuo Matsumoto
István Juhász	Asparukh Donev	Ryuichi Sugiyama
Lajos Kocsis	Georgi Vassilev	Masakatsu Miyamoto
László Keglovich	Kiril Christov	Shigeo Yaegashi
István Sárközi	Mikhail Giionin	Yasuyuki Kuwahara
István Basti	Yantcho Dimitrov	
	Georgi Ivanov	
	Ivan Zafirov	
	Todor Nikolov	
1972 **POLAND**	**HUNGARY**	**EAST GERMANY**[1]
Hubert Kostka	Istvan Geczi	Jürgen Croy
Zbigniew Gut	Peter Vepi	Manfred Zapf
Jerzy Gorgon	Miklós Pancsics	Konrad Weise
Zygmunt Anczok	Peter Juhasz	Bernd Bransch
Leslaw Cmikiewicz	Lajos Szucs	Jürgen Pommerenke
Jerzy Kraska	Mihaly Kozma	Jürgen Sparwasser
Kazimierz Deyna	Antal Dunai	Hans-Jürgen Kreische
Zygfryd Szoltysik	Lajos Ku	Achim Streich
Wlodzimierz Lubanski	Bela Varadi	Wolfgang Seguin
Robert Gadocha	Ede Dunai	Peter Ducke
Ryszard Szymczak	Laszlo Balint	Frank Ganzera
Antoni Szymanowski	Lajos Kocsis	Lothar Kurbjuweit
Marian Ostafinski	Kalman Toth	Eberhard Vogel
Kazimierz Kmiecik	Jozsef Kovacs	Ralf Schulenberg
Zygmunt Maszczyk	Laszlo Branikovics	Reinhard Häfner
Joachim Marx	Csaba Vidacs	Harald Irmscher
Grzegorz Lato	Adam Rothermel	Siegmar Wätzlich
		U.S.S.R.[1]
		Oleg Blohin
		Murtaz Hurcilava
		Yuri Istomin
		Vladimir Kaplichnyi
		Viktor Kolotov
		Evgeniy Lovchev
		Sergei Olshanskiy
		Evgeniy Rudakov
		Viacheslav Semenov
		Gennadi Yevrushikhin
		Oganes Zanazanian
		Andrei Yakubik
		Arkadiy Andriasian
		Revaz Dsodzuashvili
		Iojef Sabo
		Vladimir Onischenko
		Anatoliy Kuksov
		Yuri Eliseev
		Vladimir Pilguy

---

[1]Third place declared a tie after extra time played.

This British soccer team took home the gold medal in 1912 with a final victory of 18 to 1 over Denmark.

The Italian goalkeeper protects his team's 2-to-1 edge from Austrian attack in the 1936 soccer final.

	GOLD	SILVER	BRONZE
1976	**EAST GERMANY**	**POLAND**	**U.S.S.R.**
	Jurgen Croy	Jan Tomaszewski	Vladimir Astapovski
	Hans Jurgen Dorner	Piotr Mowlik	Viktor Matvienko
	Konrad Weise	Antoni Szymanowski	Mikhail Fomenko
	Lothar Kurbjuweit	Wladyslaw Zmuda	Stefan Reshko
	Reinhard Lauck	Zygmunt Maszczyk	Vladimir Troshkin
	Reinhard Häfner	Grzegorz Lato	Vladimir Onischenko
	Hans Jurgen Riediger	Henryk Kasperczak	Leonid Nazarenko
	Bernd Bransch	Kazimierz Deyna	Viktor Kolotov
	Martin Hoffmann	Andrzej Szarmach	Oleg Blokhin
	Gerd Kische	Kazimierz Kmiecik	Leonid Buriak
	Wolfram Lowe	Henryk Wawrowski	Aleksandr Minayev
	Wilfried Grobner	Henryk Wieczorek	Viktor Zviagintsev
	Hartmut Schade		
1980	**CZECHOSLOVAKIA**	**EAST GERMANY**	**U.S.S.R.**
	Stanislav Seman	Bodo Rudwaleit	Rinat Dasayev
	Ludek Macela	Artur Ullrich	Tengiz Sulakvelidze
	Josef Mazura	Lothar Hause	Aleksandr Chivadze
	Libor Radimec	Frank Baum	Vagiz Khidiyatullin
	Zdenek Rygel	Rudiger Schnuphase	Oleg Romantsev
	Petr Nemec	Frank Terletzki	Sergey Shavlo
	Ladislav Vizek	Wolfgang Steinbach	Sergey Andreyev
	Jan Berger	Werner Peter	Vladimir Bessonov
	Jindrich Svoboda	Dieter Kuhn	Yuriy Gavrilov
	Lubos Pokluda	Norbert Trieloff	Feodor Chernenkov
	Werner Licka	Matthias Muller	Valeriy Gazzayev
	Rostislav Vaclavicek	Matthias Liebers	Sergey Baltacha
	Jaroslav Netolicka	Wolf-Rudiger Netz	Khoren Oganesyan
	Oldrich Rott	Frank Uhlig	Vladimir Pilgu
	Frantisek Stambacher	Jurgen Bahringer	Sergey Nikulin
	Frantisek Kunzo	Bernd Jakubowski	Aleksandr Prokopenko
1984	**FRANCE**	**BRAZIL**	**YUGOSLAVIA**
	Albert Rust	Gilmar Rinaldi	Ivan Pudar
	William Ayache	Ronaldo Silva	Vlado Capljic
	Michel Bibard	Jorge Luiz Brum	Mirsad Baljic
	Dominique Bjotat	Mauro Galvao	Srecko Katanec
	Francois Brisson	Ademir Kaeser	Marko Elsner
	Patrick Cubaynes	Andre Luiz Ferreira	Ljubomir Radanovic
	Patrice Garande	Paulo Santos	Admir Smajic
	Philippe Jeannol	Carlos Verri	Nenad Gracan
	Guy Lacombe	Joao Leiehardt Neto	Milko Djurovski
	Jean-Claude Lemoult	Augilmar Oliveira	Mehmed Bazdarevic
	Jean-Philippe Rohr	Silvio Paiva	Borislav Cvetkovic
	Didier Senac	Luiz Dias	Tomislav Ivkovic
	Jean-Christoph	Luiz Carlos Winck	Jovica Nikolic
	Thouvenel	Davi Cortez Silva	Stjepan Deveric
	Jose Toure	Antonio Jose Gil	Branko Miljus
	Daniel Xoureb	Francisco Vidal	Dragan Stojkovic
	Jean-Louis Zanon	Milton Cruz	Mitar Mrkela
	Michel Bensoussan		

	GOLD	SILVER	BRONZE
1988	**U.S.S.R.**	**BRAZIL**	**WEST GERMANY**
	Dmitry Kharine	Claudio Taffarel	Oliver Reck
	Guela Ketachvili	Jorge Campos	Michael Schulz
	Igor Sklyarov	Joao Santos	Armin Görtz
	Alexey Cherednik	Ricardo Raimundo	Wolfgang Funkel
	Arvidas Yanonis	Ademir Kaefer	Thomas Hörster
	Vadim Tichtchenko	Iomar Nascimento	Olaf Janssen
	Yevgeny Kuznetsov	Valdo Candido	Rudi Bommer
	Igor Ponomaryev	Geovani Silva	Holger Fach
	Alexandr Borodyuk	Edmar Santos	Jürgen Klinsmann
	Igor Dobrovolsky	Hamilton Souza	Wolfram Wuttke
	Vladimir Lyuty	Romario Farias	Frank Mill
	Yevgeny Yarovenko	Jose Araujo	Uwe Kamps
	Sergey Fokine	Andre Cruz	Roland Grahammer
	Vladimir Tatarchuk	Luiz Winck	Thomas Hässler
	Alexey Mikhailichenko	Aloisio Alves	Christian Schreier
	Alexey Prudnikov	Jose Ferreira	Fritz Walter
	Viktor Lossev	Sergio Luiz	Ralf Sievers
	Sergey Gorlukovich	Jorge Silva	Gerhard Kleppinger
	Yuriy Savichev	Jose Oliveira	Karl Heinz Riedle
	Arminas Narbekovas	Milton Souza	Gunnar Sauer

---

18. Swimming and Diving (Men)

50 METERS FREE-STYLE (54 yd 2 ft)

1896–1984	Event not held		
1988	Matt Biondi (USA) 22.14*	Tom Jager (USA) 22.36	Gennady Prigoda (URS) 22.71

100 METERS FREE-STYLE (109 yd. 1 ft.)

1896	Alfréd Hajós (HUN) 1:22.2*	Efstathios Choraphas (GRE) 1:23.0	Otto Herschmann (AUT) d.n.a.
1900–1904	Event not held		
1906	Charles M. Daniels (USA) 1:13.4*	Zoltán von Halmay (HUN) 1:14.2	Cecil Healy (AUS) d.n.a.
1908	Charles M. Daniels (USA) 1:05.6*	Zoltán von Halmay (HUN) 1:06.2	Harald Julin (SWE) 1:08.0
1912	Duke P. Kahanamoku (USA) 1:03.4	Cecil Healy (AUS/NZL) 1:04.6	Kenneth Huszagh (USA) 1:05.6
1920	Duke P. Kahanamoku (USA) 1:01.4	Pua K. Kealoha (USA) 1:02.2	William W. Harris (USA) 1:03.0
1924	Johnny Weissmuller (USA) 59.0*	Duke P. Kahanamoku (USA) 1:01.4	Samuel Kahanamoku (USA) 1:01.8
1928	Johnny Weissmuller (USA) 58.6*	István Bárány (HUN) 59.8	Katsuo Takaishi (JPN) 1:00.0
1932	Yasuji Miyazaki (JPN) 58.2	Tatsugo Kawaishi (JPN) 58.6	Albert Schwartz (USA) 58.8
1936	Ferenc Csik (HUN) 57.6	Masanori Yusa (JPN) 57.9	Shigeo Arai (JPN) 58.0

TIMETABLE OF THE XVIth WINTER OLYMPIC GAMES—ALBERTVILLE, FRANCE (FEBRUARY 8–23 1992)

Date	Event	Venue
February 8	OPENING CEREMONY	Albertville Ice Hall

Alpine Skiing

Date	Event	Venue
Feburary 9	Men's Downhill	Val d'Isere
Feburary 10	Men's Combined, Downhill	Val d'Isere
February 11	Men's Combined, Slalom	Val d'Isere
February 12	Women's Combined, Downhill	Meribel
Feburary 13	Women's Combined, Slalom	Meribel
February 15	Women's Downhill	Meribel
Feburary 16	Men's Super Giant Slalom	Val d'Isere
Feburary 17	Women's Super Giant Slalom	Meribel
Feburary 18	Men's Giant Slalom	Val d'Isere
February 19	Women's Giant Slalom	Meribel
February 20	Women's Slalom	Meribel
February 22	Men's Slalom	Les Menuires

Freestyle Skiing

Date	Event	Venue
February 9	Ballet, heats (Men & Women)	Tignes
February 10	Ballet, Finals (Men & Women)	Tignes
February 12	Moguls, heats (Men & Women)	Tignes
February 13	Moguls, Finals (Men & Women)	Tignes
February 15	Aerials, heats (Men & Women)	Tignes
February 16	Aerials, Finals (Men & Women)	Tignes

Speed Skiing (Demonstration Sport)

Date	Event	Venue
February 18	Pool 1 (Men & Women)	Les Arcs
February 19	Pool 2 (Men & Women)	Les Arcs
February 21	Semifinals (Men & Women)	Les Arcs
Feabrury 22	Finals (Men & Women)	Les Arcs

Bobsleigh

February 15	2-Man, 1st & 2nd runs	La Plagne
February 16	2-Man, 3rd & 4th runs	La Plagne
February 21	4-Man, 1st & 2nd runs	La Plagne
February 22	4-Man, 3rd & 4th runs	La Plagne

Luge

February 9	Men's Single, 1st & 2nd runs	La Plagne
February 10	Men's Single, 3rd & 4th runs	La Plagne
February 11	Women's Single, 1st & 2nd runs	La Plagne
February 12	Women's Single, 3rd & 4th runs	La Plagne
February 14	Men's Doubles, 1st & 2nd runs	La Plagne

Curling (Demonstration Sport)

February 17	Preliminary matches	Pralognan-la-Vanoise
February 18	Preliminary matches	Pralognan-la-Vanoise
February 19	Preliminary matches	Pralognan-la-Vanoise
February 20	Preliminary matches	Pralognan-la-Vanoise
February 21	Semifinals	Pralognan-la-Vanoise
February 22	Finals	Pralognan-la-Vanoise

Ice Hockey

February 8	Preliminary matches	Meribel
February 9	Preliminary matches	Meribel
February 10	Preliminary matches	Meribel
February 11	Preliminary matches	Meribel
February 12	Preliminary matches	Meribel
February 13	Preliminary matches	Meribel
February 14	Preliminary matches	Meribel
February 15	Preliminary matches	Meribel
February 16	Preliminary matches	Meribel
February 17	Preliminary matches	Meribel
February 18	Preliminary matches	Meribel
February 19	Preliminary matches	Meribel
February 20	Preliminary matches	Meribel
February 21	Preliminary matches	Meribel
February 22	Preliminary matches	Meribel
February 23	Finals	Meribel

Figure Skating

~~v 9	Pairs, original program	Albertville Ice Hall
	Pairs, free program	Albertville Ice Hall
	Men, original program	Albertville Ice Hall

hedule

February 14	Ice Dance, compulsory program	Albertville Ice Hall
February 15	Men, free program	Albertville Ice Hall
February 16	Ice Dance, original program	Albertville Ice Hall
February 17	Ice Dance, free program	Albertville Ice Hall
February 19	Women, original program	Albertville Ice Hall
February 21	Women, free program	Albertville Ice Hall
February 22	Exhibition	Albertville Ice Hall

Speed Skating

February 9	Women's 3000 m	Albertville Ice Hall
February 10	Women's 500 m	Albertville Ice Hall
February 12	Women's 1500 m	Albertville Ice Hall
February 13	Men's 5000 m	Albertville Ice Hall
February 14	Women's 1000 m	Albertville Ice Hall
February 15	Men's 500 m	Albertville Ice Hall
February 16	Men's 1500 m	Albertville Ice Hall
February 17	Women's 5000 m	Albertville Ice Hall
February 18	Men's 1000 m	Albertville Ice Hall
February 20	Men's 10000 m	Albertville Ice Hall

Short Track Speed Skating

February 18	Preliminaries (Men & Women)	Albertville Ice Hall
February 20	Men's 3000 m	Albertville Ice Hall
February 20	Women's relay	Albertville Ice Hall
February 22	Women's 500 m	Albertville Ice Hall
February 22	Men's relay	Albertville Ice Hall

Nordic Skiing

February 9	Women's 15 km	Les Saisies
February 10	Men's 30 km	Les Saisies
February 13	Women's 5 km	Les Saisies
February 13	Men's 10 km	Les Saisies
February 15	Women's 10 km	Les Saisies
February 15	Men's 15 km	Les Saisies
February 17	Women's 4 × 5 km relay	Les Saisies
February 18	Men's 4 × 10 km relay	Les Saisies
February 21	Women's 30 km	Les Saisies
February 22	Men's 50 km	Les Saisies

Nordic Combined

February 11	70 m Hill, individual	Courchevel
February 12	15 km, individual	Courchevel
February 17	70 m hill, team	Courchevel
February 18	3 × 10 km relay, team	Courchevel

Ski Jumping

February 9	70 m Hill, individual	Courchevel
February 14	90 m Hill, team	Courchevel
February 16	90 m Hill, individual	Courchevel

Biathlon

February 11	Women's 7.5 km	Les Saisies
February 12	Men's 10 km	Les Saisies
February 14	Women's 3 × 7.5 km relay	Les Saisies
February 16	Men's 4 × 7.5 km relay	Les Saisies
February 19	Women's 15 km	Les Saisies
February 20	Men's 20 km	Les Saisies
February 23	CLOSING CEREMONY	Albertville Ice Hall

TIMETABLE OF THE XXVth OLYMPIC GAMES—BARCELONA, SPAIN (JULY 25–AUGUST 9, 1992)

OPENING CEREMONY Montjuic Olympic Stadium July 25

Date	Event

Archery (at Vall d'Hebron Archery Field)

Date	Event
July 31	70 m women, 90 m men 60 m women, 70 m men
August 1	50 m women, 50 m men 30 m women, 30 m men
August 2	men 90, 70, 50, 30 m women 70, 60, 50, 30 m men and women, quarterfinals
August 3	men and women, semifinals men and women, finals
August 4	men and women, team contests men and women, team finals

Badminton (at Badminton Pavilion)

Date	Event
July 28	Singles, Men—Preliminary matches Singles, Women—Preliminary matches Doubles, Men—Preliminary matches Doubles, Women—Preliminary matches
July 29	Singles, Men—Preliminary matches Singles, Women—Preliminary matches Doubles, Men—Preliminary matches Doubles, Women—Preliminary matches
July 30	Singles, Men—Preliminary matches Singles, Women—Preliminary matches Doubles, Men—Preliminary matches Doubles, Women—Preliminary matches
July 31	Singles, Men—Preliminary matches Singles, Women—Preliminary matches Doubles, Men—Preliminary matches Doubles, Women—Preliminary matches
August 1	Singles, Men—Preliminary matches Singles, Women—Preliminary matches Doubles, Men—Preliminary matches Doubles, Women—Preliminary matches
August 2	Singles, Men—Quarterfinals Singles, Women—Quarterfinals Doubles, Men—Quarterfinals Doubles, Women—Quarterfinals
August 3	Singles, Men—Semifinals Singles, Women—Semifinals

	Doubles, Men—Semifinals
	Doubles, Women—Semifinals
August 4	Singles, Men—Finals
	Singles, Women—Finals
	Doubles, Men—Finals
	Doubles, Women—Finals

Baseball (at Hospitalet and Viladecans Municipal Stadiums)

July 26	Preliminary games
July 27	Preliminary games
July 28	Preliminary games
July 29	Preliminary games
August 1	Preliminary games
August 2	Preliminary games
August 4	Semifinals
August 5	Finals (3rd–4th places)
	Finals

Basketball (at Badalona Municipal Hall)

July 26	Preliminary games, Men
July 27	Preliminary games, Men
July 29	Preliminary games, Men
July 30	Preliminary games, Women
July 31	Preliminary games, Men
August 1	Preliminary games, Women
August 2	Preliminary games, Men
August 3	Preliminary games, Women
August 4	Classification games, Men
	Quarterfinals, Men
August 5	Classification games, Women
	Semifinals, Women
August 6	Finals (11th–12th places), Men
	Finals (9th–10th places), Men
	Classification games, Men
	Semifinals, Men
August 7	Finals (5th–6th places), Women
	Finals (3rd–4th places), Women
	Finals (7th–8th places), Women
	Finals, Women
August 8	Finals (5th–6th places), Men
	Finals (3rd–4th places), Men
	Finals (7th–8th places), Men
	Finals, Men

Boxing (at Penya Pavilion, Club Joventut Badalona)

July 26	Preliminary bouts
July 27	Preliminary bouts
July 28	Preliminary bouts
July 29	Preliminary bouts
July 30	Preliminary bouts
July 31	Preliminary bouts
August 1	Preliminary bouts
August 2	Preliminary bouts
August 3	Quarterfinals
August 4	Quarterfinals
August 6	Semifinals
August 7	Semifinals
August 8	Finals (6)
August 9	Finals (6)

Canoeing

Wild Water (at Segre Park Slalom Canal)

July 31	Nonstop
August 1	Women, K1
	Men, C1
August 2	Men, K1
	Men, C2

Flat Water (at Castelldelfels Speed Canal)

August 3	500 m, Men—heats
	(K1, C1, K2, C2)
	500 m, Women—heats
	(K1, K2)
	500 m, Men—repechages
	(K1, C1, K2, C2)
	500 m, Women—repechages
	(K1, K2)
August 4	500 m, Women—heats (K4)
	1000 m, Men—heats
	(K1, C1, K2, C2, K4)
	1000 m, Men—repechages
	(K1, C1, K2, C2, K4)
	500 m, Women—repechages (K4)
August 5	500 m, Men—Semifinals
	(K1, C1, K2, C2)
	500 m, Women—Semifinals
	(K1, K2)
August 6	1000 m, Men—Semifinals
	(K1, C1, K2, C2, K4)
	500 m, Women—Semifinals (K4)
August 7	500 m, Men—Finals
	(K1, DC1, K2, C2)
	500 m, Women—Finals
	(K1, K2)
August 8	1000 m, Men—Finals
	(K1, C1, K2, C2, K4)
	500 m, Women—Finals (K4)

Cycling

Road Events

July 26	100 km Team time trial, Finals
	A-17 Motorway
	Individual road race, Women—Finals
	Collserola Circuit
August 2	Individual road race, Men—Finals
	Collserola Circuit

Track Events (at Horta Municipal Velodrome)

July 27	Individual pursuit, Men—1st round
	Km time trials—Finals
July 28	Sprint—qualifications, Men & Women
	Individual pursuit, Men—2nd round
	Individual sprint, Men—1/16 Finals
	Individual sprint, Women—1/8 Finals
	Individual points race—qualifications
	Individual sprint—repechage, Men & Women
July 29	Individual pursuit, Men—Semifinals
	Individual sprint, Men—1/8 Finals
	Individual sprint—Quarterfinals, Men & Women
	Individual sprint, Men—repechages
	Individual pursuit, Men—Finals

July 30	Team pursuit—qualifications
	Individual pursuit,
	Women—qualifications
	Individual sprint—Semifinals,
	Men & Women
	Team pursuit—Quarterfinals
	Individual pursuit,
	Women—Quarterfinals
July 31	Team pursuit—Semifinals
	Individual pursuit, Women—Semifinals
	Individual sprint—Finals,
	Men & Women
	Team pursuit—Finals
	Individual pursuit, Women—Finals
	Individual points race (50 km)—Finals

Equestrian Sports

July 27	Three-day event, Dressage
	Equestrian Stadium
July 28	Three-day event, Dressage
	Equestrian Stadium
July 29	Three-day event, Endurance
	El Muntanyá
July 30	Three-day event, Jumping—Finals
	Equestrian Stadium
August 1	Jumping Training
	Equestrian Stadium
August 2	Team Dressage
	Equestrian Stadium
August 3	Team Dressage—Finals
	Equestrian Stadium
August 4	Team Jumping—Finals
	Equestrian Stadium
August 5	Individual Dressage—Finals
	Equestrian Stadium
August 7	Qualifying for Individual Jumping
	Equestrian Stadium
August 9	Individual Jumping—Finals
	Olympic Stadium

Fencing (at Metallurgy Hall)

July 30	Individual foil, Women
July 31	Individual foil, Men
August 1	Individual épée, Men
August 2	Individual sabre, Men
August 3	Team foil, Women—preliminaries
August 4	Team foil, Men—preliminaries
	Team foil, Women—direct elimination
	Team foil, Women—Finals
August 5	Team épée, Men—preliminaries
	Team foil, Men—direct elimination
	Team foil, Men—Finals
August 6	Team sabre, Men—preliminaries
	Team épée, Men—direct elimination
	Team épée, Men—Finals
August 7	Team sabre, Men—direct elimination
	Team sabre, Men—Finals

Soccer (Barcelona, Zaragoza, Valencia, Sabadell)

July 25	Preliminary matches
July 26	Preliminary matches
July 27	Preliminary matches
July 28	Preliminary matches
July 29	Preliminary matches
July 30	Preliminary matches
August 1	Quarterfinals
August 2	Quarterfinals
August 5	Semifinals (Barcelona and Valencia)
August 7	3rd–4th place match (Barcelona)
August 8	Finals (Barcelona)

Gymnastics (Artistic at Sant Jordi Hall, Rhythmic at Municipal Sports Hall)

July 26	Compulsory exercises, Team, Women
July 27	Compulsory exercises, Team, Men
July 28	Optional exercises, Team, Women
July 29	Optional exercises, Team, Men
July 30	Individual all-around Finals, Men
July 31	Individual all-around Finals, Women
August 1	Apparatus Finals, Women
August 2	Apparatus Finals, Men
August 6	Rhythmic preliminaries, Women
August 7	Rhythmic preliminaries, Women
August 8	Rhythmic Finals, Women

Handball

July 27	Preliminaries, Men Granollers Municipal Hall
July 29	Preliminaries, Men Granollers Municipal Hall
July 30	Preliminaries, Women North Hospitalet Hall
July 31	Preliminaries Men Granollers Municipal Hall
August 1	Preliminaries, Women North Hospitalet Hall
August 2	Preliminaries, Men Granollers Municipal Hall
August 3	Preliminaries, Women North Hospitalet Hall
August 4	Preliminaries, Men Granollers Municipal Hall
August 6	Semifinals, Men & Women Granollers Municipal Hall
August 7	7th–8th places, Women Granollers Municipal Hall 5th–6th places, Women Granollers Municipal Hall 11th–12th places, Men Granollers Municipal Hall 9th–10th places, Men Granollers Municipal Hall 7th–8th places, Men Granollers Municipal Hall 5th–6th places, Men Granollers Municipal Hall

August 8	3rd–4th places, Women
	Sant Jordi Hall
	Finals, Women
	Sant Jordi Hall
	3rd–4th places, Men
	Sant Jordi Hall
	Finals, Men
	Sant Jordi Hall

Hockey (at Abat Mercat Sports Center)

July 26	Preliminary matches, Men
July 27	Preliminary matches, Women
July 28	Preliminary matches, Men
July 29	Preliminary matches, Women
July 30	Preliminary matches, Men
August 1	Preliminary matches, Men
August 2	Preliminary matches, Women
August 3	Preliminary matches, Men
August 4	Classification matches, Women
August 4	Semifinals, Women
August 5	Classification matches, Men
	Semifinals, Men
August 6	5th–8th place matches, Women
	5th–12th place matches, Men
August 7	5th–12th place matches, Men
	3rd–4th place matches, Women
	Finals, Women
August 8	3rd–4th place matches, Men
	Finals, Men

Judo (at Blaugrana Hall)

July 27	Heavyweight (95 kg)
July 28	Half heavyweight (95 kg)
July 29	Middleweight (86 kg)
July 30	Half middleweight (78 kg)
July 31	Lightweight (71 kg)
August 1	Half lightweight (65 kg)
August 2	Extra lightweight (60 kg)

Modern Pentathlon

July 26	Fencing at Metallurgy Hall
July 27	Swimming at Picornell Swimming Pools
	Shooting at Mollet de Vallés Shooting Range
July 28	Cross-country at Midgia Park Cross-Country Circuit
July 29	Riding at Equestrian Stadium

Rowing (at Banyoles Lake)

July 27	Elimination heats, Men & Women
July 28	Elimination heats, Men & Women
July 29	Repechages, Men & Women
July 30	Semifinals, Men & Women
July 31	Repechages/Semifinals, Men & Women
August 1	Coxless Fours, 7th–12th places, Women
	Double Sculls, 7th–12th places, Women
	Coxless Pairs, 7th–12th places, Women
	Coxed Fours, 7th–12th places, Men
	Double Sculls, 7th–12th places, Men
	Coxless Pairs, 7th–12th places, Men
	Single Sculls, 7th–12th places, Men
	Coxless Fours, Women—Finals
	Double Sculls, Women—Finals
	Coxless Pairs, Women—Finals
	Coxed Fours, Men—Finals
	Double Sculls, Men—Finals
	Coxless Pairs, Men—Finals
	Single Sculls, Men—Finals
August 2	Single Sculls, 7th–12th places, Women
	Quadruple Sculls, 7th–12th places, Women
	Eights, 7th–12th places, Women
	Coxed Pairs, 7th–12th places, Men
	Coxless Fours, 7th–12th places, Men
	Quadruple Sculls, 7th–12th places, Men
	Eights, 7th–12th places, Men
	Single Sculls, Women—Finals
	Quadruple Sculls, Women—Finals
	Eights, Women—Finals
	Coxed Pairs, Men—Finals
	Coxless Fours, Men—Finals
	Quadruple Sculls, Men—Finals
	Eights, Men—Finals

Shooting (at Mollet del Vallés Shooting Range)

July 26	Air Rifle, Women
	Free Pistol, Men
	Skeet (75 targets)
July 27	Sport Pistol, Women
	Air Rifle, Men
	Skeet (75 targets)
July 28	Air Pistol, Men
	Skeet (50 targets), Semifinals
	Skeet (25 targets), Finals
July 29	Small-bore Rifle, English Match, Men
	Rapid-Fire Pistol, Men (30 shots)
July 30	Rapid-Fire Pistol, Men (30 shots)
	Rapid-Fire Pistol, Men—Semifinals
	Rapid-Fire Pistol, Men—Finals
	Small-Bore Rifle, 3 pos, Women
July 31	Small-Bore Rifle, 3 pos, Men
	10 m Running Target (slow run), Men
	Trap (75 targets)
August 1	Air Pistol, Women
	10 m Running Target (fast run), Men
	Trap (75 targets)
August 2	Trap (50 targets), Semifinals
	Trap (25 targets), Finals

Swimming (at Bernat Picornell Swimming Pools)

July 26	100 m Freestyle, Women
	100 m Breaststroke, Men
	400 m Individual medley, Women
	200 m Freestyle, Men

July 27	100 m Butterfly, Men
	200 m Freestyle, Women
	400 m Individual medley, Women
	200 m Breaststroke, Women
	4 × 200 m Freestyle relay, Men
July 28	400 m Freestyle, Women
	100 m Freestyle, Men
	100 m Backstroke, Women
	200 m Backstroke, Men
	4 × 100 m Freestyle relay, Women
July 29	800 m Freestyle, Women—heats
	400 m Freestyle, Men
	100 m Butterfly, Women
	200 m Breaststroke, Men
	100 m Breaststroke, Women
	4 × 100 m Freestyle relay, Men
July 30	1500 m Freestyle, Men—heats
	200 m Butterfly, Men
	200 m Individual medley, Women
	100 m Backstroke, Men
	4 × 100 m Individual medley relay, Women
	50 m Freestyle, Men
	800 m Freestyle, Women—Finals
July 31	200 m Butterfly, Women
	200 m Individual medley, Men
	200 m Backstroke, Women
	4 × 100 m Individual medley relay, Men
	50 m Freestyle, Women
	1500 m Freestyle, Men—Finals

Diving (at Montjuic Municipal Swimming Pool)

July 26	Platform—preliminaries, Women
July 27	Platform—Finals, Women
July 28	Springboard—preliminaries, Men
July 29	Springboard—Finals, Men
August 1	Springboard—preliminaries, Women
August 2	Platform—preliminaries, Men
August 3	Springboard—Finals, Women
August 4	Platform—Finals, Men

Synchronized Swimming (at Bernat Picornell Swimming Pools)

August 2	Solo—preliminaries
August 3	Duets—preliminaries
August 5	Figures
August 6	Solo—Finals
August 7	Duet—Finals

Water Polo (at Montjuic Municipal and Bernat Picornell Swimming Pools)

August 1	Preliminary rounds
August 2	Preliminary rounds
August 3	Preliminary rounds
August 5	Preliminary rounds
August 6	Preliminary rounds
August 8	Finals rounds (4 games)
	Semifinals (2 games)
August 9	Finals rounds (4 games)
	Finals (2 games)

Table Tennis (at North Station Sports Complex)

July 28	Doubles, Women—preliminaries Doubles, Men—preliminaries
July 29	Singles, Women—preliminaries Doubles, Women—preliminaries Doubles, Men—preliminaries
July 30	Singles, Women—preliminaries Singles, Men—preliminaries Doubles, Men—preliminaries Doubles, Women—preliminaries
July 31	Singles, Men—preliminaries Singles, Women—preliminaries Doubles, Women—K.O. 1/4 Doubles, Men—preliminaries
August 1	Singles, Men—preliminaries Singles, Women—K.O. 1/8 Doubles, Men—K.O. 1/4 Doubles, Women—K.O. 1/2
August 2	Singles, Men—K.O. 1/8
August 3	Doubles, Women—Finals Singles, Women—Quarterfinals Doubles, Men—Semifinals
August 4	Doubles, Men—Finals Singles, Men—Quarterfinals Singles, Women—Semifinals
August 5	Singles, Women—Finals Singles, Men—Semifinals
August 6	Singles, Men—Finals

Tennis (at Vall d'Hebron Municipal Tennis Center)

July 29	Singles, Men (1/32) Singles, Women (1/32)
July 30	Singles, Men (1/32) Singles, Women (1/32)
July 31	Singles, Men (1/16) Doubles, Men (1/16)
July 31	Singles, Women (1/16) Doubles, Women (1/16)
August 1	Singles, Men (1/16) Doubles, Men (1/16)
August 1	Singles, Women (1/16) Doubles, Women (1/16)
August 2	Singles, Men (1/8) Doubles, Men (1/8) Doubles, Women (1/8) Doubles, Men (1/8)
August 3	Doubles, Men—Quarterfinals Singles—Quarterfinals
August 4	Singles, Men—Quarterfinals Doubles, Women—Quarterfinals
August 5	Doubles, Men—Semifinals Singles, Women—Semifinals
August 6	Singles, Men—Semifinals Doubles, Women—Semifinals
August 7	Doubles, Men—Finals Singles, Women—Finals
August 8	Doubles, Women—Finals Singles, Men—Finals

Track and Field (at Olympic Stadium, Olympic Road Walking Circuit and Barcelona Marathon Circuit)

TRACK AND FIELD FINALS PRINTED IN CAPITALS

July 31	100m (W) 1st and 2nd rounds, SHOT PUT (M), 100m (M) 1st and 2nd rounds, 800m (W) 1st round, javelin (W) qualifying, high jump (M) qualifying, MARATHON (W), 800 m (M) 1st round, 3000m (W) 1st round, 10000m (M) heats
August 1	100m heptathlon (W), 400m (W) 1st round, high jump heptathlon (M), 400m hurdles (W) 1st round, hammer (M) qualifying, shot put heptathlon (W), 100m (W) semifinals, 100m (M) semifinals, triple jump (M) qualifying, 800m (M) 2nd round, 800m (W) semifinals, 20KM WALK (M), JAVELIN (W), 100M (W), 100M (M), 200m heptathlon (W), 10000m (W) heats.
August 2	110m hurdles (M) 1st and 2nd rounds, long jump heptathlon (W), discus (W) qualifying, 400m (W) 1st round, HAMMER (M), HIGH JUMP (M), javelin heptathlon (W), 400m (M) 2nd round, 400m hurdles (W) semifinals, 800m (M) semifinals, 800M (W), 3000M (W), 800M HEPTATHLON (W)
August 3	discus (M) qualifying, 200 m (W) 1st and 2nd rounds, 200m (M) 1st and 2nd rounds, 1500m (M) 1st round, 400m hurdles (M) 1st round, 110 hurdles (M) semifinals, DISCUS (W), 400m (W) 2nd round, TRIPLE JUMP (M), 400m (M) semifinals, 10KM WALK (W), 110M HURDLES (M), 3000m steeplechase (M) 1st round, 400M HURDLES (W), 10000M (M)
August 4	Rest day
August 5	100m decathlon (M), pole vault (M) qualifying, 15000m (W) 1st round, long jump decathlon (M), 100m hurdles (W) 1st and 2nd rounds, shot put decathlon (M), shot put (W) qualifying, high jump decathlon (M), 200m (W) semifinals, long jump (M) qualifying, 200m (M) semifinals, 400m hurdles (M) semifinals, DISCUS (M), 400m (W) semifinals, 3000m steeplechase (M) semifinals, 400M (M) 200M (W), 200M (M), 800M (M), 400m decathlon (M), 5000m (M) 1st round
August 6	100m decathlon (M), high jump (W) qualifying, discus decathlon (M), long jump (W) qualifying, pole vault decathlon (M), javelin decathlon (M), 110m hurdles (M) semifinals, 400M, (W) LONG JUMP (M), 400M HURDLES (M), 1500m (W) semifinals, 1500m (M) semifinals, 100M HURDLES (W), 5000 (M) semifinals, 1500m decathlon (M)
August 7	50KM WALK (M), 4 × 100m (M) 1st round and semifinals, javelin (M) qualifying, 4 × 100m (W) 1st round and semifinals, 4 × 400m (M) 1st round and semifinals, POLE VAULT (M), SHOT PUT (W), LONG JUMP (W), 4 × 400m (W) 1st round and semifinals, 3000M STEEPLECHASE (M), 10000M (W)
August 8	HIGH JUMP (W), JAVELIN (M), 4 × 100m (W), 4 × 100M (M), 1500M (W), 1500M (M), 5000M (M), 4 × 400M (W), 4 × 400M (M)
August 9	MARATHON (M)

Volleyball

July 26	Preliminaries, Men, Municipal Hall
July 27	Preliminaries, Men, Municipal Hall
July 29	Preliminaries, Women, Municipal Hall
July 30	Preliminaries, Men, Municipal Hall
July 31	Preliminaries, Women, Municipal Hall
August 1	Preliminaries, Men, Municipal Hall and Vall d'Hebron
August 2	Preliminaries, Women, Municipal Hall
August 3	Preliminaries, Men, Municipal Hall and Vall d'Hebron
August 4	7th–8th places, Women, Vall d'Hebron Quarterfinals, Women, Vall d'Hebron
August 5	Quarterfinals, Men, Sant Jordi Hall 11th–12th places, Men, Vall d'Hebron 9th–10th places, Men, Vall d'Hebron

August 6	5th–6th places, Women, Vall d'Hebron
	Classifications, Men, Vall d'Hebron
	Semifinals, Women, Sant Jordi Hall
August 7	Semifinals, Men, Sant Jordi Hall
	3rd–4th places, Women, Sant Jordi Hall
	7th–8th places, Men, Vall d'Hebron
	5th–6th places, Men, Vall d'Hebron
	Semifinals, Men, Sant Jordi Hall
	Finals, Women, Sant Jordi Hall
August 9	3rd–4th places, Men, Sant Jordi Hall
	Finals, Men, Sant Jordi Hall

Weightlifting (at España Industrial Hall)

July 26	Flyweight
July 27	Bantamweight
July 28	Featherweight
July 29	Lightweight
July 30	Middleweight
July 31	Light heavyweight
August 1	Middle heavyweight
August 2	First heavyweight
August 3	Second heavyweight
August 4	Super heavyweight

Wrestling (at Catalan National Institute of Education)

Greco-Roman Style

July 26	Preliminaries—52, 68, 100 kg
July 27	Preliminaries—48, 74, 100+, 52, 68, 100 kg
July 28	Preliminaries—57, 62, 82, 90, 48, 74, 100+,
	52, 68, 100 kg
	Finals—52, 68, 100 kg
July 29	Preliminaries—48, 74, 100+, 57, 62, 82, 90 kg
	Finals—48, 74, 100+
July 30	Preliminaries—57, 62, 82, 90 kg
	Finals—57, 62, 82, 90 kg

Freestyle

August 3	Preliminaries—52, 68, 100 kg
August 4	Preliminaries—48, 74, 100+, 52, 68, 100 kg
August 5	Preliminaries—57, 62, 82, 90, 52, 68, 48, 74,
	100 kg +
	Finals—52, 68, 100 kg
August 6	Preliminaries—48, 100+, 74, 57, 62, 82, 90 kg
	Finals—48, 74, 100 kg +
August 7	Preliminaries—57, 62, 82, 90 kg
	Finals—57, 62, 82, 90 kg

Yachting (at Barcelona Harbor)

July 27	First and second races, Board sailing
	First races, all other classes
July 28	Third and fourth races, Board sailing
	Second races, all other classes
July 29	Fifth and sixth races, Board sailing
	Third races, all other classes
July 30	Seventh and eight races, Board sailing
	Fourth races, all other classes
July 31	Fifth races, Soling
	Reserve day, all other classes

August 1	Ninth race, Board sailing
	Sixth race, Soling
	Fifth race, all other classes
August 2	Tenth race, all other classes
	Reserve day, Soling
	Sixth race, all other classes
August 3	Match race, Soling
	Seventh race, all other classes
August 4	Match race, Soling
	Reserve day, all other classes
August 5–6	Reserve days

Demonstration Sports

Roller Hockey (at Reus, Sant Sadurni, Vic and Blaugrana Halls)

July 26–30	Preliminary Games
August 1–5	Semifinals/positioning games
August 7	Finals

Pelota (Colom Fronton and Municipal Pelota Sports Complex)

July 25–31	Preliminary matches
August 1–3	Semifinals
August 3–4	Finals (3rd–4th places)
August 5	Finals

Tae Kwon Do (Blaugrana Hall)

August 3	Bantamweight, Men & Women
	Welterweight, Men & Women
	Heavyweight, Men & Women
August 4	Flyweight, Men & Women
	Lightweight, Men & Women
	Middleweight, Men & Women
August 5	Finweight, Men & Women
	Featherweight, Men & Women

Exhibition Events

Events for Disabled People (at Olympic Stadium)

August 2	800 m Wheelchair, Women	
	1500 m Wheelchair, Men	
August 9	CLOSING CEREMONY	Montjuic Olympic Stadium

GOLD	SILVER	BRONZE
1948 Walter Ris (USA) 57.3*	Alan Ford (USA) 57.8	Géza Kádas (HUN) 58.1
1952 C. Clarke Scholes (USA) 57.4	Hiroshi Suzuki (JPN) 57.4	Göran Larsson (SWE) 58.2
1956 Jon Henricks (AUS) 55.4*	John Devitt (AUS) 55.8	Gary Chapman (AUS) 56.7
1960 John Devitt (AUS) 55.2*	Lance M. Larson (USA) 55.2*	Manuel dos Santos (BRA) 55.4
1964 Donald Schollander (USA) 53.4*	Robert McGregor (GBR) 53.5	Hans-Joachim Klein (GER) 54.0
1968 Michael V. Wenden (AUS) 52.2*	Kenneth Walsh (USA) 52.8	Mark A. Spitz (USA) 53.0
1972 Mark A. Spitz (USA) 51.22*	Jerry Heidenreich (USA) 51.65	Vladimir Bure (URS) 51.77
1976 Jim Montgomery (USA) 49.99*	Jack Babashoff (USA) 50.81	Peter Nocke (GER) 51.31
1980 Jorg Woithe (GDR) 50.40	Per Holmertz (SWE) 50.91	Per Johansson (SWE) 51.29
1984 Ambrose Gaines (USA) 49.80*	Mark Stockwell (AUS) 50.24	Per Johansson (SWE) 50.31
1988 Matt Biondi (USA) 48.63*	Chris Jacobs (USA) 49.08	Stephan Caron (FRA) 49.62

The following Olympic records were set in addition to those medal-winning performances marked with an asterisk*.

1:08.2	von Halmay 1908	1:00.4	Kahanamoku 1920	57.5	Ris 1948
1:05.8	Daniels 1908		(in a final prior	57.1	Scholes 1952
1:04.8	Perry McGillivray (USA) 1912		to a re-swim)	56.8	L. Reid Patterson (USA) 1956
		58.6	Weissmuller 1928		
		58.0	Miyazaki 1932	55.7	Henricks 1956
1:02.6	Kahanamoku 1912	57.7	Peter Fick (USA) 1936	54.0	Gary Ilman (USA) 1964
1:02.4	Kahanamoku 1912	57.7	Arai 1936	53.9	Ilman 1964
		57.5	Masaharu Taguchi (JPN) 1936	53.4	Zachary Zorn (USA) 1968
1:01.8	Kahanamoku 1920			52.9	Wenden 1968
1:01.4	Kahanamoku 1920	57.5	Yusa 1936	50.39	Montgomery 1976
				49.20	Jacobs (USA) 1988
				49.04	Biondi (USA) 1988

200 METERS FREE-STYLE (218 yd 2 ft)

GOLD	SILVER	BRONZE
1896 Event not held		
1900 Frederick C. V. Lane (AUS) 2:25.2	Zóltán von Halmay (HUN) 2:31.4	Karl Ruberl (AUT) 2:32.0
1904–1964 Event not held		
1968[1] Michael V. Wenden (AUS) 1:55.2*	Donald A. Schollander (USA) 1:55.8	John M. Nelson (USA) 1:58.1
1972 Mark A. Spitz (USA) 1:52.78*	Steven Genter (USA) 1:53.73	Werner Lampe (GER) 1:53.99
1976 Bruce Furniss (USA) 1:50.29*	John Naber (USA) 1:50.50	Jim Montgomery (USA) 1:50.58
1980 Sergei Kopliakov (URS) 1:49.81*	Andrei Krylov (URS) 1:50.76	Graeme Brewer (AUS) 1:51.60
1984 Michael Gross (FRG) 1:47.44*	Michael Heath (USA) 1:49.10	Thomas Fahrner (FRG) 1:49.69
1988 Duncan Armstrong (AUS) 1:47.25*	Anders Holmertz (SWE) 1:47.89	Matt Biondi (USA) 1:47.99

Michael Gross of West Germany set two world records in the 1984 Olympics at Los Angeles in the 200 meters free-style and the 100 meters butterfly.

LEFT: Mark Spitz (USA) won 7 gold medals at the Munich Games in 1972, an Olympic record for a single year in any sport.

ABOVE: The dominant free-style swimmers at 400 meters and 1,500 meters in 1956 and 1960 were (left to right) George Breen (USA), I. Murray Rose (AUS) and Tsuyoshi Yamanaka (JPN).

The following Olympic records were set in addition to those medal-winning performances already marked with an asterisk*.

1:59.5	Nelson	1968	1:51.41 Klaus	1:50.93 Furniss	1976
1:59.3	Wenden	1968	Steinbach	1:48.03 Michael	
1:52.71	Bogdanov	1976	(GER) 1976	Gross (FRG)	
	(URS)				1984

400 METERS FREE-STYLE (437 yd 1 ft)

	GOLD	SILVER	BRONZE
1896–1904	Event not held		
1906	Otto Scheff (AUT) 6:23.8*	Henry Taylor (GBR) 6:24.4	John A. Jarvis (GBR) 6:27.2
1908	Henry Taylor (GBR) 5:36.8*	Frank E. Beaurepaire (AUS/NZL) 5:44.2	Otto Scheff (AUT) 5:46.0
1912	George R. Hodgson (CAN) 5:24.4*	John G. Hatfield (GBR) 5:25.8	Harold H. Hardwick (AUS/NZL) 5:31.2
1920	Norman Ross (USA) 5:26.8	Ludy Langer (USA) 5:29.2	George Vernot (CAN) 5:29.8
1924	Johnny Weissmuller (USA) 5:04.2*	Arne Borg (SWE) 5:05.6	Andrew M. Charlton (AUS) 5:06.6
1928	V. Alberto Zorilla (ARG) 5:01.6*	Andrew M. Charlton (AUS) 5:03.6	Arne Borg (SWE) 5:04.6
1932	Clarence L. Crabbe (USA) 4:48.4*	Jean Taris (FRA) 4:48.5	Tautomu Oyokota (JPN) 4:52.3
1936	Jack Medica (USA) 4:44.5*	Shumpei Uto (JPN) 4:45.6	Shozo Makino (JPN) 4:48.1
1948	William Smith (USA) 4:41.0*	James McLane (USA) 4:43.4	John B. Marshall (AUS) 4:47.7
1952	Jean Boiteaux (FRA) 4:30.7*	Ford Konno (USA) 4:31.3	Per-Olof Ostrand (SWE) 4:35.2
1956	I. Murray Rose (AUS) 4:27.3*	Tsuyoshi Yamanaka (JPN) 4:30.4	George T. Breen (USA) 4:32.5
1960	I. Murray Rose (AUS) 4:18.3*	Tsuyoshi Yamanaka (JPN) 4:21.4	John Konrads (AUS) 4:21.8
1964	Donald A. Schollander (USA) 4:12.2*	Frank Wiegand (GER) 4:14.9	Allan Wood (AUS) 4:15.1
1968	Michael J. Burton (USA) 4:09.0*	Ralph W. Hutton (CAN) 4:11.7	Alain Mosconi (FRA) 4:13.3
1972[1]	Bradford P. Cooper (AUS) 4:00.27*	Steven Genter (USA) 4:01.94	Tom McBreen (USA) 4:02.64
1976	Brian Goodell (USA) 3:51.93*	Tim Shaw (USA) 3:52.54	Vladimir Raskatov (URS) 3:55.76
1980	Vladimir Salnikov (URS) 3:51.31*	Andrei Krylov (URS) 3:53.24	Ivar Stukolkin (URS) 3:53.95
1984	George Dicarlo (USA) 3:51.23*	John Mykkanen (USA) 3:51.49	Justin Lemberg (AUS) 3:51.79
1988	Uwe Dassler (GDR) 3:46.95*	Duncan Armstrong (AUS) 3:47.15	Artur Wojdat (POL) 3:47.34

---

[1] Rick DeMont (USA) finished first but was subsequently disqualified.

The following Olympic records were set in addition to those medal-winning performances already marked with an asterisk*.

5:48.8	T. Sydney Battersby (GBR)	1908	5:13.6	Weissmuller	1924	4:17.2	Wiegand 1964
5:42.2	Taylor	1908	4:53.2	Takashi Yokoyama (JPN)	1932	4:15.8	Schollander 1964
5:40.6	Scheff	1908				4:06.59	Bengt Gingsjoe (SWE) 1972
5:36.0	Hardwick	1912	4:51.4	Yokoyama	1932	4:05.89	Genter 1972
5:34.0	Cecil Healy (AUS/NZL)	1912	4:45.5	Uto	1936	4:04.59	Cooper 1972
			4:42.2	McLane	1948	3:59.62	Djan Madruga (BRA) 1976
5:25.4	Hodgson	1912	4:38.6	Ostrand	1952	3:57.56	Raskatov 1976
5:22.4	Breyer (USA)	1924	5:33.1	Boiteaux	1952	3:56.40	Shaw 1976
5:22.2	Weissmuller	1924	4:21.0	Yamanaka	1960	3:55.24	Goodell 1976
			4:19.2	Alan Somers (USA)	1960	3:50.91	Thomas Fahrner (FRG) 1984
						3:49.51	Mariusz Podkoscielny (POL) 1988

1,500 METERS FREE-STYLE (1,640 yd 1 ft)

	GOLD	SILVER	BRONZE
1896–1906	Event not held		
1908	Henry Taylor (GBR) 22:48.4*	T. Sydney Battersby (GBR) 22:51.2	Frank E. Beaurepaire (AUS/NZL) 22:56.2
1912	George R. Hodgson (CAN) 22:00.0*	John G. Hatfield (GBR) 22:39.0	Harold Hardwick (AUS/NZL) 23:15.4
1920	Norman Ross (USA) 22:23.2	George Vernot (CAN) 22:36.4	Frank E. Beaurepaire (AUS) 23:04.0
1924	Andrew M. Charlton (AUS) 20:06.6*	Arne Borg (SWE) 20:41.4	Frank E. Beaurepaire (AUS) 21:48.4
1928	Arne Borg (SWE) 19:51.8*	Andrew M. Charlton (AUS) 20:02.6	Clarence L. Crabbe (USA) 20:28.8
1932	Kusuo Kitamura (JPN) 19:12.4*	Shozo Makino (JPN) 19:14.1	James C. Christy (USA) 19:39.5
1936	Noboru Terada (JPN) 19:13.7	Jack Medica (USA) 19:34.0	Shumpei Uto (JPN) 19:34.5
1948	James McLane (USA) 19:18.5	John B. Marshall (AUS) 19:31.3	György Mitró (HUN) 19:43.2
1952	Ford Konno (USA) 18:30.0*	Shiro Hashizume (JPN) 18:41.4	Tetsuo Okamoto (BRA) 18:51.3
1956	I. Murray Rose (AUS) 17:58.9	Tsuyoshi Yamanaka (JPN) 18:00.3	George T. Breen (USA) 18:08.2
1960	John Konrads (AUS) 17:19.6*	I. Murray Rose (AUS) 17:21.7	George T. Breen (USA) 17:30.6
1964	Robert Windle (AUS) 17:01.7*	John Nelson (USA) 17:03.0	Allan Wood (AUS) 17:07.7
1968	Michael J. Burton (USA) 16:38.9*	John Kinsella (USA) 16:57.3	Gregory Brough (AUS) 17:04.7
1972	Michael J. Burton (USA) 15:52.58*	Graham Windeatt (AUS) 15:58.48	Douglas Northway (USA) 16:09.25
1976	Brian Goodell (USA) 15:02.40*	Bobby Hackett (USA) 15:03.91	Stephen Holland (AUS) 15:04.66
1980	Vladimir Salnikov (URS) 14:58.27*	Alexandr Chaev (URS) 15:14.30	Max Metzker (AUS) 15:14.49
1984	Michael O'Brien (USA) 15:05.20	George Dicarlo (USA) 15:10.59	Stefan Pfeiffer (FRG) 15:12.11
1988	Vladimir Salnikov (URS) 15:00.40	Stefan Pfeiffer (FRG) 15:02.69	Uwe Dassler (GDR) 15:06.15

The following Olympic records were set in addition to those medal-winning performances already marked with an asterisk*.

25:02.6	Paul Radmilovic (GBR) 1908	21:11.4	Borg 1924	17:15.9	Windle 1964
23:45.8	Beaurepaire 1908	19:51.6	Kitamura 1932	16:34.63	Hans-Joachim Fassnacht (GER) 1972
23:42.8	Battersby 1908	19:38.7	Makino 1932		
23:24.4	Taylor 1908	18:34.0	Hashizume 1952	15:59.63	Windeatt 1972
22:54.0	Taylor 1908	18:04.1	Rose 1956	15:37.61	Zoltan Wladar (HUN) 1976
22:23.0	Hodgson 1912	17:52.9	Breen 1956		
21:20.4	Charlton 1924	17:46.5	Yamanaka 1960	15:20.74	Paul Hartloff (USA) 1976
		17:32.8	Rose 1960		

Michael Burton of the United States doubled in 1968 in the 400 meters and 1,500 meters free-style, and won a third gold medal in 1972, again in the 1,500 meters free-style.

100 METERS BACK STROKE (109 yd 1 ft)

GOLD	SILVER	BRONZE
1896–1906 Event not held		
1908 Arno Bieberstein (GER) 1:24.6*	Ludvig Dam (DEN) 1:26.6	Herbert Haresnape (GBR) 1:27.0
1912 Harry J. Hebner (USA) 1:21.2	Otto Fahr (GER) 1:22.4	Paul Kellner (GER) 1:24.0
1920 Warren P. Kealoha (USA) 1:15.2	Ray Kegeris (USA) 1:16.2	Gérard Blitz (BEL) 1:19.0
1924 Warren P. Kealoha (USA) 1:13.2*	Paul Wyatt (USA) 1:15.4	Károly Bartha (HUN) 1:17.8
1928 George H. Kojac (USA) 1:08.2*	Walter Laufer (USA) 1:10.0	Paul Wyatt (USA) 1:12.0
1932 Masaji Kiyokawa (JPN) 1:08.6	Toshio Irie (JPN) 1:09.8	Kentaro Kawatsu (JPN) 1:10.0
1936 Adolf Kiefer (USA) 1:05.9*	Albert Van de Weghe (USA) 1:07.7	Masaji Kiyokawa (JPN) 1:08.4
1948 Allen Stack (USA) 1:06.4	Robert Cowell (USA) 1:06.5	Georges Vallerey (FRA) 1:07.8
1952 Yoshinobu Oyakawa (USA) 1:05.4*	Gilbert Bozon (FRA) 1:06.2	Jack Taylor (USA) 1:06.4
1956 David Thiele (AUS) 1:02.2*	John Monckton (AUS) 1:03.2	Frank E. McKinney (USA) 1:04.5

	GOLD	SILVER	BRONZE
1960	David Thiele (AUS) 1:01.9*	Frank E. McKinney (USA) 1:02.1	Robert E. Bennett (USA) 1:02.3
1964	Event not held		
1968	Roland Matthes (GDR) 58.7*	Charles Hickcox (USA) 1:00.2	Ronnie P. Mills (USA) 1:00.5
1972	Roland Matthes (GDR) 56.58*	Mike Stamm (USA) 57.70	John Murphy (USA) 58.35
1976	John Naber (USA) 55.49*	Peter Rocca (USA) 56.34	Roland Matthes (GDR) 57.22
1980	Bengt Baron (SWE) 56.53	Viktor Kuznetsov (URS) 56.99	Vladimir Dolgov (URS) 57.63
1984	Rick Carey (USA) 55.79	David Wilson (USA) 56.35	Mike West (CAN) 56.49
1988	Daichi Suzuki (JPN) 55.05	David Berkoff (USA) 55.18	Igor Polyanski (URS) 55.20

The following Olympic records were set in addition to those medal-winning performances already marked with an asterisk*.

1:25.6 (twice)	Bieberstein	1908	1:06.9	Kiefer	1936	1:01.9	Larry Barbiere (USA)	1968
1:21.1	Hebner	1912	1:06.8	Kiefer	1936	1:01.0	Matthes	1968
1:20.8	Hebner	1912	1:05.7	Oyakawa	1952	58.63	Stamm	1972
1:17.8	Ray Kegeris (USA)	1920	1:04.2	Robert Christophe (FRA)	1956	58.15	Mitchell Ivey (USA)	1972
1:14.8	Kealoha	1920	1:03.4	Monckton	1956	57.99	Ivey	1972
1:13.4	Kealoha	1924	1:02.0	Bennett	1960	56.30†	Matthes	1972
1:09.2	Kojac	1928				56.19	Naber	1976
						55.04	Polyanski (URS)	1988
						54.51	Berkoff (USA)	1988

---

†In medley relay.

200 METERS BACK STROKE (218 yd 2 ft)

	GOLD	SILVER	BRONZE
1896	Event not held		
1900	Ernst Hoppenberg (GER) 2:47.0*	Karl Ruberl (AUT) 2:56.0	Johannes Drost (HOL) 3:01.0
1904–1960	Event not held		
1964	Jed Graef (USA) 2:10.3*	Gary Dilley (USA) 2:10.5	Robert E. Bennett (USA) 2:13.1
1968	Roland Matthes (GDR) 2:09.6*	Mitchell Ivey (USA) 2:10.6	Jack Horsley (USA) 2:10.9
1972	Roland Matthes (GDR) 2:02.82*	Mike Stamm (USA) 2:04.09	Mitchell Ivey (USA) 2:04.33
1976	John Naber (USA) 1:59.19*	Peter Rocca (USA) 2:00.55	Don Harrigan (USA) 2:01.35
1980	Sandor Wladar (HUN) 2:01.93	Zoltan Verraszto (HUN) 2:02.40	Mark Kerry (AUS) 2:03.14
1984	Rick Carey (USA) 2:00.23	Frederic Delcourt (FRA) 2:01.75	Cameron Henning (CAN) 2:02.37
1988	Igor Polyanski (URS) 1:59.37	Frank Baltrusch (GDR) 1:59.60	Paul Kingsman (NZL) 2:00.48

The following Olympic records were set in addition to those medal-winning performances already marked with an asterisk*.

2:16.1	Bennett	1964	2:14.5	Graef	1964	2:07.51	Stamm	1972
2:14.7	Shigeo Fukushima (JPN)	1964	2:14.2	Dilley	1964	2:06.62	Matthes	1972
			2:13.8	Dilley	1964	2:02.25	Harrigan	1976
			2:13.7	Graef	1964	2:02.01	Naber	1976
						1:58.99	Carey	1984

100 METERS BREAST STROKE (109 yd 1 ft)

	GOLD	SILVER	BRONZE
1896–1964	Event not held		
1968	Donald McKenzie (USA) 1:07.7*	Vladimir Kossinsky (URS) 1:08.0	Nickolay Pankin (URS) 1:08.0
1972	Nobutaka Taguchi (JPN) 1:04.94*	Tom Bruce (USA) 1:05.43	John Hencken (USA) 1:05.61
1976	John Hencken (USA) 1:03.11*	David Wilkie (GBR) 1:03.43	Arvidas Iuozaytis (URS) 1:04.23
1980	Duncan Goodhew (GBR) 1:03.34	Arsen Miskarov (URS) 1:03.82	Peter Evans (AUS) 1:03.96
1984	Steve Lundquist (USA) 1:01.65*	Victor Davis (CAN) 1:01.99	Peter Evans (AUS) 1:02.97
1988	Adrian Moorhouse (GBR) 1:02.04	Karoly Guttler (HUN) 1:02.05	Dmitry Volkov (URS) 1:02.20

The following Olympic records were set in addition to those medal-winning performances already marked with an asterisk*.

1:08.9	Pankin	1968	1:05.68	Hencken	1972	1:03.88	Hencken	1976
1:08.1	McKenzie	1968	1:05.13	Taguchi	1972	1:03.62	Hencken	1976
1:08.1	Pankin	1968	1:04.92	Duncan		1:02.87	Evans	1984
1:07.9	Kossinsky	1968		Goodhew		1:02.16	Lundquist	1984
1:05.89	Mark Chatfield			(GBR)	1976			
	(USA)	1972	1:04.78	Iuozaytis	1976			

200 METERS BREAST STROKE (218 yd 2 ft)

	GOLD	SILVER	BRONZE
1896–1906	Event not held		
1908	Frederick Holman (GBR) 3:09.2*	William W. Robinson (GBR) 3:12.8	Pontus Hansson (SWE) 3:14.6
1912	Walter Bathe (GER) 3:01.8*	Wilhelm Lützow (GER) 3:05.0	Kurt Malisch (GER) 3:08.0
1920	Häken Malmroth (SWE) 3:04.4	Thor Henning (SWE) 3:09.2	Arvo Aaltonen (FIN) 3:12.2
1924	Robert D. Skelton (USA) 2:56.5	Joseph de Combe (BEL) 2:59.2	William Kirschbaum (USA) 3:01.0
1928	Yoshiyuki Tsuruta (JPN) 2:48.8*	Erich Rademacher (GER) 2:50.6	Teofilo Yldefonzo (PHI) 2:56.4
1932	Yoshiyuki Tsuruta (JPN) 2:45.4	Reizo Koike (JPN) 2:46.4	Teofilo Yldefonzo (PHI) 2:47.1
1936	Tetsuo Hamuro (JPN) 2:42.5*	Erwin Sietas (GER) 2:42.9	Reizo Koike (JPN) 2:44.2
1948	Joseph Verdeur (USA) 2:39.3*	Keith Carter (USA) 2:40.2	Robert Sohl (USA) 2:43.9
1952	John Davies (AUS) 2:34.4*	Bowen Stassforth (USA) 2:34.7	Herbert Klein (GER) 2:35.9
1956	Masura Furukawa (JPN) 2:34.7*	Masahiro Yoshimura (JPN) 2:36.7	Charis Yunitschev (URS) 2:36.8
1960	William D. Mulliken (USA) 2:37.4	Yoshihiko Osaki (JPN) 2:38.0	Wieger E. Mensonides (HOL) 2:39.7
1964	Ian O'Brien (AUS) 2:27.8*	Georgy Prokopenko (URS) 2:28.2	Chester Jastremski (USA) 2:29.6
1968	Felipe Muñoz (MEX) 2:28.7	Vladimir Kossinsky (URS) 2:29.2	Brian Job (USA) 2:29.9
1972	John Hencken (USA) 2:21.55*	David A. Wilkie (GBR) 2:23.67	Nobutaka Taguchi (JPN) 2:23.88
1976	David Wilkie (GBR) 2:15.11*	John Hencken (USA) 2:17.26	Rick Colella (USA) 2:19.20
1980	Robertas Zulpa (URS) 2:15.85	Alban Vermes (HUN) 2:16.93	Arsen Miskarov (URS) 2:17.41
1984	Victor Davis (CAN) 2:13.34*	Glenn Beringen (AUS) 2:15.79	Etienne Dagon (SUI) 2:17.41
1988	Jozsef Szabo (HUN) 2:13.52	Nick Gillingham (GBR) 2:14.12	Sergio Lopez (ESP) 2:15.21

Two of the greatest back stroke experts ever seen in Olympic competition are Roland Matthes (GDR) at left and John Naber (USA) at right. Matthes won the gold medal at 100 meters and 200 meters in both 1968 and 1972. Naber set Olympic and world records at both distances at the 1976 Games.

In the 100 meters breast stroke event in 1976, John Hencken (USA) in lane 3 beat David Wilkie (GBR) in lane 5 by just over half a second. At 200 meters Wilkie beat the defending champion Hencken.

The following Olympic records were set in addition to those medal-winning performances already marked with an asterisk*.

3:10.0	Holman	1908	2:46.2	Koike	1932	2:38.0	Mulliken	1960
3:10.6	Holman	1908	2:44.9	Koike	1932	2:37.2	Mulliken	1960
3:07.4	Lützow	1912	2:42.5	Hamuro	1936	2:31.4	O'Brien	1964
3:03.4	Bathe	1912	2:40.0†	Verdeur	1948	2:30.1	Egon	
3:02.2	Bathe	1912	2:38.9†	L. Komadel			Henninger	
2:56.0	Skelton	1924		(TCH)	1952		(GER)	1964
2:52.0	Rademacher			G. Holan		2:28.7	O'Brien	1964
		1928		(USA)	1952	2:26.32	Klaus Katzur	
2:50.0	Tsuruta	1928	2:36.8†	Davies	1952		(GDR)	1972
2:49.2	Tsuruta	1928	2:36.1†	Furukawa		2:23.45	Taguchi	1972
2:46.2	Tsuruta	1932			1956	2:21.08	Colella	1976
						2:18.29	Wilkie	1976

†In the 1948 and 1952 Games the records for this event were achieved by the then permissible butterfly stroke. Furukawa's 1956 record was achieved by the now also disallowed underwater technique.

100 METERS BUTTERFLY (109 yd 1 ft)

	GOLD	SILVER	BRONZE
1896–1964	Event not held		
1968	Douglas A. Russell (USA) 55.9*[1]	Mark A. Spitz (USA) 56.4	Ross Wales (USA) 57.2
1972	Mark A. Spitz (USA) 54.27*	Bruce Robertson (CAN) 55.56	Jerry Heidenreich (USA) 55.74
1976	Matt Vogel (USA) 54.35	Joseph Bottom (USA) 54.50	Gary Hall (USA) 54.65
1980	Par Arvidsson (SWE) 54.92	Roger Pyttel (GDR) 54.94	David Lopez (ESP) 55.13
1984	Michael Gross (FRG) 53.08*	Pedro Morales (USA) 53.23	Glenn Buchanan (AUS) 53.85
1988	Anthony Nesty (SUR) 53.00*	Matt Biondi (USA) 53.01	Andy Jameson (GBR) 53.30

[1]In 1968 Russell set an inaugural record of 57.3 which he improved to 55.9 in the semi-finals.
Olympic record performances: 54.02 by Michael Gross 1984, and 53.78 by Pedro Morales 1984.

200 METERS BUTTERFLY (218 yd 2 ft)

1896–1952	Event not held		
1956	William Yorzyk (USA) 2:19.3	Takashi Ishimoto (JPN) 2:23.8	György Tumpek (HUN) 2:23.9
1960	Michael F. Troy (USA) 2:12.8*	Neville Hayes (AUS) 2:14.6	J. David Gillanders (USA) 2:15.3
1964	Kevin J. Berry (AUS) 2:06.6*	Carl Robie (USA) 2:07.5	Fred Schmidt (USA) 2:09.3
1968	Carl Robie (USA) 2:08.7	Martyn Woodroffe (GBR) 2:09.0	John Ferris (USA) 2:09.3
1972	Mark A. Spitz (USA) 2:00.70*	Gary Hall (USA) 2:02.86	Robin Backhaus (USA) 2:03.23

GOLD	SILVER	BRONZE
1976 Michael Bruner (USA) 1:59.23*	Steven Gregg (USA) 1:59.54	William Forrester (USA) 1:59.96
1980 Sergei Fesenko (URS) 1:59.76	Philip Hubble (GBR) 2:01.20	Roger Pyttel (GDR) 2:01.39
1984 Jon Sieben (AUS) 1:57.04*	Michael Gross (FRG) 1:57.40	Rafael Vidal Castro (VEN) 1:57.51
1988 Michael Gross (FRG) 1:56.94*	Benny Nielsen (DEN) 1:58.24	Anthony Mosse (NZL) 1:58.28

There were six record butterfly performances (then permissible) in the 1948 and 1952 breast stroke events culminating in John Davies' (AUS) 2:34.4 in 1952. Thereafter the non-medal-winning records were:

2:18.6	Yorzyk	1956	2:09.3	Robie	1964	2:00.24	Gregg	1976
2:15.5	Troy	1960	2:03.70	Hall	1972	1:59.19	Pedro Morales	
2:10.0	Robie	1964	2:03.11	Backhaus	1972		(USA)	1984
			2:02.11	Spitz	1972	1:58.72	Gross	1984

200 METERS INDIVIDUAL MEDLEY

GOLD	SILVER	BRONZE
1896–1964 Event not held		
1968 Charles Hickcox (USA) 2:12.0	Greg Buckingham (USA) 2:13.0	John Ferris (USA) 2:13.3
1972 Gunnar Larsson (SWE) 2:07.17*	Tim McKee (USA) 2:08.37	Steve Furniss (USA) 2:08.45
1976–1980 Event not held		
1984 Alex Baumann (CAN) 2:01.42*	Pedro Morales (USA) 2:03.05	Neil Cochran (GBR) 2:04.38
1988 Tamas Darnyi (HUN) 2:00.17*	Patrick Kühl (GDR) 2:01.61	Vadim Yarochtchuk (URS) 2:02.40

400 METERS INDIVIDUAL MEDLEY (437 yd 1 ft)

GOLD	SILVER	BRONZE
1896–1960 Event not held		
1964 Richard Roth (USA) 4:45.4*	Roy Saari (USA) 4:47.1	Gerhard Hetz (GER) 4:51.0
1968 Charles Hickcox (USA) 4:48.4	Gary Hall (USA) 4:48.7	Michael Holthaus (GER) 4:51.4
1972 Gunnar Larsson (SWE) 4:31.98*	Tim McKee (USA) 4:31.98*	Andras Hargitay (HUN) 4:32.70
1976 Rod Strachan (USA) 4:23.68*	Tim McKee (USA) 4:24.62	Andrei Smirnov (URS) 4:26.90
1980 Aleksandr Sidorenko (URS) 4:22.89*	Sergei Fesenko (URS) 4:23.43	Zoltan Verraszto (HUN) 4:24.24
1984 Alex Baumann (CAN) 4:17.41*	Ricardo Prado (BRA) 4:18.45	Robert Woodhouse (AUS) 4:20.50
1988 Tamas Darnyi (HUN) 4:14.75*	David Wharton (USA) 4:17.36	Stefano Battistelli (ITA) 4:18.01

The following non-medal-winning performances were also Olympic Records:

4:52.0	Robie	1964	4:34.99	Larsson	1972	4:27.15	Strachan	1976
4:37.51	Hargitay	1972	4:27.76	Steve Furniss (USA)	1976	4:16.55	Darnyi	1988

4 × 100 METERS MEDLEY RELAY (4 × 109 yd 1 ft)
(Order of strokes: back-stroke, breast stroke, butterfly, free-style.)

GOLD	SILVER	BRONZE
1896–1956 Event not held		
1960 UNITED STATES 4:05.4*	AUSTRALIA 4:12.0	JAPAN 4:12.2
Frank E. McKinney	David Theile	Kazuo Tomita
Paul W. Hait	Terry Gathercole	Koichi Hirakida
Lance M. Larson	Neville Hayes	Yoshihiko Osaki
F. Jeffrey Farrell	Gary Shipton	Keigo Shimizu
1964 UNITED STATES 3:58.4*	GERMANY 4:01.6	AUSTRALIA 4:02.3
Harold T. Mann	Ernst-Joachim Küppers	Peter Reynolds
William Craig	Egon Henninger	Ian O'Brien
Fred Schmidt	Horst-Günther Gregor	Kevin J. Berry
Stephen Clark	Hans-Joachim Klein	David Dickson
1968 UNITED STATES 3:54.9*	EAST GERMANY 3:57.5	U.S.S.R. 4:00.7
Charles Hickcox	Roland Matthes	Yuri Gromak
Donald McKenzie	Egon Henninger	Vladimir Kossinsky
Douglas A. Russell	Horst-Günther Gregor	Vladimir Nemshilov
Kenneth Walsh	Frank Wiegand	Leonid Ilyichev
1972 UNITED STATES 3:48.16*	EAST GERMANY 3:52.12	CANADA 3:52.26
Mike Stamm	Roland Matthes	Eric Fish
Tom Bruce	Klaus Katzur	William Mahony
Mark A. Spitz	Hartmut Floeckner	Bruce Robertson
Jerry Heidenerich	Lutz Unger	Robert A. Kasting
1976 UNITED STATES 3:42.22*	CANADA 3:45.94	WEST GERMANY 3:47.29
John Naber	Stephen Pickell	Klaus Steinbach
John Hencken	Graham Smith	Walter Kusch
Matt Vogel	Clay Evans	Michael Kraus
Jim Montgomery	Gary MacDonald	Peter Nocke
1980 AUSTRALIA 3:45.70	U.S.S.R. 3:45.92	GREAT BRITAIN 3:47.71
Mark Kerry	Viktor Kuznetsov	Gary Abraham
Peter Evans	Arsen Miskarov	Duncan Goodhew
Mark Tonelli	Yevgeniy Seredin	David Lowe
Neil Brooks	Sergei Kopliakov	Martin Smith
1984 UNITED STATES 3:39.30*	CANADA 3:43.23	AUSTRALIA 3:43.25
Rick Carey	Mike West	Mark Kerry
Steve Lundquist	Victor Davis	Peter Evans
Pedro Morales	Tom Ponting	Glenn Buchanan
Ambrose Gaines	Sandy Goss	Mark Stockwell
1988 UNITED STATES 3:36.93*	CANADA 3:39.28	U.S.S.R. 3:39.96
David Berkoff	Mark Tewksbury	Igor Polyanski
Richard Schroeder	Victor Davis	Dmitry Volkov
Matt Biondi	Tom Ponting	Vadim Yarochtchuk
Chris Jacobs	Sandy Goss	Gennady Prigoda

The following Olympic records were set in addition to those medal-winning performances already marked with an asterisk*.

4:14.8	Australia 1960	4:05.1	United States 1964	3:51.98	United States 1972
4:08.2	United States 1960			3:47.28	United States 1976

4 × 100 METERS FREE-STYLE RELAY (4 × 109 yd 1 ft)

GOLD	SILVER	BRONZE
1896–1960 Event not held		
1964 USA 3:33.2	**GERMANY** 3:37.2	**AUSTRALIA** 3:39.1
Steve Clark	Horst Loffler	David Dickson
Mike Austin	Frank Wiegand	Peter Doak
Gary Ilman	Uwe Jacobsen	John Ryan
Don Schollander	Hans-Joachim Klein	Robert Windle
1968 USA 3:31.7*	U.S.S.R. 3:34.2	**AUSTRALIA** 3:34.7
Zachary Zorn	Semyon Belits-Geiman	Greg Rogers
Steve Rerych	Viktor Mazanov	Robert Windle
Mark Spitz	Georgy Kulikov	Robert Cusack
Ken Walsh	Leonid Ilichev	Mike Wenden
1972 USA 3:26.42*	U.S.S.R. 3:29.72	GDR 3:32.42
David Edgar	Vladimir Bure	Roland Matthes
John Murphy	Viktor Mazanov	Wilfried Hartung
Jerry Heidenreich	Viktor Aboimov	Peter Bruch
Mark Spitz	Igor Grivennikov	Lutz Unger
1976–1980 Event not held		
1984 USA 3:19.03*	**AUSTRALIA** 3:19.68	**SWEDEN** 3:22.69
Chris Cavanaugh	Greg Fasala	Thomas Leidstrom
Michael Heath	Neil Brooks	Bengt Baron
Matthew Bond	Michael Delany	Mikael Orn
Ambrose Gaines	Mark Stockwell	Per Johansson
1988 USA 3:16.53*	U.S.S.R. 3:18.33	**EAST GERMANY** 3:19.82
Chris Jacobs	Gennady Prigoda	Dirk Richter
Troy Dalbey	Yuriy Bachtakov	Thomas Flemming
Tom Jager	Nikolai Yevseyev	Lars Hinneburg
Matt Biondi	Vladimir Tkashenko	Steffen Zesner

4 × 200 METERS FREE-STYLE RELAY (4 × 218 yd 2 ft)

GOLD	SILVER	BRONZE
1896–1906 Event not held		
1908 **GREAT BRITAIN** 10:45.6	**HUNGARY** 10:59.0	**UNITED STATES** 11:02.8
John H. Derbyshire	József Munk	Harry Hebner
Paul Radmilovic	Imre Zachár	Leo Goodwin
William Foster	Béla von Las Torres	Charles M. Daniels
Henry Taylor	Zóltán von Halmay	Leslie G. Rich
1912 **AUSTRALIA** 10:11.6*	**UNITED STATES** 10:20.2	**GREAT BRITAIN** 10:28.2
Cecil Healy	Kenneth Huszagh	William Foster
Malcolm Champion[1]	Harry J. Hebner	T. Sydney Battersby
Leslie Boardman	Perry McGillivray	John Hatfield
Harold Hardwick	Duke P. Kahanamoku	Henry Taylor
1920 **UNITED STATES** 10:04.4*	**AUSTRALIA** 10:25.4	**GREAT BRITAIN** 10:37.2
Perry McGillivray	Henry Hay	Leslie Savage
Pua K. Kealoha	William Herald	E. Percy Peter
Norman Ross	Ivan Stedman	Henry Taylor
Duke P. Kahanamoku	Frank E. Beaurepaire	Harold E. Annison
1924 **UNITED STATES** 9:53.4*	**AUSTRALIA** 10:02.2	**SWEDEN** 10:06.8
Wallace O'Connor	Maurice Christie	George Werner
Harry Glancy	Ernest Henry	Orvar Trolle
Ralph Breyer	Frank E. Beaurepaire	Åke Borg
Johnny Weissmuller	Andrew M. Charlton	Arne Borg
1928 **UNITED STATES** 9:36.2*	**JAPAN** 9:41.4	**CANADA** 9:47.8
Austin Clapp	Hiroshi Yoneyama	F. Munro Bourne
Walter Laufer	Nobuo Arai	James Thompson
George Kojac	Tokuhei Sada	Garnet Ault
Johnny Weissmuller	Katsuo Takaishi	Walter Spence

---

[1] A New Zealander; the other three members of the team were Australians. The two countries entered a composite team in the Olympic Games until 1920.

GOLD	SILVER	BRONZE
1932 JAPAN 8:58.4*	UNITED STATES 9:10.5	HUNGARY 9:31.4
Yasuji Miyazaki	Frank Booth	András Wannié
Masanori Yusa	George Fissier	László Szabados
Takashi Yokoyama	Marola Kalili	András Székely
Hisakichi Toyoda	Manuella Kalili	István Bárány
1936 JAPAN 8:51.5*	UNITED STATES 9:03.0	HUNGARY 9:12.3
Masanori Yusa	Ralph Flanagan	Arpád Lengyel
Shigeo Sugiura	John Macionis	Oszkár Abay-Nemes
Masaharu Taguchi	Paul Wolf	Ödön Gróf
Shigeo Arai	Jack Medica	Ferenc Csik
1948 UNITED STATES 8:46.0*	HUNGARY 8:48.4	FRANCE 9:08.0
Walter Ris	Elemér Szathmári	Joseph Bernardo
James McLane	György Mitró	Henri Padou
Wallace Wolf	Imre Nyéki	René Cornu
William Smith	Géza Kádas	Alexandre Jany
1952 UNITED STATES 8:31.1*	JAPAN 8:33.5	FRANCE 8:45.9
Wayne Moore	Hiroshi Suzuki	Joseph Bernardo
William Woolsey	Yoshihiro Hamaguchi	Aldo Eminente
Ford Konno	Toru Goto	Alexandre Jany
James McLane	Teijiro Tanikawa	Jean Boiteaux
1956 AUSTRALIA 8:23.6*	UNITED STATES 8:31.5	U.S.S.R. 8:34.7
Kevin O'Halloran	Richard Hanley	Vitaliy Sorokin
John Devitt	George T. Breen	Vladimir Struschanov
I. Murray Rose	William Woolsey	Gennadiy Nikolayev
Jon Henricks	Ford Konno	Boris Nikitin
1960 UNITED STATES 8:10.2*	JAPAN 8:13.2	AUSTRALIA 8:13.8
George P. Harrison	Makoto Fukui	David G. Dickson
Richard A. Blick	Hiroshi Ishii	John Devitt
Michael F. Troy	Tsuyoshi Yamanaka	I. Murray Rose
F. Jeffrey Farrell	Tatsuo Fujimoto	John Konrads
1964 UNITED STATES 7:52.1*	GERMANY 7:59.3	JAPAN 8:03.8
Stephen Clark	Horst-Günther Gregor	Makoto Fukui
Roy Saari	Gerhard Hetz	Kunihiro Iwasaki
Gary Ilman	Frank Wiegand	Toshio Shoji
Donald A. Schollander	Hans-Joachim Klein	Yukiaki Okabe
1968 UNITED STATES 7:52.3	AUSTRALIA 7:53.7	U.S.S.R. 8:01.6
John M. Nelson	Gregory Rogers	Vladimir Bure
Stephen Rerych	Graham White	Semyon Belitz-Geiman
Mark A. Spitz	Robert Windle	Georgy Kulikov
Donald A. Schollander	Michael V. Wenden	Leonid Ilyichev
1972 UNITED STATES 7:35.78*	WEST GERMANY 7:41.69	U.S.S.R. 7:45.76
John Kinsella	Klaus Steinbach	Igor Grivennilkov
Frederick Tyler	Werner Lampe	Viktor Mazanov
Steven Genter	Hans-Günter Vosseler	Georgy Kulikov
Mark Spitz	Hans-Joachim Fassnacht	Vladimir Bure
1976 UNITED STATES 7:23.22*	U.S.S.R. 7:27.97	GREAT BRITAIN 7:32.11
Michael Bruner	Vladimir Raskatov	Alan McClatchey
Bruce Furniss	Andrei Bogdanov	David Dunne
John Naber	Sergei Kopliakov	Gordon Downie
Jim Montgomery	Andrei Krylov	Brian Brinkley
1980 U.S.S.R. 7:23.50	EAST GERMANY 7:28.60	BRAZIL 7:29.30
Sergei Kopliakov	Frank Pfutze	Jorge Fernades
Vladimir Salnikov	Jorg Woithe	Marcus Mattioli Laborne
Ivar Stukolkin	Detlef Grabs	Cyro Delgado Marques
Andrei Krylov	Rainer Strohbach	Djan Madruga Garrido

GOLD	SILVER	BRONZE
1984 **UNITED STATES** 7:15.69*	**WEST GERMANY** 7:15.73	**GREAT BRITAIN** 7:24.78
Michael Heath	Thomas Fahrner	Neil Cochran
David Larson	Dirk Korthals	Paul Easter
Jeff Float	Alexander Schowtka	Paul Howe
Lawrence Hayes	Michael Gross	Andrew Astbury
1988 **UNITED STATES** 7:12.51*	**EAST GERMANY** 7:13.68	**WEST GERMANY** 7:14.35
Troy Dalbey	Uwe Dassler	Erik Hochstein
Matt Cetlinski	Sven Lodziewski	Thomas Fahrner
Douglas Giertsen	Thomas Flemming	Rainer Henkel
Matt Biondi	Steffen Zesner	Michael Gross

The following Olympic records were set in addition to those medal-winning performances already marked with an asterisk*.

11:35.0	Australia 1908	9:59.4	United States 1924	8:09.0	United States 1964
10.53.4	Great Britain 1908	9:38.8	United States 1928	7:49.03	Australia 1972
10:26.4	United States 1912	8:56.1	Japan 1936	7:46.42	United States 1972
10:14.0	Australia 1912	8:42.1	Japan 1952	7:33.21	U.S.S.R. 1976
		8:17.1	Japan 1960	7:30.33	USA 1976
		8:09.7	Germany 1964	7:18.87	U.S.A. 1984

SPRINGBOARD DIVING

1896–1906 Event not held

1908	Albert Zurner (GER) 85.5	Kurt Behrens (GER) 85.3	George Gaidzik (USA) 80.8 Gottlob Walz (GER) 80.8
1912	Paul Günther (GER) 79.23	Hans Luber (GER) 76.78	Kurt Behrens (GER) 73.73
1920	Louis E. Kuehn (USA) 675.4	Clarence Pinkston (USA) 655.3	Louis J. Balbach (USA) 649.5
1924	Albert C. White (USA) 696.4	Peter Desjardins (USA) 693.2	Clarence Pinkston (USA) 653
1928	Peter Desjardins (USA) 185.04	Michael Galitzen (USA) 174.06	Farid Simaika (EGY) 172.46
1932	Michael Galitzen (USA) 161.38	Harold Smith (USA) 158.54	Richard Degener (USA) 151.82
1936	Richard Degener (USA) 163.57	Marshall Wayne (USA) 159.56	Al Greene (USA) 146.29
1948	Bruce Harlan (USA) 163.64	Miller Anderson (USA) 157.29	Samuel Lee (USA) 145.52
1952	David Browning (USA) 205.29	Miller Anderson (USA) 199.84	Robert Clotworthy (USA) 184.92
1956	Robert Clotworthy (USA) 159.56	Donald Harper (USA) 156.23	Joaquin Capilla Pérez (MEX) 150.69
1960	Gary M. Tobian (USA) 170.00	Samuel N. Hall (USA) 167.08	Juan Botella (MEX) 162.30
1964	Kenneth Sitzberger (USA) 159.90	Francis Gorman (USA) 157.63	Larry Andreasen (USA) 143.77
1968	Bernard Wrightson (USA) 170.15	Klaus Dibiasi (ITA) 159.74	James Henry (USA) 158.09
1972	Vladimir Vasin (URS) 594.09	Franco Cagnotto (ITA) 591.63	Craig Lincoln (USA) 577.29
1976	Philip Boggs (USA) 619.05	Franco Cagnotto (ITA) 570.48	Aleksandr Kosenkov (URS) 567.24
1980	Aleksandr Portnov (URS) 905.025	Carlos Giron (MEX) 892.140	Franco Cagnotto (ITA) 871.500
1984	Greg Louganis (USA) 754.41	Tan Liangde (CHN) 662.31	Ronald Merriott (USA) 661.32
1988	Greg Louganis (USA) 730.80	Tan Liangde (CHN) 704.88	Li Deliang (CHN) 665.28

PLATFORM DIVING

	GOLD	SILVER	BRONZE
1896-1904	Event not held		
1906	Gottlob Walz (GER) 156.00	Georg Hoffman (GER) 150.20	Otto Satzinger (AUT) 147.40
1908	Hjalmar Johansson (SWE) 83.75	Karl Malström (SWE) 78.73	Arvid Spångberg (SWE) 74.00
1912	Erik Adlerz (SWE) 73.94	Albert Zürner (GER) 72.60	Gustaf Blomgren (SWE) 69.56
1920	Clarence Pinkston (USA) 100.67	Erik Adlerz (SWE) 99.08	Haig Prieste (USA) 93.73
1924	Albert C. White (USA) 97.46	David Fall (USA) 97.30	Clarence Pinkston (USA) 94.60
1928	Peter Desjardins (USA) 98.74	Farid Simaika (EGY) 99.58	Michael Galitzen (USA) 92.34
1932	Harold Smith (USA) 124.80	Michael Galitzen (USA) 124.28	Frank Kurtz (USA) 121.98
1936	Marshall Wayne (USA) 113.58	Elbert Root (USA) 110.60	Hermann Stork (GER) 110.31
1948	Samuel Lee (USA) 130.05	Bruce Harlan (USA) 122.30	Joaquin Capilla Pérez (MEX) 113.52
1952	Samuel Lee (USA) 156.28	Joaquin Capilla Pérez (MEX) 145.21	Günther Haase (GER) 141.31
1956	Joaquin Capilla Pérez (MEX) 152.44	Gary M. Tobian (USA) 152.41	Richard Connor (USA) 149.79
1960	Robert D. Webster (USA) 165.56	Gary M. Tobian (USA) 165.25	Brian E. Phelps (GBR) 157.13
1964	Robert D. Webster (USA) 148.58	Klaus Dibiasi (ITA) 147.54	Thomas Gompf (USA) 146.57
1968	Klaus Dibiasi (ITA) 164.18	Alvaro Gaxiola (MEX) 154.49	Edwin Young (USA) 153.93
1972	Klaus Dibiasi (ITA) 504.12	Richard Rydze (USA) 480.75	Franco Cagnotto (ITA) 475.83
1976	Klaus Dibiasi (ITA) 600.51	Gregory Louganis (USA) 576.99	Vladimir Aleynik (URS) 548.61
1980	Falk Hoffmann (GDR) 835.65	Vladimir Aleinik (URS) 819.705	David Ambartsumyan (URS) 817.44
1984	Greg Louganis (USA) 710.91	Bruce Kimball (USA) 643.40	Li Kungzheng (CHN) 638.28
1988	Greg Louganis (USA) 638.61	Ni Xiong (CHN) 637.47	Jesus Mena (MEX) 594.39

Greg Louganis (USA), considered the world's best diver today, earned perfect 10's in competition several times in world championship meets. In the 1984 Olympics he won 2 gold medals and set new world records for springboard and platform diving.

Swimming and Diving (Women)

50 METERS FREE-STYLE (54 yd 2 ft)

GOLD	SILVER	BRONZE
1896–1984 Event not held		
1988 Kristin Otto (GDR) 25.49*	Yang Wenyi (CHN) 25.64	Katrin Meissner (GDR) 25.71 Jill Sterkel (USA) 25.71

100 METERS FREE-STYLE (109 yd 1 ft)

GOLD	SILVER	BRONZE
1896–1908 Event not held		
1912 Fanny Durack (AUSTRALASIA) 1:22.2	Wilhelmina Wylie (AUSTRALASIA) 1:25.4	Jennie Fletcher (GBR) 1:27.0
1920 Ethelda M. Bleibtrey (USA) 1:13.6*	Irene M. Guest (USA) 1:17.0	Frances C. Schroth (USA) 1:17.2
1924 Ethel Lackie (USA) 1:12.4	Mariechen Wehselau (USA) 1:12.8	Gertrude C. Ederle (USA) 1:14.2
1928 Albina Osipowich (USA) 1:11.0*	Eleanor A. Gerratti (USA) 1:11.4	M. Joyce Cooper (GBR) 1:13.6
1932 Helene Madison (USA) 1:06.8*	Willemijntje den Ouden (HOL) 1:07.8	Eleanor A. Saville (USA) 1:08.2
1936 Hendrika W. Mastenbroek (HOL) 1:05.9*	Jeanette Campbell (ARG) 1:06.4	Gisela Arendt (GER) 1:06.6
1948 Greta M. Andersen (DEN) 1:06.3	Ann E. Curtis (USA) 1:06.5	Marie-Louise J. Vaessen (HOL) 1:07.6
1952 Katalin Szöke (HUN) 1:06.8	Johanna Termeulen (HOL) 1:07.0	Judit Temes (HUN) 1:07.1
1956 Dawn Fraser (AUS) 1:02.0*	Lorraine J. Crapp (AUS) 1:02.3	Faith Leech (AUS) 1:05.1
1960 Dawn Fraser (AUS) 1:01.2*	S. Christine von Saltza (USA) 1:02.8	Natalie Steward (GBR) 1:03.1
1964 Dawn Fraser (AUS) 59.5*	Sharon Stouder (USA) 59.9	Kathleen Ellis (USA) 1:00.8
1968 Jan M. Henne (USA) 1:00.0	Susan Pedersen (USA) 1:00.3	Linda Gustavson (USA) 1:00.3
1972 Sandra Neilson (USA) 58.59*	Shirley Babashoff (USA) 59.02	Shane E. Gould (AUS) 59.06
1976 Kornelia Ender (GDR) 55.65*	Petra Priemer (GDR) 56.49	Enith Brigitha (HOL) 56.65
1980 Barbara Krause (GDR) 54.78*	Caren Metschuck (GDR) 55.16	Ines Diers (GDR) 55.65
1984 Carrie Steinseifer (USA) 55.92 Nancy Hogshead (USA) 55.92	—	Annemarie Verstappen (HOL) 56.08
1988 Kristin Otto (GDR) 54.93	Zhuang Yong (CHN) 55.47	Catherine Plewinski (FRA) 55.49

The following Olympic records were set in addition to those medal-winning performances already marked with an asterisk*.

1:29.8	Bella Moore (GBR)	1912	1:08.5	Saville	1932	59.9	Fraser 1964
1:23.6	Daisy Curwen (GBR)	1912	1:07.6	den Ouden	1932	59.5 (.47)	Magdolna Patoh (HUN) 1972
1:19.8	Durack	1912	1:06.4	Mastenbroek (twice)	1936	59.5 (.51)	Neilson 1972
1:18.0	Schroth	1920	1:05.9	Andersen	1948	59.5 (.51)	Babashoff 1972
1:14.4	Bleibtrey	1920	1:05.5	Temes	1952	59.44	Gould 1972
1:12.2	Wehselau	1924	1:03.4	Crapp	1956	59.05	Babashoff 1972
1:12.2	Osipowich	1928	1:02.4	Fraser	1956	56.95	Priemer 1976
1:11.4	Gerratti	1928	1:01.9	von Saltza	1960	56.61	Brigitha 1976
1:09.0	Cooper	1932	1:01.4	Fraser	1960	55.81	Ender 1976
1:08.9	Madison	1932	1:00.6	Fraser	1964	54.98	Krause 1980

200 METERS FREE-STYLE (218 yd 2 ft)

	GOLD	SILVER	BRONZE
1896–1964	Event not held		
1968	Debbie Meyer (USA) 2:10.5*	Jan M. Henne (USA) 2:11.0	Jane Barkman (USA) 2:11.2
1972	Shane E. Gould (AUS) 2:03.56*	Shirley Babashoff (USA) 2:04.33	Keena Rothhammer (USA) 2:04.92
1976	Kornelia Ender (GDR) 1:59.26*	Shirley Babashoff (USA) 2:01.22	Enith Brigitha (HOL) 2:01.40
1980	Barbara Krause (GDR) 1:58.33*	Ines Diers (GDR) 1:59.64	Carmela Schmidt (GDR) 2:01.44
1984	Mary Wayte (USA) 1:59.23	Cynthia Woodhead (USA) 1:59.50	Annemarie Verstappen (HOL) 1:59.69
1988	Heike Friedrich (GDR) 1:57.65*	Silvia Poll (CRC) 1:58.67	Manuela Stellmach (GDR) 1:59.01

The following Olympic records were set in addition to those medal-winning performances already marked with an asterisk*.

2:13.1	Meyer	1968	2:07.48	Rothhammer	1972
2:08.12	Ann Marshall (USA)	1972	2:07.05	Andrea Eife (GDR)	1972
			2:01.54	Brigitha	1976

The first time women's swimming made the Olympic schedule was in 1912 at Stockholm. This is the final of the 100 meters free-style event.

At the 1976 Montreal Games, Kornelia Ender (GDR) became one of only 3 women to win 4 Olympic gold medals in swimming.

400 METERS FREE-STYLE (437 yd 1 ft)

	GOLD	SILVER	BRONZE
1896–1920	Event not held		
1924	Martha Norelius (USA) 6:02.2*	Helen Wainwright (USA) 6:03.8	Gertrude C. Ederle (USA) 6:04.8
1928	Martha Norelius (USA) 5:42.8*	Marie J. Braun (HOL) 5:57.8	Josephine McKim (USA) 6:00.2
1932	Helene Madison (USA) 5:28.5*	Lenore Kight (USA) 5:28.6	Jennie Maakal (SAF) 5:47.3
1936	Hendrika W. Maestenbrock (HOL) 5:26.4*	Ragnhild Hveger (DEN) 5:27.5	Lenore Wingard (USA) 5:29.0
1948	Ann E. Curtis (USA) 5:17.8*	Karen-Margrete Harup (DEN) 5:21.2	Catherine Gibson (GBR) 5:22.5
1952	Valéria Gyenge (HUN) 5:12.1*	Eva Novák (HUN) 5:13.7	Evelyn T. Kawamoto (USA) 5:14.6
1956	Lorraine J. Crapp (AUS) 4:54.6*	Dawn Fraser (AUS) 5:02.5	Sylvia Ruuska (USA) 5:07.1
1960	S. Christine von Saltza (USA) 4:50.6*	Jane Cederqvist (SWE) 4:53.9	Catharina Lagerberg (HOL) 4:56.9
1964	Virginia Duenkel (USA) 4:43.3*	Marilyn Ramenofsky (USA) 4:44.6	Terri L. Stickles (USA) 4:47.2
1968	Debbie Meyer (USA) 4:31.8*	Linda Gustavson (USA) 4:35.5	Karen L. Moras (AUS) 4:37.0
1972	Shane E. Gould (AUS) 4:19.04*	Novella Calligaris (ITA) 4:22.44	Gudrun Wegner (GDR) 4:23.11
1976	Petra Thuemer (GDR) 4:09.89*	Shirley Babashoff (USA) 4:10.46	Shannon Smith (CAN) 4:14.60
1980	Ines Diers (GDR) 4:08.76*	Petra Schneider (GDR) 4:09.16	Carmela Schmidt (GDR) 4:10.86
1984	Tiffany Cohen (USA) 4:07.10*	Sarah Hardcastle (GBR) 4:10.27	June Croft (GBR) 4:11.49
1988	Janet Evans (USA) 4:03.85*	Heike Friedrich (GDR) 4:05.94	Anke Möhring (GDR) 4:06.62

The following Olympic records were set in addition to those medal-winning performances already marked with an asterisk*.

6:12.2	Ederle	1924	5:02.5	Fraser	1956	4:27.53	Jenny Wylie	
5:45.4	Norelius	1928	5:00.2	Crapp	1956		(USA)	1972
5:40.9	Kight	1932	4:53.6	von Saltza	1960	4:24.14	Calligaris	1972
5:28.0	Hveger	1936	4:48.6	Duenkel	1964	4:15.71	Rebecca	
5:25.7	Harup	1948	4:47.7	Ramenofsky	1964		Perrott	
5:16.6	Kawamoto	1952	4:35.0	Meyer	1968		(NZL)	1976
5:07.6	Marley L.							
	Shriver							
	(USA)	1956						

800 METERS FREE-STYLE (874 yd 2 ft)

	GOLD	SILVER	BRONZE
1896–1964	Event not held		
1968	Debbie Meyer (USA) 9:24.0*	Pamela Kruse (USA) 9:35.7	Maria T. Ramirez (MEX) 9:38.5
1972	Keena Rothhammer (USA) 8:53.68*	Shane E. Gould (AUS) 8:56.39	Norvella Calligaris (ITA) 8:57.46
1976	Petra Thuemer (GDR) 8:37.14*	Shirley Babashoff (USA) 8:37.59	Wendy Weinberg (USA) 8:42.60
1980	Michelle Ford (AUS) 8:28.90*	Ines Diers (GDR) 8:32.55	Heike Dahne (GDR) 8:33.48
1984	Tiffany Cohen (USA) 8:24.95*	Michele Richardson (USA) 8:30.73	Sarah Hardcastle (GBR) 8:32.60
1988	Janet Evans (USA) 8:20.20*	Astrid Strauss (GDR) 8:22.09	Julie McDonald (AUS) 8:22.93

The following Olympic records were set in addition to those medal-winning performances already marked with an asterisk*.

9:42.8	Meyer	1968	9:02.96	Calligaris 1972	8:46.81	Nicole Kramer	
9:38.3	Karen L. Moras		8:59.69	Rothhammer		(USA)	1976
	(AUS)	1968		1972	8:46.58	Thuemer	1976

Shane Gould (AUS) dominated women's swimming in 1972 with a bronze, a silver and 3 gold medals in the six events she entered.

100 METERS BACK STROKE (109 yd 1 ft)

1896–1920 Event not held

Year	Gold	Silver	Bronze
1924	Sybil Bauer (USA) 1:23.2*	Phyllis Harding (GBR) 1:27.4	Aileen Riggin (USA) 1:28.2
1928	Marie J. Braun (HOL) 1:22.0	Ellen King (GBR) 1:22.2	M. Joyce Cooper (GBR) 1:22.8
1932	Eleanor Holm (USA) 1:19.4	Philomena Mealing (AUS) 1:21.3	Elizabeth V. Davies (GBR) 1:22.5
1936	Dina W. J. Senff (HOL) 1:18.9	Hendrika W. Maestenbroek (HOL) 1:19.2	Alice Bridges (USA) 1:19.4
1948	Karen M. Harup (DEN) 1:14.4*	Suzanne W. Zimmermann (USA) 1:16.0	Judy-Joy Davies (AUS) 1:16.7
1952	Joan C. Harrison (SAF) 1:14.3	Geertje Wielema (HOL) 1:14.5	Jean Stewart (NZL) 1:15.8
1956	Judith B. Grinham (GBR) 1:12.9*	Carin Cone (USA) 1:12.9*	Margaret Edwards (GBR) 1:13.1
1960	Lynn E. Burke (USA) 1:09.3	Natalie Steward (GBR) 1:10.8	Satoko Tanaka (JPN) 1:11.4
1964	Cathy Ferguson (USA) 1:07.7*	Christine Caron (FRA) 1:07.9	Virginia Duenkel (USA) 1:08.0
1968	Kaye Hall (USA) 1:06.2*	Elaine B. Tanner (CAN) 1:06.7	Jane Swaggerty (USA) 1:08.1
1972	Melissa Belote (USA) 1:05.78*	Andrea Gyarmati (HUN) 1:06.26	Susie Atwood (USA) 1:06.34
1976	Ulrike Richter (GDR) 1:01.83*	Birgit Treiber (GDR) 1:03.41	Nancy Garapick (CAN) 1:03.71
1980	Rica Reinisch (GDR) 1:00.86*	Ina Kleber (GDR) 1:02.07	Petra Reidel (GDR) 1:02.64
1984	Theresa Andrews (USA) 1:02.55	Betsy Mitchell (USA) 1:02.63	Jolanda De Rover (HOL) 1:02.91
1988	Kristin Otto (GDR) 1:00.89	Krisztina Egerszegi (HUN) 1:01.56	Cornelia Sirch (GDR) 1:01.57

The following Olympic records were set in addition to those medal-winning performances already marked with an asterisk*.

1:24.0	Bauer	1924	1:13.0	Edwards	1956	1:07.6	Tanner	1968
1:22.0	King	1928	1:12.0	Laura Ranwell		1:07.4	Tanner	1968
1:21.6	Braun	1928		(SAF)	1960	1:06.08	Belote	1972
1:18.3	Holm	1932	1:09.4	Burke	1960	1:05.00	Tauna	
1:16.6	Senff	1936	1:09.0	Burke			Vandeweghe	
1:15.6	Harup	1948		(relay leg)	1960		(USA)	1976
1:15.5	Harup	1948	1:08.9	Duenkel	1964	1:03.28	Garapick	1976
1:13.8	Wielema	1952	1:08.8	Ferguson	1964	1:02.39	Richter	1976
1:13.1	Grinham	1956	1:08.5	Caron	1964	1:01.50	Reinisch	1980

200 METERS BACK STROKE (218 yd 2 ft)

1896–1964 Event not held

Year	Gold	Silver	Bronze
1968	Lillian D. Watson (USA) 2:24.8*	Elaine B. Tanner (CAN) 2:27.4	Kaye Hall (USA) 2:28.9
1972	Melissa Belote (USA) 2:19.19*	Susie Atwood (USA) 2:20.38	Donna Marie Gurr (CAN) 2:23.22
1976	Ulrike Richter (GDR) 2:13.43*	Birgit Treiber (GDR) 2:14.97	Nancy Garapick (CAN) 2:15.60
1980	Rica Reinisch (GDR) 2:11.77*	Cornelia Polit (GDR) 2:13.75	Birgit Treiber (GDR) 2:14.14
1984	Jolanda De Rover (HOL) 2:12.38	Amy White (USA) 2:13.04	Aneta Patrascoiu (ROM) 2:13.29
1988	Krisztina Egerszegi (HUN) 2:09.29*	Kathrin Zimmermann (GDR) 2:10.61	Cornelia Sirch (GDR) 2:11.45

The following Olympic records were set in addition to those medal-winning performances already marked with an asterisk*.

2:31.1	Hall	1968	2:29.2	Watson	1968	2:20.58	Belote	1972
2:30.9	Tanner	1968	2:22.13	Atwood	1972	2:16.49	Garapick	1976
						2:11.01	Egerszegi	1988
						2:10.46	Sirch	1988

100 METERS BREAST STROKE (109 yd 1 ft)

	GOLD	SILVER	BRONZE
1896–1964	Event not held		
1968	Djurdjica Bjedov (YUG) 1:15.8*	Galina Prozumenshchikova (URS) 1:15.9	Sharon Wichman (USA) 1:16.1
1972	Catherine Carr (USA) 1:13.58*	Galina Stepanova (URS) 1:14.99	Beverley J. Whitfield (AUS) 1:15.73
1976	Hannelore Anke (GDR) 1:11.16	Lyubov Rusanova (URS) 1:13.04	Marina Koshevaia (URS) 1:13.30
1980	Ute Geweniger (GDR) 1:10.22	Elvira Vasilkova (URS) 1:10.41	Susanne Nielsson (DEN) 1:11.16
1984	Petra Van Staveren (HOL) 1:09.88*	Anne Ottenbrite (CAN) 1:10.69	Catherine Poirot (FRA) 1:10.70
1988	Tania Dangalakova (BUL) 1:07.95*	Antoaneta Frenkova (BUL) 1:08.74	Silke Hörner (GDR) 1:08.83

The following Olympic records were set in addition to those medal-winning performances already marked with an asterisk*.

1:18.8	Catie Ball (USA)	1968	1:17.4	Ana Maria Norbis (URU)	1968	1:16.7	Norbis	1968
1:17.7	Bjedov	1968	1:16.8	Wichman	1968	1:15.00	Carr	1972
						1:11.11	Anke	1976
						1:10.86	Anke	1976
						1:10.11	Geweniger	1980
						1:08.35	Dangalakova	1988
						1:08.35	Hörner	1988

200 METERS BREAST STROKE (218 yd 2 ft)

	GOLD	SILVER	BRONZE
1896–1920	Event not held		
1924	Lucy Morton (GBR) 3:33.2	Agnes Geraghty (USA) 3:34.0	Gladys H. Carson (GBR) 3:35.4
1928	Hilde Schrader (GER) 3:12.6	Mietje Baron (HOL) 3:15.2	Lotte Mühe (GER) 3:17.6
1932	Claire Dennis (AUS) 3:06.3*	Hideko Maehata (JPN) 3:06.4	Else Jacobson (DEN) 3:07.1
1936	Hideko Maehata (JPN) 3:03.6	Martha Genenger (GER) 3:04.2	Inge Sörensen (DEN) 3:07.8
1948	Petronella van Vliet (HOL) 2:57.2	Beatrice Lyons (AUS) 2:57.7	Éva Novák (HUN) 2:00.2
1952	Éva Székely (HUN) 2:51.7*†	Éva Novák (HUN) 2:54.4	Helen O. Gordon (GBR) 2:57.6
1956	Ursula Happe (GER) 2:53.1*‡	Éva Székely (HUN) 2:54.8	Éva-Maria ten Elsen (GER) 2:55.1
1960	Anita Lonsbrough (GBR) 2:49.5*	Wiltrud Urselmann (GER) 2:50.0	Barbara Göbel (GER) 2:53.6
1964	Galina Prozumenshchikova (URS) 2:46.4*	Claudia A. Kolb (USA) 2:47.6	Svetlana Babanina (URS) 2:48.6
1968	Sharon Wichman (USA) 2:44.4*	Djurdjica Bjedov (YUG) 2:46.4	Galina Prozumenshchikova (URS) 2:47.0
1972	Beverley J. Whitfield (AUS) 2:41.71*	Dana Schoenfield (USA) 2:42.05	Galina Stepanova (URS) 2:42.36

GOLD	SILVER	BRONZE
1976 Marina Koshevaia (URS) 2:33.35*	Marina Iurchenia (URS) 2:36.08	Lyubov Rusanova (URS) 2:36.22
1980 Lina Kachushite (URS) 2:29.54*	Svetlana Varganova (URS) 2:29.61	Yulia Bogdanova (URS) 2:32.39
1984 Anne Ottenbrite (CAN) 2:30.38	Susan Rapp (USA) 2:31.15	Ingrid Lempereur (BEL) 2:31.40
1988 Silke Hörner (GDR) 2:26.71*	Huang Xiaomin (CHN) 2:27.49	Antoaneta Frenkova (BUL) 2:28.34

The following Olympic records were set in addition to those medal-winning performances already marked with an asterisk*.

3:27.6	Geraghty	1924	2:57.4	van Vliet	1948	2:48.3	Babanina	1964
3:11.6	Schrader	1928	2:57.0	van Vliet	1948	2:43.13	Agnes Kissne-	
3:11.2	Schrader	1928	2:54.0	Novák	1952		Kaczander	
3:08.2	Dennis	1932	2:54.0†	Székely	1952		(HUN)	1972
3:03.0	Genenger	1936	2:52.0	Urselmann	1960	2:35.14	Koshevaia	1976
3:01.9	Machata	1936	2:48.6	Bärbel Grimmer		2:29.77	Varganova	1980
3:01.2†	Székely	1948		(GER)	1964			
						2:28.94	Yulia Bogatcheva (URS)	1988
						2:27.63	Hörner	1988

†Butterfly stroke (then permitted) used.
‡Underwater technique (then permitted) used.

100 METERS BUTTERFLY (109 yd 1 ft)

1896–1952   Event not held

GOLD	SILVER	BRONZE
1956 Shelley Mann (USA) 1:11.0	Nancy J. Ramey (USA) 1:11.9	Mary J. Sears (USA) 1:14.4
1960 Carolyn J. Schuler (USA) 1:09.5*	Marianne Heemskerk (HOL) 1:10.4	Janice Andrew (AUS) 1:12.2
1964 Sharon Stouder (USA) 1:04.7*	Aagje Kok (HOL) 1:05.6	Kathleen Ellis (USA) 1:06.0
1968 Lynette McClements (AUS) 1:05.5	Ellie Daniel (USA) 1:05.8	Susan Shields (USA) 1:06.2
1972 Mayumi Aoki (JPN) 1:03.34*	Roswitha Beier (GDR) 1:03.61	Andrea Gyarmati (HUN) 1:03.73
1976 Kornelia Ender (GDR) 1:00.13*	Andrea Pollack (GDR) 1:00.98	Wendy Boglioli (USA) 1:01.17
1980 Caren Metschuck (GDR) 1:00.42	Andrea Pollack (GDR) 1:00.90	Christiane Knacke (GDR) 1:01.44
1984 Mary Meagher (USA) 59.26	Jenna Johnson (USA) 1:00.19	Karin Seick (FRG) 1:01.36
1988 Kristin Otto (GDR) 59.00*	Birte Weigang (GDR) 59.45	Qian Hong (CHN) 59.52

The following Olympic records were set in addition to those medal-winning performances already marked with an asterisk*.

1:11.2	Mann	1956	1:07.0	Stouder	1964	1:01.84	Boglioli	1976
1:09.8	Schuler	1960	1:05.6	Stouder	1964	1:01.43	Pollack	1976
1:07.8	Ellis	1964	1:04.00	Aoki	1972	1:01.03	Ender	1976
1:07.5	Donna De Varona (USA)	1964	1:03.80	Gyarmati	1972	0:59.05	Meagher	1984

Aagje Kok (HOL) won the 200 meters butterfly when it was introduced in the Olympic program in 1968.

200 METERS BUTTERFLY (218 yd 2 ft)

	GOLD	SILVER	BRONZE
1896–1964	Event not held		
1968	Aagje Kok (HOL) 2:24.7*	Helga Lindner (GDR) 2:24.8	Ellie Daniel (USA) 2:25.9
1972	Karen Moe (USA) 2:15.57*	Lynn Colella (USA) 2:16.34	Ellie Daniel (USA) 2:16.74
1976	Andrea Pollack (GDR) 2:11.41*	Ulrike Tauber (GDR) 2:12.50	Rosemarie Gabriel (GDR) 2:12.86
1980	Ines Geissler (GDR) 2:10.44*	Sybille Schonrock (GDR) 2:10.45	Michelle Ford (AUS) 2:11.66
1984	Mary Meagher (USA) 2:06.90*	Karen Phillips (AUS) 2:10.56	Ina Beyermann (FRG) 2:11.91
1988	Kathleen Nord (GDR) 2:09.51	Birte Weigang (GDR) 2:09.91	Mary Meagher (USA) 2:10.80

The following Olympic records were set in addition to those medal-winning performances already marked with an asterisk *. The butterfly stroke was permissible in the 1948 and 1952 breast stroke competition. The fastest time then recorded was 2:54.0 by Éva Székely in 1952.

2:33.0	Diane Giebel (USA)	1968	2:26.3	Kok	1968	2:14.53 Karen Thornton (USA) 1976
2:29.4	Daniel	1968	2:18.32	Rosemarie Kother (GDR)	1972	2:14.39 Tamara Shelofastova (URS) 1976
2:29.1	Toni Hewitt (USA)	1968	2:17.18	Daniel	1972	2:11.56 Pollack 1976

200 METERS INDIVIDUAL MEDLEY

	GOLD	SILVER	BRONZE
1896–1964	Event not held		
1968	Claudia Kolb (USA) 2:24.7	Susan Pedersen (USA) 2:28.8	Jan Henne (USA) 2:31.4
1972	Shane Gould (AUS) 2:23.07*	Kornelia Ender (GDR) 2:23.59	Lynn Vidali (USA) 2:24.06
1976–1980	Event not held		
1984	Tracy Caulkins (USA) 2:12.64*	Nancy Hogshead (USA) 2:15.17	Michele Pearson (AUS) 2:15.92
1988	Daniela Hunger (GDR) 2:12.59*	Yelena Dendeberova (URS) 2:13.31	Noemi Ildiko Lung (ROM) 2:14.85

400 METERS INDIVIDUAL MEDLEY

	GOLD	SILVER	BRONZE
1896–1960	Event not held		
1964	Donna De Varona (USA) 5:18.7*	Sharon Finneran (USA) 5:24.1	Martha Randall (USA) 5:24.2
1968	Claudia A. Kolb (USA) 5:08.5*	Lynn Vidali (USA) 5:22.2	Sabine Steinbach (GDR) 5:25.3
1972	Gail Neall (AUS) 5:02.97*	Leslie Cliff (CAN) 5:03.57	Novella Calligaris (ITA) 5:03.99
1976	Ulrike Tauber (GDR) 4:42.77*	Cheryl Gibson (CAN) 4:48.10	Becky Smith (CAN) 4:50.48
1980	Petra Schneider (GDR) 4:36.29*	Sharron Davies (GBR) 4:46.83	Agnieszka Czopek (POL) 4:48.17
1984	Tracy Caulkins (USA) 4:39.24	Suzanne Landells (AUS) 4:48.30	Petra Zindler (FRG) 4:48.57
1988	Janet Evans (USA) 4:37.76	Noemi Ildiko Lung (ROM) 4:39.46	Daniela Hunger (GDR) 4:39.76

The following Olympic records were set in addition to those medal-winning performances already marked with an asterisk *.

5:30.6	Anita Lonsbrough (GBR)	1964	5:26.8	Veronika Holletz (GDR)	1964	5:17.2	Kolb 1968
						5:06.96	Evelin Stolze (GDR) 1972
5:27.8	Randall	1964	5:24.2	De Varona	1964	4:52.90	Smith 1976
						4:51.24	Tauber 1976

4 × 100 METERS FREE-STYLE RELAY

	GOLD	SILVER	BRONZE
1896–1908	Event not held		
1912	GREAT BRITAIN 5:52.8*	GERMANY 6:04.6	AUSTRIA 6:17.0
	Bella Moore	Wally Dressel	Margarete Adler
	Jennie Fletcher	Louise Otto	Klara Milch
	Annie Spiers	Hermine Stindt	Josephine Sticker
	Irene Steer	Grete Rosenberg	Berta Zahourek
1920	UNITED STATES 5:11.6*	GREAT BRITAIN 5:40.8	SWEDEN 5:43.6
	Margaret D. Woodbridge	Hilda James	Aina Berg
	Frances C. Schroth	Constance M. Jeans	Emy Machnow
	Irene M. Guest	Charlotte Radcliffe	Karin Nilsson
	Ethelda M. Bleibtrey	Grace McKenzie	Jane Gylling
1924	UNITED STATES 4:58.8*	GREAT BRITAIN 5:17.0	SWEDEN 5:35.6
	Gertrude C. Ederle	Florence Barker	Aina Berg
	Euphrasia Donnelly	Grace McKenzie	Vivan Petersson
	Ethel Lackie	Iris V. Tanner	Gulli Everlund
	Mariechen Wehselau	Constance M. Jeans	Hjördis Töppel
1928	UNITED STATES 4:47.6*	GREAT BRITAIN 5:02.8	SOUTH AFRICA 5:13.4
	Adelaide Lambert	M. Joyce Cooper	Katharine Russell
	Eleonora Gerratti	Sarah Stewart	Rhoda Rennie
	Albina Osipowich	Iris V. Tanner	Marie Bedford
	Martha Norelius	Ellen E. King	Frederica J. van der Goes
1932	UNITED STATES 4:38.0*	NETHERLANDS 4:47.5	GREAT BRITAIN 4:52.4
	Josephine McKim	Maria Vierdag	Elizabeth V. Davies
	Helen Johns	Maria Oversloot	Helen Varcoe
	Eleonora Saville	Cornelia Ladde	M. Joyce Cooper
	Helene Madison	Willemijntje den Ouden	Edna Hughes

GOLD	SILVER	BRONZE
1936 **NETHERLANDS** 4:36.0*	**GERMANY** 4:36.8	**UNITED STATES** 4:40.2
Johanna K. Selbach	Ruth Halbsguth	Katherine L. Rawls
Catherina W. Wagner	Leni M. Lohmar	Bernice R. Lapp
Willemijntje den Ouden	Ingeborg Schmitz	Mavis Freeman
Hendrika W. Mastenbroek	Gisela Arendt	Olive M. McKean
1948 **UNITED STATES** 4:29.2*	**DENMARK** 4:29.6	**NETHERLANDS** 4:31.6
Marie L. Corridon	Eva J. Riise	Irma Schuhmacher
Thelma M. Kalama	Karen M. Harup	Margot Marsman
Brenda M. Helser	Greta M. Andersen	Marie-Louise J. Vaessen
Ann E. Curtis	Fritze W. Carstensen	Johanna M. Termeulen
1952 **HUNGARY** 4:24.4*	**NETHERLANDS** 4:29.0	**UNITED STATES** 4:30.1
Ilona Novák	Marie-Louise Linssen	Jacqueline La Vine
Judit Temes	Koosje van Voorn	Marilee Stepan
Éva Novák	Johanna M. Termeulen	Joan Alderson
Katalin Szöke	Irma Heijting	Evelyn Kawamoto
1956 **AUSTRALIA** 4:17.1*	**UNITED STATES** 4:19.2	**SOUTH AFRICA** 4:25.7
Dawn Fraser	Sylvia Ruuska	Jeanette Myburgh
Faith Leech	Shelley Mann	Susan Roberts
Sandra Morgan	Nancy Simons	Natalie Myburgh
Lorraine J. Crapp	Joan Rosazza	Moira Abernethy
1960 **UNITED STATES** 4:08.9*	**AUSTRALIA** 4:11.3	**GERMANY** 4:19.7
Joan A. Spillane	Dawn Fraser	Christel Steffin
Shirley A. Stobs	Ilsa Konrads	Heidi Pechstein
Carolyn V. Wood	Lorraine J. Crapp	Gisela Weiss
S. Christine von Saltza	Alva Colquhoun	Ursula Brunner
1964 **UNITED STATES** 4:03.8*	**AUSTRALIA** 4:06.9	**NETHERLANDS** 4:12.0
Sharon Stouder	Robyn Thorn	Paulina van der Wildt
Donna De Varona	Janice Murphy	Catharina Beumer
Lillian Watson	Lynette Bell	Winnie Van Weerdenburg
Kathleen Ellis	Dawn Fraser	Erica Terpstra
1968 **UNITED STATES** 4:02.5*	**EAST GERMANY** 4:05.7	**CANADA** 4:07.2
Jane Barkman	Gabriele Wetzko	Angela Coughlan
Linda Gustavson	Roswitha Krause	Marilyn Corson
Susan Pedersen	Uta Schmuck	Elaine B. Tanner
Jan M. Henne	Martina Grunert	Marion Lay
1972 **UNITED STATES** 3:55.19*	**EAST GERMANY** 3:55.55	**WEST GERMANY** 3:57.93
Sandra Neilson	Gabriele Wetzko	Jutta Weber
Jennifer Kemp	Andrea Eife	Heidemarie Reineck
Jane Barkman	Elke Sehmisch	Gudrun Beckmann
Shirley Babashoff	Kornelia Ender	Angela Steinbach
1976 **UNITED STATES** 3:44.82*	**EAST GERMANY** 3:45.50	**CANADA** 3:48.81
Kim Peyton	Kornelia Ender	Gail Amundrud
Wendy Boglioli	Petra Priemer	Barbara Clark
Jill Sterkel	Andrea Pollack	Becky Smith
Shirley Babashoff	Claudia Hempel	Anne Jardin
1980 **EAST GERMANY** 3:42.71*	**SWEDEN** 3:48.93	**NETHERLANDS** 3:49.51
Barbara Krause	Carina Ljungdahl	Conny van Bentum
Caren Metschuck	Tina Gustafsson	Wilma van Velsen
Ines Diers	Agneta Martensson	Reggie de Jong
Sarina Hulsenbeck	Agneta Eriksson	Annelies Maas
1984 **UNITED STATES** 3:43.43	**NETHERLANDS** 3:44.40	**WEST GERMANY** 3:45.56
Jenna Johnson	Annemarie Verstappen	Iris Zscherpe
Carrie Steinseifer	Elles Voskes	Susanne Schuster
Dara Torres	Desi Reijers	Christiane Pielke
Nancy Hogshead	Conny Van Bentum	Karin Seick

Tracy Caulkins (USA), here wearing 5 World Championship gold medals and one silver from 1978, added 2 Olympic golds in 1984 in the 200 and 400 meters individual medleys.

Shirley Babashoff (USA) holds a total of 8 Olympic medals, including 2 golds in the 4 × 100 meters free-style relay events in 1972 and 1976 and 6 silvers in team and individual competition.

GOLD	SILVER	BRONZE
1988 EAST GERMANY 3:40.63* Kristin Otto Katrin Meissner Daniela Hunger Manuela Stellmach	NETHERLANDS 3:43.39 Marianne Muis Mildred Muis Cornelia Van Bentum Karin Brienesse	UNITED STATES 3:44.25 Mary Wayte Mitzi Kremer Laura Walker Dara Torres

The following Olympic records were set in addition to those medal-winning performances already marked with an asterisk *.

4:55.6	United States 1928	4:28.1	United States 1952	3:50.27	United States 1976
4:33.5	Denmark 1948	3:58.11	East Germany 1972	3:48.95	East Germany 1976
4:31.3	Netherlands 1948				

4 × 100 METERS MEDLEY RELAY

(Order of strokes: back stroke, breast stroke, butterfly, free-style.)

1896–1956 Event not held

GOLD	SILVER	BRONZE
1960 UNITED STATES 4:41.1* Lynn E. Burke Patty Kempner Carolyn J. Schuler S. Christine von Saltza	AUSTRALIA 4:45.9 Marilyn Wilson Rosemarie Lassig Janice Andrew Dawn Fraser	GERMANY 4:47.6 Ingrid Schmidt Ursula Küper Bärbel Fuhrmann Ursula Brunner
1964 UNITED STATES 4:33.9* Cathy Ferguson Cynthia Goyette Sharon Stouder Kathleen Ellis	NETHERLANDS 4:37.0 Kornelia Winkel Klena Bimolt Aagje Kok Erica Terpstra	U.S.S.R. 4:39.2 Tatyana Savelieva Svetlana Babanina Tatyana Deviatova Natalya Ustinova
1968 UNITED STATES 4:28.3* Kaye Hall Catie Ball Ellie Daniel Susan Pedersen	AUSTRALIA 4:30.0 Lynette P. Watson Lynette McClements Judy Playfair Janet Steinbeck	WEST GERMANY 4:36.4 Angelika Kraus Uta Frommater Heike Hustede Heidi Reineck
1972 UNITED STATES 4:20.75* Melissa Belote Catherine Carr Deena Deardurff Sandra Neilsen	EAST GERMANY 4:24.91 Christine Herbst Renate Vogel Roswitta Beier Kornelia Ender	WEST GERMANY 4:26.46 Silke Pielen Verena Eberle Gudrun Beckmann Heidi Reineck
1976 EAST GERMANY 4:07.95* Ulrike Richter Hannelore Anke Andrea Pollack Kornelia Ender	UNITED STATES 4:14.55 Linda Jeszek Lauri Siering Camille Wright Shirley Babashoff	CANADA 4:15.22 Wendy Hogg Robin Corsiglia Susan Sloan Anne Jardin
1980 EAST GERMANY 4:06.67* Rica Reinisch Ute Geweniger Andrea Pollack Caren Metschuck	GREAT BRITAIN 4:12.24 Helen Jameson Margaret Kelly Ann Osgerby June Croft	U.S.S.R. 4:13.61 Yelena Kruglova Elvira Vasilkova Alla Grishchenkova Natalya Strunnikova
1984 UNITED STATES 4:08.34 Theresa Andrews Tracy Caulkins Mary Meagher Nancy Hogshead	WEST GERMANY 4:11.97 Svenja Schlicht Ute Hasse Ina Beyermann Karin Seick	CANADA 4:12.98 Reema Abdo Anne Ottenbrite Michelle MacPherson Pamela Rai

GOLD	SILVER	BRONZE
1988 **EAST GERMANY** 4:03.74*	**UNITED STATES** 4:07.90	**CANADA** 4:10.49
Kristin Otto	Beth Barr	Lori Melien
Silke Horner	Tracey McFarlane	Allison Higson
Birte Weigang	Janel Jorgensen	Jane Kerr
Katrin Meissner	Mary Wayte	Andrea Nugent

The following Olympic records were set in addition to those medal-winning performances already marked with an asterisk*.

4:49.0	Gt. Britain	1960	4:27.58	East Germany 1972	4:20.10	Canada	1976	
4:47.7	Holland	1960			4:13.98	East Germany 1976		
4:39.1	U.S.S.R.	1964	4:27.57	United States 1972				

SYNCHRONIZED SWIMMING—SOLO

1896–1980 Event not held		
1984 Tracie Ruiz (USA) 198.467	Carolyn Waldo (CAN) 195.300	Miwako Motoyoshi (JPN) 187.050
1988 Carolyn Waldo (CAN) 200.150	Tracie Ruiz-Conforto (USA) 197.633	Mikako Kotani (JPN) 191.850

SYNCHRONIZED SWIMMING—DUET

1896–1980 Event not held		
1984 USA 195.584	CANADA 194.234	JAPAN 187.992
Candy Costie	Sharon Hambrock	Saeko Kimura
Tracie Ruiz	Kelly Kryczka	Miwako Motoyoshi
1988 CANADA 197.717	USA 197.284	JAPAN 190.159
Michelle Cameron	Sarah Josephson	Miyako Tanaka
Carolyn Waldo	Karen Josephson	Mikako Kotani

SPRINGBOARD DIVING

1896–1912 Event not held		
1920 Aileen M. Riggin (USA) 539.9	Helen·E. Wainwright (USA) 534.8	Thelma R. Payne (USA) 534.1
1924 Elizabeth Becker (USA) 474.5	Aileen M. Riggin (USA) 460.4	Caroline Fletcher (USA) 434.4
1928 Helen Meany (USA) 78.62	Dorothy Poynton (USA) 75.62	Georgia Coleman (USA) 73.38
1932 Georgia Coleman (USA) 87.52	Katherine Rawls (USA) 82.56	Jane Fauntz (USA) 82.12
1936 Marjorie Gestring (USA) 89.27	Katherine Rawls (USA) 88.35	Dorothy Hill (USA) 82.36
1948 Victoria Draves (USA) 108.74	Zoe Ann Olsen (USA) 108.23	Patricia Elsener (USA) 101.30
1952 Patricia McCormick (USA) 147.30	Madeleine Moreau (FRA) 139.34	Zoe Ann Jensen (USA) 127.57
1956 Patricia McCormick (USA) 142.36	Jeanne Stunyo (USA) 125.89	Irene Macdonald (CAN) 121.40
1960 Ingrid Krämer (GER) 155.81	Paula J. Pope (USA) 141.24	Elizabeth Ferris (GBR) 139.09
1964 Ingrid Engel (GER) 145.00	Jeanne Collier (USA) 138.36	Mary Willard (USA) 138.18
1968 Sue Gossick (USA) 150.77	Tamara Pogozheva (URS) 145.30	Keala O'Sullivan (USA) 145.23
1972 Micki J. King (USA) 450.03	Ulrika Knape (SWE) 434.19	Marina Janicke (GDR) 430.92
1976 Jennifer Chandler (USA) 506.19	Christa Kohler (GDR) 469.41	Cynthia McIngvale (USA) 466.83

GOLD	SILVER	BRONZE
1980 Irina Kalinina (URS) 725.910	Martina Proeber (GDR) 698.895	Karin Guthke (GDR) 685.245
1984 Sylvie Bernier (CAN) 530.70	Kelly McCormick (USA) 527.46	Christina Seufert (USA) 422.07
1988 Gao Min (CHN) 580.23	Li Qing (CHN) 534.33	Kelly Anne McCormick (USA) 533.19

PLATFORM DIVING

GOLD	SILVER	BRONZE
1896–1908 Event not held		
1912 Greta Johansson (SWE) 39.9	Lisa Regnell (SWE) 36.0	Isabelle White (GBR) 34.0
1920 Stefani Fryland-Clausen (DEN) 34.6	Eileen Armstrong (GBR) 33.3	Eva Ollivier (SWE) 33.3
1924 Caroline Smith (USA) 10.5	Elizabeth Becker (USA) 11.0	Hjördis Töpel (SWE) 15.5
1928 Elizabeth Pinkston (USA) 31.6	Georgia Coleman (USA) 30.6	Lala Sjöqvist (SWE) 29.2
1932 Dorothy Poynton (USA) 40.26	Georgia Coleman (USA) 35.56	Marion Roper (USA) 35.22
1936 Dorothy Hill (USA) 33.93	Velma Dunn (USA) 33.63	Käthe Köhler (GER) 33.43
1948 Victoria Draves (USA) 68.87	Patricia Elsener (USA) 66.28	Birte Christoffersen (DEN) 66.04
1952 Patricia McCormick (USA) 79.37	Paula J. Myers (USA) 71.63	Juno Irwin (USA) 70.49
1956 Patricia McCormick (USA) 84.85	Juno Irwin (USA) 81.64	Paula J. Myers (USA) 81.58
1960 Ingrid Krämer (GER) 91.28	Paula J. Pope (USA) 88.94	Ninel Krutova (URS) 86.99
1964 Lesley Bush (USA) 99.80	Ingrid Engel (GER) 98.45	Galina Alekseyeva (URS) 97.60
1968 Milena Duchková (TCH) 109.59	Natalia Lobanova (URS) 105.14	Ann Peterson (USA) 101.11
1972 Ulrika Knape (SWE) 390.00	Milena Duchková (TCH) 370.92	Marina Janicke (GDR) 360.54
1976 Elena Vaytsekhovskaya (URS) 406.59	Ulrika Knape (SWE) 402.60	Deborah Wilson (USA) 401.07
1980 Martina Jaschke (GDR) 596.250	Servard Emirzyan (URS) 576.465	Liana Tsotadze (URS) 575.925
1984 Zhou Jihong (CHN) 435.51	Michele Mitchell (USA) 431.19	Wendy Wyland (USA) 422.07
1988 Xu Yanmei (CHN) 445.20	Michele Mitchell (USA) 436.95	Wendy Williams (USA) 400.44

The following married medalists also won medals under their maiden names:

Eleanor Saville, formerly Gerratti

Lenore Wingard, formerly Kight

Marie-Louise Linssen, formerly Vaessen

Irma Heijting, formerly Schuhmacher

Paula Pope, formerly Myers

Dorothy Hill, formerly Poynton

Elizabeth Pinkston, formerly Becker

Zoe Ann Jensen, formerly Olsen

Ingrid Engel, formerly Krämer

Water Polo

Water Polo tournaments were held in 1900 and 1904 but entries were Clubs rather than International teams.

	GOLD	SILVER	BRONZE
1908	**GREAT BRITAIN** Charles S. Smith George Nevinson George Cornet Thomas Thould George Wilkinson Paul Radmilovic Charles G. E. Forsyth	**BELGIUM** Albert Michant Herman Meyboom Victor Boin Joseph Pletincx Fernand Feyaerts Oscar Grégoire Herman Donners	**SWEDEN** Thorsten Kumfeldt Axel Runström Harald Julin Pontus Hansson Gunnar Wennerström Robert Andersson Erik Bergvall
1912	**GREAT BRITAIN** Charles S. Smith George Cornet Charles Bugbee Arthur Hill George Wilkinson Paul Radmilovic Isaac Bentham	**SWEDEN** Thorsten Kumfeldt Harald Julin Max Gumpel Pontus Andersson Wilhelm Andersson Robert Andersson Eric Bergqvist	**BELGIUM** Albert Durant Herman Donners Victor Boin Joseph Pletincx Oscar Grégoire Herman Meyboom Félicien Courbet Jean Hoffman Pierre Nijs
1920	**GREAT BRITAIN** Charles S. Smith Paul Radmilovic Charles Bugbee Noel M. Purcell Christopher Jones William Peacock William H. Dean	**BELGIUM** Gérard Blitz Maurice Blitz Albert Durant Joseph Pletincx Paul Gailly Pierre Nijs René Bauwens Pierre Dewin	**SWEDEN** Harald Julin Robert Andersson Wilhelm Andersson Eric Bergqvist Max Gumpel Pontus Hansson Erik Andersson Nils Backlund Theodor Nauman
1924	**FRANCE** Paul Dujardin Henri Padou Georges Rigal Albert Deborgies Nöel Delberghe Robert Desmettre Albert Mayraud	**BELGIUM** Gérard Blitz Maurice Blitz Albert Durant Joseph Pletincx Joseph Cludts Joseph de Combe Pierre Dewin Georges Fleurix Paul Gailly Jules Thiry Pierre Vermetten	**UNITED STATES** Arthur Austin Oliver Horn Frederick Lauer Clarence Mitchell John Norton Wallace O'Connor George Schroth Herbert Vollmer Johnny Weissmuller
1928	**GERMANY** Erich Rademacher Fritz Gunst Otto Cordes Emil Benecke Joachim Rademacher Karl Bähre Max Amann Johann Blank	**HUNGARY** István Barta Sándor Ivády Márton Hommonay Alajos Keserü Olivér Halasy József Vértesy Ferenc Keserü	**FRANCE** Paul Dujardin Henri Padou Jules Keignaert Emile Bulteel Achille Tribouillet Henri Cuvelier Ernest Rogez Albert van de Plancke Albert Thévenon

GOLD	SILVER	BRONZE
1932 HUNGARY	**GERMANY**	**UNITED STATES**
György Bródy	Erich Rademacher	Herbert Wildman
Sándor Ivády	Fritz Gunst	Wallace O'Connor
Márton Hommonay	Otto Cordes	Calvert Strong
Olivér Halasy	Emil Benecke	Philip Daubenspeck
József Vértesy	Joachim Rademacher	Harold McCallister
János Németh	Heiko Schwartz	Charles Finn
Ferenc Keserü	Hans Schulze	Austin Clapp
Alajos Keserü	Hans Eckstein	
István Barta		
Miklós Sárkány		
1936 HUNGARY	**GERMANY**	**BELGIUM**
György Bródy	Paul Klingenburg	Albert Castelens
Kálmán Hazai	Bernhard Baier	Gérard Blitz
Márton Hommonay	Gustav Schürger	Pierre Coppieters
Olivér Halasy	Fritz Gunst	Fernand Isselé
Jenö Brandi	Josef Hauser	Joseph de Combe
János Németh	Hans Schneider	Henry Stoelen
György Kutasi	Hans Schulze	Henry Disy
Mihály Bozsi	Alfred Kienzle	Henri de Pauw
István Molnár	Heinrich Krug	Edmond Michiels
Sándor Tarics	Helmuth Schwenn	
Miklós Sárkány	Fritz Stolze	
1948 ITALY	**HUNGARY**	**NETHERLANDS**
Pasquale Buonocore	László Jenei	Johannes J. Rohner
Emilio Bulgarelli	Miklós Holop	Cornelius Korevaar
Cesare Rubini	Dezsö Gyarmati	Cor Braasem
Geminio Ognio	Károly Szittya	Hans Stam
Ermenegildo Arena	Oszkár Csuvik	Alfred F. Ruimschotel
Aldo Ghira	István Szivós	Rudolph van Feggelen
Tulio Pandolfini	Dezsö Lemhényi	Frits Smol
Mario Majoni	Jenö Brandi	Hendrikus Z. Keetelaar
Gianfranco Pandolfini	Dezsö Fábián	Pieter J. Salomons
	Endre Györfi	
1952 HUNGARY	**YUGOSLAVIA**	**ITALY**
László Jenei	Zdravko Kovačić	Raffaello Gambino
György Vizvári	Veljiko Bakašun	Cesare Rubini
Dezsö Gyarmati	Ivo Stakula	Maurizio Mannelli
Kálmán Markovits	Ivo Kurtini	Geminio Ognio
Antal Bolvári	Boško Vuksanović	Ermenegildo Arena
István Szivós	Zdravko Ježić	Renato de Sanzuane
György Kárpáti	Lovro Radonić	Carlo Peretti
Róbert Antal	Vlado Ivković	Renato Traiola
Dezsö Fábián	Marko Brainović	Vincenzo Polito
Károly Szittya		Salvatore Gionta
Dezsö Lemhényi		
Miklós Martin		
István Hosznos		
1956 HUNGARY	**YUGOSLAVIA**	**U.S.S.R.**
Ottó Boros	Zdravko Kovačić	Boris Goikhman
Dezsö Gyarmati	Hrvoje Kačić	Vyacheslav Kurrenoy
Kálmán Markovits	Marijan Žužej	Yuriy Schlyapin
István Hevesi	Ivo Cipci	Valentin Prokopov
György Kárpáti	Tomislav Franjković	Boris Markarov
Mihály Mayer	Lovro Radonić	Petr Mchvenieradze
Antal Bolvári	Zdravko Ježić	Petr Breus
László Jenei	Vlado Ivković	Mikhail Ryzhak
Tivadar Kanisza		Viktor Ageyev
István Szivós		Nodar Gvakharia
Ervin Zádor		

GOLD	SILVER	BRONZE
1960 **ITALY**	**U.S.S.R.**	**HUNGARY**
Danio Bardi	Vladimir Semyenov	Ottó Boros
Giuseppe d'Altrui	Anatoliy Kartashyov	István Hevesi
Franco Lavoratori	Vladimír Novikov	Mihály Mayer
Gianni Lonzi	Petr Mchvenieradze	Kálmán Markovits
Rosario Parmegiani	Yuriy Grigorovskiy	Tivadar Kanizsa
Eraldo Pizzo	Viktor Ageyev	Zoltán Dömötör
Dante Rossi	Givi Chikvanaya	György Kárpáti
Amadeo Ambron	Leri Gogoladze	László Jenei
Salvatore Gionta	Vyacheslav Kurrenoy	Péter Rusorán II
Luigi Mannelli	Boris Goikhman	András Katona
Brunello Spinelli	Evgeniy Saltsyn	Dezső Gyarmati
Giancario Guerrini		László Felkai
		János Konrád
		András Bodnár
1964 **HUNGARY**	**YUGOSLAVIA**	**U.S.S.R.**
Miklós Ambrus	Milan Muškatirović	Igor Grabovsky
László Felkai	Ivo Trumbić	Vladimir Kuznetsov
János Konrád	Vinco Rosić	Boris Grishin
Zoltán Dömötör	Slatco Šimenč	Boris Popov
Tivadar Kanizsa	Božidor Stanišić	Nikolay Kalashnikov
Péter Rusorán II	Ante Nardeli	Zenon Bortevich
György Kárpáti	Zoran Janković	Nicolay Kuznetsov
Dezső Gyarmati	Frane Nonković	Vladimir Semyenov
Dénes Pócsik	Karlo Stipanić	Viktor Ageyev
Mihály Mayer	Mirko Sandič	Leonid Ossipov
András Bodnár	Ozren Bonačic	Eduard Yegorov
Ottó Boros		
1968 **YUGOSLAVIA**	**U.S.S.R.**	**HUNGARY**
Karlo Stipanić	Vadim Gulyaev	Endre Molnár
Ivo Trumbić	Givi Chikvanaya	Mihály Mayer
Ozren Bonačić	Boris Grishin	István Szivós
Uroš Marović	Alexandr Dolgushin	János Konrád II
Ronald Lopatny	Alexei Barkalov	László Sárosi
Zoran Janković	Yuriy Grigorovskiy	László Felkai
Miroslav Poljak	Vladimir Semyenov	Ferenc Konrád III
Dejan Dabović	Alexandr Shidlovski	Dénes Pócsik
Djordje Perišić	Vjacheslav Skok	András Bodnár
Mirko Sandič	Leonid Ossipov	Zoltán Dömötör
Zdravko Hebel	Oleg Bovin	János Steinmetz
1972 **U.S.S.R.**	**HUNGARY**	**UNITED STATES**
Vadim Gulyaev	Endre Molnár	James Slatton
Anatoli Akimov	András Bodnár	Stanley Cole
Alexandr Dreval	István Goergenyi	Russell Webb
Alexandr Dolgushin	Zoltàn Kasas	Barry Weitzenberger
Vladimir Shmudski	Tamás Fárágo	Gary Sheerer
Alexandr Kabanov	László Sárosi	Bruce Bradley
Alexei Barkalov	István Szivós	Peter Asch
Alexandr Shidlovski	István Magas	James Ferguson
Nikolai Melnikov	Dénes Pócsik	Steven Barnett
Leonid Ossipov	Ferenc Konrád	John Parker
Vyacheslav Sobchenko	Tibor Czervenyak	Eric Lindroth
1976 **HUNGARY**	**ITALY**	**HOLLAND**
Endre Molnár	Alberto Alberani	Evert Kroon
István Szivós	Roldano Simeoni	Nico Landeweerd
Tamás Fárágo	Silvio Baracchini	Jan Evert Veer
László Sárosi	Sante Marsili	Hans van Zeeland
Gyorgy Horkai	Marcello del Duca	Ton Buunk
Gábor Csapó	Gianni de Magistris	Piet de Zwarte
Attila Sudár	Alessandro Ghibellini	Hans Smit
Gyorgy Kenéz	Luigi Castagnola	Rik Toonen
Gyorgy Gerendás	Riccardo de Magistris	Gyze Stroboer
Ferenc Konrád	Vincenzo d'Angelo	Andy Hoepelman
Tibor Czervenyák	Umberto Panerai	Alex Boegschoten

	GOLD	SILVER	BRONZE
1980	**U.S.S.R.**	**YUGOSLAVIA**	**HUNGARY**
	Yevgeniy Sharanov	Luka Vezilic	Endre Molnár
	Sergey Kotenko	Zoran Gopcevic	István Szivós Jr
	Vladimir Akimov	Damir Polić	Attila Sudár
	Yevgeniy Grischin	Ratko Rudić	Gyorgy Gerendás
	Mait Riisman	Zoran Mustur	Gyorgy Horkai
	Aleksandr Kabanov	Zoran Roje	Gábor Csapó
	Aleksey Barkalov	Milivoj Bebic	István Kiss
	Erkin Shagayev	Slobodan Trifunovic	István Udvardi
	Georgy Mshvenieradze	Bosko Lozica	László Kuncz
	Mikhail Ivanov	Predrag Manojlović	Tamás Fáragó
	Vyacheslav Sobchenko	Milorad Krivokapic	Károly Hauszler
1984	**YUGOSLAVIA**	**UNITED STATES**	**WEST GERMANY**
	Milorad Krivokapic	Craig Wilson	Peter Rohle
	Deni Lusic	Kevin Robertson	Thomas Loebb
	Zoran Petrovic	Gary Figueroa	Frank Otto
	Bozo Vuletic	Peter Campbell	Rainer Hoppe
	Veselin Djuho	Douglas Burke	Armando Fernandez
	Zoran Roje	Joseph Vargas	Thomas Huber
	Milivoj Bebic	Jon Svendsen	Jurgen Schroeder
	Perica Bukic	John Siman	Rainer Osselmann
	Goran Sukno	Andrew McDonald	Hagen Stamm
	Tomislav Paskvalin	Terry Schroeder	Roland Freund
	Igor Milanovic	Jody Campbell	Dirk Theismann
	Dragan Andric	Timothy Shaw	Santiago Chalmovsky
	Andrija Popovic	Christopher Dorst	Werner Obschernikat
1988	**YUGOSLAVIA**	**UNITED STATES**	**U.S.S.R.**
	Aleksandar Sostar	Craig Wilson	Yevgeny Charonov
	Deni Lusic	Kevin Robertson	Nourlan Mendygalyev
	Dubravko Simenc	James Bergeson	Yevgeny Grichine
	Perica Bukic	Peter Campbell	Alexandr Kolotov
	Veselin Djuho	Douglas Kimbell	Sergey Naoumov
	Dragan Andric	Edward Klass	Viktor Berendyuga
	Mirko Vicevic	Alan Mouchawar	Sergey Kotenko
	Igor Gocanin	Jody Campbell	Dmitry Apanasenko
	Mislav Bezmalimovic	Jeff Campbell	Georgy Mchvenyeradze
	Tomislav Paskvalin	Greg Boyer	Mikhail Ivanov
	Igor Milanovic	Terry Schroeder	Sergey Markotch
	Goran Radjenovic	Chris Duplanty	Nikolai Smirnov
	Renco Posinkovic	Michael Evans	Mikhail Giorgadze

19. Table Tennis (Introduced in 1988)

MEN'S SINGLES

1988	Yoo Nam-Kyu (KOR)	Kim Ki-Taik (KOR)	Erik Lindh (SWE)

MEN'S DOUBLES

1988	**CHINA**	**YUGOSLAVIA**	**KOREA**
	Chen Longcan	Ilua Lupuleski	Ahn Jae-Hyung
	Wei Qingguang	Zoran Primorac	Yoo Nam-Kyu

WOMEN'S SINGLES

	GOLD	SILVER	BRONZE
1988	Chen Jing (CHN)	Li Huifen (CHN)	Jiao Zhimin (CHN)

WOMEN'S DOUBLES

1988	**KOREA** Hyun Jung-Hwa Yang Young-Ja	**CHINA** Chen Jing Jiao Zhimin	**YUGOSLAVIA** Jasna Fazlic Gordana Perkucin

---

20. Tennis

MEN'S SINGLES

			[1]
1896	John Boland (GBR)	Demis Kasdaglis (GRE)	(GBR)
1900	Hugh Doherty (GBR)	Harold Mahony (GBR)	Reginald Doherty (GBR) A.B. Norris (GBR)
1904	Beals Wright (USA)	Robert LeRoy (USA)	Alonzo Bell (USA) Edgar Leonard (USA)
1906	Max Decugis (FRA)	Maurice Germot (FRA)	Zdenek Zemla (BOH)
1908	Josiah Ritchie (GBR)	Otto Froitzheim (GER)	Wilberforce Eves (GBR)
1908[1]	Wentworth Gore (GBR)	George Caridia (GBR)	Josiah Ritchie (GBR)
1912	Charles Winslow (SAF)	Harold Kitson (SAF)	Oscar Kreuzer (GER)
1912[1]	Andre Gobert (FRA)	Charles Dixon (GBR)	Anthony Wilding (NZL)
1920	Louis Raymond (SAF)	Ichiya Kumagae (JPN)	Charles Winslow (GBR)
1924	Vincent Richards (USA)	Henri Cochet (FRA)	Umberto De Morpurgo (ITA)
1928–1984 Event not held			
1988	Miloslav Mecir (TCH)	Tim Mayotte (USA)	Stefan Edberg (SWE) Brad Gilbert (USA)

---

[1] Indoor tournaments.

Jean Borontra (France), one of the leading players of his time, won the bronze with Reno Lacoste as his partner, in the 1924 doubles, when his career was just beginning. He made his 35th appearance at Wimbledon in 1964, just 40 years later.

MEN'S DOUBLES

	GOLD	SILVER	BRONZE
1896	**GBR/GERMANY** John Boland Fritz Traun	**GREECE** Demis Kasdaglis Demetrios Petrokokkinos	—
1900	**GREAT BRITAIN** Reginald Doherty Hugh Doherty	**USA/FRANCE** Basil Spalding dc Garmendia Max Decugis	**FRANCE** A. Prevost G. de la Chapelle **GREAT BRITAIN** Harold Mahony A.B. Norris
1904	**USA** Edgar Leonard Beals Wright	**USA** Alonzo Bell Robert LeRoy	**USA** Joseph Wear Allen West **USA** Clarence Gamble Arthur Wear
1906	**FRANCE** Max Decugis Maurice Germot	**GREECE** Xenophon Kasdaglis Ioannis Ballis	**BOHEMIA** Zdenek Zemla Ladislav Zemla
1908	**GREAT BRITAIN** George Hillyard Reginald Doherty	**GREAT BRITAIN** Josiah Ritchie James Parke	**GREAT BRITAIN** Charles Cazalet Charles Dixon
1908[1]	**GREAT BRITAIN** Wentworth Gore Herbert Barrett	**GREAT BRITAIN** George Simond George Caridia	**SWEDEN** Gunnar Setterwall Wollmar Bostrom
1912	**SOUTH AFRICA** Charles Winslow Harold Kitson	**AUSTRIA** Felix Pipes Arthur Zborzil	**FRANCE** Albert Canet Marc Meny de Marangue
1912[1]	**FRANCE** Andre Gobert Maurice Germot	**SWEDEN** Gunnar Setterwall Carl Kempe	**GREAT BRITAIN** Charles Dixon Arthur Beamish

[1]Indoor tournaments.

GOLD	SILVER	BRONZE
1920 **GREAT BRITAIN** Noel Turnball Max Woosnam	**JAPAN** Ichiya Kumagae Seiichiro Kashio	**FRANCE** Max Decugis Pierre Albarran
1924 **UNITED STATES** Vincent Richards Frank Hunter	**FRANCE** Jacques Brugnon Henri Cochet	**FRANCE** Jean Borotra Rene Lacoste
1928–1984 Event not held		
1988 **UNITED STATES** Ken Flach Robert Seguso	**SPAIN** Emilio Sanchez Sergio Casal	**CZECHOSLOVAKIA** Miloslav Mecir Milan Sreiber **SWEDEN** Stefan Edberg Anders Jarryd

MIXED DOUBLES

GOLD	SILVER	BRONZE
1896 Event not held		
1900 **GREAT BRITAIN** Charlotte Cooper Reginald Doherty	**FRANCE/GBR** Helene Prevost Harold Mahony	**BOHEMIA/GBR** Hedwig Rosenbaum Archibald Walden **USA/GBR** Marion Jones Hugh Doherty
1904 Event not held		
1906 **FRANCE** Marie Decugis Max Decugis	**GREECE** Sophia Marinow Georgios Simiriotis	**GREECE** Aspasia Matsa Xenophon Kasdaglis
1908 Event not held		
1912 **GERMANY** Dora Koring Heinrich Schomburg	**SWEDEN** Sigrid Fick Gunnar Setterwall	**FRANCE** Marguerite Broquedis Albert Canet
1912[1] **GREAT BRITAIN** Edith Hannam Charles Dixon	**GREAT BRITAIN** Helen Aitchison Herbert Barrett	**SWEDEN** Sigrid Fick Gunnar Setterwall
1920 **FRANCE** Suzanne Lenglen Max Decugis	**GREAT BRITAIN** Kathleen McKane Max Woosnam	**CZECHOSLOVAKIA** Milada Skrbova Ladislav Zemla
1924 **UNITED STATES** Hazel Wightman Norris Williams	**UNITED STATES** Marion Jessup Vincent Richards	**NETHERLANDS** Cornelia Bouman Hendrik Timmer
1928–1988 Event not held		

[1]Indoor tournament.

WOMEN'S SINGLES

1896 Event not held		
1900 Charlotte Cooper (GBR)	Helene Prevost (FRA)	Marion Jones (USA)
1904 Event not held		
1906 Esmee Simiriotou (GRE)	Sophia Marinou (GRE)	Euphrosine Paspati (GRE)
1908 Dorothea Chambers (GBR)	Dorothy Boothby (GBR)	Joan Winch (GBR)
1908[1] Gwen Eastlake-Smith (GBR)	Angela Greene (GBR)	Martha Adlerstrahle (SWE)
1912 Marguerite Broquedis (FRA)	Dora Koring (GER)	Molla Bjurstedt (SWE)
1912[1] Ethel Hannam (GBR)	Thora Castenschiold (DEN)	Mabel Parton (GBR)
1920 Suzanne Lenglen (FRA)	Dorothy Holman (GBR)	Kathleen McKane (GBR)

[1]Indoor tournaments.

Charlotte Cooper (GBR) was the first female Olympic gold medalist, when she won the women's tennis singles in 1900. She went on to 5 Wimbledon titles after that.

GOLD	SILVER	BRONZE
1924 Helen Wills (USA)	Julie Vlasto (FRA)	Kathleen McKane (GBR)
1928–1984 Event not held		
1988 Steffi Graf (FRG)	Gabriela Sabatini (ARG)	Zina Garrison (USA) Manuela Maleyeva (BUL)

WOMEN'S DOUBLES

1896–1912 Event not held		
1920 GREAT BRITAIN Winifred McNair Kathleen McKane	GREAT BRITAIN Geraldine Beamish Dorothy Holman	FRANCE Suzanne Lenglen Elisabeth d'Ayen
1924 UNITED STATES Hazel Wightman Helen Wills	GREAT BRITAIN Edith Covell Kathleen McKane	GREAT BRITAIN Dorothy Shepherd-Barron Evelyn Colyer
1928–1984 Event not held		
1988 UNITED STATES Pam Shriver Zina Garrison	CZECHOSLOVAKIA Jana Novotna Helena Sukova	AUSTRALIA Elizabeth Smylie Wendy Turnbull WEST GERMANY Steffi Graf Claudia Kohde-Kilsch

21. Track and Field Athletics (Men)

100 METERS (109 yd 1 ft)

	GOLD	SILVER	BRONZE
1896	Thomas E. Burke (USA) 12.0	Fritz Hofmann (GER) d.n.a.	Alajos Szokolyi (HUN) d.n.a.
1900	Francis W. Jarvis (USA) 11.0	J. Walter B. Tewksbury (USA) 1 ft.	Stanley Rowley (AUS/NZL) inches
1904	Archie Hahn (USA) 11.0	Nathaniel J. Cartmell (USA) d.n.a.	William Hogenson (USA) d.n.a.
1906	Archie Hahn (USA) 11.2	Fay R. Moulton (USA) 11.3	Nigel Barker (AUS) 11.3
1908	Reginald E. Walker (SAF) 10.8*	James A. Rector (USA) 2 ft.	Robert Kerr (CAN) inches
1912	Ralph C. Craig (USA) 10.8	Alvah Meyer (USA) 10.9	Donald F. Lippincott (USA) 10.9
1920	Charles W. Paddock (USA) 10.8	Morris M. Kirksey (USA) 1 ft.	Harry F. V. Edward (GBR) d.n.a.
1924	Harold M. Abrahams (GBR) 10.6*	Jackson V. Scholz (USA) 2 ft.	Arthur E. Porritt (NZL) d.n.a.
1928	Percy Williams (CAN) 10.8	Jack E. London (GBR) 2 ft.	Georg Lammers (GER) inches
1932	Eddie Tolan (USA) 10.3*	Ralph H. Metcalfe (USA) 10.3*	Arthur Jonath (GER) 10.4
1936	Jesse Owens (USA) 10.3	Ralph H. Metcalfe (USA) 10.4	Martinus B. Osendarp (HOL) 10.5
1948	W. Harrison Dillard (USA) 10.3	H. Norwood Ewell (USA) 10.4	Lloyd B. LaBeach (PAN) 10.4
1952	Lindy J. Remigino (USA) 10.4	Herbert H. McKenley (JAM) 10.4	Emmanuel McDonald Bailey (GBR) 10.4
1956	Bobby-Joe Morrow (USA) 10.5	W. Thane Baker (USA) 10.5	Hector D. Hogan (AUS) 10.6
1960	Armin Hary (GER) 10.2*	David W. Sime (USA) 10.2*	Peter F. Radford (GBR) 10.3
1964	Robert L. Hayes (USA) 10.0*	Enrique Figuerola (CUB) 10.2	Harry W. Jerome (CAN) 10.2
1968	James R. Hines (USA) 9.9*	Lennox Miller (JAM) 10.0	Charles E. Greene (USA) 10.0
1972	Valeriy Borzov (URS) 10.14	Robert Taylor (USA) 10.24	Lennox Miller (JAM) 10.33
1976	Hasely Crawford (TRI) 10.06	Donald Quarrie (JAM) 10.08	Valeriy Borzov (URS) 10.14
1980	Allan Wells (GBR) 10.25	Silvio Leonard (CUB) 10.25	Petar Petrov (BUL) 10.39
1984	Carl Lewis (USA) 9.99	Sam Graddy (USA) 10.19	Ben Johnson (CAN) 10.22
1988	Carl Lewis[1] (USA) 9.92*	Linford Christie (GBR) 9.97	Calvin Smith (USA) 9.99

[1] Ben Johnson (Can) won in 9.79 but was subsequently disqualified.

The performances listed below were Olympic Records set additionally in preliminaries.

11.8	Burke	1896	10.6	Williams	1928	10.3	Ira J. Murchison	
10.8	Jarvis	1900	10.6	Robert			(USA)	1956
10.8	Tewksbury	1900		MacAllister		10.3	Morrow	1956
10.8	Rector	1908		(USA)	1928	10.2	Hary	1960
10.8	Walker	1908	10.6	London	1928	10.0	Greene	1968
10.8	Rector	1908	10.4	Tolan	1932	10.0	Hermes Ramirez	
10.6	Lippincott	1912	10.3	Owens	1936		(CUB)	1968
10.6	(twice)		10.3	Morrow	1956	10.0	Greene	1968
	Abrahams	1924				10.0	Hines	1968

Jim Hines (USA) won the 1968 Olympic 100 meters in the world record time of 9.9 seconds. High altitude helped sprinters because of reduced air resistance.

Jesse Owens (USA) captured public attention by winning 4 gold medals in the 1936 Games at Berlin. Owens was the top vote-getter in an election held to select 20 charter members of the U.S. Olympic Hall of Fame.

Carl Lewis (USA) won 4 gold medals in the 1984 Olympics, emulating the feat of his hero, Jesse Owens, the star of the 1936 Olympics in Berlin. Lewis won the 100 and 200 meters sprints, the long jump (28 ft 0¼ in) and was anchor man in the 4 × 100 meters relay.

Performances of 10.2 and 10.3 (final) by Owens in 1936 and 9.9 by Hayes in 1964 were wind assisted. The performance by Hines in 1968 was automatically timed at 9.95.

200 METERS (218 yd 2 ft)

	GOLD	SILVER	BRONZE
1896	Event not held		
1900	J. Walter B. Tewksbury (USA) 22.2*	Norman G. Pritchard (IND) 5 yd.	Stanley Rowley (AUS/NZL) 1 yd.
1904	Archie Hahn (USA) 21.6*[1]	Nathaniel J. Cartmell (USA) 2 yd.	William Hogenson (USA) d.n.a.
1906	Event not held		
1908	Robert Kerr (CAN) 22.6	Robert Cloughen (USA) 1 ft.	Nathaniel J. Cartmell (USA) 1 ft.
1912	Ralph C. Craig (USA) 21.7	Donald F. Lippincott (USA) 21.8	William R. Applegarth (GBR) 22.0
1920	Allen Woodring (USA) 22.0	Charles W. Paddock (USA) d.n.a.	Harry F. V. Edward (GBR) d.n.a.
1924	Jackson V. Scholz (USA) 21.6*	Charles W. Paddock (USA) ½ yd.	Eric H. Liddell (GBR) 1½ yd.
1928	Percy Williams (CAN) 21.8	Walter Rangeley (GBR) 2 ft.	Helmut Körnig[2] (GER) 1 ft.
1932	Eddie Tolan (USA) 21.2*	George Simpson (USA) 21.4	Ralph H. Metcalfe[3] (USA) 21.5
1936	Jesse Owens (USA) 20.7*	Mack M. Robinson (USA) 21.1	Martinus B. Osendarp (HOL) 21.3
1948	Melvin E. Patton (USA) 21.1	H. Norwood Ewell (USA) 21.1	Lloyd B. LaBeach (PAN) 21.2
1952	Andrew W. Stanfield (USA) 20.7*	W. Thane Baker (USA) 20.8	James Gathers (USA) 20.8

[1] Race run over straight course.
[2] Awarded bronze medal when Scholz refused to re-run after third place tie.
[3] Metcalfe's lane was later found to be 1½ meters too long.

	GOLD	SILVER	BRONZE
1956	Bobby-Joe Morrow (USA) 20.6*	Andrew W. Stanfield (USA) 20.7	W. Thane Baker (USA) 20.9
1960	Livio Berruti (ITA) 20.5*	Lester N. Carney (USA) 20.6	Abdoulaye Seye (FRA) 20.7
1964	Henry Carr (USA) 20.3*	O. Paul Drayton (USA) 20.5	Edwin Roberts (TRI) 20.6
1968	Tommie C. Smith (USA) 19.8*	Peter G. Norman (AUS) 20.0	John W. Carlos (USA) 20.0
1972	Valeriy Borzov (URS) 20.00	Larry J. Black (USA) 20.19	Pietro Mennea (ITA) 20.30
1976	Donald Quarrie (JAM) 20.23	Millard Hampton (USA) 20.29	Dwayne Evans (USA) 20.43
1980	Pietro Mennea (ITA) 20.19	Allan Wells (GBR) 20.21	Donald Quarrie (JAM) 20.29
1984	Carl Lewis (USA) 19.80*	Kirk Baptiste (USA) 19.96	Thomas Jefferson (USA) 20.26
1988	Joe DeLoach (USA) 19.75*	Carl Lewis (USA) 19.79	Robson da Silva (BRA) 20.04

The performances listed below were Olympic Records set additionally in preliminaries.

22.2	Hahn	1904	21.4	Arthur Jonath		20.3	Smith	1968
21.6	Körnig	1928		(GER)	1932	20.2	Norman	1968
21.5	Metcalfe	1932	21.1	(twice) Owens	1936	20.2	Smith	1968
21.5	Tolan	1932	21.1	Robinson	1936	20.1	Carlos	1968
21.4	Carlos B. Luti		20.5	Berutti	1960	20.1	Smith	1968
	(ARG)	1932	20.5	Drayton	1964			

400 METERS (437 yd 1 ft)

1896	Thomas E. Burke (USA) 54.2*	Herbert Jamison (USA) 15 yd.	Fritz Hofmann (GER) d.n.a.
1900	Maxwell W. Long (USA) 49.4*	William J. Holland (USA) 1 yd.	Ernst Schultz (DEN) 15 yd.
1904	Harry L. Hillman (USA) 49.2*	Frank Waller (USA) 5 yd.	Herman C. Groman (USA) 1 yd.
1906	Paul H. Pilgrim (USA) 53.2	Wyndham Halswell (GBR) 53.8	Nigel Barker (AUS) 54.1
1908	Wyndham Halswell (GBR) 50.0	No other competitors[1]	
1912	Charles D. Reidpath (USA) 48.2*	Hanns Braun (GER) 48.3	Edward F. Lindberg (USA) 48.4
1920	Bevil G. d'U. Rudd (SAF) 49.6	Guy M. Butler (GBR) d.n.a.	Nils Engdahl (SWE) d.n.a.
1924	Eric H. Liddell (GBR) 47.6*	Horatio M. Fitch (USA) 48.4	Guy M. Butler (GBR) 48.6
1928	Raymond J. Barbuti (USA) 47.8	James Ball (CAN) 48.0	Joachim Büchner (GER) 48.2
1932	William A. Carr (USA) 46.2*	Benjamin B. Eastman (USA) 46.4	Alexander Wilson (CAN) 47.4
1936	Archie F. Williams (USA) 46.5	A. Godfrey K. Brown (GBR) 46.7	James E. LuValle (USA) 46.8
1948	Arthur S. Wint (JAM) 46.2*	Herbert H. McKenley (JAM) 46.4	Malvin G. Whitfield (USA) 46.6
1952	V. George Rhoden (JAM) 45.9*	Herbert H. McKenley (JAM) 45.9*	Ollie A. Matson (USA) 46.8
1956	Charles L. Jenkins (USA) 46.7	Karl-Friedrich Haas (GER) 46.8	Voitto V. Hellsten (FIN) 47.0 Ardalion V. Ignatyev (URS) 47.0

---

[1]Re-run ordered after J. C. Carpenter (USA) disqualified in original final. Only Halswell showed up and "walked over" for the title.

	GOLD	SILVER	BRONZE
1960	Otis C. Davis (USA) 44.9*	Carl Kaufmann (GER) 44.9*	Malcolm C. Spence (SAF) 4.55
1964	Michael D. Larrabee (USA) 45.1	Wendell A. Mottley (TRI) 45.2	Andrzej Badenski (POL) 45.6
1968	Lee E. Evans[1] (USA) 43.8*	G. Lawrence James (USA) 43.9	Ronald J. Freeman (USA) 44.4
1972	Vincent E. Matthews (USA) 44.66	Wayne C. Collett (USA) 44.80	Julius Sang (KEN) 44.92
1976	Alberto Juantorena (CUB) 44.26	Fred Newhouse (USA) 44.40	Herman Frazier (USA) 44.95
1980	Viktor Markin (URS) 44.60	Richard Mitchell (AUS) 44.84	Frank Schaffer (GDR) 44.87
1984	Alonzo Babers (USA) 44.27	Gabriel Tiacoh (CIV) 44.54	Antonio McKay (USA) 44.71
1988	Steve Lewis (USA) 43.87	Harry Reynolds (USA) 43.93	Danny Everett (USA) 44.09

[1]Automatically timed at 43.86, the current record.

The performances listed below were Olympic Records set additionally in preliminaries.

50.4	Long	1900	47.8	Fitch	1924	45.5	Davis	1960
48.4	Halswell	1908	47.2	Carr	1932	44.8	Evans	1968
48.0	Josef Imbach (SUI)	1924						

800 METERS (874 yd 2 ft)

	GOLD	SILVER	BRONZE
1896	Edwin H. Flack (AUS/NZL) 2:11.0	Nándor Dáni (HUN) 2:11.8	Demitrios Golemis (GRE) 100 yd.
1900	Alfred E. Tysoe (GBR) 2:01.2	John F. Cregan (USA) 1 yd.	David C. Hall (USA) d.n.a.
1904	James D. Lightbody (USA) 1:56.0*	Howard V. Valentine (USA) 2 yd.	Emil W. Breitkreutz (USA) d.n.a.

Alberto Juantorena (CUB), known as "The Horse," defeated 2 USA runners for the gold medal at 400 meters in 1976. He also won the gold at 800 meters.

	GOLD	SILVER	BRONZE
1906	Paul H. Pilgrim (USA) 2:01.5	James D. Lightbody (USA) 2:01.6	Wyndham Halswell (GBR) 2:03.0
1908	Melvin W. Sheppard (USA) 1:52.8*	Emilio Lunghi (ITA) 1:54.2	Hanns Braun (GER) 1:55.4
1912	James E. Meredith (USA) 1:51.9*	Melvin W. Sheppard (USA) 1:52.0	Ira N. Davenport (USA) 1:52.0
1920	Albert G. Hill (GBR) 1:53.4	Earl W. Eby (USA) 1 yd.	Bevil G. d'U. Rudd (SAF) d.n.a.
1924	Douglas G. A. Lowe (GBR) 1:52.4	Paul Martin (SUI) 1:52.6	Schuyler C. Enck (USA) 1:53.0
1928	Douglas G. A. Lowe (GBR) 1:51.8*	Erik Byléhn (SWE) 1:52.8	Hermann Engelhardt (GER) 1:53.2
1932	Thomas Hampson (GBR) 1:49.7*	Alexander Wilson (CAN) 1:49.9	Philip A. Edwards (CAN) 1:51.5
1936	John Y. Woodruff (USA) 1:52.9	Mario Lanzi (ITA) 1:53.3	Philip A. Edwards (CAN) 1:53.6
1948	Malvin G. Whitfield (USA) 1:49.2*	Arthur S. Wint (JAM) 1:49.5	Marcel Hansenne (FRA) 1:49.8
1952	Malvin G. Whitfield (USA) 1:49.2*	Arthur S. Wint (JAM) 1:49.4	Heinz Ulzheimer (GER) 1:49.7
1956	Thomas W. Courtney (USA) 1:47.7*	Derek J. N. Johnson (GBR) 1:47.8	Audun Boysen (NOR) 1:48.1
1960	Peter G. Snell (NZL) 1:46.3*	Roger Moens (BEL) 1:46.5	George E. Kerr (BWI) 1:47.1
1964	Peter G. Snell (NZL) 1:45.1*	William Cothers (CAN) 1:45.6	Wilson Kiprugut (KEN) 1:45.9
1968	Ralph D. Doubell (AUS) 1:44.3*	Wilson Kiprugut (KEN) 1:44.5	Thomas F. Farrell (USA) 1:45.4
1972	David J. Wottle (USA) 1:45.9	Evgeni Arzhanov (URS) 1:45.9	Michael Boit (KEN) 1:46.0
1976	Alberto Juantorena (CUB) 1:43.5*	Ivo Van Damme (BEL) 1:43.9	Richard Wohlhuter (USA) 1:44.1
1980	Steven Ovett (GBR) 1:45.4	Sebastian Coe (GBR) 1:45.9	Nikolai Kirov (URS) 1:46.0
1984	Joaquim Cruz (BRA) 1:43.00*	Sebastian Coe (GBR) 1:43.64	Earl Jones (USA) 1:43.83
1988	Paul Ereng (KEN) 1:43.45	Joaquim Cruz (BRA) 1:43.90	Saïd Aouita (MAR) 1:44.06

The performances listed below were Olympic Records set additionally in the preliminaries.

2:10.0	Flack	1896	1:47.1	Kerr	1960	1:46.1 Kiprugut	1964
1:59.0	Hall	1900	1:46.1	Kerr	1964		

1,500 METERS (1,640 yd 1 ft)

1896	Edwin H. Flack (AUS/NZL) 4:33.2*	Arthur Blake (USA) d.n.a.	Albin Lermusiaux (FRA) d.n.a.
1900	Charles Bennett (GBR) 4:06.2*	Henri Deloge (FRA) 2 yd	John Bray (USA) d.n.a.
1904	James D. Lightbody (USA) 4:05.4*	W. Frank Verner (USA) d.n.a.	Lacey E. Hearn (USA) d.n.a.
1906	James D. Lightbody (USA) 4:12.0	John McGough (GBR/IRL) 4:12.6	Kristian Hellström (SWE) 4:13.4
1908	Melvin W. Sheppard (USA) 4:03.4*	Harold A. Wilson (GBR) 4:03.6	Norman F. Hallows[1] (GBR) 4:04.0
1912	Arnold N. S. Jackson[2] (GBR) 3:56.8*	Abel R. Kiviat (USA) 3:56.9	Norman S. Taber (USA) 3:56.9

[1] The Olympic record has only been set in those winning performances marked * with the exception of Hallows, who achieved 4:03.4 in the 1908 preliminaries.
[2] A. N. S. Jackson (1912) changed name to A. N. S. Strode-Jackson and P. J. Baker (1920) changed name to P. J. Noel-Baker.

LEFT: Lauri Lehtinen (FIN) (left) was rightly awarded the gold medal in 1932 for the 5,000 meters run, although both he and runner-up Ralph Hill were clocked at the same Olympic record time. RIGHT: Kip Keino (KEN) won the 1,500 meters by the remarkable margin of nearly 20 yards at Mexico City in 1968.

Lasse Viren of Finland (number 301) repeated his 1972 gold medal success at 5,000 meters in Montreal. Earlier that week he had won the gold medal at 10,000 meters for the second consecutive time.

GOLD	SILVER	BRONZE
1920	Albert G. Hill (GBR) 4:01.8	Philip J. Baker[2] (GBR) 4:02.4	M. Lawrence Shields (USA) d.n.a.
1924	Paavo J. Nurmi (FIN) 3:53.6*	Willy Schärer (SUI) 3:55.0	Henry B. Stallard (GBR) 3:55.6
1928	Harri E. Larva (FIN) 3:53.2*	Jules Ladoumègue (FRA) 3:53.8	Eino Purje (FIN) 3:56.4
1932	Luigi Beccali (ITA) 3:51.2*	John F. Cornes (GBR) 3:52.6	Philip A. Edwards (CAN) 3:52.8
1936	John E. Lovelock (NZL) 3:47.8*	Glenn Cunningham (USA) 3:48.4	Luigi Beccali (ITA) 3:49.2
1948	Henry Eriksson (SWE) 3:49.8	Lennart Strand (SWE) 3:50.4	Willem F. Slijkhuis (HOL) 3:50.4
1952	Josef Barthel (LUX) 3:45.1*	Robert E. McMillen (USA) 3:45.2	Werner Lueg (GER) 3:45.4
1956	Ron Delany (IRL) 3:41.2*	Klaus Richtzenhain (GER) 3:42.0	John M. Landy (AUS) 3:42.0
1960	Herbert J. Elliott (AUS) 3:35.6*	Michel Jazy (FRA) 3:38.4	István Rózsavölgyi (HUN) 3:39.2
1964	Peter G. Snell (NZL) 3:38.1	Josef Odložil (TCH) 3:39.6	John Davies (NZL) 3:39.6
1968	H. Kipchoge Keino (KEN) 3:34.9*	James R. Ryun (USA) 3:37.8	Bodo Tümmler (GER) 3:39.0
1972	Pekka Vasala (FIN) 3:36.3	H. Kipchoge Keino (KEN) 3:36.8	Rodney Dixon (NZL) 3:37.5
1976	John Walker (NZL) 3:39.2	Ivo Van Damme (BEL) 3:39.3	Paul Heinz Wellmann (GER) 3:39.3
1980	Sebastian Coe (GBR) 3:38.4	Jurgen Straub (GDR) 3:38.8	Steven Ovett (GBR) 3:39.0
1984	Sebastian Coe (GBR) 3:32.53*	Steve Cram (GBR) 3:33.40	Jose Abascal (ESP) 3:34.30
1988	Peter Rono (KEN) 3:35.96	Peter Elliott (GBR) 3:36.15	Jens-Peter Herold (GDR) 3:36.21

5,000 METERS (3 miles 188 yd)

	GOLD	SILVER	BRONZE
1896–1908	Event not held		
1912	Hannes Kolehmainen (FIN) 14:36.6*	Jean Bouin (FRA) 14:36.7	George W. Hutson (GBR) 15:07.6
1920	Joseph Guillemot (FRA) 14:55.6	Paavo J. Nurmi (FIN) 15:00.0	Erik Backman (SWE) 15:13.0
1924	Paavo J. Nurmi (FIN) 14:31.2*	Ville Ritola (FIN) 14:31.4	Edvin Wide (SWE) 15:01.8
1928	Ville Ritola (FIN) 14:38.0	Paavo J. Nurmi (FIN) 14:40.0	Edvin Wide (SWE) 14:41.2
1932	Lauri A. Lehtinen (FIN) 14:30.0*	Ralph Hill (USA) 14:30.0*	Lauri J. Virtanen (FIN) 14:44.0
1936	Gunnar Höckert (FIN) 14:22.2*	Lauri A. Lehtinen (FIN) 14:25.8	Henry Jonsson (SWE) 14:29.0
1948	Gaston E. G. Reiff (BEL) 14:17.6*	Emil Zátopek (TCH) 14:17.8	Willem F. Slijkhuis (HOL) 14:26.8
1952	Emil Zátopek (TCH) 14:06.6*	Allain Mimoun-o-Kacha (FRA) 14:07.4	Herbert Schade (GER) 14:08.6
1956	Vladimir P. Kuts (URS) 13:39.6*	D. A. Gordon Pirie (GBR) 13:50.6	G. Derek Ibbotson (GBR) 13:54.4
1960	Murray G. Halberg (NZL) 13:43.4	Hans Grodotzki (GER) 13:44.6	Kazimierz Zimny (POL) 13:44.8
1964	Robert K. Schul (USA) 13:48.8	Harald Norpoth (GER) 13:49.6	William Dellinger (USA) 13:49.8
1968	Mohamed Gammoudi (TUN) 14:05.0	H. Kipchoge Keino (KEN) 14:05.2	Naftali Temu (KEN) 14:06.4
1972	Lasse Viren (FIN) 13:26.4*	Mohamed Gammoudi (TUN) 13:27.4	Ian Stewart (GBR) 13:27.6
1976	Lasse Viren (FIN) 13:24.8	Dick Quax (NZL) 13:25.2	Klaus-Peter Hildenbrand (GER) 13:25.4
1980	Miruts Yifter (ETH) 13:21.0	Suleiman Nyambui (TAN) 13:21.6	Kaarlo Maaninka (FIN) 13:22.0

Juan Carlos Zabala of Argentina, winner of the 1932 marathon, being helped off the track exhausted. He was 2 months short of his 21st birthday, the youngest Olympic champion ever at track.

Saïd Aouita of Morocco won the 5,000 meters run in the 1984 Olympics and now currently holds world records in the 1,500 and 5,000 meters races.

	GOLD	SILVER	BRONZE
1984	Saïd Aouita (MAR) 13:05.59*	Markus Ryffel (SUI) 13:07.54	Antonio Leitao (POR) 13:09.20
1988	John Ngugi (KEN) 13:11.70	Dieter Baumann (FRG) 13:15.52	Hans-Jörg Kunze (GDR) 13:15.73

The Olympic record has only been set in those medal-winning performances marked
* with the exception of Emiel Puttemans (BEL), 13:31.8 in the 1972 preliminaries
and Brendan Foster (GBR), 13:20.3 in the 1976 preliminaries.

10,000 METERS (6 miles 376 yd)

	GOLD	SILVER	BRONZE
1896–1908	Event not held		
1912	Hannes Kolehmainen (FIN) 31:20.8*	Lewis Tewanima (USA) 32:06.6	Albin O. Stenroos (FIN) 32:21.8
1920	Paavo J. Nurmi (FIN) 31:45.8	Joseph Guillemot (FRA) 31:47.2	James Wilson (GBR) 31:50.8
1924	Ville Ritola (FIN) 30:23.2*	Edvin Wide (SWE) 30:55.2	Eero E. Berg (FIN) 31:43.0
1928	Paavo J. Nurmi (FIN) 30:18.8*	Ville Ritola (FIN) 30:19.4	Edvin Wide (SWE) 31:00.8
1932	Janusz Kusocinski (POL) 30:11.4*	Volmari Iso-Hollo (FIN) 30:12.6	Lauri J. Virtanen (FIN) 30:35.0
1936	Ilmari Salminen (FIN) 30:15.4	Arvo Askola (FIN) 30:15.6	Volmari Iso-Hollo (FIN) 30:20.2
1948	Emil Zátopek (TCH) 29:59.6*	Alain Mimoun-o-Kacha (FRA) 30:47.4	Bertil Albertsson (SWE) 30:53.6
1952	Emil Zátopek (TCH) 29:17.0*	Alain Mimoun-o-Kacha (FRA) 29:32.8	Aleksandr A. Anufriyev (URS) 29:48.2
1956	Vladimir P. Kuts (URS) 28:45.6*	József Kovács (HUN) 28:52.4	Allan Lawrence (AUS) 28:53.6
1960	Pyotr G. Bolotnikov (URS) 28:32.2*	Hans Grodotzki (GER) 28:37.0	W. David Power (AUS) 28:38.2
1964	William M. Mills (USA) 28:24.4*	Mohamed Gammoudi (TUN) 28:24.8	Ronald W. Clarke (AUS) 28:25.8
1968	Naftali Temu (KEN) 29:27.4	Mamo Wolde (ETH) 29:28.0	Mohamed Gammoudi (TUN) 29:34.2
1972	Lasse Viren (FIN) 27:38.4*	Emiel Puttemans (BEL) 27:39.6	Meruts Yifter (ETH) 27:41.0
1976	Lasse Viren (FIN) 27:40.4	Carlos Lopes (POR) 27:45.2	Brendan Foster (GBR) 27:54.9
1980	Miruts Yifter (ETH) 27:42.7	Kaarlo Maaninka (FIN) 27:44.3	Mohammed Kedir (ETH) 27:44.7
1984	Alberto Cova (ITA) 27:47.54	Mike McLeod (GBR) 28:06.22	Mike Musyoki (KEN) 28:06.46
1988	Brahim Boutayeb (MAR) 27:21.46*	Salvatore Antibo (ITA) 27:23.55	Kipkemboi Kimeli (KEN) 27:25.16

The Olympic record has only been set in those medal-winning performances marked
* with the exception of: 33:49.0 by Kolehmainen, and 32:30.8 by Len Richardson
(SAF) both in 1912; and 27:53.4 by Puttemans in 1972.

MARATHON (42,195 meters—26 miles 385 yd)

The length of a Marathon was standardized at the 1908 distance of 26 miles 385
yards (42 195 m) from 1924.

The distances run in other years were:

1896 & 1904	24 miles 1,503 yards *40 000 m*	1912	24 miles 1,723 yards *40 200 m*
1900	25 miles 28 yards *40 260 m*	1920	26 miles 991 yards *42 750 m*
1906	26 miles 18 yards *41 860 m*		

GOLD	SILVER	BRONZE
1896 Spyridon Louis (GRE) 2h 58:50.0	Charilaos Vasilakos (GRE) 3h 06:03.0	Gyula Kellner (HUN) 3h 09:35.0
1900 Michel Theato (FRA) 2h 59:45.0	Émile Champion (FRA) 3h 04:17.0	Ernst Fast (SWE) 3h 37:14.0
1904 Thomas J. Hicks (USA) 3h 28:35.0	Albert J. Coray (FRA) 3h 34:52.0	Arthur L. Newton (USA) 3h 47:33.0
1906 William J. Sherring (CAN) 2h 51:23.6	John Svanberg (SWE) 2h 58:20.8	William Frank (USA) 3h 00:46.8
1908 John J. Hayes[1] (USA) 2h 55:18.4*	Charles A. Hefferon (SAF) 2h 56:06.0	Joseph Foreshaw (USA) 2h 57:10.4
1912 Kenneth K. McArthur (SAF) 2h 36:54.8	Christian W. Gitsham (SAF) 2h 37:52.0	Gaston Strobino (USA) 2h 38:42.4
1920 Hannes Kolehmainen (FIN) 2h 32:35.8*	Jüri Lossman (EST) 2h 32:48.6	Valerio Arri (ITA) 2h 36:32.8
1924 Albin O. Stenroos (FIN) 2h 41:22.6	Romeo Bertini (ITA) 2h 47:19.6	Clarence H. DeMar (USA) 2h 48:14.0
1928 Mohamed El Ouafi (FRA) 2h 32:57.0	Miguel Plaza (CHI) 2h 33:23.0	Martti Marttelin (FIN) 2h 35:02.0
1932 Juan Carlos Zabala (ARG) 2h 31:36.0*	Samuel Ferris (GBR) 2h 31:55.0	Armas A. Toivonen (FIN) 2h 32:12.0
1936 Kitei Son (JPN) 2h 29:19.2*	Ernest Harper (GBR) 2h 31:23.2	Shoryu Nan (JPN) 2h 31:42.0
1948 Delfo Cabrera (ARG) 2h 34:51.6	Thomas Richards (GBR) 2h 35:07.6	Etienne Gailly (BEL) 2h 35:33.6
1952 Emil Zátopek (TCH) 2h 23:03.2*	Reinaldo B. Gorno (ARG) 2h 25:35.0	Gustaf N. Jansson (SWE) 2h 26:07.0
1956 Alain Mimoun-o-Kacha (FRA) 2h 25:00.0	Franjo Mihalič (YUG) 2h 26:32.0	Veikko Karvonen (FIN) 2h 27:47.0
1960 Abebe Bikila (ETH) 2h 15:16.2*	Rhadi Ben Abdesselem (MAR) 2h 15:41.6	A. Barry Magee (NZL) 2h 17:18.2
1964 Abebe Bikila (ETH) 2h 12:11.2*	Basil B. Heatley (GBR) 2h 16:19.2	Kokichi Tsuburaya (JPN) 2h 16:22.8
1968 Mamo Wolde (ETH) 2h 20:26.4	Kenji Kimihara (JPN) 2h 23:31.0	Michael Ryun (NZL) 2h 23:45.0
1972 Frank Shorter (USA) 2h 12:19.8	Karel Lismont (BEL) 2h 14:31.8	Mamo Wolde (ETH) 2h 15:08.4
1976 Waldemar Cierpinski (GDR) 2h 09:55.0*	Frank Shorter (USA) 2h 10:45.8	Karel Lismont (BEL) 2h 11:12.6
1980 Waldemar Cierpinski (GDR) 2h 11:03	Gerard Nijboer (HOL) 2h 11:20	Setymkul Dzhumanazarov (URS) 2h 11:35
1984 Carlos Lopes (POR) 2h 09:21*	John Treacy (IRL) 2h 09:56	Charles Spedding (GBR) 2h 09:58
1988 Gelindo Bordin (ITA) 2:10.32	Douglas Wakiihuri (KEN) 2:10.47	Ahmed Salah (DJI) 2:10.59

[1]Dorando Pietri (ITA) finished 1st but was disqualified for assistance by officials over the final few hundred yards.

4 × 100 METERS (109 yd 1 ft) RELAY

1896–1908 Event not held		
1912 **GREAT BRITAIN** 42.4	SWEDEN 42.6	
David H. Jacobs	Ivan Möller	
Harold M. Macintosh	Charles Luther	
Victor H. A. D'Arcy	Ture Persson	
William R. Applegarth	Knut Lindberg	
1920 **UNITED STATES** 42.2*	FRANCE 42.6	SWEDEN d.n.a.
Charles W. Paddock	René Tirard	Agne Holmström
Jackson V. Scholz	René Lorain	William Pettersson
Loren C. Murchison	René Mourlon	Sven Malm
Morris M. Kirksey	Emile Ali Khan	Nils Sandström

GOLD	SILVER	BRONZE
1924 **UNITED STATES** 41.0*	**GREAT BRITAIN** 41.2	**NETHERLANDS** 41.8
Francis Hussey	Harold M. Abrahams	Jakob Boot
Louis A. Clarke	Walter Rangeley	Henricus Broos
Loren C. Murchison	Lancelot C. Royle	Jan de Vries
J. Alfred Le Coney	William P. Nichol	Marinus van den Berge
1928 **UNITED STATES** 41.0*	**GERMANY** 41.2	**GREAT BRITAIN** 41.8
Frank C. Wykoff	Georg Lammers	Cyril W. Gill
James F. Quinn	Richard Corts	Eric R. Smouha
Charles E. Borah	Hubert Houben	Walter Rangeley
Henry A. Russell	Helmut Körnig	Jack E. London
1932 **UNITED STATES** 40.0*	**GERMANY** 40.9	**ITALY** 41.2
Robert A. Kiesel	Helmut Körnig	Giuseppe Castelli
Emmett Toppino	Walter Hendrix	Ruggero Maregatti
Hector M. Dyer	Erich Borchmeyer	Gabriele Salviati
Frank C. Wykoff	Arthur Jonath	Edgardo Toetti
1936 **UNITED STATES** 39.8*	**ITALY** 41.1	**GERMANY** 41.2
Jesse Owens	Orazio Mariani	Wilhelm Leichum
Ralph H. Metcalfe	Gianni Caldana	Erich Borchmeyer
Foy Draper	Elio Ragni	Erwin Gillmeister
Frank C. Wykoff	Tullio Gonnelli	Gerd Hornberger
1948 **UNITED STATES**[1] 40.6	**GREAT BRITAIN** 41.3	**ITALY** 41.5
H. Norwood Ewell	John Archer	Carlo Monti
Lorenzo C. Wright	John A. Gregory	Enrico Perucconi
W. Harrison Dillard	Alistair McCorquodale	Antonio Siddi
Melvin E. Patton	Kenneth J. Jones	Michele Tito
1952 **UNITED STATES** 40.1	**U.S.S.R.** 40.3	**HUNGARY** 40.5
F. Dean Smith	Boris Tokaryev	László Zarándi
W. Harrison Dillard	Levan Kalyayev	Géza Varasdi
Lindy J. Remigino	Levan Sanadze	György Csányi
Andrew W. Stanfield	Vladimir Sukharyev	Béla Goldoványi
1956 **UNITED STATES** 39.5	**U.S.S.R.** 39.8	**GERMANY** 40.3
Ira J. Murchison	Boris Tokaryev	Lothar Knörzer
Leamon King	Vladimir Sukharyev	Leonhard Pohl
W. Thane Baker	Leonid Bartenyev	Heinz Fütterer
Bobby-Joe Morrow	Yuriy Konovalov	Manfred Germar
1960 **GERMANY** 39.5*	**U.S.S.R.** 40.1	**GREAT BRITAIN** 40.2
Bernd Cullmann	Gusman Kosanov	Peter F. Radford
Armin Hary	Leonid Bartenyev	David H. Jones
Walter Mahlendorf	Yuriy Konovalov	David H. Segal
Martin Lauer	Edvin Ozolin	J. Neville Whitehead
1964 **UNITED STATES** 39.0*	**POLAND** 39.3	**FRANCE** 39.3
O. Paul Drayton	Andrzej Zielinski	Paul Genevay
Gerald A. Ashworth	Wieslaw Maniak	Bernard Laidebeur
Richard V. Stebbins	Marian Foik	Claude Piquemal
Robert L. Hayes	Marian Dudziak	Jocelyn Delecour
1968 **UNITED STATES** 38.2*	**CUBA** 38.3	**FRANCE** 38.4
Charles E. Greene	Hermes Ramirez	Gérard Fenouil
Melvin Pender	Juan Morales	Jocelyn Delecour
Ronnie Ray Smith	Pablo Montes	Claude Piquemal
James R. Hines	Enriques Figuerola	Roger Bambuck
1972 **UNITED STATES** 38.19*	**U.S.S.R.** 38.50	**WEST GERMANY** 38.79
Larry J. Black	Alexandr Korneliuk	Jobst Hirscht
Robert Taylor	Vladimir Lovetski	Karl-Heinz Klotz
Gerald Tinker	Yuri Silov	Gerhard Wucherer
Eddie J. Hart	Valeriy Borzov	Klaus Ehl

---

[1]USA was disqualified but later reinstated.

GOLD	SILVER	BRONZE
1976 **UNITED STATES** 38.33	**EAST GERMANY** 38.66	**U.S.S.R.** 38.78
Harvey Glance	Manfred Kokot	Alexandr Aksinin
John Jones	Jorg Pfeifer	Nikolai Kolesnikov
Millard Hampton	Klaus-Dieter Kurrat	Yuri Silov
Steven Riddick	Alexander Thieme	Valeriy Borzov
1980 **U.S.S.R.** 38.26	**POLAND** 38.33	**FRANCE** 38.53
Vladimir Muravyov	Krzysztof Zwolinski	Antoine Richard
Nikolai Sidorov	Zenon Licznerski	Pascal Barré
Aleksandr Aksinin	Leszek Dunecki	Patrick Barré
Andre Prokofiev	Marian Woronin	Hermann Panzo
1984 **UNITED STATES** 37.83*	**JAMAICA** 38.62	**CANADA** 38.70
Sam Graddy	Al Lawrence	Ben Johnson
Ron Brown	Greg Meghoo	Tony Sharpe
Calvin Smith	Don Quarrie	Desai Williams
Carl Lewis	Ray Stewart	Sterling Hinds
1988 **U.S.S.R.** 38.19	**GREAT BRITAIN** 38.28	**FRANCE** 38.40
Viktor Bryzgin	Elliot Bunney	Bruno Marie-Rose
Vladimir Krylov	John Regis	Daniel Sangouma
Vladimir Muravyev	Mike McFarlane	Gilles Queneherve
Vitaliy Savin	Linford Christie	Max Moriniere

The performances listed below were Olympic Records set additionally in preliminaries.

43.0	Great Britain	1912	42.0	Netherlands	1924	38.6	Jamaica 1968
42.5	Sweden	1912	41.2	United States	1924		(Errol Stewart,
42.3	Germany	1912	41.0	United States	1924		Michael Fray,
	(K. Halt,		40.6	United States	1932		Clifton Forbes,
	M. Hermann,		40.0	United States	1936		Lennox Miller)
	E. Kern,		39.5	Germany	1960	38.3	Jamaica 1968
	Richard Rau)		39.5	United States	1964		
42.0	Great Britain	1924	38.7	Cuba	1968		

4 × 400 METERS (437 yd 1 ft) RELAY

1896–1908 Event not held		
1912 **UNITED STATES** 3:16.6*	**FRANCE** 3:20.7	**GREAT BRITAIN** 3.23.2
Melvin W. Sheppard	Charles L. Lelong	George Nicol
Edward F. Lindberg	Robert Schurrer	Ernest J. Henley
James E. Meredith	Pierre Failliot	James T. Soutter
Charles D. Reidpath	Charles A. C. Poulenard	Cyril N. Seedhouse
1920 **GREAT BRITAIN** 3:22.2	**S. AFRICA** d.n.a.	**FRANCE** d.n.a.
Cecil R. Griffiths	Harry Davel	George André
Robert A. Lindsay	Clarence W. Oldfield	Gaston Féry
John C. Ainsworth-Davis	Jack K. Oosterlaak	Maurice Delvart
Guy M. Butler	Bevil G. d'U. Rudd	Jean Devaux
1924 **UNITED STATES** 3:16.0*	**SWEDEN** 3:17.0	**GREAT BRITAIN** 3:17.4
Con S. Cochrane	Artur Svensson	Edward J. Toms
Alan B. Helffrich	Erik Byléhn	George R. Renwick
James O. McDonald	Gustaf Wejnarth	Richard N. Ripley
William E. Stevenson	Nils Engdahl	Guy M. Butler
1928 **UNITED STATES** 3:14.2*	**GERMANY** 3:14.8	**CANADA** 3:15.4
George Baird	Otto Neumann	Alexander Wilson
Emerson Spencer	Richard Krebs	Philip A. Edwards
Frederick P. Alderman	Harry Storz	Stanley Glover
Raymond J. Barbuti	Hermann Engelhard	James Ball

GOLD	SILVER	BRONZE
1932 UNITED STATES 3:08.2*	GREAT BRITAIN 3:11.2	CANADA 3:12.8
Ivan Fuqua	Crew H. Stoneley	Raymond Lewis
Edgar A. Ablowich	Thomas Hampson	James Ball
Karl D. Warner	Lord Burghley	Philip A. Edwards
William A. Carr	Godfrey L. Rampling	Alexander Wilson
1936 GREAT BRITAIN 3:09.0	UNITED STATES 3:11.0	GERMANY 3:11.8
Frederick F. Wolff	Harold Cagle	Helmut Hamann
Godfrey L. Rampling	Robert C. Young	Friedrich von Stülpnagel
William Roberts	Edward T. O'Brien	Harry C. Voigt
A. Godfrey K. Brown	Alfred L. Fitch	Rudolf Harbig
1948 UNITED STATES 3:10.4	FRANCE 3:14.8	SWEDEN 3:16.3
Arthur H. Harnden	Jean Kerebel	Kurt Lundqvist
Clifford F. Bourland	Francis Schewetta	Lars-Enk Wolfbrandt
Roy B. Cochran	Robert C. Chef d'Hôtel	Folke Alnevik
Malvin G. Whitfield	Jacques J. Lunis	Rune Larsson
1952 JAMAICA 3:03.9*	UNITED STATES 3:04.0	GERMANY 3:06.6
Arthur S. Wint	Ollie A. Matson	Hans Geister
Leslie A. Laing	G. Eugene Cole	Günther Steines
Herbert H. McKenley	Charles H. Moore	Heinz Ulzheimer
V. George Rhoden	Malvin G. Whitfield	Karl-Friedrich Haas
1956 UNITED STATES 3:04.8	AUSTRALIA 3:06.2	GREAT BRITAIN 3:07.2
Lou Jones	Leslie S. Gregory	John E. Salisbury
Jesse W. Mashburn	David F. Lean	Michael K. V. Wheeler
Charles L. Jenkins	Graham Gipson	F. Peter Higgins
Thomas W. Courtney	Kevin V. Gosper	Derek J. N. Johnson
1960 UNITED STATES 3:02.2*	GERMANY 3:02.7	BRITISH W.I. 3:04.0
Jack L. Yerman	Hans-Joachim Reske	Malcolm Spence
Earl V. Young	Manfred Kinder	James Wedderburn
Glenn A. Davis	Johannes Kaiser	Keith A. St. H. Gardner
Otis C. Davis	Carl Kaufmann	George E. Kerr

Harry Hillman (USA) had the unique distinction of winning the 400 meters foot race and the 400 meters hurdles in the 1904 Olympics.

	GOLD	SILVER	BRONZE
1964	**UNITED STATES** 3:00.7*	**GREAT BRITAIN** 3:01.6	**TRINIDAD** 3:01.7
	Ollan C. Cassell	Timothy J. M. Graham	Edwin Skinner
	Michael D. Larrabee	Adrian P. Metcalfe	Kent Bernard
	Ulis C. Williams	John H. Cooper	Edwin Roberts
	Henry Carr	Robbie I. Brightwell	Wendell A. Mottley
1968	**UNITED STATES**[1] 2:56.1*	**KENYA** 2:59.6	**WEST GERMANY** 3:00.5
	Vincent E. Matthews	Daniel Rudisha	Helmar Müller
	Ronald J. Freeman	Munyoro L. Nyamau	Manfred Kinder
	G. Lawrence James	Naftali Bon	Gerhard Hennige
	Lee E. Evans	Charles Asati	Martin Jellinghaus
1972	**KENYA** 2:59.8	**GREAT BRITAIN** 3:00.5	**FRANCE** 3:00.7
	Charles Asati	Martin E. Reynolds	Gilles Bertould
	Hezakiah Nyamau	Alan P. Pascoe	Daniel Velasques
	Robert Ouko	David P. Hemery	Francis Kerbiriou
	Julius Sang	David A. Jenkins	Jacques Carette
1976	**UNITED STATES** 2:58.7	**POLAND** 3:01.4	**WEST GERMANY** 3:02.0
	Herman Frazier	Ryszard Podlas	Franz-Peter Hofmeiste
	Benjamin Brown	Jan Werner	Lothar Krieg
	Fred Newhouse	Zbigniew Jaremski	Harald Schmid
	Maxie Parks	Jerzy Pietrzyk	Bernd Herrmann
1980	**U.S.S.R.** 3:01.1	**EAST GERMANY** 3:01.3	**ITALY** 3:04.3
	Remigius Valyulis	Klaus Thiele	Stefano Malinverni
	Michail Linge	Andreas Knebel	Mauro Zuliani
	Nikolai Chernyetsky	Frank Schaffer	Roberto Tozzi
	Viktor Markin	Volker Beck	Pietro Mennea
1984	**UNITED STATES** 2:57.91	**GREAT BRITAIN** 2:59.13	**NIGERIA** 2:59.32
	Sunder Nix	Kriss Akabusi	Sunday Uti
	Ray Armstead	Gary Cook	Moses Ugbusie
	Alonzo Babers	Todd Bennett	Rotimi Peters
	Antonio McKay	Phil Brown	Innocent Egbunike
1988	**UNITED STATES** 2:56.16*	**JAMAICA** 3:00.30	**WEST GERMANY** 3:00.56
	Danny Everett	Howard Davis	Norbert Dobeleit
	Steve Lewis	Devon Morris	Edgar Itt
	Kevin Robinzine	Winthrop Graham	Jörg Vaihinger
	Harry Reynolds	Bert Cameron	Ralf Lubke

[1] Automatically timed at 2:56.16.

The Olympic record has only been set in those winning performances marked * with the exception of:

3:19.0	Great Britain	1912
3:11.8	United States	1932
3:00.7	United States	1968

110 METERS (120 yd 1 ft) HURDLES

1896	Thomas P. Curtis (USA) 17.6	Grantley T. Goulding (GBR) 17.7	—[1]
1900	Alvin C. Kraenzlein (USA) 15.4*	John McLean (USA) 1½ ft.	Fred G. Moloney (USA) d.n.a.
1904	Frederick W. Schule (USA) 16.0	Thaddeus Shideler (USA) 2 yd.	L. Ashburner (USA) d.n.a.
1906	R. G. Leavitt (USA) 16.2	A. H. Healey (GBR) 16.2	Vincent DeV. Duncker (SAF) d.n.a.
1908	Forrest C. Smithson (USA) 15.0*	John C. Garrels (USA) 5 yd.	Arthur B. Shaw (USA) d.n.a.
1912	Frederick W. Kelly (USA) 15.1	James I. Wendell (USA) 15.2	Martin W. Hawkins (USA) 15.3

	GOLD	SILVER	BRONZE
1920	Earl J. Thomson (CAN) 14.8*	Harold E. Barron (USA) 2½ yd.	Frederick S. Murray (USA) d.n.a.
1924	Daniel C. Kinsey (USA) 15.0	Sydney J. M. Atkinson (SAF) inches	Sten Pettersson (SWE) d.n.a.
1928	Sydney J. M. Atkinson (AF) 14.8	Stephen E. Anderson (USA) 14.8	John S. Collier (USA) 15.0
1932	George J. Saling (USA) 14.6	Percy M. Beard (USA) 14.7	Donald O. Finlay (GBR) 14.8
1936	Forrest G. Towns (USA) 14.2	Donald O. Finlay (GBR) 14.4	Frederick D. Pollard (USA) 14.4
1948	William F. Porter (USA) 13.9*	Clyde L. Scott (USA) 14.1	Craig K. Dixon (USA) 14.1
1952	W. Harrison Dillard (USA) 13.7*	Jack W. Davis (USA) 13.7*	Arthur Barnard (USA) 14.1
1956	Lee Q. Calhoun (USA) 13.5*	Jack W. Davis (USA) 13.5*	Joel W. Chankle (USA) 14.1
1960	Lee Q. Calhoun (USA) 13.8	Willie L. May (USA) 13.8	Hayes W. Jones (USA) 14.0
1964	Hayes W. Jones (USA) 13.6	H. Blaine Lindgren (USA) 13.7	Anatoly Mikhailov (URS) 13.7
1968	Willie Davenport (USA) 13.3*	Ervin Hall (USA) 13.4	Eddy Ottoz (ITA) 13.4
1972	Rodney Milburn (USA) 13.24*	Guy Drut (FRA) 13.34	Thomas L. Hill (USA) 13.48
1976	Guy Drut (FRA) 13.30	Alejandro Casanas (CUB) 13.33	Willie Davenport (USA) 13.38
1980	Thomas Munkelt (GDR) 13.39	Alejandro Casanas (CUB) 13.40	Aleksandr Puchkov (URS) 13.44
1984	Roger Kingdom (USA) 13.20*	Greg Foster (USA) 13.23	Arto Bryggare (FIN) 13.40
1988	Roger Kingdom (USA) 12.98*	Colin Jackson (GBR) 13.28	Tonie Campbell (USA) 13.38

[1]Only two finalists.

Willie Davenport, the 1968 hurdles champion, shows his strong form in Mexico City.

The performances listed below were Olympic records set additionally in preliminaries.

15.6	Kraenzlein	1900	14.8	Leighton Dye		14.1	Towns	1936
15.4	Smithson	1908		(USA)	1928	14.1	Porter	1948
15.0	Barron	1920	14.8	Anderson	1928	13.9	Dillard	1952
15.0	Thomson	1920	14.6	Weightman-Smith		13.5	Ottoz	1968
14.8	George C.				1928	13.3	Hall	1968
	Weightman-Smith		14.5	Jack Keller		13.24	Foster	1984
	(SAF)	1928		(USA)	1932	13.24	Kingdom	1984
			14.4	Saling	1932	13.17	Kingdom	1988

400 METERS (437 yd 1 ft) HURDLES

	GOLD	SILVER	BRONZE
1896	Event not held		
1900	J. Walter B. Tewksbury (USA) 57.6*	Henri Tauzin (FRA) d.n.a.	George W. Orton (CAN) d.n.a.
1904[1]	Harry L. Hillman (USA) 53.0	Frank Waller (USA) 2 yd.	George Poage (USA) d.n.a.
1906	Event not held		
1908	Charles J. Bacon (USA) 55.0*	Harry L. Hillmann (USA) 1½ yd.	Leonard F. Tremeer (GBR) d.n.a.
1912	Event not held		
1920	Frank F. Loomis (USA) 54.0*	John K. Norton (USA) d.n.a.	August G. Desch (USA) d.n.a.
1924	F. Morgan Taylor (USA) 52.6[2]	Erik Vilén (FIN) 53.8*	Ivan H. Riley (USA) 54.2
1928	Lord Burghley (GBR) 53.4*	Frank J. Cuhel (USA) 53.6	F. Morgan Taylor (USA) 53.6
1932	Robert M. N. Tisdall (IRL) 51.7[2]	Glenn F. Hardin (USA) 51.9*	F. Morgan Taylor (USA) 52.0
1936	Glenn F. Hardin (USA) 52.4	John W. Loaring (CAN) 52.7	Miguel S. White (PHI) 52.8
1948	Roy B. Cochran (USA) 51.1*	Duncan White (CEY) 51.8	Rune Larsson (SWE) 52.2
1952	Charles H. Moore (USA) 50.8*	Yuriy N. Lituyev (URS) 51.3	John McF. Holland (NZL) 52.2
1956	Glenn A. Davis (USA) 50.1*	S. Eddie Southern (USA) 50.8	Joshua Culbreath (USA) 51.6
1960	Glenn A. Davis (USA) 49.3*	Clifton E. Cushman (USA) 49.6	Richard W. Howard (USA) 49.7
1964	Warren Cawley (USA) 49.6	John H. Cooper (GBR) 50.1	Salvadore Morale (ITA) 50.1
1968	David P. Hemery (GBR) 48.1*	Gerhard Hennige (GER) 49.0	John Sherwood (GBR) 49.0
1972	John Akii-bua (UGA) 47.82*	Ralph V. Mann (USA) 48.51	David P. Hemery (GBR) 48.52
1976	Edwin Moses (USA) 47.64*	Michael Shine (USA) 48.69	Evgeniy Gavrilenko (URS) 49.45
1980	Volker Beck (GDR) 48.70	Vasily Arkhipenko (URS) 48.86	Gary Oakes (GBR) 49.11
1984	Edwin Moses (USA) 47.75	Danny Harris (USA) 48.13	Harald Schmid (FRG) 48.19
1988	Andre Phillips (USA) 47.19*	Amadou Dia Ba (SEN) 47.23	Edwin Moses (USA) 47.56

[1]Hurdles only 2 ft 6 in *75,9 cm* high instead of more usual 3 ft 0 in *91,1 cm*.
[2]Record not allowed because a hurdle was knocked down.

The performances listed below were Olympic records set additionally in preliminaries.

57.0	Bacon	1908	52.8	Tisdall	1932	50.1	Southern	1956
56.4	Hillman	1908	51.9	Larsson	1948	49.0	Ronald Whitney	
53.4	Taylor	1928	51.9	Cochran	1948		(USA)	1968
52.8	Hardin	1932	50.8	Moore	1952			

Andre Phillips (USA, left) won the 400 meters hurdles at the 1988 Games in an Olympic record time of 47.19 sec, ahead of Amadou Dia Ba (SEN) and the reigning champion Ed Moses (USA).

3,000 METERS (1 mile 1,520 yd 1 ft) STEEPLECHASE

Steeplechases were held in 1900 (two races), 1904 and 1908 but none were over obstacles or at distances comparable with the existing event. No steeplechase event was held in 1896, 1906 or 1912.

	GOLD	SILVER	BRONZE
1920	Percy Hodge (GBR) 10:00.4*	Patrick J. Flynn (USA) 100 yd.	Ernesto Ambrosini (ITA) 40 yd.
1924	Ville Ritola (FIN) 9:33.6*	Elias Katz (FIN) 9:44.0	Paul Bontemps (FRA) 9:45.2
1928	Toivo A. Loukola (FIN) 9:21.8*	Paavo J. Nurmi (FIN) 9:31.2	Ove Andersen (FIN) 9:35.6
1932[1]	Volmari Iso-Hollo (FIN) 10:33.4	Thomas Evenson (GBR) 10:46.0	Joseph P. McCluskey (USA) 10:46.2
1936	Volmari Iso-Hollo (FIN) 9:03.8*	Kaarlo Tuominen (FIN) 9:06.8	Alfred Dompert (GER) 9:07.2
1948	Tore Sjöstrand (SWE) 9:04.6	Erik Elmsäter (SWE) 9:08.2	Göte Hagström (SWE) 9:11.8
1952	Horace Ashenfelter (USA) 8:45.4*	Vladimir V. Kazantsev (URS) 8:51.6	John I. Disley (GBR) 8:51.8
1956	Christopher W. Brasher (GBR) 8:41.2*	Sándor Rozsnyói (HUN) 8:43.6	Ernst Larsen (NOR) 8:44.0
1960	Zdzislaw Krzyszkowiak (POL) 8:34.2*	Nikolay Sokolov (URS) 8:36.4	Semyon Rzhishchin (URS) 8:42.2
1964	Gaston Roelants (BEL) 8:30.8*	Maurice Herriott (GBR) 8:32.4	Ivan Belyayev (URS) 8:33.8
1968	Amos Biwott (KEN) 8:51.0	Benjamin Kogo (KEN) 8:51.6	George Young (USA) 8:51.8
1972	H. Kipchoge Keino (KEN) 8:23.6*	Benjamin W. Jipcho (KEN) 8:24.6	Tapio Kantanen (FIN) 8:24.8
1976	Anders Garderud (SWE) 8:08.0*	Bronislaw Malinowski (POL) 8:09.1	Frank Baumgartl (GDR) 8:10.4
1980	Bronislaw Malinowski (POL) 8:09.7	Filbert Bayi (TAN) 8:12.5	Eshetu Tura (ETH) 8:13.6
1984	Julius Korir (KEN) 8:11.80	Joseph Mahmoud (FRA) 8:13.31	Brian Diemer (USA) 8:14.06
1988	Julius Kariuki (KEN) 8:05.51*	Peter Koech (KEN) 8:06.79	Mark Rowland (GBR) 8:07.96

[1]Distance in final was 3,460 meters due to error on part of lap-scoring official.

The performances listed below were Olympic records set additionally in preliminaries.

10:17.4	Hodge	1920	8:51.0	Ashenfelter		8:24.8	Kantanen	1972
9:43.8	Katz	1924			1952	8:23.8	Biwott	1972
9:18.8	Evenson	1932	8:33.0	Herriott	1964	8:18.6	Bronislaw	
9:14.6	Iso-Hollo	1932	8:31.8	Adolfas			Malinowski	
8:58.0	Kazantsev			Aleksiejunas				1976
		1952		(URS)	1964			

20,000 METERS (12 miles 752 yd) ROAD WALK

	GOLD	SILVER	BRONZE
1896–1952	Event not held		
1956	Leonid Spirin (URS) 1h 31:27.4*	Antonas Mikenas (URS) 1h 32:03.0	Bruno Junk (URS) 1 h 32.12.0
1960	Vladimir Golubnichiy (URS) 1 h 34:07.2	Noel F. Freeman (AUS) 1h 34:16.4	Stanley F. Vickers (GBR) 1h 34:56.4
1964	Kenneth J. Matthews (GBR) 1h 29:34.0*	Dieter Lindner (GER) 1h 31:13.2	Vladimir Golubnichiy (URS) 1h 31:59.4
1968	Vladimir Golubnichiy (URS) 1h 33:58.4	José Pedraza (MEX) 1h 34:0.0	Nickolay Smaga (URS) 1h 34:03.4
1972	Peter Frenkel (GDR) 1h 26:42.4*	Vladimir Golubnichiy (URS) 1h 26:55.2	Hans Reimann (GDR) 1h 27:16.6
1976	Daniel Bautista (MEX) 1h 24:40.6*	Hans Reimann (GDR) 1h 25:13.8	Peter Frenkel (GDR) 1h 25:29.4
1980	Maurizio Damilano (ITA) 1h 23:35.5*	Pyotr Pochinchuk (URS) 1h 24:45.4	Roland Wieser (GDR) 1h 25:58.2
1984	Ernesto Canto (MEX) 1h 23:13*	Raul Gonzalez (MEX) 1h 23:20	Maurizio Damilano (ITA) 1h 23:26
1988	Jozef Pribilinec (TCH) 1:19.57*	Ronald Weigel (GDR) 1:20.00	Maurizio Damilano (ITA) 1:20.14

50,000 METERS (31 miles 120 yd) ROAD WALK

1896–1928	Event not held		
1932	Thomas Green (GBR) 4h 50:10.0*	Janis Dalinsh (LAT) 4h 47:20.0	Ugo Frigerio (ITA) 4h 59:06.0
1936	Harold Whitlock (GBR) 4h 30:41.1*	Arthur Schwab (SUI) 4h 32:09.2	Adalberts Bubenko (LAT) 4h 32:42.2
1948	John Ljunggren (SWE) 4h 41:52.0	Gaston Godel (SUI) 4h 48:17.0	Tebbs Lloyd Johnson (GBR) 4h 48:31.0
1952	Guiseppe Dordoni (ITA) 4h 28:07.8*	Josef Dolezal (TCH) 4h 30:17.8	Antal Roka (HUN) 4h 31:27.2
1956	Norman Read (NZL) 4h 30:42.8	Yevgeniy Maskinskov (URS) 4h 32:57.0	John Ljunggren (SWE) 4h 35:02.0
1960	Don Thompson (GBR) 4h 25:30.0*	John Ljunggren (SWE) 4h 25:47.0	Abdon Pamich (ITA) 4h 27:55.4
1964	Abdon Pamich (ITA) 4h 11:12.4*	Paul Nihill (GBR) 4h 11:31.2	Ingvar Pettersson (SWE) 4h 14:17.4
1968	Christoph Höhne (GDR) 4h 20:13.6	Antal Kiss (HUN) 4h 30:17.0	Larry Young (USA) 4h 31:55.4
1972	Bernd Kannenberg (GER) 3h 56:11.6*	Veniamin Soldatenko (URS) 3h 58:24.0	Larry Young (USA) 4h 00:46.0
1976	Event not held		
1980	Hartwig Gauder (GDR) 3h 49:24.0*	Jorge Liopart (ESP) 3h 51:25.0	Yevgeny Ivchenko (URS) 3h 56:32.0
1984	Raul Gonzalez (MEX) 3h 47:26*	Bo Gustafsson (SWE) 3h 53:19	Sandro Bellucci (ITA) 3h 53:45
1988	Vyacheslav Ivanenko (URS) 3:38.29*	Ronald Weigel (GDR) 3:38.56	Hartwig Gauder (GDR) 3:39.45

HIGH JUMP

	GOLD	SILVER	BRONZE
1896	Ellery H. Clark (USA) 5′11″ *1,81 m**	[1]	[1]
1900	Irving K. Baxter (USA) 6′2¾″ *1,90 m**	Patrick J. Leahy (GBR) 5′ 10″ *1,78 m*	Lajos Gönczy (HUN) 5′ 8¾″ *1,75 m*
1904	Samuel S. Jones (USA) 5′ 11″ *1,80 m*	Garrett P. Serviss (USA) 5′ 10″ *1,77 m*	Paul Weinstein (GER) 5′ 10″ *1,77 m* [2]
1906	Con Leahy (GBR/IRL) 5′ 9¾″ *1,77 m*	Lajos Gönczy (HUN) 5′8¾″ *1,75 m*	
1908	Harry F. Porter (USA) 6′ 3″ *1,905 m**	[3]	[3]
1912	Alma W. Richards (USA) 6′ 4″ *1,93 m**	Hans Liesche (GER) 6′ 3¼″ *1,91 m*	George L. Horine (USA) 6′ 2½″ *1,89 m*
1920	Richmond W. Landon (USA) 6′ 4¼″ *1,94 m**	Harold P. Muller (USA) 6′ 2¾″ *1,90 m*	Bo Ekelund (SWE) 6′ 2¾″ *1,90 m*
1924	Harold M. Osborn (USA) 6′ 6″ *1,98 m*	Leroy T. Brown (USA) 6′ 4¾″ *1,95 m*	Pierre Lewden (FRA) 6′ 3¼″ *1,92 m*
1928	Robert W. King (USA) 6′ 4¼″ *1,94 m*	Ben Van D. Hedges (USA) 6′ 3¼″ *1,91 m*	Claude Ménard (FRA) 6′ 3¼″ *1,91 m*
1932	Duncan McNaughton (CAN) 6′ 5½″ *1,97 m*	Robert L. Van Osdel (USA) 6′ 5½″ *1,97 m*	Simeon G. Toribio (PHI) 6′ 5½″ *1,97 m*

[1]Tie for second place between James B. Connolly (USA) and Robert S. Garrett (USA) at 5′ 4¾″ *1,65 m.*
[2]Tie for third place between Herbert Kerrigan (USA) and Themistoklis Diakidis (GRE) at 5′ 7½″ *1,72 m.*
[3]Con Leahy (GBR/IRL), István Somodi (HUN) and Geo André (FRA) tied for second place at 6′ 2″ *1,88 m.*

Dick Fosbury (USA), whose back flop style in winning the high jump in 1968 at 7 feet 4¼ inches caught the imagination of the stadium and television viewers all over the world.

	GOLD	SILVER	BRONZE
1936	Cornelius C. Johnson (USA) 6′ 7¾″ *2,03 m**	David D. Albritton (USA) 6′ 6¾″ *2,00 m*	Delos P. Thurber (USA) 6′ 6¾″ *2,00 m*
1948	John A. Winter (AUS) 6′ 6″ *1,98 m*	Björn Paulsen (NOR) 6′ 4¾″ *1,95 m*	George A. Stanich (USA) 6′ 4¾″ *1,95 m*
1952	Walter F. Davis (USA) 6′ 8¼″ *2,04 m**	Kenneth G. Wiesner (USA) 6′ 7″ *2,01 m*	Jose Telles da Conceicao (BRA) 6′ 6″ *1,98 m*
1956	Charles E. Dumas (USA) 6′ 11½″ *2,12 m**	Charles Porter (AUS) 6′ 10½″ *2,10 m*	Igor Kashkarov (URS) 6′ 9¾″ *2,08 m*
1960	Robert Shavlakadze (URS) 7′ 1″ *2,16 m**	Valeriy N. Brumel (URS) 7′ 1″ *2,16 m**	John C. Thomas (USA) 7′ 0¼″ *2,14 m*
1964	Valeriy N. Brumel (URS) 7′ 1¾″ *2,18 m**	John C. Thomas (USA) 7′ 1¾″ *2,18 m**	John Rambo (USA) 7′ 1″ *2,16 m*
1968	Richard Fosbury (USA) 7′ 4¼″ *2,24 m**	Edward J. Caruthers (USA) 7′ 3½″ *2,22 m*	Valentin Gavrilov (URS) 7′ 2½″ *2,20 m*
1972	Yuri Tarmak (URS) 7′ 3¾″ *2,23 m*	Stefan Junge (GDR) 7′ 3″ *2,21 m*	Dwight E. Stones (USA) 7′ 3″ *2,21 m*
1976	Jacek Wszola (POL) 7′ 4½″ *2,25 m**	Greg Joy (CAN) 7′ 3¾″ *2,23 m*	Dwight E. Stones (USA) 7′ 3″ *2,21 m*
1980	Gerd Wessig (GDR) 7′ 8¾″ *2,36 m**	Jacek Wszola (POL) 7′ 7″ *2,31 m*	Jorg Freimuth (GDR) 7′ 7″ *2,31 m*
1984	Dietmar Mogenburg (FRG) 7′ 8½″ *2.35m*	Patrik Sjöberg (SWE) 7′ 7¾″ *2.33m*	Zhu Jianbua (CHN) 7′ 7″ *2.31m*
1988	Gennady Avdeyenko (URS) 7′9¾″ *2,38 m**	Hollis Conway (USA) 7′8¾″ *2,36 m*	Rudolf Povarnitsin (URS) 7′8¾″ *2,36 m* Patrik Sjöberg (SWE) 7′8¾″ *2,36 m*

POLE VAULT

1896	William W. Hoyt (USA) 10′ 9¾″ *3,30 m**	Albert C. Tyler (USA) 10′ 7¾″ *3,25 m*	Evangelos Damaskos (GRE) 9′ 4″ *2,85 m*
1900	Irving K. Baxter (USA) 10′ 9¾″ *3,30 m**	M. B. Colkett (USA) 10′ 7¾″ *3,25 m*	Carl-Albert Andersen (NOR) 10′ 5¾″ *3,20 m*
1904	Charles E. Dvorak (USA) 11′ 6″ *3,50 m**	Leroy Samse (USA) 11′ 3″ *3,43 m*	L. Wilkins (USA) 11′ 3″ *3,43 m*
1906	Fernand Gonder (FRA) 11′ 1¾″ *3,40 m*	Bruno Söderström (SWE) 11′ 1¾″ *3,40 m*	Ernest C. Glover (USA) 10′ 11¾″ *3,35 m*
1908	Edward T. Cooke (USA) 12′ 2″ *3,70 m**	Alfred C. Gilbert[1] (USA) 12′ 2″ *3,70 m**	[2]
1912	Harry S. Babcock (USA) 12′ 11½″ *3,95 m**	[3]	
1920	Frank K. Foss (USA) 13′ 5″ *4,09 m**	Henry Petersen (DEN) 12′ 1½″ *3,70 m*	Edwin E. Meyers (USA) 11′ 9½″ *3,60 m*
1924	Lee S. Barnes (USA) 12′ 11½″ *3,95 m*	Glenn Graham (USA) 12′ 11½″ *3,95 m*	James K. Brooker (USA) 12′ 9½″ *3,90 m*
1928	Sabin W. Carr (USA) 13′ 9¼″ *4,20 m**	William Droegemuller (USA) 13′ 5¼″ *4,10 m*	Charles E. McGinnis (USA) 12′ 11½″ *3,95 m*
1932	William W. Miller (USA) 14′ 1¾″ *4,31 m**	Shuhei Nishida (JPN) 14′0″ *4,26 m*	George G. Jefferson (USA) 13′ 9″ *4,19 m*
1936	Earle Meadows (USA) 14′ 3¼″ *4,35 m**	Shuhei Nishida (JPN) 13′ 11¼″ *4,25 m*	Sueo Oe (JPN) 13′ 11¼″ *4,25 m*
1948	O. Guinn Smith (USA) 14′ 1¼″ *4,30 m*	Erkki O. Kataja (FIN) 13′ 9¼″ *4,20 m*	Robert E. Richards (USA) 13′ 9¼″ *4,20 m*
1952	Robert E. Richards (USA) 14′ 11″ *4,55 m**	Donald D. R. Laz (USA) 14′ 9″ *4,50 m*	Ragnar T. Lundberg (SWE) 14′ 5″ *4,40 m*
1956	Robert E. Richards (USA) 14′ 11½″ *4,56 m**	Robert A. Gutowski (USA) 14′ 10¼″ *4,53 m*	Georgios Roubanis (GRE) 14′ 9″ *4,50 m*
1960	Donald G. Bragg (USA) 15′ 5″ *4,70 m**	Ronald H. Morris (USA) 15′ 1″ *4,60 m*	Eeles Landström (FIN) 14′ 11″ *4,55 m*

---

[1]Tied for gold medal.
[2]Tie for bronze medal between Edward B. Archibald (CAN), Charles S. Jacobs (USA) and Bruno Söderström (SWE) at 11′ 9″ *3,58 m*.
[3]Tie for silver medal between Frank T. Nelson (USA) and Marcus S. Wright (USA) at 12′ 7½″ *3,85 m*.

GOLD	SILVER	BRONZE
1964 Frederick M. Hansen (USA) 16' 8¾" *5,10 m**	Wolfgang Reinhardt (GER) 16' 6¾" *5,05 m*	Klaus Lehnertz (GER) 16' 4¾" *5,00 m*
1968 Robert L. Seagren (USA) 17' 8½" *5,40 m**	Claus Schiprowski (GER) 17' 8½" *5,40 m**	Wolfgant Nordwig (GDR) 17' 8½" *5,40 m**
1972 Wolfgang Nordwig (GDR) 18' 0½" *5,50 m**	Robert L. Seagren (USA) 17' 8½" *5,40 m*	Jan E. Johnson (USA) 17' 6½" *5,35 m*
1976 Tadeusz Slusarski (POL) 18' 0½" *5,50 m**	Antti Kalliomaki (FIN) 18' 0½" *5,50 m**	David Roberts (USA) 18' 0½" *5,50 m**
1980 Wladyslaw Kozakiewicz (POL) 18' 11½" *5,78 m**	Konstantin Volkov (URS) 18' 6½" *5,65 m*	Tadeusz Slusarski (POL) 18' 6½" *5,65 m*
1984 Pierre Quinon (FRA) 18' 10¼" *5,75m*	Mike Tully (USA) 18' 6½" *5,65m*	Earl Bell (USA) 18' 4½" *5,60m* Thierry Vigneron (FRA) 18' 4½" *5,60m*
1988 Sergey Bubka (URS) 19'4¼" *90 m**	Rodion Gataullin (URS) 19'2¼" *5,85 m*	Grigory Yegorov (URS) 19'0¼" *5,80 m*

Bob Seagren retained the USA unbeaten gold medal run in the pole vault, but only on the "count back" from two Germans who also cleared 17 feet 8½ inches in 1968.

BROAD JUMP (LONG JUMP)

1896 Ellery H. Clark (USA) 20' 10" *6,35 m**	Robert S. Garrett (USA) 20' 3¼" *6,18 m*	James B. Connolly (USA) 20' 0½" *6,11 m*
1900 Alvin C. Kraenzlein (USA) 23' 6¾" *7,18 m**	Myer Prinstein (USA) 23' 6¼" *7,17 m*	Patrick J. Leahy (GBR) 22' 9½" *6,95 m*
1904 Myer Prinstein (USA) 24' 1" *7,34 m**	Daniel Frank (USA) 22' 7¼" *6,89 m*	Robert S. Stangland (USA) 22' 7" *6,88 m*
1906 Myer Prinstein (USA) 23' 7¼" *7,20 m*	Peter O'Connor (GBR/IRL) 23' 0½" *7,02 m*	Hugo Friend (USA) 22' 10" *6,96 m*
1908 Francis C. Irons (USA) 24' 6½" *7,48 m**	Daniel J. Kelly (USA) 23' 3¼" *7,09 m*	Calvin D. Bricker (CAN) 23' 3" *7,08 m*
1912 Albert L. Gutterson (USA) 24' 11" *7,60 m**	Calvin D. Bricker (CAN) 23' 7¾" *7,21 m*	Georg Aberg (SWE) 23' 6½" *7,18 m*
1920 William Petterson (SWE) 23' 5¼" *7,15 m*	Carl E. Johnson (USA) 23' 3¼" *7,09 m*	Erik Abrahamsson (SWE) 23' 2½" *7,08 m*

RIGHT: Bob Beamon (USA) achieving the star performance of the 1968 Olympics with a world-record-shattering long jump of 29 feet 2½ inches. This record is confidently predicted as one that will last into the 21st century.

	GOLD	SILVER	BRONZE
1924[1]	William De Hart Hubbard (USA) 24′ 5″ *7,44 m*	Edward O. Gourdin (USA) 23′ 10¼″ *7,27 m*	Sverre Hansen (NOR) 23′ 9¾″ *7,26 m*
1928	Edward B. Hamm (USA) 25′ 4¼″ *7,73 m**	Silvio Cator (HAI) 24′ 10¼″ *7,58 m*	Alfred H. Bates (USA) 24′ 3¼″ *7,40 m*
1932	Edward L. Gordon (USA) 25′ 0¾″ *7,63 m*	C. Lambert Redd (USA) 24′ 11¼″ *7,60 m*	Chuhei Nambu (JPN) 24′ 5¼″ *7,44 m*
1936	Jesse Owens (USA) 26′ 5¼″ *8,06 m**	Luz Long (GER) 25′ 9¾″ *7,87 m*	Naoto Tajima (JPN) 25′ 4½″ *7,74 m*
1948	William S. Steele (USA) 25′ 7¾″ *7,82 m*	Thomas Bruce (AUS) 24′ 9″ *7,55 m*	Herbert P. Douglas (USA) 24′ 8¾″ *7,54 m*
1952	Jerome C. Biffle (USA) 24′ 10″ *7,57 m*	Meredith C. Gourdine (USA) 24′ 8¼″ *7,53 m*	Ödön Földessy (HUN) 23′ 11¼″ *7,30 m*
1956	Gregory C. Bell (USA) 25′ 8¼″ *7,83 m*	John D. Bennett (USA) 25′ 2¼″ *7,68 m*	Jorma Valkama (FIN) 24′ 6¼″ *7,48 m*
1960	Ralph H. Boston (USA) 26′ 7½″ *8,12 m**	Irvin Roberson (USA) 26′ 7¼″ *8,11 m*	Igor A. Ter-Ovanesyan (URS) 26′ 4½″ *8,04 m*
1964	Lynn Davies (GBR) 26′ 5½″ *8,07 m*	Ralph H. Boston (USA) 26′ 4″ *8,03 m*	Igor A. Ter-Ovanesyan (URS) 26′ 2½″ *7,99 m*
1968	Robert Beamon (USA) 29′ 2½″ *8,90 m**	Klaus Beer (GDR) 26′ 10¼″ *8,19 m*	Ralph H. Boston[2] (USA) 26′ 9¼″ *8,16 m*
1972	Randy L. Williams (USA) 27′ 0¼″ *8,24 m*	Hans Baumgartner (GER) 26′ 10″ *8,18 m*	Arnie Robinson (USA) 26′ 4″ *8,03 m*
1976	Arnie Robinson (USA) 27′ 4¾″ *8,35 m*	Randy L. Williams (USA) 26′ 7¼″ *8,11 m*	Frank Wartenberg (GDR) 26′ 3¾″ *8,02 m*
1980	Lutz Dombrowski (GDR) 28′ 0¼″ *8,54 m*	Frank Paschek (GDR) 26′ 11¼″ *8,21 m*	Valery Podluzhnyi (URS) 26′ 10″ *8,18 m*
1984	Carl Lewis (USA) 28′ 0¼″ *8,54 m*	Gary Honey (AUS) 27′ 0½″ *8,24 m*	Giovanni Evangelisti (ITA) 27′ 0½″ *18,24 m*
1988	Carl Lewis (USA) 28′ 7½″ *8,72 m*	Michael Powell (USA) 27′ 10¼″ *8,49 m*	Larry Myricks (USA) 27′ 1¾″ *8,27 m*

[1]In the 1924 Pentathlon Robert LeGendre (USA) had jumped 25′ 5¾″ *7,76 m* but this was not classed as the Olympic broad jump record.
[2]Set Olympic record of 27′ 1¼″ *8,27 m* in qualifying round.

TRIPLE JUMP[1]

1896[2] James B. Connolly (USA) 44' 11¾" *13,71 m* *	Alexandre Tuffere (FRA) 41' 8" *12,70 m*	Joannis Persakis (GRE) 41' 0¾" *12,52 m*
1900 Myer Prinstein (USA) 47' 5½" *14,47 m* *	James B. Connolly (USA) 45' 10" *13,97 m*	Lewis P. Sheldon (USA) 44' 9" *13,64 m*
1904 Myer Prinstein (USA) 47' 1" *14,35 m*	Frederick Englehardt (USA) 45' 7¼" *13,90 m*	Robert S. Stangland (USA) 43' 10¼" *13,36 m*
1906 Peter O'Connor (GBR/IRL) 46' 2" *14,07 m*	Con Leahy (GBR/IRL) 45' 10¼" *13,98 m*	Thomas Cronan (USA) 44' 11¼" *13,70 m*
1908 Timothy J. Ahearne (GBR) 48' 11¼" *14,91 m* *	J. Garfield McDonald (CAN) 48' 5¼" *14,76 m*	Edvard Larsen (NOR) 47' 2¾" *14,39 m*
1912 Gustaf Lindblom (SWE) 48' 5" *14,76 m*	Georg Åberg (SWE) 47' 7¼" *14,51 m*	Erik Almlöf (SWE) 46' 5¾" *14,17 m*
1920 Vilho Tuulos (FIN) 47' 7" *14,50 m*	Folke Jansson (SWE) 47' 6" *14,48 m*	Erik Almlöf (SWE) 46' 9¾" *14,27 m*
1924 Anthony W. Winter (AUS) 50' 11¼" *15,52 m* *	Luis Brunetto (ARG) 50' 7¼" *15,42 m*	Vilho Tuulos (FIN) 50' 5" *15,37 m*
1928 Mikio Oda (JPN) 49' 10¾" *15,21 m*	Levi Casey (USA) 49' 9" *15,17 m*	Vilho Tuulos (FIN) 49' 6¾" *15,11 m*
1932 Chuhei Nambu (JPN) 51' 7" *15,72 m* *	Erik Svensson (SWE) 50' 3¼" *15,32 m*	Kenkichi Oshima (JPN) 49' 7¼" *15,12 m*
1936 Naoto Tajima (JPN) 52' 5¾" *16,00 m* *	Masao Harada (JPN) 51' 4½" *15,66 m*	John P. Metcalfe (AUS) 50' 10" *15,50 m*
1948 Arne Åhman (SWE) 50' 6¼" *15,40 m*	George G. Avery (AUS) 50' 4¾" *15,36 m*	Ruhi Sarialp (TUR) 49' 3½" *15,02 m*
1952 Adhemar Ferreira da Silva (BRA) 53' 2½" *16,22 m* *	Leonid Shcherbakov (URS) 52' 5" *15,98 m*	Arnoldo Devonish (VEN) 50' 11" *15,52 m*
1956 Adhemar Ferreira da Silva (BRA) 53' 7½" *16,35 m* *	Vilhjálmur Einarsson (ISL) 53' 4" *16,26 m*	Vitold Kreyer (URS) 52' 6½" *16,02 m*
1960 Józef Schmidt (POL) 55' 1¾" *16,81 m* *	Vladimir Goryayev (URS) 54' 4½" *16,63 m*	Vitold Kreyer (URS) 53' 10¾" *16,43 m*
1964 Józef Schmidt (POL) 55' 3¼" *16,85 m* *	Olyeg Fyedoseyev (URS) 54' 4¾" *16,58 m*	Viktor Kravchenko (URS) 54' 4¼" *16,57 m*
1968 Viktor Saneyev (URS) 57' 0¾" *17,39 m* *	Nelson Prudencio (BRA) 56' 7¾" *17,27 m*	Giuseppe Gentile (ITA) 56' 5¾" *17,22 m*
1972 Viktor Saneyev (URS) 56' 11" *17,35 m*	Joerg Drehmel (GDR) 56' 9¼" *17,31 m*	Nelson Prudencio (BRA) 55' 11¼" *17,05 m*
1976 Viktor Saneyev (URS) 56' 8¾" *17,29 m*	James Butts (USA) 56' 8½" *17,18 m*	Joao de Oliveira (BRA) 55' 5½" *16,90 m*

[1]Formerly known as the Hop, Step and Jump.
[2]Winner took two hops with his right foot, contrary to present rule.

Leo Sexton (USA), the 1932 gold medal winner in the shot put, is one of a long line of American champions in this event.

GOLD	SILVER	BRONZE
1980	Jaak Uudmae (URS) 56' 11" *17,35 m*	Viktor Saneyev (URS) 56' 6¾" *17,24 m*	Joao de Oliveira (BRA) 56' 6" *17,22 m*
1984	Al Joyner (USA) 56' 7½" *17,26 m*	Mike Conley (USA) 56' 4½" *17,18 m*	Keith Connor (GBR) 55' 4½" *16,87 m*
1988	Khristo Markov (BUL) 57' 9½" *17,61 m*	Igor Lapshin (URS) 57' 5¾" *17,52 m*	Alexandr Kovalenko (URS) 57' 2" *17,42 m*

SHOT PUT

1896[1]	Robert S. Garrett (USA) 36' 9½" *11,22 m**	Miltiades Gouskos (GRE) 36' 6¾" *11,15 m*	Georgios Papasideris (GRE) 33' 11¾" *10,36 m*
1900[1]	Richard Sheldon (USA) 46' 3" *14,10 m**	Josiah C. McCracken (USA) 42' 1¾" *12,85 m*	Robert S. Garrett (USA) 40' 7" *12,37 m*
1904[1]	Ralph W. Rose (USA) 48' 7" *14,80 m**	W. Wesley Coe (USA) 47' 3" *14,40 m*	Leon E. J. Feuerbach (USA) 43' 10½" *13,37 m*
1906	Martin Sheridan (USA) 40' 5" *12,32 m*	Mihály Dávid (HUN) 38' 9½" *11,83 m*	Erik V. Lemming (SWE) 36' 11¼" *11,26 m*
1908	Ralph W. Rose (USA) 46' 7½" *14,21 m*	Dennis Horgan (GBR) 44' 8¼" *13,61 m*	John C. Garrels (USA) 43' 3" *13,18 m*
1912	Patrick J. McDonald (USA) 50' 4" *15,34 m*	Ralph W. Rose (USA) 50' 0¼" *15,25 m*	Lawrence A. Whitney (USA) 46' 5" *14,15 m*
1920	Ville Pörhölä (FIN) 48' 7" *14,81 m*	Elmer Niklander (FIN) 46' 5¼" *14,155 m*	Harry B. Liversedge (USA) 46' 5" *14,15 m*
1924	Clarence L. Houser (USA) 49' 2" *14,99 m*	Glenn Hartranft (USA) 49' 1¾" *14,98 m*	Ralph G. Hills (USA) 48' 0¼" *14,64 m*
1928	John Kuck (USA) 52' 0¾" *15,87 m**	Herman H. Brix (USA) 51' 8" *15,75 m*	Emil Hirschfeld (GER) 51' 6¾" *15,72 m*
1932	Leo J. Sexton (USA) 52' 5¾" *16,00 m**	Harlow P. Rothert (USA) 51' 5" *15,67 m*	František Douda (TCH) 51' 2½" *15,60 m*
1936	Hans Woelke (GER) 53' 1¾" *16,20 m**	Sulo Bärlund (FIN) 52' 10½" *16,12 m*	Gerhard Stöck (GER) 51' 4½" *15,66 m*
1948	Wilbur M. Thompson (USA) 56' 2" *17,12 m**	F. James Delaney (USA) 54' 8½" *16,68 m*	James E. Fuchs (USA) 53' 10¼" *16,42 m*
1952	W. Parry O'Brien (USA) 57' 1¼" *17,41 m**	C. Darrow Hooper (USA) 57' 0½" *17,39 m*	James E. Fuchs (USA) 55' 11½" *17,06 m*
1956	W. Parry O'Brien (USA) 60' 11" *18,57 m**	William H. Nieder (USA) 59' 7½" *18,18 m*	Jiří Skobla (TCH) 57' 10¾" *17,65 m*
1960	William H. Nieder (USA) 64' 6¾" *19,68 m**	W. Parry O'Brien (USA) 62' 8¼" *19,11 m*	Dallas C. Long (USA) 62' 4¼" *19,01 m*
1964	Dallas C. Long (USA) 66' 8¼" *20,33 m**	J. Randel Matson (USA) 66' 3¼" *20,20 m*	Vilmos Varju (HUN) 63' 7¼" *19,39 m*
1968	J. Randel Matson[2] (USA) 67' 4½" *20,54 m*	George R. Woods (USA) 66' 0" *20,12 m*	Eduard Gushchin (URS) 65' 10¾" *20,09 m*
1972	Wladyslaw Komar (POL) 69' 6" *21,18 m**	George R. Woods (USA) 69' 5½" *21,17 m*	Hartmut Briesenick (GDR) 69' 4¼" *21,14 m*
1976	Udo Beyer (GDR) 69' 0¾" *21,05 m*	Evgeniy Mironov (URS) 69' 0" *21,03 m*	Alexandr Baryshnikov[3] (URS) 68' 10¾" *21,00 m*
1980	Vladimir Kiselyov (URS) 70' 0½" *21,35 m**	Alexandr Baryshnikov (URS) 69' 2" *21,08 m*	Udo Beyer (GDR) 69' 1¼" *21,06 m*
1984	Alessandro Andrei (ITA) 69' 9" *21,26 m*	Michael Carter (USA) 69' 2½" *21,09 m*	Dave Laut (USA) 68' 9¾" *20,97 m*
1988	Ulf Timmermann (GDR) 73' 8¾" *22,47 m**	Randy Barnes (USA) 73' 5½" *22,39 m*	Werner Günthör (SUI) 72' 1¾" *21,99 m*

[1]The shot was put from a 7 foot *2,13 m* square.
[2]Set Olympic record of 67' 10¼" *20,68 m* in qualifying round.
[3]Set Olympic record of 69' 11½" *21,32 m* in qualifying round.

DISCUS THROW

1896	Robert S. Garrett (USA) 95' 7½" *29,15 m**	Panagiotis Paraskevopoulos (GRE) 94' 11½" *28,95 m*	Sotirios Versis (GRE) 94' 5" *28,78 m*
1900	Rudolf Bauer (HUN) 118' 2½" *36,04 m**	František Janda-Suk (BOH) 115' 7½" *35,25 m*	Richard Sheldon (USA) 113' 6" *34,60 m*

	GOLD	SILVER	BRONZE
1904	Martin J. Sheridan[1] (USA) 128' 10½" 39,28 m*	Ralph W. Rose (USA) 128' 10½" 39,28 m*	Nicolaos Georgantas (GRE) 123' 7½" 37,68 m
1906	Martin J. Sheridan (USA) 136' 0" 41,46 m*	Nicolaos Georgantas (GRE) 124' 10" 38,06 m	Werner Järvinen (FIN) 120' 9½" 36,82 m
1908	Martin J. Sheridan (USA) 134' 2" 40,89 m	Merritt H. Giffin (USA) 133' 6½" 40,70 m	Marquis F. Horr (USA) 129' 5" 39,44 m
1912	Armas R. Taipale (FIN) 148' 3½" 45,21 m*	Richard L. Byrd (USA) 138' 10" 42,32 m	James H. Duncan (USA) 138' 8½" 42,28 m
1920	Elmer Niklander (FIN) 146' 7" 44,68 m	Armas R. Taipale (FIN) 144' 11½" 44,19 m	Augustus R. Pope (USA) 138' 2½" 42,13 m
1924	Clarence L. Houser (USA) 151' 5" 46,15 m*	Vilho A. Niittymaa (FIN) 147' 5½" 44,95 m	Thomas J. Lieb (USA) 147' 0½" 44,83 m
1928	Clarence L. Houser (USA) 155' 2½" 47,32 m*	Antero Kivi (FIN) 154' 11" 47,23 m	James Corson (USA) 154' 6" 47,10 m
1932	John F. Anderson (USA) 162' 4½" 49,49 m*	Henri J. Laborde (FRA) 159' 0½" 48,47 m	Paul Winter (FRA) 157' 0" 47,85 m
1936	Kenneth K. Carpenter (USA) 165' 7" 50,48 m*	Gordon G. Dunn (USA) 161' 11" 49,36 m	Giorgio Oberweger (ITA) 161' 6" 49,23 m
1948	Adolfo Consolini (ITA) 173' 1½" 52,78 m*	Giuseppe Tosi (ITA) 169' 10½" 51,78 m	Fortune E. Gordien (USA) 166' 6½" 50,77 m
1952	Sim G. Iness (USA) 180' 6½" 55,03 m*	Adolfo Consolini (ITA) 176' 5" 53,78 m	James L. Dillion (USA) 174' 9½" 53,28 m
1956	Alfred A. Oerter (USA) 184' 10½" 56,36 m*	Fortune E. Gordien (USA) 179' 9½" 54,81 m	Desmond Koch (USA) 178' 5½" 54,40 m
1960	Alfred A. Oerter (USA) 194' 1½" 59,18 m*	Richard A. Babka (USA) 190' 4" 58,02 m	Richard L. Cochran (USA) 187' 6" 57,16 m
1964	Alfred A. Oerter (USA) 200' 1½" 61,00 m*	Ludvik Danek (TCH) 198' 6½" 60,52 m	David Weill (USA) 195' 2" 59,49 m
1968	Alfred A. Oerter (USA) 212' 6" 64,78 m*	Lothar Milde (GDR) 206' 11" 63,08 m	Ludvik Danek (TCH) 206' 5" 62,92 m
1972	Ludvik Danek (TCH) 211' 3" 64,40 m	L. Jay Silvester (USA) 208' 4" 63,50 m	Rickard Bruch (SWE) 208' 0" 63,40 m
1972	Ludvik Danek (TCH) 211' 3" 64,40 m	L. Jay Silvester (USA) 208' 4" 63,50 m	Rickard Bruch (SWE) 208' 0" 63,40 m
1976	Maurice MacWilkins (USA) 221' 5" 67,50 m[2]	Wolfgang Schmidt (GDR) 217' 3" 66,22 m	John Powell (USA) 215' 7" 65,70 m
1980	Viktor Rasshchupkin (URS) 218' 7" 66,64 m	Imrich Bugar (TCH) 217' 9" 66,38 m	Luis Delis (CUB) 217' 7" 66,32 m
1984	Rolf Danneberg (FRG) 218' 6" 66,60 m	Mac Wilkins (USA) 217' 6" 66,30 m	John Powell (USA) 214' 9" 65,46 m
1988	Jurgen Schult (GDR) 225' 9" 68,82 m*	Romas Ubartas (URS) 221' 5" 67,48 m	Rolf Danneberg (FRG) 221' 1" 67,38 m

[1]First place decided by a throw-off.
[2]Set Olympic record of 224' 0" 68,28 m in qualifying round.

HAMMER THROW

	GOLD	SILVER	BRONZE
1896	Event not held		
1900[1]	John J. Flanagan (USA) 163' 1½" 49,73 m	Truxton T. Hare (USA) 161' 2" 49,13 m	Josiah C. McCracken (USA) 139' 3½" 42,46 m
1904	John J. Flanagan (USA) 168' 0½" 51,23 m*	John R. DeWitt (USA) 164' 10½" 50,26 m	Ralph W. Rose (USA) 150' 0" 45,73 m
1906	Event not held		
1908	John J. Flanagan (USA) 170' 4" 51,92 m*	Matthew J. McGrath (USA) 167' 11" 51,18 m	Cornelius Walsh (CAN) 159' 1½" 48,50 m
1912	Matthew J. McGrath (USA) 179' 7" 54,74 m*	Duncan Gillis (CAN) 158' 9" 48,39 m	Clarence C. Childs (USA) 158' 0" 48,17 m
1920	Patrick J. Ryan (USA) 173' 5½" 52,87 m	Carl Johan Lind (SWE) 158' 10½" 48,43 m	Basil Bennet (USA) 158' 3½" 48,25 m
1924	Frederick D. Tootell (USA) 174' 10" 53,29 m	Matthew J. McGrath (USA) 166' 9½" 50,84 m	Malcolm C. Nokes (GBR) 160' 4" 48,87 m
1928	Patrick O'Callaghan (IRL) 168' 7" 51,39 m	Ossian Skiöld (SWE) 168' 3" 51,29 m	Edmund F. Black (USA) 160' 10" 49,03 m

[1]Thrown from a 9 foot 2,74 m instead of the now regular 7 foot 2,135 m circle.

LEFT: Hal Connolly (USA) won the hammer throw in Melbourne in 1956 with a throw of 207 feet 3½ inches.

ABOVE: Al Oerter (USA) dominated the discus competition for 4 consecutive meetings (1956 to 1968), a unique achievement in Olympic track and field.

	GOLD	SILVER	BRONZE
1932	Patrick O'Callaghan (IRL) 176' 11" *53,92 m*	Ville Pörhölä (FIN) 171' 6" *52,27 m*	Peter E. Zaremba (USA) 165' 1½" *50,33 m*
1936	Karl Hein (GER) 185' 4" *56,49 m**	Erwin Blask (GER) 180' 6½" *55,04 m*	Fred Warngård (SWE) 179' 10½" *54,83 m*
1948	Imre Németh (HUN) 183' 11" *56,07 m*	Ivan Gubijan (YUG) 178' 0½" *54,27 m*	Robert H. Bennett (USA) 176' 3" *53,73 m*
1952	József Csermák (HUN) 197' 11½" *60,34 m**	Karl Storch (GER) 193' 1" *58,86 m*	Imre Németh (HUN) 189' 5" *57,74 m*
1956	Harold V. Connolly (USA) 207' 3½" *63,19 m**	Mikhail P. Krivonosov (URS) 206' 9" *63,03 m*	Anatoliy Samotsvetov (URS) 205' 2½" *62,56 m*
1960	Vasiliy Rudenkov (URS) 220' 1½" *67,10 m**	Gyula Zsivótzky (HUN) 215' 10" *65,79 m*	Tadeusz Rut (POL) 215' 4" *65,64 m*
1964	Romuald Klim (URS) 228' 9½" *69,74 m**	Gyula Zsivótzky (HUN) 226' 8" *69,09 m*	Uwe Beyer (GER) 223' 4½" *68,09 m*
1968	Gyula Zsivótzky (HUN) 240' 8" *73,36 m**	Romuald Klim (URS) 240' 5" *73,28 m*	Lázár Lovász (HUN) 228' 11" *69,78 m*
1972	Anatoli Bondarchuk (URS) 247' 8" *75,50 m**	Jochen Sachse (GDR) 245' 11" *74,96 m**	Vasili Khmelevski (URS) 242' 10½" *74,04 m*
1976	Yuri Sedykh (URS) 254' 4" *77,52 m**	Alexei Spiridonov (URS) 249' 7" *76,08 m*	Anatoli Bondarchuk (URS) 247' 8" *75,48 m*
1980	Yuri Sedykh (URS) 268' 4" *81,80 m**	Sergei Litvinov (URS) 264' 6" *80,64 m*	Yuri Tamm 259' 0" *78,96 m*
1984	Juha Tiainen (FIN) 256' 2" *78,08 m*	Karl-Hans Riehm (FRG) 255' 10" *77,98 m*	Klaus Ploghaus (FRG) 251' 7" *76,68 m*
1988	Sergey Litvinov (URS) 278' 2" *84,80 m**	Yuri Sedykh (URS) 274' 10" *83,76 m*	Yuri Tamm (URS) 266' 3" *81,16 m*

JAVELIN THROW

1896–1904	Event not held		
1906	Erik V. Lemming (SWE) 176' 10" *53,90 m**	Knut Lindberg (SWE) 148' 2" *45,17 m*	Bruno Söerström (SWE) 147' 10½" *44,92 m*
1908	Erik V. Lemming (SWE) 179' 10½" *54,82 m**	Arne Halse (NOR) 165' 11" *50,57 m*	Otto Nilsson (SWE) 154' 6" *47,09 m*
1912	Erik V. Lemming (SWE) 198' 11" *60,64 m**	Juho Saaristo (FIN) 192' 5" *58,66 m*	Mór Kóczán (HUN) 182' 1" *55,50 m*
1920	Jonni Myyrä (FIN) 215' 9½" *65,78 m**	Urho Peltonen (FIN) 208' 4" *63,50 m*	Pekka Johansson (FIN) 207' 0" *63,09 m*
1924	Jonni Myyrä (FIN) 206' 6½" *62,96 m*	Gunnar Lindström (SWE) 199' 10" *60,92 m*	Eugene G. Oberst (USA) 191' 5" *58,35 m*
1928	Erik Lundkvist (SWE) 218' 6" *66,60 m*	Béla Szepes (HUN) 214' 1" *65,26 m*	Olav Sunde (NOR) 209' 10½" *63,97 m*
1932	Matti Järvinen (FIN) 238' 6½" *72,71 m**	Matti Sippala (FIN) 229' 0" *69,79 m*	Eino Penttila (FIN) 225' 4½" *68,69 m*
1936	Gerhard Stöck (GER) 235' 8" *71,84 m*	Yrjö Nikkanen (FIN) 232' 2" *70,77 m*	Kalervo Toivonen (FIN) 232' 0" *70,72 m*
1948	K. Tapio Rautavaara (FIN) 228' 10½" *69,77 m*	Steve A. Seymour (USA) 221' 7½" *67,56 m*	József Várszegi (HUN) 219' 10½" *67,03 m*
1952	Cyrus C. Young (USA) 242' 0½" *73,78 m**	William Miller (USA) 237' 8½" *72,46 m*	Toivo Hyytiäinen (FIN) 235' 10" *71,89 m*
1956	Egil Danielsen (NOR) 281' 2" *85,71 m**	Janusz Sidlo (POL) 262' 4½" *79,98 m*	Viktor Tsibulenko (URS) 260' 9½" *79,50 m*
1960	Viktor Tsibulenko (URS) 277' 8" *84,64 m*	Walter Krüger (GER) 260' 4" *79,36 m*	Gergely Kulcsár (HUN) 257' 9" *78,57 m*
1964	Pauli Nevala (FIN) 271' 2" *82,66 m*	Gergely Kulcsár (HUN) 270' 0½" *82,32 m*	Janis Lusis (URS) 264' 2" *80,57 m*

Bruce Jenner (USA) acknowledges the cheers of the crowd after shattering Olympic and world records in the 1976 decathlon.

Daley Thompson (GBR) won the decathlon in 1980 and repeated in 1984 with an Olympic record of 8,797 points under a new scoring system.

	GOLD	SILVER	BRONZE
1968	Janis Lusis (URS) 295' 7" 90,10 m*	Jorma V. P. Kinnunen (FIN) 290' 7" 88,58 m	Gergely Kulcsár (HUN) 285' 7½" 87,06 m
1972	Klaus Wolfermann (GER) 296' 10" 90,48 m*	Janis Lusis (URS) 296' 9" 90,46 m	William Schmidt (USA) 276' 11½" 84,42 m
1976	Miklos Nemeth (HUN) 310' 4" 94,58 m*	Hannu Siitonen (FIN) 288' 5" 87,92 m	Gheorghe Megelea (ROM) 285' 11" 87,16 m
1980	Dainis Kula (URS) 299' 2" 91,20 m	Aleksandr Makarov (URS) 294' 1" 89,64 m	Wolfgang Hanisch (GDR) 284' 6" 86,72 m
1984	Arto Härkonen (FIN) 284' 8" 86,76 m	David Ottley (GBR) 281' 3" 85,74 m	Kenth Eldebrink (SWE) 274' 8" 83,72 m
1988	Tapio Korjus (FIN) 276' 6" 84,28 m	Jan Zelezny (TCH) 276' 0" 84,12 m[2]	Seppo Räty (FIN) 273' 2" 83,26 m

[1]New javelin introduced.
[2]Olympic record 281' 10" 85,90 m by Zelezny in qualifying round.

DECATHLON[1]

(Figures refer to points scored)

	GOLD	SILVER	BRONZE
1896–1908	Event not held		
1912	Hugo Wieslander[2] (SWE) 5,965	Charles Lomberg (SWE) 5,721	Gösta Holmér (SWE) 5,768
1920	Helge Løvland (NOR) 5,803	Brutus Hamilton (USA) 5,739	Bertil Ohlson (SWE) 5,639
1924	Harold M. Osborn (USA) 6,476	Emerson Norton (USA) 6,117	Aleksander Klumberg (EST) 6,056
1928	Paavo Yrjölä (FIN) 6,587	Akilles Järvinen (FIN) 6,645	J. Kenneth Doherty (USA) 6,428
1932	James A. B. Bausch (USA) 6,735	Akilles Järvinen (FIN) 6,879	Wolrad Eberle (GER) 6,661

GOLD	SILVER	BRONZE
1936 Glenn E. Morris (USA) 7,254	Robert H. Clark (USA) 7,063	Jack Parker (USA) 6,760
1948 Robert B. Mathias (USA) 6,628	Ignace Heinrich (FRA) 6,559	Floyd M. Simmons (USA) 6,531
1952 Robert B. Mathias (USA) 7,592	Milton G. Campbell (USA) 6,995	Floyd M. Simmons (USA) 6,945
1956 Milton G. Campbell (USA) 7,614	Rafer L. Johnson (USA) 7,457	Vasiliy Kuznetsov (URS) 7,337
1960 Rafer L. Johnson (USA) 7,926	Yang Chuan-kwang (TAI) 7,839	Vasiliy Kuznetsov (URS) 7,557
1964 Willi Holdorf (GER) 7,794	Rein Aun (URS) 7,744	Hans-Joachim Walde (GER) 7,735
1968 William A. Toomey (USA) 8,144	Hans-Joachim Walde (FRG) 8,094	Kurt Bendlin (FRG) 8,071
1972 Nikolai Avilov (URS) 8,466	Leonid Litvinenko (URS) 7,970	Ryszard Katus (POL) 7,936
1976 Bruce Jenner (USA) 8,634	Guido Kratschmer (FRG) 8,407	Nikolai Avilov (URS) 8,378
1980 Daley Thompson (GBR) 8,522	Yuri Kutsenko (URS) 8,369	Sergei Zhelanov (URS) 8,135
1984 Daley Thompson (GBR) 8,847*	Jürgen Hingsen (FRG) 8,695	Siegfried Wentz (FRG) 8,416
1988 Christian Schenk (GDR) 8,488 pts	Torsten Voss (GDR) 8,399	Dave Steen (CAN) 8,328

[1]The decathlon consists of 100 m, long jump, shot put, high jump, 400 m, 110 m hurdles, discus, pole vault, javelin and 1500 m. The competition occupies 2 days (but 3 days in 1912). Scores given above are all recalculated on the 1984 tables for purposes of comparison. Note that in 3 years (1912, 1928 and 1932) the original medal order would have been different had the 1984 values then prevailed.
[2]Jim Thorpe (USA) finished first with 6,564 pts but was later disqualified for a breach of the then amateur rules. He was reinstated posthumously by the IOC in 1982, but only as joint first.

Track and Field Athletics (Women)

MARRIED NAMES
The following won medals under both their maiden and their married names:

Auerswald—Lange	Khnykina—Dvalishvili	Schaller—Klier
Becker—Mickler	Kirszenstein—Szewinska	Schlaak—Jahl
Brehmer—Lathan	Kohler—Birkemeyer	Smallwood—Cook
Eckert—Wockel	Manning—Jackson	Strickland—Delahunty
Foulds—Paul	Odam—Tyler	Vergova—Petkova
Goddard—Callender	Oelsner—Gohr	Wieczorek—Ciepla
Hunte—Oakes	Richter—Górecka	Zharkova—Maslakova
Joyner-Kersee	Romashkova—Ponomaryeva	

100 METERS (109 yd. 1 ft.)

1928 Elizabeth Robinson (USA) 12.2*	Fanny Rosenfeld (CAN) inches	Ethel Smith (CAN) inches
1932 Stanislawa Walasiewicz (POL) 11.9*	Hilda Strike (CAN) 11.9*	Wilhelmina von Bremen (USA) 12.0
1936 Helen H. Stephens (USA) 11.5	Stanislawa Walasiewicz (POL) 11.7	Kathe Krauss (GER) 11.9
1948 Francina E. Blankers-Koen (HOL) 11.9	Dorothy G. Manley (GBR) 12.2	Shirley B. Strickland (AUS) 12.2
1952 Marjorie Jackson (AUS) 11.5	Daphne L. E. Hasenjager (SAF) 11.8	Shirley B. Strickland (AUS) 11.9
1956 Betty Cuthbert (AUS) 11.5	Christa Stubnick (GER) 11.7	Marlene J. Mathews (AUS) 11.7

Wyomia Tyus (USA) successfully defends her 100 meters title in 1968 in the world record of 11.0 seconds.

Renate Stecher (No. 147) edges Raelene Boyle of Australia to become the fifth woman ever to win the 100 meters/200 meters double.

GOLD	SILVER	BRONZE
1960	Wilma G. Rudolph (USA) 11.0*	Dorothy Hyman (GBR) 11.3	Giuseppina Leone (ITA) 11.3
1964	Wyomia Tyus (USA) 11.4	Edith Maguire (USA) 11.6	Ewa Kobukowska (POL) 11.6
1968	Wyomia Tyus (USA) 11.0*	Barbara A. Ferrell (USA) 11.1	Irena Szewinska (POL) 11.1
1972	Renate Stecher (GDR) 11.07	Raelene A. Boyle (AUS) 11.23	Silvia Chivas (CUB) 11.24
1976	Annegret Richter (GER) 11.08	Renate Stecher (GDR) 11.13	Inge Helten (GER) 11.17
1980	Ludmila Kondrateva (URS) 11.06	Marlies Gohr (GDR) 11.07	Ingrid Auerswald (GDR) 11.14
1984	Evelyn Ashford (USA) 10.97*	Alice Brown (USA) 11.13	Merlene Ottey-Page (JAM) 11.16
1988	Florence Griffith-Joyner (USA) 10.54*	Evelyn Ashford (USA) 10.83	Heike Drechsler (GDR) 10.85

The performances listed below were Olympic records set additionally in preliminaries.
(Nine records were established prior to the 1928 final.)

12.2	Marie Dollinger (GER)	1932	11.4	Cuthbert	1956	10.88 Griffith-Joyner 1988
11.9	Walasiewicz		11.3	Rudolph	1960	10.62 Griffith-Joyner 1988
(twice)		1932	11.01	Richter	1976	

Performances of 11.4 and 11.5 (final) by Stephens in 1936; 11.5 (final) by Cuthbert 1956; 11.0 (final) by Rudolph 1960; 11.3 by Tyus in 1964; 11.1 by Ferrell and 11.0 by Tyus in 1968 were wind assisted.

200 METERS (218 yd 2 ft)

	GOLD	SILVER	BRONZE
1928–1936	Event not held		
1948	Francina E. Blankers-Koen (HOL) 24.4	Audrey D. Williamson (GBR) 25.1	Audrey Patterson[1] (USA) 25.2
1952	Marjorie Jackson (AUS) 23.7	Bertha Brouwer (HOL) 24.2	Nadyezhda Khnykina (URS) 24.2
1956	Betty Cuthbert (AUS) 23.4*	Christa Stubnick (GER) 23.7	Marlene J. Mathews (AUS) 23.8
1960	Wilma G. Rudolph (USA) 24.0	Jutta Heine (GER) 24.4	Dorothy Hyman (GBR) 24.7
1964	Edith Maguire (USA) 23.0*	Irena Kirszenstein (POL) 23.1	Marilyn M. Black (AUS) 23.1
1968	Irena Szewinska (POL) 22.5*	Raelene A. Boyle (AUS) 22.7	Jennifer Lamy (AUS) 22.8
1972	Renate Stecher (GDR) 22.40*	Raelene A. Boyle (AUS) 22.45	Irena Szewinska (POL) 22.74
1976	Barbel Eckert (GDR) 22.37*	Annegret Richter (GER) 22.39	Renate Stecher (GDR) 22.47
1980	Barbel Wockel (GDR) 22.03*	Natalya Bochina (URS) 22.19	Merlene Ottey (JAM) 22.20
1984	Valerie Brisco-Hooks (USA) 21.81*	Florence Griffith (USA) 22.04	Merlene Ottey-Page (JAM) 22.09
1988	Florence Griffith-Joyner (USA) 21.34*	Grace Jackson (JAM) 21.72	Heike Drechsler (GDR) 21.95

---

[1] A recently discovered photo-finish indicates that Shirley Strickland (AUS) was third.

The performances listed below were Olympic records set additionally in preliminaries.

25.7	Blankers-Koen 1948	24.3	Blankers-Koen 1948	22.9	Barbara A. Ferrell (USA) 1968
25.6	Cynthia A. Thompson (JAM) 1948	24.3	Khnykina 1952	22.9	Boyle 1968
		23.6	Jackson 1952	22.8	Ferrell 1968
		23.4	Jackson 1952	21.76	Griffith-Joyner 1988
25.3	Daphne L. E. Robb (SAF) 1948	23.2	Rudolph 1960	21.56	Griffith-Joyner 1988
		23.0	Boyle 1968		

400 METERS (437 yd 1 ft)

Year			
1928–1960	Event not held		
1964	Betty Cuthbert (AUS) 52.0*	Ann E. Packer (GBR) 52.2	Judith F. Amoore (AUS) 53.4
1968	Colette Besson (FRA) 52.0*	Lillian B. Board (GBR) 52.1	Natalya Pyechenkina (URS) 52.2
1972	Monika Zehrt (GDR) 51.08*	Rita Wilden (GER) 51.21	Kathy Hammond (USA) 51.64
1976	Irena Szewinska (POL) 49.29*	Christina Brehmer (GDR) 50.51	Ellen Streidt (GDR) 50.55
1980	Marita Koch (GDR) 48.88*	Jarmila Kratochvilova (TCH) 49.46	Christina Lathan (GDR) 49.66
1984	Valerie Brisco-Hooks (USA) 48.83*	Chandra Cheeseborough (USA) 49.05	Kathy Cook (GBR) 49.43
1988	Olga Bryzgina (URS) 48.65*	Petra Müller (GDR) 49.45	Olga Nazarova (URS) 49.90

The performances listed below were Olympic records set additionally in preliminaries.

54.4	Antonia Munkácsi (HUN)	1964	51.94	Charlene Rendina (AUS)	1972	51.68	Helga Seidler (GDR) 1972
53.1	Packer	1964	51.71	Györgyi Balogh (HUN)	1972	51.47	Zehrt 1972
52.7	Packer	1964				50.48	Szewinska 1976

Florence Griffith-Joyner (USA) won three gold medals and one silver at the 1988 Games in Seoul, setting new Olympic records for the 100 and 200 meters.

The 200 meters final in 1960 with Wilma Rudolph (USA) (far right), the gold medal winner of the 100 meters dash as well, wearing No. 117; Jutta Heine (GER), the silver medal winner wearing No. 77; and Dorothy Hyman (GBR), the bronze medal winner wearing No. 100. Also in the photo is Giuseppina Leone (ITA), No. 181, bronze medal winner in the 100 meters dash.

At the 1980 Games, Barbel Wockel (née Eckert) (GDR) successfully defended her Olympic titles at 200 meters and the 4 × 100 meters relay, thus becoming only the third woman athlete to win 4 gold medals in track and field.

800 METERS (874 yd. 2 ft.)

	GOLD	SILVER	BRONZE
1928	Lina Radke (GER) 2:16.8*	Kinuye Hitomi (JPN) 2:17.6	Inga Gentzel (SWE) 2:17.8
1932–1956	Event not held		
1960	Ludmila I. Shevtsova (URS) 2:04.3*	Brenda Jones (AUS) 2:04.4	Ursula Donath (GER) 2:05.6
1964	Ann E. Packer (GBR) 2:01.1*	Maryvonne Dupureur (FRA) 2:01.9	M. Ann M. Chamberlain (NZL) 2:02.8
1968	Madeline Manning (USA) 2:00.9*	Ilona Silai (ROM) 2:02.5	Maria F. Gommers (HOL) 2:02.6

GOLD	SILVER	BRONZE
1972 Hildegard Falck (GER) 1:58.6*	Niole Sabaite (URS) 1:58.7	Gunhild Hoffmeister (GDR) 1:59.2
1976 Tatyana Kazankina (URS) 1:54.9*	Nikolina Chtereva (BUL) 1:55.4	Elfi Zinn (GDR) 1:55.6
1980 Nadezhda Olizarenko (URS) 1:53.5*	Olga Mineyeva (URS) 1:54.9	Tatyana Providokhina (URS) 1:55.5
1984 Doina Melinte (ROM) 1:57.60	Kim Gallagher (USA) 1:58.63	Fita Lovin (ROM) 1:58.83
1988 Sigrun Wodars (GDR) 1:56.10	Christine Wachtel (GDR) 1:56.64	Kim Gallagher (USA) 1:56.91

The performances listed below were Olympic records set additionally in preliminaries.

2:10.9	Antje Gleichfeid (GER)	1960	2:07.8	Donath	1960	2:04.1	Dupureur	1964
			2:05.9	Dixie I. Willis (AUS)	1960	1:58.9	Svetla Zlateva (BUL)	1972
						1:56.5	Anita Weiss (GDR)	1976

---

[1] Automatically timed at 1:53.43.

1,500 METERS (1,640 yd 1 ft)

1928–68 Event not held		
1972 Lyudmila Bragina[1] (URS) 4:01.4*	Gunhild Hoffmeister (GDR) 4:02.8	Paola Cacchi-Pigni (ITA) 4:02.9
1976 Tatyana Kazankina (URS) 4:05.5	Gunhild Hoffmeister (GDR) 4:06.0	Ulrike Klapezynski (GDR) 4:06.1
1980 Tatyana Kazankina (URS) 3:56.6*	Christiane Wartenberg (GDR) 3:57.8	Nadezhda Olizarenko (URS) 3:59.6
1984 Gabriella Dorio (ITA) 4:03.25	Doina Melinte (ROM) 4:03.76	Maricica Puica (ROM) 4:04.15
1988 Paula Ivan (ROM) 3:53.96*	Laima Baikauskaite (URS) 4:00.24	Tatyana Samolenko (URS) 4:00.30

---

[1] Set Olympic Records of 4:06.5 and 4:05.1 in preliminaries.

3,000 METERS (3,280 yd 2 ft)

1984 Maricica Puica (ROM) 8:35.96*	Wendy Sly (GBR) 8:39.47	Lynn Williams (CAN) 8:42.14
1988 Tatyana Samolenko (URS) 8:26.53*	Paula Ivan (ROM) 8:27.15	Yvonne Murray (GBR) 8:29.02

10,000 METERS (6 miles 376 yd)

1988 Olga Bondarenko (URS) 31:05.21*	Liz McColgan (GBR) 31:08.44	Yelena Zhupiyeva (URS) 31:19.82

MARATHON

1984 Joan Benoit (USA) 2h 24:52*	Grete Waitz (NOR) 2h 26:18	Rosa Mota (POR) 2h 26:57
1988 Rosa Mota (POR) 2:25.40	Lisa Martin (AUS) 2:25.53	Kathrin Dörre (GDR) 2:26.21

4 × 100 METERS (109 yd 1 ft) RELAY

1928 **CANADA** 48.4*	**UNITED STATES** 48.8	**GERMANY** 49.2
Fanny Rosenfeld	Mary Washburn	Rosa Kellner
Ethel Smith	Jessie Gross	Leni Schmidt
Florence Bell	Loretta McNeil	Anni Holdmann
Myrtle Cook	Elizabeth Robinson	Leni Junker
1932 **UNITED STATES** 47.0*	**CANADA** 47.0*	**GREAT BRITAIN** 47.6
Mary L. Carew	Mildred Frizell	Eileen M. Hiscock
Evelyn Furtsch	Lilian Palmer	Gwendoline A. Porter
Annette J. Rogers	Mary Frizell	Violet R. Webb
Wilhelmina Von Bremen	Hilda Strike	Nellie Halstead
1936 **UNITED STATES** 46.9	**GREAT BRITAIN** 47.6	**CANADA** 47.8
Harriet C. Bland	Eileen M. Hiscock	Dorothy E. Brookshaw
Annette J. Rogers	Violet Olney	Mildred J. Dolson
Elizabeth Robinson	Audrey K. Brown	Hilda M. Cameron
Helen H. Stephens	Barbara H. A. Burke	Aileen A. Meagher
1948 **NETHERLANDS** 47.5	**AUSTRALIA** 47.6	**CANADA** 47.8
Xenia Stad-de-Jong	Shirley B. Strickland	Viola Myers
Jeanette J. M. Witziers-Timmers	Joy E. Maston	Nancy Mackay
Gerda J. M. Van der Kade Koudijs	Betty L. McKinnon	Doris P. Foster
Francina E. Blankers-Koen	Joyce A. King	Patricia Jones
1952 **UNITED STATES** 45.9*	**GERMANY** 45.9*	**GREAT BRITAIN** 46.2
Mae Faggs	Ursula Knab	Sylvia Cheeseman
Barbara P. Jones	Maria Sander	June F. Foulds
Janet T. Moreau	Helga Klein	Jean C. Desforges
Catherine Hardy	Marga Peterson	Heather J. Armitage
1956 **AUSTRALIA** 44.5*	**GREAT BRITAIN** 44.7	**UNITED STATES** 44.9
Shirley B. Delahunty	Anne Pashley	Mae Faggs
Norma Crocker	Jean E. Scrivens	Margaret Matthews
Fleur Mellor	June F. Paul	Wilma G. Rudolph
Betty Cuthbert	Heather J. Armitage	Isabelle Daniels
1960 **UNITED STATES** 44.5	**GERMANY** 44.8	**POLAND** 45.0
Martha Hudson	Martha Langbein	Tereza B. Wieczorek
Lucinda Williams	Anni Biechl	Barabara Janiszewska
Barbara P. Jones	Brunhilde Hendrix	Celina Jesionowska
Wilma G. Rudolph	Jutta Heine	Halina Richter
1964 **POLAND** 43.6*	**UNITED STATES** 43.9	**GREAT BRITAIN** 44.0
Tereza B. Ciepla	Willye D. White	Janet M. Simpson
Irena Kirzsenstein	Wyomia Tyus	Mary D. Rand
Halina Górecka	Marilyn White	Daphne Arden
Ewa Klobukowska	Edith Maguire	Dorothy Hyman
1968 **UNITED STATES** 42.8*	**CUBA** 43.3	**U.S.S.R.** 43.4
Barbara A. Ferrell	Marlene Elejarde	Ludmila Zharkova
Margaret A. Bailes	Fulgencia Romay	Galina Bukharina
Mildrette Netter	Violeta Quesada	Vyera Popkova
Wyomia Tyus	Miguelina Cobián	Ludmila Samotyesova
1972 **WEST GERMANY** 42.81*	**EAST GERMANY** 42.95	**CUBA** 43.36
Christine Krause	Evelyn Kaufer	Marlene Elejarde
Ingrid Mickler	Christina Heinich	Carmen Valdes
Annegret Richter	Barbel Struppert	Fulgencia Romay
Heidemarie Rosendahl	Renate Stecher	Silvia Chivas
1976 **EAST GERMANY** 42.55*	**WEST GERMANY** 42.59	**U.S.S.R.** 43.09
Marlies Oelsner	Elvira Possekel	Tatyana Prorochenko
Renate Stecher	Inge Helten	Ludmila Maslakova
Carla Bodendorf	Annegret Richter	Nadezda Besfamilnaya
Barbel Eckert	Annegret Kroniger	Vera Anisimova
1980 **EAST GERMANY** 41.60*	**U.S.S.R.** 42.10	**GREAT BRITAIN** 42.43
Romy Muller	Vera Komissova	Heather Hunte
Barbel Wockel	Ludmila Maslakova	Kathryn Smallwood
Ingrid Auerswald	Vera Anissimova	Beverley Goddard
Marlies Gohr	Natalya Bochina	Sonia Lannaman

Close finish in the 4 × 100 meters relay in 1956, which produced a world record and gold medals for Australia, with Betty Cuthbert (middle) the winner over Great Britain's anchor runner Heather Armitage.

	GOLD	SILVER	BRONZE
1984	**USA** 41.65	**CANADA** 42.77	**GREAT BRITAIN** 43.11
	Alice Brown	Angela Bailey	Simone Jacobs
	Jeanette Bolden	Marita Payne	Kathy Cook
	Chandra Cheeseborough	Angella Taylor	Bev Callender
	Evelyn Ashford	France Gareau	Heather Oakes
1988	**USA** 41.98	**EAST GERMANY** 42.09	**U.S.S.R.** 42.75
	Alice Brown	Silke Möller	Ludmila Kondratyeva
	Sheila Echols	Kerstin Behrendt	Galina Malchugina
	Florence Griffith-Joyner	Ingrid Lange	Marina Jirova
	Evelyn Ashford	Marlies Gohr	Natalya Pomoshnikova

The performances listed below were Olympic records set additionally in preliminaries.

49.4	Canada	1928	44.9	Australia	1956	43.4	United States	1968
46.4	Germany	1936	44.9	Germany	1956	43.4	Netherlands	1968
46.1	Australia	1952	44.4	United States	1960	42.61	West Germany	1976

4 × 400 METERS (437 yd 1 ft) RELAY

	GOLD	SILVER	BRONZE
1928–68	Event not held		
1972	**EAST GERMANY** 3:23.0*	**UNITED STATES** 3:25.2	**WEST GERMANY** 3:26.5
	Dagmar Kasling	Mable Fergerson	Annette Ruckes
	Rita Kuhne	Madeline Jackson	Inge Bödding
	Helga Seidler	Cheryl Toussaint	Hildegard Falck
	Monika Zehrt	Kathy Hammond	Rita Wilden
1976	**EAST GERMANY** 3:19.2*	**UNITED STATES** 3:22.8	**U.S.S.R.** 3:24.2
	Doris Maletzki	Debra Sapenter	Inta Klimovicha
	Brigitte Rohde	Sheila Ingram	Ludmila Aksenova
	Ellen Streidt	Pam Jiles	Natalia Sokolova
	Christina Brehmer	Rosalyn Bryant	Nadezda Ilina

GOLD	SILVER	BRONZE
1980 U.S.S.R. 3:20.2	EAST GERMANY 3:20.4	GREAT BRITAIN 3:27.5
Tatyana Prorochenko	Gabriele Lowe	Linsey MacDonald
Tatyana Goichik	Barbara Krug	Michelle Probert
Nina Zuskova	Christina Lathan	Joslyn Hoyte-Smith
Irina Nazarova	Marita Koch	Janine MacGregor
1984 UNITED STATES 3:18.29*	CANADA 3:21.21	WEST GERMANY 3:22.98
Lillie Leatherwood	Charmaine Crooks	Heike Schulte-Mattler
Sherri Howard	Jillian Richardson	Ute Thimm
Valerie Brisco-Hooks	Molly Killingbeck	Heide Gaugel
Chandra Cheeseborough	Marita Payne	Gaby Bussmann
1988 U.S.S.R. 3:15.17*	UNITED STATES 3:15.51	EAST GERMANY 3:18.29
Tatyana Ledovskaya	Denean Howard	Dagmar Neubauer
Olga Nazarova	Diane Dixon	Kirsten Emmelmann
Maria Pinigina	Valerie Brisco	Sabine Busch
Olga Bryzgina	Florence Griffith-Joyner	Petra Müller

The following record times were set in the preliminaries of the 1972 Games: 3:29.3 West Germany, 3:28.5 East Germany.

100 METERS (109 yd 1 ft) HURDLES

1928–68 Event not held		
1972 Annelie Ehrhardt (GDR) 12.59*	Valeria Bufanu (ROM) 12.84	Karin Balzer (GDR) 12.90
1976 Johanna Schaller (GDR) 12.77	Tatyana Anisimova (URS) 12.78	Natalia Lebedeva (URS) 12.80
1980 Vera Komisova (URS) 12.56*	Johanna Klier (GDR) 12.63	Lucyna Langer (POL) 12.65
1984 Benita Fitzgerald-Brown (USA) 12.84	Shirley Strong (GBR) 12.88	Kim Turner (USA) 13.06 Michele Chardonnet (FRA) 13.06
1988 Yordanka Donkova (BUL) 12.38*	Gloria Siebert (GDR) 12.61	Claudia Zaczkiewicz (FRG) 12.75

The following record times were set in the preliminaries: 12.0 and 12.73 by Ehrhardt 1972; 12.47 Donkova 1988.

400 METERS HURDLES

1928–1980 Event not held		
1984 Nawal El Moutawakel (MAR) 54.61*	Judi Brown (USA) 55.20	Cristina Cojocaru (ROM) 55.41
1988 Debbie Flintoff-King (AUS) 53.17*	Tatyana Ledovskaya (URS) 53.18	Ellen Fiedler (GDR) 53.63

The following record times were set in the preliminaries: 54.58 Fiedler 1988; 54.00 Flintoff-King 1988.

HIGH JUMP

1928 Ethel Catherwood (CAN) 5' 2½" 1,59 m*	Carolina A. Gisolf (HOL) 5' 1¼" 1,56 m	Mildred Wiley (USA) 5' 1¼" 1,56 m
1932 Jean M. Shiley (USA) 5' 5" 1,65 m*	Mildred Didrikson (USA) 5' 5" 1,65 m*	Eva Dawes (CAN) 5' 3" 1,60 m
1936 Ibolya Csák (HUN) 5' 3" 1,60 m	Dorothy J.B. Odam (GBR) 5' 3" 1,60 m	Elfriede Kaun (GER) 5' 3" 1,60 m

	GOLD	SILVER	BRONZE
1948	Alice Coachman (USA) 5' 6" *1,68 m**	Dorothy J.B. Tyler (GBR) 5' 6" *1,68 m**	Micheline O. M. Ostermeyer (FRA) 5' 3¼" *1,61 m*
1952	Esther C. Brand (SAF) 5' 5½" *1,67 m*	Sheila W. Lerwill (GBR) 5' 5" *1,65 m*	Alexandra G. Chudina (URS) 5' 4" *1,63 m*
1956	Mildred McDaniel (USA) 5' 9¼" *1,76 m**	[1]	—
1960	Iolanda Balas (ROM) 6' 0¾" *1,85 m**	[2]	—
1964	Iolanda Balas (ROM) 6' 2¾" *1,90 m**	Michele Brown (AUS) 5' 10¾" *1,80 m*	Taisia Chenchik (URS) 5' 10" *1,78 m*
1968	Miloslava Rezkova (TCH) 5' 11½" *1,82 m*	Antonina Okorokova (URS) 5' 10¾" *1,80 m*	Valentina Kozyr (URS) 5' 10¾" *1,80 m*
1972	Ulrike Meyfarth (GER) 6' 3½" *1,92 m**	Yordanka Blagoyeva (BUL) 6' 2" *1,88 m*	Ilona Gusenbauer (AUT) 6' 2" *1,88 m*
1976	Rosemarie Ackermann (GDR) 6' 4" *1,93 m**	Sara Simeoni (ITA) 6' 3¼" *1,91 m*	Yordanka Blagoyeva (BUL) 6' 3¼" *1,91 m*
1980	Sara Simeoni (ITA) 6' 5½" *1,97 m**	Urszula Kielan (POL) 6' 4½" *1,94 m*	Jutta Kirst (GDR) 6' 4½" *1,94 m*
1984	Ulrike Meyfarth (FRG) 6' 7½" *2,02 m**	Sara Simeoni (ITA) 6' 6¾" *2,00 m*	Joni Huntley (USA) 6' 5½" *1,97 m*
1988	Louise Ritter (USA) 6' 8" *2,03 m**	Stefka Kostadinova (BUL) 6' 7" *2,01 m*	Tamara Bykova (URS) 6' 6¼" *1,99 m*

[1] Tie for second place by Thelma E. Hopkins (GBR) and Maria Pissrayeva (URS) at 5' 5½" *1,67 m.*

[2] Tie for second place by Jaroslawa Józwiakowska (POL) and Dorothy A. Shirley (GBR) at 5' 7¼" *1,71 m.*

LONG JUMP

	GOLD	SILVER	BRONZE
1928–1936	Event not held		
1948	V. Olga Gyarmati (HUN) 18' 8" *5,69 m**	Noemi Simonetto de Portela (ARG) 18' 4¼" *5,60 m*	B. Ann-Britt Leyman (SWE) 18' 3¼" *5,57 m*
1952	Yvette W. Williams (NZL) 20' 5½" *6,24 m**	Alexandra G. Chudina (URS) 20' 1½" *6,14 m*	Shirley Cawley (GBR) 19' 5" *5,92 m*
1956	Elzbieta Krzesinska (POL) 20' 10" *6,35 m**	Willye D. White (USA) 19' 11¾" *6,09 m*	Nadyezhda Dvalishvili (URS) 19' 10¾" *6,07 m*
1960	Vyera Krepkina (URS) 20' 10¾" *6,37 m**	Elzbieta Krzesinska (POL) 20' 6¾" *6,27 m*	Hildrun Claus (GER) 20' 4¼" *6,21 m*
1964	Mary D. Rand (GBR) 22' 2¼" *6,76 m**	Irena Kirszenstein (POL) 21' 7¾" *6,60 m*	Tatyana S. Schelkanova (URS) 21' 0¾" *6,42 m*
1968	Viorica Viscopoleanu (ROM) 22' 4½" *6,82 m**	Sheila Sherwood (GBR) 21' 10¾" *6,68 m*	Tatyana Talysheva (URS) 21' 10" *6,66 m*
1972	Heidemarie Rosendahl[1] (GER) 22' 3" *6,78 m*	Diana Yorgova (BUL) 22' 2½" *6,77 m*	Eva Suranova (TCH) 21' 10¾" *6,67 m*
1976	Angela Voigt (GDR) 22' 0¾" *6,72 m*	Kathy McMillan (USA) 21' 10¼" *6,66 m*	Lidia Alfeyeva (URS) 21' 8" *6,60 m*
1980	Tatiana Kolpakova (URS) 23' 2" *7,06 m**	Brigitte Wujak (GDR) 23' 1¼" *7,04 m*	Tatiana Skachko (URS) 23' 0" *7,01 m*
1984	Anisoara Stanciu (ROM) 22' 10" *6,96 m*	Vali Ionescu (ROM) 22' 4¼" *6,81 m*	Susan Hearnshaw (GBR) 22' 3¾" *6,80 m*
1988	Jackie Joyner-Kersee (USA)[2] 24' 3½" *7,40 m**	Heike Drechsler (GDR) 23' 8¼" *7,22 m*	Galina Chistiakova (URS) 23' 4" *7,11 m*

[1] Set Olympic record of 22' 5" *6,83 m* in Pentathlon.
[2] Set Olympic record 23' 10¼" *7,27 m* in heptathlon.

SHOT PUT

1928–1936	Event not held		
1948	Micheline O. M. Ostermeyer (FRA) 45′ 1¼″ *13,75 m**	Amelia Piccinini (ITA) 42′ 11½″ *13,09 m*	Ina Schäffer (AUT) 42′ 10¾″ *13,08 m*
1952	Galina I. Zybina (URS) 50′ 1½″ *15,28 m**	Marianne Werner (GER) 47′ 9½″ *14,57 m*	Klavdia Tochenova (URS) 47′ 6¾″ *14,50 m*
1956	Tamara Tyshkyevich (URS) 54′ 5″ *16,59 m**	Galina I. Zybina (URS) 54′ 2¾″ *16,53 m*	Marianne Werner (GER) 51′ 2½″ *15,61 m*
1960	Tamara N. Press (URS) 56′ 9¾″ *17,32 m**	Johanna Lüttge (GER) 54′ 5¾″ *16,61 m*	Earlene I. Brown (USA) 53′ 10¼″ *16,42 m*
1964	Tamara N. Press (URS) 59′ 6″ *18,14 m**	Renate Garisch (GER) 57′ 9¼″ *17,61 m*	Galina I. Zybina (URS) 57′ 3″ *17,45 m*
1968	Margitta Gummel (GDR) 64′ 4″ *19,61 m**	Marita Lange (GDR) 61′ 7¼″ *18,78 m*	Nadyezhda Chizhova *(URS) 59′ 8″ 18,19 m*
1972	Nadyezhda Chizhova (URS) 69′ 0″ *21,03 m**	Margitta Gummel (GDR) 66′ 4¼″ *20,22 m*	Ivanka Khristova (BUL) 63′ 6″ *19,35 m*
1976	Ivanka Khristova (BUL) 69′ 5¼″ *21,16 m**	Nadyezhda Chizhova (URS) 68′ 9¼″ *20,96 m*	Helena Fibingerova (TCH) 67′ 9¾″ *20,67 m*
1980	Ilona Slupianek (GDR) 73′ 6¼″ *22,41m**	Svetlana Krachevskaya (URS) 70′ 3¼″ *21,42 m*	Margitta Pufe (GDR) 69′ 6¾″ *21,20 m*
1984	Claudia Losch (FRG) 67′ 2¼″ *20,48 m*	Mihaela Loghin (ROM) 67′ 2″ *20,47 m*	Gael Martin (AUS) 62′ 11½″ *19,19 m*
1988	Natalya Lisovskaya (URS) 72′ 11¾″ *22,24 m*	Kathrin Neimke (GDR) 69′ 1½″ *21,07 m*	Li Meisu (CHN) 69′ 1¼″ *21,06 m*

Tamara Andreyevna Tyschkyevich, the Russians' 244-lb. gold medal winner in the shot put in 1956.

DISCUS THROW

	GOLD	SILVER	BRONZE
1928	Helena Konopacka (POL) 129′ 11½″ *39,62m**	Lillian Copeland (USA) 121′ 7½″ *37,08 m*	Ruth Svedberg (SWE) 117′ 10″ *35,92 m*
1932	Lillian Copeland (USA) 133′ 1½″ *40,58 m**	Ruth Osburn (USA) 131′ 7½″ *40,11 m*	Jadwiga Wajsówna (POL) 127′ 1″ *38,73 m*
1936	Gisela Mauermayer (GER) 156′ 3″ *47,63 m**	Jadwiga Wajsówna (POL) 151′ 7½″ *46,22 m*	Paula Mollenhauer (GER) 130′ 6½″ *39,80 m*
1948	Micheline O. M. Ostermeyer (FRA) 137′ 6″ *41,92 m*	Edera C. Gentile (ITA) 135′ 0½″ *41,17 m*	Jacqueline Mazeas (FRA) 132′ 9″ *40,47 m*

	GOLD	SILVER	BRONZE
1952	Nina Romashkova (URS) 168' 8" *51,42 m*	Yelizaveta Bagryantseva (URS) 154' 5½" *47,08 m*	Nina Dumbadze (URS) 151' 10" *46,29 m*
1956	Olga Fikotová (TCH) 176' 1½" *53,69 m*	Irina Beglyakova (URS) 172' 4½" *52,54 m*	Nina Ponomaryeva (URS) 170' 8" *52,02 m*
1960	Nina Ponomaryeva (URS) 180' 9" *55,10 m*	Tamara N. Press (URS) 172' 6" *52,59 m*	Lia Manoliu (ROM) 171' 9" *52,36 m*
1964	Tamara N. Press (URS) 187' 10½" *57,27 m*	Ingrid Lotz (GER) 187' 8" *57,21 m*	Lia Manoliu (ROM) 186' 10½" *56,97 m*
1968	Lia Manoliu (ROM) 191' 2" *58,28 m*	Liesel Westermann (GER) 189' 6" *57,76 m*	Jolán Kleiber (HUN) 180' 1" *54,90 m*
1972	Faina Melnik (URS) 218' 7" *66,62 m*	Argentina Menis (ROM) 213' 5" *65,06 m*	Vassilka Stoyeva (BUL) 211' 1" *64,34 m*
1976	Evelin Schlaak (GDR) 226' 4" *69,00 m*	Maria Vergova (BUL) 220' 9" *67,30 m*	Gabriele Hinzmann (GDR) 219' 3" *66,84 m*
1980	Evelin Jahl (GDR) 229' 6" *69,96 m*	Maria Petkova (BUL) 222' 9" *67,90 m*	Tatyana Lesovaya (URS) 221' 1" *67,40 m*
1984	Ria Stalman (HOL) 214' 5" *65,36 m*	Leslie Deniz (USA) 212' 9" *64,86 m*	Florenta Craiunescu (ROM) 208' 9" *63,64 m*
1988	Martina Hellmann (GDR) 237' 2" *72,30 m*	Diana Gansky (GDR) 235' 10" *71,88 m*	Tsvetanka Khristova (BUL) 228' 10" *69,74 m*

JAVELIN THROW

	GOLD	SILVER	BRONZE
1928	Event not held		
1932	Mildred Didrikson (USA) 143' 4" *43,68 m*	Ellen Braumüller (GER) 142' 8½" *43,49 m*	Tilly Fleischer (GER) 142' 1¼" *43,40 m*
1936	Tilly Fleischer (GER) 148' 2½" *45,18 m*	Luise Krüger (GER) 142' 0" *43,29 m*	Marja Kwasniewska (POL) 137' 1½" *41,80 m*
1948	Herma Bauma (AUT) 149' 6" *45,57 m*	Kaisa V. Parviainen (FIN) 143' 8" *43,79 m*	Lily M. L. Carlstedt (DEN) 140' 6½" *42,08 m*
1952	Dana Zátopková (TCH) 165' 7" *50,47 m*	Alexandra G. Chudina (URS) 164' 0½" *50,01 m*	Yelena Y. Gorchakova (URS) 163' 3" *49,76 m*
1956	Inese Jaunzeme (URS) 176' 8" *53,86 m*	Marlene Ahrens (CHI) 165' 3" *50,38 m*	Nadyezhda E. Konyayeva (URS) 164' 11½" *50,28 m*
1960	Elvira A. Ozolina (URS) 183' 7½" *55,98 m*	Dana Zátopková (TCH) 176' 5" *53,78 m*	Birute Kalediene (URS) 175' 4" *53,45 m*
1964	Mihaela Penes (ROM) 198' 7" *60,54 m*	Martá Rudase (HUN) 191' 2" *58,27 m*	Yelena Y. Gorchakova (URS) 187' 2" *57,06 m*[1]
1968	Angéla Németh (HUN) 198' 0" *60,36 m*	Mihaela Penes (ROM) 196' 7" *59,92 m*	Eva Janko (AUT) 190' 5" *58,04 m*

ABOVE: Ruth Fuchs (GDR) was a convincing winner in the 1972 javelin throw, beating the previous Olympic record by nearly 5 feet.

ABOVE: Dana Zatopkova (Czechoslovakia), whose husband won 4 gold medals, won a gold medal in the javelin throw herself in the 1952 Olympics.

RIGHT: Powerful Nadezhda Tkachenko (URS) turned in a world record performance in capturing the women's pentathlon gold medal in 1980.

	GOLD	SILVER	BRONZE
1972	Ruth Fuchs (GDR) 209' 7" 63,88m*	Jacqueline Todten (GDR) 205' 2" 62,54 m	Kathy Schmidt (USA) 196' 8" 59,94 m
1976	Ruth Fuchs (GDR) 216' 4" 65,94 m*	Marion Becker (GDR) 212' 3" 64,70 m²	Kathy Schmidt (USA) 209' 10" 63,96 m
1980[3]	Maria Colon (CUB) 224' 5" 68,40 m*	Saida Gunba (URS) 222' 2" 67,76 m	Ute Hommola (GDR) 218' 4" 66,56 m
1984	Tessa Sanderson (GBR) 228' 2" 69,56 m*	Tiina Lillak (FIN) 226' 4" 69,00 m	Fatima Whitbread (GBR) 220' 67,14 m
1988	Petra Felke (GDR) 245' 0" 74,68 m*	Fatima Whitbread (GBR) 230' 8" 70,32 m	Beate Koch (GDR) 220' 9" 67,30 m

PENTATHLON[1]
(Figures refer to points scored)

	GOLD	SILVER	BRONZE
1928–1960	Event not held		
1964	Trina R. Press (URS) 5,246*	Mary D. Rand (GBR) 5,035	Galina Bystrova (URS) 4,956
1968	Ingrid Becker (GER) 5,098	Liese Prokop (AUT) 4,966	Annamária Tóth (HUN) 4,959
1972	Mary E. Peters (GBR) 4,801*[2]	Heidemarie Rosendahl (GER) 4,791	Burglinde Pollak (GDR) 4,768
1976	Sigrun Siegl (GDR) 4,745[3]	Christine Laser (GDR) 4,745	Burglinde Pollak (GDR) 4,740
1980	Nadezhda Tkachenko (URS) 5,083*	Olga Rukavishnikova (URS) 4,937	Olga Kuragina (URS) 4,875

[1]The Pentathlon consisted of 100 m hurdles, shot put, high jump, long jump and 200 m from 1964 to 1976. In 1980 the 200 m was replaced by 800 m.
[2]New scoring tables introduced in May 1971.
[3]Siegl finished ahead of Laser in three events.

HEPTATHLON (Replaced Pentathlon)[1]
(Figures refer to points scored)

1984[2]	Glynis Nunn (AUS) 6,387 pts*	Jackie Joyner (USA) 6,363	Sabine Everts (FRG) 6,388
1988	Jackie Joyner-Kersee (USA) 7,291 pts*	Sabine John (GDR) 6,897	Anke Behmer (GDR) 6,958

[1]The heptathlon consists of 100 m hurdles, high jump, shot put, 200 m on the first day; long jump, javelin and 800 m on the second day.
[2]Rescored with 1986 tables.

---

22. Volleyball (Men)

1896–1960 Event not held

1964	U.S.S.R.	CZECHOSLOVAKIA	JAPAN
	Yury Chesnokov	Václav Šmidl	Yataka Demachi
	Yury Vengerovsky	Josef Labuda	Tsutomu Koyama
	Eduard Sibiryakov	Josef Musil	Sadatoshi Sugahara
	Dmitry Voskoboynikov	Petr Kop	Naohiro Ikeda
	Vazha Kacharava	Milan Čuda	Yasutaka Sato
	Stanislaw Ljugailo	Karel Paulus	Toshiaki Kosedo
	Vitaly Kovalenko	Bohumil Golián	Tokihiko Higuchi
	Yury Poyarkov	Boris Perušič	Masayuki Minami
	Ivan Bugaenkov	Pavel Schenk	Takeshi Tokutomi
	Nikolay Burobin	Ladislav Toman	Teruhisa Moriyama
	Valery Kalachikhin	Zdenek Humhal	Yuzo Nakamura
	Georgy Mondzolevsky	Josef Šorim	Katsutoshi Nekoda
1968	U.S.S.R.	JAPAN	CZECHOSLOVAKIA
	Eduard Sibiryakov	Naohiro Ikeda	Antonin Procházka
	Valery Kravchenko	Masayuki Minami	Jiri Svoboda
	Vladimir Belyaev	Katsutoshi Nekoda	Lubomir Zajíček
	Evgeny Lapinsky	Mamoru Shiragami	Josef Musil
	Oleg Antropov	Isao Koizumi	Josef Smolka
	Vasilijus Matushevas	Kenji Kimura	Vladimir Petlak
	Victor Mikhalchuk	Yasuaki Mitsumori	Petr Kop
	Yury Poyarkov	Jungo Morita	František Sokol
	Boris Tereshuk	Tadayoshi Yokota	Bohumil Golián
	Vladimir Ivanov	Seiji Oko	Zdenek Groessl
	Ivan Bugaenkov	Tetsuo Sato	Pavel Schenk
	Georgy Mondzolevsky	Kenji Shimaoka	Drahomir Koudelka
1972	JAPAN	EAST GERMANY	U.S.S.R.
	Katsutoshi Nekoda	Arnold Schulz	Valery Kravchenko
	Kenji Kimura	Wolfgang Webner	Efim Tchulak
	Yoshihide Fukao	Siegfried Schneider	Vladimir Poutiatov
	Jungo Morita	Wolfgang Weise	Vladimir Patkin
	Tadayoshi Yokota	Rudi Schumann	Leonid Zaiko
	Seiji Oko	Eckehard Pietzsch	Yuri Starunski
	Kenji Shimaoka	Wolfgang Löwe	Vladimir Kondra
	Yuzo Nakamura	Wolfgang Maibohm	Viatcheslav Domani
	Masayuki Minami	Rainer Tscharke	Victor Borsch
	Tetsuo Sato	Jürgen Maune	Alexandre Saprykine
	Yasuhiro Noguchi	Horse Peter	Evgeny Lapinsky
	Tetsuo Nishimoto	Horse Hagen	Yury Poyarkov

	GOLD	SILVER	BRONZE
1976	**POLAND**	**U.S.S.R.**	**CUBA**
	Wlodzimierz Stefanski	Anatoli Polishuk	Leonel Marshall
	Bronislaw Bebel	Viacheslav Zaitsev	Victoriano Sarmientos
	Lech Lasko	Efim Tchulak	Ernesto Martinez
	Tomasz Wojtowicz	Vladimir Dorohov	Victor Garcia
	Edward Skorek	Aleksandr Ermilov	Carlos Salas
	Wieslaw Gawlowski	Pavel Selivanov	Raul Vilches
	Miroslaw Rybaczewski	Oleg Moliboga	Jesus Savigne
	Zbigniew Lubiejewski	Vladimir Kondra	Lorenzo Martinez
	Ryszard Bosek	Yuri Starunski	Diego Lapera
	Wlodzimierz Sadalski	Vladimir Chernyshov	Antonio Rodriguez
	Zbigniew Zarzycki	Vladimir Ulanov	Alfredo Figueredo
	Marek Karbarz	Aleksandr Savin	Jorge Perez
1980	**U.S.S.R.**	**BULGARIA**	**ROMANIA**
	Yuriy Panchenko	Stoyan Guntchev	Corneliu Oros
	Viacheslav Zaitsev	Kristo Stoyanov	Laurentiu Dumanoiu
	Aleksandr Savin	Dimitar Zlatanov	Dan Girleanu
	Vladimir Dorohov	Stefan Dimitrov	Nicu Stoian
	Aleksandr Ermilov	Tzano Tzanov	Sorin Macavei
	Pavel Selivanov	Petko Petkov	Constantin Sterea
	Oleg Moliboga	Mitko Todorov	Neculae Vasile Pop
	Vladimir Kondra	Emil Valchev	Gunter Enescu
	Vladimir Chernyshov	Kristo Iliyev	Valter-Corneliu Chifu
	Feodor Lashchenov	Yordan Anghelov	Marius Cata-Chitiga
	Vilyar Loor	Dimitar Dimitrov	Florin Mina
	Valeriy Krivov	Kaspar Simeonov	Viorel Manole
1984	**UNITED STATES**	**BRAZIL**	**ITALY**
	Dusty Dvorak	Bernardo Rezende	Marco Negri
	Dave Saunders	Mario Oliveira Neto	Pier Paolo Lucchetta
	Steve Salmons	Antonio Ribiero	Gian Carlo Dametto
	Paul Sunderland	Jose Montanaro Jr	Franco Bertoli
	Rich Duwelius	Ruy Campos Nascimento	Francesco Dall'Olio
	Steve Timmons	Renan Dal Zotto	Piero Rebaudengo
	Craig Buck	William Silva	Giovanni Errichiello
	Marc Waldie	Amauri Ribiero	Guido De Luigi
	Chris Marlowe	Marcus Freire	Fabio Vullo
	Aldis Berzins	Domingo Lampariello	Giovanni Lanfranco
	Pat Powers	Neto	Paolo Vecchi
	Karch Kiraly	Bernard Rajzman	Andrea Lucchetta
		Fernando D'Avila	
1988	**UNITED STATES**	**U.S.S.R.**	**ARGENTINA**
	Troy Tanner	Yuriy Pantchenko	Claudio Zulianello
	Dave Saunders	Andrey Kuznetsov	Daniel Castellani
	Jon Root	Vyacheslav Zaitsev	Eduardo Martinez
	Robert Ctvrtlik	Yevgeny Krasilnikov	Alejandro Diz
	Robert Partie	Raimond Vilde	Daniel Colla
	Steve Timmons	Valeriy Lossev	Carlos Weber
	Craig Black	Yuriy Sapega	Hugo Conte
	Scott Fortune	Alexandr Sorokolet	Waldo Kantor
	Ricci Luyties	Yaroslav Antonov	Raul Quiroga
	Jeff Stork	Yuriy Tcherednik	Jon Uriarte
	Eric Sato	Igor Rounov	Estiban De Palma
	Karch Kiraly	Vladimir Chkourine	Juan Cuminetti

Volleyball (Women)

GOLD	SILVER	BRONZE
1896–1960 Event not held		
1964 JAPAN	**U.S.S.R.**	**POLAND**
Masae Kasai	Antonina Ryzhova	Krystyna Czajkowska
Emiko Miyamoto	Astra Biltauer	Jozefa Ledwigowa
Kinuko Tanida	Ninel Lukanina	Maria Golimowska
Yuriko Handa	Ljudmila Buldakova	Jadwiga Rutkowska
Yoshiko Matsumara	Nelly Abramova	Danuta Kordaczuk
Sata Isobe	Tamara Tikhonina	Krystyna Jakobowska
Masako Kondo	Valentina Kamenek	Jadwiga Marko
Ayano Shibuki	Inna Ryskal	Maria Sliwkowa
Katsumi Matsumara	Marita Katusheva	Zofia Szczesniewska
Yoko Shinozaki	Tatyana Roschina	Krystyna Krupowa
Yuko Fujimoto	Valentina Mishak	
Setsuko Sasaki	Ludmila Gureeva	
1968 U.S.S.R.	**JAPAN**	**POLAND**
Ljudmila Buldakova	Setsuko Yoshika	Krystyna Czajkowska
Ljudmila Mikhailovskaya	Suzue Takayama	Jozefa Ledwigowa
Vera Lantratova	Toyoko Iwahara	Elzbieta Porzec
Vera Galushka	Yukiyo Kojima	Wanda Wiecha
Tatyana Sarycheva	Sachiko Fukunaka	Zofia Szczesniewska
Tatyana Ponyaeva	Kunie Shiskikura	Krystyna Jakobowska
Nina Smoleeva	Setsuko Inoue	Lidia Chmielnicka
Inna Ryskal	Sumie Oinuma	Barbara Niemczyk
Galina Leantieva	Keiko Hama	Krystyna Krupowa
Roza Salikhova		Halina Aszkielowicz
Valentina Vinogradova		Jadwiga Ksiazek
		Krystyna Ostromecka
1972 U.S.S.R.	**JAPAN**	**N. KOREA**
Inna Ryskal	Sumie Oinuma	Chun Ok Ri
Vera Douiounova	Noriko Yamashita	Myong Suk Kim
Tatyana Tretiakova	Seiko Shimakage	Zung Bok Kim
Nina Smoleeva	Makiko Furukawa	Ok Sun Kang
Roza Salikhova	Takako Iida	Yeun Ja Kim
Ljudmila Buldakova	Katsumi Matsumura	He Suk Hwang
Tatyana Gonobobleva	Michiko Shiokawa	Ok Rim Jang
Lubov Turina	Takako Shirai	Myong Suk Paek
Galina Leontieva	Mariko Okamoto	Chun Ja Ryom
Tatyana Sarycheva	Keiko Hama	Su Dae Kim
Ludmila Borozna	Yaeko Yamazaki	Ok Jin Jong
Natalia Koudreva	Toyoko Iwahara	
1976 JAPAN	**U.S.S.R.**	**KOREA**
Takako Iida	Anna Rostova	Soonbok Lee
Mariko Okamoto	Ludmila Shetinina	Junghye Yu
Echiko Maeda	Lilia Osadchaya	Kyungja Byon
Noriko Matsuda	Natalia Kushnir	Soonok Lee
Takako Shirai	Olga Kozakova	Myungsun Baik
Kiyomi Kato	Nina Smoleeva	Heesook Chang
Yuko Arakida	Lubov Rudovskaya	Kumja Ma
Katsuko Kanesaka	Larisa Bergen	Youngnae Yun
Mariko Yoshida	Inna Ryskal	Kyunghwa Yu
Shoko Takayanagi	Ludmila Chernysheva	Mikum Park
Hiromi Yano	Zoya Iusova	Soonok Jung
Juri Yokoyamma	Nina Muradian	Heajung Jo
1980 U.S.S.R.	**EAST GERMANY**	**BULGARIA**
Nadyezda Radzevich	Ute Kostrzeva	Tania Dimitrova
Natalya Razumova	Andrea Heim	Silva Petrunova
Olga Solovova	Annette Schultz	Anka Khristolova
Yelena Akhaminova	Christine Mummhardt	Verka Borissova
Irina Makagonova	Heike Lehmann	Roumiana Kaicheva
Lubov Kozyreva	Barbara Czekalla	Maya Gheorghieva
Svetlana Nikishina	Karla Roffeis	Tania Gogova
Ludmila Chernysheva	Martina Schmidt	Tzevetana Bojourina
Svetlana Badulina	Anke Westendorf	Valentina Iliyeva
Lidiya Loginova	Karin Puschel	Galina Stantcheva
Larisa Pavlova	Brigitte Fetzer	Margarita Gerasimova
Yelena Andreyuk	Katharina Bullin	Rossitza Dimitrova

GOLD	SILVER	BRONZE
1984 **CHINA**	**UNITED STATES**	**JAPAN**
Ping Lang	Paula Weishoff	Yumi Egami
Yan Liang	Susan Woodstra	Kimie Morita
Ling Zhu	Rita Crockett	Yuko Mitsuya
Yuzhu Hou	Laurie Flachmeier	Miyoko Hirose
Xiaolan Zhou	Carolyn Becker	Kyoko Ishida
Xilan Yang	Flo Hyman	Yoko Kagabu
Huijuan Su	Rosie Magers	Norie Hiro
Ying Jiang	Julie Vollertsen	Kayoko Sugiyama
Yanjun Li	Debbie Green	Sachiko Otani
Xiaojun Yang	Kimberley Ruddins	Keiko Miyajima
Meizhu Zheng	Jeanne Beauprey	Emiko Odaka
Rongfang Zhang	Linda Chisholm	Kumi Nakada
1988 **U.S.S.R.**	**PERU**	**CHINA**
Valentina Oguyenko	Katherine Horny	Li Guojun
Yelena Volkova	Cenaida Uribe	Zhao Hong
Irina Smirnova	Rosa Garcia	Hou Yuzhu
Marina Kumych	Miriam Gallardo	Wang Yajun
Tatyana Sidorenko	Gabriela Perez	Yang Xilan
Irina Parkomtchuk	del Solar	Su Huijuan
Tatyana Krainova	Isabel Heredia	Jiang Ying
Olga Chkurnova	Cecilia Tiit	Cui Yongmei
Marina Nikulina	Luisa Cervera	Yang Xiaojun
Yelena Ovchinnikova	Demisse Fajardo	Zheng Meizhu
Olga Krivocheyeva	Alejandra de la	Wu Dan
Svetlana Korytova	Guerra	Li Yueming
	Gina Torrealva	
	Natalya Malaga	

23. Weightlifting

This sport became standardized in 1928 with the result depending on the aggregate weight of three two-handed overhead lifts: the Press, the Snatch and Jerk. But from 1976 the competition is decided by the aggregate of the Snatch and the Jerk only. The present Middleweight, Light-Heavyweight and Middle Heavyweight were previously called Welterweight, Middleweight and Light-Heavyweight respectively.

FLYWEIGHT
(Weight up to *52 kg* 114½ lb)

1928–1968	Event not held		
1972	Zygmunt Smalcerz (POL) 744 lb *337,5 kg*	Lajos Szuecs (HUN) 727½ lb *330 kg*	Sandor Holczreiter (HUN) 722 lb *327,5 kg*
1976	Alexandr Voronin (URS) 534½ lb *242,5 kg*	Gyorgy Koszegi (HUN) 523½ lb *237,5 kg*	Mohammad Nassiri (IRN) 518 lb *235,0 kg*
1980	Kanybek Osmanoliev (URS) 540 lb *245 kg*	Bong Chol Ho (PRK) 540 lb *245 kg*	Gyong Si Han (PRK) 540 lb *245 kg*
1984	Zeng Guoqiang (CHN) 518 lb *235 kg*	Zhou Peishun (CHN) 518 lb *235 kg*	Kazushito Manabe (JPN) 512½ lb *232,5 kg*
1988	Sevdalin Marinov (BUL) 595 lb *270 kg**	Chun Byung-Kwan (KOR) 573 lb *260 kg*	He Zhuogiang (CHN) 567½ lb *257,5 kg*

BANTAMWEIGHT

(Weight up to *56 kg* 123½ lb)

1928–1936	Event not held		
1948	Joseph de Pietro (USA) 678 lb *307,5 kg*	Julian Creus (GBR) 655¾ lb *297,5 kg*	Richard Tom (USA) 650¼ lb *295 kg*
1952	Ivan Udodov (URS) 694¼ lb *315 kg*	Mahmoud Namdjou (IRN) 678 lb *307,5 kg*	Ali Mirzai (IRN) 661¼ lb *300 kg*
1956	Charles Vinci (USA) 755 lb *342,5 kg*	Vladimir Stogov (URS) 744 lb *337,5 kg*	Mahmoud Namdjou (IRN) 733 lb *332,5 kg*
1960	Charles Vinci (USA) 760½ lb *345 kg*	Yoshinobu Miyake (JPN) 744 lb *337,5 kg*	Esmail E. Khan (IRN) 727½ lb *330 kg*
1964	Alexey Vakhonin (URS) 788 lb *357,5 kg*	Imre Földi (HUN) 782½ lb *355 kg*	Shiro Ichinoseki (JPN) 766 lb *347,5 kg*
1968	Mohammad Nassiri (IRN) 810 lb *367,5 kg*	Imre Földi (HUN) 810 lb *367,5 kg*	Henryk Trebicki (POL) 788 lb *357,5 kg*
1972	Imre Földi (HUN) 832 lb *377,5 kg*	Mohammad Nassiri (IRN) 815½ lb *370 kg*	Gennadi Chetin (URS) 810 lb *367,5 kg*
1976	Norair Nurikyan (BUL) 578½ lb *262,5 kg*	Grzegorz Cziura (POL) 556½ lb *252,5 kg*	Kenkichi Ando (JPN) 551 lb *250 kg*
1980	Daniel Nunez (CUB) 606¼ lb *275 kg*	Yurik Sarkisian (URS) 595 lb *270 kg*	Tadeusz Dembonczyk (POL) 584 lb *265 kg*
1984	Wu Shude (CHN) 589½ lb *267,5 kg*	Lai Runming (CHN) 584 lb *265 kg*	Masahito Kotaka (JPN) 556½ lb *252,5 kg*
1988	Oxen Mirzoyan (URS) 644¾ lb *292,5 kg**	He Yingqiang (CHN) 633¾ lb *287,5 kg*	Liu Shoubin (CHN) 589¼ lb *267,5 kg*

[1]Mitko Grablev (BUL) finished in first place with 655¾ lb *297,5 kg* but was subsequently disqualified.

FEATHERWEIGHT

(Weight up to *60 kg* 132 lb)

1928	Franz Andrysek (AUT) 633¾ lb *287,5 kg*	Pierino Gabetti (ITA) 622¾ lb *282,5 kg*	Hans Wölpert (GER) 622¾ lb *282,5 kg*
1932	Raymond Suvigny (FRA) 633¾ lb *287,5 kg*	Hans Wölpert (GER) 622¾ lb *282,5 kg*	Anthony Terlazzo (USA) 617¼ lb *280 kg*
1936	Anthony Terlazzo (USA) 688¾ lb *312,5 kg*	Saleh Moh Soliman (EGY) 672¼ lb *305 kg*	Ibrahim H. Shams (EGY) 661¼ lb *300 kg*
1948	Mahmoud Fayad (EGY) 733 lb *332,5 kg*	Rodney Wilkes (TRI) 699¾ lb *317,5 kg*	Jaffar Salmassi (IRN) 688¾ lb *312,5 kg*
1952	Rafael Chimishkyan (URS) 774 lb *337,5 kg*	Nikolay Saksonov (URS) 733 lb *332,5 kg*	Rodney Wilkes (TRI) 711 lb *322,5 kg*
1956	Isaac Berger (USA) 777 lb *352,5 kg*	Evgeniy Minayev (URS) 755 lb *342,5 kg*	Marian Zielinski (POL) 738½ lb *355 kg*
1960	Evgeniy Minayev (URS) 821 lb *372,5 kg*	Isaac Berger (USA) 799 lb *362,5 kg*	Sebastiano Mannironi (ITA) 777 lb *352,5 kg*
1964	Yoshinobu Miyake (JPN) 876¼ lb *397,5 kg*	Isaac Berger (USA) 843¼ lb *382,5 kg*	Mieczyslaw Nowak (POL) 832 lb *377,5 kg*
1968	Yoshinobu Miyake (JPN) 865¼ lb *392,5 kg*	Dito Shanidze (URS) 854¼ lb *387,5 kg*	Yoshiyuki Miyake (JPN) 848¾ lb *385 kg*
1972	Norair Nurikyan (BUL) 887¼ lb *402,5 kg*	Dito Shanidze (URS) 881¾ lb *400 kg*	Janos Benedek (HUN) 859¾ lb *390 kg*
1976	Nikolai Kolesnikov (URS) 628¼ lb *285 kg*	Georgi Todorov (BUL) 617¼ lb *280 kg*	Kuzumasa Hirai (JPN) 606¼ lb *275 kg*
1980	Viktor Mazin (URS) 639¼ lb *290 kg*	Stefan Dimitrov (BUL) 633¾ lb *287,5 kg*	Marek Seweryn (POL) 622¾ lb *282,5 kg*
1984	Chen Weiqiang (CHN) 622¾ lb *282,5 kg*	Gelu Radu (ROM) 617¼ lb *280 kg*	Wen-Yee Tsai (TPE) 600¾ lb *272,5 kg*
1988	Naim Suleymanoglu (TUR) 755 lb *342,5 kg**	Stefan Topourov (BUL) 688¾ lb *312,5 kg*	Ye Huanming (CHN) 633¾ lb *287,5 kg*

LIGHTWEIGHT

(Weight up to *67,5 kg* 149 lb)

	GOLD	SILVER	BRONZE
1928[1]	Kurt Helbig (GER) 711 lb *322,5 kg* Hans Haas (AUT) 711 lb *322,5 kg*	—	Fernand Arnout (FRA) 666¾ lb *302,5 kg*
1932	René Duverger (FRA) 716½ lb *325 kg*	Hans Haas (AUT) 678 lb *307,5 kg*	Gastone Pierini (ITA) 666¾ lb *302,5 kg*
1936[1]	Anwar Mohammed Mesbah (EGY) 755 lb *342,5 kg* Robert Fein (AUT) 755 lb *342,5 kg*		Karl Jansen (GER) 722 lb *327,5 kg*
1948	Ibrahim H. Shams (EGY) 793½ lb *360 kg*	Attia Hamouda (EGY) 793½ lb *360 kg*	James Halliday (GBR) 749½ lb *340 kg*
1952	Thomas Kono (USA) 799 lb *365,5 kg*	Yevgeniy Lopatin (URS) 771½ lb *350 kg*	Verne Barberis (AUS) 771½ lb *350 kg*
1956	Igor Rybak (URS) 837¾ lb *380 kg*	Ravil Khabutdinov (URS) 821 lb *372,5 kg*	Chang-Hee Kim (KOR) 815½ lb *370 kg*
1960	Viktor Bushuyev (URS) 876¼ lb *397,5 kg*	Howe-Liang Tan (SIN) 837¾ lb *380 kg*	Abdul Wahid Aziz (IRQ) 837¾ lb *380 kg*
1964	Waldemar Baszanowski (POL) 953¼ lb *432,5 kg*	Vladimir Kaplunov (URS) 953¼ lb *432,5 kg*	Marian Zielinski (POL) 925¾ lb *420 kg*
1968	Waldemar Baszanowski (POL) 964½ lb *437,5 kg*	Parviz Jalayer (IRN) 931¼ lb *422,5 kg*	Marian Zielinski (POL) 925¾ lb *420 kg*
1972	Mukharbi Kirzhinov (URS) 1,014 lb *460 kg*	Mladen Koutchev (BUL) 992 lb *450 kg*	Zbigniew Kaczmarek (POL) 964½ lb *437,5 kg*
1976[2]	Piotr Korol (URS) 672¼ lb *305 kg*	Daniel Senet (FRA) 661¼ lb *300 kg*	Kazimierz Czarnecki (POL) 650¼ lb *295 kg*
1980	Yanko Roussev (URS) 755 lb *342,5 kg*	Joachim Kunz (GDR) 738½ lb *335 kg*	Mintcho Pachov (BUL) 716 lb *325 kg*
1984	Yao Jingyuan (CHN) 705¼ lb *320 kg*	Andrei Socaci (ROM) 688¾ lb *312,5 kg*	Jouni Grenman (FIN) 688¾ lb *312,5 kg*
1988	Joachim Kunz (GDR) 749½ lb *340 kg*	Israil Militossyan (URS) 744 lb *337,5 kg*	Li Jinhe (CHN) 716½ lb *325 kg*

[1]Results and bodyweights being equal both were declared champions.
[2]Zbigniew Kaczmarek (POL) finished in first place with 677¾ lb *307,5 kg* but was subsequently disqualified.

MIDDLEWEIGHT

(Weight up to *75 kg* 165¼ lb)

1928	Roger François (FRA) 738½ lb *335 kg*	Carlo Galimberti (ITA) 733 lb *332,5 kg*	August Scheffer (HOL) 722 lb *327,5 kg*
1932	Rudolf Ismayr (GER) 760½ lb *345 kg*	Carlo Galimberti (ITA) 749½ lb *340 kg*	Karl Hipfinger (AUT) 744 lb *337,5 kg*
1936	Khadr S. El Touni (EGY) 854¼ lb *387,5 kg*	Rudolf Ismayr (GER) 777 lb *352,5 kg*	Adolf Wagner (GER) 777 lb *352,5 kg*
1948	Frank Spellman (USA) 859¾ lb *390 kg*	Peter George (USA) 843¼ lb *382,5 kg*	Sung-Jip Kim (KOR) 837¾ lb *380 kg*
1952	Peter George (USA) 881¾ lb *400 kg*	Gérard Gratton (CAN) 859¾ lb *390 kg*	Sung-Jip Kim (KOR) 843¼ lb *382,5 kg*
1956	Fyodor Bogdanovskiy (URS) 925¾ lb *420 kg*	Peter George (USA) 909¼ lb *412,5 kg*	Ermanno Pignatti (ITA) 843¼ lb *382,5 kg*
1960	Aleksandr Kurynov (URS) 964½ lb *437,5 kg*	Thomas Kono (USA) 942¼ lb *427,5 kg*	Gyözö Veres (HUN) 892¾ lb *405 kg*
1964	Hans Zdražila (TCH) 981 lb *445 kg*	Viktor Kurentsov (URS) 970 lb *440 kg*	Masashi Ouchi (JPN) 964½ lb *437,5 kg*
1968	Viktor Kurentsov (URS) 1,047 lb *475 kg*	Masashi Ouchi (JPN) 1,003 lb *455 kg*	Károly Bakos (HUN) 970 lb *440 kg*
1972	Yordan Bikov (BUL) 1,069 lb *485 kg*	Mohamed Trabulsi (LIB) 1,041½ lb *472,5 kg*	Anselmo Silvino (ITA) 1,036 lb *470 kg*
1976	Yordan Mitkov (BUL) 738½ lb *335 kg*	Vartan Militosyan (URS) 727½ lb *330 kg*	Peter Wenzel (GDR) 722 lb *327,5 kg*

	GOLD	SILVER	BRONZE
1980	Assen Zlatev (BUL) 793½ lb *360 kg*	Alexandr Pervy (URS) 788 lb *357,5 kg*	Nedeltcho Kolev (BUL) 760½ lb *345 kg*
1984	Karl-Heinz Radschinsky (FRG) 749½ lb *340 kg*	Jacques Demers (CAN) 738½ lb *335 kg*	Dragomir Cioroslan (ROM) 733 lb *332,5 kg*
1988	Borislav Guidikov (BUL) 826½ lb *375 kg*	Ingo Steinhöfel (GDR) 793½ lb *360 kg*	Alexandr Varbanov (URS) 788 lb *357,5 kg*

LIGHT-HEAVYWEIGHT

(Weight up to *82,5 kg* 182 lb)

1928	Said Nosseir (EGY) 782½ lb *355 kg*	Louis Hostin (FRA) 777 lb *352,5 kg*	Johannes Verheijen (HOL) 744 lb *337,5 kg*
1932	Louis Hostin (FRA) 804½ lb *365 kg*	Svend Olsen (DEN) 793½ lb *360 kg*	Henry Duey (USA) 727½ lb *330 kg*
1936	Louis Hostin (FRA) 821 lb *372,5 kg*	Eugen Deutsch (GER) 804½ lb *365 kg*	Ibrahim Wasif (EGY) 793½ lb *360 kg*
1948	Stanley Stanczyk (USA) 920¼ lb *417,5 kg*	Harold Sakata (USA) 837¾ lb *380 kg*	Gösta Magnusson (SWE) 826½ lb *375 kg*
1952	Trofim Lomakin (URS) 920¼ lb *417,5 kg*	Stanley Stanczyk (USA) 914¾ lb *415 kg*	Arkhadiy Vorobyov (URS) 898¼ lb *407,5 kg*
1956	Thomas Kono (USA) 986½ lb *447,5 kg*	Vasiliy Stepanov (URS) 942¼ lb *427,5 kg*	James George (USA) 920¼ lb *417,5 kg*
1960	Ireneusz Palinski (POL) 975½ lb *442,5 kg*	James George (USA) 947¾ lb *430 kg*	Jan Bochenek (POL) 925¾ lb *420 kg*
1964	Rudolf Plukfelder (URS) 1,047 lb *475 kg*	Géza Tóth (HUN) 1,030½ lb *467,5 kg*	Győző Veres (HUN) 1,030½ lb *467,5 kg*
1968	Boris Selitsky (URS) 1,069 lb *485 kg*	Vladimir Belyaev (URS) 1,069 lb *485 kg*	Norbert Ozimek (POL) 1,041½ lb *472,5 kg*
1972	Leif Jenssen (NOR) 1,118¾ lb *507,5 kg*	Norbert Ozimek (POL) 1,096¾ lb *497,5 kg*	György Horvath (HUN) 1,091¼ lb *495 kg*
1976[1]	Valeri Schary (URS) 804½ lb *365 kg*	Trendachil Stoichev (BUL) 793½ lb *360 kg*	Peter Baczako (HUN) 760½ lb *345 kg*
1980	Yurik Vardanyan (URS) 881¾ lb *400 kg*	Blagoi Blagoev (BUL) 821 lb *372,5 kg*	Dusan Poliacik (TCH) 810 lb *367,5 kg*
1984	*Petre Becheru (ROM) 782½ lb 355 kg*	*Robert Kabbas* (AUS) 755 lb *342,5 kg*	*Ryoji Isaoka* (JPN) 749½ lb *340 kg*
1988	Israil Arsamakov (URS) 832 lb *377,5 kg*	Istvan Messzi (HUN) 815½ lb *370 kg*	Lee Hyung-Kun (KOR) 810 lb *367,5 kg*

[1]Blagoi Blagoev (BUL) finished in second place with 799 lb *362,5 kg* but was subsequently disqualified.

MIDDLE-HEAVYWEIGHT

(Weight up to *90 kg* 198¼ lb)

1928–1948	Event not held		
1952	Norbert Shemansky (USA) 981 lb *445 kg*	Grigoriy Novak (URS) 903¾ lb *410 kg*	Lennox Kilgour (TRI) 887¼ lb *402,5 kg*
1956	Arkhadiy Vorobyov (URS) 1,019½ lb *462,5 kg*	David Sheppard (USA) 975½ lb *442,5 kg*	Jean Debuf (FRA) 936¾ lb *425 kg*
1960	Arkhadiy Vorobyov (URS) 1,041½ lb *472,5 kg*	Trofim Lomakin (URS) 1,008½ lb *457,5 kg*	Louis Martin (GBR) 981 lb *445 kg*
1964	Vladimir Golovanov (URS) 1,074¾ lb *487,5 kg*	Louis Martin (GBR) 1,047 lb *475 kg*	Ireneusz Palinski (POL) 1,030½ lb *467,5 kg*
1968	Kaarlo Kangasniemi (FIN) 1,140¾ lb *517,5 kg*	Jan Talts (URS) 1,118¾ lb *507,5 kg*	Marek Golab (POL) 1,091¼ lb *495 kg*
1972	Andon Nikolav (BUL) 1,157¼ lb *525 kg*	Atanas Shopov (BUL) 1,140¾ lb *517,5 kg*	Hans Bettembourg (SWE) 1,129¾ lb *512,5 kg*
1976	David Rigert (URS) 843¼ lb *382,5 kg*	Lee James (USA) 799 lb *362,5 kg*	Atanas Shopov (BUL) 793½ lb *360 kg*
1980	Peter Baczako (URS) 832 lb *377,5 kg*	Roumen Alexandrov (BUL) 826½ lb *375 kg*	Frank Mantek (GDR) 815½ lb *370 kg*

GOLD	SILVER	BRONZE
1984 Nicu Vlad (ROM) 865¼ lb *392,5 kg**	Dumitru Petre (ROM) 793½ lb *360 kg*	David Mercer (GBR) 771 lb *352,5 kg*
1988 Anatoly Khrapatyi (URS) 909¼ lb *412,5 kg**	Nail Moukhamediarov (URS) 881¾ lb *400 kg*	Slawomir Zawada (POL) 881¾ lb *400 kg*

100 kg
(Weight up to *100 kg* 220½ lb)

GOLD	SILVER	BRONZE
1928–1976 Event not held		
1980 Ota Zaremba (TCH) 870¾ lb *395 kg*	Igor Nikitin (URS) 865¼ lb *392,5 kg*	Alberto Blanco (CUB) 848¾ lb *385 kg*
1984 Rolf Milser (FRG) 848¾ lb *385 kg*	Vasile Gropa (ROM) 843¼ lb *382,5 kg*	Pekka Niemi (FIN) 810 lb *367,5 kg*
1988 Pavel Kuznetsov (URS) 936¾ lb *425 kg*	Nicu Vlad (ROM)[1] 887¼ lb *402,5 kg*	Peter Immesberger (FRG) 870¾ lb *395 kg*

---

[1] Andor Szanyi (HUN) finished in second place with 898¼ lb *407,5 kg* but was subsequently disqualified.

HEAVYWEIGHT

From 1928 to 1952 Heavyweight had to be over *82,5 kg* 182 lb. From 1956 to 1968 the limit was *90,0 kg* 198¼ lb. Since 1972 the top weight has been *110 kg* 242 lb.

GOLD	SILVER	BRONZE
1928 Josef Strassberger (GER) 821 lb *372,5 kg*	Arnold Luhaäär (EST) 793½ lb *360 kg*	Jaroslav Skobla (TCH) 788 lb *357,5 kg*
1932 Jaroslav Skobla (TCH) 837¾ lb *380 kg*	Václav Pšenička (TCH) 832 lb *377,5 kg*	Josef Strassberger (GER) 832 lb *377,5 kg*
1936 Josef Manger (AUT) 903¾ lb *410 kg*	Václav Pšenička (TCH) 887¼ lb *402,5 kg*	Arnold Luhaäär (EST) 881¾ lb *400 kg*
1948 John Davis (USA) 997½ lb *452,5 kg*	Norbert Schemansky (USA) 936¾ lb *425 kg*	Abraham Charité (HOL) 909¼ lb *412,5 kg*
1952 John Davis (USA) 1,014 lb *460 kg*	James Bradford (USA) 964½ lb *437,5 kg*	Humberto Selvetti (ARG) 953¼ lb *432,5 kg*
1956 Paul Anderson (USA) 1,102 lb *500 kg*	Humberto Selvetti (ARG) 1,102 lb *500 kg*	Alberto Pigaiani (ITA) 997½ lb *452,5 kg*
1960 Yuriy Vlassov (URS) 1,184¾ lb *537,5 kg*	James Bradford (USA) 1,129¾ lb *512,5 kg*	Norbert Schemansky (USA) 1,102 lb *500 kg*

LEFT: In 1980, Sultan Rakhmanov (URS) earned the super-heavyweight gold medal, succeeding the famous former two-time champion, Vassili Alexeev.

1964	Leonid Zhabotinsky (URS) 1,262 lb *572,5 kg*	Yuriy Vlassov (URS) 1,256½ lb *570 kg*	Norbert Schemansky (USA) 1,184¾ lb *537,5 kg*
1968	Leonid Zhabotinsky (URS) 1,262 lb *572,5 kg*	Serge Reding (BEL) 1,223½ lb *555 kg*	Joseph Dube (USA) 1,223½ lb *555 kg*
1972	Jan Talts (URS) 1,278½ lb *580 kg*	Alexandre Kraitchev (BUL) 1,240 lb *562,5 kg*	Stefan Gruetzner (GDR) 1,223½ lb *555 kg*
1976[1]	Yuri Zaitsev (URS) 848¾ lb *385 kg*	Krastio Semerdjiev (BUL) 848¾ lb *385 kg*	Tadeusz Rutkowski (POL) 832 lb *377,5 kg*
1980	Leonid Taranenko (URS) 931¼ lb *422,5 kg*	Valentin Khristov (BUL) 892¾ lb *405 kg*	Gyorgy Szlai (HUN) 859 ¾ lb *390 kg*
1984	Norberto Oberburger (ITA) 859¾ lb *390 kg*	Stefan Tasnadi (ROM) 837¾ lb *380 kg*	Guy Carlton (USA) 832 lb *377,5 kg*
1988	Yuriy Zakharevich (URS) 1,003 lb *455 kg**	Jozsef Jacso (HUN) 942½ lb *427,5 kg*	Ronny Weller (GDR) 936¾ lb *425 kg*

[1]Valentin Khristov (BUL) finished in first place with 881¾ lb *400 kg*, but was subsequently disqualified.

SUPER-HEAVYWEIGHT

(Weight limit over *110 kg* 242½ lb)

	GOLD	SILVER	BRONZE
1928–1968	Event not held		
1972	Vassili Alexeev (URS) 1,410¾ lb *640 kg*	Rudolf Mang (GER) 1,344¾ lb *610 kg*	Gerd Bonk (GDR) 1,262 lb *572,5 kg*
1976	Vassili Alexeev (URS) 970 lb *440 kg*	Gerd Bonk (GDR) 892¾ lb *405 kg*	Helmut Losch (GDR) 854¼ lb *387,5 kg*
1980	Sultan Rakhmanov (URS) 970 lb *440 kg*	Jurgen Heuser (GDR) 903¾ lb *410 kg*	Tadeusz Rutkowski (POL) 898¼ lb *407,5 kg*
1984	Dinko Lukin (AUS) 909¼ lb *412,5 kg*	Mario Martinez (USA) 903¾ lb *410 kg*	Manfred Nerlinger (FRG) 876¼ lb *397,5 kg*
1988	Alexandr Kourlovich (URS) 1,019 lb *462,5 kg**	Manfred Nerlinger (FRG) 947¾ lb *430 kg*	Martin Zawieja (FRG) 914¾ lb *415 kg*

Paul Anderson (USA) set an Olympic record in winning the heavyweight class gold medal in 1956. A year later he raised 6,270 lb. on his back.

24. Wrestling

The contemporary descriptions of some bodyweight classes have varied during the history of the Games. Current descriptions are used in the lists below.

FREE-STYLE—LIGHT FLYWEIGHT
(Weight up to *48 kg* 105¾ lb)

	GOLD	SILVER	BRONZE
1896–1900	Event not held		
1904	Robert Curry (USA)	John Heim (USA)	Gustav Thiefenthaler (USA)
1906–1968	Event not held		
1972	Roman Dmitriev (URS)	Ognian Nikolov (BUL)	Ebrahim Javadpour (IRN)
1976	Khassan Issaev (BUL)	Roman Dmitriev (URS)	Akira Kudo (JPN)
1980	Claudio Pollio (ITA)	Se Hong Jang (PRK)	Sergei Kornilaev (URS)
1984	Robert Weaver (USA)	Takashi Irie (JPN)	Son Gab-Do (KOR)
1988	Takashi Kobayashi (JPN)	Ivan Tzonov (BUL)	Sergey Karamtchakov (URS)

FREE-STYLE—FLYWEIGHT

Note: 1904 weight up to 115 lb *52,16 kg*. From 1948 weight up to *52 kg* 114½ lb.

1896–1900	Event not held		
1904	George Mehnert (USA)	Gustave Bauers (USA)	William Nelson (USA)
1906–1936	Event not held		
1948	Lennart Viitala (FIN)	Halit Balamir (TUR)	Thure Johansson (SWE)
1952	Hasan Gemici (TUR)	Yushu Kitano-Ali (JPN)	Mahmoud Mollaghassemi (IRN)
1956	Mirian Tsalkalamanidze (URS)	Mohamad-Ali Khojastehpour (IRN)	Hüseyin Akbas (TUR)
1960	Ahmet Bilek (TUR)	Masayuki Matsubara (JPN)	Mohamad Saifpour Saidabadi (IRN)
1964	Yoshikatsu Yoshida (JPN)	Chang-sun Chang (KOR)	Said Aliaakbar Haydari (IRN)
1968	Shigeo Nakata (JPN)	Richard Sanders (USA)	Surenjav Sukhbaatar (MGL)
1972	Kiyomi Kato (JPN)	Arsen Alakhverdiev (URS)	Hyong Kim Gwong (PRK)
1976	Yuji Takada (JPN)	Alexandr Ivanov (URS)	Jeon Hae-Sup (KOR)
1980	Anatoly Beloglazov (URS)	Wladyslaw Stecyk (POL)	Nermedin Selimov (BUL)
1984	Saban Trstena (YUG)	Kim Jong-Kyu (KOR)	Yuji Takada (JPN)
1988	Mitsuru Sato (JPN)	Saban Trstena (YUG)	Vladimir Toguzov (URS)

FREE-STYLE—BANTAMWEIGHT

Note: The weight limit for this event has been: 1908, 125 lb *56,70 kg;* 1980, 119 lb *54 kg;* 1924–1936, *56 kg* 123½ lb and from 1948, *57 kg* 125¾ lb.

	GOLD	SILVER	BRONZE
1896–1900	Event not held		
1904	Isaac Niflot (USA)	August Wester (USA)	Z. B. Strebler (USA)
1906	Event not held		
1908	George Mehnert (USA)	William Press (GBR)	Aubert Côté (CAN)
1912–1920	Event not held		
1924	Kustaa Pihlajamäki (FIN)	Kaarlo Mäkinen (FIN)	Bryant Hines (USA)
1928	Kaarlo Mäkinen (FIN)	Edmond Spapen (BEL)	James Trifunov (CAN)
1932	Robert Pearce (USA)	Ödön Zombori (HUN)	Aatos Jaskari (FIN)
1936	Ödön Zombori (HUN)	Ross Flood (USA)	Johannes Herbert (GER)
1948	Nasuk Akar (TUR)	Gerald Leeman (USA)	Charles Kouyos (FRA)
1952	Shohachi Ishii (JPN)	Rashid Mamedbekov (URS)	Kha-Shaba Jadav (IND)
1956	Mustafa Dagistanli (TUR)	Mohamad Yaghoubi (IRN)	Mikhail Chakhov (URS)
1960	Terrence McCann (USA)	Nejdet Zalev (BUL)	Tadeusz Trojanowski (POL)
1964	Yojiro Uetake (JPN)	Hüseyin Akbas (TUR)	Aidyn Ibragimov (URS)
1968	Yojiro Uetake (JPN)	Donald Behm (USA)	Abutaleb Gorgori (IRN)
1972	Hideaki Yanagide (JPN)	Richard Sanders (USA)	László Klinga (HUN)
1976	Vladimir Umin (URS)	Hans-Dieter Bruchert (GDR)	Masao Arai (JPN)

A free-style bout between bantamweights at Empress Hall, Earls Court, London in the 1948 Olympics. Nasuk Akar (TUR), the eventual gold medal winner, is on top of Charles Kouyos (FRA), who won the bronze medal.

GOLD	SILVER	BRONZE
1980 Sergei Beloglazov (URS)	Li Ho Pyong (PRK)	Dugarsuren Quinbold (MGL)
1984 Hideyaki Tomiyama (JPN)	Barry Davis (USA)	Kim Eui-Kon (KOR)
1988 Sergey Beloglazov (URS)	Askari Mohammadian (IRN)	Noh Kyung-Sun (KOR)

FREE-STYLE—FEATHERWEIGHT

Note: The weight limit for this event has been: 1904, 135 lb *61,24 kg;* 1908, 133 lb *60,30 kg;* 1920, 132¼ lb *60 kg;* 1924–1936, 134½ lb *61 kg;* 1948–1960, and 1972, *62 kg* 136½ lb; 1964–1968, *63 kg* 138¾ lb.

1896–1900 Event not held		
1904 Benjamin Bradshaw (USA)	Theodore McLear (USA)	Charles Clapper (USA)
1906 Event not held		
1908 George Dole (USA)	James P. Slim (GBR)	William McKie (GBR)
1912 Event not held		
1920 Charles E. Ackerly (USA)	Samuel Gerson (USA)	P. W. Bernard (GBR)
1924 Robin Reed (USA)	Chester Newton (USA)	Katsutoshi Naito (JPN)
1928 Allie Morrison (USA)	Kustaa Pihlajamäki (FIN)	Hans Minder (SUI)
1932 Hermanni Pihlajamäki (FIN)	Edgar Nemir (USA)	Einar Karlsson (SWE)
1936 Kustaa Pihlajamäki (FIN)	Francis Millard (USA)	Gösta Jönsson (SWE)
1948 Gazanfer Bilge (TUR)	Ivar Sjölin (SWE)	Adolf Müller (SUI)
1952 Bayram Sit (TUR)	Nasser Guivehtchi (IRN)	Josiah Henson (USA)
1956 Shozo Sasahara (JPN)	Joseph Mewis (BEL)	Erkki Penttilä (FIN)
1960 Mustafa Dagistanli (TUR)	Stantcho Ivanov (BUL)	Vladimir Rubashvili (URS)
1964 Osamu Watanabe (JPN)	Stantcho Ivanov (BUL)	Nodar Khokhashvili (URS)
1968 Masaaki Kaneko (JPN)	Enyu Todorov (BUL)	Shamseddin Seyed-Abbassi (IRN)
1972 Zagalav Abdulbekov (URS)	Vehbi Akdag (TUR)	Ivan Krastev (BUL)
1976 Yang Jung-Mo (KOR)	Zeveg Oidov (MGL)	Gene Davis (USA)
1980 Magomedgasan Abushev (URS)	Mikho Doukov (BUL)	Georges Hadjioannidis (GRE)
1984 Randy Lewis (USA)	Kosei Akaishi (JPN)	Lee Jung-Keun (KOR)
1988 John Smith (USA)	Stepan Sarkissian (URS)	Simeon Chterev (BUL)

FREE-STYLE—LIGHTWEIGHT

Note: The weight limit for this event has been: 1904, 145 lb *65,77 kg;* 1908, 146¾ lb *66,60 kg;* 1920, 148¾ lb *67,50 kg;* 1924 to 1936, 145½ lb *66 kg;* 1948 to 1960, *67 kg* 147½ lb; 1964 and 1968, *70 kg* 154 lb; and from 1972, *68 kg* 149¾ lb.

1896–1900 Event not held		
1904 Otto Roehm (USA)	R. Tesing (USA)	Albert Zirkel (USA)
1906 Event not held		
1908 G. de Relwyskow (GBR)	William Wood (GBR)	Albert Gingell (GBR)

	GOLD	SILVER	BRONZE
1912	Event not held		
1920	Kalle Anttila (FIN)	Gottfrid Svensson (SWE)	Peter Wright (GBR)
1924	Russell Vis (USA)	Volmart Wickström (FIN)	Arvo Haavisto (FIN)
1928	Osvald Käpp (EST)	Charles Pacôme (FRA)	Eino Leino (FIN)
1932	Charles Pacôme (FRA)	Károly Kárpáti (HUN)	Gustaf Klarén (SWE)
1936	Károly Kárpáti (HUN)	Wolfgang Ehrl (GER)	Hermanni Pihlajamäki (FIN)
1948	Celal Atik (TUR)	Gösta Frändfors (SWE)	Hermann Baumann (SUI)
1952	Olle Anderberg (SWE)	J. Thomas Evans (USA)	Djahanbakte Tovfighe (IRN)
1956	Emamali Habibi (IRN)	Shigeru Kasahara (JPN)	Alimberg Bestayev (URS)
1960	Shelby Wilson (USA)	Viktor Sinyavskiy (URS)	Enyu Dimov (BUL)
1964	Enyu Valtschev[1] (BUL)	Klaus-Jürgen Rost (GER)	Iwao Horiuchi (JPN)
1968	Abdollah Movahed Ardabili (IRN)	Enyu Valtschev[1] (BUL)	Sereeter Danzandarjaa (MGL)
1972	Dan Gable (USA)	Kikuo Wada (JPN)	Ruslan Ashuraliev (URS)
1976	Pavel Pinigin (URS)	Lloyd Keaser (USA)	Yasaburo Sagawara (JPN)
1980	Saipulla Absaidov (URS)	Ivan Yankov (BUL)	Saban Sejdi (YUG)
1984	You In-Tak (KOR)	Andrew Rein (USA)	Jukka Rauhala (FIN)
1988	Arsen Fadzayev (URS)	Park Jang-Soon (KOR)	Nate Carr (USA)

[1]Valtschev competed as Dimov in 1960.

FREE-STYLE—WELTERWEIGHT

Note: The weight limit for this event has been: 1904, 158 lb *71,67 kg;* 1924 to 1936, 158½ lb *72 kg;* 1948 to 1960, *73 kg* 160¾ lb; from 1972, *74 kg* 163 lb.

	GOLD	SILVER	BRONZE
1896–1900	Event not held		
1904	Charles Erickson (USA)	William Beckmann (USA)	Jerry Winholtz (USA)
1906–1920	Event not held		
1924	Hermann Gehri (SUI)	Eino Leino (FIN)	Otto Müller (SUI)
1928	Arvo Haavisto (FIN)	Lloyd Appleton (USA)	Maurice Letchford (CAN)
1932	Jack van Bebber (USA)	Daniel MacDonald (CAN)	Eino Leino (FIN)
1936	Frank Lewis (USA)	Ture Andersson (SWE)	Joseph Schleimer (CAN)
1948	Yasar Dogu (TUR)	Richard Garrard (AUS)	Leland Merrill (USA)
1952	William Smith (USA)	Per Berlin (SWE)	Abdullah Modjtabavi (IRN)
1956	Mitsuo Ikeda (JPN)	Ibrahim Zengin (TUR)	Vakhtang Balavadze (URS)
1960	Douglas Blubaugh (USA)	Ismail Ogan (TUR)	Mohammad Bashir (PAK)
1964	Ismail Ogan (TUR)	Guliko Sagaradze (URS)	Mohamad-Ali Sanatkaran (IRN)
1968	Mahmut Atalay (TUR)	Daniel Robin (FRA)	Dagvasuren Purev (MGL)

	GOLD	SILVER	BRONZE
1972	Wayne Wells (USA)	Jan Karlsson (SWE)	Adolf Seger (GER)
1976	Jiichiro Date (JPN)	Mansour Barzegar (IRN)	Stanley Dziedzic (USA)
1980	Valentin Raitchev (BUL)	Jamtsying Davaajav (MGL)	Dan Karabin (TCH)
1984	David Schultz (USA)	Martin Knosp (FRG)	Saban Sejdi (YUG)
1988	Kenneth Monday (USA)	Adlan Varayev (URS)	Rakhmad Sofindi (BUL)

FREE-STYLE—MIDDLEWEIGHT

Note: The weight limit for this event has been: 1908, 161 lb *73 kg;* 1920, 165¼ lb *75 kg;* 1924 to 1960, 174 lb *79 kg;* 1964 and 1968, *87 kg* 191¾ lb; from 1972, *82 kg* 180¾ lb.

1896–1906	Event not held		
1908	Stanley Bacon (GBR)	George de Relwyskow (GBR)	Frederick Beck (GBR)
1912	Event not held		
1920	Eino Leino (FIN)	Väinö Penttala (FIN)	Charles Johnson (USA)
1924	Fritz Hagmann (SUI)	Pierre Ollivier (BEL)	Vilho Pekkala (FIN)
1928	Ernst Kyburz (SUI)	Donald P. Stockton (CAN)	Samuel Rabin (GBR)
1932	Ivar Johansson (SWE)	Kyösti Luukko (FIN)	József Tunyogi (HUN)
1936	Emile Poilvé (FRA)	Richard Voliva (USA)	Ahmet Kireiçci (TUR)
1948	Glen Brand (USA)	Adil Candemir (TUR)	Erik Lindén (SWE)
1952	David Tsimakuridze (URS)	Gholamheza Takhti (IRN)	György Gurics (HUN)
1956	Nikola Stautscher (BUL)	Daniel Hodge (USA)	Georgiy Skhirtladze (URS)
1960	Hasan Güngör (TUR)	Georgiy Skhirtladze (URS)	Hans Y. Antonsson (SWE)
1964	Prodan Gardschev (BUL)	Hasan Güngör (TUR)	Daniel Brand (USA)
1968	Boris Gurevitch (URS)	Munkbat Jigjid (MGL)	Prodan Gardschev (BUL)
1972	Levan Tediashvili (URS)	John Peterson (USA)	Vasile Jorga (ROM)
1976	John Peterson (USA)	Viktor Novojilov (URS)	Adolf Seger (GER)
1980	Ismail Abilov (BUL)	Magomedhan Aratsilov (URS)	Istvan Kovacs (HUN)
1984	Mark Schultz (USA)	Hideyuki Nagashima (JPN)	Chris Rinke (CAN)
1988	Han Myung-Woo (KOR)	Necmi Gencalp (TUR)	Josef Lohyna (TCH)

FREE-STYLE—LIGHT-HEAVYWEIGHT

Note: The weight limit for this event has been: 1920, 181¾ lb *82,5 kg;* 1924 to 1960, *87 kg* 191¾ lb; 1964 and 1968, *97 kg* 213¾ lb; from 1972, *90 kg* 198¼ lb.

1896–1912	Event not held		
1920	Anders Larsson (SWE)	Charles Courant (SUI)	Walter Maurer (USA)
1924	John Spellman (USA)	Rudolf Svensson (SWE)	Charles Courant (SUI)

John Peterson (right side up), the only American wrestler to win a gold medal at the 1976 Games, here defeats Mehmet Uzun (TUR) in a semi-final bout.

	GOLD	SILVER	BRONZE
1928	Thure Sjöstedt (SWE)	Anton Bögli (SUI)	Henri Lefèbre (FRA)
1932	Peter Mehringer (USA)	Thure Sjöstedt (SWE)	Eddie Scarf (AUS)
1936	Knut Fridell (SWE)	August Neo (EST)	Erich Siebert (GER)
1948	Henry Wittenberg (USA)	Fritz Stöckli (SUI)	Bengt Fahlkvist (SWE)
1952	Wiking Palm (SWE)	Henry Wittenberg (USA)	Adil Atan (TUR)
1956	Gholam Reza Tahkti (IRN)	Boris Kulayev (URS)	Peter S. Blair (USA)
1960	Ismet Atli (TUR)	Gholam Reza Tahkti (IRN)	Anatoliy Albul (URS)
1964	Alexander Medved (URS)	Ahmet Ayik (TUR)	Said Mustafafov (BUL)
1968	Ahmet Ayik (TUR)	Shota Lomidze (URS)	József Csatári (HUN)
1972	Ben Peterson (USA)	Gennadi Strakhov (URS)	Karoly Bajko (HUN)
1976	Levan Tediashvili (URS)	Ben Peterson (USA)	Stelica Morcov (ROM)
1980	Sanasar Oganesyan (URS)	Uwe Neupert (GDR)	Aleksander Cichon (POL)
1984	Ed Banach (USA)	Akira Ota (JPN)	Noel Loban (GBR)
1988	Makharbek Khadartsev (URS)	Akira Ota (JPN)	Kim Tae-Woo (KOR)

FREE-STYLE—HEAVYWEIGHT

Note: The weight limit for this event has been: 1904, over 158 lb *71,6 kg;* 1908, over 161 lb *73 kg;* 1920, over 181¾ lb *82,5 kg;* 1924 to 1960, over *87 kg* 191¾ lb; 1964 and 1968, over *97 kg* 213¾ lb; from 1972, up to *100 kg* 220¼ lb.

1896–1900	Event not held		
1904	B. Hansen (USA)	Frank Kungler (USA)	F. C. Warmbold (USA)
1906	Event not held		
1908	George C. O'Kelly (GBR/IRL)	Jacob Gundersen (NOR)	Edmond Barrett (GBR/IRL)
1912	Event not held		
1920	Robert Roth (SUI)	Nathan Pendleton (USA)	Ernst Nilsson (SWE) Frederick Meyer (USA)
1924	Harry Steele (USA)	Henry Wernli (SUI)	Andrew McDonald (GBR)
1928	Johan Richthoff (SWE)	Aukusti Sihovla (FIN)	Edmond Dame (FRA)
1932	Johan Richthoff (SWE)	John Riley (USA)	Nikolaus Hirschl (AUT)
1936	Kristjan Palusalu (EST)	Josef Klapuch (TCH)	Hjalmar Nyström (FIN)
1948	Gyula Bóbis (HUN)	Bertil Antonsson (SWE)	Joseph Armstrong (AUS)
1952	Arsen Mekokishvili (URS)	Bertil Antonsson (SWE)	Kenneth Richmond (GBR)
1956	Hamit Kaplan (TUR)	Hussein Mekhmedov (BUL)	Taisto Kangasniemi (FIN)
1960	Wilfried Dietrich (GER)	Hamit Kaplan (TUR)	Savkus Dzarassov (URS)
1964	Alexandr Ivanitsky (URS)	Liutvi Djiber (BUL)	Hamit Kaplan (TUR)
1968	Alexander Medved (URS)	Osman Duraliev (BUL)	Wilfried Dietrich (GER)
1972	Ivan Yarygin (URS)	Khorloo Baianmunkh (MGL)	József Csatáti (HUN)
1976	Ivan Yarygin (URS)	Russell Hellickson (USA)	Dimo Kostov (BUL)
1980	Ilya Mate (URS)	Slavtcho Tchervenkov (BUL)	Julius Strnisko (TCH)
1984	Lou Banach (USA)	Joseph Atiyeh (SYR)	Vasile Pascasu (ROM)
1988	Vasile Puscasu (ROM)	Leriy Khabelov (URS)	William Scherr (USA)

FREE-STYLE—SUPER-HEAVYWEIGHT
(Weight over 220¼ lb *100 kg*)

1896–1968	Event not held		
1972	Alexander Medved (URS)	Osman Duraliev (BUL)	Chris Taylor (USA)
1976	Soslan Andiev (URS)	Jozsef Balla (HUN)	Ladislau Simon (ROM)
1980	Soslan Andiev (URS)	Jozsef Balla (HUN)	Adam Sandruski (POL)
1984	Bruce Baumgartner (USA)	Bob Molle (CAN)	Ayhan Taskin (TUR)
1988	David Gobedjichvili (URS)	Bruce Baumgartner (USA)	Andreas Schröder (GDR)

GRECO-ROMAN—LIGHT-FLYWEIGHT
(Weight up to *48 kg* 105¾ lb)

1896–1968   Event not held

1972	Gheorghe Berceanu (ROM)	Rahim Ahabadi (IRN)	Stefan Anghelov (BUL)
1976	Alexei Shumakov (URS)	Gheorghe Berceanu (ROM)	Stefan Anghelov (BUL)
1980	Zaksylik Ushkempirov (URS)	Constantin Alexandru (ROM)	Ferenc Seres (HUN)
1984	Vincenzo Maenza (ITA)	Markus Scherer (FRG)	Ikazo Saito (JPN)
1988	Vicenzo Maenza (ITA)	Andrzej Glab (POL)	Bratan Tzenov (BUL)

GRECO-ROMAN—FLYWEIGHT
(Weight up to 114½ lb *52 kg*)

1896–1936   Event not held

1948	Pietro Lombardi (ITA)	Kenan Olcay (TUR)	Reino Kangasmäki (FIN)
1952	Boris Gurevich (URS)	Ignazio Fabra (ITA)	Leo Honkala (FIN)
1956	Nikolay Solovyov (URS)	Ignazio Fabra (ITA)	Durum Ali Egribas (TUR)
1960	Dumitru Pirvulescu (ROM)	Osman Sayed (UAR)	Mohamad Paziraye (IRAN)
1964	Tsutomu Hanahara (JPN)	Angel Kerezov (BUL)	Dumitru Pirvulescu (ROM)
1968	Petar Kirov (BUL)	Vladimir Bakulin (URS)	Miroslav Zeman (TCH)
1972	Petar Kirov (BUL)	Koichiro Hirayama (JPN)	Giuseppe Bognanni (ITA)
1976	Vitali Konstantinov (URS)	Nicu Ginga (ROM)	Koichiro Hirayama (JPN)
1980	Vakhtang Blagidze (URS)	Lajos Racz (HUN)	Mladen Mladenov (BUL)
1984	Atsuji Miyahara (JPN)	Daniel Aceves (MEX)	Dae-Du Bang (KOR)
1988	Jon Ronningen (SWE)	Atsuji Miyahara (JPN)	Lee Jae-Suk (KOR)

GRECO-ROMAN—BANTAMWEIGHT

Note: The weight limit for this event has been: 1924 to 1928, 127¾ lb *58 kg;* 1932 to 1936, 123¼ lb *56 kg;* since 1948, 125½ lb *57 kg.*

1896–1920   Event not held

1924	Eduard Pütsep (EST)	Anselm Ahlfors (FIN)	Väinö Ikonen (FIN)
1928	Kurt Leucht (GER)	Jindrich Maudr (TCH)	Giovanni Gozzi (ITA)
1932	Jakob Brendel (GER)	Marcello Nizzola (ITA)	Louis François (FRA)
1936	Márton Lörincz (HUN)	Egon Svensson (SWE)	Jakob Brendel (GER)
1948	Kurt Pettersén (SWE)	Aly Mahmoud Hassan (EGY)	Habil Kaya (TUR)
1952	Imre Hódos (HUN)	Zakaria Chihab (LIB)	Artem Teryan (URS)
1956	Konstantin Vyrupayev (URS)	Evdin Veseterby (SWE)	Francisc Horvat (ROM)
1960	Olyeg Karavayev (URS)	Ion Cernea (ROM)	Petrov Dinko (BUL)
1964	Masamitsu Ichiguchi (JPN)	Vladlen Trostiansky (URS)	Ion Cernea (ROM)

GOLD	SILVER	BRONZE
1968 János Varga (HUN)	Ion Baciu (ROM)	Ivan Kochergin (URS)
1972 Rustem Kazakov (URS)	Hans-Júrgen Veil (GER)	Risto Björlin (FIN)
1976 Pertti Ukkola (FIN)	Ivan Frgic (YUG)	Farhat Mustafin (URS)
1980 Shamil Serikov (URS)	Josef Lipien (POL)	Benni Ljungbeck (SWE)
1984 Pasquale Passarelli (FRG)	Masaki Eto (JPN)	Haralambos Holidis (GRE)
1988 Andras Sike (HUN)	Stoyan Balov (BUL)	Charalambos Holidis (GRE)

GRECO-ROMAN—FEATHERWEIGHT

Note: The weight limit for this event has been: 1912 to 1920, 132¼ lb *60 kg;* 1924 to 1928, 1948 to 1960 and since 1972, *62 kg* 136½ lb; 1932 to 1936, *61 kg* 134¼ lb; 1964 to 1968, *63 kg* 138¾ lb.

1896–1908   Event not held

1912 Kaarlo Koskelo (FIN)	Georg Gerstacker (GER)	Otto Lasanen (FIN)
1920 Oskari Friman (FIN)	Hekki Kähkönen (FIN)	Fridtjof Svensson (SWE)
1924 Kalle Antila (FIN)	Aleksanteri Toivola (FIN)	Erik Malmberg (SWE)
1928 Voldemar Väli (EST)	Erik Malmberg (SWE)	Giacomo Quaglia (ITA)
1932 Giovanni Gozzi (ITA)	Wolfgang Ehrl (GER)	Lauri Koskela (FIN)
1936 Yasar Erkan (TUR)	Aarne Reini (FIN)	Einar Karlsson (SWE)
1948 Mehmet Oktav (TUR)	Olle Anderberg (SWE)	Ferenc Tóth (HUN)
1952 Yakov Punkin (URS)	Imre Polyák (HUN)	Abdel Rashed (EGY)
1956 Rauno Mäkinen (FIN)	Imre Polyák (HUN)	Roman Dzneladze (URS)
1960 Müzahir Sille (TUR)	Imre Polyák (HUN)	Konstantin Vyrupayev (URS)
1964 Imre Polyák (HUN)	Roman Rurua (URS)	Branko Martinovič (YUG)
1968 Roman Rurua (URS)	Hideo Fujimoto (JPN)	Simeon Popescu (ROM)
1972 Gheorghi Markov (BUL)	Heinz-Helmut Wehling (GDR)	Kazimierz Lipien (POL)
1976 Kazimierz Lipien (POL)	Nelson Davidian (URS)	Laszlo Reczi (HUN)
1980 Stilianos Migiakis (GRE)	Istvan Toth (HUN)	Boris Kramorenko (URS)
1984 Kim Weon-Kee (KOR)	Kentolle Johansson (SWE)	Hugo Dietsche (SUI)
1988 Kamandar Madjidov (URS)	Jivko Vanguelov (BUL)	An Dae-Hyun (KOR)

GRECO-ROMAN—LIGHTWEIGHT

Note: The weight limit for this event has been: 1906, 165¼ lb *75 kg;* 1908, 146¾ lb *66,6 kg;* 1912 to 1928, 148¾ lb *67.5 kg;* 1932 to 1936, 145½ lb *66 kg;* 1948 to 1960, 147½ lb *67 kg;* 1964 to 1968, 154¼ lb *70 kg;* since 1972, 149¾ lb *68 kg.*

1896–1904	Event not held		
1906	Rudolf Watzl (AUT)	Karl Karlsen (DEN)	Ferenc Holuban (HUN)
1908	Enrico Porro (ITA)	Nikolay Orlov (URS)	Avid Lindén-Linko (FIN)
1912	Eemil Wäre (FIN)	Gustaf Malmström (SWE)	Edvin Matiasson (SWE)
1920	Eemil Wäre (FIN)	Taavi Tamminen (FIN)	Fritjof Andersen (NOR)
1924	Oskari Friman (FIN)	Lajos Keresztes (HUN)	Kalle Westerlund (FIN)
1928	Lajos Keresztes (HUN)	Eduard Sperling (GER)	Eduard Westerlund (FIN)
1932	Erik Malmberg (SWE)	Abraham Kurland (DEN)	Eduard Sperling (GER)
1936	Lauri Koskela (FIN)	Josef Herda (TCH)	Voldemar Väli (EST)
1948	Gustaf Freij (SWE)	Aage Eriksen (NOR)	Károly Ferencz (HUN)
1952	Shazam Safin (URS)	Gustaf Freij (SWE)	Mikuláš Athanasov (TCH)
1956	Kyösti Lehtonen (FIN)	Riza Dogan (TUR)	Gyul Tóth (HUN)
1960	Avtandil Koridze (URS)	Branislav Martinovič (YUG)	Gustaf Freij (SWE)
1964	Kazim Ayvaz (TUR)	Valeriu Bularca (ROM)	David Gvantseladze (URS)
1968	Munji Mumemura (JPN)	Stevan Horvat (YUG)	Petros Galaktopoulos (GRE)
1972	Shamil Khisamutdinov (URS)	Stoyan Apostolov (BUL)	Gian Matteo Ranzi (ITA)
1976	Suren Nalbandyan (URS)	Stefan Rusu (ROM)	Heinz-Helmut Wehling (GDR)
1980	Stefan Rusu (ROM)	Andrzej Supron (POL)	Lars-Erik Skiold (SWE)
1984	Vlado Lisjak (YUG)	Tapio Sipila (FIN)	James Martinez (USA)
1988	Levon Djoulfalakian (URS)	Kim Sung-Moon (KOR)	Tapio Sipila (FIN)

GRECO-ROMAN—WELTERWEIGHT

Note: The weight limit for this event has been: 1932 to 1936, 158½ lb *72 kg;* 1948 to 1960, 160¾ lb *73 kg;* 1964 to 1968, 171¾ lb *78 kg;* since 1972, 163 lb *74 kg.*

1896–1928	Event not held		
1932	Ivar Johansson (SWE)	Väinö Kajander (FIN)	Ercole Gallegatti (ITA)
1936	Rudolf Svedberg (SWE)	Frit Schäfer (GER)	Eino Virtanen (FIN)
1948	Gösta Andersson (SWE)	Miklós Szilvási (HUN)	Henrik Hansen (DEN)
1952	Miklós Szilvási (HUN)	Gösta Andersson (SWE)	Khalil Taha (LIB)
1956	Mithat Bayrak (TUR)	Vladimir Maneyev (URS)	Per Berlin (SWE)
1960	Mithat Bayrak (TUR)	Günther Maritschnigg (GER)	René Schiermeyer (FRA)
1964	Anatoly Kolesov (URS)	Cyril Todorov (BUL)	Bertil Nyström (SWE)

	GOLD	SILVER	BRONZE
1968	Rudolf Vesper (GDR)	Daniel Robin (FRA)	Károly Bajkó (HUN)
1972	Vitezslav Mache (TCH)	Petros Galaktopoulos (GRE)	Jan Karlsson (SWE)
1976	Alexandr Bykov (URS)	Vitezslav Macha (TCH)	Karlheinz Helbing (GER)
1980	Ferenc Kocsis (HUN)	Anatoly Bykov (URS)	Mikko Huntala (FIN)
1984	Jouko Salomaki (FIN)	Roger Tallroth (SWE)	Stefan Rusu (ROM)
1988	Kim Young-Nam (KOR)	Daoulet Tourlykhanov (URS)	Jozef Tracz (POL)

GRECO-ROMAN—MIDDLEWEIGHT

Note: The weight limit for this event has been: 1906, 187¼ lb *85 kg;* 1908, 160¾ lb *73 kg;* 1912 to 1928, 165¼ lb *75 kg;* 1932 to 1960, 174 lb *79 kg;* 1964 to 1968, 191¾ lb *87 kg;* since 1972, 180¾ lb *82 kg.*

	GOLD	SILVER	BRONZE
1896–1904	Event not held		
1906	Verner Weckman (FIN)	Rudolf Lindmayer (AUT)	Robert Bebrens (DEN)
1908	Frithiof Mårtensson (SWE)	Mauritz Andersson (SWE)	Anders Andersen (DEN)
1912	Claes Johansson (SWE)	Martin Klein[1] (URS)	Alfred Asikainen (FIN)
1920	Carl Westergren (SWE)	Artur Lindfors (FIN)	Matti Perttila (FIN)
1924	Eduard Westerlund (FIN)	Artur Lindfors (FIN)	Roman Steinberg (EST)
1928	Väinö Kokkinen (FIN)	László Papp (HUN)	Albert Kusnetz (EST)
1932	Väinö Kokkinen (FIN)	Jean Földeák (GER)	Axel Cadier (SWE)
1936	Ivar Johansson (SWE)	Ludwig Schweikert (GER)	József Palotás (HUN)
1948	Axel Grönberg (SWE)	Muhlis Tayfur (TUR)	Ercole Gallegatti (ITA)
1952	Axel Grönberg (SWE)	Kalervo Rauhala (FIN)	Nikolay Byelov (URS)
1956	Guivi Kartozia (URS)	Dimiter Dobrev (BUL)	Rune Jansson (SWE)
1960	Dimiter Dobrev (BUL)	Lothar Metz (GER)	Ion Taranu (ROM)
1964	Branislav Simic (YUG)	Jiri Kormanik (TCH)	Lothar Metz (GER)
1968	Lothar Metz (GDR)	Valentin Olenik (URS)	Bransislav Simič (YUG)
1972	Csaba Hegedus (HUN)	Anatoli Nazarenko (URS)	Milan Nenadic (YUG)
1976	Momir Petkovic (YUG)	Vladimir Cheboksarov (URS)	Ivan Kolev (BUL)
1980	Gennady Korban (URS)	Jan Dolgowicz (POL)	Pavel Pavlov (BUL)
1984	Ion Draica (ROM)	Dimitrios Thanapoulos (GRE)	Soren Claeson (SWE)
1988	Mikhail Mamiachvili (URS)	Tibor Komaromi (HUN)	Kim Sang-Kyu (KOR)

---

[1] In fact án Estonian.

Verner Weckman and Yrjo Saarela, both of Finland, battled out the final match of the 1908 light-heavyweight Greco-Roman competition.

GRECO-ROMAN—LIGHT-HEAVYWEIGHT

Note: The weight limit in this event has been: 1908, 205 lb *93 kg;* 1912 to 1928, 181¾ lb *82.5 kg;* 1932 to 1960, 191¾ lb *87 kg;* 1964 to 1968, 213¾ lb *97 kg;* since 1972, 198¼ lb *90 kg.*

	GOLD	SILVER	BRONZE
1896–1906	Event not held		
1908	Verner Weckman (FIN)	Yrjö Saarela (FIN)	Carl Jensen (DEN)
1912	—	Anders Ahlgren† (SWE) Ivar Böhling (FIN)	Béla Varga (HUN)
1920	Claes Johansson (SWE)	Edil Rosenqvist (FIN)	Johannes Eriksen (DEN)
1924	Carl Westergren (SWE)	Rudolf Svensson (SWE)	Onni Pellinen (FIN)
1928	Ibrahim Moustafa (EGY)	Adolf Rieger (GER)	Onni Pellinen (FIN)
1932	Rudolf Svensson (SWE)	Onni Pellinen (FIN)	Mario Gruppioni (ITA)
1936	Axel Cadier (SWE)	Edwins Bietags (LITH)	August Néo (EST)
1948	Karl-Erik Nilsson (SWE)	Kaelpo Gröndahl (FIN)	Ibrahim Orabi (EGY)
1952	Kaelpo Gröndahl (FIN)	Shalva Shikhladze (URS)	Karl-Erik Nilsson (SWE)
1956	Valentin Nikolayev (URS)	Petko Sirakov (BUL)	Karl-Erik Nilsson (SWE)
1960	Tevfik Kis (TUR)	Krali Bimbalov (BUL)	Givy Kartozlya (URS)
1964	Boyan Radev (BUL)	Pev Sfensson (SWE)	Heinz Kiehl (GER)
1968	Boyan Radev (BUL)	Nikolai Yakovenko (URS)	Nicolae Martinescu (ROM)
1972	Valeri Rezantsev (URS)	Josip Corak (YUG)	Czeslaw Kwiecinski (POL)
1976	Valeri Rezantsev (URS)	Stoyan Ivanov (BUL)	Czeslaw Kwiecinski (POL)

GOLD	SILVER	BRONZE
1980 Norbert Nottny (HUN)	Igor Kanygin (URS)	Petre Dicu (ROM)
1984 Steven Fraser (USA)	Ilie Matei (ROM)	Frank Andersson (SWE)
1988 Atanas Komchev (BUL)	Harri Koskela (FIN)	Vladimir Popov (URS)

†Declared equal second after 9 hours of wrestling—no gold medal awarded.

GRECO-ROMAN—HEAVYWEIGHT

Note: The weight limit for this event has been: 1896, open: 1906, over 187¼ lb *85 kg;* 1908, over 205 lb *93 kg;* 1912 to 1928, over 181¾ lb *82,5 kg;* 1932 to 1960, over 191¾ lb *87 kg;* 1964 to 1968, over 213¾ lb *97 kg;* since 1972, up to 202¼ lb *100 kg.*

GOLD	SILVER	BRONZE
1896 Carl Schuhmann (GER)	Georgios Tsitas (GRE)	Stephanos Christopoulos (GRE)
1900–1904 Event not held		
1906 Sören M. Jensen (DEN)	Heari Baur (AUT)	Marcel Dubois (BEL)
1908 Richard Weisz (HUN)	Aliksandr Petrov (URS)	Sören M. Jensen (DEN)
1912 Yrjö Saarela (FIN)	Johan Olin (FIN)	Sören M. Jensen (DEN)
1920 Adolf Lindfors (FIN)	Poul Hansen (DEN)	Martti Nieminen (FIN)
1924 Henri Deglane (FRA)	Edil Rosenqvist (FIN)	Raymund Badó (HUN)
1928 Rudolf Svensson (SWE)	Hjalmar E. Nyström (FIN)	Georg Gehring (GER)
1932 Carl Westergren (SWE)	Josef Urban (TCH)	Nikolaus Hirschl (AUT)
1936 Kirstjan Palusalu (EST)	John Nyman (SWE)	Kurt Hornfischer (GER)
1948 Ahmet Kireçci (TUR)	Tor Nilsson (SWE)	Guido Fantoni (ITA)
1952 Johannes Kotkas (URS)	Josef Ružička (TCH)	Tauno Kovanen (FIN)
1956 Anatoliy Parfenov (URS)	Wilfried Dietrich (GER)	Adelmo Bulgarelli (ITA)
1960 Ivan Bogdan (URS)	Wilfried Dietrich (GER)	Bohumil Kubat (TCH)
1964 István Kozma (HUN)	Anatoly Roshin (URS)	Wilfried Dietrich (GER)
1968 István Kozma (HUN)	Anatoly Roshin (URS)	Petr Kment (TCH)
1972 Nicolae Martinescu (ROM)	Nikolai Yakovenko (URS)	Ferenc Kiss (HUN)
1976 Nikolai Bolboshin (URS)	Kamen Goranov (BUL)	Andrzej Skrzylewski (POL)
1980 Gheorgi Raikov (BUL)	Roman Bierla (POL)	Vasile Andrei (ROM)
1984 Vasile Andrei (ROM)	Greg Gibson (USA)	Jozef Tertelje (YUG)
1988 Andrzej Wronski (POL)	Gerhard Himmel (FRG)	Dennis Koslowski (USA)

GRECO-ROMAN—SUPER-HEAVYWEIGHT
(Weight over *100 kg* 202¼ lb)

	GOLD	SILVER	BRONZE
1896–1968	Event not held		
1972	Anatoly Roshin (URS)	Alexandre Tomov (BUL)	Victor Dolipschi (ROM)
1976	Alexandr Kolchinski (URS)	Alexandre Tomov (BUL)	Roman Codreanu (ROM)
1980	Alexandr Kolchinski (URS)	Alexandre Tomov (BUL)	Hassan Bchara (LIB)
1984	Jeffrey Blatnick (USA)	Refik Memisevic (YUG)	Victor Dolipschi (ROM)
1988	Alexandr Kareline (URS)	Ranguel Guerovski (BUL)	Tomas Johansson (SWE)

25. Yachting

INTERNATIONAL SOLING CLASS

	GOLD	SILVER	BRONZE
1896–1968	Event not held		
1972	**UNITED STATES** Harry Melges, Jr. William Bentsen William Allen	SWEDEN Stig Wennerstroem Bo Knape Stefan Krook	CANADA David Miller John Ekels Paul Cote
1976	**DENMARK** Paul Jensen Vald Bandolowski Erik Hansen	UNITED STATES John Kolius Walter Glasgow Richard Hoepfner	EAST GERMANY Dieter Below Michael Zachries Olaf Engelhardt
1980	**DENMARK** Paul Jensen Vald Bandolowski Erik Hansen	U.S.S.R Boris Budnikov Aleksandr Budnikov Nikolai Polyakov	GREECE Anastassios Boudouris Anastassios Gavrilis Aristidis Rapanakis
1984	**UNITED STATES** Robert Haines Jr Edward Trevelyan Roderick Davis	BRAZIL Torben Grael Daniel Adler Ronaldo Senfft	CANADA Hans Fogh John Kerr Steve Calder
1988	**EAST GERMANY** Jochen Schümann Thomas Flach Bernd Jäkel	UNITED STATES John Kostecki William Baylis Robert Billingham	DENMARK Jesper Bank Jan Mathiasen Steen Secher

INTERNATIONAL STAR CLASS

	GOLD	SILVER	BRONZE
1896–1928	Event not held		
1932	**UNITED STATES** Gilbert Gray Andrew Libano, Jr.	GREAT BRITAIN Colin Ratsey Peter Jaffe	SWEDEN Gunnar Asther Daniel Sunden-Cullberg
1936	**GERMANY** Peter Bischoff Hans-Joachim Weise	SWEDEN Arved Laurin Uno Wallentin	NETHERLANDS Adriaan Maas Willem de Vries Lentsch
1948	**UNITED STATES** Hilary Smart Paul Smart	CUBA Carlos de Cardenas Carlos de Cardenas, Jr.	NETHERLANDS Adriaan Maas Edward Stutterheim
1952	**ITALY** Agostino Straulino Nicolo Rode	UNITED STATES John Reid John Price	PORTUGAL Francisco de Andrade Joaquim Fiuza
1956	**UNITED STATES** Herbert Williams Lawrence Low	ITALY Agostino Straulino Nicolo Rode	BAHAMAS Durward Knowles Sloan Farrington

	GOLD	SILVER	BRONZE
1960	U.S.S.R.	PORTUGAL	UNITED STATES
	Timir Pinegin	Mario Quina	William Parks
	Fyedor Shutkov	José Quina	Robert Halperin
1964	BAHAMAS	UNITED STATES	SWEDEN
	Durward Knowles	Richard Stearns	Pelle Pettersson
	Cecil Cooke	Lynn Williams	Holger Sundstrom
1968	UNITED STATES	NORWAY	ITALY
	Lowell North	Peder Lunde	Franco Cavallo
	Peter Barrett	Per Olav Wiken	Camillo Gargano
1972	AUSTRALIA	SWEDEN	WEST GERMANY
	David Forbes	Pelle Pettersson	Willi Kuhweide
	John Anderson	Stellan Westerdahl	Karsten Meyer
1976	Event not held		
1980	U.S.S.R.	AUSTRIA	ITALY
	Valentin Mankin	Hubert Raudaschl	Giorgio Gorla
	Aleksandr Muzychenko	Karl Ferstl	Alfio Peraboni
1984	UNITED STATES	WEST GERMANY	ITALY
	William E. Buchan	Joachim Griese	Giorgio Gorla
	Stephen Erikson	Michael Marcour	Alfio Peraboni
1988	GREAT BRITAIN	UNITED STATES	BRAZIL
	Michael McIntyre	Mark Reynolds	Torben Grael
	Philip Vaile	Hal Haenel	Nelson Falcao

INTERNATIONAL FLYING DUTCHMAN CLASS

	GOLD	SILVER	BRONZE
1896–1956	Event not held		
1960	NORWAY	DENMARK	GERMANY
	Peder Lunde Jr.	Hans Fogh	Rolf Mulka
	Björn Bergvall	Ole Erik Petersen	Ingo von Bredow
1964	NEW ZEALAND	GREAT BRITAIN	UNITED STATES
	Helmer Pedersen	Franklyn Musto Jr.	Harry Melges Jr.
	Earle Wells	Arthur Morgan	William Bentsen
1968	GREAT BRITAIN	WEST GERMANY	BRAZIL
	Rodney Pattisson	Ullrich Libor	Reinaldo Conrad
	Iain Macdonald-Smith	Peter Naumann	Burkhard Cordes
1972	GREAT BRITAIN	FRANCE	WEST GERMANY
	Rodney Pattisson	Yves Pajot	Ullrich Libor
	Christopher Davies	Marc Pajot	Peter Naumann
1976	WEST GERMANY	GREAT BRITAIN	BRAZIL
	Jorg Diesch	Rodney Pattisson	Reinaldo Conrad
	Eckart Diesch	Julian Brooke	Peter Ficker
		Houghton	
1980	SPAIN	IRELAND	HUNGARY
	Alejandro Abascal	David Wilkins	Szabolcs Detre
	Miguel Noguer	James Wilkinson	Zsolt Detre
1984	UNITED STATES	CANADA	GREAT BRITAIN
	Jonathan McKee	Terry McLaughlin	Jonathan Richards
	William C. Buchan	Evert Bastet	Peter Allam
1988	DENMARK	NORWAY	CANADA
	Jorgen Bojsen-Moller	Ole-Petter Pollen	Frank McLaughlin
	Christian Gronberg	Erik Bjorkum	John Millen

INTERNATIONAL 470 CLASS

	GOLD	SILVER	BRONZE
1896–1972	Event not held		
1976	WEST GERMANY	SPAIN	AUSTRALIA
	Frank Huebner	Antonio Gorostegui	Ian Brown
	Harro Bode	Pedro Millet	Ian Ruff
1980	BRAZIL	EAST GERMANY	FINLAND
	Marcos Soares	Jorn Borowski	Jouko Lindgren
	Eduardo Penido	Egbert Swensson	Georg Tallberg
1984	SPAIN	UNITED STATES	FRANCE
	Luis Doreste	Stephen Benjamin	Thierry Peponnet
	Roberto Molina	Christopher Steinfeld	Luc Pillot
1988	FRANCE	U.S.S.R.	UNITED STATES
	Thierry Peponnet	Tynou Tyniste	John Shadden
	Luc Pillot	Toomas Tyniste	Charlie McKee

INTERNATIONAL FINN CLASS

GOLD	SILVER	BRONZE
1896–1948 Event not held		
1952 Paul Elvström (DEN)	Charles Currey (GBR)	Rickard Sarby (SWE)
1956 Paul Elvström (DEN)	André Nelis (BEL)	John Marvin (USA)
1960 Paul Elvström (DEN)	Aleksandr Chuchelov (URS)	André Nelis (BEL)
1964 Willi Kuhweide (GER)	Peter Barrett (USA)	Henning Wind (DEN)
1968 Valentin Mankin (URS)	Hubert Raudaschl (AUT)	Fabio Albarelli (ITA)
1972 Serge Maury (FRA)	Ilias Hatzipavlis (GRE)	Victor Potapov (URS)
1976 Jochen Schumann (GDR)	Andrei Balashov (URS)	John Bertrand (AUS)
1980 Esko Rechardt (FIN)	Wolfgang Mayrhofer (AUT)	Andrei Balashov (URS)
1984 Russell Coutts (NZL)	John Bertrand (USA)	Terry Neilson (CAN)
1988 Soe Luis Doreste (ESP)	Peter Holmberg (ISV)	John Cutler (NZL)

INTERNATIONAL TORNADO CLASS

GOLD	SILVER	BRONZE
1896–1972 Event not held		
1976 **GREAT BRITAIN** Reginald White John Osborn	**UNITED STATES** David McFaull Michael Rothwell	**WEST GERMANY** Jorg Spengler Jorg Schmall
1980 **BRAZIL** Alexandre Welter Lars Bjorkstrom	**DENMARK** Peter Due Per Kjergard	**SWEDEN** Goran Marstrom Jorgen Ragnarsson
1984 **NEW ZEALAND** Rex Sellers Christopher Timms	**UNITED STATES** Randy Smyth Jay Glaser	**AUSTRALIA** Chris Cairns John Anderson
1988 **FRANCE** Jean-Yves Le Deroff Nicolas Henard	**NEW ZEALAND** Chris Timms Rex Sellers	**BRAZIL** Lars Grael Clinio Freitas

WINDGLIDER CLASS

GOLD	SILVER	BRONZE
1984 Steve Van Den Berg (HOL)	Randall Steele (USA)	Bruce Kendall (NZL)
1988 Bruce Kendall (NZL)	Jan Boersma (AHO)	Michael Gebhardt (USA)

WOMEN'S INTERNATIONAL 470 CLASS
(Introduced in 1988)

GOLD	SILVER	BRONZE
1988 **UNITED STATES** Allison Jolly Lynne Jewell	**SWEDEN** Marit Söderström Birgitta Bengtsson	**U.S.S.R.** Larissa Moskalenko Irina Tchounikhovskaya

WINTER OLYMPIC GAMES
TABLE OF MEDAL WINNERS
BY NATIONS 1908–1988

(including ice events in 1908 and 1920)

Note: These totals include all first, second and third places including those in events no longer on the current schedule. Results of demonstration events are not included.

	GOLD	SILVER	BRONZE	TOTAL
1. U.S.S.R.	79	57	59	195
2. Norway	54	60	54	168
3. USA	42	46	35	123
4. East Germany[1]	39	36	35	110
5. Sweden	36	25	31	92
6. Finland	33	43	34	110
7. Austria	28	38	32	98
8. Germany[2]	26	26	23	75
9. Switzerland	23	25	25	73
10. Canada	14	12	18	44
11. Italy	14	10	9	33
12. Netherlands	13	17	12	42
13. France	13	10	16	39
14. Great Britain	7	4	10	21
15. Czechoslovakia	2	8	13	23
16. Liechtenstein	2	2	5	9

[1] East Germany (GDR) 1968–1988.
[2] Germany 1908–1964, West Germany (FRG) 1968–1988.

DEVELOPMENT OF THE
WINTER OLYMPIC GAMES

These figures relate to the Winter Games, and Ice Events in 1908 and 1920.

GAMES	NO. OF COUNTRIES	NO. OF SPORTS	NO. OF COMPETITORS	
			Male	Female
London (IVth Summer)	6	1	14	7
Antwerp (VIIth Summer)	10	2	73	12
I Chamonix	16	5	281	13
II St. Moritz	25	6	468	27
III Lake Placid	17	5	274	32
IV Garmisch	28	6	675	80
V St. Moritz	28	7	636	77
VI Oslo	30	6	623	109
VII Cortina	32	6	687	132
VIII Squaw Valley	30	5	521	144
IX Innsbruck	36	7	986	200
X Grenoble	37	7	1,081	228
XI Sapporo	35	7	1,015	217
XII Innsbruck	37	7	900	228
XIII Lake Placid	37	7	833	234
XIV Sarajevo	49	7	1,002	276
XV Calgary	57	7	1,113	315
XVI Albertville	—	—	—	—
XVII Lillehammer	—	—	—	—

THE WINTER OLYMPICS

Although the Winter Games were not inaugurated until 1924—28 years after the Modern Olympics were first held in Athens in 1896—there were ice rink events held in both the IVth Games in 1908 and the VIIth Games in 1920. Indeed ice skating was on the draft program for the IInd 1900 Games at Paris.

In London in 1908 there were four ice skating events to which six nations—Argentina, Germany, Great Britain, Russia, Sweden and the United States—sent competitors. The Swedes dominated the men's competition with the great Ulrich Salchow showing why he was 10 times world champion. Britain's Madge Syers won the ladies championships. In a special figure contest Nikolai Panin of Russia won the gold medal.

In 1920 at Antwerp there were individual figure skating events won by Sweden and the pairs by Finland. An ice hockey tournament was won by Canada. Ten countries sent competitors.

Nikolai Panin, winner of a special figure skating title of 1908, was the only Russian to win an Olympic gold medal prior to the 1952 Games.

1924—Ist Winter Games, Chamonix-Mont Blanc, France

The success of the 1920 events assisted the advocates of a separate Winter Games against Nordic opposition. Sixteen nations sent teams to the Games which were only retrospectively recognized as the Ist Winter Olympics. The heroes were the Finnish speed skater Clas Thunberg who won 3 gold, 1 silver and 1 bronze medal and Thorleif Haug (Norway) who won 3 gold and a bronze medal for Nordic skiing. Little noticed was a tiny 11-year-old Norwegian figure skater who came last—Sonja Henie. The Canadians trounced all ice hockey opposition, scoring 85 goals in three games.

1928—IInd Winter Games, St. Moritz, Switzerland

All real opposition to a series of Winter Olympics was subdued by the success of the Chamonix celebration. This time 25 countries including, for example, Japan and Mexico, appeared. The unwelcome warm weather nearly spoiled the Games—one speed skating event was canceled and the bobsleigh program curtailed. The top skier proved to be the Norwegian Johan Gröttumsbraaten while Thunberg collected two more speed skating golds. In figure skating the Swede Grafström won his third gold medal and the 15-year-old Sonja Henie opened her massive account.

North America dominated the bobsleigh with two USA crews and the ice hockey with the Canadians harvesting 38 goals to nil in three games.

1932—IIIrd Winter Games, Lake Placid, New York, USA

The world economic recession coupled with the long trans-Atlantic traveling time that would be necessary for Europeans, who have always numerically predominated, depleted the competitors from 495 to 306.

Again the weather spoiled some events: snow had to be transported to repair the cross-country skiing courses. The Nordic skiers maintained their Olympic monopoly as the inevitable introduction of Alpine skiing was still four years away but Norway's stranglehold was broken by the Swedes and Finns. In the speed skating North Americans predominated because of their successful insistence on imposing their bunched start rules which invited bodily contact instead of the more clinical European pair starts. The figure skating saw the eclipse of Grafström by Austria's Karl Schäfer and the high noon of Sonja Henie's talent.

1936—IVth Winter Games, Garmisch-Partenkirchen, Germany

The Winter Olympics hit the "big time" in 1936 with half a million paying spectators, which was more than the first three Games in aggregate. Twenty-eight countries, now including, for example, Australia and Turkey, sent 755 competitors. The weather smiled on this prestige exercise by the Nazi State and the level of competition hit new heights. The introduction of Alpine skiing events was sensational as two Nordics, the Norwegians Birger Ruud, the great ski jumper, and Laila Schou Nilsen, a sixteen-year-old girl who held all five speed skating records, won the downhill races. These remarkable performances only earned them a fourth place and a bronze medal respectively because the only Alpine championship was a combined event with a slalom section (watched by a record 70,000 people) in which the Central Europeans recovered their lost ground. The Norwegian speed skater Ivan Ballangrud dominated the rink with 3 golds; in figure skating Schäfer (Austria) and Sonja Henie (Norway) gained their final Olympic laurels; and a British team sensationally won the ice hockey tournament largely thanks to recruiting a number of Anglo-Canadians.

ABOVE: Canada, in white, won the 1932 ice hockey gold medal.

LEFT: Sonja Henie, a Norwegian who later became wealthy from professional ice shows, won the second of her 3 gold medals at Lake Placid in 1932.

1948—Vth Winter Games, St. Moritz, Switzerland

The Games in 1940 were originally intended for Sapporo, Japan, but the Sino-Japanese war put an end to that. The situation then became highly confused because of the open hostilities between the International Skiing Federation (FIS), who wanted to allow ski instructors to appear in the Games, and the International Olympic Committee (IOC), who regarded them as professionals. In the context of this battle, Oslo, Helsinki, St. Moritz and Garmisch all in turn offered to host the Games. The war clouds overshadowed this conflict and also eclipsed thoughts as to the best site for 1944. On a postal vote the IOC granted the Vth Winter Games of 1948 to St. Moritz and twenty-eight countries sent 713 competitors.

Alpine skiing with six championships now attracted a far wider entry than the five Nordic skiing titles.

The most successful Alpine skier was Henri Oreiller (France) with two golds and a bronze. Gretchen Fraser (USA) by winning the slalom achieved the first ever non-European skiing success. North America grabbed both individual figure skating titles through Richard Button (USA) and the glamorous Barbara Ann Scott (Canada). The Norwegians dominated the speed skating as did the Americans and Swiss the bob races. The ice hockey tournament was marred by a blazing row over which of two USA teams should represent their country. The Canadians won very narrowly over the Czechs.

1952—VIth Winter Games, Oslo, Norway

It is perhaps extraordinary that the Games of 1952 are the only ones to be held in a Nordic country. Norway is the top medal-winning nation and Finland and Sweden are also in the top six countries as regards successes in these Games.

There was a record number of 30 countries present—with Germany and Japan being allowed back into the fold—and a new attendance record of 541,407 paying spectators.

The Norwegians excelled on their home ground with Stein Erikson even winning the less familiar Alpine skiing event, the giant slalom. Hjalmar Andersen with 3 golds was the most successful speed skater in the packed Bislet Stadium. Figure skating saw the master, Richard Button (USA), retain his crown while Britain's Jeanette Altwegg's impeccable compulsory figures survived the onslaught of several more dramatic free skaters.

The two winning German bob teams were so grotesquely heavy (they averaged over 260 lb a man) that the International Federation legislated for a maximum weight limit in future contests. The Canadians again won the ice hockey but the quality of their opposition was rising steadily.

1956—VIIth Winter Games, Cortina d'Ampezzo, Italy

These Games were paradoxically largely financed by Italian soccer, via pools. New ground was broken in the first appearance since 1908 of Russians who promptly won the men's 4 × 10 km relay and took three out of the first four places in the women's 10 km race, harvested many speed skating successes and sensationally won the ice hockey tournament. The hero of the Games was Toni Sailer (Austria), who won a grand slam in the three Alpine skiing events— all by an imperious margin.

The USA triumphed in both the men's and the women's individual figure skating. These Winter Games were the first to be televised and so enjoyed by record numbers of people, but the price for spreading the interest in this way was some loss in the gate money from spectators actually attending the Games.

1960—VIIIth Winter Games, Squaw Valley, California, USA

In 1955 these Games were awarded by two votes to this then virtually non-existent ski resort in preference to the famous established center of Innsbrück. In the end, despite furious objections from the bobsleighers who were not provided for, and by the Nordic skiers, because they disliked the great altitude of their courses (2,000 meters or over 6,500 feet), the Games were a remarkable success. One strong feature was the compactness of the sites, which made it possible for spectators to see a large variety of the competitions.

The program was extended by the addition of speed skating for women and the Winter Biathlon (cross-country skiing and shooting). The Swedish iron man Sixten Jernberg added to his Cortina successes by winning the tough 30 km Nordic race. The Russian women's four entrants in the 10 km event took the first four places. For the first time ever a non-Scandinavian, Georg Thoma (Germany), won the combined event, while another German, Helmut Recknagel, decisively won the special ski jump.

No one skier established personal ascendancy in the very tightly contested Alpine events. The speed skating times were sensational especially in the 10,000 meters in which Knut Johannesen (Norway) beat the world's record by some 46 seconds.

David Jenkins (USA), extracting a rare six points (the maximum possible) from one judge, won the gold medal for figure skating. The USA and Canada shunted the USSR, the winners at Cortina, to third place in the ice hockey tournament.

Jean-Claude Killy (FRA) achieved the triple in Alpine skiing of downhill, slalom, and giant slalom before a home crowd at Grenoble in 1968.

1964—IXth Winter Games, Innsbrück, Austria

These Games hit new high water marks regarding the number of competitors present, the number of nations represented and the number of paying spectators—nearly a million.

The U.S.S.R. collected 25 medals, the USA, with the largest team, only 6, and neighboring Switzerland an embarrassing nil.

The heroine of the Games was a Russian lady, Lydia Skoblikova, who won a Winter Games record of four golds. She was a speed skater with a superb style, who had already won two previous golds in 1960.

To the French contingent the Goitschel sisters Christine, 19 (slalom gold) and Marielle, 18 (giant slalom gold) were goddesses, especially as each was a runner-up to the other in these events. Austria and France were 3-all over the six Alpine titles. The Scandinavians allowed not one trespasser in the men's Nordic events but the Russians monopolized the women's cross-country program and the Russian men recaptured the ice hockey title which they had won in 1956 and lost in 1960.

Two lowland nations, the Netherlands and Britain, each had a popular success. Sjoukje Dijkstra, in front of her Queen, won the women's figure skating and so Netherlands' first gold. Britain's Tony Nash and the Hon. Robin Dixon won the boblet gold.

1968—Xth Winter Games, Grenoble, France

These Games were Jean-Claude Killy's. The handsome hotelier's rather disputatious Alpine skiing grand slam was hard fought with winning margins for the downhill, slalom and giant slalom being 8/100th, 9/100th and 2.3 seconds respectively. The outstanding Nordic skier was a Swedish lady—Toini Gustafsson—who collected two individual golds and a relay silver. The East German ladies were disqualified from the Luge event for secretly heating their runners.

The speed skating, despite pessimistic forecasts, produced fast times and three golds for the Netherlands, but only one out of eight for the Russians. The Soviets, however, retained their ice hockey title despite losing a very tense match 4-5 to the Czechs.

1972—XIth Winter Games, Sapporo, Japan

These Games, which cost the Japanese $61 million to stage, reflected the mounting strain that international sport suffers as the competitive screw turns. The magic of the Japanese-style opening ceremony seemed however to quell the endless behind-the-scenes rows about the alleged professionalism of full-time skiers who are inevitably regarded as commercial models by equipment and clothing manufacturers. Austria's hero, Karl Schranz, was sent home by the Committee before the Games opened.

The Alpine nations were stunned when the slalom title went to a Spaniard—"Paquito" Fernandez Ochoa. There was an unexpected but popular double gold by a seventeen-year-old Swiss miss—Marie-Therese Nadig—leaving the slalom for Barbara Cochran, the United States' first skiing gold medalist for twenty years.

The Russians won 4 out of the 6 Nordic cross-country titles includ-

Ard Schenk (HOL) was the hero of the Sapporo Games in 1972, winning 3 out of the 4 speed-skating events.

ing an individual double by Galina Kulakova, who won a third gold in the relay. The Japanese by dint of endless practice were able to achieve a grand slam in the 70 meter hill ski jumping. Individual star of Asia's first Winter Games was Ard Schenk, the Dutch speed skater, who outclassed the world and won three gold medals.

1976—XIIth Winter Games, Innsbrück, Austria

The citizens of Colorado, USA, by referendum, forced the Denver organizing committee to withdraw its application for the allocation of the XIIth Games to that city. Innsbrück, host for the second time, kept it "simple." An influenza epidemic could not stop Germany's Rosi Mittermaier becoming the personality of these Games, with only 13/100ths of a second in the giant slalom between her and an unprecedented Alpine skiing grand slam by a woman.

1980—XIIIth Winter Games, Lake Placid, New York, USA

Lake Placid had been applying for the Games unsuccessfully since 1962 and finally was rewarded in 1974. With remarkable foresight speed skater Eric Heiden was selected to take the oath. Mainland China and Cyprus made their Winter Games debuts. There were many complaints about the organization of the Games, the prime one being in the field of transportation. Spectators in particular found it very difficult to get to sites.

Eric Heiden (USA) won the most medals at the Games with an unprecedented sweep of all five speed skating gold medals, all in Olympic record times. His sister Beth also won a bronze in the women's events.

Galina Kulakova (URS) won a silver in the Nordic relay to bring her total to a women's Winter Games record of eight medals, comprising four golds, two silvers and two bronze, in the four Games since 1968.

At the end of the Lake Placid Games only Great Britain, Sweden and the United States could claim to have been represented in all Winter events of the Modern Olympics, including those of 1908 and 1920.

1984—XIVth Winter Games, Sarajevo, Yugoslavia

The first Winter Games held in Eastern Europe was awarded to Sarajevo, which previously was famous as the site of the assassination of Archduke Ferdinand in 1914—an act which historians argue caused World War I. A record 49 countries attended and though the weather was not good, the enthusiasm of the organizers and local populace overcame most difficulties.

The outstanding competitor was Marja Liisa Hamalainen of Finland, who won all three ladies' individual events as well as a team bronze in Nordic skiing. However, Britain's Jayne Torvill and Christopher Dean gained most media attention with their superb ice dancing routines—their artistic interpretation of Ravel's *Bolero* was awarded nine perfect sixes. American Alpine skiers made a major impact with Bill Johnson winning the downhill with a record average speed. Twin teammates Phil and Steve Mahre won gold and silver medals in the slalom, while Italy's Michela Figini became the youngest-ever Alpine skiing gold medalist, and the Soviet Union equaled Canada's record of six hockey titles. Just prior to the Games two defending champions, Ingemar Stenmark of Sweden and Hanni Wenzel of Liechtenstein were banned as "professionals."

1988—XVth Winter Games, Calgary, Canada

The Games were finally awarded to Calgary in 1981, after three previously unsuccessful bids. Most of the venues were close together, except for the sites for Alpine and Nordic skiing, which were some 90 km away. The programme was stretched to 16 days to include three weekends for the benefit of television—for which ABC paid $309 million for the North American rights. There were a number of new events; Nordic Combination for teams, Team Jumping, Alpine Combination, Super Giant Slaloms for men and women, and a 5,000 m speed skating event for women. In all there were 46 events, as well as demonstration sports of curling, short track speed skating and free-style skiing. A dramatic climatic change gave springlike weather, and strong winds, which badly affected the bob, luge and ski-jumping events. Despite some excellent performances in all events, the "star" of these Games was the lone British ski jumper "Eddie the Eagle" Edwards, who, perhaps because he was so totally inept by world standards, stole the media attention from the great and the famous. He finished last in both jumps, some 20 m behind the rest of the field. The most successful competitors were Yvonne Van Gennip (HOL) with three speed skating titles, and Matti Nykänen (FIN), who totally dominated the ski jumping, winning three golds. There was criticism of Katarina Witt (GDR) for her skimpy costumes, but not for her skating ability, as she retained her title. In speed skating the circuit proved to be sensationally fast with records falling en masse. Only one competitor in Calgary failed a drug test, a Polish hockey player. A record number of 1,428 competitors from a record 57 countries attended.

1992—XVIth Winter Games, Albertville, France

In October 1986 the IOC awarded the Games to Albertville, ahead of six other sites in six countries. The events will be staged over a fairly wide area of Savoie. There will be nine additional events comprising, free-style mogul skiing for men and women, short track speed skating for men and women (two events each), and three biathlon events for women. In figure skating compulsory exercises have been eliminated. Speed skiing will be a demonstration sport. This will be the last Winter Games to be held in the same year as the Summer celebration. In future the Winter Games will be held in the even-numbered years between the editions of the Summer Games. Thus the next celebration will be in 1994, and thence in 1998 etc. The remarkable political changes of 1990 mean that beginning with Albertville there will be a unified German team competing in the Olympic Games once more.

1994—XVIIth Winter Games, Lillehammer, Norway

This will be the first Winter Games not held in the same year as the main Summer celebration. These Games were awarded to Lillehammer during the 1988 Games in Seoul. The small Norwegian town, only 22,000 population, lying some 180 km north of Oslo, had previously made a bid for the 1992 Games.

ROLL OF OLYMPIC MEDAL WINNERS IN THE WINTER EVENTS SINCE 1908

1. Alpine Skiing (Men)

DOWNHILL

1908–1936 Event not held		
1948 Henri Oreiller (FRA) 2:55.0	Franz Gabl (AUT) 2:59.1	Karl Molitor (SUI) 3:00.3 Rolf Olinger (SUI) 3:00.3
1952 Zeno Colo (ITA) 2:30.8	Othmar Schneider (AUT) 2:32.0	Christian Pravda (AUT) 2:32.4
1956 Anton Sailer (AUT) 2:52.2	Raymond Fellay (SUI) 2:55.7	Andreas Molterer (AUT) 2:56.2
1960 Jean Vuarnet (FRA) 2:06.0	Hans-Peter Lanig (GER) 2:06.5	Guy Perillat (FRA) 2:06.9
1964 Egon Zimmermann (AUT) 2:18.16	Leo Lacroix (FRA) 2:18.90	Wolfgang Bartels (GER) 2:19.48
1968 Jean-Claude Killy (FRA) 1:59.85	Guy Périllat (FRA) 1:59.93	J. Daniel Daetwyler (SUI) 2:00.32
1972 Bernhard Russi (SUI) 1:51.43	Roland Collombin (SUI) 1:52.07	Heinrich Messner (AUT) 1:52.40
1976 Franz Klammer (AUT) 1:45.73	Bernhard Russi (SUI) 1:46.06	Herbert Plank (ITA) 1:46.59
1980 Leonhard Stock (AUT) 1:45.50	Peter Wirnsberger (AUT) 1:46.12	Stephen Podborski (CAN) 1:46.62
1984 Bill Johnson (USA) 1:45.59	Peter Mueller (SUI) 1:45.86	Anton Steiner (AUT) 1:45.95
1988 Pirmin Zurbriggen (SUI) 1:59.63	Peter Müller (SUI) 2:00.14	Franck Piccard (FRA) 2:01.24

SLALOM

1908–1936 Event not held		
1948 Edi Reinalter (SUI) 2:10.3	James Couttet (FRA) 2:10.8	Henri Oreiller (FRA) 2:12.8
1952 Othmar Schneider (AUT) 2:00.0	Stein Eriksen (NOR) 2:01.2	Guttorm Berge (NOR) 2:01.7
1956 Anton Sailer (AUT) 3:14.7	Chiharu Igaya (JPN) 3:18.7	Stig Sollander (SWE) 3:20.2
1960 Ernst Hinterseer (AUT) 2:08.9	Matthias Lietner (AUT) 2:10.3	Charles Bozon (FRA) 2:10.4
1964 Josef Stiegler (AUT) 2:21.13	William Kidd (USA) 2:21.27	James Heuga (USA) 2:21.52
1968 Jean-Claude Killy (FRA) 1:39.73	Herbert Huber (AUT) 1:39.82	Alfred Matt (AUT) 1:40.09

Toni Sailer (AUT) dominated the Alpine skiing in the 1956 Games at Cortina, winning all 3 gold medals.

Although he regularly dominated the Alpine World Cup competition, Ingemar Stenmark (SWE) was frustrated in his desire for an Olympic gold medal until he swept the slalom and giant slalom events at Lake Placid in 1980.

Phil Mahre (USA) beat his twin brother Steve by 21/100ths of a second in the Giant Slalom in the 1984 Olympics, to win the gold and silver medals between them.

	GOLD	SILVER	BRONZE
1972	Francisco Fernandez Ochoa (ESP) 1:49.27	Gustavo Thoeni (ITA) 1:50.28	Rolando Thoeni (ITA) 1:50.30
1976	Piero Gros (ITA) 2:03.29	Gustavo Thoeni (ITA) 2:03.73	Willy Frommelt (LIE) 2:04.28
1980	Ingemar Stenmark (SWE) 1:44.26	Phil Mahre (USA) 1:44.76	Jacques Luethy (SUI) 1:45.06
1984	Phil Mahre (USA) 1:39.21	Steve Mahre (USA) 1:39.62	Didier Bouvet (FRA) 1:40.20
1988	Alberto Tomba (ITA) 1:39.47	Frank Wörndl (FRG) 1:39.53	Paul Frommelt (LIE) 1:39.84

GIANT SLALOM

	GOLD	SILVER	BRONZE
1908–1948	Event not held		
1952	Stein Erikson (NOR) 2:25.0	Christian Pravda (AUT) 2:26.9	Toni Spiss (AUT) 2:28.8
1956	Anton Sailer (AUT) 3:00.1	Andreas Molterer (AUT) 3:06.3	Walter Schuster (AUT) 3:07.2
1960	Roger Staub (SUI) 1:48.3	Josef Stiegler (AUT) 1:48.7	Ernst Hinterseer (AUT) 1:49.1
1964	Francois Bonlieu (FRA) 1:46.71	Karl Schranz (AUT) 1:47.09	Josef Stiegler (AUT) 1:48.05
1968	Jean-Claude Killy (FRA) 3:29.28	Willy Favre (SUI) 3:31.50	Heinrich Messner (AUT) 3:31.83
1972	Gustavo Thoeni (ITA) 3:09.62	Edmund Bruggmann (SUI) 3:10.75	Werner Mattle (SUI) 3:10.99
1976	Heini Hemmi (SUI) 3:26.97	Ernst Good (SUI) 3:27.17	Ingemar Stenmark (SWE) 3:27.41
1980	Ingemar Stenmark (SWE) 2:40.74	Andreas Wenzel (LIE) 2:41.49	Hans Enn (AUT) 2:42.51
1984	Max Julen (SUI) 2:41.18	Juriy Franko (YUG) 2:41.41	Andreas Wenzel (LIE) 2:41.75
1988	Alberto Tomba (ITA) 2:06.37	Hubert Strolz (AUT) 2:07.41	Pirmin Zurbriggen (SUI) 2:08.39

SUPER GIANT SLALOM
(Introduced in 1988)

	GOLD	SILVER	BRONZE
1988	Franck Piccard (FRA) 1:39.66	Helmut Mayer (AUT) 1:40.96	Lars-Börje Eriksson (SWE) 1:41.08

ALPINE COMBINATION (Downhill and Slalom)

	GOLD	SILVER	BRONZE
1908–1932	Event not held		
1936	Franz Pfnür (GER) 99.25 pts	Gustav Lantschner (GER) 96.26	Emile Allais (FRA) 94.69
1948	Henri Oreiller (FRA) 3.27pts	Karl Molitor (SUI) 6.44	James Couttet (FRA) 6.95
1952–1984	Event not held		
1988	Hubert Strolz (AUT) 36.55 pts	Bernhard Gstrein (AUT) 43.45	Paul Accola (SUI) 48.24

Alpine Skiing (Women)

DOWNHILL

1908–1936	Event not held		
1948	Hedy Schlunegger (SUI) 2:28.3	Trude Beiser (AUT) 2:29.1	Resi Hammerer (AUT) 2:30.2
1952	Trude Jochum-Beiser (AUT) 1:47.1	Annemarie Buchner (GER) 1:48.0	Giuliana Minuzzo (ITA) 1:49.0
1956	Madeleine Berthod (SUI) 1:40.7	Frieda Dänzer (SUI) 1:45.4	Lucile Wheeler (CAN) 1:45.9
1960	Heidi Biebl (GER) 1:37.6	Penelope Pitou (USA) 1:38.6	Traudl Hecher (AUT) 1:38.9
1964	Christl Haas (AUT) 1:55.39	Edith Zimmerman (AUT) 1:56.42	Traudl Hecher (AUT) 1:56.66
1968	Olga Pall (AUT) 1:40.87	Isabelle Mir (FRA) 1:41.33	Christl Haas (AUT) 1:41.41
1972	Marie-Therese Nadig (SUI) 1:36.68	Annemarie Pröll (AUT) 1:37.00	Susan Corrock (USA) 1:37.68
1976	Rosi Mittermaier (GER) 1:46.16	Brigitte Totschnig (AUT) 1:46.68	Cindy Nelson (USA) 1:47.50
1980	Annemarie Moser-Pröll (AUT) 1:37.52	Hanni Wenzel (LIE) 1:38.22	Marie-Therese Nadig (SUI) 1:38.36
1984	Michela Figini (SUI) 1:13.36	Maria Walliser (SUI) 1:13.41	Olga Chartova (TCH) 1:13.53
1988	Marina Kiehl (FRG) 1:25.86	Brigitte Oertli (SUI) 1:26.61	Karen Percy (CAN) 1:26.62

SLALOM

1908–1936	Event not held		
1948	Gretchen Fraser (USA) 1:57.2	Antoinette Meyer (SUI) 1:57.0	Erika Mahringer (AUT) 1:58.0
1952	Andrea Lawrence-Mead (USA) 2:10.6	Ossi Reichert (GER) 2:11.4	Annemarie Buchner (GER) 2:13.3
1956	Renée Colliard (SUI) 1:52.3	Regina Schöpf (AUT) 1:55.4	Jevginija Sidorova (URS) 1:56.7
1960	Anne Heggtveit (CAN) 1:49.6	Betsy Snite (USA) 1:52.9	Barbi Henneberger (GER) 1:56.6
1964	Christine Goitschel (FRA) 1:29.86	Marielle Goitschel (FRA) 1:30.77	Jean Saubert (USA) 1:31.36
1968	Marielle Goitschel (FRA) 1:25.86	Nancy Greene (CAN) 1:26.15	Annie Famose (FRA) 1:27.89
1972	Barbara Cochran (USA) 1:31.24	Danielle Debernard (FRA) 1:31.26	Florence Steurer (FRA) 1:32.69
1976	Rosi Mittermaier (GER) 1:30.54	Claudia Giordani (ITA) 1:30.87	Hanny Wenzel (LIE) 1:32.20
1980	Hanni Wenzel (LIE) 1:25.09	Christa Kinshofer (GER) 1:26.50	Erika Hess (SUI) 1:27.89

Gretchen Fraser (USA) won the women's slalom race the first time it was contested, in 1948 at St. Mortiz.

Rosi Mittermaier of West Germany won 2 golds and one silver in women's Alpine skiing events at Innsbruck in 1976.

GOLD	SILVER	BRONZE
1984 Paolette Magoni (ITA) 1:36.47	Perrine Pelen (FRA) 1:37.38	Ursula Konsett (LIE) 1:37.50
1988 Vreni Schneider (SUI) 1:36.69	Mateja Svet (YUG) 1:38.37	Christa Kinshofer-Gütlein (FRG) 1:38.40

GIANT SLALOM

1908–1948 Event not held		
1952 Andrea Lawrence-Mead (USA) 2:06.8	Dagmar Rom (AUT) 2:09.0	Annemarie Buchner (GER) 2:10.0
1956 Ossi Reichert (GER) 1:56.5	Josefine Frandl (AUT) 1:57.8	Dorothea Hochleitner (AUT) 1:58.2
1960 Yvonne Rüegg (SUI) 1:39.9	Penelope Pitou (USA) 1:40.0	Giuliana Chenal-Minuzzo (ITA) 1:40.2
1964 Marielle Goitschel (FRA) 1:52.24	Christine Goitschel (FRA) 1:53.11	Jean Saubert (USA) 1:53.11
1968 Nancy Greene (CAN) 1:51.97	Annie Famose (FRA) 1:54.61	Fernande Bochatay (SUI) 1:54.74
1972 Marie-Therese Nadig (SUI) 1:29.90	Annemarie Pröll (AUT) 1:30.75	Wiltrud Drexel (AUT) 1:32.35
1976 Kathy Kreiner (CAN) 1:29.13	Rosi Mittermaier (GER) 1:29.25	Danielle Debernard (FRA) 1:29.95
1980 Hanni Wenzel (LIE) 2:41.66	Irene Epple (GER) 2.42.12	Perrine Pelen (FRA) 2:42.41
1984 Debbie Armstrong (USA) 2:20.98	Christin Cooper (USA) 2:21.38	Perrine Pelen (FRA) 2:21.40
1988 Vreni Schneider (SUI) 2:06.49	Christa Kinshofer-Gütlein (FRG) 2:07.42	Maria Walliser (SUI) 2:07.72

SUPER GIANT SLALOM
(Introduced in 1988)

1988 Sigrid Wolf (AUT) 1:19.03	Michela Figini (SUI) 1:20.03	Karen Percy (CAN) 1:20.29

ALPINE COMBINATION

1908–1932 Event not held		
1936 Christel Cranz (GER) 97.06 pts	Kathe Grasegger (GER) 95.26	Laila Schou Nilsen (NOR) 93.48
1948 Trude Beiser (AUT) 6.58 pts	Gretchen Fraser (USA) 6.95	Erika Mahringer (AUT) 7.04
1952–1984 Event not held		
1988 Anita Wachter (AUT) 29.25 pts	Brigitte Oertli (SUI) 29.48	Maria Walliser (SUI) 51.28

RIGHT: Hanni Wenzel, from the tiny Principality of Liechtenstein (66 sq. miles), won gold medals in the slalom and giant slalom, as well as the silver medal in the downhill, at the 1980 Winter Games.

2. Nordic Skiing (Men)

15 km (9.3 miles) CROSS-COUNTRY

GOLD	SILVER	BRONZE
1908–1920 Event not held		
1924[1] Thorleif Haug (NOR) 1h 14:31.0	Johan Gröttumsbraaten (NOR) 1h 15:51.0	Tipani Niku (FIN) 1h 26:26.0
1928[2] Johan Gröttumsbraaten (NOR) 1h 37:01.0	Ole Hegge (NOR) 1h 39:01.0	Reidar Ödegaard (NOR) 1h 40:11.0
1932[3] Sven Utterström (SWE) 1h 23:07.0	Axel T. Wikström (SWE) 1h 25:07.0	Veli Saarinen (FIN) 1h 25:24.0
1936[1] Erik-August Larsson (SWE) 1h 14:38.0	Oddbjörn Hagen (NOR) 1h 15:33.0	Pekka Niemi (FIN) 1h 16:59.0
1948[1] Martin Lundström (SWE) 1h 13:50.0	Nils Östensson (SWE) 1h 14:22.0	Gunnar Eriksson (SWE) 1h 16:06.0
1952[1] Hallgeir Brenden (NOR) 1h 1:34.0	Tapio Mäkelä (FIN) 1h 2:09.0	Paavo Lonkila (FIN) 1h 2:20.0
1956 Hallgeir Brenden (NOR) 49:39.0	Sixten Jernberg (SWE) 50:14.0	Pavel Koltschin (URS) 50:17.0
1960 Haakon Brusveen (NOR) 51:55.5	Sixten Jernberg (SWE) 51:58.6	Veikko Hakulinen (FIN) 52:03.0
1964 Eero Mäntyranta (FIN) 50:54.1	Harald Grönningen (NOR) 51:34.8	Sixten Jernberg (SWE) 51:42.2
1968 Harald Grönningen (NOR) 47:54.2	Eero Mäntyranta (FIN) 47:56.1	Gunnar Larsson (SWE) 48:33.7
1972 Sven-Åke Lundback (SWE) 45:28.24	Fedor Simaschov (URS) 46:00.84	Ivar Formo (NOR) 46:02.86
1976 Nikolay Bajukov (URS) 43:58.47	Evgeniy Beliayev (URS) 44:01.10	Arto Koivisto (FIN) 44:19.25
1980 Thomas Wassberg (SWE) 41:57.63	Juha Mieto (FIN) 41:57.64	Ove Aunli (NOR) 42:28.62
1984 Gunde Swan (SWE) 41:25.6	Aki Karvonen (FIN) 41:34.9	Harri Kirvesniemi (FIN) 41:45.6
1988 Michael Deviatyarov (URS) 41:18.9	Pal Mikkelsplass (NOR) 41:33.4	Vladimir Smirnov (URS) 41:48.5

[1] The distance was 18 km.
[2] The distance was 19,7 km.
[3] The distance was 18,2 km.

30 km (18.6 miles) CROSS-COUNTRY

GOLD	SILVER	BRONZE
1908–1952 Event not held		
1956 Veikko Hakulinen (FIN) 1h 44:06.0	Sixten Jernberg (SWE) 1h 44:30.0	Pavel Koltschin (URS) 1h 45:45.0
1960 Sixten Jernberg (SWE) 1h 51:03.9	Rolf Rämgård (SWE) 1h 51:61.9	Nikolay Anikin (URS) 1h 52:28.2
1964 Eero Mäntyranta (FIN) 1h 30:50.7	Harald Grönningen (NOR) 1h 32:02.3	Igor Voronchikin (URS) 1h 32:15.8
1968 Franco Nones (ITA) 1h 35:39.2	Odd Martinsen (NOR) 1h 36:28.9	Eero Mäntyranta (FIN) 1h 36:55.3
1972 Viaceslav Vedenine (URS) 1h 36:31.2	Paal Tyldum (NOR) 1h 37:25.3	Johs Harviken (NOR) 1h 37:32.4
1976 Sergei Savelyev (URS) 1h 30:29.38	William Koch (USA) 1h 30:57.84	Ivan Garanin (URS) 1h 31:09.29
1980 Nikolai Simyatov (URS) 1h 27:02.80	Vasiliy Rochev (URS) 1h 27:34.22	Ivan Lebanov (BUL) 1h 28:03.87
1984 Nikolai Simyatov (URS) 1h 28:56.3	Aleksdandr Savyalov (URS) 1h 29:23.3	Gunde Swan (SWE) 1h 29:35.7
1988 Alexey Prokororov (URS) 1:24:26.3	Vladimir Smirnov (URS) 1:24:35.1	Vegard Ulvang (NOR) 1:25:11.6

Gunde Swan of Sweden set an Olympic record for the 15 km cross-country Nordic ski race in the 1984 Winter Games.

50 km (31 miles) CROSS-COUNTRY

1908–1920	Event not held		
1924	Thorleif Haug (NOR) 3h 44:32.0	Thoralf Strömstad (NOR) 3h 46:23.0	Johan Gröttumsbraaten (NOR) 3h 47:46.0
1928	Per Erik Hedlund (SWE) 4h 52:03.0	Gustaf Jonsson (SWE) 5h 05:30.0	Volger Andersson (SWE) 5h 05:46.0
1932	Veli Saarinen (FIN) 4h 28:00.0	Väinö Likkanen (FIN) 4h 28:20.0	Arne Rustadstuen (NOR) 4h 31:53.0
1936	Elis Wiklund (SWE) 3h 30:11.0	Axel Wikström (SWE) 3h 33:20.0	Nils-Joel Englund (SWE) 3h 34:10.0
1948	Nils Karlsson (SWE) 3h 47:48.0	Harald Eriksson (SWE) 3h 52:20.0	Benjamin Vanninen (FIN) 3h 57:28.0
1952	Veikko Hakulinen (FIN) 3h 33:33.0	Eero Kolehmainen (FIN) 3h 38:11.0	Magnar Estenstad (NOR) 3h 38:28.0
1956	Sixten Jernberg (SWE) 2h 50:27.0	Veikko Hakulinen (FIN) 2h 51:45.0	Fyedor Terentyeve (URS) 2h 53:32.0
1960	Kalevi Hämäläinen (FIN) 2h 59:06.3	Veikko Hakulinen (FIN) 2h 59:26.7	Rolf Rämgård (SWE) 3h 02:46.7
1964	Sixten Jernberg (SWE) 2h 43:52.6	Assar Roennlund (SWE) 2h 44:58.2	Arto Tiainen (FIN) 2h 45:30.4
1968	Olle Ellefsaeter (NOR) 2h 28:45.8	Viaceslav Vedenine (URS) 2h 29:02.5	Josef Haas (SUI) 2h 29:14.8
1972	Paal Tyldrum (NOR) 2h 43:14.75	Magne Myrmo (NOR) 2h 43:29.45	Viaceslav Vedenine (URS) 2h 44:00.19

	GOLD	SILVER	BRONZE
1976	Ivar Formo (NOR) 2h 37:30.50	Gert-Dietmar Klause (GDR) 2h 38:13.21	Benny Soedergren (SWE) 2h 39:39.21
1980	Nikolai Simyatov (URS) 2h 27:24.60	Juha Mieto (FIN) 2h 30:20.52	Aleksandr Savyalov (URS) 2h 30:51.52
1984	Thomas Wassberg (SWE) 2h 15:55.8	Gunde Swan (SWE) 2h 16:00.7	Aki Karvonen (FIN) 2h 17:04.7
1988	Gunde Svan (SWE) 2:04:30.9	Maurilio De Zolt (ITA) 2:05:36.4	Andy Grünenfelder (SUI) 2:06:01.9

RELAY RACE 4 x 10 km (6 miles 376 yd.)

1908–1932   Event not held

	GOLD	SILVER	BRONZE
1936	FINLAND 2h 41:33.0	NORWAY 2h 41:39.0	SWEDEN 2h 43:03.0
	Sulo Nurmela	Oddbjörn Hagen	John Berger
	Klaes Karppinen	Olaf Hoffsbakken	Erik-August Larsson
	Matti Lahde	Sverre Brodahl	Artur Häggblad
	Kalle Jalkanen	Bjarne Iversen	Martin J. Matsbo
1948	SWEDEN 2h 32:08.0	FINLAND 2h 41:06.6	NORWAY 2h 44:33.0
	Nils Östensson	Lauri Silvennoinen	Erling Evensen
	Nils Täpp	Teuvo Laukkanen	Olav Ökern
	Gunnar Eriksson	Sauli Rytky	Reidar Nyborg
	Martin Lundström	August Kiuru	Olav Hagen
1952	FINLAND 2h 20:16.0	NORWAY 2h 23:13.0	SWEDEN 2h 24:13.0
	Heikki Hasu	Magnar Estenstad	Nils Täpp
	Paavon Lonkila	Mikal Kirkholt	Sigurd Andersson
	Urho Korhonen	Martin Stokken	Enar Josefsson
	Tapio Mäkelä	Hallgeir Brenden	Martin Lundström
1956	U.S.S.R. 2h 15:30.0	FINLAND 2h 16:31.0	SWEDEN 2h 17:42.0
	Fhedor Terentyev	August Kiuru	Lennart Larsson
	Pavel Koltschin	Jorma Kortelainen	Gunnar Samuelsson
	Nikolay Anikin	Arvo Viitanen	Per-Erik Larsson
	Vladimir Kusin	Veikko Hakulinen	Sixten Jernberg
1960	FINLAND 2h 18:45.6	NORWAY 2h 18:46.4	U.S.S.R. 2h 21:21.6
	Toimi Alatalo	Harald Grönningen	Anatoliy Schelyuchin
	Eero Mäntyranta	Hallgeir Brenden	Gennadiy Vaganov
	Vaino Huhtala	Einar Ostby	Aleksey Kusnetsov
	Veikko Hakulinen	Haakon Brusveen	Nikolay Anikin
1964	SWEDEN 2h 18:34.6	FINLAND 2h 18:42.4	U.S.S.R. 2h 18:46.9
	Karl-Ake Asph	Vaino Huhtala	Ivan Utrobin
	Sixten Jernberg	Arto Tiainen	Gennadiy Vaganov
	Janne Stefansson	Kalevi Laurila	Igor Voronchikin
	Assar Roennlund	Eero Mäntyranta	Pavel Koltschin
1968	NORWAY 2h 08:33.5	SWEDEN 2h 10:13.2	FINLAND 2h 10:56.7
	Odd Martinsen	Jan Halvarsson	Kalevi Oikarainen
	Paal Tyldrum	Bjarne Andersson	Hannu Taipale
	Harald Grönningen	Gunnar Larsson	Kalevi Laurila
	Olle Ellefsaeter	Assar Roennlund	Eero Mäntyranta
1972	U.S.S.R. 2h 04:47.94	NORWAY 2h 04:57.06	SWITZERLAND 2h 07:00.06
	Vladimir Voronkov	Oddvar Braa	Alfred Kaflin
	Yuri Skobov	Paal Tyldrum	Albert Giger
	Fedor Simaschov	Ivor Formo	Alois Kaelin
	Viaceslav Vedenine	Johs Harviken	Edi Hauser
1976	FINLAND 2h 07:59.72	NORWAY 2h 09:58.36	U.S.S.R. 2h 10:51.46
	Matti Pitkaenen	Paal Tyldum	Eveniy Beliayev
	Juha Mieto	Einar Sagstuen	Nikolay Bajukov
	Pertti Teurajaervi	Ivar Formo	Sergei Savelyev
	Arto Koivisto	Odd Martinsen	Ivan Garanin
1980	U.S.S.R. 1h 57:03.46	NORWAY 1h 58:45.77	FINLAND 2h 00:00.18
	Vasiliy Rochev	Lars Erik Eriksen	Harri Kirvesniemi
	Nikolai Bajukov	Per Knut Aalund	Pertti Teurajaervi
	Eveniy Beliayev	Ove Aunli	Matti Pitkaenen
	Nikolai Simyatov	Oddvar Bra	Juha Mieto

Sixten Jernberg of Sweden has won more medals in winter Olympic competition than any other athlete—4 gold, 3 silver and 2 bronze.

	GOLD	SILVER	BRONZE
1984	**SWEDEN** 1h 55:06.3	U.S.S.R. 1h 55:16.5	FINLAND 1h 56:31.4
	Thomas Wassberg	Aleksandr Batuk	Kari Ristanen
	Benny Kohlberg	Aleksandr Savyalov	Juha Mieto
	Jan Bo Ottosson	Vladimir Nikitin	Harri Kirvesniemi
	Gunde Swan	Nikolai Zimyatov	Aki Karvonen
1988	**SWEDEN** 1h 43:58.6	U.S.S.R. 1h 44:11.3	CZECHOSLOVAKIA 1h 45:22.7
	Jan Ohosson	Vladimir Smirnov	Radim Nyc
	Thomas Wassberg	Vladimir Sakhnov	Vaclav Korunda
	Gunde Svan	Mikhail Deviatyarov	Pavel Benc
	Nils Mogren	Alexey Prokororov	Ladislav Svanda

Ski Jumping

1924–1960 Held on one hill only.

SMALL HILL (70 meters)

1964	Veikko Kankkonen (FIN) 229.90	Toralf Engan (NOR) 226.30	Torgeil Brandtzaeg (NOR) 222.90
1968	Jiri Raska (TCH) 216.5	Reinhold Bachler (AUT) 214.2	Baldur Preiml (AUT) 212.6
1972	Yukio Kasaya (JPN) 244.2	Akitsugo Konno (JPN) 234.8	Seiji Aochi (JPN) 229.5
1976	Hans-Georg Aschenbach (GDR) 252.0	Jochen Danneberg (GDR) 246.2	Karl Schnabl (AUT) 242.0

GOLD	SILVER	BRONZE
1980 Toni Innauer (AUT) 266.3	Manfred Deckert (GDR) 249.2 Hirokazu Yagi (JPN) 249.2	—
1984 Jens Weissflog (GDR) 215.2	Matti Nykänen (FIN) 214.0	Jari Puikkonen (FIN) 212.8
1988 Matti Nykänen (FIN) 229.1	Pavel Ploc (TCH) 212.1	Jiri Malec (TCH) 211.8

BIG HILL (90 meters)

GOLD	SILVER	BRONZE
1964 Toralf Engan (NOR) 230.70	Veikko Kankkonen (FIN) 228.90	Torgeir Brandtzaeg (NOR) 227.20
1968 Vladimir Beloussov (URS) 231.3	Jiri Raska (TCH) 229.4	Lars Grini (NOR) 214.3
1972 Wojciech Fortuna (POL) 219.9	Walter Steiner (SUI) 219.8	Rainer Schmidt (GDR) 219.3
1976 Karl Schnabl (AUT) 234.8	Anton Innauer (AUT) 232.9	Henry Glass (GDR) 221.7
1980 Jouko Tormanen (FIN) 271.0	Hubert Neuper (AUT) 262.4	Jari Puikkonen (FIN) 248.5
1984 Matti Nykänen (FIN) 231.2	Jens Weissflog (GDR) 213.7	Pavel Ploc (TCH) 202.9
1988 Matti Nykänen (FIN) 224.0	Erik Johnsen (NOR) 207.9	Matjaz Debelak (YUG) 207.7

90 METER—TEAM COMPETITION

GOLD	SILVER	BRONZE
1988 FINLAND 634.4 Ari Pekka Nikkola Matti Nykänen Tuomo Ylipulli Jari Puikkonen	YUGOSLAVIA 625.5 Primoz Ulaga Matjaz Zupan Matjaz Debelak Miran Tepes	NORWAY 596.1 Ole Eidhammer Jon Kiorum Ole Fidjestol Erik Johnsen

Karl Schnabl of Austria won a gold medal on the 90 meter hill at Innsbruck in 1976, and a bronze medal on the 70 meter hill.

NORDIC COMBINED (15 km[2] and jumping)

	GOLD	SILVER	BRONZE
1908–1920	Event not held		
1924[1]	Thorleif Haug (NOR)	Thoralf Strömstad (NOR)	Johan Gröttumsbraaten (NOR)
1928[1]	Johan Gröttumsbraaten (NOR)	Hans Vinjarengen (NOR)	John Snersrud (NOR)
1932	Johan Gröttumsbraaten (NOR) 446.0	Ole Stenen (NOR) 436.05	Hans Vinjarengen (NOR) 434.60
1936	Oddbjörn Hagen (NOR) 430.30	Olaf Hoffsbakken (NOR) 419.80	Sverre Brodahl (NOR) 408.10
1948	Heikki Hasu (FIN) 448.80	Martti Huhtala (FIN) 433.65	Sfen Israelsson (SWE) 433.40
1952	Simon Slåttvik (NOR) 451.621	Heikki Hasu (FIN) 447.5	Sverre Stenersen (NOR) 436.335
1956	Sverre Stenersen (NOR) 455.0	Bengt Eriksson (SWE) 473.4	Franciszek Gron-Gasienica (POL) 436.8
1960	Georg Thoma (GER) 457.952	Tormod Knutsen (NOR) 453.0	Nikolay Gusakow (URS) 452.0
1964	Tormod Knutsen (NOR) 469.28	Nikolai Kiselev (URS) 453.04	Georg Thoma (GER) 452.88
1968	Frantz Keller (GER) 449.04	Alois Kaelin (SUI) 447.94	Andreas Kunz (GDR) 444.10
1972	Ulrich Wehling (GDR) 413.34	Rauno Mittinen (FIN) 405.55	Karl-Heinz Luck (GDR) 398.80
1976	Ulrich Wehling (GDR) 423.39	Urban Hettich (GR) 418.90	Konrad Winkler (GDR) 417.47
1980	Ulrich Wehling (GDR) 432.20	Jouko Karjalainen (FIN) 429.50	Konrad Winkler (GDR) 425.32
1984	Tom Sandberg (NOR) 422.595	Kuoko Karjalainen (FIN) 416.900	Jukka Ylipulli (FIN) 410.825
1988	Hippolyt Kempf (SUI)	Klaus Sulzenbacher (AUT)	Allar Levandi (URS)

[1]In 1924 and 1928, the scoring was decided upon a different basis from that used from 1932 onwards.
[2]From 1924–1952 distance was 18 km.

NORDIC COMBINED—TEAM
(Introduced in 1988)

1988	WEST GERMANY Hans Pohl Hubert Schwarz Thomas Müller	SWITZERLAND Andreas Schaad Hippolyt Kempf Fredy Glanzmann	AUSTRIA Günther Csar Hansjörg Aschenwald Klaus Sulzenbacher

Biathlon

10 km

1908–1976	Event not held		
1980	Frank Ullrich (GDR) 32:10.69	Vladimir Alikin (URS) 32:53.10	Anatoliy Alyabiev (URS) 33:09.16
1984	Eirik Kvalfoss (NOR) 30:53.8	Peter Angerer (FRG) 31:02.4	Matthias Jacob (GDR) 31:10.5
1988	Frank-Peter Rötsch (GDR) 25:08.1	Valeriy Medvedtsev (URS) 25:23.7	Sergey Tchepikov (URS) 25:29.4

20 km

BIATHLON RELAY (4 × 7.5 km)

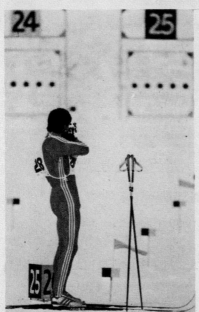

The 4 × 7.5 kilometer biathlon relay has been contested four times since its insertion in the 1968 program, and Soviet bi-athlete Alexander Tikhimov has been on the gold medal team at each Celebration.

Galina Kulakova (URS) set a women's Winter Games record with 8 total medals (4 gold, 2 silver and 2 bronze) in the 4 Games since 1968.

Nordic Skiing (Women)

5 km CROSS-COUNTRY (3 miles 188 yd.)

	GOLD	SILVER	BRONZE
1908–1960	Event not held		
1964	Klaudia Boyarskikh (URS) 17:50.5	Mirja Lehtonen (FIN) 17:52.9	Alevtina Koltschina (URS) 18:08.4
1968	Toini Gustafsson (SWE) 16:45.2	Galina Kulakova (URS) 16:48.4	Alevtina Koltschina (URS) 16:51.6
1972	Galina Kulakova (URS) 17:00.50	Marjatta Kajosmaa (FIN) 17:05.50	Helena Sikolova (TCH) 17:07.32
1976	Helena Takalo (FIN) 15:48.69	Raisa Smetanina (URS) 15:49.73	Nina Baldicheva[1] (URS) 16:12.82
1980	Raisa Smetanina (URS) 15:06.92	Hilkka Riihivuori (FIN) 15:11.96	Kvetslava Jeriova (TCH) 15:23.44
1984	Marja-Liisa Hamalainen (FIN) 17:04.0	Berit Aunli (NOR) 17:14.1	Kvetoslava Jeriova (TCH) 17:18.3
1988	Marjo Matikainen (FIN) 15:04.0	Tamara Tikhonova 15:05.3	Vida Ventsene (URS) 15:11.1

[1]Third finisher Galina Kulakova (URS) disqualified.

10 km CROSS-COUNTRY (6.2 miles)

1908–1948	Event not held		
1952	Lydia Widemen (FIN) 41:40.0	Mirja Hietamies (FIN) 42:39.0	Siiri Rantanen (FIN) 42:50.0
1956	Lyubov Kosyryeva (URS) 38:11.0	Radya Yeroschina (URS) 38:16.0	Sonja Edström (SWE) 38:23.0
1960	Maria Gusakova (URS) 39:46.6	Lyubov Baranova-Kosyryeva (URS) 40:04.2	Radya Yeroschina (URS) 40:06.0
1964	Klaudia Boyarskikh (URS) 40:24.3	Eudokia Mekshilo (URS) 40:26.6	Maria Gusakova (URS) 40:46.6
1968	Toini Gustafsson (SWE) 36:46.5	Berit Moerdre (NOR) 37:54.6	Inger Aufles (NOR) 37:59.9
1972	Galina Kulakova (URS) 34:17.8	Alevtina Olunina (URS) 34:54.1	Marjatta Kajosmaa (FIN) 34:56.5
1976	Raisa Smetanina (URS) 30:13.41	Helena Takalo (FIN) 30:14.28	Galina Kulakova (URS) 30:38.61
1980	Barbara Petzold (GDR) 30:31.54	Hilkka Riihivuori (FIN) 30:35.05	Helena Takalo (FIN) 30:45.25
1984	Marja-Liisa Hamalainen (FIN) 31:442.	Raisa Smetanina (URS) 32:02.9	Brit Pettersen (NOR) 32:12.7
1988	Vida Ventsene (URS) 30:08.3	Raisa Smetanina (URS) 30:17.0	Marjo Matikainen (FIN) 30:20.5

20 km CROSS-COUNTRY

1984	Marja-Liisa Hamalainen (FIN) 1h 01:45.0	Raisa Smetanina (URS) 1h 02:26.7	Anne Jahren (NOR) 1h 03:13.6
1988	Tamara Tikhonova (URS) 55:53.6	Anfissa Reztsova (URS) 56:12.8	Raisa Smetanina (URS) 57:22.1

Marja-Lisa Haemaelainen (FIN) dominated the women's skiing events, taking all three individual gold medals in the 1984 Olympics.

4 × 5 km RELAY[1]

	GOLD	SILVER	BRONZE
1908–1952	Event not held		
1956	FINLAND 1:9:01.0	U.S.S.R. 1h 9:28.0	SWEDEN 1h 9:48.0
	Sirkka Polkunen	Lyubov Kosyryeva	Irma Johansson
	Mirja Hietamies	Alevtina Koltschina	Anna-Lisa Eriksson
	Siiri Rantanen	Radya Yeroschina	Sonja Edström
1960	SWEDEN 1h 4:21.4	U.S.S.R. 1h 5:2.6	FINLAND 1h 6:27.5
	Irma Johansson	Radya Yeroschina	Siiri Rantanen
	Britt Strandberg	Maria Gusakova	Eeva Ruoppa
	Sonja	Lyubov	Toini Pöysti
	Ruthström-Edström	Baranova-Kosyryeva	
1964	U.S.S.R. 59:20.2	SWEDEN 1h:27.0	FINLAND 1h 2:45.1
	Alevtina Koltschina	Barbo Martinsson	Senja Pusula
	Eudokia Mekshilo	Britt Strandberg	Toini Pöysti
	Klaudia Boyarskikh	Toini Gustafsson	Mirja Lehtonen
1968	NORWAY 57:30.0	SWEDEN 57:51.0	U.S.S.R. 58:13.6
	Inger Aufles	Britt Strandberg	Alevtina Koltschina
	Babben Enger Damon	Toini Gustafsson	Rita Achkina
	Berit Moerdre	Barbo Martinsson	Galina Kulakova
1972	U.S.S.R. 48:46.15	FINLAND 49:19.37	NORWAY 49:51.49
	Lyubov Moukhateva	Helena Takalo	Inger Aufles
	Alevtina Olunina	Hilkka Kuntola	Aslaug Dahl
	Galina Kulakova	Marjatta Kajosmaa	Berit Lammedal
1976	U.S.S.R. 1h 07:49.75	FINLAND 1h 08:36.57	EAST GERMANY
			1h 09:57.95
	Nina Baldicheva	Liisa Suihkonen	Monika Debertshaeuser
	Zinaida Amosova	Marjatta Kajosmaa	Sigrun Krause
	Raisa Smetanina	Hilkka Kuntola	Barbara Petzold
	Galina Kulakova	Helena Takalo	Veronika Schmid
1980	EAST GERMANY	U.S.S.R. 1h 03:18.30	NORWAY 1h 04:13.50
	1h 02:11.10		
	Marlies Rostock	Nina Baldicheva	Brit Pettersen
	Carola Anding	Nina Rocheva	Anette Boe
	Veronika Hesse	Galina Kulakova	Marit Myrmael
	Barbara Petzold	Raisa Smetanina	Berit Aunli
1984	NORWAY 1h 06:49.7	CZECHOSLOVAKIA	FINLAND 1h 07:36.7
		1h 07:34.7	
	Inger Nygraaten	Dagmar Schvubova	Pirkko Maatta
	Anne Jahren	Blanka Paulu	Eija Hyytiainen
	Brit Pettersen	Gabriela Svobodova	Marjo Matikainen
	Berit Aunli	Kvetoslava Jeriova	Marja-Liisa Hämäläinen
1988	U.S.S.R. 59:51.1	NORWAY 1h 01:33.0	FINLAND 1h 01:53.8
	Svetlana Naguekina	Trude Dydendahl	Pirkko Maatta
	Nina Gavrilyuk	Marit Wold	Marja-Liisa Kirvesniemi
	Tamara Tikhonova	Anne Jahren	Marjo Matikainen
	Anfissa Reztsova	Marianne Dahlmo	Jaana Savolainen

[1]Race over three stages before 1976.

3. Figure Skating (Men)

	GOLD	SILVER	BRONZE
1908	Ulrich Salchow	Richard Johansson	Per Thorén
	(SWE) 1,886.5 pts	(SWE) 1,826.0 pts	(SWE) 1,787.0 pts
1920	Gillis Grafström	Andreas Krogh	Martin Stixrud
	(SWE) 2,838.5	(NOR) 2,634	(NOR) 2,561.5

	GOLD	SILVER	BRONZE
1924	Gillis Grafström (SWE) 2,575.25 pts	Willy Böckl (AUT) 2,518.75 pts	Georges Gautschi (SUI) 2,233.5 pts
1928	Gillis Grafström (SWE) 2,698.25	Willy Böckl (AUT) 2,682.50	Robert v. Zeebroeck (BEL) 2,578.75
1932	Karl Schäfer (AUT) 2,602.0	Gillis Grafström (SWE) 2,514.5	Montgomery Wilson (CAN) 2,448.3
1936	Karl Schäfer (AUT) 2,959.0	Ernst Baier (GER) 2,805.3	Felix Kaspar (AUT) 2,801.0
1948	Richard Button (USA) 1,720.6	Hans Gerschwiler (SUI) 1,630.1	Edi Rada (AUT) 1,603.2
1952	Richard Button (USA) 1,730.3	Helmut Seibt (AUT) 1,621.3	James Grogan (USA) 1,627.4
1956	Hayes Alan Jenkins (USA) 1,497.95	Ronald Robertson (USA) 1,492.15	David Jenkins (USA) 1,465.41
1960	David Jenkins (USA) 1,440.2	Jarol Divin (TCH) 1,414.3	Donald Jackson (CAN) 1,401.0
1964	Manfred Schnelldorfer (GER) 1,916.9	Alain Calmat (FRA) 1,876.5	Scott Allen (USA) 1,873.6
1968	Wolfgang Schwartz (AUT) 1,094.1	Timothy Wood (USA) 1,891.6	Patrick Péra (FRA) 1,864.5
1972	Ondrej Nepela (TCH) 2,739.1	Sergei Chetverukhin (URS) 2,672.4	Patrick Péra (FRA) 2,653.1
1976	John Curry (GBR) 192.74	Vladimir Kovalev (URS) 187.64	Toller Cranston (CAN) 187.38
1980	Robin Cousins (GBR) 189.48	Jan Hoffmann (GDR) 189.72	Charles Tickner (USA) 187.06
1984	Scott Hamilton (USA) 3.4 pl	Brian Orser (CAN) 5.6 pl	Jozef Sabovtchik (TCH) 7.4 pl
1988	Brian Boitano (USA) 3.0 pl	Brian Orser (CAN) 4.2 pl	Viktor Petrenko (URS) 7.8 pl

Figure Skating (Women)

	GOLD	SILVER	BRONZE
1908	E. Madge Syers (GBR) 1,262.5 pts	Elsa Rendschmidt (GER) 1,055.0 pts	Dorothy Greenhough-Smith (GBR) 960.5 pts
1920	Magda Julin-Mauroy (SWE) 913.5	Svea Norén (SWE) 887.75	Theresa Weld (USA) 898.0
1924	Herma Planck-Szabo (AUT) 2,094.25	Beatrix Loughran (USA) 1,959.0	Ethel Muckelt (GBR) 1,750.50
1928	Sonja Henie (NOR) 2,452.25	Fritzi Burger (AUT) 2,248.50	Beatrix Loughran (USA) 2,254.50
1932	Sonja Henie (NOR) 2,302.5	Fritzi Burger (AUT) 2,167.1	Maribel Vinson (USA) 2,158.5
1936	Sonja Henie (NOR) 2,971.4	Cecilia Colledge (GBR) 2,926.8	Vivi-Anne Hultén (SWE) 2,763.2
1948	Barbara Scott (CAN) 1,467.7	Efa Pawlik (AUT) 1,418.3	Jeanette Altwegg (GBR) 1,405.5
1952	Jeanette Altwegg (GBR) 1,455.8	Tenley Albright (USA) 1,432.2	Jacqueline du Bief (FRA) 1,422.0
1956	Tenley Albright (USA) 1,866.39	Carol Heiss (USA) 1,848.24	Ingrid Wendl (AUT) 1,753.91
1960	Carol Heiss (USA) 1,490.1	Sjoukje Dijkstra (HOL) 1,424.8	Barbara Roles (USA) 1,414.8
1964	Sjoukje Dijkstra (HOL) 2,018.5	Regine Heitzer (AUT) 1,945.5	Petra Burka (CAN) 1,940.0
1968	Peggy Fleming (USA) 1,970.5	Gabrielle Seyfert (GDR) 1,882.3	Hana Maskova (TCH) 1,828.8
1972	Beatrix Schuba (AUT) 2,751.5	Karen Magnussen (CAN) 2,673.2	Janet Lynn (USA) 2,663.1
1976	Dorothy Hamill (USA) 193.80	Dianne De Leeuw (HOL) 190.24	Christine Errath (GDR) 188.16
1980	Anett Poetzsch (GDR) 189.00	Linda Fratianne (USA) 188.30	Dagmar Lurz (GER) 183.04

	GOLD	SILVER	BRONZE
1984	Katarina Witt (GDR) 3.2 pl	Rosalyn Sumners (USA) 4.6 pl	Kira Ivanova (URS) 9.2 pl
1988	Katarina Witt (GDR) 4.2 pl	Elizabeth Manley (CAN) 4.6 pl	Debra Thomas (USA) 6.0 pl

PAIRS

	GOLD	SILVER	BRONZE
1908	Anna Hübler Heinrich Burger (GER) 56.0 pts	Phyllis W. Johnson James H. Johnson (GBR) 51.5 pts	Madge Syers Edgar Syers (GBR) 48.0 pts
1920	Ludovika Jakobsson Walter Jakobsson (FIN) 80.75	Alexia Bryn Yngvar Bryn (NOR) 72.75	Phyllis W. Johnson Basi Williams (GBR) 66.25
1924	Helene Engelmann Alfred Berger (AUT) 74.50	Ludovika Jakobsson Walter Jakobsson (FIN) 71.75	Andrée Joly Pierre Brunet (FRA) 69.25
1928	Andrée Joly Pierre Brunet (FRA) 100.50	Lilly Scholz Otto Kaiser (AUT) 99.25	Melitta Brunner Ludwig Wrede (AUT) 93.25
1932	Andrée Brunet Pierre Brunet (FRA) 76.7	Beatrix Loughran Sherwin Badger (USA) 77.5	Emilia Rotter László Szollás (HUN) 76.4
1936	Maxi Herber Ernst Baier (GER) 103.3	Ilse Pausin Erik Pausin (AUT) 102.7	Emilia Rotter László Szollás (HUN) 97.6
1948	Micheline Lannoy Pierre Baugniet (BEL) 123.5	Andrea Kékessy Ede Király (HUN) 122.2	Suzanne Morrow Wallace Diestelmeyer (CAN) 121.0
1952	Ria Falk Paul Falk (GER) 102.6	Karol Estelle Kennedy Michael Kennedy (USA) 100.6	Marianna Nagy László Nagy (HUN) 97.4
1956	Elisabeth Schwarz Kurt Oppelt (AUT) 101.8	Frances Dafoe Norris Bowden (CAN) 101.9	Marianna Nagy László Nagy (HUN) 99.3
1960	Barbara Wagner Robert Paul (CAN) 80.4	Marika Kilius Hansjürgen Bäumler (GER) 76.8	Nancy Ludington Ronald Ludington (USA) 76.2
1964[1]	Ludmilla Belousova Oleg Protopopov (URS) 104.4	Debbie Wilkes Guy Revell (CAN) 98.5	Vivian Joseph Ronald Joseph (USA) 98.2
1968	Ludmilla Belousova Oleg Protopopov (URS) 315.2	Tatiana Chesternyava Alexander Gorelik (URS) 312.3	Margo Glockshuber Wolfgang Danne (GER) 304.4
1972	Irina Rodnina Alexei Ulanov (URS) 420.4	Ludmila Smirnova Andrei Suraikin (URS) 419.4	Manuela Gross Uwe Kagelmann (GDR) 411.8
1976	Irina Rodnina Aleksander Zaitsev (URS) 140.54	Romy Kermer Rolf Oesterreich (GDR) 136.35	Manuela Grosse Uwe Kagelmann (GDR) 134.57
1980	Irina Rodina Aleksander Zaitsev (URS) 147.26	Marina Tcherkosova Sergey Shakrai (URS) 143.80	Manuela Mager Uwe Bewersdorff (GDR) 140.52
1984	Elena Valova Oleg Vassilyev (URS) 1.4 pl	Kitty Carruthers Peter Carruthers (USA) 2.8 pl	Larissa Selezneyva Oleg Makarov (URS) 3.8 pl
1988	Yekaterina Gordeyeva Sergey Grinkov (URS) 1.4 pl	Elena Valova Oleg Vassilyev (URS) 2.8 pl	Jill Watson Peter Oppegard (USA) 4.2 pl

[1] Marika Kilius and Hansjürgen Bäumler (GER) finished second but were subsequently disqualified.

Scott Hamilton (USA) dazzled the 1984 Olympic spectators with his performance in figure skating, and won the gold medal.

ICE DANCE

GOLD	SILVER	BRONZE
1908–1972 Event not held		
1976 Ludmila Pakhomova Aleksander Gorshkov (URS) 209.92 pts	Irina Moiseyeva Andrei Minenkov (URS) 204.88 pts	Colleen O'Connor James Millns (USA) 202.64 pts
1980 Natalya Linichuk Gennadiy Karponosov (URS) 205.48 pts	Krisztina Regoczy Andras Sallay (HUN) 204.52 pts	Irina Moiseyeva Andrei Minenkov (URS) 201.86 pts
1984 Jayne Torvill Christopher Dean (GBR) 2.0 pl	Natalya Bestemyanova Andrei Bukin (URS) 4.0 pl	Marina Klimova Sergey Ponomarenko (URS) 7.0 pl
1988 Natalya Bestemyanova Andrei Bukin (URS) 2.0 pl	Marina Klimova Sergey Ponomarenko (URS) 4.0 pl	Tracy Wilson Robert McCall (CAN) 6.0 pl

4. Speed Skating (Men)

500 METERS

	GOLD	SILVER	BRONZE
1908–1920	Event not held		
1924	Charles Jewtraw (USA) 44.0*	Oskar Olsen (NOR) 44.2	Roald Larsen (NOR) 44.8 Clas Thunberg (FIN) 44.8
1928	Clas Thunberg (FIN) 43.4* Bernt Evensen (NOR) 43.4*		John O'Neil Farrell (USA) 43.6 Roald Larsen (NOR 43.6 Jaako Friman (FIN) 43.6
1932	John Amos Shea (USA) 43.4*	Bernt Evensen (NOR) d.n.a.	Alexander Hurd (CAN) d.n.a.
1936	Ivar Ballangrud (NOR) 43.4*	Georg Krog (NOR) 43.5	Leo Freisinger (USA) 44.0
1948	Finn Helgesen (NOR) 43.1*	Kenneth Bartholomew (USA) 43.2 Thomas Byberg (NOR) 43.2 Robert Fitzgerald (USA) 43.2	
1952	Kenneth Henry (USA) 43.2	Donald McDermott (USA) 43.9	Arne Johansen (NOR) 44.0 Gordon Audley (CAN) 44.0
1956	Yevgeniy Grischin (URS) 40.2*	Rafael Gratsch (URS) 40.8	Alv Gjestvang (NOR) 41.0
1960	Yevgeniy Grischin (URS) 40.2*	William Disney (USA) 40.3	Rafael Gratsch (URS) 40.4
1964	Richard McDermott (USA) 40.1*	Yevgeniy Grischin (URS) 40.6 Vladimir Orlov (URS) 40.6 Alv Gjestvang (NOR) 40.6	
1968	Erhard Keller (GER) 40.3	Richard McDermott (USA) 40.5 Magne Thomassen (NOR) 40.5	
1972	Erhard Keller (GER) 39.44*	Hasse Borjes (SWE) 39.69	Valeriy Muratov (URS) 39.80
1976	Evgeniy Kulikov (URS) 39.17*	Valeriy Muratov (URS) 39.25	Daniel Immerfall (USA) 39.54
1980	Eric Heiden (USA) 38.03*	Yevgeniy Kulikov (URS) 38.37	Lieuwe de Boer (HOL) 38.48
1984	Sergey Fokitchev (URS) 38.19	Yoshihiro Kitazawa (JPN) 38.30	Gaetan Boucher (CAN) 38.39
1988	Jens-Uwe Mey (GDR) 36.45$	Jan Ykema (HOL) 36.76	Akira Kuriowa (JPN) 36.77

1,000 METERS

	GOLD	SILVER	BRONZE
1909–1972	Event not held		
1976	Peter Mueller (USA) 1:19.32*	Jorn Didriksen (NOR) 1:20.45	Valeriy Muratov (URS) 1:20.57

	GOLD	SILVER	BRONZE
1980	Eric Heiden (USA) 1:15.18*	Gaetan Boucher (CAN) 1:16.68	Frode Ronning (NOR) 1:16.91 Vladimir Lobanov (URS) 1:16.91
1984	Gaetan Boucher (CAN) 1:15.80	Sergey Khlebnikov (URS) 1:16.63	Kai Arne Engelstad (NOR) 1:16.75
1988	Nikolai Gouliayev (URS) 1:13.03*	Jens-Uwe Mey (GDR) 1:13.11	Igor Gelezovsky (URS) 1:13.19

1,500 METERS

	GOLD	SILVER	BRONZE
1908–1920	Event not held		
1924	Clas Thunberg (FIN) 2:20.8*	Roald Larsen (NOR) 2:22.0	Sigurd Moen (NOR) 2:25.6
1928	Clas Thunberg (FIN) 2:21.1	Bernt Evensen (NOR) 2:21.9	Ivar Ballangrud (NOR) 2:22.6
1932	John Amos Shea (USA) 2:57.5	Alexander Hurd (CAN) d.n.a.	William F. Logan (CAN) d.n.a.
1936	Charles Mathiesen (NOR) 2:19.2*	Ivar Ballangrud (NOR) 2:20.2	Birger Wasenius (FIN) 2:20.9
1948	Sverre Farstad (NOR) 2:17.6*	Ake Seyffarth (SWE) 2:18.1	Odd Lundberg (NOR) 2:18.9
1952	Hjalmar Andersen (NOR) 2:20.4	Willem van der Voort (HOL) 2:20.6	Roald Aas (NOR) 2:21.6
1956	Yevgeniy Grischin (URS) 2:08.6 Yuriy Michailov (URS) 2:08.6		Toivo Salonen (FIN) 2:09.4
1960	Roald Aas (NOR) 2:10.4 Yevgeniy Grischin (URS) 2:10.4		Boris Stenin (URS) 2:11.5
1964	Ants Antson (URS) 2:10.3	Cornelis Verkerk (HOL) 2:10.6	Villy Haugen (NOR) 2:11.25
1968	Cornelis Verkerk (HOL) 2:03.4*	Ard Schenk (HOL) 2:05.0 Ivar Eriksen (NOR) 2:05.0	
1972	Ard Schenk (HOL) 2:02.96*	Roar Gronvold (NOR) 2:04.26	Goran Clässon (SWE) 2:05.89
1976	Jan Egil Storholt (NOR) 1:59.38*	Yuriy Kondakov (URS) 1:59.97	Hans Van Helden (HOL) 2:00.87
1980	Eric Heiden (USA) 1:53.44*	Kai Stenshjemmet (NOR) 1:56.81	Terje Andersen (NOR) 1:56.92
1984	Gaetan Boucher (CAN) 1:58.36	Sergey Khlebnikov (URS) 1:58.83	Oleg Bogiev (URS) 1:58.89
1988	Andre Hoffmann (GDR) 1:52.06*	Eric Flaim (USA) 1:52.12	Michael Hadschieff (AUT) 1:52.31

5,000 METERS

	GOLD	SILVER	BRONZE
1908–1920	Event not held		
1924	Clas Thunberg (FIN) 8:39.0*	Julius Skutnabb (FIN) 8:48.4	Roald Larsen (NOR) 8:50.2
1928	Ivar Ballangrud (NOR) 8:50.5	Julius Skutnabb (FIN) 8:59.1	Bernt Evensen (NOR) 9:01.1
1932	Irving Jaffee (USA) 9:40.8	Edward S. Murphy (USA) d.n.a.	William F. Logan (CAN) d.n.a.
1936	Ivar Ballangrud (NOR) 8:19.6*	Birger Wasenius (FIN) 8:23.3	Antero Ojala (FIN) 8:30.1
1948	Reidar Liaklev (NOR) 8:29.4	Odd Lundberg (NOR) 8:32.7	Göthe Hedlund (SWE) 8:34.8
1952	Hjalmar Andersen (NOR) 8:10.6*	Kees Broekman (HOL) 8:21.6	Sverre Haugli (NOR) 8:22.4

GOLD	SILVER	BRONZE
1956 Boris Schilkov (URS) 7:48.7*	Sigvard Ericsson (SWE) 7:56.7	Oleg Gontscharenko (URS) 7:57.5
1960 Viktor Kositschkin (URS) 7:51.3	Knut Johannesen (NOR) 8:00.8	Jan Pesman (HOL) 8:05.1
1964 Knut Johannesen (NOR) 7:38.4*	P. Moe (NOR) 7:38.6	F. Anton Maier (NOR) 7:42.0
1968 F. Anton Maier (NOR) 7:22.4*	Cornelis Verkerk (HOL) 7:23.2	Petrus Nottet (HOL) 7:25.5
1972 Ard Schenk (HOL) 7:23.6	Roar Gronvold (NOR) 7:28.18	Sten Stensen (NOR) 7:33.39
1976 Sten Stensen (NOR) 7:24.48	Piet Kleine (HOL) 7:26.47	Hans Van Helden (HOL) 7:26.54
1980 Eric Heiden (USA) 7:02.29*	Kai Stenshjemmet (NOR) 7:03.28	Tom Oxholm (NOR) 7:05.59
1984 Tomas Gustafsson (SWE) 7:12.28	Igor Malkov (URS) 7:12.30	Rene Schoefisch (GDR) 7:17.49
1988 Tomas Gustafsson (SWE) 6:44.63*	Leendert Visser (HOL) 6:44.98	Gerard Kemkers (HOL) 6:45.92

10,000 METERS

1908–1920 Event not held		
1924 Julius Sknutnabb (FIN) 18:04.8*	Clas Thunberg (FIN) 18:07.8	Roald Larsen (NOR) 18:12.2
1928 Event abandoned		
1932 Irving Jaffee (USA) 19:13.6	Ivar Ballangrud (NOR) d.n.a.	Frank Stack (CAN) d.n.a.
1936 Ivar Ballangrud (NOR) 17:24.3*	Birger Wasenius (FIN) 17:28.2	Max Stiepl (AUT) 17:30.0
1948 Ake Seyffarth (SWE) 17:26.3	Lauri Parkkinen (FIN) 17:36.0	Pentti Lammio (FIN) 17:42.7

Eric Heiden (USA) earned an unprecedented sweep of all five speed skating gold medals at Lake Placid, setting an Olympic record in each event.

GOLD	SILVER	BRONZE
1952 Hjalmar Andersen (NOR) 16:45.8*	Kees Broekman (HOL) 17:10.6	Carl-Erik Asplund (SWE) 17:16.6
1956 Sigvard Ericsson (SWE) 16:35.9*	Knut Johannesen (NOR) 16:36.9	Oleg Gontscharenko (URS) 16:42.3
1960 Knut Johannesen (NOR) 15:46.6*	Viktor Kositschkin (URS) 15:49.2	Kjell Bäckman (SWE) 16:14.2
1964 Johnny Nilsson (SWE) 15:50.1	F. Anton Maier (NOR) 16:06.0	Knut Johannesen (Nor) 16:06.3
1968 Johnny Hoeglin (SWE) 15:23.6*	F. Anton Maier (NOR) 15:23.9	Orejan Sandler (SWE) 15:31.8
1972 Ard Schenk (HOL) 15:01.35*	Cornelis Verkerk (HOL) 15:04.70	Sten Stensen (NOR) 15:07.08
1976 Piet Kleine (HOL) 14:50.59*	Sten Stensen (NOR) 14:53.30	Hans Van Helden (HOL) 15:02.02
1980 Eric Heiden (USA) 14:28.13*	Piet Kleine (HOL) 14:36.03	Tom Oxholm (NOR) 14:36.60
1984 Igor Malkov (URS) 14:39.90	Tomas Gustafsson (SWE) 14:39.95	Rene Schoefisch (GDR) 14:46.91
1988 Tomas Gustafsson (SWE) 13:48.20*	Michael Hadschieff (AUT) 13:56.11	Leendert Visser (HOL) 14:00.55

Former world cycling champion Sheila Young (USA) won gold, silver and bronze medals in the 1976 speed skating competition.

Speed Skating (Women)

1908–1956 Events not held, but in 1932 there were three demonstration events for women speed skaters.

The Russian speed skater Lydia Skoblikova won a record 6 Olympic gold medals in the 1960 and 1964 Games.

500 METERS

	GOLD	SILVER	BRONZE
1960	Helga Hasse (GER) 45.9*	Natalie Dontschenko (URS) 46.0	Jeanne Ashworth (USA) 46.1
1964	Lydia Skoblikova (URS) 45.0*	Irina Yegorova (URS) 45.4	Tatyana Sidorova (URS) 45.5
1968	Ludmila Titova (URS) 46.1	Mary Meyers (USA) 46.3 Dianne Holum (USA) 46.3 Jennifer Fish (USA) 46.3	No bronze award
1972	Anne Henning (USA) 43.33*	Vera Krasnova (URS) 44.01	Ludmila Titova (URS) 44.45
1976	Sheila Young (USA) 42.76*	Catherine Priestner (CAN) 43.12	Tatyana Averina (URS) 43.17
1980	Karin Enke (GDR) 41.78*	Leah Mueller (USA) 42.26	Natalya Petruseva (URS) 42.42
1984	Christa Rothenburger (GDR) 41.02*	Karin Enke (GDR) 41.28	Natalya Chive (URS) 41.50
1988	Bonnie Blair (USA) 39.10*	Christa Rothenburger (GDR) 39.12	Karin Enke-Kania (GDR) 39.24

1,000 METERS

1960	Klala Guseva (URS) 1:34.1*	Helga Haase (GER) 1:34.3	Tamara Rylova (URS) 1:34.8
1964	Lydia Skoblikova (URS) 1:33.2*	Irina Yegorova (URS) 1:34.3	Kaija Mustonen (FIN) 1:34.8
1968	Carolina Geijssen (HOL) 1:32.6	Ludmila Titova (URS) 1:32.9	Dianne Holum (USA) 1:33.4
1972	Monika Pflug (GER) 1:31.40*	Atje Keulen-Deelstra (HOL) 1:31.61	Anne Henning (USA) 1:31.62
1976	Tatyana Averina (URS) 1:28.43*	Leah Poulos (USA) 1:28.57	Sheila Young (USA) 1:29.14
1980	Natalya Petruseva (URS) 1:24.10*	Leah Mueller (USA) 1:25.41	Sylvia Albrecht (GDR) 1:26.46
1984	Karin Enke (GDR) 1:21.61*	Andrea Schoene (GDR) 1:22.83	Natalya Petruseva (URS) 1:23.21
1988	Christa Rothenburger (GDR) 1:17.65*	Karin Enke-Kania (GDR) 1:17.70	Bonnie Blair (USA) 1:18.31

Karin Enke Kania of East Germany, after winning her first Olympic gold at 500 meters in 1980, won 2 more golds in 1984 at 1,000 and 1,500 meters and silvers at 50 and 2,000 meters.

1,500 METERS

	GOLD	SILVER	BRONZE
1960	Lydia Skoblikova (URS) 2:25.2*	Elvira Seroczynska (POL) 2:25.7	Helena Pilejeyk (POL) 2:27.1
1964	Lydia Skoblikova (URS) 2:22.6*	Kaija Mustonen (FIN) 2:25.5	Berta Kolokoltseva (URS) 2:27.1
1968	Kaija Mustonen (FIN) 2:22.4*	Carolina Geijssen (HOL) 2:22.7	Christina Kaiser (HOL) 2:24.5
1972	Dianne Holum (USA) 2:20.85*	Christina Baas-Kaiser (HOL) 2:21.05	Atje Keulen-Deelstra (HOL) 2:22.05
1976	Galina Stepanskaya (URS) 2:16.58*	Sheila Young (USA) 2:17.06	Tatyana Averina (URS) 2:17.96
1980	Annie Borckink (HOL) 2:10.95*	Ria Visser (HOL) 2:12.35	Sabine Becker (GDR) 2:12.38
1984	Karin Enke (GDR) 2:03.42*	Andrea Schoene (GDR) 2:05.29	Natalya Petruseva (URS) 2:05.78
1988	Yvonne Van Gennip (HOL) 2:00.68*	Karin Enke-Kania (GDR) 2:00.82	Andrea Schoene-Ehrig (GDR) 2:01.49

3,000 METERS

	GOLD	SILVER	BRONZE
1960	Lydia Skoblikova (URS) 5:14.3*	Valentina Stenina (URS) 5:16.9	Eevi Huttunen (FIN) 5:21.0
1964	Lydia Skoblikova (URS) 5:14.9	Valentina Stenina (URS) 5:18.5 Pil-Hwa Han (PRK) 5:18.5	
1968	Johanna Schut (HOL) 4:56.2*	Kaija Mustonen (FIN) 5:01.0	Christina Kaiser (HOL) 5:01.3
1972	Christina Baas-Kaiser (HOL) 4:52.14*	Dianne Holum (USA) 4:58.67	Atje Keulen-Deelstra (HOL) 4:59.91
1976	Tatyana Averina (URS) 4:45.19*	Andrea Mitscherlich (GDR) 4:45.23	Lisbeth Korsmo (NOR) 4:45.24
1980	Bjorg Eva Jensen (NOR) 4:32.13*	Sabine Becker (GDR) 4:32.79	Beth Heiden (USA) 4:33.77
1984	Andrea Schoene (GDR) 4:24.79*	Karin Enke (GDR) 4:26.33	Gabi Schoenbrunn (GDR) 4:33.13
1988	Yvonne Van Gennip (HOL) 4:11.94*	Andrea Schoene-Ehrig (GDR) 4:12.09	Gabi Schoenbrunn-Zange (GDR) 4:16.92

1988	Yvonne Van Gennip	Andrea Schoene-Ehrig	Gabi Schoenbrunn-Zange
	(HOL) 7:14.13*	(GDR) 7:17.12	(GDR) 7:21.61

---

5. Bobsleigh

2-MAN BOB

1908–1928 Event not held

1932	**UNITED STATES I** 8:14.74	**SWITZERLAND II** 8:16.28	**UNITED STATES II** 8:29.15
	J. Hubert Stevens Curtis P. Stevens	R. Capadrutt O. Geier	J. R. Heaton R. Minton
1936	**UNITED STATES I** 5:29.29	**SWITZERLAND II** 5:30.64	**UNITED STATES II** 5:33.96
	Ivan Brown Alan Washbond	F. Feierabend J. Beerli	G. Colgate R. Lawrence
1948	**SWITZERLAND II** 5:29.2	**SWITZERLAND I** 5:30.4	**UNITED STATES II** 5:35.3
	Felix Endrich Friedrich Waller	F. Feierabend P. Eberhard	F. Fortune S. Carron
1952	**GERMANY I** 5:24.54	**UNITED STATES I** 5:26.89	**SWITZERLAND I** 5:27.71
	Andreas Ostler Lorenz Nieberl	S. Benham P. Martin	F. Feierabend S. Waser
1956	**ITALY I** 5:30.14	**ITALY II** 5:31.45	**SWITZERLAND I** 5:37.46
	Lamberto Dall Costa Giacomo Conti	Eugenio Monti R. Alvera	M. Angst H. Warburton
1960	Event not held		
1964	**GREAT BRITAIN** 4:21.90	**ITALY II** 4:22.02	**ITALY I** 4:22.63
	Anthony J. D. Nash The Hon. Robin Dixon	S. Zardini R. Bonagura	Eugenio Monti S. Siorpaes
1968	**ITALY I** 4:41.54	**WEST GERMANY I** 4:41.54	**ROMANIA I** 4:44.46
	Eugenio Monti Luciano de Paolis	Horst Floth Pepi Bader	Ion Panturu Nicolae Neagoe
1972	**WEST GERMANY II** 4:57.07	**WEST GERMANY I** 4:58.84	**SWITZERLAND I** 4:59.33
	Wolfgang Zimmerer Peter Utzschneider	Horst Floth Pepi Bader	Jean Wicki Egy Hubacher

The winning USA 4-man bobsled team of 1932, with Eddie Eagen in second position. Eagen, later head of the NY State Boxing Commission, is the only athlete to win gold medals in both Summer and Winter Games—his other medal being as light-heavyweight boxing champion in 1920.

GOLD	SILVER	BRONZE
1976 **EAST GERMANY II** 3:444.2	**WEST GERMANY I** 3:449.9	**SWITZERLAND I** 3:457.0
Meinhard Nehmer	Wolfgang Zimmerer	Erich Schaerer
Bernard Germeshausen	Manfred Schumann	Josef Benz
1980 **SWITZERLAND II** 4:09.36	**EAST GERMANY II** 4:10.93	**EAST GERMANY I** 4:11.08
Erich Shaerer	Bernhard	Meinhard Nehmer
Josef Benz	Germeshausen	Bogdan Musiol
	Hans-Jurgen Gerhardt	
1984 **GDR II** 3:25.56	**GDR I** 3:26.04	**U.S.S.R. II** 3:26.16
Wolfgang Hoppe	Bernhard Lehmann	Zintis Ekmanis
Dietmar Schauerhammer	Bogdan Musiol	Vladimir Aleksandrov
1988 **U.S.S.R. I** 3:53.48	**EAST GERMANY** 3:54.19	**EAST GERMANY II** 3:54.64
Yanis Kipurs	Wolfgang Hoppe	Bernhard Lehmann
Vladimir Kozlov	Bogdan Musiol	Mario Hoyer

4-MAN BOB

GOLD	SILVER	BRONZE
1908–1920 Event not held		
1924 **SWITZERLAND I** 5:45.54	**GREAT BRITAIN II** 5:48.83	**BELGIUM I** 6:02.29
Eduard Scherrer	R. H. Broome	C. Mulder
Alfred Neveu	T. A. Arnold	R. Mortiaux
Alfred Schläppi	H. A. W. Richardson	P. v. d. Broeck
Heinrich Schläppi	R. E. Soher	V. A. Verschueren or
		H. P. Willems
1928 **UNITED STATES II** 3:20.5 (5-man event)	**UNITED STATES I** 3:21.0	**GERMANY II** 3:21.9
William Fiske	J. Heaton	H. Kilian
Nion Tocker	D. Granger	V. Krempl
Charles Mason	L. Hine	H. Hess
Clifford Gray	T. Doe	S. Huber
Richard Parke	J. O'Brien	H. Nägle
1932 **UNITED STATES I** 7:53.68	**UNITED STATES II** 7:55.70	**GERMANY I** 8:00.04
William Fiske	H. Homburger	H. Kilian
Edward Eagen	P. Bryant	M. Ludwig
Clifford Gray	F. P. Stevens	Dr. H. Mehlhorn
Jay O'Brien	E. Horton	S. Huber
1936 **SWITZERLAND II** 5:19.85	**SWITZERLAND II** 5:22.73	**GREAT BRITAIN** 5:23.41
Pierre Mussy	R. Capadrutt	F. McEvoy
Arnold Gartmann	H. Aichele	J. Cardno
Charles Bouvier	F. Feierabend	G. Dugdale
Joseph Beerli	H. Bütikofer	C. Green
1948 **UNITED STATES II** 5:20.1	**BELGIUM** 5:21.3	**UNITED STATES I** 5:21.5
Francis Tyler	M. Houben	J. Bickford
Patrick Martin	F. Mansveld	T. Hicks
Edward Rimkus	G. Niels	D. Dupree
William D'Amico	J. Mouvet	W. Dupree
1952 **GERMANY** 5:07.84	**UNITED STATES I** 5:10.48	**SWITZERLAND I** 5:11.70
Andreas Ostler	S. Benham	F. Feierabend
Friedrich Kuhn	P. Martin	A. Madörin
Lorenz Nieberl	H. Crossett	A. Filippini
Franz Kemser	J. Atkinson	S. Waser
1956 **SWITZERLAND I** 5:10.44	**ITALY II** 5:12.10	**UNITED STATES** 5:12.39
Franz Kapus	Eugenio Monti	A. Tyler
Gottfried Diener	U. Girardi	W. Dodge
Robert Alt	R. Alvera	C. Butler
Heinrich Angst	R. Mocellini	J. Lamy

	GOLD	SILVER	BRONZE
1960	Event not held		
1964	CANADA I 4:14.46	AUSTRIA I 4:15.48	ITALY II 4:15.60
	Victor Emery	Erwin Thaler	Eugenio Monti
	Peter Kirby	A. Knoxeder	S. Siorpaes
	Douglas Anakin	J. Nairz	B. Rigoni
	John Emery	Reinhold Durnthaler	G. Siorpaes
1968	ITALY I 2:17.39	AUSTRIA I 2:17.48	SWITZERLAND 2:18.04
	Eugenio Monti	Erwin Thaler	Jean Wicki
	Luciano De Paolis	Reinhold Durnthaler	Hans Candrian
	Roberto Zandonella	Herbert Gruber	Willi Hofmann
	Mario Armano	Josef Eder	Walter Graf
1972	SWITZERLAND I 4:43.07	ITALY I 4:43.83	WEST GERMANY I 4:43.92
	Jean Wicki	Nevio de Zordo	Wolfgang Zimmerer
	Edy Hubacher	G. Bonichon	Peter Utzschneider
	Hans Leutenegger	Adriano Frassinelli	Stefan Gaisreister
	Werner Camichel	C. dal Fabbo	Walter Steinbauer
1976	EAST GERMANY I 3:40.43	SWITZERLAND II 3:40.89	WEST GERMANY I 3:41.37
	Meinhard Nehmer	Erich Schaerer	Wolfgang Zimmerer
	Jochen Babok	Ulrich Baechli	Peter Utzschneider
	Bernhard Germeshausen	Rudolf Marti	Bodo Bittner
	Bernhard Lehmann	Josef Benz	Manfred Schumann
1980	EAST GERMANY I 3:59.92	SWITZERLAND I 4:00.87	EAST GERMANY II 4:00.97
	Meinhard Nehmer	Erich Shaerer	Horst Schonau
	Bogdan Musiol	Ulrich Baechli	Roland Wetzig
	Bernhard Germeshausen	Rudolf Marti	Detlef Richter
	Hans-Jurgen Gerhardt	Josef Benz	Andreas Kirchner
1984	WEST GERMANY I 3:20.22	WEST GERMANY II 3:20.78	SWITZERLAND I 3:21.39
	Wolfgang Hoppe	Bernhard Lehmann	Silvio Giobellina
	Roland Wetzig	Bogdan Musiol	Heinz Stettler
	Dietmar Schauerhammer	Ingo Voge	Urs Salzmann
	Andreas Kirchner	Eberhard Weise	Rico Freiermuth
1988	SWITZERLAND I 3:47.51	EAST GERMANY I 3:47.58	U.S.S.R. I 3:48.26
	Ekkehard Fasser	Wolfgang Hoppe	Yanis Kipurs
	Kurt Meier	Dietmar Schuaerhammer	Gountis Ossis
	Marcel Faessler	Bogdan Musiol	Yuriy Tone
	Werner Stocker	Ingo Voge	Valdimir Kozlov

---

6. Lugeing (Tobogganing)

SINGLE SEATER—MEN

1908–1960	Event not held		
1964	Thomas Koehler (GER) 3:26.77	Klaus Bonsack (GER) 3:27.04	Hans Plenk (GER) 3:30.15
1968	Manfred Schmid (AUT) 2:52.48	Thomas Koehler (GDR) 2:52.66	Klaus Bonsack (GDR) 2:53.33
1972	Wolfgang Scheidel (GDR) 3:27.58	Harald Ehrig (GDR) 3:28.39	Wolfram Fiedler (GDR) 3:28.73
1976	Detlef Guenther (GDR) 3:27.688	Josef Fendt (GER) 3:28.196	Hans Rinn (GER) 3:28.574
1980	Bernhard Glass (GDR) 2:54.796	Paul Hildgartner (ITA) 2:55.372	Anton Winkler (GER) 2:56.545

	GOLD	SILVER	BRONZE
1984	Paul Hildgartner (ITA) 3:04.258	Sergey Danilin (URS) 3:04.962	Valeriy Dudin (URS) 3:05.012
1988	Jens Müller (GDR) 3:05.548	Georg Hackl (FRG) 3:05.916	Yuriy Khartchenko (URS) 3:06.274

TWO-SEATER—MEN

1908–1960 Event not held			
1964	AUSTRIA 1:41.62	AUSTRIA 1:41.91	ITALY 1:42.87
	Josef Feistmantl	Reinhold Senn	W. Aussendorfer
	Manfred Stengl	H. Thaler	S. Mair
1968	EAST GERMANY 1:35.85	AUSTRIA 1:36.34	WEST GERMANY 1:37.29
	Klaus Bonsack	Manfred Schmid	Wolfgang Winkler
	Thomas Koehler	Ewald Walch	Fritz Nachmann
1972	ITALY 1:28.35		EAST GERMANY 1:29.16
	Paul Hildgartner		Klaus Bonsack
	Walter Plaikner		Wolfram Fiedler
	EAST GERMANY 1:28.35		
	Horst Hornlein		
	Reinhard Bredow		
1976	EAST GERMANY 1:25.604	WEST GERMANY 1:25.889	AUSTRIA 1:25.919
	Hans Rinn	Hans Brandner	Rudolf Schmid
	Norbert Hahn	Balthasar Schwarm	Franz Schachner
1980	EAST GERMANY 1:19.331	ITALY 1:19.606	AUSTRIA 1:19.795
	Hans Rinn	Peter Gschitzer	Georg Fluckinger
	Norbert Hahn	Karl Brunner	Karl Schrott
1984	WEST GERMANY 1:23.620	U.S.S.R. 1:23.660	EAST GERMANY 1:23.887
	Hans Stangassinger	Evgeni Beloussov	Jörg Hoffmann
	Franz Wembacher	Aleksandr Belyakov	Jochen Pietzsch
1988	EAST GERMANY 1:31.940	EAST GERMANY 1:32.039	WEST GERMANY 1:32.274
	Jörg Hoffmann	Stefan Krause	Thomas Schwab
	Jochen Pietsch	Jan Behrendt	Wolfgang Staudinger

SINGLE-SEATER—WOMEN

1908–1960 Event not held			
1964	Otrun Enderlein (GER) 3:24.67	Ilse Geisler (GER) 3:27.42	Helene Thurner (AUT) 3:29.06
1968	Erica Lechner (ITA) 2:28.66	Christa Schmuck (GER) 2:29.37	Angelika Duenhaupt (GER) 2:29.56
1972	Anna-Maria Muller (GDR) 2:59.18	Ute Ruehrold (GDR) 2:59.49	Margit Schumann (GDR) 2:59.54
1976	Margit Schumann (GDR) 2:50.621	Ute Ruehrold (GDR) 2:50.846	Elisabeth Demleitner (GER) 2:51.056
1980	Vera Sosulya (URS) 2:36.537	Melitta Sollmann (GDR) 2:37.657	Ingrida Amantova (URS) 2:37.817
1984	Steffi Martin (GDR) 2:46.570	Bettine Schmidt (GDR) 2:46.873	Ute Weiss (GDR) 2:47.248
1988	Steffi Martin-Walter (GDR) 3:03.973	Ute Weiss-Oberhoffner (GDR) 3:04.105	Cerstin Schmidt (GDR) 3:04.181

7. Ice Hockey

GOLD	SILVER	BRONZE
1908	Event not held		
1920	**CANADA**	**UNITED STATES**	**CZECHOSLOVAKIA**
	Robert J. Benson	Raymond L. Bonney	Dr. Adolf Dusek
	Wally Byron	Anthony J. Conroy	Dr. Karel Hartmann
	Frank Frederickson	Herbert L. Drury	Vilém Loos
	Chris Fridfinnson	J. Edward Fitzgerald	Jan Pallausch
	Mike Goodman	George P. Geran	Jan Peka
	Haldor Halderson	Frank X. Goheen	Dr. Karel Pesek
	Konrad Johannesson	Joseph McCormick	Josef Sroubek
	A. "Huck" Woodman	Lawrence J. McCormick	Otakar Vindyš
		Frank A. Synott	
		Leon P. Tuck	
		Cyril Weidenborner	
1924	**CANADA**	**UNITED STATES**	**GREAT BRITAIN**
	Jack A. Cameron	Clarence J. Abel	W. H. Anderson
	Ernest J. Collett	Herbert L. Drury	Lorne H. Carr-Harris
	Albert J. McCaffery	Alphonse A. Lacroix	Colin G. Carruthers
	Harold E. McMunn	John A. Langley	Eric D. Carruthers
	Duncan B. Munro	John J. Lyons	Guy E. Clarkson
	W. Beattie Ramsay	Justin J. McCarthy	Ross Cuthbert
	Cyril S. Slater	Willard W. Rice	George Holmes
	Reginald J. Smith	Irving W. Small	Hamilton D. Jukes
	Harry E. Watson	Frank A. Synott	Edward B. Pitblado
			Blane N. Sexton
1928	**CANADA**	**SWEDEN**	**SWITZERLAND**
	Charles Delahay	Carl Abrahamsson	Giannin Andreossi
	Frank Fisher	Emil Bergman	Mezzi Andreossi
	Dr. Louis Hudson	Birger Holmqvist	Robert Breiter
	Norbert Mueller	Gustaf Johansson	Louis Dufour
	Herbert Plaxton	Henry Johansson	Charles Fasel
	Hugh Plaxton	Nils Johansson	Albert Geromini
	Roger Plaxton	Ernst Karlberg	Fritz Kraatz
	John G. Porter	Erik Larsson	Arnold Martignoni
	Frank Sullivan	Bertil Linde	Heini Meng
	Dr. Joseph Sullivan	Sigurd Oberg	Anton Morosani
	Ross Taylor	Vilhelm Petersen	Dr. Luzius Rüedi
	David Trottier	Kurt Sucksdorff	Richard Torriani
1932	**CANADA**	**UNITED STATES**	**GERMANY**
	William H. Cockburn	Osborn Anderson	Rudi Ball
	Clifford T. Crowley	John B. Bent	Alfred Heinrich
	Albert G. Duncanson	John Chase	Erich Herker
	George F. Garbutt	John E. Cookman	Gustav Jaenecke
	Roy Hinkel	Douglas N. Everett	Werner Korff
	C. Victor Lindquist	Franklin Farrell	Walter Leinwever
	Norman J. Malloy	Joseph F. Fitzgerald	Erich Römer
	Walter Monson	Edward M. Frazier	F. Marquardt Slevogt
	Kenneth S. Moore	John B. Garrison	Martin Schröttle
	N. Romeo Rivers	Gerard Hallock III	Georg Strobl
	Harold A. Simpson	Robert C. Livingston	
	Hugh R. Sutherland	Francis A. Nelson	
	W. Stanley Wagner	Winthrop H. Palmer	
	J. Aliston Wise	Gordon Smith	

GOLD	SILVER	BRONZE
1936 GREAT BRITAIN	**CANADA**	**UNITED STATES**
Alexander Archer	Maxwell Deacon	John B. Garrison
James Borland	Hugh Farquharson	August F. Kammer
Edgar Brenchley	Kenneth Farmer	Philip W. LaBatte
James Chappell	James Haggarty	John C. Lax
John Coward	Walter Kitchen	Thomas H. Moone
Gordon Dailley	Raymond Milton	Eldridge B. Ross
John Davey	Francis W. Moore	Paul E. Rowe
Carl Erhardt	Herman Murray	Francis J. Shaugnessy
James Foster	Arthur Nash	Gordon Smith
John Kilpatrick	David Neville	Francis J. Spain
Archibald Stinchcombe	Ralph St. Germain	Frank R. Stubbs
Robert Wyman	Alexander Sinclair	
	William Thomson	
1948 CANADA	**CZECHOSLOVAKIA**	**SWITZERLAND**
Murray-Alb Dowey	Vladimir Bouzek	Hans Bänninger
Bernard Dunster	Augustin Bubnik	Alfred Bieler
Orval Gravelle	Jaroslav Drobny	Heinrich Boller
Patrick Guzzo	Premsyl Hajny	Ferdinand Cattini
Walter Halder	Zdenek Jarkovsky	Hans Cattini
Thomas Hibbert	Stanislav Konopásek	Hans Dürst
Ross King	Bohumil Modry	Walter Dürst
Henri-André Laperrire	Miloslav Pokorny	Emil Handschin
John Lecompte	Vaclav Rozinak	Heini Lohrer
George A. Mara	Dr. Mirosláv Sláma	Werner Lohrer
Albert Renaud	Karel Stibor	Reto Perl
Reginald Schroeter	Vilém Stovik	Gebhard Poltera
	Ladislav Troják	Ulrich Poltera
	Josef Trousilek	Beat Ruedi
	Oldrich Zábrodsky	Otto Schubinger
	Vladimir Zábrodsky	Richard Torriani
		Hans Trepp
1952 CANADA	**UNITED STATES**	**SWEDEN**
George G. Able	Ruben E. Bjorkman	Gote Almqvist
John F. Davies	Leonard S. Ceglarski	Hans Andersson
William Dawe	Joseph J. Czarnota	S. "Tvilling" Andersson
Robert B. Dickson	Richard J. Desmond	Ake Andersson
Donald V. Gauf	Andre P. Gambucci	Lars Bjorn
William J. Gibson	Clifford N. Harrison	Gote Blomqvist
Ralph L. Hansch	Gerald W. Kilmartin	Thord Flodqvist
Robert R. Meyers	John F. Mulhern	Erik Johansson
David E. Miller	Joyn M. Noah	Gosta Johansson
Eric E. Paterson	Arnold C. Oss, Jr.	Rune Johansson
Thomas A. Pollock	Robert E. Rompre	Sven Johansson
Allan R. Purvis	James W. Sedin	Ake Lassas
Gordon Robertson	Allen A. Van	Holger Nurmela
Louis J. Secco	Donald F. Whiston	Hans Oberg
Francis C. Sullivan	Kenneth J. Yackel	Lars Pettersson
Robert Watt		Lars Svensson
		Sven Thunman

GOLD	SILVER	BRONZE
1956 U.S.S.R.	**UNITED STATES**	**CANADA**
Yevgeniy Babitsch	Wendell Anderson	Denis Brodeur
Usevolod Bobrov	Wellington Burnett	Charles Brooker
Nikolay Chlystov	Eugene Campbell	William Colvin
Aleksey Guryschev	Gordon Christian	Alfred J. Horne
Juriy Krylov	William Cleary	Arthur Hurst
Alfred Kutschewskiy	Richard Dougherty	Byrle Klinck
Vlanetin Kusin	Willard Ikola	Paul Knox
Grigoriy Mkrttschan	John Matchefts	Kenneth Laufman
Viktor Nikiforov	John Mayasich	Howard Lee
Juriy Pantjuchov	Daniel McKinnon	James Logan
Nikolay Putschkov	Richard Meredith	Floyd Martin
Viktor Schuwalov	Weldon Olson	Jack McKenzie
Genrich Sidorenkov	John E. Petroske	Donald Rope
Nikolay Sologubov	Kenneth Purpur	Georges Scholes
Ivan Tregubov	Ronald Rigazio	Gerald Theberge
Dmitriy Ukolov	Richard Rodenhiser	Robert White
Aleksandr Uwarov	Edward Sampson	Keith Woodall
1960 UNITED STATES	**CANADA**	**U.S.S.R.**
Roger A. Christian	Bob Attersley	Veniamin Aleksandrov
William Christian	Moe Benoit	Aleksandr Aljimetov
Robert B. Cleary	Jim Connelly	Juriy Baulin
William J. Cleary	Jack Douglas	Michail Bytschkov
Eygene Grazia	Fred Etcher	Vladimir Grebennikov
Paul Johnson	Bob Forhan	Yevgeniy Groschev
John Kirrane	Don Head	Viktor Jakuschev
John Mayasich	Harold Hurley	Yevgeniy Jerkin
Jack McCartan	Kenneth Laufman	Nikolay Karpov
Robert McVey	Floyd Martin	Alfred Kutschewskiy
Richard Meredith	Bob McKnight	Konstantin Loktev
Weldon Olson	Clifford Pennington	Stanislav Petuchov
Edwyn Owen	Donald Rope	V. Prjaschtschnikov
Rodney Paavola	Bob Rousseau	Nikolay Putschkov
Lawrence Palmer	George Samolenko	Genrich Sidorenkov
Richard Rodenhiser	Harry Sinden	Nikolay Sologybov
Thomas Williams	Darryl Sly	Juriy Tsitsinov
1964 U.S.S.R.	**SWEDEN**	**CZECHOSLOVAKIA**
Viktor Konovalenko	K. Svensson	Vlado Dzurila
Boris Zaitsev	L. Haeggroth	Vlado Nadrchal
Viktor Kuzkin	G. Blome	F. Gregor
Eduard Ivanov	R. Stoltz	R. Potsch
Vitaliy Davidov	N. Johansson	F. Tikal
Aleksandr Ragulin	B. Nordlander	S. Sventek
Olyeg Zatisev	N. Nilsson	L. Smid
Aleksandr Almetov	U. Sterner	J. Walter
Viktor Yakushev	T. Johansson	Josef Golonka
Vyacheslav Starchinov	R. Pettersson	Jiri Holik
Konstantin Loktev	E. Maeaettae	V. Bubnik
Boris Mayorov	L. Johansson	Jan Klapac
Anatoliy Firsov	L. Lundvall	J. Dolana
Stanislav Petuchov	C. Oeberg	S. Pryl
Veniamin Aleksandrov	A. Andersson	M. Vlach
Evgeniy Maiorov	U. Oehrlund	Jaroslav Jirik
Leonid Volkov	H. Mild	Josef Cerny

GOLD	SILVER	BRONZE
1968 U.S.S.R.	**CZECHOSLOVAKIA**	**CANADA**
Viktor Zinger	Vladimir Nadrchal	Wayne Stephenson
Viktor Konovalenko	Vlado Dzurila	Kenneth Broderick
Vitaliy Davidov	Oldrich Machac	Marshall Johnston
Viktor Blinov	Jan Suchy	Brian Glennie
Igor Romishevskiy	Josef Horesovsky	Barry Mckenzie
Olyeg Zaitsev	Frantisek Pospisil	Paul Conlin
Aleksandr Ragulin	Karel Masopust	Edward Hargreaves
Viktor Kuzkin	Frantisek Sevcik	Terence O'Malley
Boris Mayorov	Jan Havel	Raymond Cadieux
Anatoliy Firsov	Jan Hrbaty	Stephen Monteith
Evgeniy Zymin	Vaclav Nedomansky	William Macmillan
Viktor Polupanov	Josef Golonka	Francis Huck
Anatoliy Ionov	Petr Hejma	Garry Dineen
Vyacheslav Starchinov	Jiri Kochta	Danny O'Shea
Evgeniy Michakov	Jaroslav Jirik	Morris Mott
Vladimir Vikulov	Jiri Holik	Herbert Pinder
Yuriy Moiseyev	Josef Cerny	Rogert Bourbonnais
Venyamin Aleksandrov	Jan Klapac	Gerry Pinder
1972 U.S.S.R.	**UNITED STATES**	**CZECHOSLOVAKIA**
Vladislav Tretiak	Michael Curran	Vado Dzurila
Aleksandr Pachkov	Peter Sears	Jiri Holocek
Viktor Kuzkin	James McElmury	Rudolf Tajcnar
Vitaliy Davidov	Thomas Mellor	Jaroslav Holik
Yevgeniy Michalkov	Frank Sanders	Vaclav Nedomansky
Aleksandr Maltsev	Charles Brown	Vladimir Bednar
Aleksandr Iakuchev	Richard McGlynn	Frantisek Pospisil
Vladimir Lutchenko	Walter Old	Jiri Holik
Aleksandr Ragulin	Kenneth Ahearn	Karal Vohralik
Igor Romichevskiy	Stuart Irving	Josef Horesovsky
Gennadiy Tsygankov	Mark Howe	Oldrich Machac
Valeri Kharlamov	Henry Bucha	Josef Cerny
Yuriy Blinov	Keith Christiansen	Bohuslav Stastny
Vladimir Petrov	Robbie Ftorek	Richard Farda
Anatoliy Firsov	Ronald Marsland	Ivan Hlinka
Boris Mikhailov	Craig Farmer	Jiri Kochta
Vladimir Vikulov	Timothy Sheehy	Vladimir Martinec
1976 U.S.S.R.	**CZECHOSLOVAKIA**	**WEST GERMANY**[1]
Alexandr Sidelnikov	Jiri Holecek	Erich Weishaupt
Vladislav Tretiak	Pavel Svitana	Anton Kehle
Alexiandr Gusev	Oldrich Machac	Rudolf Thanner
Vladimir Lutchenko	Milan Chalupa	Josef Voelk
Sergei Babinov	Frantisek Pospisil	Udo Kiessling
Yuriy Liapkin	Miroslav Dvorak	Stefan Metz
Valeriy Vasilyev	Milan Kajkl	Klans Auhuber
Gennadiy Tsygankov	Jiri Bubla	Ignaz Berndaner
Sergei Kapustin	Milan Novy	Rainer Philipp
Victor Shalimov	Vladimir Martinec	Lorenz Funk
Alexandr Maltsev	Jiri Novak	Wolfgang Boos
Boris Alexandrov	Bohuslav Stastny	Ernst Koepf
Boris Mikhailov	Jiri Holik	Ferenc Vozar
Alexandr Iakuchev	Ivan Hlinka	Walter Koeberle
Vladimir Petrov	Eduard Novak	Erich Kuehnhackl
Valeriy Kharlamov	Jaroslav Pouzar	Alois Schloder
Vladimir Shadrin	Bohuslav Ebermann	Martin Hinterstocker
Victor Jlutkov	Josef Augusta	Franz Reindl

---

[1]Three-way tie for bronze with USA and Finland decided on goal average.

	GOLD	SILVER	BRONZE
1980	**UNITED STATES**	**U.S.S.R.**	**SWEDEN**
	Steven Janaszak	Vladimir Mischkin	Pelle Lindbergh
	James Craig	Vladislav Tretiak	William Lofqvist
	Kenneth Morrow	Vyacheslav Fetissov	Tomas Jonsson
	Michael Ramsey	Vasiliy Pervuchin	Sture Andersson
	William Baker	Valeriy Vassilyev	Ulf Weinstock
	John O'Callahan	Aleksey Kasanotov	Jan Eriksson
	Bob Suter	Sergey Starikov	Tommy Samuelsson
	David Silk	Zinetula Bilyaletdinov	Mats Waltin
	Neal Broten	Vladimir Krutov	Thomas Eriksson
	Mark Johnson	Alexandr Maltsev	Per Lundqvist
	Steven Christoff	Yuriy Lebedyev	Mats Ahlberg
	Mark Wells	Boris Mikhailov	Hakan Eriksson
	Mark Pavelich	Vladimir Petrov	Mats Naslund
	Eric Strobel	Valeriy Kharlamov	Lennart Norberg
	Michael Eruzione	Helmut Balderis	Bengt Lundholm
	David Christain	Victor Jlutkov	Leif Holmgren
	Robert McLanahan	Aleksandr Golikov	Bo Berglund
	William Schneider	Sergey Makarov	Harald Luckner
	Philip Verchota	Vladimir Golikov	Dan Soderstrom
	John Harrington	Aleksandr Skvortzov	Lars Molin
1984	**U.S.S.R.**	**CZECHOSLOVAKIA**	**SWEDEN**
	Vyatcheslav Fetissov	Milan Chalupa	Arne Michael Thelven
	Aleksey Kassatonov	Jaroslav Benak	Bo Ericsson
	Sergey Makarov	Jiri Lala	Jens Erik Ohling
	Igor Larionov	Vladimir Kyhos	Per-Erik Eklung
	Vladimir Kroutov	Frantischek Tchernik	Peter Gradin
	Vassili Pervukhin	Arnold Kadlec	Thomas Ahlen
	Zenetoula Bilyatletdinov	Miloslav Horava	Mats Thelin
	Sergey Chepelev	Igor Liba	Karl Soedergren
	Aleksandr Guerasimov	Darius Rusnak	Mats Waltin
	Andrei Khomoutov	Vincent Lukatch	Tommy Motrh
	Igor Stelnov	Radoslav Svoboda	Goeran Lindblom
	Sergey Starikov	Eduard Uvira	Leif Nordin
	Nikolai Drozdetsky	Pavel Richter	Tomas Sandstroem
	Viktor Tumenyev	Vladimir Ruzsitchka	Lars Eriksson
	Aleksandr Kozhevnikov	Vladimir Cladr	Thom Eklund
	Aleksandr Skvortsov	Jiri Hrdina	Peter Hjalm
	Vladimir Kovin	Duschan Paschek	Thomas Rundquist
	Mikhail Vasilyev	Jaroslav Korbela	Mats Hessel
	Valdimir Zoubkov		
1988	**U.S.S.R.**	**FINLAND**	**SWEDEN**
	Vladimir Krutov	Timo Blomqvist	Peter Andersson
	Igor Larionov	Kari Eloranta	Anders Eldebrink
	Vyacheslav Fetisov	Jyrki Lumme	Lars Ivarsson
	Sergey Makarov	Jukka Virtanen	Lars Karlsson
	Alexey Kasatonov	Arto Ruotanen	Mats Kihlstrom
	Valeriy Kamensky	Reijo Ruotsalainen	Tommy Samuelsson
	Andrei Khomutov	Simo Saarinen	Mikael Andersson
	Anatoliy Semenyov	Kai Suikkanen	Bo Berglund
	Alexandr Mogilny	Raimo Helminen	Jonas Bergqvist
	Vyacheslav Bykov	Iiro Jarvi	Peter Eriksson
	Sergey Svetlov	Esa Keskinen	Michael Hjalm
	Ilya Byakin	Erkki Laine	Mikael Johansson
	Sergey Yachin	Kari Laitinen	Lars Molin
	Alexandr Tchernykh	Erkki Lehtonen	Lars Pettersson
	Andrey Lomakin	Reijo Mikkolainen	Thomas Rundqvist
	Alexey Gusarov	Janne Ojanen	Ulf Sandstrom
	Alexandr Kozhevnikov	Timo Susi	Hakan Sodergren
	Igor Stelnov	Pekka Tuomisto	Jens Ohling
	Sergey Starikov	Teppo Numminen	Thomas Eriksson
	Igor Kravchuk	Jari Torkki	Thom Eklund
	Sergey Mylnikov	Jukka Tammi	Peter Ahslin
	Vitaliy Samoilov	Jarmo Myllys	Peter Lindmark
			Anders Bergman

The USA hockey team celebrated wildly after its 4–3 upset victory in the semi-finals against the heavily favored Soviet team in 1980. A 4–2 victory over Finland in the final game secured the gold medal for the American skaters.

OLYMPIC RECORDS

ARCHERY

EVENT	POINTS	NAME & COUNTRY	YEAR
Men's Double FITA	2,616	Darrell Pace (USA)	1984
Women's Double FITA	2,683	Kim Soo-Nyung (KOR)	1988

CYCLING

EVENT	MIN/SEC	NAME & COUNTRY	YEAR
1000 meters time trial	1:02.955	Lothar Thoms (GDR)	1980
4000 meters individual pursuit	4:32.00	Gintautas Umaras (URS)	1988
4000 meters team pursuit	4:13.31	USSR	1988

SHOOTING

EVENT	POINTS	NAME & COUNTRY	YEAR
Small-bore rifle (3 pos)	1,181	Alister Allan (GBR)	1988
Small-bore (prone)	600	Miroslav Varga (TCH)	1988
Free pistol	581	Alexandr Melentev (URS)	1980
Rapid fire pistol	598	Afanasi Kuzmine (URS)	1988
Running game	591	Gennady Avramenko (URS)	1988
	591	Tor Heiestad (NOR)	1988
Trap	199	Angelo Scalzone (ITA)	1972
Skeet	198	Yevgeny Petrov (URS)	1968
	198	Romano Garagnani (ITA)	1968
	198	Konrad Wirnhier (GER)	1968
	198	Josef Panacek (TCH)	1976
	198	Eric Swinkels (HOL)	1976
	198	Luciano Giovannetti (ITA)	1980
	198	Matthew Dryke (USA)	1984
	198	Axel Wagner (GDR)	1988
	198	Alfonso De Iruarrizaga (CHI)	1988
Air rifle	594	Goran Maksimovic (YUG)	1988
Air pistol	590	Erich Buljung (USA)	1988

WOMEN

EVENT	POINTS	NAME & COUNTRY	YEAR
Sport pistol	591	Nino Saloukvadze (URS)	1988
	591	Jasna Sekaric (YUG)	1988
Standard rifle	590	Silvia Sperber (FRG)	1988
Air pistol	390	Nino Saloukvadze (URS)	1988
Air rifle	395	Launi Meili (USA)	1988
	395	Irina Chilova (URS)	1988
	395	Zhang Qiuping (CHN)	1988

SWIMMING

MEN

EVENT	MIN/SEC	NAME & COUNTRY	YEAR
50 meters freestyle	22.14	Matt Biondi (USA)	1988
100 meters freestyle	48.63	Matt Biondi (USA)	1988
200 meters freestyle	1 47.25	Duncan Armstrong (AUS)	1988
400 meters freestyle	3 46.95	Uwe Dassler (GDR)	1988
1,500 meters freestyle	14 58.27	Vladimir Salnikov (URS)	1980
4 × 100 meters freestyle relay	3 16.53	USA	1988
4 × 200 meters freestyle relay	7 12.51	USA	1988
100 meters breaststroke	1 01.65	Steve Lundquist (USA)	1984
200 meters breaststroke	2 13.34	Victor Davis (CAN)	1984
100 meters backstroke	54.51*	David Berkoff (USA)	1988
200 meters backstroke	1 58.99	Richard Carey (USA)	1984
100 meters butterfly	53.00	Anthony Nesty (SUR)	1988
200 meters butterfly	1 56.94	Michael Gross (FRG)	1988
200 meters medley	2 00.17	Tamas Darnyi (HUN)	1988
400 meters medley	4 14.75	Tamas Darnyi (HUN)	1988
4 × 100 meters medley relay	3 36.93	USA	1988

WOMEN

EVENT	MIN/SEC	NAME & COUNTRY	YEAR
50 meters freestyle	25.49	Kristin Otto (GDR)	1988
100 meters freestyle	54.79	Barbara Krause (GDR)	1980
200 meters freestyle	1 57.65	Heike Friedrich (GDR)	1988
400 meters freestyle	4 03.85	Janet Evans (USA)	1988
800 meters freestyle	8 20.20	Janet Evans (USA)	1988
4 × 100 meters freestyle relay	3 40.63	GDR	1988
100 meters breaststroke	1 07.95	Tania Dangalakova (URS)	1988
200 meters breaststroke	2 26.71	Silke Hoerner (GDR)	1988
100 meters backstroke	1 00.86	Rica Reinisch (GDR)	1980
200 meters backstroke	2 09.29	Krisztina Egerzegi (HUN)	1988
100 meters butterfly	59.00	Kristin Otto (GDR)	1988
200 meters butterfly	2 06.90	Mary Meagher (USA)	1984
200 meters medley	2 12.59	Daniela Hunger (GDR)	1988
400 meters medley	4 36.29	Petra Schneider (GDR)	1980
4 × 100 meters medley relay	4 03.74	GDR	1988

TRACK & FIELD ATHLETICS

MEN

EVENT	HR	MIN	SEC	NAME & COUNTRY	YEAR
100 meters			9.92	Carl Lewis (USA)	1988
200 meters			19.75	Joe DeLoach (USA)	1988
400 meters			43.86	Lee Evans (USA)	1968
800 meters		1	43.00	Joaquim Cruz (BRA)	1984
1500 meters		3	32.53	Sebastian Coe (GBR)	1984
5000 meters		13	05.59	Said Aouita (MAR)	1984
10000 meters		27	21.46	Brahim Boutayeb (MOR)	1988
Marathon	2	09	21.0	Carlos Lopes (POR)	1984
20 km walk	1	19	57.0	Jozef Pribilinec (TCH)	1988
50 km walk	3	38	29.0	Vyacheslav Ivanenko (URS)	1988
110 meters hurdles			12.98	Roger Kingdom (USA)	1988
400 meters hurdles			47.19	Andre Philips (USA)	1988
3000 meters steeplechase		8	05.51	Julius Kariuki (KEN)	1988
4 × 100 meters relay			37.83	USA	1984
4 × 400 meters relay		2	56.16	USA	1968
		2	56.16	USA	1988

High jump	2.38	Gennadiy Avdeyenko (URS)	1988
Pole vault	5.90	Sergei Bubka (URS)	1988
Long jump	8.90	Bob Beamon (USA)	1968
Triple jump	17.61	Khristo Markov (BUL)	1988
Shot put	22.47	Ulf Timmermann (GDR)	1988
Discus throw	68.82	Jurgen Schult (GDR)	1988
Hammer throw	84.80	Sergei Litvinov (URS)	1988
Javelin throw	85.90	Jan Zelezny (TCH)	1988
Decathlon	8847 points*	Daley Thompson (GBR)	1984

*In qualifying round.

<table>
<tr><td>WOMEN</td><td colspan="2">MIN/ SEC</td><td></td><td></td></tr>
<tr><td>100 meters</td><td></td><td>10.62*/10.54w</td><td>Florence Griffith-Joyner (USA)</td><td>1988</td></tr>
<tr><td>200 meters</td><td></td><td>21.34</td><td>Florence Griffith-Joyner (USA)</td><td>1988</td></tr>
<tr><td>400 meters</td><td></td><td>48.65</td><td>Olga Bryzgina (URS)</td><td>1988</td></tr>
<tr><td>800 meters</td><td>1</td><td>53.43</td><td>Nadezda Olizarenko (URS)</td><td>1980</td></tr>
<tr><td>1500 meters</td><td>3</td><td>53.96</td><td>Paula Ivan (ROM)</td><td>1988</td></tr>
<tr><td>3000 meters</td><td>8</td><td>26.53</td><td>Tatyana Samolenko (URS)</td><td>1988</td></tr>
<tr><td>10,000 meters</td><td>31</td><td>05.21</td><td>Olga Bondarenko (URS)</td><td>1988</td></tr>
<tr><td>Marathon</td><td>2 24</td><td>52.0</td><td>Joan Benoit (USA)</td><td>1984</td></tr>
<tr><td>100 meters hurdles</td><td></td><td>12.38</td><td>Yordanka Donkova (BUL)</td><td>1988</td></tr>
<tr><td>400 meters hurdles</td><td></td><td>53.17</td><td>Debbie Flintoff-King (AUS)</td><td>1988</td></tr>
<tr><td>4 × 100 meters relay</td><td></td><td>41.60</td><td>GDR</td><td>1980</td></tr>
<tr><td>4 × 400 meters relay</td><td>3</td><td>15.17</td><td>USSR</td><td>1988</td></tr>
<tr><td>10 km walk</td><td></td><td>——</td><td>Not previously held</td><td></td></tr>
<tr><td>High jump</td><td></td><td>2.03</td><td>Louise Ritter (USA)</td><td>1988</td></tr>
<tr><td>Long jump</td><td></td><td>7.40</td><td>Jackie Joyner-Kersee (USA)</td><td>1988</td></tr>
<tr><td>Shot put</td><td></td><td>22.41</td><td>Ilona Slupianek (GDR)</td><td>1980</td></tr>
<tr><td>Discus throw</td><td></td><td>72.30</td><td>Martina Hellmann (GDR)</td><td>1988</td></tr>
<tr><td>Javelin throw</td><td></td><td>74.68</td><td>Petra Felke (GDR)</td><td>1988</td></tr>
<tr><td>Heptathlon</td><td colspan="2">7291 points*</td><td>Jackie Joyner-Kersee (USA)</td><td>1988</td></tr>
</table>

*In preliminary round.   w—wind-assisted.

WEIGHTLIFTING

EVENT	TOTAL WEIGHT (KG)	NAME & COUNTRY	YEAR
52 kg class	270.0	Svdalin Marinov (BUL)	1988
56 kg class	292.5	Oxen Mirzoyan (URS)	1988
60 kg class	342.5	Naim Suleymanoglu (TUR)	1988
67.5 kg class	342.5	Yanko Rusev (BUL)	1980
75 kg class	375.0	Borislav Guidikov (BUL)	1988
82.5 kg class	400.0	Yurik Vardanyan (URS)	1980
90 kg class	412.5	Anatoli Khrapatyi (URS)	1988
100 kg class	425.0	Pavel Kuznetsov (URS)	1988
110 kg class	455.0	Yuriy Zakharevich (URS)	1988
100+ kg class	462.5	Alexandr Kurlovich (URS)	1988

SPEED SKATING

EVENT	MIN/ SEC		NAME & COUNTRY	YEAR
500 meters		36.45	Jens-Uwe Mey (GDR)	1988
1000 meters	1	13.03	Nikolai Gouliayev (URS)	1988
1500 meters	1	52.06	Andre Hoffmann (GDR)	1988
5000 meters	6	44.63	Tomas Gustafsson(SWE)	1988
10,000 meters	13	48.20	Tomas Gustafsson (SWE)	1988

WOMEN

500 meters		39.10	Bonnie Blair (USA)	1988
1000 meters	1	17.65	Christa Rothenburger (GDR)	1988
1500 meters	2	00.68	Yvonne Van Gennip (HOL)	1988
3000 meters	4	11.94	Yvonne Van Gennip (HOL)	1988
5000 meters	7	14.13	Yvonne Van Gennip (HOL)	1988